AMERICA'S GAME

AMERICA'S GAME

A History of Major League Baseball through World War II

Bryan Soderholm-Difatte

ROWMAN & LITTLEFIELD
Lanham • Boulder • New York • London

Published by Rowman & Littlefield
A wholly owned subsidiary of The Rowman & Littlefield Publishing Group, Inc.
4501 Forbes Boulevard, Suite 200, Lanham, Maryland 20706
www.rowman.com

Unit A, Whitacre Mews, 26-34 Stannary Street, London SE11 4AB

British Library Cataloguing in Publication Information Available

Library of Congress Cataloging-in-Publication Data

Name: Soderholm-Difatte, Bryan, author.
Title: America's game : a history of major league baseball through World War II / Bryan Soderholm-
    Difatte.
Description: Lanham, Maryland : ROWMAN & LITTLEFIELD, [2018] | Includes bibliographical
    references and index.
Identifiers: LCCN 2017048325 (print) | LCCN 2017050748 (ebook) | ISBN 9781538110638 (elec-
    tronic) | ISBN 9781538110621 (hardcover : alk. paper)
Subjects: LCSH: Baseball—United States—History—20th century.
Classification: LCC GV863.A1 (ebook) | LCC GV863.A1 S687 2018 (print) | DDC 796.357/64—
    dc23
LC record available at https://lccn.loc.gov/2017048325

Printed in the United States of America

CONTENTS

AUTHOR'S NOTE

A popular exhibit, especially for kids, at the 1939–40 New York World's Fair was the Academy of Sport, which included a "School of Baseball" featuring prominent contemporary and former ballplayers as "Instructors of the Day." Among those instructors were Babe Ruth, Charlie Keller, Dominic DiMaggio, Vince DiMaggio, Elbie Fletcher, and Ossie Bluege. One 11-year-old boy who got their autographs on cards certifying he attended their "instruction" was my dad. He grew up with the Yankees teams led by Joe DiMaggio that won seven pennants and six World Series in eight years, from 1936 to 1943. He loved baseball, and they were his guys. I mention this because my dad's recollections of the players he watched and the games he saw in person and listened to on the radio, his command of the statistical record, and his putting them in the context of what he knew had come before his time—although mostly from reading about it in newspapers and books rather than learning about it from *his* dad, the son of an immigrant, who did not grow up in love with the game—all of that gave me a deep understanding of and appreciation for the relevance of baseball history. It's what made me a baseball guy.

An important part of the game's appeal is its history and tradition. Indeed, a strong argument can be made that the history of Major League Baseball, and also the history of the Negro Leagues before major-league integration, is what provides the connective tissue from one generation of baseball fans and followers to the next. Ballplayers are larger-than-life, mythic heroes. They may be gone from the scene, but they live for us in the present because of what they did, the standards they set, and the teams they represented. They are more than mere mortals. At least they are to the tens of millions of Americans, past and present, who have been and are captivated by baseball played at the highest level. The great players, managers, and teams of the past are the touchstones against which the best players, managers, and teams of today are compared. History is the reason why the Chicago Cubs winning the 2016 World Series caught the imagination of Americans across the country, because the Cubs had not won one since way back in 1908.

This book is about Major League Baseball from the beginning of the twentieth-century birth of the current structure of two leagues—the new-born American League and the well-established National League—until 1947, when Branch Rickey, the Brooklyn Dodgers, and Jackie Robinson integrated the major leagues. With the possible exception of boxing and notwithstanding the highly specific seasonal popularity of college foot-ball, baseball was without question America's national sports obses-sion—the national pastime—in the years this book covers. The major leagues' prehistory is not a subject of this inquiry. Suffice it to say that the origins of the American game of baseball can be traced to any number of variants derived from English games involving a ball, batting, and running to bases that were played as early as the pre–Revolutionary War era. The basic outlines of the current game of baseball were clearly estab-lished before the Civil War, when the game was popular in the northeast-ern United States. Major League Baseball came into being in the last quarter of that century, setting the foundation for what became known for a very long time as the "modern era," which began in 1901 when Ban Johnson declared the American League a major-league rival of the Na-tional League.

The "modern era" beginning in 1901? A quaint term now, more than a century later when so much has changed about the major-league game—including the end of racial exclusion; the introduction of divisional align-ments, wild-card teams, designated hitters, and interleague play; players coming from baseball-enthused Caribbean Basin and East Asian coun-tries to play in the majors; and the World Series extending into Novem-ber.

STATISTICAL SOURCES

My primary statistical source is the website baseball-reference.com, which buttresses the traditional record of annual player and team statistics with multiple data aggregations, including batter and pitcher splits, derived from the long-standing and painstaking efforts of Retrosheet researchers to provide as comprehensive a record as possible of every game played, at least as far as the box score. As of January 1 2018, comprehensive splits data was not available on baseball-reference for the years before 1913. For relief pitching data before 1913, I relied on the "Relief Pitcher Register" in the third edition of *Total Baseball*, edited by baseball historians John Thorn and Pete Palmer and published in 1993.

Because official statistics are the prime currency for comparative analysis, it is important to remember they can be misleading about player performance, especially in comparisons across time, because of differences in context, including the era and even the dimensions of their home ballpark. There have been several advanced metrics developed over the years to assess every player's unique overall value to his team. Probably the best known is "wins above replacement" (WAR), which measures the totality of a player's performance in terms of how many additional wins that player contributed to his team over what a "replacement player" from the highest minor-league level would have contributed instead. Although there are three competing versions of WAR that yield differing player values, they generally are consistent in the year-to-year patterns they show of the same player's performance. I have chosen the WAR variant used in baseball-reference.com.

INTRODUCTION
Ruining a Good Thing

The National League—Major League Baseball's *only* league at the time—entered the twentieth century besieged. By now the game was well established as both a business and a sporting event played on a daily basis during the summer months that attracted sufficiently large numbers of paying customers to make it profitable, especially for franchise owners and star players. As a sporting event, Organized Baseball inspired fierce loyalty, often reflected in gambling and even fisticuffs over the outcome of games, by devoted *fan*atics to their home-city teams. While the quality and even the style of play were certainly more primeval than today, the basic geometry and rules of the game that are recognizable today were set. Baseball was already America's "national pastime."

Indicative of the game's place in American culture, basic statistics were kept and the games were covered by local newspapers. Although major-league baseball as defined by the National League had existed for only a quarter of a century—exactly 25 years—as the centuries turned, its past was already being revered. Star players had sex appeal and followings among grown-ups and kids alike. Hero worship of baseball players was anything but unheard of. Even though there remained a widespread perspective in the Calvinistic mode of American thinking, particularly within the growing professional class, that baseball was a frivolous pursuit, a worthy recreational activity perhaps, but hardly a meaningful or even reputable profession, many a boy playing the game in the sandlots aspired to be like their baseball heroes in the professional game. To be like Cap Anson, or Billy Hamilton, or Hugh Duffy, or Ed Delahanty, or Kid Nichols, or Cy Young, or even any of the ruffian Baltimore Orioles (although their mothers most certainly did not approve), whose worshipped heroes featured John McGraw and Hughie Jennings, Willie Keeler and Joe Kelley.

Although only 25 years had passed since the National League was born, great teams—as well as great players—were already the yardstick against which the present and future were being measured. By dominating the National League in the 1890s, between them winning every pennant from 1891 to 1898, the Boston Beaneaters with five championships, and the Orioles with three, vied with the 1880s St. Louis Browns and Chicago White Stockings in the argument about the best team in baseball history. But as popular as the game now was, Major League Baseball—represented by only the National League—was being undermined by its own recent history. Established in 1876, the National League of Professional Baseball Clubs was the brainchild of William Hulbert and Harry Wright. Rather than the collective of affiliated clubs lacking an effective superstructure for imposing the rigor and coherence necessary for sustained success that was the then-existing National Association, Hulbert and Wright conceived of professional baseball being run as a business enterprise of stable franchises with adherence to governing rules and procedures and set schedules.

Historically considered the first "major league" because in 1871 it became the first association of baseball clubs all of whose players were paid professionals, the National Association was on the verge of imploding just five years later. There were no standardized processes and procedures to manage relationships between teams, or between teams and their players, or to ensure the integrity of schedules or even the games. Affiliated clubs came and went, some failing to complete their schedules if there was more money to be made playing local or regional exhibitions rather than league games involving expensive travel. In reality, the National Association was professional only in the sense that players were paid, unless their clubs went bankrupt and they weren't. With the exception of some powerhouse clubs that cornered the market on the best players and stayed both financially viable and committed to providing their paying customers high-quality baseball worthy of paid professionals, the National Association's business practices were amateurish.

Harry Wright had organized the first openly professional baseball team in Cincinnati in 1869 and is thus considered the father of professional baseball. William Hulbert, a successful commodities broker in Chicago, thought investing in a professional baseball team was a good business proposition. Both were consummate professionals frustrated by the chaos and hints of scandal in National Association operations, including over whether some games were rigged. Wright was immediately attracted to Hulbert's proposal that a new league be formed in which rules and standards obligated all member franchises. The team he had assembled and was now managing in Boston was the best team in baseball, and Wright recognized that the organizational weaknesses of the National Association would ultimately undercut the prestige and potential profits that could be earned if his club competed instead in a league where there was franchise continuity from one year to the next; where player talent was more uniform—although there would always be stars and mediocrities; and where schedules that were balanced, published in advance, and reliably adhered to meant that all games counted. Hulbert became president of the new National League and was also an owner of the league's Chicago franchise. Wright switched the allegiance of his famed Boston Red Stockings from the National Association to the National League, as did four other clubs, putting an end to baseball's first "major" league.

As a start-up, the National League faced some difficult initial years. Although some franchises ultimately failed—the league went from eight teams its first year to six the next two before going back to eight in 1879—no clubs folded in midseason. Weather permitting, all scheduled games were played. The league also introduced a "reserve clause" to player contracts so that players were tied to their teams to ensure there was roster continuity from one year to the next. Quickly proving its for-profit business model to be a success, the National League inspired competition. By the turn of the century, however, the other "major" leagues that once were had been swept away, including the American Association (in existence from 1882 to 1891) and the one league that was considered a grave existential threat to the profit-making prerogatives of franchise owners—the Players' League.

In a workers-of-the-baseball-world-unite moment (Marxist ideas had made headway among American laborers increasingly organizing into unions), the Players' League was the outgrowth of star players' anger and resentment at being bound to their teams by the reserve clause preventing them from being paid fair market value for their baseball skills and accomplishments, which franchise owners exploited to boost their own earnings from the game. Organized in 1890, the Players' League lasted just one year before lack of financial wherewithal doomed its existence. The Players' League failure led ultimately to the demise of the American Association as well, four of whose franchises—including Baltimore—were picked up by the National League to make a 12-team league in 1892. Now there was just one major league.

By consolidating their control over all of Major League Baseball, the franchise owners who ruled the roost in the 1890s ushered in a robber-baron era in baseball, which by the end of the century led directly to contraction of the National League and contributed to the climate that allowed the American League to emerge as a *major* league rival. This was a time in American history where there was considerable social and political agitation against business tycoons who were taking advantage of the escalating, unstoppable momentum of prodigious economic growth made possible by the rapid pace of technological innovation, the country's vast reserves of profitable raw materials to fuel the creation and growth of new industries, and the labor of countless immigrants who came to the United States of America for greater opportunities and a better life. Baseball's magnates sought to monopolize their own industry, just as Andrew Carnegie did with steel, J. P. Morgan did with finance, John D. Rockefeller did with oil, and Cornelius Vanderbilt did with railroads. They imposed a salary cap for players—not for each team, but a maximum salary any one player could be paid, which was well below fair market value for the game's best players—and rode roughshod over the minor leagues, a part of Organized Baseball recognized as controlled by the major leagues, in ways that made it difficult for minor-league clubs to operate effectively. They certainly did not amass the wealth and political clout of the men who were at the forefront of profiting from America's economic boom, but baseball's "robber barons" considered themselves just as entitled to do whatever they wanted with their industry, and they were every bit as resented.

* * *

The collapse of the Players' League and the end of the American Association left players powerless in the face of the National League's owner-barons, who nonetheless proceeded to badly overplay their hand. By the end of the decade the owners' robber-baron pretensions were destroying the league. Twelve teams was proving unmanageable, particularly at a time when the US economy was in a depression sparked by the stock market crash of 1893. With no rival league as a challenge to channel their energies, and with a weak league president, National League owners became embroiled in palace intrigues that undermined the whole enterprise. It clearly was a problem that a league with so many teams condemned some to be perennial bottom-dwellers. The franchises in Washington, St. Louis, and Louisville were consistently among the worst teams in baseball. Brooklyn went from middle of the pack in the mid-1890s to way out of the running as the decade advanced. It didn't help that owners were permitted to own stock in other teams, and in 1899 this conflict of interest was carried to the extreme when Cleveland owner Frank Robison bought controlling interest in the financially struggling St. Louis franchise and Baltimore owner Harry Von der Horst became an equal partner in Brooklyn. In 1900 Barney Dreyfuss, whose Louisville club was in dire straits despite stars such as Honus Wagner and player-manager Fred Clarke, hedged his bets by securing half ownership in Pittsburgh.

Syndicated ownership of major-league teams nearly destroyed the integrity of the game. Upon securing controlling or half interest in a second franchise, both Robison and Von der Horst immediately strip-mined the best players and their managers—Patsy Tebeau in Cleveland and Ned Hanlon in Baltimore—from their financially weaker team to bolster their other, potentially more profitably one. On the Robison front, St. Louis went from dead last in 1898 with a 39–111 record to fifth place and a substantially better 84–67 mark in 1899, while Cleveland, having lost the likes of Hall of Famers Cy Young, Jesse Burkett, and Bobby Wallace to St. Louis, fell from fourth place and 81–68 to last place and the major league's worst ever record at 20–134. On the Von der Horst front, Brooklyn, which had finished 10th with a 54–91 record in the 12-team league the previous year, became an instant pennant winner in 1899 with a 100–47 mark after being blessed with former Orioles outfielders Willie Keeler and Joe Kelley and shortstop Hughie Jennings. Because third baseman John McGraw and catcher Wilbert Robinson refused to go to Brooklyn so they could attend to their outside business interests in Baltimore, the Orioles stayed respectable, dropping from a competitive second to a noncompetitive fourth.

Von der Horst's dismantling of the Baltimore Orioles to benefit Brooklyn so soon after their three straight pennants from 1894 to 1896, followed by a pair of runner-up years to Boston's Beaneaters, was stunning in its audacity and disregard for legacy—specifically that an owner with interests in two franchises would transfer the best players on a championship-caliber team rather than build toward reclaiming the top spot and establishing an enduring dynasty. Although they finished six games behind Boston in 1898, after losing out by just two games the previous year, most of the Orioles' best players were still in their prime, while the Beaneaters had a more veteran, aging roster. Only one of Baltimore's core players in 1898 was over 30—Robinson, who was 34—and McGraw, Keeler, and Kelley were only in their mid-20s. Over in Boston, four of the Beaneaters' core regulars were over 30—including outfielders Hugh Duffy and Billy Hamilton—and two other star players, pitching ace Kid Nichols and third baseman Jimmy Collins, were in their late 20s.

The Orioles were a formidable team with perhaps the largest number of the best players in the game on their roster at any one time in the nineteenth century. The mid- to late 1890s were an offensive era that played well to the Orioles' strengths. They were tenacious and innovative on offensive, developing or fine-tuning strategies that would come to define Deadball Era baseball. They always seemed to have runners on base and were aggressive and skilled in taking extra bases and scoring runs. Whether with the Baltimore chop as a tactic to get on base, using the hit-and-run play and stealing bases with abandon to advance runners, or placing hits between infielders and into the outfield gaps, the Orioles had a perpetual-motion offense that kept pressure on opposing pitchers and the defense.

Their in-your-face, win-at-any-cost style of play is part of the mystique that came to define the 1890s Baltimore Orioles, both contemporaneously and historically. In addition to being outstanding ballplayers, they were a team of roughnecks looking for any advantage they could get. That included skirting the rules and the ethics of fair play. The Orioles were not above impeding opposing runners on the bases, hiding baseballs in the tall grass for when necessary to make a stunning defensive play to cut down unwitting baserunners, and bullying and intimidating the usually lone umpire working the game. They were crude and they were rude, hardly paragons of virtue however admired they were for how—and how well—they played the game. They were hated and loved, despised and admired. Attitudes toward the Orioles reflected a dichotomy in American society that embraced both a tough-minded whatever-it-takes approach to making a mark in the world, on the one hand, and an ethos of fair play and civility, including frowning on drunkenness and rowdiness, on the other.

Because syndicate ownership allowed the wholesale transfer of players from one franchise to another, and with league owners increasingly concerned that 12 teams were four too many, the Orioles' ultimate fate was all but inevitable after Von der Horst broke up the team. Cleveland, Louisville, and Washington were obvious candidates for contraction because all three franchises had long been laggards in attendance. There was not an obvious fourth, however, although St. Louis would have been but for the complete roster overhaul in 1899 bringing on board all of Cleveland's best players thanks to their new interlocking ownership. None of those cities had a history of winning success, except for St. Louis a decade earlier in the American Association. Baltimore certainly did, but after attendance dropped by more than half from 273,000 the previous year to just 123,400 in 1898, despite finishing second, the die was cast. Although Brooklyn, along with Cleveland and Washington, drew fewer fans than Baltimore, the city was a thriving and growing metropolis that had just been incorporated into greater New York City. Having bought into the franchise in Brooklyn, there was where Von der Horst, with an ownership stake in both clubs, decided to place his bet on the future.

Notwithstanding the Orioles' minidynasty of the mid-1890s, Baltimore, like Cleveland and Louisville—the two other clubs under syndicate ownership—was dismissed from the National League in 1900. Washington was the other team to suffer that fate. As Von der Horst and Robison had done, Barney Dreyfuss, predictably, made certain that all the best players on his now-defunct Louisville club found their way to his other club in Pittsburgh. Thus reinforced, the seventh-place Pirates of 1899 became the second-place Pirates in 1900, finishing behind Brooklyn in a league pared down to eight teams. Pittsburgh won the next three National League pennants. But the National League now faced the challenge of a new major league—one that it could not contract out of existence, unlike the four teams it cavalierly erased from the ledger in 1900.

Part I

Deadball Baseball

1

THE AMERICAN LEAGUE START-UP

Like many American boys, Byron Bancroft Johnson grew up in love with baseball, but being from a well-heeled family for whom baseball was not a reputable livelihood, he did the next best thing by becoming a top sportswriter in Cincinnati. In 1892, just after the demise of the American Association as a major-league competitor to the National League, Johnson took over as president of the Western League, a minor league on the brink of dissolution. His ambition and connections helped the Western League grow and prosper. So too did the 1895 arrival of Charles A. Comiskey, one of baseball's biggest stars in the 1880s, to take over as owner and manager of the Western League's struggling franchise in St. Paul, Minnesota.

Charlie Comiskey's baseball fame derived from his being a dangerous hitter, a deft defensive first baseman who popularized playing off the bag when there was nobody on first, and a very successful player-manager for the American Association's St. Louis Browns. His leadership skills evident very early on, Comiskey was in only his third year as a big-leaguer when he was named manager of the Browns late in the 1884 season. As player-manager beginning the next year, he led the Browns to four consecutive American Association pennants. Comiskey was among the many star players who took their chance in the Players' League in 1890 and returned to their former teams after its collapse. When the American Association went under a year later, Comiskey left the Browns—one of the association's four franchises transferred to the National League—to take over as first baseman–manager of the Cincinnati Reds until deciding after his team's 10th-place finish in 1894 that he would rather be a club owner himself, even if in the minor leagues. Comiskey's baseball gravitas as both player and manager, and his business acumen, helped Johnson's Western League gain the credibility needed to attract quality ballplayers.

As the quality of Western League baseball improved, its players became a frequent target of National League clubs asserting their right under agreements governing "Organized Baseball" to draft players from minor-league teams. Exercising their "captains of industry" prerogatives, NL owners in the same year Comiskey went west unilaterally cut in half the price they would pay minor-league teams for their players. Not only was this a significant financial blow to the increasingly successful Western League, but the league's pennant races were disrupted by the increasing propensity of National League owners to draft many of its players and farm their own underperforming players to Western League teams as their needs dictated. Cincinnati Reds owner John T. Brush was a particularly egregious offender because he also owned the Western League's Indianapolis franchise and shifted players back and forth between his major-league and minor-league teams depending on which was having more competitive success. While the Reds were a good team, they were not a contender. His Western League team, however, won three pennants between 1895 and 1899—all in the odd-numbered years. (In addition to his minor-league club, Brush also owned stock in another major-league franchise—the New York Giants—as did several other NL owners.)

Johnson did not knuckle under to the National League's efforts to keep the Western League in its appropriate place. Instead, he successfully upped the ante. Bolstered by many players from the four NL clubs excised from the league in 1900, Johnson was able to secure the financial backing of one of America's richest men, Ohio coal magnate Charles Somers. Miffed about Cleveland having to endure a horrific 20–134 season because syndicate owners had transferred all of the team's best players—including Cy Young—to their *other* team in St. Louis and then being summarily eliminated from the National League, Somers wanted to see major-league baseball back in Cleveland and was willing to use his extensive wealth to help make that happen. Comiskey, meanwhile, wore down the owner of the Chicago Orphans (soon enough to be nicknamed the "Cubs") to acquiesce to his establishing a Western League team in the Windy City, even though the Orphans had territorial rights. In 1900, as the National League subtracted to eight teams, the Western League moved into Chicago and, in a savvy public relations move telegraphing his intentions, Johnson renamed his league the "American League." It was, however, still a *minor* league.

But Johnson's—and Comiskey's—ambitions were greater than that.

For the start-up American League to challenge the established National League as a *major* league, it was essential that the quality of play be on par *and* that the infant league be successful in the major cities of America. This being long before cross-country air travel, the "major cities of America" for Major League Baseball meant east of the Mississippi. The hard line National League owners were taking on player salaries and contractual rights played into Johnson's hands. National League owners were themselves in disarray over a proposal by Brush and three other owners in 1901 to take the concept of syndicate baseball to a whole new level. They proposed that NL franchises not be individually owned but instead controlled by a small oligarchy—Brush and his three pals—that would run the league's entire operation, including the assignment of players and managers. That plan went nowhere because of opposition from the four other National League owners, who would have lost their stake in the game to Brush and his three pals. And now, because of Brush's gambit, there was widespread distrust among the National League owners.

After Comiskey's successful move into Chicago in 1900, which included his White Sox winning the American League (still officially a minor league) pennant, and with the financial clout of Somers behind him, Johnson went for the jugular. The new league announced franchises in three of the four cities the National League had abandoned—Cleveland, Baltimore, and Washington. Detroit, an up-and-coming city that had not had a major-league team since 1888, was also awarded a franchise. Detroit's Wolverines were forced to disband because of financial insolvency just a year after winning the National League pennant in 1886. The city's population had increased by 40 percent since then, according to the 1900 US census, making Detroit now the 13th-largest city in the country.

Even more alarming to the established major-league order, Johnson's infant league intended to take on the National League directly in three of its most important cities in 1901, with Chicago being joined by new AL franchises in Philadelphia and Boston. Milwaukee would be the only American League franchise remaining from Johnson's original Western League, and that would turn out to be for just one year. The National League tried to head off AL expansion into their cities by reestablishing the American Association as an affiliated minor league populated by players from NL reserve rosters with franchises in all of the American League cities, but a late start and lack of financial backing quickly doomed that plan to failure.

Ban Johnson wasted little time in declaring that come 1901 the American League would be a "major" league. As the necessary foundation for its success, the new major league turned its attention to stealing away as many of the best National League players as possible. Having already been told by Johnson that the new league would take into account the many player grievances that had festered since the late 1880s, a nascent players union that had been organized in June of 1900 instructed its player-members after the season not to sign new contracts until after the union had met with National League owners to press their demands for a much higher minimum base salary and significant concessions on how their contracts were handled, including the selling of players back and forth between the NL and the minor leagues.

National League owners, however, underestimated the players' resolve, did not sufficiently appreciate how formidable an adversary Johnson's new "major" league was, and refused to give an inch. They thought they could steamroll the players' resolve flat as a pancake because they were the *established* league. They made the hubristic mistake of assuming they were the only game in town for the players. But the National League was no longer the only game in town; the American League's roster of "major-league" cities and ability and willingness to pay higher salaries made its presence credible to established veteran players, especially star players, who believed they were being shortchanged by their franchise owners. It was the perfect storm of opportunity for Ban Johnson and his self-declared new "major" league.

* * *

Two other founding fathers of the American League took center stage with Johnson, Comiskey, and Somers in the winter of 1900–01—the actual turn of the twentieth century—to make their new "major" league not only a reality, but a competitive success. The first was Connie Mack. A taciturn, dignified leader, so much a gentleman that he managed the Philadelphia Athletics for 50 years in a suit, straw hat, and button-down collar rather than a baseball uniform, Mack was perfect for the new league that Johnson wanted to distinguish from the National League with a less rowdy brand of baseball suitable for fair play and family viewing. The other was Clark Griffith. One of the premier pitchers in baseball at the turn of the century—he had six straight 20-win seasons for the Chicago Orphans from 1894 to 1899—Griffith was bitterly resentful of National League owners suppressing players' market value.

Mack had come to the Western League in 1897 after a pedestrian 11-year career as a catcher, which—like Comiskey—included defecting to the player-organized Players' League. While Comiskey's defensive innovations included playing off the bag at first, Mack's innovations behind the plate were subtle and technically a violation of the rules, such as tipping the hitter's bat to throw off his swing and mimicking the sound of a foul ball on pitches that the umpire really should have called a ball. The last three of his big-league seasons as a catcher were also as the player-manager of the Pittsburgh Pirates, a middle-of-the-pack team that he managed to a winning record each year. After being dismissed for his efforts following the 1896 season, Mack jumped at the opportunity to buy a 25 percent share in the Western League's Milwaukee Brewers franchise, putting him into baseball ownership.

Connie Mack had an affinity for administration and strategic planning that, for all intents and purposes, made him effectively the chief operating officer of the Milwaukee franchise. His organizational talents caught the attention of Johnson, who made Mack part of the brain trust he and Comiskey assembled as they pushed for their minor league to go major. Johnson was impressed by Mack's assertiveness and astuteness in strategic planning discussions on the committee that was deciding in what cities to challenge the National League. Even more impressive from Johnson's perspective must have been Mack's demonstrated aggressiveness in pursuing established National League players for his Western League team that he also managed. After all, Johnson and Comiskey's league had to attract *major* league players to lay claim to being a *major* league.

He may have cultivated the image of a gentleman, and was in fact a gentleman, but Connie Mack was cutthroat in baseball business dealings and usually got what he was after. Even while managing the Brewers to second place in 1900—the year the Western League was renamed the American League—Mack invested himself fully in seeing the new league become a major-league rival of the National League. The Brewers stayed in place as one of the AL's original "major-league" franchises, but Johnson in particular understood that Milwaukee was not a "major-league" American city, not yet anyway. Mr. Johnson wanted Mr. Mack in Philadelphia for 1901, and Mack was brilliant in making that happen.

At first benefiting from Mr. Somers helping bankroll the effort, it was Connie Mack who worked the local business community to find funding to finance the American League's Philadelphia operation. It was he who persuaded Ben Shibe, a prominent local entrepreneur and partner of Al Reach in the country's foremost sporting goods company, to invest in becoming majority owner of the new franchise. And it was he—Connie Mack—who found the location for a new ballpark and commissioned for it to be built. Mack purchased a 25 percent share in the ownership of the new Philadelphia franchise, whose nom de guerre would be the "Athletics"—Shibe controlled 50 percent, and two local sportswriters held the remaining 25 percent—and assumed control of all baseball decisions. He also appointed himself manager.

The Somers-Mack duo was also instrumental in organizing the American League entry into Boston. As he did in Philadelphia, Mack helped to locate grounds to build a ballpark for the new team. Recognizing the importance of Boston to Johnson's grand strategy for making the American League a major league, Somers took responsibility as the interim owner of the Boston franchise until someone else could be found. To avoid the appearance of a conflict of interest—syndicate baseball having been discredited by the National League's embrace of that concept—Somers temporarily transferred his ownership of the Cleveland team to his partner in that franchise. It would not be until two years later that Somers was able to give up his stake in Boston and reclaim ownership of his club in Cleveland.

Just as critical as Mack in helping make Johnson's scheme a reality was Clark Griffith. If he was not the actual "first" National League recruit of the new league in the winter of 1900–01, Griffith was the most important because without him there would not have been as many prominent players who jumped the established major league for an ambitious upstart. As a star player acting the role of a labor agitator, it was he who urged players to wait things out after the 1900 season before signing new contracts while he led a delegation to the National League owners meeting in December to press their demands. Once his proposals were predictably spurned, Griffith wasted no time in becoming an avid apostle for the infant league over the winter as the centuries turned.

The American League proved wildly successful in raiding the National League for players. The new league opened its first season as a declared "major" league having enticed five of baseball's biggest stars at the turn of the century to defect from their National League teams. In addition to Griffith, they included Cy Young, already with 286 major-league victories, mostly with the Cleveland Spiders, on his way to a career total of 511; John McGraw, the Orioles' great third baseman in the 1890s; the Beaneaters' Jimmy Collins, whose athletic quickness enabled him to pioneer the art of charging in for bunts and who by 1900 had eclipsed McGraw as the game's best third baseman; and Napoleon Lajoie of the Phillies, the game's best second baseman.

Signing Griffith, Collins, and Lajoie was a particular coup for the new league because they stayed in the same city in which they had been stars for their National League team. Their fans could still enjoy their exploits merely by going to the ballpark of the rival American League team in town. Moreover, Griffith in Chicago and Collins in Boston were both named player-managers of their new teams, adding to their own and their new team's stature. Both used their credibility as great players and prominence as outspoken critics of National League owners being misers to aggressively and successfully pursue stars from the established league. McGraw, meanwhile, was named player-manager of the American League Orioles in the same city where he had made his name as the fiery third baseman of the National League's once-upon-a-dynasty team in Baltimore.

While not as high profile, many of the other players who jumped to the American League were also highly rated and significant losses for the

National League clubs they had belonged to. Their defections not only solidified the credibility of the American League as a major rival to the National League, but diminished the luster of the teams they had left. This was particularly problematic for the NL teams in Boston, Philadelphia, and Chicago because many of the AL's most prominent new stars now played for the American League teams in their cities. Indeed, the new league built strongly competitive teams in all three cities, and while it might be too much to say this was how Johnson planned it, in fact, Chicago won the American League's first pennant as a major league in 1901, Philadelphia the second in 1902, Boston the third and fourth in 1903 and '04, Philadelphia the fifth in 1905, and Chicago the sixth in '06.

The American League's inaugural season as a major league was a major success. The National League outdrew their new rival 1.9 million fans to 1.7 million in 1901, but was in trouble in two of the three cities the two leagues shared. In Chicago, Comiskey's White Sox, managed by Griffith, won the pennant; the Orphans finished sixth. The AL club outdrew the NL team by nearly 150,000. In Boston, the new AL team finished second while the established NL club came in fifth. The American League won the attendance battle in that city, too, by nearly 143,000. Only in Philadelphia among the three cities that had a team in each league did the National League prevail in their league standings—the NL Phillies finished second, the AL Athletics fourth—and in attendance, although the difference was only about 28,600 fans. Former Phillies star Lajoie won the American League's first batting title with a .426 average, which was the best in both leagues, playing for Philadelphia's Athletics. Cy Young, now pitching for Boston's Americans (who would not be known as the Red Sox for another seven years), led the majors in victories with 33.

It got worse for the NL in 1902. Once again, the National League lost numerous players to the American League, including five more of baseball's biggest turn-of-the-century stars. Abandoning the league that made them famous were Ed Delahanty, baseball's best hitter since the mid-1890s with three .400 seasons between 1894 and 1899; Jesse Burkett, who twice hit .400 in the mid-1890s and had just won the 1901 National League batting title; George Davis, the best shortstop in baseball—(the versatile Honus Wagner, said to have been tempted to also jump leagues but didn't, had yet to play shortstop on a regular basis); Bobby Wallace, another top-tier shortstop still at the beginning of his career; and Elmer Flick, one of baseball's premier outfielders after only four seasons. Delahanty, now playing for Washington, went on to lead the American League with a .376 batting average in 1902.

And that was not all. The American League was now in four National League cities, having left Milwaukee for St. Louis, where the newly minted AL Browns benefited from nearly all of the NL Cardinals' best players—including Burkett and Wallace—joining their team. While the Cardinals finished sixth in their league, the Browns finished second in theirs and had an attendance advantage of nearly 46,000. In fact, in all four cities the two leagues had in common in 1902—Philadelphia, St. Louis, Boston, and Chicago, in the order the AL teams finished—the American League's entry finished ahead of the National League club in both the league standings and attendance. Overall, the American League swamped the National League in attendance by half a million fans, 2.2 to 1.7 million.

* * *

If the situation wasn't already bad enough for the National League, Johnson announced when the season was over that in 1903 the American League would have a team in a fifth National League city—none other than New York, the largest and most important city in the country. Ban Johnson had been looking for this opportunity, and it was John McGraw who opened the door.

The ruffian, aggressive McGraw was precisely the personality type Johnson did *not* want representative of his new league. Johnson presented the American League as committed to playing pure baseball unsullied by rowdy behavior, including threatening and otherwise intimidating umpires, and cheating on the field that often also translated to boorishness by fans in the stands. McGraw was emblematic of both those vices, as were his teammates, when he was the star third baseman of the Orioles' dynasty in the mid-1890s. But with a mission to build a credible challenge to the National League, Johnson was willing to overlook McGraw's very objectionable qualities because McGraw was a popular player and, most important, identifiable with Baltimore—the sixth-largest metropolis in the United States, according to the 1900 census, and home of the legendary Orioles.

Johnson's marriage of convenience with McGraw for the purpose of advancing his American League project quickly soured, as was certainly predictable. Call it creative differences between two strong-willed individuals; McGraw was constantly clashing with the umpires, and then with Johnson. By June of 1902 the situation had become untenable, with Johnson repeatedly suspending McGraw for being abusive toward umpires. McGraw, meanwhile, began working behind the scenes to return to the National League, and specifically to New York to rebuild and manage the then-hapless Giants. The two strong-willed individuals parted officially in July, no love lost between them. Hardly blameless in their messy breakup, McGraw nonetheless offered an interesting—and relevant—insight when he accused Johnson's policy of being "everything for Boston,

Chicago, and Philadelphia," with all the other AL franchises having to fend for themselves. At the time, of course, those were precisely the three cities where the new American League was going head-to-head with the established National League, although there were now four shared cities between the two leagues, including St. Louis.

McGraw's departure from Baltimore amounted to a scorched-earth policy. He took with him several of the Orioles' most important players—notably Joe McGinnity and Roger Bresnahan, both in the Hall of Fame, and Dan McGann. The move was made possible because the Orioles' owner, who agreed with McGraw that Johnson was acting against Baltimore's baseball interests, sold his ownership shares to Andrew Freedman, principal owner of the New York Giants. Some of Baltimore's players went to Cincinnati in midseason after McGraw left thanks to the Reds owner, John Brush, also being part of the Giants' ownership group. Johnson was able to ensure the Orioles finished the 1902 season by revamping the team's roster, but also set in motion his plan to replace Baltimore with a franchise in New York City the very next year.

Not only was there no stopping the American League from going into New York, but the defection of National League stars continued. Willie Keeler, a .373 hitter since becoming a regular with the Orioles in 1894, and Pittsburgh pitching stars Jack Chesbro and Jesse Tannehill jumped the NL ship after the 1902 season to play for the new New York team, and Sam Crawford, one of baseball's young rising stars, defected to the American League franchise in Detroit. Although the National League Phillies had won a temporary court injunction in Pennsylvania the previous year prohibiting their former star Napoleon Lajoie, then with the Philadelphia Athletics, from playing in any American League games in the state, it was too little too late. Undaunted, Johnson and Mack resolved the situation by arranging for Lajoie to play for Cleveland, although he still could not play any of his team's games in Philadelphia. Lajoie's situation did nothing to deter AL teams from continuing to seek out NL players, especially the best players, nor did it deter Keeler, Chesbro, Crawford, and many lesser lights from accepting American League offers for 1903.

With their league in danger of becoming increasing irrelevant in Major League Baseball and their franchise investments threatened, National League owners in January 1903 finally sued for peace. It was in the American League's interest, too, to bring order and stability to the national pastime and end what amounted to a bidding war for players that could ultimately drive up player costs to prohibitive levels. A new National Agreement was negotiated that put in place a National Commission to serve as the governing body for Organized Baseball, whose members were the presidents of the two leagues and a commission chairman. The two leagues agreed there would be no further incursions into each other's territory—effectively limiting the number of shared cities to five; agreed to respect each other's player contracts, which included the player-hated reserve clause; and agreed that the rules of the game would be the same in both leagues. Most specifically, the American League adopted a National League rule change that went into effect in 1901 that foul balls counted as strikes up until there were two strikes on the batter. Had that rule been in effect in the AL in 1901, it is very unlikely Lajoie's league-leading batting average would have been as high as .426. As the 1903 season progressed, the two leagues also agreed to Johnson's proposal that the pennant winners in each league meet at the end of the season in a series to determine the champion of the baseball world. Much to the shock of the National League, the American League pennant winner—the Boston Americans—beat the presumed superior Pittsburgh Pirates in the first World Series.

What became known as Major League Baseball's "modern era" had begun, although that classification in recent years has sometimes been reinterpreted. Major League Baseball would remain unchanged in its geographic sweep for 50 years and in its basic competitive structure of two-league, two-pennant races for another 66 years, although with an asterisk for two years of the Federal League in 1914 and 1915—the next, and last, time a new league attempted to force the issue by unilaterally declaring itself a "major" league. The hated reserve clause would remain in effect, antagonizing players, for nearly three-quarters of a century.

And one other thing, although this was not a part of any agreement and was not even discussed, because nobody would have even thought to—Organized Baseball, the major and minor leagues both, would be entirely white. There would be allowance for Native Americans and white Hispanics, perhaps, but not for black Americans, notwithstanding that the 14th and 15th Amendments to the Constitution had given them full rights of citizenship since 1868. That would not change in the minor leagues for another 43 years, and a year after that for the majors.

* * *

Ratified by the National Agreement before the 1903 season began, the American League's move into New York was the capstone of Johnson's maneuverings. It was an audacious move opposed at every turn by the Giants. Even after the National League conceded as part of the peace settlement between the two major leagues that the new league would have a New York team, the Giants used their Tammany Hall political connections to stymie American League efforts to procure land for a ballpark. Johnson was forced finally to forge his own Tammany connections through men of questionable ethics whom he approved as the new owners of the AL's New York entry—Frank Farrell, a gambling kingpin and crony of corrupt Tammany politicians, and Bill Devery, a corrupt police official who was similarly connected. They were able to secure land on high ground in Manhattan for a ballpark in time for the 1903 season, giving the team that would eventually become the Yankees its first nickname, the Highlanders.

Johnson, however, had long since taken care to ensure the New York team's new manager was not ethically challenged. It was not coincidental that White Sox manager Clark Griffith was the man Johnson wanted to take charge in New York. Although he was as fiery and contentious with umpires as McGraw, Griffith was more restrained. He knew and respected boundaries. More importantly, he had credibility as a proven winner—his White Sox won the first American League pennant in 1901—and in his ability to recruit and attract players. Griffith was probably the one man(ager) at Ban Johnson's disposal who could take on the tour de force in New York that was John McGraw. Charles Comiskey, Griffith's employer, knew this as well. In any event, a transaction of some mystery occurred that sent Griffith from Chicago to New York almost immediately after the 1902 season ended, and Griffith began the task at hand to entice dissatisfied star players to defect from the National League to his new team even as momentum was building for the peace agreement that would put an end to player raids.

Notwithstanding Johnson's manipulations to ensure a competitive team in New York, McGraw's Giants used their half-season head start to quickly take pride of place in the Big City. The Giants shot up from last in the National League in 1902 to second in 1903, while the Highlanders finished fourth in their first year of operation. The Giants also crushed the Highlanders at the gate, with nearly 580,000 fans coming to their games in New York—a new major-league attendance record—compared to just under 212,000 for the Highlanders, the second-worst attendance showing in the American League.

The next year, however, when the Highlanders were in contention for the 1904 American League pennant until the last day of the season, McGraw and Brush—now the Giants' principal owner, having bought out Freedman—were sufficiently concerned about not allowing their uptown, hilltop rivals to gain any momentum for the city's affections that they peremptorily announced in midsummer that the Giants, who were running away with the National League pennant, would not play in any World Series with the American League champion. It didn't matter that Boston instead of New York won the 1904 AL pennant, the NL champion Giants refused to play in a World Series. For the next 16 years until 1920, it was the Giants who were the favored baseball team in New York. They won five more pennants and played in five World Series; in 1905,

McGraw and Brush conceded to the inevitable that a playoff between the two leagues' pennant winners for the championship of the baseball world was precisely what fans wanted to see. The Highlanders, meanwhile, took a long time getting on a competitive track, even after they changed their name to the Yankees in 1913.

Until the arrival of Babe Ruth in 1920 upended New York baseball, the only year the Highlanders outdrew the Giants was in 1906, when Griffith had his team in the pennant hunt in a three-team race until the final week of the season, while McGraw's Giants—despite winning 96 games to the Highlanders' 90—finished a distant second because the Chicago Cubs effectively ended the pennant race early in the summer on their way to a record-setting 116 wins. It should be noted for accuracy that the Yankees also drew more fans than the Giants to their games in 1918. That season was cut short by a month because of the First World War, however, costing McGraw's team 21 home games, whereas the Yankees were deprived of only 11 games at home; the Giants actually drew more fans per game than the Yankees to the Polo Grounds, which the two New York teams had shared since 1912.

The Giants may have dominated the New York baseball scene, but the American League beat out the National in overall attendance every year without exception from 1904 until 1926. New York was the only one of the five cities the two leagues had in common with rival franchises where the National League had the attendance advantage. In Philadelphia, Boston, and St. Louis, the American League club consistently drew more than its NL counterpart. Chicago was the only swing city when it came to attendance. The AL may have been the more fan-favored major league because of outstanding players like Lajoie, Jimmy Collins, Young, Keeler, Crawford, and George Davis swiped from the National League, and because a greater number of the compelling new stars who burst into the baseball world in the first decade and the teens—Ty Cobb, Walter Johnson, Eddie Collins, Home Run Baker, Tris Speaker, Shoeless Joe Jackson, and Babe Ruth—played for American League clubs.

* * *

The men who were the founding fathers of the American League, and arguably of modern baseball, could rightfully be proud of their accomplishment. Connie Mack and Clark Griffith would stay around for half a century or longer (in Griffith's case) as managers, owners, or in both capacities, becoming two of the most consequential shapers not only of the American League but of twentieth-century major-league baseball. But in the first decade of the new league, the two men provided the ballast of gravitas that helped the American League to flourish. In late twentieth-century terms, they provided adult supervision to a game renowned for

Connie Mack, manager of the Athletics, and Clark Griffith, manager of the Senators, before the first game of the 1919 season. Both remained powerbrokers in the game until midcentury. *National Photo Company Collection (Library of Congress).*

aggressive, roughneck behavior (although Griffith was himself prone to both vices). By their professionalism, the two managers were instrumental in giving the new league both integrity and credibility. Griffith and Mack gave the game a patina of respectability that was just as advantageous to the start-up American League becoming a successful business enterprise as the star players picked off from the National League. After all, while winning games and pennants might seem like the bottom line for baseball teams, the real bottom line (as in any business) was revenue.

Ban Johnson and Charles Comiskey, without whose ambitious vision and drive none of this would have happened, ultimately went from being allies in a start-up venture to bitter enemies. Even as the new league was consolidating its success, once it became certain their venture would not fail, the two men began drifting apart. Part of it was ego. Johnson resented the relatively widespread public perception in the early years of the American League that Comiskey played a greater role than he in establishing their league as a credible rival to the National League. Part of it was boundaries derived from their different roles. Johnson was the league president; Comiskey one of eight franchise owners. The disciplinary rules that Johnson enforced applied to all, but Comiskey took umbrage at some of the suspensions Johnson handed down to his players for abusive behavior toward umpires during the 1905 pennant race, which he felt cost his team the pennant. And part of it was Johnson not letting go, no doubt tied to his ego, as he continued trying to manipulate events behind the scenes, especially concerning player transactions and franchise competitiveness, for as long as he was league president.

2

AL TEAMS PLAYING FOR KEEPS

It was a wild ride for the American League in the first decade of its history. The lack of a dominant team made for thrilling pennant races. After Boston finished 14½ games ahead of second-place Philadelphia in 1903 and gave the infant league first bragging rights in a postseason World Series by defeating the NL champion Pittsburgh Pirates, every American League pennant race from 1904 to 1909 was decided by 3½ games or less.

Although it would be wrong to say this was the beginning of the New York–Boston rivalry that captivates us today, the new league's first great pennant race in 1904 was in fact between the two East Coast cities. It was Boston's Americans, occasionally called the Pilgrims, as the future Red Sox were then nicknamed, against New York's presumptuous Highlanders, as the Yankees were then known. Shades of the compelling drama that unfolded exactly one century later in the American League Championship Series of 2004, the team from Boston stunned the team from New York to win the pennant in a most tortuous way. Boston repeating as AL champions ultimately turned on a wild pitch by Highlanders pitching ace Jack Chesbro that allowed the pennant-winning run to score in the ninth inning of the next-to-last game (it was a doubleheader) on the last day of the season.

Led by player-manager Jimmy Collins, whose defection from the Beaneaters gave the new American League team in Boston instant credibility, the Americans had left the rest of the league in the dust the previous year, taking a 9½-game lead into September. They scored the most runs and had the best pitching staff in baseball. Paced by Cy Young leading the league in wins for the third straight year with a 28–9 record, following 33–10 and 32–11 in '01 and '02, three Boston pitchers won 20 games.

One was former Beaneaters pitcher Bill Dinneen, who bolted from the National League team in Boston the year before to win 21 games for the American League team in Boston and did so again in 1903. The third was Tom Hughes, whose 20–7 record gave him the second-best winning percentage in the league after Young. Outfielder Buck Freeman, who jumped from the Beaneaters along with Collins in 1901, was the power bat in the lineup, with 39 doubles, 20 triples, and a league-leading 13 home runs and 104 runs batted in. Shortstop Freddy Parent, however, was Boston's best position player based on wins above replacement.

Trying to become the first American League team to follow up a pennant with a pennant in 1904, the Americans faced stiff competition from the Highlanders—a franchise in only its second year of play made possible by AL founding father Ban Johnson's determination not only that his new league needed a franchise in the most important city of the country, but that the team needed to be good. In 1904, with Clark Griffith transplanted from Chicago to manage the Highlanders, they were. Willie Keeler had the last outstanding year of his storied career, batting .343— second in the league. The Highlanders had their own star shortstop in the feisty Kid Elberfeld. The generously listed 5-foot-9 Jimmy Williams, the only player of consequence to come over from Baltimore when the Orioles franchise was abandoned by the American League in favor of New York, complemented the Kid in the middle of the infield.

Boston's superior pitching staff was ultimately the difference in the 1904 pennant race. For the second year in a row the Americans had a trio of 20-game winners, a back-to-back accomplishment matched by the 1904–05 New York Giants that would not be again until the 1951–52 Cleveland Indians. Young threw a career-high 10 shutouts on his way to a 26–16 record; Dinneen, completing every one of his 37 starts, was a 20-game winner for the third straight year; and Jesse Tannehill, acquired from New York in exchange for Hughes, was 21–11. Boston's pitchers combined for the league's lowest earned run average for the third straight year.

Notwithstanding an extraordinary year by Jack Chesbro, pitching was more problematic for the 1904 Highlanders, whose 2.57 team earned run average was fifth in the league. Leaving Pittsburgh for New York in 1903, Chesbro and Tannehill were among the last players to make the jump before the peace settlement between the two leagues put an end to such things. After having thrown 938⅔ innings in his four years with the Pirates, an average of 235 a year, Chesbro worked 779⅓ innings in just his first two years as a Highlander—324⅔ of them in 1903, when he led his new team with 21 wins, and 130 more than that in 1904. Pitching in 55 of the Highlanders' 155 games in 1904 and completing 48 of his 51 starts, Chesbro won 41 and lost only 12 to become the first of only two pitchers to win 40 games since the 60 feet, 6 inches distance from the rubber to the plate was set in 1893. Pitching one-third of his team's innings, Chesbro personally accounted for 45 percent of the Highlanders' 92 victories. Jack Powell, picked up from the St. Louis Browns before the season, worked almost as hard, throwing 390⅓ innings while making 45 starts and posting a 23–19 record. Between them, they started 62 percent of the Highlanders' games and claimed 70 percent of their victories.

New York and Boston dueled fiercely for the top spot in the final two months of the 1904 season in a heated race that had included Griffith's former team in Chicago until the White Sox faltered at the end of August and beginning of September. After August 11, when the Americans trailed the White Sox by 1½ games and the Highlanders were 2½ games behind, both teams played 62 games in the final 60 days of the season, including games that ended in ties because of darkness or weather. The Americans spent 29 days in first place, the Highlanders 21. Neither club was ever more than two games out the rest of the way—Boston twice and New York just once, after a doubleheader loss to Cleveland in late September. Most days began with the two clubs no more than a game ahead or a game behind in the standings.

The pennant-race rivals played each other 11 times in the final four weeks of the 1904 season. Boston won five, New York four, and the two games that ended in a tie because of darkness were replayed. The season came down to both teams playing their last five games against each other. Boston held a half-game lead, meaning whichever club won at least three of the five would win the pennant. Chesbro won the first game in New York to vault the Highlanders into first, after which the series moved to Boston the next day where the Americans won both games of a double-header—clobbering Chesbro in the opener and benefiting from a 1–0 shutout by Young in the nightcap—to take a 1½-game lead. Then it was back to New York for a season-ending doubleheader with the burden on the Highlanders to win both. Although the Highlanders won the second game, that didn't matter because the boys from Boston beat the New Yorkers, 3–2, in the opener on Chesbro's infamous ninth-inning wild pitch to seize the league championship. The Americans, however, were not given an opportunity to defend their World Series honor from the year before because John McGraw refused to allow his National League pennant-winning Giants to play the winner of what he considered to be an inferior league.

By 1905 Jimmy Collins was managing the oldest team in the league. He himself was 35, and Cy Young was 38. In his 16th year, Young had the first losing season of his career at 18–19, although he did not pitch badly; his 1.82 earned run average was third in the league. Seven of Boston's eight position regulars were 30 years or older, and the other—

shortstop Freddy Parent—was 29. The Americans played poorly and were out of the running by June. Despite their lackluster 78–74 fourth-place performance in 1905, Boston still had the best winning percentage of any team in the first five years of the American League's history.

The following year, Collins assumed executive responsibilities for running the ballclub, as if being field manager and his team's star, if not its best player, was not enough to handle. As a player, third baseman Collins was soon out of the lineup with a knee injury. As an executive, Collins was learning on the job (not very well, it turned out), and as a manager, Collins was overmatched in rebuilding mode, became disinterested, and temporarily left his club in midsummer. Boston fell into the American League basement and Collins failed to last out the season as manager even after returning from his sabbatical. It was his last year as a manager, and in 1907 he was traded away. While his teammates on the 1903 and '04 pennant-winning Americans faded away with age, old Cy Young soldiered on. He recovered from his back-to-back losing seasons in '05 and '06 with back-to-back 20-win seasons his last two years in Boston and had an earned run average both years under 2.00.

* * *

Connie Mack's Philadelphia Athletics, meanwhile, had fallen off the table after winning the 1902 pennant, finishing a distant second and then fifth while Boston was winning two in a row. With neither of the 1904 pennant-race finalists in the running the next year, and their earlier core largely intact, the Athletics reemerged as a force in 1905. Leading the league in runs, extra-base hits, and total bases, the Athletics had the most imposing offense in the American League. First baseman Harry Davis topped the league in runs, homers, and runs batted in.

The Athletics' pitching was even more formidable than their hitting. Their 895 strikeouts not only broke the record they had set the previous year, but were 243 more than any other American League team; the Giants, with 760, were the only other major-league club with more than 700 strikeouts. In a year when major-league pitchers averaged 3.9 strikeouts per nine innings, the Athletics had four pitchers strike out more than five for every nine innings of work. Southpaw Rube Waddell's 287 strikeouts were by far the most in baseball, and his ratio of 7.9 Ks every nine innings was likewise the best. With a 27–10 record, Waddell led the league in both wins and winning percentage, and his 1.48 ERA was also the best. Fellow lefty Eddie Plank's 24 wins were second in the league, and his 210 strikeouts second best in the majors. Right-handers Andy Coakley and Chief Bender both won 18 games and also averaged more than five strikeouts per nine innings. While none of the 1905 Athletics' position players are baseball immortals, Waddell, Plank, and Bender are all historically great pitchers enshrined in the Hall of Fame.

Spending most of the first half of the season trailing Cleveland and Chicago, Philadelphia went into first place for good in early August, but still had to fight off the White Sox till the end. Even though both clubs won the same number of games (92), the Athletics had four fewer losses, and therein was their two-game margin of victory for the pennant. They benefited from league rules then in effect that did not require all games that were postponed or ended in ties to be made up. The Athletics were famously upended in the 1905 World Series against the Giants, losing in five games. Christy Mathewson had probably the most dominating pitching performance in World Series history with three complete-game shutouts against them. The Athletics sent 94 men to the plate in the games Mathewson pitched, only 15 of whom reached base, just 13 on hits.

The next year it was the rejuvenated Highlanders battling the White Sox late into the season. With Keeler, Williams, and Elberfeld from their 1904 club still core position players, second-year first baseman Hal Chase leading the team in batting with a .323 average, and Al Orth leading the league with 27 victories to go along with Chesbro's 23 wins, New York finished second, just three games behind Chicago. It turned out to be New York's last best shot at a pennant until the 1920 arrival of Babe Ruth. The Highlanders dropped to fifth in 1907 and were last in 1908. Their 103 losses that year are still the most in "Yankees" franchise history. By then, Clark Griffith, who was brought to New York by Ban Johnson to give the new franchise credibility and, it was hoped, win some championships, was shown the door; Willie Keeler at 36 was near the end of the road; and having pitched more than 1,400 innings in his first four years in New York from 1903 to 1906—nearly 50 percent of his career total innings—Jack Chesbro was burned out and would pitch in only 10 more games before calling it quits in 1909.

Although a single great year is not by itself supposed to merit inclusion in the Hall of Fame, baseball's highest honor—few disagree, for example, that the 61 homers Roger Maris hit in one year and 100 over two years does not a Hall of Fame career make—it does appear that the 41 games won by Jack Chesbro in 1904 is the only reason for *his* eternal residency in Cooperstown. He was a very good pitcher to be sure, but there are lots of very good pitchers not in the Hall of Fame with Chesbro's approximate resume. He did not win 200 games, falling two victories short, and even the years when he was at his best, Chesbro did not stand out in a pitchers' era—except for his one exceptional season in 1904. That was the only year he was in his league's top five in pitching wins above replacement, and he was only second best to Waddell.

The 1906 White Sox that beat out the Highlanders for the pennant were, of course, the famed "Hitless Wonders" who had the worst team batting average and the fewest homers in the American League and then went on to beat the far more formidable Cubs in the World Series. A 19-game winning streak in August that began with the White Sox 7½ games behind in fourth place and ended with them up by 5½ games—a 13-game swing in their fortunes—was decisive in turning their season around, even though they fell out of first place at the beginning of September and spent most of the final weeks playing from behind. Their 19 straight wins was unmatched by any American League club until the 1947 Yankees, and not surpassed as the AL record until nearly a full century later when the 2002 Oakland Athletics won 20 in a row. Although the Hitless Wonders averaged only 3.67 runs per game, in August they scored at a pace of 4.5 runs a game while being extraordinarily stingy, giving up just 44 runs all month. Ten of their 19 consecutive wins were shutouts.

* * *

The next three years—1907 to 1909—belonged to the Detroit Tigers, although all were competitive pennant races. For the first six years of their existence, the Tigers were more housecat than jungle predator. They were never in realistic contention for the pennant and had only two winning seasons. But as early as 1903, three key defectors from the National League had given Detroit the nucleus for a potential contender. The pitching staff was bolstered by George Mullin reneging on a contract he signed with Brooklyn to pitch instead for the Tigers in 1902 and Bill Donovan jumping Brooklyn to play in Detroit in 1903, just two years after his 25 wins were tops in the National League. The two right-handers teamed to give the Tigers a formidable one-two in the rotation, with Mullin having back-to-back 20-win seasons in '05 and '06. Also abandoning the National League for Detroit in 1903 was Cincinnati outfielder Sam Crawford. Although having only three full seasons behind him, which included batting .330 and .333 for the Reds in 1901 and 1902, Crawford quickly became one of the American League's premier players. And in late August 1905, Ty Cobb came to Detroit.

It all came together for the Tigers when Hughie Jennings became manager in 1907 after the club had backslid from third in 1905 to sixth. A teammate of John McGraw's and the star shortstop on the Baltimore Orioles' championship teams of the 1890s, Jennings may have impressed many observers as a loudmouth nuisance for his antics in the third-base coaching box—which famously included his signature "Eee-Yah!" cheer, shrill whistling, and what might have passed for a radical new dance step—but his Orioles pedigree and his club's talents made the Tigers the first American League team to win three consecutive pennants. They also lost three consecutive World Series, but that's beside the point.

At the start of the 1907 season, the 20-year-old Cobb was still a kid feeling his oats after having mixed success in '06 trying to break into the starting lineup. From the beginning, Cobb's personality and fierce ambition proved divisive on the club. It was not just that he was an upstart, self-important kid with a temper, but that the vigor, ferocity, and impetuous creativity with which he played the game was viewed by many veterans on the club as unprofessional. Nonetheless, Ty Cobb emerging as an unyielding force of nature was the catalyst to Detroit's success. Batting .350 in his first year as a core regular, Cobb captured the first of the 12 batting titles he would win in his career—or it might really have been only 11, depending on how one views the controversy that surfaced in more ways than one over whether he *really was* the batting champion in 1910. Cobb also led the league in slugging percentage and on-base plus slugging for the first of six straight years. By now, Cobb's hard-nosed, take-no-prisoners style of play was earning him a reputation as a dirty player he would never live down.

The 1907 Tigers came from 7½ games back in mid-July to join what, by the beginning of September, had become a four-team race also involving the White Sox, Athletics, and the Cleveland team then known as the Naps after Napoleon Lajoie, their star second baseman. Detroit finished 1½ games ahead of Philadelphia, only to be quickly dispatched in the World Series by the far-superior Cubs, four games to none, after the first game ended in a 12-inning tie because of darkness. Cobb was stymied by the Cubs' superior pitching, getting just four hits in 20 at-bats.

Although largely forgotten because of the drama of the Cubs, Giants, and Pirates fighting to the bitter end in the National League, the American League pennant race in 1908 also involved three teams in contention till last call. The Tigers held a 1½-game lead over second-place Cleveland when they arrived in Chicago for their final three games of the season. Going head-to-head in their final series of the season with the Tigers was exactly what the White Sox needed because, although 2½ back in the standings, they still had a shot at the pennant—but only if they could win all three against Detroit. Doc White and Ed Walsh, Chicago's two best pitchers, won the first two games to pull the Sox within a half-game of Detroit. Walsh's victory gave him 40 for the season against 15 losses in 66 games, bringing him within one of Jack Chesbro's 41 wins just four years earlier.

Thus did the American League chapter of the Great '08 Race come down to the final game of the year between Detroit and Chicago. Like the White Sox, the Cleveland Naps were also just a half-game out of first place, but win or lose in their own final game against the St. Louis

Browns, Cleveland could not finish first regardless of the outcome in Chicago. The reason was that the Naps had gotten to play 154 games to a decision, while neither the Tigers nor the White Sox would be required to make up games postponed earlier in the season—one for Detroit and two for Chicago. While a final-day victory by both Chicago and Cleveland would have eliminated the Tigers and left the Naps with the most wins, their 90–64 record would have given them a .584 winning percentage just shy of the .586 winning percentage by virtue of the 89–63 record the White Sox would have had, had they beaten the Tigers. A final-day victory by both Detroit and Cleveland, on the other hand, would have left both teams with 90 wins, but the Tigers would win the pennant with one fewer loss. As it happened, both Detroit and Cleveland *did* win. The final standings show the Tigers in first place by a half-game over the Naps and a game and a half over the White Sox.

Detroit won in 1908 by dominating the league offensively in a pitchers' year. Their team batting average of .263 was 24 percentage points better than the league average (.239) and 18 points higher than the Browns and Red Sox (.245), who tied for second in batting. The Tigers' 1,775 total bases were not only the most in the league, but they were the only team with more than 1,600. Detroit had the top three players in runs, hits, and doubles, and the top four in total bases. Cobb and Crawford were first and second in batting average, and two of only three players in the American League to bat over .300. Their offense was the necessary condition for winning in 1908 because Detroit's pitching staff made little contribution to that pitchers' year. The Tigers were the only team in the majors to give up more than 1,300 hits; opposing teams hit .255 against them when the league batting average was .239. The 1908 World Series proved both the adage that great pitching can stop great hitting and that mediocre pitching can't; the Cubs—who had both great pitching and a potent offense—beat the Tigers again in five games, although this time Detroit actually won a game.

After securing the 1907 pennant with 92 wins and requiring only 90 to win in 1908, Detroit won 98 in '09 to take their third straight pennant by 3½ games over the Philadelphia Athletics, a team on the threshold of a dynasty. Ahead virtually the entire year, the Tigers were paced by Cobb's Triple Crown, another great year at the plate by Crawford, and a terrific year by rookie shortstop Donie Bush. Detroit's pitching was significantly better than the previous year, with Mullin posting a 29–8 record. Ed Willett, in his second full season, won 21, and Ed Summers just missed 20 wins with a 19–8 record. This time Cobb and the Tigers faced off in the World Series against the Pittsburgh Pirates and their star, Honus Wagner—probably still the best player in baseball, even taking into account Cobb's accomplishments. The Series went seven games. The outcome was the same for Detroit—no World Series championship. Wagner played better than Cobb, batting .333 and stealing six bases to Ty's two stolen bases and .231 average.

* * *

Although it would have seemed improbable at the time, the 1909 World Series was the last for Ty Cobb, who was still at the beginning of his career and who, in his first three full years as a regular, had led Detroit to the pennant each time. The Tigers did not plunge to the depths of extended baseball impoverishment and were rarely a bad team for the remainder of Cobb's career with them, but it would not be until 1934—25 years later—that they returned to the fall classic. Hughie Jennings's 14 years as Detroit's manager that began with three straight pennants ended in 1920 with him never winning another. His next-to-last "Eee-Yah!" came in 1915 when, after a pair of sixth-place endings and finishing fourth in 1914, he unexpectedly brought Detroit back into the thick of the American League pennant race and managed his team to 100 wins. That was only good enough for second place, however, 2½ games off Boston's pace, making Detroit one of only eight teams in history—four in each league—to win 100 games and *not* make it into the postseason.

Sam Crawford, now in his mid-30s, had his last outstanding season in 1915, leading the league with 19 triples—baseball's true power currency before the Babe—for the third straight year and the sixth time in his career. He also led the league in RBIs. As right fielder Crawford was entering his twilight years, left fielder Bobby Veach, in just his third year, was entering his prime. Veach led the league in doubles and matched Crawford for the league lead in RBIs. The Tigers also had a pair of 20-game winners in Hooks Dauss (24–13) and Harry Coveleski (22–13). The left-handed older brother of Stan Coveleski, a righty who made the Hall of Fame, Harry was in the middle of three straight 20-win seasons in which his pitching 940⅓ innings took such a toll on his arm that his career was essentially over less than two years later.

But the star of the Detroit Tigers' 1915 show was none else but Ty Cobb. Most famously, this was the year Cobb set a post-1900 major-league record for stolen bases with 96 that would stand for 47 years until Maury Wills swiped 102 in 1962. (Wills had only 93 in his team's first 154 games, but there was not much ado about his having the benefit of an eight-games-longer schedule in which to break the record the way there was about Roger Maris eclipsing Babe Ruth's 60 home runs the previous year.) Cobb was also caught 38 times, giving him a stolen-base success rate of 72 percent—not quite up to the over-80-percent level of elite base stealers in today's Major League Baseball. Cobb's .369 batting average in 1915 was good for at least his fifth, or perhaps his ninth, consecutive batting title, depending on how one views the 1910 controversy. Either way, he broke the record of four straight set by Wagner from 1906 to 1909. Cobb's string of batting titles, however long, included back-to-back .400 seasons in 1911 (.420) and 1912 (.409).

By most accounts, including Major League Baseball's official record book, Cobb won nine batting titles in a row between 1907 and 1915, but it is now indisputable that his *official* .385 to .384 advantage over Napoleon Lajoie in 1910 double-counted a game in which he went 2-for-3, meaning he actually hit .383 to Lajoie's .384. The issue is further muddied by the fact that the St. Louis Browns conspired to let Lajoie win the batting title in a doubleheader on the final day of the season by playing their third baseman back on the outfield grass, allowing the widely despised (even hated) Cobb's much-better-liked Cleveland rival to dump seven bunt singles onto the infield grass among eight hits for the day. Plus, Cobb sat out the final two games of the 1910 season in an effort to preserve his lead. The Browns' manager and a coach were permanently banned from baseball by American League president Ban Johnson for their action on behalf of Lajoie. Cobb died believing he had won nine batting titles in a row, and 12 overall, because the clerical error was not discovered—or perhaps not acknowledged—till after his death. It would be a matter of some significance to the ultracompetitive Cobb, however, because if his 1910 title does not count, then Rogers Hornsby would hold the record for most consecutive batting titles with six in the National League from 1920 to 1925. Either way, Ty Cobb still holds the record for most batting championships in a career.

Jennings's last "Eee-Yah!" came in 1916. The Tigers fought from fourth place and seven games behind in mid-August into first place three weeks later. With just 11 games left on Detroit's schedule, they were tied at the top with Boston when the Red Sox came to town for a three-game series. The Red Sox swept the three games, limiting the Tigers to just six runs, effectively ending what proved to be Detroit's last serious bid for a pennant for nearly two decades.

Generating offense was rarely a problem for the Tigers in Cobb's remaining 16 years in Detroit following their three straight pennants. One year after his consecutive batting titles streak was halted at nine (officially), or perhaps just five, Cobb reeled off three more consecutive batting championships from 1917 to 1919, giving him a final total of 11 (or 12) for his career. But tyrannical Ty had close seconds in 1921 (.389 to teammate Harry Heilmann's .394) and 1922 (.401 to George Sisler's .420). Cobb's third .400 season in 1922 brought his career batting average to a high of .373. By now Cobb was also the manager, having replaced Jennings in 1921. Cobb's run in Detroit ended in 1926 amid allegations he was involved in a betting-on-baseball escapade seven years before.

Cobb was cleared by the commissioner and played two more years for the Philadelphia Athletics before leaving the game with a lifetime .367 batting average and 4,191 hits, until two were taken away as a result of that double-counting in 1910, leaving him with 4,189. Exactly 3,900 of those hits—not including any double-counting—came in Ty Cobb's 22 years in Detroit, for whom he hit .368 in 2,806 games.

Another in a long line of terrific Detroit outfielders, and one of baseball's best pure hitters in the 1920s, Harry Heilmann is perhaps best known for the oddity of winning four batting titles, one every odd-numbered year between 1921 and 1927, never with an average lower than .393. Not that his even-numbered years should be considered off years; Heilmann was never below .346 in any of the between years. Heilmann's .403 mark to win the 1923 crown was the last time an American League batter would hit .400 until Ted Williams in 1941, although "Slug," as he was also known for his batting prowess, fell exactly one hit short of a second .400 season when his .398 average led the league in 1927. That capped a stretch of seven years in which he averaged .380.

Pitching was a fundamental problem for Detroit throughout the Cobb era. Even when they competed for the pennant in 1915 and '16, the Tigers were in the bottom half of the league in giving up runs. Hooks Dauss was Detroit's only pitcher of lasting consequence in the 20 years between 1910 and 1930, but he was rarely among the league's best pitchers. His 21 victories in both 1919 and 1923 were the only times a Tigers pitcher won 20 games between Harry Coveleski in 1916 and Schoolboy Rowe and Tommy Bridges in 1934—the year Detroit finally got back to the World Series.

3

NATIONAL LEAGUE RUNAWAYS AND THE GREAT '08 RACE

In contrast to the American League's competitive pennant races in the first decade of Major League Baseball's so-called modern era, the National League was dominated by three teams that jockeyed for the top spot and, sequentially and with some overlap, won every NL pennant between 1901 and 1913. The Pittsburgh Pirates won the first three and the New York Giants the next two with little difficulty. But it was the Chicago Cubs who were the dominant team in all of Major League Baseball, with four National League flags and two World Series championships between 1906 and 1910. The Pirates won their fourth pennant and first World Series in 1909. There were no other teams in the National League that were remotely as competitive. Boston and St. Louis crossed the .500 plateau just twice those 13 years, and Boston not once after 1902. And only one National League pennant race, famously in 1908, was close. All the others were blowouts by historically outstanding teams. The Pirates were the only major-league team not to have a losing record between 1901 and 1910. Pittsburgh averaged nearly 95 wins and only twice, in 1904 and 1910, failed to win 90. Honus Wagner at shortstop, left fielder Fred Clarke as player-manager, and Tommy Leach, who played third base and the outfield, were the Pirates' cornerstone players for the entire decade.

The foundation for Pittsburgh's success was the competitive corruption in baseball inherent in syndicated ownership and the National League's decision in 1900 to contract from 12 to eight clubs. Until then, the Pirates had been at best a second-rate team that began in 1882 under the nickname "Alleghenys" as an original franchise of the American Association and switched allegiances to the National League in 1888. The

Alleghenys became the "Pirates" in 1891—taking prideful liking to a smear—when they were accused of behaving as such by pilfering a player whose team inadvertently failed to "reserve" his contract after the collapse of the Players' League, to which he had defected along with countless other big-leaguers in 1890. Having just finished the 1890 season with a 23–113 record for the second-worst winning percentage in any major-league season exceeding 100 games—only the 1899 Cleveland Spiders (20–134), denuded of all their best players by syndicate ownership, were worse—it was perhaps understandable if Pittsburgh resorted to an unseemly raid on an exposed high-value asset in an effort to improve a terrible team. The Pirates were neither competitive nor terrible the rest of the 1890s, generally finishing middle of the pack.

Meanwhile, persistently near the bottom of the standings since joining the National League when its parent league—the American Association—disbanded in 1892, and one of the weakest draws when it came to attendance (probably not helped by being less than 100 miles from Cincinnati, one of the league's highest-drawing teams), were the Louisville Colonels. When it became apparent to Colonels owner Barney Dreyfuss that his club was a prime candidate to be dumped once the National League decided to eliminate four franchises, he bought into the Pirates and immediately proceeded to transfer Louisville's best players to Pittsburgh in lopsided trades. And Louisville had some very good players. The most notable were the versatile Wagner, who played all over the field before settling in at shortstop in 1903, and Clarke, who was named player-manager of the Colonels in 1897 at the age of only 24. Both were already acknowledged to be great players. Fred Clarke slid seamlessly into both his outfield and manager positions in Pittsburgh, and Honus Wagner wasted little time establishing himself in the top tier of the greatest players in baseball history. Anyone who was any good still in Louisville when the Colonels were downsized out of major-league existence was assigned to Pittsburgh. The Louisville Colonels would live on in the high minor leagues.

The arrivals of Wagner, Clarke, Leach, second baseman Claude Ritchey, and pitcher Deacon Phillippe from Louisville in 1900 instantly made the Pirates, who were not competitive in the years preceding contraction, one of the best teams in baseball. Pittsburgh went from seventh in a 12-team league in 1899, just two games ahead of the Colonels, to second place behind Brooklyn, then an emerging power. Paced by their core five Colonels from Louisville, the Pirates won the next three National League pennants by comfortable 7½-, 27½-, and 6½-game margins. The Pirates so dominated the National League from 1901 to 1903 that they rarely were not in first place. In each of their pennant-winning seasons, Pittsburgh was at the top of the NL heap to stay by the Fourth of July, and for all practical purposes all three pennant races were decided by September. The Pirates' 103–36 record in 1902, when the schedule was only 140 games, remains the major leagues' second-best winning percentage since the start of the twentieth century after the 1906 Cubs.

Being able to integrate Louisville's best players was an enormous benefit for Pittsburgh. Although the Pirates probably would have had the NL's best team regardless, the National League was a relatively weak league all around when they won their three straight pennants because of the impact of star-player defections. Indeed, through the first two decades of the twentieth century (and of the upstart American League)—the "Deadball Era" from 1901 to 1919—just one of the eight major-league position players to have at least 30 wins above replacement over any five-year period played in the National League. His name—Honus Wagner, whose 49 wins above replacement from 1905 to 1909 was the most of any the major-league position player in the Deadball Era. Ty Cobb, in his five best consecutive years from 1909 to 1913, had a player value marginally below Wagner's with 47.6 wins above replacement.

The Pirates suffered far less than other NL teams when the AL enticed star players to leave for bigger paychecks. The NL's other would-be contenders were forced to rebuild to compensate for the stars they lost, and the teams that had been less competitive to begin with took far longer to recover from their player defections. The 1899 and 1900 defending NL champion Brooklyn Superbas (for whom the nickname "Dodgers" would not be their regular calling card until the 1930s) were particularly hard hit, losing their ace Joe McGinnity (28–8 in 1900), center fielder Fielder Jones, and third baseman Lave Cross in 1901 and falling to third. In 1903 the Superbas lost another top pitcher, Bill Donovan, and star outfielder Willie Keeler abandoned Brooklyn for Manhattan to join the new High-landers team. The Pirates' core regulars, by contrast—Wagner, Clarke, Leach, Ritchey, and center fielder Ginger Beaumont—stayed in Pittsburgh, whatever the AL temptations that came their way.

It's not entirely true that the Pirates were not hurt by player defections. Just not right away. The Pirates did lose promising young third baseman Jimmy Williams in 1901, but Williams had only two years of experience and was easily replaced at third by Tommy Leach. More difficult to overcome were the defections of two of the Pirates' three 20-game win-ners in 1902—Jack Chesbro, whose 28–6 record was the best in the National League, and Jesse Tannehill, who was 20–6. Both were enticed by bigger bucks to leave Pittsburgh and pitch for the new American League team in New York City. Too late for Pittsburgh was the 1903 agreement between the two leagues that put an end to such talent raids and established the two-league structure that adheres to this day. Al-though Pittsburgh won again in 1903, the defections of Chesbro and

Tannehill caused the sands to shift from under Pittsburgh's command of the National League and paved the way for the emergence of John McGraw's would-be New York dynasty.

* * *

On the heels of Pittsburgh's three in a row from 1901 to 1903, the New York Giants were the National League's next outstanding team. This was the beginning of baseball's "Napoleonic Wars" occasioned by McGraw's fierce determination to win at all costs. He took over an abysmal franchise when he abandoned the American League team he was managing in July 1902 to come to New York and built it into baseball's first extended-generational dynasty.

For New Yorkers, it had been a long time since the Giants won back-to-back National League pennants in 1888 and '89, which they followed up both years by winning lengthy unofficial postseason exhibitions against the American Association pennant winners. Their star players then included Hall of Famers Buck Ewing, Roger Connor, Tim Keefe, and Mickey Welch. Ewing was considered baseball's best catcher at least until the arrivals of Mickey Cochrane and Gabby Hartnett in the 1920s; Connor was overshadowed by contemporary first baseman Cap Anson; Welch won 307 major-league games and Keefe won 342, both mostly in the 1880s *before* the present distance of 60 feet, 6 inches was set from the pitching rubber to home plate.

New York's time at the top of the baseball world came to an abrupt end in 1890 when Connor, Ewing, Keefe, and others defected to the short-lived Players' League. Although they did finish second in 1894 and third in 1897, the Giants spent most of the 1890s in the bottom half of the league. Their two best players were both future Hall of Famers—shortstop George Davis and pitcher Amos Rusie. Coming to New York in 1893, Davis blossomed into a star with the Giants and was surpassed in shortstop stature only by the Orioles' Hughie Jennings. The hard-throwing right-handed Rusie won 234 games, never failed to win at least 20, had four straight 30-win seasons, and led the league in strikeouts five times. The fear factor from the speed of his fastball and lack of control—Rusie averaged nearly 4.4 walks every nine innings and led the league in bases on balls five straight years from 1890 to 1894—was a major impetus for moving the pitcher's rubber farther from the plate. With Rusie sitting out both the 1899 and 1900 seasons because of arm trouble and contract disputes, Davis was the Giants' only outstanding player as the centuries turned, and in 1902 he jumped leagues to play for the Chicago White Sox. The New York Giants by now were one of the worst teams in baseball, in part because principal owner Andrew Freedman had decided in 1899 not to field competitive teams just to spite fellow National League owners who despised his arrogance and overbearing attitude.

The Giants seemed hopeless when McGraw arrived to take charge in July 1902. They had lost 27 of their previous 32 games. In part bolstered by players McGraw brought with him from Baltimore, the Giants played better the rest of the way in 1902, but still had the third-worst record in the league after his arrival. They ended up last, a very distant 53½ games behind the Pirates, with 40 more losses than victories. While they no longer had either Davis or Rusie, the Giants did have a priceless asset in right-hander Christy Mathewson, acquired from Cincinnati in exchange for Rusie—a deal no doubt facilitated by virtue of syndicated ownership, Brush at the time being the majority owner of the Reds in addition to his smaller stake in the Giants. Mathewson won 20 games for the Giants as a rookie in 1901 for a team that had just 52 victories, and was their only pitcher with a winning record that year.

Having brought Joe McGinnity—an elite pitcher—the versatile Roger Bresnahan, and first baseman Dan McGann with him from Baltimore in 1902, McGraw wasted little time in turning the Giants into a powerhouse. With the stingiest pitching in the league, the Giants improved from 48 wins to 84 in 1903 and finished second, 6½ games behind the Pirates. McGinnity had the first of back-to-back 30-win seasons with a 31–20 record, and Mathewson's 30–13 mark was his first of three straight 30-win years. The Giants also became a far more formidable offensive club in their first full year under McGraw. Bresnahan, playing mostly in center field, hit .350, just five percentage points behind league leader Honus Wagner, and left fielder Sam Mertes, who McGraw had enticed to defect the other way from the American League, led the league with 104 runs batted in.

The Giants made their push for greatness the next year when McGraw acquired Bill Dahlen from Brooklyn to play shortstop and Art Devlin, a rookie, took over at third base. In August, the Giants obtained six-year veteran outfielder Mike Donlin from the Reds. Dahlen, Devlin, and Bresnahan were clutch players and more valuable to McGraw, however, if for no other reason than they were tough, resilient, and quintessential team players, whereas Donlin was a bit of a prima donna who loved theater and vaudeville, married a Broadway actress, and sat out the 1907 season in a salary dispute while performing on the vaudeville circuit with his wife.

With newcomers Dahlen, Devlin, and Donlin, Bresnahan in center field in 1904 and catching in 1905, and pitchers Mathewson and McGinnity as McGraw's cornerstone players, the Giants won 106 games in 1904 and 105 in '05—the first two seasons the major leagues played a 154-game schedule. They ran away with the pennant both years, winning by 13 games over the second-place Cubs in 1904 and by nine games over the runner-up Pirates in 1905. In both years, the Giants had three pitchers win at least 20 games, something no National League club has done since. Mathewson was 33–12, McGinnity 35–8, and Dummy Taylor 21–15 in 1904, and in 1905 it was Mathewson at 31–9, McGinnity with a 21–15 record, and Red Ames was 22–8.

While McGraw and the Giants refused in advance to play the upstart American League pennant winner in any kind of "World Series" in 1904, unlike the Pirates the previous year, they got into the spirit of the new major-league structure in 1905. It surely satiated the revenge-is-sweet aspect of McGraw's competitive juices that his Giants wiped out Connie Mack's Philadelphia Athletics in five games in the World Series that year, particularly since it was expected to be closely fought. Pitching every other game and coming through with three complete-game shut-outs, Christy Mathewson cemented his good fortune and fame.

With both the 1904 and 1905 pennant races locked up by mid-July, there was little reason to believe the Giants would not continue to domi-nate the National League. McGraw was looking forward to his Giants always being the team to beat. They followed up their 1905 championship season with 96 victories, but as impressive as 96 wins are, that was still 20 fewer than the 1906 Chicago Cubs. Donlin's preference for show business over baseball (it was about the money), and the age-related declining performances of 37-year-old shortstop Dahlen and 36-year-old right-hander McGinnity, were not helpful to McGraw in 1907, as his team crumbled into fourth place with 25 fewer victories than the Cubs.

* * *

Now it was Chicago's turn to dominate the National League. For five years—1906 to 1910—the Chicago Cubs were the best team in baseball. They won four of the next five pennants, three by double-digit blowout margins. They won nearly 70 percent of their games. They did so having to face off against New York and Pittsburgh, both clubs winning 90 games four times in those five years, which is typically a benchmark for pennant contention. The Pirates and Giants were in fact the two other best teams in baseball. The 1906–10 Cubs played 23 percent of their games against 90-win Pittsburgh and New York pennant-race rivals, and won 56 percent of them. Chicago won 100 games four times, including 1909 when they did not win the pennant.

Indicative of a dynasty, the Cubs had remarkable stability among their core regulars. The infield with player-manager Frank Chance at first base, Johnny Evers at second, Joe Tinker at short, Harry Steinfeldt at third, and Johnny Kling behind the plate was the best in baseball and held together all five years, except for 1909 when Kling quit the team to focus on an outside business venture before returning the next year. Jimmy Sheckard in left and Frank "Wildfire" Schulte in right were regulars in the outfield all five years. Jimmy Slagle was the center fielder until he retired after the 1908 season and was replaced by Solly Hofman, who could play anywhere in the infield or outfield. Mordecai "Three Finger" Brown, Ed Reulbach, Orval Overall, and Jack Pfiester were the heart of the best overall pitching staff in Major League Baseball.

The Cubs kick-started their five-year dynasty in 1906 with 116 wins—still the major-league record—earning Chance accolades around Chicago town as the "Peerless Leader." Reulbach with a 19–4 record and Brown at 26–6 had the two best winning percentages among major-league pitchers. The season started off as a battle for supremacy between the Giants and Cubs, which lasted only till the end of May. After losing both games of a doubleheader on May 30, the Cubs went more than seven weeks before the next time they lost two in a row. They were now four games ahead of Pittsburgh and 6½ over New York. They were on a pace to win 105 games. And then they really got hot. From July 24 until the end of the season the unstoppable Cubs lost only eight games, never more than one at a time, while winning 55 to establish the highest single-season winning percentage (.763) of any team in modern baseball history. Including their back-to-back losses in July, Chance's "peerless" Cubs went 88–21 (.807) after their doubleheader loss on May 30. They did not lose two in a row again after July until the worst possible time—Games Five and Six to the White Sox in the 1906 fall classic, which cost them the only all-Chicago World Series in history.

The Cubs made it two pennants in a row in 1907 with 107 wins to finish a comfortable 17 games ahead of second-place Pittsburgh. They took over first place for good on May 28, and on July 4 already held an insurmountable 11½-game lead. All five of Chicago's principal starters had earned runs averages under 1.70. Pfiester, Carl Lundgren, and Brown had the three best ERAs in the league, and Reulbach (17–4), Brown (20–6), and Overall (23–7) had the three best winning percentages in the National League. The Cubs beat the Tigers handily in the World Series.

In 1908, they won what many baseball historians still consider the greatest pennant race of all time by one game over both their archrivals in New York and Pittsburgh as a result of one of the most controversial games in history. This was the only year of the five that the Cubs failed to win 100 games; they won 99. Reulbach with a 24–7 record led National League pitchers in winning percentage for the third straight year. He was third in wins behind Brown (29–9), who won eight fewer than Mathewson. Tinker was the second-best player in the National League after Wagner, based on the WAR metric, and had the best defensive WAR in baseball. Evers batted an even .300, the fifth-best average in the league in what was very much a pitchers' year. Once again, the Cubs had little difficulty dispatching Detroit in the World Series.

The Cubs boosted their victory total back over 100 to 104 in 1909, but that, for once, was not good enough to win the pennant because the Pirates won 110 to finish 6½ games ahead of them. In 236 pennant races in the two major leagues from 1901 to 1993 before the wild-card format went into effect, when finishing first was an ironclad requirement to advance to the postseason, only eight of the 70 clubs that won 100 games did not finish on top of the standings in their league or division and went home for the winter. The 1909 Chicago Cubs were the first of those teams.

Chicago won 104 again in 1910, which this time was more than enough to secure the pennant. The 1910 Cubs were the inspiration for the Franklin Pierce Adams ode to that "trio of bear cubs"—Tinker-to-Evers-to-Chance—the best known, even if not the most literary, of baseball poetry. Ironically, Chance played only 88 games at first base that year. Suitably titled "Baseball's Sad Lexicon," Adams's prose was printed in the *New York Evening Mail* on July 10, when the Giants were in Chicago, trailing the Cubs by only 1½ games, but with the writing perhaps apparent on the wall. Although the Giants won that day to close within half a game, their loss to the Cubs the next day was the first of five straight defeats, and nine losses in 12 games, that effectively finished them for the season and allowed the Cubs to cruise thereafter to their fourth pennant in five years. They were no match for the Philadelphia Athletics in the World Series. It had now been two years since Chicago's Cubs were last champions of the baseball world.

The only tough time the Cubs had winning the pennant and, for that matter, the only National League pennant race in the first decade of the twentieth century that was not a foregone conclusion by mid-September, was the taut three-team race involving the Cubs, Pirates, and Giants in 1908 that went down to the final day—and then one—because Chicago got a do-over on the outcome of the Merkle game. The story of the Great '08 Race is well known and has been told very well several times. It made an otherwise nondescript player named Fred Merkle, then at the beginning of his career, an infamous (and increasingly sympathetic) figure in baseball history, never to be forgotten.

The Giants rebounded from their disappointing 1907 season to win 98 games in 1908, only to lose the pennant to Chicago on an end-of-season makeup game necessitated by Merkle's "boner" in the bottom of the ninth on September 23 at the Polo Grounds in New York City, causing millions of New Yorkers to ask, how could you not win a game that you actually won?

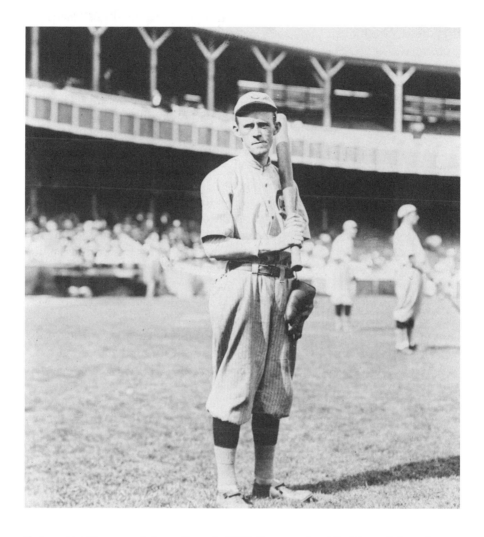

Cubs second baseman Johnny Evers in 1910, the year Franklin Pierce Adams immortalized his name with the words "These are the saddest of possible words, Tinker to Evers to Chance." *George Grantham Bain Collection (Library of Congress).*

The answer? By young Merkle, all of 19 years old, inexperienced, and in the game because the Giants' regular first baseman was unable to play, failing to complete his journey of 90 feet from first to second base after the winning run scored on the presumed walk-off game-winning hit, of course.

It was a rookie mistake that apparently was not all that uncommon in those early-century days, even by veteran players, at least according to historical accounts. With fans storming the playing field after walk-off hits, players had a survivalist interest in leaving the field posthaste lest they be mobbed, even if by their deliriously happy home crowd. Heady Cubs players, however, most notably Johnny Evers, demanded of the umpires that the rules are the rules and should be enforced, and the unfortunate Merkle was called out. By this time, New York's fan(atic)s had swamped the field, preventing the game from continuing. The National League president decreed that the game would be replayed at the end of the season only if the two teams were tied for first.

As fate would have it, the pennant rested on the outcome of that one game, and with the Giants and Cubs tied for first when the regular season officially ended, the Merkle game had to be replayed. The rest is history. The Cubs won the replayed game to win the pennant and went on to win the World Series. Fred Merkle went on to have a decent career. John McGraw went on to win more pennants than any other manager in National League history. And the Cubs did not win another World Series for more than a century—108 years, to be exact—perhaps Merkle's curse for what he had to endure.

Up on the mound, no more could possibly have been asked of Mathewson by the Giants than what he gave. In addition to leading the league with 37 wins against just 11 losses, Matty had the lowest earned run average (1.43), pitched in the most games (56) and started the most games (44), threw more complete games (34) and shutouts (11) than anyone else, and saved five of the nine games he finished in relief. In 390⅔ innings, also tops in the league, Mathewson walked just 42 batters and led the league in strikeouts for the fifth time with 259. With McGinnity a whisper of his former self, southpaw Hooks Wiltse (24–13) was the only other Giants pitcher of any consequence that year. But the National League pennant was not to be for the Giants in 1908.

Neither was it to be for the Pittsburgh Pirates, who also won 98 games, their most since 1902, for their highest winning percentage since the schedule was bumped to 154 games five years earlier. The Pirates had successfully transitioned from the team that won three straight pennants between 1901 and 1903, thanks to three foundation players from those pennants—Wagner, Fred Clarke, and Tommy Leach—still there to continue Pittsburgh's winning ways. Honus Wagner was at his best, winning four consecutive batting titles between 1906 and 1909 and leading the league in doubles all four years, on-base percentage and slugging percentage three times each, runs batted in twice, and stolen bases twice—all while playing an exemplary shortstop. Clarke, still player-manager, was the National League's second-best player after Wagner from 1907 to 1909, based on his cumulative wins above replacement. Leach, having the three best years of his career, was not far behind.

The Pirates' pitching staff was, if anything, better in the second half of the decade than when they won three straight pennants to begin the new century. Their ace was veteran right-hander Vic Willis, whose Hall of Fame career went back to 1898 and the last pennant won by the great Boston Beaneaters of the 1890s. By 1902, when the Beaneaters finished a distant third behind the Pirates, he had won 20 four times in five years, including 27 wins in both 1899 and 1902, but then was forced to endure three straight losing seasons—including leading the league with 25 and 29 losses in '04 and '05—pitching for terrible Boston clubs that lost two-thirds of their games. Finally rescued when the always-competitive Pirates traded for him in 1906, and pitching once again for a winning ballclub, Willis returned to prominence as a top-tier pitcher by putting together four consecutive 20-win seasons, including 23–11 in 1908. Second-year pitcher Nick Maddox also won 23 for the '08 Pirates, and Howie Camnitz, in his third year, was 16–9.

* * *

At the close of play on America's 132nd birthday—July 4, 1908—only a game and a half separated the first-place Cubs from the third-place Giants. The Pirates were second, a half-game behind, but it was they who spent most of July and August on top, although never by a comfortable margin. The Giants, for their part, were the team with the hot hand going into September. McGraw had his team surging since a sluggish start that put them in a 6½-game hole with a .500 record in mid-June. Going into Chicago for three games at the end of August having just swept the Pirates four straight in Pittsburgh, the Giants were poised to break open the pennant race. They had won eight in a row and held a 3½-game lead. But now the Cubs were again playing well. The Cubs swept the Giants, and when the season turned to September, New York and Chicago were nominally tied for first with Pittsburgh a half-game behind.

Chicago began September with a 14–6 surge, and Pittsburgh was nearly just as good at 15–7. The Giants, however, recovering from being swept in Chicago, won 18 of 19 games to grab a 4½-game lead over the Cubs on September 18. Following their doubleheader loss to the Giants at the Polo Grounds on that day, the Pirates were now five back. That was as far behind as Pittsburgh had been since trailing by four games in mid-June. It was, in fact, their largest deficit of the season, and with only 15 games remaining, it seemed improbable the Pirates could overtake the Giants. And with only 16 games remaining for the Cubs, even the never-say-die Evers was thinking that 4½ games back was too large a margin to overcome and that his team's chances of winning a third straight pennant were effectively over.

Then the Giants went into a tailspin that made it a nailbiter of a pennant race once again. It began with the Giants losing their next two games at home to the Pirates and the two games after that when the Cubs came into the Polo Grounds. It seemed their four-game skid came to an end the next day against the Cubs, except for the part about Merkle forgetting to touch second base. Now it was their rivals' turn to get hot. The Cubs won 12 of their next 14 games, and the Pirates were even better, winning 13 of 14 to take over first place and bring a half-game lead over Chicago (and a 1½-game lead over New York) into their final game of the regular season. At this point, depending on whether the Merkle game would need to be replayed, the Pirates and Cubs both had one game left—against each other in Chicago—and the Giants had three at home against Boston, a bad team safely ensconced in sixth place.

There were three possible outcomes predicated on the fact that the rules at the time did not require games that ended in a tie to be replayed even if the outcome would have a direct bearing on the pennant race. The Pirates could win the pennant outright by beating Chicago. They had 98 wins and the Cubs had 97, but because both had 55 losses, whichever team lost its 56th game in their season-finale matchup would be eliminated from contention. Should the Pirates win their 99th game, they would clinch the pennant regardless of what New York did the next three days because the Giants, with a 95–55 record, could win at most 98 games if they swept Boston. In this case, Pittsburgh's pennant-winning margin of victory would be a half-game over Chicago and possibly also New York. Alternately, a Cubs victory over the Pirates would secure them the pennant by a half-game over Pittsburgh should the Giants lose any of their games against Boston. *Only if* Chicago beat Pittsburgh *and* New York swept Boston, leaving the Giants and Cubs with identical 98–55 records, would the Merkle game be replayed, and that's exactly what happened. Three Finger Brown outdueled Vic Willis, officially eliminating the Pirates, and the Cubs had to await the outcome of New York's could-be final games the next three days. The Giants won all three, the Cubs returned to the scene of the Merkle crime, and Brown, entering the game in relief in the very first inning, beat Mathewson to give the Chicago Cubs their third straight National League pennant.

Ending in failure, the 1908 season was the end of the line for the would-be dynasty John McGraw had been building since defecting from the American League to come to New York. In the five years from 1904 to 1908, the Giants averaged 97 wins a year—even taking into account that they won only 82 in 1907. Their dominance in '04 and '05 put the Giants on the threshold of a dynasty that would have rivaled that of the contemporary Chicago Cubs. Instead of winning the 1908 pennant to cement that legacy, McGraw had to endure Chance and the Cubs ending that dream with a more dominating and longer-lasting one of their own. Of the team's star players from the 1904 and 1905 pennants, only Christy Mathewson remained after 1908. He and second baseman Larry Doyle, in only his second year in 1908, were the foundation for the team McGraw rebuilt that would succeed Chicago in seizing a stranglehold on first place after 1910, winning three straight pennants.

* * *

As for the Pirates, they left nothing to chance in 1909. Even though the Cubs followed their 1908 National League and World Series championships by winning 104 games, the Pirates outdid them by 6½ games with a 110–42 record and were 18½ games better than the third-place Giants, whose 92 victories were hardly an embarrassment. The Pirates also celebrated the opening of their new ballpark—one of baseball's first "modern" stadiums—which would not be named for team owner Barney Dreyfuss who financed the project, as was the practice, but instead be called Forbes Field in honor of the British general whose forces liberated the strategically located outpost that would be renamed "Pittsburgh" in one of the decisive battles that turned the French and Indian War in favor of the British colonies in America. In their postseason skirmish with the Tigers of Detroit, it was three victories by rookie right-hander Babe Adams, who had only 30 games of big-league experience to call upon, that proved decisive in turning the World Series in favor of the Pirates from Pittsburgh.

Even at 35, Honus Wagner was by far the best position player in the National League in 1909. His .339 batting average led the league for the fourth consecutive year. Fred Clarke, who was even older at 36, had the second-best season of his career as measured by WAR, his best having come as a 24-year-old playing for Louisville back in 1897, his first year as a playing manager. After having caught 143 games in 1908, an unprecedented feat in an era when a catcher's protective armor was rudimentary at best, George Gibson, now in his fifth year, continued his "iron man" act by catching 150 of Pittsburgh's 154 games in 1909. He not only threw out 53 percent of the runners who tried to steal on the Pirates, but hit a robust (for a catcher) .265. Camnitz won 25 and Willis 22.

Only four teams since have matched the '09 Pirates' 110 wins—the iconic 1927 Yankees, also with 110; the 111-win 1954 Cleveland Indians; the 1998 Yankees with 114 victories; and the 2001 Seattle Mariners, whose 116-win season proved to be an anomaly and is basically forgotten. Pittsburgh's .724 winning percentage in 1909 remains the third highest in modern history, after the 1906 Cubs, and their own .741 mark in 1902 (when the schedule was 140 games), and ahead of the 1927 Yankees and 1954 Indians, both of whom played all 154 games on their schedule, and the 1998 Yankees and 2001 Mariners, who played 162-game schedules. Lacking the depth their rivals in Chicago and New York had in quality players, however, especially with Wagner and Clarke nearing the end of their playing careers, the Pirates faded rapidly from prominence. After their 1909 triumphs, it would be more than a decade before they were seriously competitive again, and they did not return to the World Series until 1925, the equivalent of about two players' generations in the context of career longevity.

Honus Wagner won his eighth and final batting title in 1911. He retired after the 1917 season having been every bit as dominant in his era as Babe Ruth would become in a few short years. In the first decade of the twentieth century, Wagner led his league in every meaningful offensive category. He had the highest batting average, scored the most runs, had the most hits, most home runs, most runs batted in, and most stolen bases. Except for the home runs—this was the Deadball Era, after all—his totals in all those categories stack up among the best of any player in any era. And Wagner did all this at a time when pitchers were clearly dominant over hitters. Moreover, Wagner was consistently very good. He never had a bad year. There was not a single season between 1899 and 1912 that his player value was below the five wins above replacement standard considered to be an all-star-level quality of performance. From 1901 to 1909, Wagner's annual player value was always at least seven wins above replacement, and for six consecutive years—1904 to 1909—never fewer than eight wins above replacement, the benchmark for an MVP-level of performance. He may not have revolutionized the game the way Ruth did, which by itself makes the Babe the *greatest* ever to play the game, but given that he played a much more demanding and defensively important position—shortstop—played it very well, and by all accounts is considered even today to have been one of the very best defensive shortstops to ever take the field, whereas Ruth was a good-enough but not great defensive outfielder, it would not be unreasonable to argue that Honus Wagner, and not Babe Ruth, was the *best* baseball player ever. (Willie Mays is legitimately in that argument, too.)

Fred Clarke retired as a player after the 1911 season, but continued on as manager until 1915. Based on longevity and performance—both his own as a player and the records of the teams he managed—Clarke was probably the most successful player-manager in baseball history. Including three years leading Louisville's Colonels, Clarke was a playing manager for 15 major-league seasons. In his 12 years as player-manager in Pittsburgh, the Pirates won four pennants, had a .622 winning percentage—the equivalent of 96 wins in a 154-game season—and never once had a losing record, while he personally batted exactly .300. Clarke stepped aside as a player after 1911 despite having hit .324 that year, his highest average since batting .351 in 1903, in part because he was about to celebrate his 39th birthday, but also because Max Carey had a promising rookie season in 1911 and represented for the future Pirates what Clarke had been in the past—a premier player, if not quite a superstar.

For the rest of the decade, Max Carey was the only position regular on the Pirates of historical, or even contemporary, consequence. He led the National League in stolen bases five times in six years between 1913 and 1918, averaging more than 50 per year. Although he was already in his 30s when the Lively Ball Era kicked in around 1920, Carey took advantage by becoming a consistent .300 hitter in his concluding years with the Pirates, including batting a career-high .343 in 1925 when Pittsburgh finally won another National League pennant. He also kept up with the running game, averaging 49 stolen bases and leading both leagues every year from 1922 to 1925.

The Pirates' pitching during their lean teen years was insufficient to compensate for their offensive deficiencies. Their best pitcher in the first half of the 1910s was Babe Adams, hero of the 1909 World Series, until arm and shoulder problems caused the Pirates to release him in 1916. Two years of pitching rehabilitation in the minors enticed the Pirates to bring Adams back to Pittsburgh at the end of the war-shortened 1918 season, and he was one of the best pitchers in the National League the next three years. Southpaw Wilbur Cooper, however, was by now the ace of the Pittsburgh staff, and one of the premier pitchers in baseball. With the exception of Grover Cleveland Alexander and possibly Hippo Vaughn, another lefty, there was no better pitcher in the National League than Cooper in the seven years from 1916 to 1922. Cooper had three straight 20-win seasons from 1920 to 1922 and would likely have had five in a row were it not for shortened seasons in 1918 and 1919—both years in which he won 19 games—because of World War I. Wilbur Cooper is likely the best pitcher for sustained excellence over any five-year period to ever take the mound in Pittsburgh, yet is not much remembered today. Never having pitched in a postseason game, which at the time would have required his team to win the pennant, has not helped the cause of his legacy. Ironically, after 13 years and a 202–159 record for the Pirates, and despite having just won 20 games again, Cooper was traded to the Cubs in 1925, the very year Pittsburgh returned to—and won—the World Series.

4

THE ALMIGHTY CUBS AND THE PUNCHLESS WONDERS

How the White Sox Stunned Baseball
in the 1906 World Series

There have been 14 World Series exclusive to New York City—seven between the Yankees and Dodgers (Brooklyn and the Bronx, both New York City boroughs), six between the Yankees and Giants, and one between the Yankees and Mets. There has been just one each exclusive to Chicago, in 1906, and St. Louis, in 1944. The only all-Chicago World Series in history is one of baseball's great David vs. Goliath stories. In the 1906 World Series, David—the Chicago White Sox, American League pennant winners despite having the lowest batting average in the league and hitting only seven home runs all year—knocked off Goliath—the Chicago Cubs, who had great pitching, terrific defense, and baseball's most imposing offense and had won 76 percent of their games with a 116–36 record. That's all anybody seems to remember about those White Sox, that they were the "Hitless Wonders" that beat the powerhouse Cubs in the World Series. And that's one of the foundation stories of the Cubs' more-than-a-century-long drought without a World Series championship.

In fact, however, the White Sox, who had won the very first American League pennant in 1901, were exactly in the middle of a five-year stretch from 1904 to 1908 in which they were—based on their record alone—the best team in the American League, despite having finished first only once. Their .591 winning percentage was the equivalent of a 91–63 record over a single 154-game season, which would have put them five games ahead of Cleveland and six ahead of the Philadelphia Athletics, whose winning percentages were the second and third highest during those five years. Moreover, their overall record from 1904 to 1908 was the best of any American League team in the first decade of the new league's history. They were one game better than the 1901–05 Boston Americans, two better than the 1906–10 Detroit Tigers, and three better than the 1901–05 Athletics. All three of those clubs won more pennants than the White Sox—Detroit took three, and Boston and Philadelphia both had two. Chicago's White Sox, however, were the only one of those teams that never finished worse than third. They were not as successful in finishing first only because their offense was an enduring weakness, and indeed they would be completely lost to history were it not for their stunning triumph over the heavily favored Cubs in the 1906 World Series.

And once upon a time, whatever misfortunes plagued the Cubs for more than 100 years—108, to be exact—whatever curse devoted Cubs fans may believe had stricken their team because they had not won a World Series since 1908 and not even been to one since 1945, yes, once upon a time Chicago's Cubs were a baseball dynasty. From 1906 to 1910 the Cubs were baseball's most dominant team, winning four pennants but only two World Series. In 1909, the one year they did not win the pennant, they still won 104 games. Their .693 winning percentage that year was the equivalent of 107 wins over a single 154-game schedule. The National League's two other best teams that decade—the 1901–05 Pirates and the 1904–08 Giants—would have finished eight and nine games behind the Cubs, respectively, in their five best years consolidated into a single season.

The Cubs were a well-balanced team with few weaknesses, strong in every facet of the game. They outscored their opponents by a phenomenal 53 percent from 1906 to 1910, compared to the Giants outscoring theirs by 37 percent and the Pirates theirs by 35 percent in their five best years. The 1904–08 White Sox, by contrast, with great pitching and defense and an anemic offense, outscored their opponents by just 24 percent. Yet, the Chicago Cubs of this era might also be lost to history were it not for an enduring limerick celebrating their famed double-play combination, their improbable defeat by the Hitless Wonders in the 1906 World Series, and the fact that 1908 became etched in history—seemingly never to be erased—as the last year the Cubs were baseball's champions . . . until, finally, they won it all in 2016.

* * *

The two teams restored Chicago to what some would have said was its rightful place as the premier city in Major League Baseball. It was a Chicago businessman, William Hulbert, who organized the National League in 1876 as an alternative to the chaos and corruption of the existing National Association, and it was the National League that effectively made Major League Baseball an enduring American institution. Of the eight original National League franchises, Hulbert's Chicago White Stockings and the Boston Red Stockings were the only two whose historical lineage has continued to this day, as the Cubs and Braves, without interruption. The White Stockings won six of the first 11 National League pennants, including in the league's debut season, giving the city of Chicago claim to being Major League Baseball's first dynasty. Their best player was Adrian "Cap" Anson, who without question was baseball's most important figure in baseball's most important city in the nineteenth century.

A first baseman, Anson was the game's first superstar player. He was also the game's first superstar manager, although that stature derived in part from his excellence as a player. But by the late 1890s, Anson had overstayed his welcome as manager, and the White Stockings—who had become the Colts in 1890 and the Orphans in 1898 before becoming the Cubs in 1903—spent the rest of the nineteenth century and the first years of the twentieth mired in relative mediocrity. Cap Anson retired in 1897 after a 27-year career, 22 in Chicago, with a .334 career batting average, 3,435 hits, and 2,075 runs batted in. He had been the all-time hits leader since 1880 and would remain so for 43 years until Ty Cobb surpassed him in 1923. Anson became the career RBI leader in 1881 and held that record until Babe Ruth passed him in 1933, 52 years later.

Chicago endured 15 years without a major-league pennant between 1886 and 1901 until the White Sox won the first American League pennant. The future Cubs—then still the Orphans—might have been the established major-league franchise in Chicago, but the upstart White Sox had the more compelling roster, beginning with Clark Griffith, a star pitcher for the Colts/Orphans in the 1890s before abandoning the club to become player-manager of the White Sox in their inaugural season because of his antipathy toward National League owners conspiring to hold down player salaries. While Griffith left to take over the new American League franchise in New York in 1903, the White Sox remained the more favored club in Chicago going into the 1906 season.

Chicago's National League club, meanwhile, had its worst year in franchise history in 1901, winning just 38 percent of their games. Representing the future, however, were Frank Chance, then a reserve outfielder, and rookie catcher Johnny Kling. The following year the Orphans hired Frank Selee, who managed the Beaneaters to five pennants in the 1890s, to take charge and turn things around. Rookie Joe Tinker took over at shortstop in 1902, Johnny Evers made his debut at second base in the beginning of September, and the Orphans moved to within a game of .500. The next year the Orphans became the Cubs and finished third, winning nearly 60 percent of their games, and in 1904 they finished second with 93 wins, the third most among the major league's 16 teams. The famous Tinker-to-Evers-to-Chance double-play combination was now in place, Chance having become the full-time first baseman. Three Finger Brown was now pitching in Chicago and hard-hitting outfielder Frank "Wildfire" Schulte made his debut. Righty Ed Reulbach came on board in 1905 to complement Brown. Selee had nearly completed building what would prove to be a Cubs dynasty when he was forced to step down as manager 63 games into the 1905 season for health reasons. Suffering from tuberculosis, he died four years and eight days later in July 1909. Frank Chance, now the Cubs' 28-year-old first baseman, was named player-manager and led them to a second straight 90-win season.

Before the start of the 1906 season, the Cubs acquired Jimmy Sheckard from Brooklyn to team with Schulte in the outfield, third baseman Harry Steinfeldt from Cincinnati to complete their Tinker-to-Evers-to-Chance infield, and rookie southpaw Jack Pfiester joined Brown and Reulbach on the mound. Orval Overall, obtained in a trade in June, made for an impressive pitching foursome. The foundation of their dynasty now in place, Chicago's Cubs were by far baseball's best team the rest of the decade, winning four of the next five National League pennants and two of the four World Series they played. They were the first great team of the twentieth century. Although the 1891–98 Boston Beaneaters—five pennants in eight years—and the 1894–98 Baltimore Orioles—three pennants, all in a row, in five years—might have a case to make on their own behalf, the 1906–10 Chicago Cubs were more likely the greatest team so far in baseball history.

Exceptional pitching and defense was what most separated the Cubs from tough and worthy opponents in the Pittsburgh Pirates and New York Giants, who were the second and third best teams in baseball, respectively, between 1906 and 1910. Four times in five years, the Cubs led the league in fewest runs allowed, and they did so by substantial margins. They were the only National League team with an earned run average under 2.00 in any season, and they did that three times. Their ERA for the five years was 1.98. Chicago led the league in percentage of outs on balls hit into play every year except 1908, and did so by a significant 4 percent margin over the league average. "Tinker-to-Evers-to-Chance" deserved to have a poem written about them for their defensive prowess, notwithstanding that the Cubs never led the league in double plays as the prose might imply, thanks in large part to the stinginess of their pitchers and defense in allowing baserunners.

Three Finger Brown was the only rival to Mathewson as the best pitcher in baseball at the time. Each year of that run Brown's ERA was below 2.00, never once exceeding 1.86 (in 1910), and each year of that run he won at least 20 games. He completed 133 of 155 starts and was also the Cubs' go-to reliever if his manager needed a new pitcher to secure a victory, earning 25 saves. From 1906 to 1910, Brown won 127 and lost just 44 for a .743 winning percentage, his earned run average was 1.42, and he allowed just 8.4 batters to reach base by walk or hit for every nine innings he pitched. Mathewson was equally impressive with a 135–50 record—a .730 winning percentage—a 1.85 ERA, and allowing 8.9 baserunners per nine innings. Matty made 183 starts, completing 140, and added 10 saves. Brown's 1,460⅔ innings pitched were 105 fewer than Mathewson threw. Prorating their cumulative pitching wins above replacement for a single season, Brown is in a dead heat with Mathewson.

Pfiester was one of two pitchers to earn the sobriquet "Giant Killer," during the Great '08 Race. He was "Jack the Giant Killer" for two complete-game victories against the visiting Giants three days apart at the end of August in a three-game sweep that started with Chicago 3½ games back of first-place New York and ended with them just a half-game behind. (The other "Giant Killer" was Phillies rookie Harry Coveleski, who beat the Giants three times in one week as the season was winding down, forcing the issue with regard to the Giants having to make up the Merkle game.) In the final week of the season, Reulbach pitched complete-game shutouts against Brooklyn in both games of a doubleheader to keep the Cubs a slim half-game ahead of the Giants, who also swept a doubleheader that day, and one up on the Pirates with just seven games to go, including the Merkle makeup game.

The Cubs' offense during these years was more impressive than is generally thought, especially with the excellence of their pitching and terrific defense. They had by far the best scoring ratio of any team in the National League from 1906 to 1910 relative to both hits and total baserunners, besting the league average by 13 and 12 percent, respectively. Tinker, Evers, Chance, and Steinfeldt—their entire infield—were among the 10 best National League position players based on their cumulative wins above replacement during the five years of the Cubs' dynasty. Chance at first base, Evers at second, and catcher Johnny Kling were the best all-around players in the National League at their positions the first 10 years of the new century. Joe Tinker would have been too if not for Honus Wagner, Pittsburgh's Flying Dutchman (a nickname based on both his German heritage and an opera of the same name popular at that time, by Richard *Wagner*).

There has been some retrospective sentiment among baseball historians that Tinker-to-Evers-to-Chance are in the Hall of Fame, all three elected in 1946 by the Old-Timers Committee, only by virtue of "Baseball's Sad Lexicon"—the prose that immortalized their names—rather than by merit. Of the three, Frank Chance, in addition to being a very good defensive first baseman, was the most dangerous and productive batter. Frequently hurt, however, Chance played more than 100 games in only six seasons and had a relatively short peak to his career. His best years were 1903 to 1907, and by 1908, the midpoint of the Cubs' dynasty, Chance was no longer the top first baseman in the National League; at 31 years old, he had endured more than his fair share of baseball-related injuries—he was hit by a pitch 68 times the previous five years. Although he played fewer than 100 games in both 1909 and 1910, Chance nonetheless remained one of the most capable players in the game and was, after all, their "Peerless Leader" as player-manager.

While not great players, Tinker and Evers, the heart of the double-play combination despite their famously not talking to each other for years over some misunderstanding or other, were certainly very good with a tough-minded commitment to winning. Wagner's all-around excellence obscures how good Tinker really was defensively. By advanced metrics, Tinker was not only the better shortstop in the field, but may have been the best defensive shortstop ever, taking into account the significant differences between eras, including the size and suppleness of gloves and even official scoring. Whatever advanced metrics might say about the merits of their Hall of Fame selection, the three infielders were nonetheless top-tier players on one of the greatest teams in history over any five-year period.

* * *

Great pitching and terrific defense also defined the contemporaneous South Side team in Chicago. (Both clubs' ballparks were geospatially named, the White Sox playing in South Side Park, and the Cubs in West Side Grounds.) The 1904–08 White Sox surrendered the fewest runs in the American League three straight years from 1905 to 1907, and their 2.17 ERA over the entire five years was by far the best among American League teams. The White Sox made the fewest errors and had the highest fielding percentage in the league every year except, ironically, when they won the pennant in 1906. Making outs on balls in play was particularly important because White Sox pitchers were collectively below the league average in percentage of outs they were able to get by striking out opposing batters.

Ed Walsh, the pitcher most associated with the 1906 Hitless Wonders, didn't have his breakout season of greatness till the next year. The right-handed Walsh had pitched in just 40 major-league games with a modest 14–6 record over two seasons when the 1906 season got under way. With right-hander Frank Smith, winner of 35 games the two previous years, struggling to be effective, Walsh stepped up with a 17–13 record, led the league with 10 shutouts, and his 1.88 ERA was the first of five straight years his earned run average was under 2.00. That Nick Altrock (20–13) and Doc White (18–6 with a league-best 1.52 ERA) got the first two starts in the World Series and Walsh didn't pitch until Game Three might well have been because they were southpaws and three of the Cubs' starting position players—Sheckard, Schulte, and Evers—batted left-handed. White, whose nickname derived from his medical training as a dentist, had jumped the Phillies to join the White Sox just before the two leagues agreed to settle their differences in 1903.

If anyone deserved the "Iron Man" appellation, it was Big Ed Walsh for the next two years. He started 95 of the White Sox' 313 games in 1907 and 1908, relieved in 27 others, and hurled 886⅓ innings with a 1.50 ERA. The real "Iron Man," the Giants' Joe McGinnity, earned his nickname with the 842 innings he threw for McGraw in 1903 and 1904. As for outcomes, Walsh was 24–18 and led the league with a 1.60 ERA in 1907, and in 1908 he won 40, with 11 shutouts, and lost 15 with an earned run average of 1.42. Walsh's extraordinary workload may have been influenced by both Frank Owen, who won 21 for the 1906 White Sox, and Altrock sliding into relative ineffectiveness and limited innings in 1907. That left it up to Walsh, White—whose 27 wins tied Addie Joss for the most in baseball—and Smith, who rebounded to 23 wins from five the year before, to carry the staff. The White Sox were ultimately unable to keep pace with Detroit because, while White, Walsh, and Smith won 74 games, the rest of the staff won just 13. The same three pitchers combined for 74 wins again in 1908, when the White Sox missed the pennant by a game and a half, accounting for all but 14 of their team's 88 victories.

In contrast to their pitching, the 1904–08 White Sox in general had lesser-caliber core position players than their rivals for the American League pennant. With two exceptions, none were better than about average in the spectrum of performance for a typical position regular starting in the major leagues. The two exceptions, however—shortstop George Davis and center fielder Fielder Jones—were two of the best position players in the American League in the first decade of the twentieth century. Of the others, only left fielder Patsy Dougherty made baseball historian Bill James's cut for the 100 best players at their position through the end of the twentieth.

After nine years playing in New York as a top-tier shortstop for the Giants, George Davis abandoned the National League in 1902 to play for more pay in Chicago with the White Sox. He hit over .300 in each of his Giants seasons and was arguably baseball's best defensive shortstop at the turn of the century. The White Sox dropped from first to fourth in his first year with the team, but Davis was by far their best player. That attracted the attention of John McGraw, who had taken over as Giants manager in July 1902 and needed a quality shortstop in his mission to build a powerhouse team. McGraw offered Davis a better deal to return to the Giants. Reneging on his Chicago contract to move back to New York, Davis found himself benched for the entire 1903 by a federal court order pending adjudication of the White Sox' claim that he and the Giants must honor the reserve clause binding players to their teams that underlay the negotiated settlement just agreed to by the two major leagues. Under league pressure to keep the peace, the Giants gave up their claim, the White Sox welcomed him back with no (or at least few) hard feelings, and George Davis returned to Chicago to pursue a strong end to an excellent career.

Until Ty Cobb emerged as a superstar for Detroit in 1907, Fielder Jones was one of the top three outfielders in the American League's short history, along with Detroit's Sam Crawford and Cleveland's Elmer Flick. One of Brooklyn's best players when they won back-to-back pennants in 1899 and 1900, Jones like Clark Griffith was vocal in his disdain for the reserve clause and was enticed by the new league's promises of greater financial return on performance. Ditching Brooklyn for the new American League team in Chicago, he played for his third consecutive pennant-winning team in 1901. After hitting .306 in his first three years with the White Sox, and with his 1903 contract inexplicably *not* including a reserve clause, *and* with McGraw now looking to strengthen his out-field, Jones signed to play for the Giants in 1904, just as Davis had the year before. And just like Davis that year, he was forced back to Chicago by National League powerbrokers who were not about to jeopardize the peace agreement between the two leagues. As with Davis, Chicago owner Charles Comiskey welcomed Jones back to the fold. Apparently holding no grudge against him, and recognizing his exceptional leadership skills, Comiskey named Jones player-manager in June 1904 once it was obvious that the team's current player-manager had lost the respect of his players.

Fielder Jones may not have been the city of Chicago's "Peerless Leader," but his taking over was the catalyst needed to boost the Sox into competitive mode. Jones rallied the White Sox from their fifth-place standing when he took charge into the heat of the 1904 pennant race before a September fade resulted in their finishing third, six games behind. The next year, a furious finish fell two games short of Philadelphia's Athletics for the pennant. Building on his team's falling-short experiences the two previous years, Jones gave Chicago an American League pennant in 1906 to go along with the National League title that Cubs' player-manager Frank Chance—the city's true "Peerless Leader"—also gave the city.

Following their improbable triumph over the Chance Cubs in the World Series, the 1907 White Sox ended up third, 5½ games behind

Detroit. The next year they again fought valiantly for the pennant in baseball's other Great '08 Race. Languishing in fourth place, seven games behind the Tigers, with an unimpressive 59–50 record in late August, the White Sox finished with the best record in the league thereafter, but that proved too little, too late to catch either Detroit or Cleveland. Losing their season series to both the Naps (8–14) and Tigers (9–13) fatally undermined their quest for a second pennant in three years, which would have meant another all-Chicago World Series as the Cubs also won a tight three-team pennant race—the one much better chronicled and recalled—that wasn't decided until the final day.

Starting from third place just three games behind the Tigers, the White Sox played 36 games from September 1 till time ran out on their season. Ed Walsh started 14 of them, nine on two days of rest, three with just one day from his previous start, and on September 21 he started and won both games of a doubleheader against the Red Sox to keep the White Sox just one game behind with five remaining on the schedule. Frank Smith started 11 games, Doc White started seven, and the rest of the staff combined for just four starts. From September 18 until October 3, either Walsh or Smith started every one of the 11 games the White Sox played, while White rested his overworked left arm. Beginning on October 4, the White Sox faced off against the Tigers at home for their final three games of the season. They trailed by 2½ games and needed a sweep to pass them by. White won the first game, Walsh the second, and with the pennant directly at stake, Jones chose to go with White on just one day of rest instead of Smith, who had pitched three days earlier. Jones may have calculated that White, a southpaw, was a better bet than Smith to shut down the Tigers' two best hitters—Ty Cobb and Sam Crawford, both left-handed batters. White failed to get out of the first inning, the White Sox were shut out 7–0, and the Tigers went to the World Series.

* * *

If one takes account of only hits and batting average, then indeed "Hitless Wonders" is an appropriate appellation for Chicago's White Sox from 1905 to 1908. But it was also misleading, because this was a team—low batting average aside—that could score runs. In 1905 the Sox batted .237, four percentage points below the league average, but were outscored by only the pennant-winning Philadelphia Athletics, and by just 11 runs. The Hitless Wonders of 1906 were third in scoring despite having the league's lowest batting average at .230, seven percentage points worse than last-place Boston and 19 points below the league average. Only the National League's last-place Boston franchise had a lower team batting average (.226) in Major League Baseball. While the Sox upped their team average to .238 in 1907, it was still the second worst in the league, but once again they were third in scoring. They hit even fewer home runs than in their Hitless Wonders year, dropping from seven to five. Chicago finished third in the standings. In 1908, however, with still fewer home runs—just three—the White Sox were not so proficient in crossing the plate; they were just fifth in runs, with an almost subterranean .224 batting average (once again, seventh in the league), and this was probably what ultimately cost them a pennant they lost by 1½ games.

The secret to Chicago's success was a very efficient offense. From 1905 to 1908, the White Sox averaged fewer than 7.5 hits per game. For a team that averaged 1.2 fewer hits than the 8.7 hits per game of their pennant-race rivals, the White Sox needed 5 percent *fewer* hits per run. But there is a paradox. And that is that their ratio of runs scored to runners earning their way on base by hits, walks, and hit-by-pitch was not as good as that of six of the American League's seven other contending teams from 1905 to 1908, suggesting the White Sox were not as efficient in capitalizing on potential scoring opportunities. The White Sox scored one run for every 2.9 runners they put on base from 1905 to 1908, compared to one run for every 2.74 baserunners by the league's other contenders, meaning that Chicago required 5 percent *more* baserunners per run than did their pennant-race rivals.

The reason for this paradoxical discrepancy between two indicators of scoring efficiency—runs relative to hits, versus runs relative to total baserunners—can be summarized by the words "total bases." The truth is that, even for the Deadball Era, the White Sox had a much more anemic offense than their primary competitors. They were not so much "hitless" wonders as "punchless" wonders. Just 18 percent of their total hits from 1905 to 1908 went for extra bases, appreciably below the league average of 20 percent. Meanwhile, the league's seven other best teams during those years averaged nearly 22 percent of their total hits going for extra bases. The four-year annual average of 162 doubles, 45 triples, and only 6.5 home runs for the White Sox was substantially fewer in all extra-base categories than the 207 doubles, 66 triples, and 17.6 home runs collective average totals of their seven rivals. Extra-base hits have a much bigger impact than singles beyond the obvious extra bases because they both set up and score more runs.

The Detroit Tigers' offense when they won three consecutive pennants from 1907 to 1909 best illustrates the point. With 21 percent of their hits going for extra bases, compared to the American League average of 19 percent those three years, the Tigers were the league's most efficient team scoring runners on base each year. Having Sam Crawford and Ty Cobb batting third and fourth was a major reason why Detroit required fewer baserunners to score runs. Both were power hitters of their day. In each of Detroit's three pennant-winning years, Cobb and Crawford were first and second in the league in total bases. They were, in fact, first and second in all of Major League Baseball in 1907 and 1909, and second and third in the majors in 1908 behind Honus Wagner. It is no accident that their total bases—that extra-base power—were productive in scoring baserunners. In 1908 and 1909, Cobb and Crawford finished first and second in the league in runs batted in, and Cobb also led the league in RBIs in 1907, with Crawford finishing fourth. This was a significant advantage for Detroit, one that Fielder Jones did not have with his "punchless wonders" in Chicago.

On balance, it is fair to conclude that the White Sox did indeed have a very efficient offense for the lineup they had. Perhaps most remarkable was that they scored as many runs as they did for as relatively few total bases they had; Chicago averaged 9 percent fewer total bases for each run scored than their fellow contenders from 1905 to 1908. But the broader point is that even in the Deadball Era, before Babe Ruth introduced the home run as its own offensive strategy, extra-base hits provided the most solid foundation for scoring runs. Chicago's no extra-base offense, requiring more runners on base for each run scored than teams that had more primarily doubles and triples power in their lineups, had to work harder to score runs through singles and walks, sacrifice hits and stolen bases, and well-timed hits with runners in scoring position. If the White Sox needed to be extraordinarily proficient in creating scoring opportunities and getting the timely hit, they were helped by being well disciplined at the plate. They were the only American League team to draw more than 400 walks in 1906, 1907, and again in 1908.

* * *

Paradoxically, the White Sox' stunning the baseball world in the 1906 World Series by defeating the Cubs reinforces the point. The 570 runs scored by the White Sox may have been third in their league but paled in comparison to the Cubs' major league–leading 704 runs. The White Sox team batting average of .230 was not only last in the American League and far below the league average of .249, but wholly anemic in comparison to the Cubs' National League–leading .262 batting mark, which was 18 percentage points better than their league's average of .244.

Second in the league in home runs with 20, tied for the lead in triples with 71, and second in doubles with 181, the Cubs were also the powerhouse team of the National League. The White Sox, by contrast, hit only seven homers all year, and only one American League team had fewer triples—which was the real power number in the Deadball Era—than Chicago's 52, and that team, the Athletics, led the league with 32 homers and had more than 24 percent of their hits go for extra bases, which was tops in the American League. Only 18.6 percent of the White Sox' hits were for extra bases, the fewest in the American League, while extra-base hits accounted for 21 percent of the Cubs' total. Because of all that, the Cubs were much more efficient than their crosstown opponent in scoring baserunners and in the productivity of their hits. The 1906 Cubs had a dynamic multidimensional offense. Besides their display of power, they stole 283 bases, exactly 100 more than the league average, and their 231 sacrifice bunts were more than 20 percent higher than the National League club with the second-most sacrifice hits.

And on top of their imposing offense, Brown, Reulbach, Pfiester, Overall, and Carl Lundgren gave the Cubs superb pitching that was at least equal, if not superior, to the White Sox. Defensively, the Cubs may have been even better than the White Sox, especially with Tinker-to-Evers-to-Chance in the infield. Perhaps the most significant indicator of the Cubs' overwhelming dominance of the baseball world in 1906 was that they outscored their game opponents during the season by a phenomenal 85 percent—705 runs for the Cubs versus 381 they allowed their opponents, of which only 270 were earned—whereas the White Sox, who also had superior pitching and defense in league context, outscored their opponents by just 24 percent, 570 runs to 460.

There is no way anyone who had watched their seasons or looked at this data in advance of the World Series could have expected the Chicago White Sox to beat the Chicago Cubs.

Yet they did.

In six games.

The White Sox did so despite batting just .198 in the Series with only 37 hits, just over six per game, and committing an uncharacteristically high 15 errors, including six in one game alone. And they did so despite collecting all of 11 hits in the first four games, hitting .097 as a team while scoring just six runs. Going nearly hitless—that's not too much of an exaggeration—it was a wonder the White Sox still managed to win two of the first four games, which they did because of their own superb pitching. Altrock pitched a four-hitter to win the opening game, 2–1, and Walsh shut out the Cubs on two hits to win Game Three. The Cubs countered each Sox win with their own stellar pitching; Reulbach limited the White Sox to one hit in the second game and Brown shut them out on two hits in Game Four.

Then the White Sox exploded, hitting .351 as a team, to win the next two games, 8–6 and 8–3, to take the World Series in six.

Both teams scored 22 runs in the Series, but the White Sox held the Cubs' seemingly imposing offensive juggernaut to one fewer hit than they were able to gather off the Cubs' own stellar staff. Perhaps the quality of White Sox pitching was such that baseball experts of the day should have considered the possibility that the dominating Cubs might lose because, after all, good pitching can stop good hitting on any given day or in a short series. But the explanation for why the Chicago White Sox beat the heavily favored Chicago Cubs is quite simple, really—the hitless, punchless wonders were uncharacteristically . . . shall we say, offensive.

The Chicago White Sox—the Hitless Wonders—would not have won the 1906 World Series were it not for their unexpectedly potent hitting for extra bases, which did exactly that—advance runners an extra base (or two) without having to work for it. The team that averaged fewer than one hit in five going for more than a mere single during the regular season had 35 percent of their 37 hits in the World Series go for extra bases—10 doubles and three triples, although still no homers. Scoring in 11 of the 55 innings they came to bat in the World Series, an extra-base hit either began a rally or drove in runs in seven of those innings and directly contributed to 15 of the 22 runs they scored in the Series. Only two of their 13 extra-base hits did not contribute to a run; seven White Sox players who had extra-base hits came around to score without having to be advanced into scoring position, but more significantly, eight of those extra-base hits drove in a total of 12 runs.

* * *

With the strength of their pitching, the White Sox might have become the first dominant team in American League history had they had more offensive clout rather than having to rely on "small ball" to score so many of their runs. They had the best cumulative record in the American League from 1904 to 1908—five games better than Cleveland, with the second-best record—but won only a single pennant. Having more punch in their lineup might have made a difference in the two pennant races the White Sox lost by two games or fewer. Or, to paraphrase Earl Weaver, an American League manager from a much later generation, White Sox manager Fielder Jones undoubtedly would have loved the two- and three-run double or triple.

The bitter ending to the 1908 pennant race proved the end of the Fielder Jones era. Frustrated by Comiskey's meddling with his team, including on key personnel decisions, and with lucrative business interests on the West Coast, Jones stepped down as both player and manager of the White Sox at the end of the season. Jones was still a top-tier player when he retired from the game, having been among the top 10 American League position players based on the WAR metric in each of his last four years. While pitching remained a strength, it would be nearly a decade before they were competitive again for the pennant. For most of those years, Chicago's team batting average remained among the worst in the league; they might still have been "hitless," but they were no longer "wonders" when it came to scoring efficiency on their hits. Despite Ed Walsh winning 27 games in both 1911 and 1912, the White Sox were not in the running even remotely either year, finishing fourth both times. Not until 1915, bolstered by the preseason acquisition of second baseman Eddie Collins from Philadelphia and the in-season deal for Cleveland's Shoeless Joe Jackson, did the White Sox reemerge as a contender. Collins and Jackson were two of baseball's elite hitters and helped the White Sox become a far more formidable offensive club. For the next five years. the White Sox played Deadball Era baseball as well as any team, but now— unlike the Hitless Wonders—they were also consistently at or near the top of the league in runs, batting average, and slugging percentage. And while Walsh was now gone, his decline in effectiveness almost certainly hastened by averaging 361 innings in seven years between 1906 and 1912, the arrivals of Eddie Cicotte in 1912 and Red Faber in 1914 ensured that the White Sox would continue to have first-rate pitching.

Thus began the tarnished golden era in White Sox history from 1916 to 1920—during which they won two pennants and a World Series, only to have eight of their players conspire to lose the 1919 World Series, condemning the franchise to 40 years in the wilderness before their next pennant.

* * *

As good as the Chicago Cubs were in 1910, winning 104 games on their way to a fourth pennant in five years, the end of the decade was also the end of their dynasty. On the right side of the infield, first baseman Frank Chance, because his history of accumulated injuries had taken its toll, and second baseman Johnny Evers, because of a nervous breakdown, both missed nearly the entire 1911 season. Thirty-two-year-old third baseman Harry Steinfeldt was released after miscalculating his leverage in demanding a long-term contract Chance was unwilling to take a chance on, especially with Heinie Zimmerman, who was eight years younger, showing such prowess in spring training. Thirty-five-year-old catcher Johnny Kling got off to a bad start and was traded shortly after the 1911 season began, leaving shortstop Joe Tinker the last man standing from the Cubs' great infield. Three Finger Brown, still at the top of his game, had his sixth straight 20-win season in 1911, but the toll of 1,730⅔ innings pitched since 1906 made this his last year as an elite pitcher. They ended up second with 92 wins, 7½ games back of the Giants. While Evers came back and had a terrific season in 1912, the Giants by now had assumed the dynasty mantle, and the Cubs' ninth consecutive 90-win season was not nearly good enough to compete with them. At the end of the year, Chance was released as both player—he appeared ineffectually in only 33 games in 1911 and 1912—and manager. Brown was also let go after nine superb seasons with the Cubs.

Frank Chance is in the Hall of Fame as a first baseman, but his historical legacy is as a great player-manager. The "Peerless Leader" managed the Cubs for seven full seasons, never winning fewer than 91 games. In his eight years as Cubs manager, Chance won 768 games and lost only 389, which figures to an average of 102 wins over 154 games each year. Had Chance never managed another game, his .664 winning percentage with the Cubs would be by far the highest in history for a major-league manager, exceeding Joe McCarthy's career-winning percentage of .615. Chance, however, did not pass up the chance to return as manager of the Yankees in 1913 and 1914, and the Red Sox in 1923. These were bad teams whose potential for improvement proved limited—and he ended up with a .593 managerial winning percentage.

The Cubs got progressively worse after Chance's departure, falling into the middle of the standings. Heinie Zimmerman won the Triple Crown in 1912, but failed to become the superstar player some thought possible, perhaps because character issues concerning his professional baseball ethics got in the way. Their best player in the teens—and one of baseball's best pitchers in the last decade of the Deadball Era—was southpaw Hippo Vaughn, who won 20 games five times in six years between 1914 and 1919, and just missed with 19 in 1920.

After finishing fifth in 1917, the Cubs made a dramatic move by trading with the Phillies for Grover Cleveland Alexander, coming off three straight 30-win seasons, to join Vaughn on their pitching staff for the 1918 season. (If Alexander was not the best pitcher in baseball, that was only because of Walter Johnson.) They also traded with the Braves for Lefty Tyler, himself a top-rated pitcher, although not in the class of either Alexander or Vaughn. Alexander pitched only three games for the Cubs in 1918 before becoming one of the first players drafted into World War I, but the Cubs leapfrogged to the pennant nonetheless, which they took by a decisive 10½ games over the defending NL champion Giants. Vaughn's 22 wins and 1.74 ERA paced both the Cubs and the National League; Tyler was 19–9.

It had been ten long years since the Cubs last won the World Series back in 1908, but 1918 was not to be their year as they lost in six games to the Boston Red Sox—another team, like the Chicago Cubs, that would embark on decades upon decades of being unable to win another championship.

* * *

Despite their accomplishments, the 1906–10 Cubs are not often in the discussion about the best teams in history over any minimum five-year period, and when they are they are often dismissed. Some count against their legacy the fact that they played in the Deadball Era. Baseball was still relatively primitive at the beginning of the last century, with far greater variability in the talent and abilities of players and teams. But comparing baseball dynasties in the context of their time, no team was as dominant as the 1906–10 Cubs, whose .693 winning percentage is by far the best of any other team, including any of the great Yankees teams, over any five-year period. And notwithstanding the continual improvement in the quality of players and teams, the 1906–10 Cubs still have the highest combined percentage of games played and winning percentage against 90-win teams of any team in any five year-period since the beginning of the twentieth century. *And* no other team over any five-year period so dominated its opponents in run differential as the 1906–10 Chicago Cubs. Extending their run to cover the seven full seasons Frank Chance was their manager, the Cubs from 1906 to 1912 won exactly two-thirds of their games. No other team over any seven-year stretch, including the Yankees at their best from 1936 to 1942 when they won six pennants and five World Series, can match that.

More problematic for their legacy is that their historical luster is diminished by the fact that they failed to cap off their finest season—baseball's best winning percentage since the start of the "modern era" in 1903—with a triumph in a World Series they were overwhelmingly favored to win. How could they possibly have lost the 1906 World Series to a team known in history as the "Hitless Wonders"?

FIRST CALL TO THE BULLPEN

The Early Days of Relief Pitching

The 1908 season was baseball's most pitching-dominant year since the distance from the pitching slab to the plate was established in 1893, and would remain so at least until 60 years later. Eighteen qualifying pitchers had an earned run average under 2.00. Teams averaged only 3.3 runs a game, the Cardinals and the Highlanders—both finishing last in their respective leagues—were the only clubs to surrender more than four runs a game, the collective ERA of major-league pitchers was 2.37, and batters hit just .239, only .0003 percentage points better than the 16 National League and American Association clubs hit 20 years earlier in 1888. Big Ed Walsh (40–15), Christy Mathewson (37–11), Three Finger Brown (29–9), and Addie Joss (24–11 with a 1.16 ERA) were indomitable. Yet, paradoxically, or at least counterintuitively for the time, complete games had plummeted to an astonishing two-thirds of all starts, and nearly 9 percent of all victories were "saved" by a relief pitcher. Relief pitchers would have to wait more than half a century to be officially awarded the "save" they so deserved, although it must be noted that their saves were counted retroactively according to a 1969 definition that credited a save for any victory completed by a relief pitcher regardless of the size lead that pitcher was asked to protect, some of which were quite big.

At the turn of the century, pitchers rarely were removed from the games they started unless they got hurt or were completely ineffective. In 1901, whether in victory or defeat, 86 percent of games pitched were complete games. By 1905, even though complete games had slipped to 80 percent, relief pitchers were rarely in the game at the end of victories, and then mostly after the starting pitcher had been routed and their team had made a big comeback. In winning the 1902 American League pennant, for example, the Philadelphia Athletics had the fewest complete games in the league (114 in a 140-game schedule), but only two of Connie Mack's pitching changes were in what would later be called "save situations," where the relief pitcher got the save by virtue of entering the game with his team in the lead.

At a time when rosters were typically about 15 players, pitching staffs were relatively small—an inherent limitation to using pitchers in relief roles. In most games when the starting pitcher did not go the distance, a manager would use only one other pitcher to either finish up a losing cause or go for the victory himself. John McGraw, however, was already changing the paradigm for the role of relief pitchers. In 1903, his first full year in charge of the Giants, McGraw began to conceive of a relief pitcher in terms other than finishing up for a starting pitcher so badly scored upon (or physically exhausted or hurting) that he was mercifully removed from the game. Despite having two of the league's most durable pitchers in Mathewson and "Iron Man" Joe McGinnity, McGraw's genius was in realizing that victories don't necessarily have to come from complete games. Sometimes bringing in a fresh arm to complete a game is the best way to secure a victory. When the Giants dominated the league in 1904 and 1905, 14 percent of their victories were "saved" by a relief pitcher, as opposed to 3.4 percent of the total wins by the seven other National League clubs. Notwithstanding an outstanding pitching staff rivaled by only the Cubs, the Giants had the *fewest* complete games in the National League in 1904, 1906, and 1907, and the second fewest in 1903, 1905, and 1908. They led the league in saves every year from 1903 to 1909 as McGraw called upon a relief pitcher to save 102 of the Giants' 663 victories. The Giants alone accounted for fully one-third of the 311 saves by National League teams in those seven years.

New York Highlanders manager Clark Griffith was perhaps as much a pioneer in making pitching changes as McGraw. Griffith called on his bullpen 177 times between 1904 and 1906 (an average of 1.2 pitching changes in games his starting pitchers did *not* complete)—more than any other manager in baseball—and his was the only team that had fewer than 100 complete games in any season (88 in 1905 and 99 in 1906). Unlike McGraw, however, Griffith did not use relief pitchers with the intent to save leads. Griffith's relievers totaled only 10 saves those three years, accounting for about 6 percent of their relief appearances. Giants relievers, by contrast, collected saves in 38 percent of their games—a total of 48 saves resulting from the 126 pitching changes McGraw made in the same three years. That Griffith made as many pitching changes as he did was probably less a calculus to preserve victories than because his pitching staff, even with workhorses Jack Chesbro, Jack Powell, and Al Orth, was not as stingy in preventing runs as Giants pitchers, nor for that matter as effective as about half the other teams in the American League. Griffith was following the pattern of other managers in removing pitchers from games when they weren't effective, but probably was more astute than others in not leaving his best pitchers in lost-cause games. In 1906, for example, when he won 23 but lost 17, Chesbro completed only 24 of his 42 starts—a paltry 57 percent for an ace in a year when American League pitchers finished 78 percent of their starts. The Highlanders lost seven of Chesbro's starts by at least five runs, including 10–0 and 10–1 blowouts.

It may have been more an evolution than a revolution, but other managers (more quickly in the National League) soon followed McGraw's lead, mostly because it made sense. By 1908, in large part because of McGraw's influence, NL complete games were down to 67 percent, and 10 percent of victories were games saved by relief pitchers. Over in the American League, while the percentage of complete games was about the same, only 7.5 percent of victories were saved. By 1911, there had been little change in the AL's percentage of complete games and saves, while in the NL complete games had fallen to 55 percent and saved victories increased to 15 percent. It would not be until 1913–14 that American League managers were in sync with their NL counterparts in using relief pitchers to replace a tired or beleaguered starting pitcher for effect—to win and "save" games.

* * *

Not only was McGraw far ahead of his contemporaries in his willingness to use a relief pitcher to ensure a victory, but he either imagined or anticipated a future of designated relief pitchers. As early as 1905, and certainly in 1906, McGraw had *one* pitcher he used mostly in relief, not necessarily often, to win or preserve victories. That one pitcher in 1905 was Claud Elliott, who made two starts and had eight relief appearances with six saves in the 31 games Giants starting pitchers failed to complete. Elliott was 28 years old in 1905 and never pitched again in the major leagues, but the next year McGraw used 22-year-old Cecil Ferguson in the same way, except more so. Starting only once and pitching a complete-game shutout when he did, Ferguson made 21 relief appearances in 1906, the most ever by a pitcher to that point in time. He finished exactly half of the 38 games McGraw's starters failed to complete, with seven saves and one victory in relief. Ferguson appeared in 15 games with the Giants the next year, 10 in relief with one save, but his future was primarily as a starter for the Boston Braves (then known as the Doves), to whom he was traded, from 1908 to 1910.

Notwithstanding his insight with Elliott and Ferguson, however, McGraw for the most part called on established starting pitchers when he went to his bullpen. Except for Ferguson in 1906, McGraw used Joe McGinnity, Hooks Wiltse, and Dummy Taylor—starting pitchers all— the most often in relief, usually to finish up games. In 1908, the year of the Great '08 Race, McGinnity was McGraw's primary workhorse in relief—17 of his 37 appearances were as a reliever—probably because, at age 37, the Iron Man had nearly exhausted his career, and indeed, 1908 was his last season in the major leagues. Undoubtedly because of the exigencies of a taut pennant race, McGraw also used Christy Mathewson in relief more often than usual that year. Mathewson pitched 12 times as a reliever, finishing nine games and tying his teammate McGinnity and rival Three Finger Brown for the league lead in saves with five.

The concept McGraw employed with Elliott and Ferguson was so radical at the time that even McGraw did not, and probably could not, stick with it. Those were the days when all pitchers were expected to have the ability, stamina, and durability to pitch the entire game, and no self-respecting pitcher or manager expected anything less. No manager at this time carried a pitcher on his staff to be used almost exclusively in relief, even as preparatory training to becoming a starting pitcher. As the value of using a relief pitcher to save a victory or to go for the win in close games gained currency among major-league managers, most went to their strength—their best starting pitchers—for many of those occasions. From 1908 to 1912, Cubs ace Three Finger Brown and White Sox ace Ed Walsh, two of the best starting pitchers in baseball, were also beyond question the two best relievers, almost certainly to the detriment of their career longevity.

Brown's performance in the dual roles of starting ace and ace reliever between 1908 and 1911 is nothing short of remarkable. He won 102 and lost only 43 in those four years while starting 123 games and making 70 relief appearances. In addition to completing 107 of his own starts, Brown either got a win, loss, or save in 52 of the 65 games he finished for other starters in relief. His record as a reliever was 12–8 with 32 retroactively awarded saves. Between his starting and relief roles, Three Finger Brown was directly involved in the outcome of fully one-third of the 406 games the Cubs won from 1908 through 1911. When Cubs manager Frank Chance chose to use Brown in relief, it was almost always with the game in the balance; Brown was credited with a decision or the save in 74 percent of his relief appearances those four years. And his were not short relief stints. Brown not only pitched complete games in 87 percent of his starts, but averaged over 2⅓ innings in relief. In the epic pennant race of 1908, had Chance not used Brown—his top starting pitcher and also his relief ace—Chicago would not have won a third straight pennant; Three

Finger was 29–9 with five saves in 50 games that year, 16 as a reliever. And in 1911, using Brown as often as he did as a reliever—26 relief appearances with a 5–3 record and 13 saves, to go along with his 16–8 record in 27 starts—was probably Chance's last best chance to win another pennant. As it turned out, the Cubs lost out to McGraw's Giants by 7½ games after fading badly in late summer.

Chance's reliance on Brown as both his ace starter and his ace reliever certainly paid dividends for the Chicago Cubs. But at what cost? Brown was never the same after pitching 53 games and working 270 innings in 1911. By finishing 24 games started by other pitchers in his 26 relief appearances, in addition to his own 21 complete games as a starting pitcher, Brown was pitching at the end of 45 of the Cubs' 157 games that year. The physical toll from all that mound work must have been great indeed; Brown appeared in just 15 games, made only eight starts, and hurled a mere 88⅔ innings in 1912, after which he was released by the Cubs for his efforts. Brown was 34 in 1911, however, old for a ballplayer in that era. He pitched for Cincinnati in 1913, was in the Federal League

Mordecai "Three Finger" Brown in 1909, when he led the league with 27 wins and seven saves as the Cubs' ace, both as a starting pitcher and as a reliever. *National Photo Company Collection (Library of Congress).*

in 1914 and 1915, and returned to the Cubs for 12 farewell appearances in 1916. Three Finger Brown never recovered his former greatness, and only against the lesser talent of the Federal League was he able to pitch 200 innings in a season after the 1,220⅓ he threw between 1908 and 1911.

Meanwhile, across Chicago town, Ed Walsh led the American League in saves five times in six years between 1907 and 1912, with 25 percent of the 316 games he pitched being in relief of another starter. He won 151 of his career 191 victories during those six years, completed 197 of his 237 starts, and was in at the finish of 75 of the 79 games he appeared in relief. The White Sox finished fourth, 28 games out of first place in 1912, but Walsh nonetheless pitched 393 innings in 62 games while winning 27 and saving 10 of his team's pedestrian 78 victories. In addition to his 32 complete games in 41 starts, Walsh worked 56 innings in 21 games as a reliever—an average of 2⅔ innings each time out of the bullpen. By the end of the 1912 season, having pitched 2,248 innings the last six years, Walsh was effectively washed up. He appeared in just 33 games and pitched only 190⅔ more innings the rest of his career, at which he kept trying until 1917. He was 31 in 1912.

* * *

McGraw would go on to use right-hander Otis "Doc" Crandall primarily as a reliever from 1909 through 1913, but not the way he used Ferguson—nearly all of whose appearances in 1906 were in relief. While Crandall is remembered for being the first pitcher to be used primarily as a "relief ace," he was the starting pitcher in 53 of the 185 games he pitched those five years for McGraw. Crandall's last season with the Giants in 1913 was the only one in which McGraw employed him as he had Ferguson—almost entirely out of the bullpen; Crandall started only two games while being called on to relieve 33 times. Despite his many starts, Crandall was McGraw's early twentieth-century version of a relief ace, although this should not be confused with today's concept of a "closer" dedicated to wrapping up a close game in the final inning in almost all circumstances. It might be more accurate to say he was a "finisher." Over 90 percent of Crandall's relief appearances for McGraw were to finish the game. Overall, Crandall finished 43 percent of the games Giants starters were unable to complete between 1909 and 1913. With a 28–10 record and 24 saves in relief, Crandall figured directly in the game's outcome in nearly half (48 percent) of his relief appearances.

John McGraw was the only manager who used a pitcher in this way. It would not be until the 1920s before any manager, including McGraw with Claude Jonnard from 1922 to 1924, would again employ a pitcher almost exclusively in relief—as he did with Elliott in 1905, Ferguson in

1906, and Crandall in 1913—and nearly half a century before this would become accepted practice. Complete games declined to below 60 percent in 1911 and held steady, typically between 55 and 60 percent, for the rest of the decade except for 1918, when many players were serving during World War I. About three-quarters of major-league victories were complete games, with the remainder won or saved by the bullpen. But no major-league pitcher was groomed specifically for the role of relief specialist. Many young pitchers, however, began their careers as primarily relievers to prove they belonged. If they were any good they soon moved into the starting rotation or became multirole pitchers, both starting and relieving. If not, they were soon out of the major leagues. This was the way it was for some of the better pitchers in baseball who came of age in the teens and early '20s. In 1915, for example, Carl Mays began his career with the Red Sox by relieving in 32 of the 38 games he pitched, leading the league with seven saves. By July the following year, he was settling in as a starting pitcher on his way to becoming one of the best pitchers of his generation.

"Saves" leaders were not necessarily the staff ace as in the days of Three Finger Brown and Ed Walsh, but starting pitchers were nonetheless called upon between their own starts to preserve victories in the late innings, or pitchers who started fewer games than their team's best pitchers and appeared more often than them in relief. The pitchers who were called upon to relieve 15 to 20 times in a year typically started at least as many games, and usually more, but their starts were often timed to go against the league's weaker competition, so managers could use their best starters against the best teams. They were true "multirole" pitchers. Of the 33 pitchers who led their league in saves (multiple saves leaders in any given year were not unusual) between 1913, when Crandall was used almost exclusively in relief but did not lead the league in saves, and 1923, the year before Firpo Marberry became baseball's first true relief ace, 19 made at least 20 starts, and two others started 19. Thirty relief appearances seem to have been the point at which a pitcher's role was almost exclusively in the bullpen. Even then, however, nearly all designated relievers started games for their teams, some quite a number of times. Crandall's 33 relief appearances in 1913 was the first time a pitcher appeared in as many as 30 games as a reliever, and six more would do so between 1915 and 1917, before the exigencies of World War I cut a month off the 1918 schedule and limited the 1919 season to 140 games.

As the Lively Ball Era got going in 1920 and games became more high scoring, managers were forced to go more often to their bullpen. Between 1920 and 1923, 22 pitchers appeared 30 times or more in relief, seven of whom also made more than 10 starts, and five others had at least five. The Cardinals' Lou North and the Giants' Slim Sallee in 1921, and the Giants' Claude Jonnard in 1922 were the first pitchers in history to work in 30 games without making a single start. Jonnard was also only the third pitcher ever to have back-to-back seasons throwing 30 games in relief, following the Browns' Bill Burwell in 1920 and 1921 and the Cardinals' Clyde Barfoot in 1922 and 1923, he was the first to do so three years in a row (1922 to 1924), and all three, including Jonnard, started at least twice in one of those years. Unlike Sallee, who started more than 300 major-league games in a career lasting from 1908 to 1921, North, Burwell, Barfoot, and Jonnard had short-lived major-league careers, although all four pitched afterward in the high minor leagues, primarily as starting pitchers rather than relievers. As important as being able to make a call to the bullpen had become to win or to save close games in the late innings, the idea of relief pitching as its own discipline for which to develop quality pitchers had still not arrived.

6

THE ROCK STAR MANAGER AND HIS WINNING IMPERATIVE

John McGraw was the first manager to assume rock star status in the baseball world. (Although the concept of "rock star" was still about a half century away—hello Elvis!—you get the point.) This had not been the case up till now, even though managers were typically centered on the covers of team programs because, after all, they were the guys in charge, except possibly for managers who were also star players on their teams, which magnified their aura, linking them and their leadership to the teams they managed. Player-managers Charlie Comiskey in the 1880s and Cap Anson in the 1880s and '90s had obvious appeal and identification with their teams. Some managers who did not take the field of play were also prominent, provided their teams were highly successful, as were Baltimore Orioles manager Ned Hanlon (a former player) and Boston Beaneaters manager Frank Selee (who had long since given up on a playing career) in the 1890s. Theirs were the dominant teams in the National League in the concluding decade of the nineteenth century, and both Hanlon and Selee gained no small measure of fame from being their managers. But neither Hanlon nor Selee were in the celestial firmament as managers alone that McGraw seized for himself very quickly upon taking over as Giants manager in July 1902.

Fred Clarke and Frank Chance, being star players on their teams as well as the managers, were the new century's successors to Anson's legacy for leadership both on the field of play and in guiding their teams in the games themselves and over the course of a season. They were populist icons in the cities their teams represented. Chance in Chicago was called the "Peerless Leader." Clarke was justifiably overshadowed on his club in Pittsburgh by the best player in baseball, a shortstop named Honus Wagner.

At only 30 years old when he began his first full season as the Giants' manager in 1903, McGraw could have continued his playing career while also managing, had he chosen to do so. He was still one of baseball's best players as recently as 1899, when he was named player-manager of the old Orioles to replace Hanlon, who was transferred by Baltimore's syndicate owner to his other team in Brooklyn, and he was a part-time player in his time as the American League Orioles' manager in 1901 and part of '02. Coming to New York, however, the emerging Little Napoleon decided instead to focus exclusively on managing, and specifically the imperative of winning. Part of that was because assorted injuries resulting from his having been an inordinately aggressive player back in the old Orioles' heyday had undoubtedly diminished his skills, and McGraw, hard-nosed and unsentimental in evaluating talent, was sufficiently self-aware to know that. Clarke, a year older, and Chance, three years younger, could be full-time playing managers and proved to be very successful in both roles, but McGraw chose not to. McGraw almost certainly calculated that by not having to attend to the discipline and rigors of maintaining his playing skills, he could concentrate on developing players, finding that extra edge to win games, and building a dynasty.

Even though he did not take the field as a player, it wasn't long before "John McGraw, manager of the New York Giants," far eclipsed both Chance and Clarke for recognition of his team being identifiable with him as manager. This was due in no small part to McGraw's notoriety, which in turn was abetted by his talent and skill for relentless self-promotion, akin to a cult of personality, around and about New York town. It helped that McGraw was controversial from the moment he betrayed Ban Johnson and the American League in 1902 by quitting on Baltimore to manage in New York. It helped that he almost immediately—in 1904— brought New York its first National League championship since 1889. Just as it did for Christy Mathewson's legacy as one of the greatest pitchers in history, the 1905 World Series secured McGraw's fame and reputation for managerial genius that would only grow as the decade advanced, even though his Giants played second fiddle to the Cubs and did not get to the World Series again until 1911. It also helped that in addition to being a very successful baseball manager, McGraw immersed himself in the social life of the Big City, including some of its less savory aspects.

And it helped that he had as foils Clarke in Pittsburgh and Chance in Chicago, whose competitive rivalry with the Giants was based on the legitimate excellence of all three teams, but was fueled by the intense dislike, bordering on hatred, of both player-managers toward McGraw.

Much of that was occasioned by McGraw's rowdy, anything-goes style that he brought from his old Orioles playing days, which provoked confrontations and bad blood between his team and theirs. And Chance and Clarke could give as well as they got. Their rivalry was not just about winning championships. It was personal. It was not pretty. But it helped produce intense, riveting baseball.

If you followed baseball in those days, it was hard to be neutral about John McGraw, often referred to as Mugsy (shades of the criminal underworld). If you didn't love him because you lived in Manhattan and were fanatic for the Giants, you probably had to hate him. Maybe it was his sudden success in turning a lousy team into a dominating one so quickly; maybe it was his insufferable arrogance; or maybe it was because he was managing the best team in New York City at a time when New York, New York, was doing its best to diminish the importance of other great American cities, like Chicago (and Philadelphia, and Boston, and even Brooklyn, which New York had only recently gobbled up). Whatever the reason, McGraw and his Giants became a magnet for attention in the baseball world, providing consistently compelling story lines. In large part because of McGraw's growing reputation for managerial brilliance and his take-no-prisoners approach to winning, the Giants became both the most popular team in baseball and the team fans in other cities most wanted to see their team beat.

* * *

If McGraw established himself as a great manager in the first decade of the new century, the second sealed his reputation in perpetuity. He won three consecutive pennants from 1911 to 1913, two decisively, and another in 1917 by a very comfortable 10-game margin. The Giants failed to win any of the subsequent World Series. The 1911 pennant race was the only one of their three in a row where the Giants were not in control by the Fourth of July; they didn't break away until September on their way to a 7½-game winning margin. There was no midsummer drama either of the next two years as the Giants won convincingly by 10 games in 1912 and 12½ in 1913. With 103 and 101 wins those two years, the 1912–13 Giants were the last National League team to win 100 games in back-to-back seasons until the Brooklyn Dodgers in 1941 and '42. Only three NL teams won 100 games in any single season between the 1913 Giants and the 1941 Dodgers.

Excelling in all facets of the game, the Giants in the early teens were a testimony to McGraw's ability to build teams that played better than the individual abilities of his players. McGraw had no historically great position players to write into his lineup. The most consequential players McGraw wrote into his starting lineup on a daily basis were catcher Chief

Meyers, second baseman Larry Doyle, and shortstop Art Fletcher. None of the Giants' other core regulars during these years were exceptional players. They were more typical of the average big-league player who was a regular in a major-league lineup. Indicative of his ability to leverage his players for effect, McGraw managed a highly potent offense that emphasized getting runners on base and relentless speed to advance runners. The Giants led the league in on-base percentage all five of those years and battered opposing pitchers for more extra-base hits—the most efficient way to drive in runs, rather than rely on singles and advancing baserunners alone—than the league average. His team led the majors in stolen bases all three years they won the pennant, averaging just over two per game. The 1911 Giants swiped 347 bases—the most since the old Orioles in 1899—followed by 319 in 1912 and 296 in 1913. No other National League team came close to running with the abandon of McGraw's Giants.

Doyle, Fletcher, and Meyers were the cornerstone position players of the 1911–13 Giants. An argument can be made that Larry Doyle—the Giants' best position player—has been historically underappreciated, notwithstanding his fame for having said, "It's great to be young and a Giant." Making his debut in July 1907 and taking over second base during the taut 1908 race, Doyle played the first half of his career under the shadow of the Cubs' Johnny Evers, the best second baseman in the league. Prized most by McGraw for his defense, Art Fletcher took over at shortstop as a rookie in July 1911 at a time when the Giants were struggling to break out from the pack. Meyers—called "Chief" instead of his first name, John, because of his Native American heritage, a practice emblematic of the times—was the best all-around catcher in baseball in the first half of the 1910s. In addition to being a solid defensive catcher, Meyers was a better hitter than any of his contemporaries at the position. He batted .334 during the Giants' stretch of three straight pennants, including .352 in 1912. At a time when body armor for catchers was still primitive, McGraw was careful in managing his catcher's playing time, frequently substituting for him late in games to reduce Meyers's exposure to fatigue and potential injury. As a result, Meyers never reached 450 plate appearances in a season or had as many as 400 official at-bats, but he did catch an average of 128 games a year for the Giants between 1910 and 1914, which was most important to McGraw.

The Giants' pitching, while not as dominant as that of the 1906–10 Cubs, has greater historical name recognition. The headliner was, of course, Christy Mathewson. Going into the 1911 season, Matty already had 263 wins against only 121 losses so far in his Giants career, to go along with a 1.97 earned run average. The next three years as the Giants won three straight pennants, Mathewson went 74–36 and had the league's

Giants manager John McGraw with his longtime ace Christy Mathewson, both wearing coats in cold weather, in 1914. *George Grantham Bain Collection (Library of Congress)*.

best ERA in 1911 (1.99) and 1913 (2.06). In between, his 2.12 earned run average in 1912 was second to rookie teammate Jeff Tesreau's 1.96. Tesreau was 17–7 that year, 22–13 in 1913, and 26–10 the year after that.

The most pleasant surprise, however, and a vindication for his manager, was southpaw Rube Marquard putting together three straight 20-win seasons from 1911 to 1913. Marquard had been much maligned for failing to live up to the $11,000 McGraw spent in 1908 to acquire him from Indianapolis, where he won 28 games that year. His purchase price set a new record for a minor-league player, and Marquard's struggles in his first two years with the Giants—he was 9–18 in the first 43 games he pitched—earned him the derisive moniker "The $11,000 Lemon." Although never again winning 20 games in a career that lasted until 1925, his 73–28 record when the 1911–13 Giants dominated the National League proved sufficient for Rube Marquard to eventually make it into the Hall of Fame despite an otherwise mediocre career.

* * *

The 1911–13 Giants have not gotten the credit they probably deserve as a great team because, despite winning all three pennants decisively, they failed to win a single World Series. In 1911 they lost the Series in six games to the Philadelphia Athletics as Frank Baker hit two home runs that played no small role in the Giants' defeat—a two-run shot off Marquard in the second game to break up a 1–1 tie and give his team the win, and a solo blast off Mathewson with one out in the ninth in the next game to even the score at 1–1 and set the stage for the Athletics to win in extra innings. Forever thereafter, Frank would be addressed as "Home Run" Baker. The Giants lost the next year's Series to the Boston Red Sox in eight games (Game Two was tied after 11 innings when the sun went down) because in the 10th inning of the Series finale, first Fred Snodgrass dropped a routine fly ball in center field, then Meyers the catcher and first baseman Fred Merkle, with Mathewson standing nearby, allowed a pop foul by Tris Speaker to drop between them, after which Speaker—one of the best hitters in baseball—with a new lease on his at-bat, delivered a single that tied the game and set up the championship-winning sacrifice fly. And in 1913 they lost the World Series to the Athletics again, in five games, this time as Baker once more battered the Giants' pitching, although not so much with the long ball (he had only one home run).

But their legacy was perhaps irrevocably damaged by what happened at the hands of the of Boston's 1914 "Miracle" Braves, who surged from last place on the Fourth of July to win the pennant by 10½ games over second-place New York. And then, the very next year, the Giants finished dead last. That had never happened to John McGraw in a full season before, and wouldn't ever again.

While the Braves' surge to win the 1914 pennant is rightly applauded on its merits as being as one of the greatest come-from-behind drives in history, it wasn't so much that the Giants collapsed and let a big lead slip away, as that they were never in command of the pennant race in the first place. Getting off to a fast start with a 21–11 record through May, McGraw's team seemed poised to break away for another dominant season. Instead, the Giants' record the rest of the way was just four games above .500 at 63–59—hardly the mark of a pennant contender. On July 18, when they began their drive from the bottom of the heap to the National League pennant, the Braves were only 11 games behind the first-place Giants in tightly bunched standings, and New York's lead over second-place Chicago was three games. The Giants were a pedestrian 38–38 thereafter while the Braves, going 59–16, were an astonishing 21 games better than the defending National League champions.

Offense wasn't the Giants' problem. For the third time in five years they led the league in scoring. The problem was that, with the exception of Tesreau, the Giants' pitching faltered badly. Mathewson had the last of his 12 consecutive 20-win seasons with a 24–13 record, but it was his least impressive performance. Age and fatigue seemed to finally catch up with the 33-year-old Mathewson in the second half of the season. The Giants had a losing 8–9 record in games started by Mathewson after July 18, when the Braves began their drive out of last place. Matty himself went 9–9, including a victory in relief, but lost four straight starts in August, including twice to the Braves, as Boston relentlessly closed the gap. His ERA in September, when the Braves took command of the race, was, for him especially, an unsightly 4.17. Rube Marquard, who won 24, 26, and 23 games when Giants were winning three in a row, fell to 12–22 in 1914. After pitching a two-hit shutout against the Reds on July 22, his record stood at a respectable 9–8 with a 2.76 earned run average. The rest of the season was a personal pitching disaster. Marquard lost 14 of his next 15 starts, including 12 in a row between the Giants' 95th and 140th games, and his ERA in that stretch was 4.14. Right-hander Jeff Tesreau was the one Giants pitcher who remained tough to beat even as the Braves went on their miracle surge. While his team struggled to a 38–38 record after July 18, Tesreau was outstanding the rest of the way with a 15–4 mark.

* * *

After being stunningly overtaken by the Braves in 1914 and enduring recovery years in 1915 (dead last) and 1916 (fourth place), the New York Giants dominated the league again in 1917, winning the pennant by 10 games. This gave the Giants four pennants for the decade, but yet again they failed to win the World Series, this time playing foil to the Chicago White Sox, helping to establish the myth that the White Sox of that era were one of the greatest teams in history, derailed only by the greed and/ or naïveté of their "eight men out." Larry Doyle, no longer young and a Giant, did not share in this pennant, having been traded for third baseman Heinie Zimmerman, a batting star for the 1917 Giants.

Their 1917 pennant was set up by a furious finish in 1916 when the Giants won 30 of their last 38 games. This included an astounding 26 consecutive victories from September 7, when the Giants had a 59–62 record and were 13½ games behind, to September 30. The Giants played all seven other National League teams during their streak, and all 26 wins came at the Polo Grounds as part of a 31-game homestand over 26 days in September. Unfortunately for the Giants, their 26-game winning streak was too little, too late, coming in the final month of the season. They were still fourth when it ended, but had narrowed the gap between them and first-place Brooklyn to five games.

As astounding as 26 in a row was, it was the Giants' second substantial winning streak of the 1916 season. After getting off to a terrible start, winning only two of their first 15 games and finding themselves already 8½ behind (making it seem like last-place 1915 all over again), McGraw's guys reeled off 17 straight from May 9 to 29, putting them within 1½ games of Brooklyn at the top. In counterpoise to the 26 straight they would win in September, this winning streak was all on the road during the Giants' first western swing of the season. It was Christy Mathewson on the mound when the Giants extended their streak to 17 straight. It was also the 371st win of his career. At 35, Mathewson made just two more starts and won only once more for the Giants (in relief) before being traded to Cincinnati in July for the opportunity to manage. Matty tacked on one final victory for his career resume in a Reds uniform.

Let's see. That's 17 in a row, and then 26 in a row . . . and the New York Giants only finished fourth? The Giants' two winning streaks accounted for fully half of their 86 victories in 1916, meaning that the rest of the year they went 43–66. That's 23 games *under* .500. If it appeared the Giants were set to compete after their 17 straight wins in May, that expectation was dashed by July 4 when they found themselves in fifth place, 8½ games in the hole.

Virtually no core players on McGraw's 1917 team played a significant role in the National League pennants that came before or after. Shortstop Art Fletcher was in his prime in 1917, and in fact had the best season of his 13-year career. A direct contemporary of Hall of Fame shortstops Rabbit Maranville of the Braves and Dave Bancroft of the Phillies, Fletcher rather than either of them was probably baseball's best all-around shortstop in the 1910s, based on his sustained excellence both defensively and with the bat in the seven years from 1913 to 1919. Left fielder George Burns had the distinction of his first year as a starting player being the last of the Giants' three straight pennants from 1911 to 1913, and his last year with the Giants being the first of their four straight pennants from 1921 to 1924. In between, Burns led the league in scoring five times and stole 327 bases, twice leading the league. Both Fletcher and Burns, by then nearing the end of their careers, proved to be valuable trade bait for McGraw to acquire a pair of topflight players to shore up the Giants' infield in the early 1920s—Fletcher to the Phillies for Bancroft in a trade of shortstops, and Burns to the Reds for third baseman Heinie Groh.

* * *

The 1917 pennant marked the exact halfway point in John McGraw's long tenure as manager of the New York Giants. Having assumed the reins of command at the Polo Grounds in July 1902, McGraw managed the Giants for 15 years before 1917, and he managed the Giants for 15 years after 1917 before stepping down 40 games into the 1932 season. With all due respect to Connie Mack, whose Philadelphia Athletics in 1917 were mired in an extended string of last-place finishes, McGraw was the highest-profile manager in baseball. And he was as high profile to the informed, and even casual, baseball public as any of the game's greatest players of the day. If he wasn't before, John McGraw was by now . . . a rock star.

But for a manager to be a "rock star"—and McGraw was the first, at least among those who did not also play—he must not only manage a highly successful team, but be seen as a dynamic leader responsible for his highly successful team's achievements and, hardest of all, have star power rivaling that of any of his players. The first two characteristics are essential. Managers who arguably were more prominent than their players could not truly be considered rock stars if their teams were not very good, like what Casey Stengel had to cope with when he managed in Brooklyn and Boston in the 1930s and 1940s, or if they themselves were too understated, as was Bill McKechnie despite leading three different teams to four pennants, or perhaps even Mr. Mack.

John McGraw emphatically embodied all three characteristics. The achievements of his teams are beyond dispute. He managed the Giants for 31 years during which they won 10 pennants—back-to-back in 1904 and 1905, three in a row from 1911 to 1913 (after being denied in 1908 because of the Merkle game), another in 1917, and finally four in a row from 1921 to 1924. And he was certainly lauded and applauded as the architect of the Giants being Major League Baseball's most prestigious franchise in the first quarter century. McGraw was a "Little Napoleon," the fiery commander of his troops, a brilliant strategist for whom defeat was not an option, a tough taskmaster who expected (indeed, demanded) perfection and wanted it known that *he* was the driver of his team's success.

Christy Mathewson, observing his manager at work, provided context and depth to McGraw's masterminding of the game in his 1912 classic *Pitching in a Pinch*—one of the earliest books by an intellectual partici-pant in the game that educated legions of baseball fans to the reality that baseball was in fact a rigorous discipline of nuanced sophistication that gave an edge to "thinking" ballplayers and managers, although, of course, player talent and mastering the necessary basic skills were the essential undergirding. McGraw called it "scientific" baseball, and Mathewson helped show how the scientist McGraw went about winning games, the playing field his daily laboratory.

McGraw was an astute observer of players' strengths and weaknesses, including those who played against his Giants. He paid careful attention to how opposing managers handled game situations and what cards his

opposing manager held on the bench. Relentless in emphasizing preparation and requiring his players to master the game's fundamentals and the
nuances of strategy, McGraw thoroughly understood game strategy and
tactics; he burnished his reputation as a baseball genius by always looking for an angle and being willing to make unconventional (for the time)
adaptations that might give his team an edge. McGraw was at the forefront of managers thinking more strategically about *how* to win games.
This led to groundbreaking insights on the value of relief pitchers to save
and win games, and to the use of his bench players as chess pieces to win
games, not merely to be available to give starting position players an
occasional day of rest, to substitute for them when injured, or to replace
them in the event of sustained poor performance.

While developing individual skills, practice, and executing plays had
always been important, where McGraw excelled was to work at perfect-
ing anticipation and an almost balletic choreography by his teams on the
field, whether executing an offensive play or playing defense with runners on base. He drilled his players incessantly on how to play the game
and to avoid costly mistakes, but expected them to use their own initiative
during games. He wanted his players to think on their own, after they had
learned how to think from him. He castigated players for mistakes (especially dumb mistakes), but was mostly forgiving if they worked hard,
learned the many nuances of the game, respected baseball as a profession,
and desired to excel at that profession. Errors would always be made—
these were the days when gloves were rudimentary and playing fields
were often poorly maintained—and were forgiven, but McGraw left little
to chance to ensure his teams sustained a high level of baseball proficiency. If the Giants lost, they lost, but they rarely beat themselves through
lack of teamwork, lack of anticipation, lack of effort, or not having their
head in the game. Beating yourself was what truly upset John McGraw.
Whether from ingrained attention to detail or fear of displeasing their
managers' volatile temperament (or both), his teams rarely did so. This
was why the Giants were so good. He expected loyalty from his players,
but was loyal to them in turn. Even as McGraw was becoming ever more
the "Little Napoleon" for his dictatorial managerial style, his teams—
including the 1911–13 Giants who won three straight pennants, and the
1921–24 Giants who won four in a row—were often better than they
perhaps should have been with the players they had, because they were so
well schooled in how to play the game and had strong on-the-field leadership inspired and nurtured by their authoritarian manager.

Until Babe Ruth took New York City by force of power and personality, McGraw was perhaps the most famous name in baseball (although Ty
Cobb, for one, might beg to differ). He was certainly synonymous with
the New York Giants, and nearly so with baseball itself. As good as his

teams were, once fan favorite (and the pastime's most popular player nationwide) Christy Mathewson left in 1916—and arguably even before—John McGraw, the *manager*, not any of his players, was the most prominent figure on the New York Giants. McGraw was *the* shining star on his team, even though he was not a player in the field and managed at the end of his career in a tailored suit instead of a baseball uniform. It is quite possible that McGraw soured on his outstanding second baseman Frankie Frisch, whom he had been grooming to be the Giants' future manager, and traded him to the Cardinals after the 1926 season precisely because the Fordham Flash (note the flashy nickname) was beginning to eclipse the Little Napoleon in star stature.

Other managers competed with McGraw for name recognition and also became synonymous with their highly successful teams, but who among them outshone his team's star players? Perhaps only Connie Mack, whose reputation for managerial excellence and identification with his team in Philadelphia grew apace with John McGraw's in New York. McGraw's 1920s contemporary and New York rival Miller Huggins? Nope, certainly not with Babe Ruth, a transcendent player, whose rules-don't-apply-to-me bombastic ego gave the appearance that Huggins was not in control of his own team. Joe McCarthy was certainly identifiable with the success of his great Yankees teams of the 1930s, but first Ruth and Lou Gehrig, and then Joe DiMaggio were brighter stars in the pinstripe firmament. Casey Stengel had Mickey Mantle and Yogi Berra. Perhaps Leo Durocher, both when he managed the Dodgers in the 1940s and the Giants in the 1950s, but that was arguably as much—if not more—attributable to his celebrity-tabloid lifestyle as to his mastery of the local baseball scene, and by 1954 he was eclipsed on his own team by Willie Mays.

Not until Billy Martin in the 1970s, at least until he had to share the limelight with Reggie Jackson, and Earl Weaver in the second half of that decade (after Brooks Robinson had retired) was there a manager who could claim to be more famous in contemporary baseball context than any of his players. They were the heirs to John McGraw—Major League Baseball's first rock star manager.

7

THE DISTINGUISHED GENTLEMAN AND HIS "A" TEAM

The Rise and Dismantling of Mack's First Dynasty

Connie Mack also assumed rock star status as manager of the Philadelphia Athletics, but he was more Paul McCartney to McGraw's Mick Jagger. He may physically remind you (he certainly does me) of the gentleman farmer with the pitchfork in Grant Wood's 1930 classic *American Gothic*, but Mr. Mack is actually more in the character of Norman Rockwell's portraits that shine a light on American values and work ethic.

Although he did not strive to outshine his star players, or any of his players, Connie Mack was as much the face of his franchise as McGraw, historically entwined with his team, and every bit as focused on preparation and strategy. As early as 1905, when they first met in a World Series, the outcome was as much about them as their teams, with McGraw earning first bragging rights. This was true even more so when the Giants and Athletics faced off twice more in the 1911 and 1913 fall classics, but this time it was Mack who proved the better manager by virtue of his superior team—and the Athletics *were* the better team by almost any measure of analysis. Implicitly contrasting their differing styles of command, Giants pitching ace Christy Mathewson suggested in a 1914 article published in *Everybody's Magazine* that his team's failure to win any of the three previous World Series was attributable to McGraw's dominating personality—"the club is McGraw"—creating "self-consciousness, overanxiety, and nervousness" that weighed on his team "like the Old Man of the Sea." Connie Mack's Athletics, on the other hand, made fewer mistakes because, being allowed "to stand on their own feet," they did not feel as much pressure. At least, so said Mathewson.

With his patrician demeanor, particularly managing in white-collar business attire, projection of unflustered authority, and mastery of the game, Mack had every bit the stature of McGraw in Major League Baseball, even if not the fame and notoriety, but his temperament was one of studied paternalism rather than volatility. Connie Mack was the dad his players did not want to disappoint. He was a teacher—the "Tall Tactician"—demanding, to be sure, and quick to cut his losses if it was clear a player was not catching on to his lesson plan, not a firebrand creative strategist like McGraw—the "Little Napoleon"—who was far more controlling and controversial. Mack instructed, then let them play, allowing them to learn from their mistakes. McGraw taught but did not have much patience for mistakes, and was quick to harshly upbraid when mistakes were made.

* * *

In a career that would ultimately include 50 years as manager of the Philadelphia Athletics—the entire first half of the twentieth century—Connie Mack managed two all-time great teams. His first, from 1910 to 1914, was the American League's first dynasty, winning four pennants with little opposition and three World Series in five years.

The Athletics were up and down in their fortunes in the first decade of the new American League, locked in a pattern where every even-numbered season was a disappointment that Mack was able to redress in the odd-numbered years. After coming in fourth in the league's inaugural season, they won the pennant in 1902 by five games; finished a distant second to Boston in 1903; endured a fifth-place finish, although with a winning record, in 1904; won their second pennant in 1905 by a two-game margin with 92 wins, only to be shut out four times by McGraw's Giants in the World Series (three times by Mathewson alone); fell to fourth with 78 wins in 1906; competed with Detroit for the pennant in 1907, finishing only a game and a half behind with 88 victories; collapsed to a dismal sixth-place showing in 1908 with a 68–85 record; and challenged the Tigers for the pennant again in 1909, winning 95 and ending up 3½ games back. Mack's 1905 pennant winners failed to live up to expectations. In 1906, 1907, and 1909, losing crucial games late in the season proved costly for the Athletics. Given the strength of their pitching and stable core of solid position regulars, the Athletics might well be said to have underachieved in winning only two pennants in their—and the league's—first nine years. Eddie Plank and Rube Waddell, both southpaws, were two of the best pitchers in baseball, and right-hander Chief Bender was consistently effective, although he started many fewer games than the two left-handed aces and would not have his best years until the Athletics became a dynasty.

Lefties, of course, are known for their eccentricities. Plank was the mature, responsible one. A rookie in 1901, Plank had four 20-win seasons in a row from 1902 to 1905 and was on his way to what might have been the best year of his career in '06 when the toll of having averaged 320 innings per year in his first five seasons sidelined him for most of the final two months with arm problems. His 19–6 record nonetheless gave him the best winning percentage in the league, and Plank was back over 340 innings the next year, when he was 24–16. Waddell also had four straight 20-win seasons from 1902 to 1905, and six straight years—1902 to 1907—that he led the league in strikeouts. Waddell's 302 strikeouts in 1903 were the most since 1892, the year before the distance from the pitcher's rubber to home plate was established at 60 feet, 6 inches, and his 349 strikeouts in 1904 would hold up as the most until Sandy Koufax whiffed 382 in 1965.

For all his exceptional talent, however, Rube Waddell was a handful—wildly eccentric, drinking to excess, often unreliable in his commitment to the team, even if invariably reliable on the mound. Many were left to wonder whether the Athletics' five-game defeat at the hands of Christy Mathewson and the Giants in the 1905 World Series would have been so decisive had Waddell pitched in the Series. Despite having an exceptional 27–10 record and a league-leading 1.48 earned run average—the best of his career—that year, Waddell was sidelined for the fall classic, either because he injured his pitching shoulder roughhousing with a teammate or, more ominously, because Mack was made aware that gamblers had tried to entice Waddell to sit out the Series. Finally unwilling to put up with Waddell's distractions, Mack sold him to the Browns in 1908.

First baseman Harry Davis, second baseman Danny Murphy, and outfielders Socks Seybold and Topsy Hartsel were the most productive hitters in Mack's lineup in the early years. Murphy was a gritty competitor, a good defensive second baseman, and a tough out. Hartsel was the table-setter; he led the league in walks five times, and his 121 bases on balls in 1905 stood as the American League record until some guy named Ruth was deemed so dangerous that he walked 150 times in 1920. Seybold was a power threat, his 16 home runs in 1902 standing as the American League record until that same Ruth guy hit 29 in 1919. Leading the league in homers four straight years from 1904 to 1907, with a career-high 12 in 1906, Davis was the first player in either league to win back-to-back home-run titles, let alone four in a row. In both 1905 and 1906, Davis claimed two-thirds of the Triple Crown by also driving in more runs than any other batter in the American League.

* * *

Although they ended the season 3½ games behind in second place, 1909 was the foundation for the four pennants the Philadelphia Athletics would win the next five years. It was in 1909 that second baseman Eddie Collins, third baseman Frank Baker, and shortstop Jack Barry established themselves as cornerstone regulars of what would become famously known as the "$100,000 infield" that defined Connie Mack's 1910 to 1914 dynasty. When age caught up with the veteran Davis in 1911, the acrobatic Stuffy McInnis took over at first base to round out the most famous *complete* infield in history. The Cubs' Tinker-to-Evers-to-Chance is arguably the more famous infield, but third baseman Harry Steinfeldt was not part of the verse, and the Athletics' $100,000 infield was indisputably better.

The 1909 season was also the year the Athletics opened baseball's first modern reinforced concrete and steel stadium—Shibe Park—just two months before the Pittsburgh Pirates began playing ball in Forbes Field, their own new modern ball yard. Until then, major-league ballparks were primarily wooden structures with relatively small attendance capacities and limited life spans. They were prone to damaging or destroying fires, but even if they didn't burn down, the fact they were made of lumber necessarily meant they didn't last long because of weathering, and

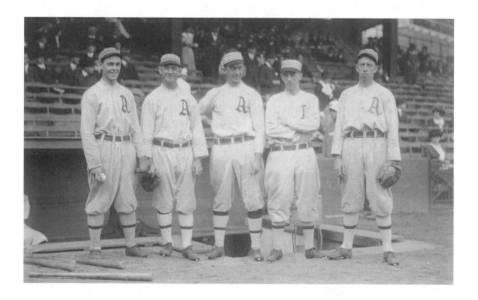

First baseman Stuffy McInnis, outfielder Eddie Murphy, third baseman Home Run Baker, shortstop Jack Barry, and second baseman Eddie Collins of the 1914 Philadelphia Athletics. *George Grantham Bain Collection (Library of Congress).*

they required constant repairs. The building materials used to construct Shibe Park gave the Athletics' new ballpark permanence and allowed for a double-deck grandstand from first to third. Named for team owner Ben Shibe, who financed its construction, Shibe Park had a distinctive architectural design that made it a landmark destination in Philadelphia. While the Pirates won the World Series in their very first year at Forbes Field, Shibe Park had to wait till 1910 for baseball's ultimate event. But then Shibe Park got to be the American League host site in four of the next five World Series, with the home team emerging as baseball champions of the world three times.

With a seating capacity of 23,000 when the Athletics first took the field there, Shibe Park could accommodate many more fans than the 13,600-seating capacity of Columbia Park, which originally opened in 1901 capable of holding just 9,500 fans. The nearly 675,000 who watched the Athletics play in their new stadium in 1909 was the most of any American League team since the White Sox drew 687,000 in 1905 while fighting for a pennant they lost to the Athletics, who were second in the league in attendance that year. Notwithstanding their brand-new stadium, the Athletics did not come anywhere close to their 1909 home attendance in any of their four pennant-winning seasons that followed—a dismaying fact not lost on Connie Mack.

Even more than a century later, the 1910–14 Philadelphia Athletics remain one of the greatest teams in baseball history. They won all four of their pennants by comfortable margins—14½ games in 1910, 13½ in 1911, 6½ in 1913, and 8½ in 1914. In the first two of those years, the Athletics confirmed their dominance of the baseball world by dispatching Chicago's Cubs in five games in the 1910 World Series, outscoring them by 20 runs, and McGraw's Giants in six games in the 1911 Series. The Athletics won 90 games for a fourth straight year in 1912, but the Boston Red Sox in their own new ball yard—the now-venerable Fenway Park— were just too good, winning 105 games. The next year, Philadelphia was back on top of the American League with another dominating performance and humiliated McGraw's Giants for the second time in a World Series, this time in five games. In 1914, the Athletics once again all but extinguished the hopes of American League challengers by midsummer, entering September with a 13-game lead on their way to 99 wins and another comfortable pennant . . . before being ignominiously, and famously, swept in the 1914 World Series by Boston's "Miracle" Braves. No team had ever been swept in the World Series before, and it couldn't have happened to a better team.

* * *

Connie Mack had an unquestionably great team. Its backbone was the $100,000 infield and a consistently solid pitching staff that included veterans Eddie Plank and Chief Bender from the 1905 pennant-winning team. Led by Collins and Baker—the team's premier stars, both historically great players—the 1910–14 Athletics were the best offensive team in the American League.

By the end of the 1914 season, Eddie Collins had displaced Napoleon Lajoie as the greatest second baseman the game had yet to see. His lifetime batting average stood at .338, and in 1,013 games for the Athletics, Collins had already stolen 367 bases, including a league-high 81 in 1910. Ty Cobb by then had played in 1,241 games, stolen 488 bases, had a much better batting average (.368) and hit for more power (a .515 slugging percentage, compared to Collins's .440), and had a slightly higher on-base percentage. But from his first full season as Philadelphia's second baseman in 1909 to 1914, Eddie Collins had a player value of 53.5 wins above replacement, marginally exceeding Cobb's 53.1. Only Honus Wagner, with 57.3 wins above replacement from 1904 to 1909, had greater value as a position player over any six-year period in the history of the game up till then. Averaging nearly nine wins above replacement per year—eight wins above replacement in any given year is considered to be an MVP level of performance—his years playing second base for Mack's first great Philadelphia team must still be considered as the best by any player at his position in the history of the American League. Only Rogers Hornsby in the 1920s and Joe Morgan in the 1970s were arguably better all-around second basemen in major-league history, but Collins has a strong case in comparison with either player. And Eddie Collins was still only 27 years old in 1914, with 13 more years as a full-time second baseman to go in his playing career.

Frank Baker, who took over at third base the same year as Collins did at second, was nearly as impressive. Deserving of being called "Home Run" Baker, he led or tied for the league lead in home runs each year from 1911 to 1914, totaling 42, while also batting .334 with 451 runs batted in. In addition to his four consecutive home-run titles, which equaled Harry Davis's record, Baker led the league in RBIs in both 1912 and 1913. Both the Cubs and Giants found him perhaps the toughest out in their World Series matchups with the Athletics. Baker had nine hits each in the 1910, 1911, and 1912 World Series, with batting averages of .409, .375, and .450. He also was the Athletics' best hitter when they were swept in the 1914 Series, batting .250 with four hits—two of them doubles—and driving in two of his team's six runs off Boston Braves pitching. Home Run Baker was the best all-around third baseman in the game's history until Eddie Mathews in the 1950s, and in the American League until George Brett in the 1970s.

The Athletics' best pitcher in 1910 and 1911 was right-handed Jack Coombs. After four undistinguished seasons, he proved a revelation in 1910 with a 31–9 record and a 1.30 earned run average. Thirteen of his 31 wins were shutouts. He followed that up by pitching three complete-game victories against the Cubs in the 1910 World Series, including the clinching Game Five. Coombs led the majors in wins again in 1911 with a 28–12 record, then outpitched Christy Mathewson in an epic 11-inning duel in Game Three of the 1911 Series in which the Giants touched him for just three hits. In 1912, Coombs had a third straight 20-win season, leading Athletics pitchers in starts and innings for the third straight year. Then came a bout with typhoid fever, which sidelined him for two years and effectively ended his career.

Mack was both astute and innovative in his use of aging pitchers Plank and Bender. The savvy manager relied on them as the spine of his staff, using both—especially Bender—often in relief to supplement a new core of young pitchers. Plank, already 34 when the 1910 season began, remained the staff ace until 1914, with superb 23–8 and 26–6 records in 1911 and 1912. Bender, eight years younger, was reaching the height of his effectiveness. He led the league in winning percentage in 1910 with a 23–5 mark, again in 1911 with a 17–5 record, and yet again in 1914 with a 17–3 performance. Bender also had a 21–10 record with 13 retroactively awarded saves in 1913, a year he started 21 games and relieved in 27 others. By 1914, however, Bob Shawkey (15–8) and Bullet Joe Bush (17–13), both in their second year, pitched the most innings and had the most decisions.

* * *

Even though the American League team in Boston intervened with a command performance to take the 1912 pennant, and the 1914 World Series debacle at the hands of the National League team in Boston spoiled the party, the Philadelphia Athletics looked to be the team to beat for at least the next several years. All four members of the $100,000 infield were still in their prime; Shawkey, Bush, and 1914 rookie southpaws Herb Pennock and Rube Bressler were primed to take over when Plank and Bender bowed out; and young catcher Wally Schang—called up in May 1913—was proving himself a budding star, having hit .278 in 186 games in 1913 and 1914. The Red Sox were the only team on the horizon that appeared capable of challenging the Athletics.

Notwithstanding their impressive 99 wins, however, 1914 marked the end of Mack's first Philadelphia dynasty. Although undoubtedly embarrassed by his team's fold against the much less imposing "Miracle" Braves—a World Series upset to rival that of Chicago's "Hitless Wonders" White Sox taking down the favored Cubs in 1906—it was financial pressures from diminishing attendance and the challenge posed by the start-up Federal League that caused Mack, who by now had secured half the ownership shares of the Philadelphia Athletics, and Shibe, who controlled the other half, to begin disbanding their great team. Taking a page from the American League's own origins, the Federal League—which lasted only two years (1914 and 1915) before financial and legal challenges forced its submission—offered higher salaries to attract the veteran major leaguers needed to build credibility. This in turn contributed to demands for more money by players staying loyal to the American and National Leagues, dollars that Mack was unable or unwilling to pay. Mack had already given Collins a sizable salary increase and a multiyear contract to ensure he was not tempted to defect prior to the 1914 season.

The Athletics' financial situation was certainly not helped by the US economy being hit with its second major recession in four years in 1913, which continued unabated into 1914. Industrial production and real income declined, and in 1914 the number of civilians in the labor force who were unemployed nearly doubled from 1.7 to 3.1 million Americans, representing about 12 percent of nonfarm workers. Tough economic times undoubtedly contributed to a dramatic 30 percent decline in attendance at major-league games, not including the Federal League, for which reliable attendance figures are not available. Notwithstanding the attraction of watching Eddie Collins and Home Run Baker, and the fact that the Athletics won the American League pennant, Mack's ledgers showed an even greater 39 percent drop in paying customers in 1914. They may have been by far the best team in baseball, but the Philadelphia Athletics were only fifth in the American League in attendance, and seventh overall among the 16 major-league clubs. This was not helping Mr. Mack pay his $100,000 infield (whose members, of course, did not collectively earn nearly that much).

It would be wrong, however, to say that Connie Mack broke up the core of his great team all at once. He did so over three years. But the heart was cut out in 1915. Mack released Plank and Bender shortly after the 1914 season ended rather than pay them their due, leaving a young pitching staff without experienced veterans. In December, he sold Eddie Collins and his expensive multiyear contract to the White Sox for $50,000, and followed up by selling Jack Barry to the Red Sox in July. Promising young pitchers Shawkey and Pennock were also gone by midseason 1915. Mack didn't get rid of Baker in 1915, but his refusal to meet Baker's salary demands caused his great third baseman to sit out the season. The next year Baker was sold to the Yankees for $37,500.

Indicative of the importance of these players, particularly Collins and Baker, the Athletics—after four pennants in five years, and six in the first 14 years of the American League's history—plunged into the first of a disheartening seven consecutive last-place finishes beginning in 1915. A carousel of players coming and going gave the Philadelphia Athletics little sense of identity in their leanest years. Many of the deals Mack made helped other American League teams to pennants with little benefit for the Athletics, aside from the all-important cash infusions he needed to keep his team in operation. McInnis and outfielder Amos Strunk, the last of the core players of the 1910–14 Athletics, were gone after 1917, as were Bush and Schang. McInnis, Strunk, Schang, and Bush went on to play vital roles in the Red Sox, winning the 1918 pennant and their last World Series of the twentieth century. Schang and Bush, along with Shawkey and Pennock, went on to become core players on pennant-winning Yankees teams in the 1920s.

It would be a full decade before Philadelphia's Athletics were competitive again. The Athletics won only 323 games—an average of 46 a season (although two years were shortened in support of the US effort in World War I)—and endured 710 losses from 1915 to 1921, amounting to their winning fewer than a third of their games (a .313 winning percentage). The 1916 Athletics were so bad, winning only 36 games the entire season with 117 losses—a .235 winning percentage—that nearly the entire rest of the league could keep its head above the .500 watermark just because Philadelphia was on the schedule. Only one of the seven other American League clubs even had a losing record—the Washington Senators at 76–77—and they might have finished with a .500 record had they been able to make up a missed game due to a rainout, which would have been against . . . Philadelphia. Mack managed back-to-back victories only six times all season; the Athletics' other 24 wins were all one-game winning streaks. Four times the Athletics endured losing streaks of at least nine games, including one that went 20 games. Even the 1962 expansion New York Mets, who famously lost 120 games in a 162-game season, did not have a winning percentage as bad as the 1916 Philadelphia Athletics.

Not surprisingly, attendance at Shibe Park plummeted immediately once Mack began breaking up his first dynasty. Connie Mack surely understood that not having a competitive club, that fielding a team that arguably was not even major-league caliber, was not going to attract fans to the stands. But Mack was more concerned with the financial travails of ownership than with the quality of the team he was showcasing and having to manage. He was willing to bide his time, however long that might be, before investing in rebuilding and not constantly dealing away his best players in an effort to stabilize his club's coffers. It would take more than a decade, but that time would come.

8

THE STALLINGS PLATOON AND HOW THE 1914 MIRACLE BRAVES WON IT ALL

Systematic platooning of starting position players did not emerge as a fully credible lineup strategy until George Stallings's masterful manipulation of all his outfielders in a three-position platoon proved indispensable to his Boston Braves, stunning the baseball world by rising from the ashes of dead last on the Fourth of July, 15 games behind the Giants, to win it all in 1914. The Braves won the pennant by 10½ games, an amazing 25½-game swing in the standings after Independence Day, and capped it all off with a World Series sweep of Connie Mack's imposing Philadelphia Athletics, champions of the baseball world in three of the four previous years. Not for nothing are they remembered as the "Miracle" Braves.

Platooning—rotating two players at the same position, usually depending on the starting pitcher—was not so much unheard of before this time as not practiced. It was already at least intuitively understood by players and managers that a batter hitting from the opposite side of the pitcher's throwing arm had a better visual and reaction-time advantage, but few teams had ever platooned. Moreover, the prevailing wisdom was that, barring injuries or poor performance, seven of the eight position players in the starting lineup were the same from day to day and played every inning of every game, the understandable exception being inevitably banged-up catchers since the very limited armored protection at the time—flimsy chest protectors, shin guards, and cage-like masks—made it nearly impossible for one player to hold down the position every day for a full season. The bench players rounding out the roster were there more for emergencies—to substitute for an injured regular, to give a regular an occasional day of rest, or to take over if the incumbent was ineffective—than for inclusion in the game at critical moments. If a team was truly blessed, its bench players might see hardly any action at all. Except for injuries, managers rarely replaced a starting position player during the game, with the understandable occasional exception of banged-up catchers. Even pinch-hitting for pitchers was rare because, for the most part, they finished what they started even if they were losing.

At first, the small size of rosters would have been a mitigating factor; managers wanted their best players on the field every day, and lesser lights were the reserves on the bench. Even after rosters got larger, the premium was still on fielding the best players, and for reasons of both pride and paydays—especially the money—no player in a starting role wanted any part of being systematically kept out of the lineup because of who was pitching for the other team. And all managers, including McGraw, preferred the certainties of a set daily lineup.

McGraw, however, paralleling his insight on bringing in a relief pitcher to "save" leads, was also ahead of his time in using his bench strategically in games. Quick to see the possibilities in his never-ending quest to gain a key advantage, McGraw was much more inclined to pinch-hit and sometimes pinch-run for a position player in pivotal moments of a game, typically in the later innings, which—if in any but the last inning—required a defensive replacement in the field. Although other managers were slow to follow his lead, by the teens, pinch-hitting or pinch-running for a starting position player for tactical advantage during games gained currency as a winning strategy. Part of this was enabled by the expansion of active rosters from 15 players, including pitchers, to 17 players in 1908.

If replacing a position player at a critical moment during the game was a savvy managerial move to gain a "platoon" advantage against the opposing pitcher, it made sense to seek such an advantage at a position of weakness from the beginning of the game by platooning a left-handed with a right-handed batter, depending on the throwing arm of the starting pitcher. The expansion of active rosters to 25 players in 1913 was almost certainly a major factor contributing to that year being the first that managers began using lefty/righty position-player platoons for all or a significant portion of the season. The larger rosters allowed managers to begin experimenting with platooning in a systematic way—"experimenting" because they could not be certain of platooning's efficacy as a starting lineup strategy, particularly over the course of a full season, despite the proven advantages of sometimes replacing a position player, typically a weak hitter, who batted from one side of the plate with one who hit from the other side to improve the odds of a timely hit during the course of a game.

It is noteworthy that none of the six clubs that platooned in 1913 began the season doing so, and in virtually every case, because of injuries, subpar performance by rookies, or the struggles of no-longer-in-their-prime veterans to hit pitchers who threw from the same side they batted, circumstances forced their managers' hand. With few exceptions, the players who were platooned in 1913 were either veterans very near the end of their careers or players coming into the year with limited major-league experience who went on to have relatively short or undistinguished journeyman careers. The most accomplished player to be platooned was left-handed-batting second baseman Johnny Evers, in his first year as player-manager of the Cubs, who decided by midsummer that he was having so much trouble hitting left-handers that it would be best if he played much less often when his Cubs faced a southpaw, perhaps so he could focus on managing the game rather than worrying about his at-bats against lefties.

Both of baseball's most prominent managers, whose teams met in the World Series, also platooned in 1913. In Philadelphia, Connie Mack decided in June to platoon his left-handed-batting everyday right fielder Eddie Murphy, even though Murphy was having a good season at the plate against both lefties and righties. That came to an end in early August, with Murphy back to being the full-time right fielder. And in New York, it was an injury in late May to starting third baseman Buck Herzog, a right-handed batter, that ultimately led McGraw to platoon for the first time at a position other than catcher. The switch-hitting Tillie Shafer did so well in his absence that McGraw decided to start him at third against right-handed pitchers even after Herzog returned to the lineup. Herzog's only starts against righties the rest of the season came only in the games where McGraw needed the versatile Shafer to play either second base or in the outfield because of injuries to starters at those positions. Ironically, after returning from his injury, the right-handed-batting Herzog hit much better (.341) in his 19 starts against right-handed pitchers when Shafer started at a position other than third base than he did (.257) in his 18 starts against lefties. There was no other year in his 13-year career that Buck Herzog was platooned.

The fact that six teams platooned in 1913 suggests that, rather than platooning being the brainchild of McGraw or any one manager alone, it seems to have been a strategy whose time had come. But of the six teams that platooned that year, only the Braves, Cardinals, and Giants did so the next, and neither McGraw nor Cardinals player-manager Miller Huggins—who, as a switch-hitter himself, always had a platoon advantage against any pitcher he faced—began the season with a platoon at any position. The one who did—McGraw's rival in the 1914 pennant race, Braves manager George Stallings—has gone down in history as the mastermind behind the concept of platooning. For Stallings, however, platooning was making a virtue of necessity, compensating for his team's positions of weakness in the outfield.

* * *

Boston was one of just two of the original 1876 National League franchises to make it to the twentieth century. Chicago was the other. Playing today in Atlanta, the Braves are also the only franchise that can trace its genesis without interruption to the very first year of professional "major" league baseball dating back to the inaugural season of the National Association in 1871.

It was the Wright brothers coming to Boston—Harry and George, not Wilbur and Orville—that set the stage for Beantown becoming, in the 1870s at least, the center of the professional baseball world. The baseball Wright brothers—Harry as the manager, center fielder, and occasional pitcher, and George as the best player at shortstop—first came to Boston in 1870 with the Cincinnati Red Stockings, baseball's first professional team taking on any and all amateur baseball clubs in the Northeast, many of which were actually semipro, that wanted to try their luck against them. From May 1869 until June 1870, the Cincinnati pros won 81 consecutive games—some accounts report 84, others 89—before finally losing in Brooklyn, soon after having soundly defeated opponents in the Boston area. As openly paid "professionals," as opposed to club players—many if not most of the best of whom were given a share of the gate receipts or monetarily rewarded with a set stipend, even if not officially paid because that was against the rules of the association that governed high-profile amateur baseball competition—the Cincinnati team was much more skilled than the club teams they (mostly) demolished. Their winning streak captivated the crowds that came to see them, inspiring the entrepreneurial bent of the men who financed the amateur clubs and nurtured competition, which accelerated the movement toward what was already an inevitability—the creation of baseball's first for-profit league of paid players. The Cincinnati team disbanded later that summer after its loss in Brooklyn, and the brothers Wright were recruited to be the foundation of a professional baseball team in Boston, which took their former Cincinnati team's nickname. The Boston Red Stockings became an original franchise in the National Association, which began league play in May 1871. As for the justifiably more famous Wright brothers, Wilbur had just turned four and Orville would be born in August.

George Wright was arguably baseball's first star player as the game transitioned from club to professional-league competition, and his older brother Harry was baseball's first "professional" manager. Although their team finished third in the first year of the first professional baseball league, the Boston Red Stockings took each of the next four National

Association pennants before the league disbanded in 1876, unable to organizationally compete with the newborn National League. The Red Stockings wasted no time in changing allegiances from the National Association to the new National League, which Harry Wright considered a more *professional* professional league.

Boston won two of the first three National League pennants, a third in 1883 (by which time both Wright brothers had left town), three in a row from 1891 to 1893, stepped aside in rebuilding mode as Baltimore took the next three, and returned to the top in 1897 and 1898. The 1890s Beaneaters were probably the best team in the first quarter century of Major League Baseball. Outfielder Hugh Duffy, a prolific hitter, and right-hander Kid Nichols, likely a better pitcher at the time than his contemporary Cy Young (both starting their careers in 1890), were the outstanding players when the Beaneaters won their first three pennants. They were joined by outfielder Billy Hamilton and third baseman Jimmy Collins, also two of the best in the game, for Boston's next two in the late 1890s. Manager Frank Selee was at the forefront as a strategist in a decade when baseball was becoming more professional and the game more sophisticated.

As the nineteenth century came to an end in 1899 and 1900, the Boston Beaneaters were displaced at the top of the National League heap by the Brooklyn Superbas, a franchise bolstered by many of the Orioles' star players from their pennant-winning years as a result of syndicated shared ownership. But the veteran Beaneaters were also more than showing their age with many core regulars in their 30s. If that was not enough to point their trajectory, the National League franchise in Boston was perhaps the hardest hit by defections of key players when the upstart American League declared itself to be "major" in 1901. Adding insult to injury, many of the Beaneaters' defectors—most notably Collins—stayed in the city to play for the team that would soon be called the Red Sox in homage to when the Beaneaters were the Red Stockings. Although by now over the hill, Duffy's defection to become player-manager of the American League entry in Milwaukee was also a significant blow.

For the first 10 years of the new century, the Beaneaters had little roster continuity and virtually no good players. They also had a bit of an identity crisis, playing as the Doves from 1907 to 1910 (not as in the bird of peace, but rather nicknamed after the team's new owners, George and John Dovey) and then as the Rustlers (after the Doveys got out of the baseball business) before finally becoming the Braves in 1912. Not until the arrival of Stallings in 1913 did the franchise have a winning record after May in any season. In six of those years, they never saw the sunny side of .500 after April. In 1905 their four principal starting pitchers each *lost* 20 games, including Vic Willis—four times a 20-game winner for the Beaneaters before they became persistent losers.

The only position players of consequence on the National League side of Beantown during those lean years were first baseman Fred Tenney, who played 15 seasons in Boston before being traded to the Giants in December 1907, and Bill Sweeney, a versatile infielder who played for Boston from 1907 to 1913. Otherwise, there was frequent turnover among position regulars. Boston often dealt for veteran players in their declining years, including former Pirates stars Claude Ritchey and Ginger Beaumont in 1907, former Giants stars Dan McGann and Bill Dahlen in 1908, and former Phillies star Roy Thomas in 1909. Only one of these players—Beaumont—was as young as 30, and none played in Boston for very long.

* * *

Stallings was said to have stated: "Give me a ballclub of only mediocre ability, and if I can get the players in the right frame of mind, they'll beat the World Champions." That's what he had, and that's what he did. In 1913, when he took over as the franchise's ninth manager in the 12 years since Selee left Beantown, Stallings inherited the worst team in baseball, one that had not *lost* fewer than 90 games since way back in 1903, when they dropped 80 in a 140-game schedule. Recasting the roster and proving a tough taskmaster, Stallings turned the team around in his first year at the helm, guiding the Braves home fifth with a 69–82 record, a substantial improvement over their eighth-place 52–101 mark the year before. He also ended up platooning at both corner outfield positions and, for a time, at third base. The Braves were clearly getting better, and even though a writer for *Baseball Magazine*, the preeminent publication on the sport at the time, claimed the Braves had a sufficiently "formidable ball club" to finish second or third in 1914, nobody expected them to beat out the Giants, still less the way they did so.

Famously last on the Fourth of July, the Braves won seven of their next 10 games to cut their deficit to 11½ games on July 15. They had played half their schedule, but were still at the bottom of the standings. They then became the "Miracle" Braves, storming to the pennant by winning 61 of their remaining 77 games. A surge of 27 wins in 33 games between July 17 and August 25 moved the Braves past six other teams into a virtual tie for first place with the Giants. After two more weeks of jockeying for position, the two teams were again knotted at the top when the Giants came into Boston for three games beginning on September 7. Beating the New Yorkers two out of three put the Braves in first place to stay; winning 12 of their next 14 decisions pushed their lead up to six games on September 23; and by the time the Braves showed up at the

Polo Grounds for their final five games with the Giants, they had already clinched the pennant.

Although Stallings couldn't be sure going into the season, pitching turned out to be a particular strength for the 1914 Braves. Hub Perdue, a right-hander, and Lefty Tyler were his most proven pitchers. Both were 16-game winners the previous year, and both were entering their fourth season. The Braves also had a promising pair of right-handers in their second season—Dick Rudolph and Bill James. Perdue got off to a bad start and was traded away in late June. Rudolph and James, however, were exceptional, both winning 26 games, and Tyler had 16 wins of his own. After July 4, Rudolph went 20–2 and James 19–1, while Tyler was 10–5, as the Braves blazed their way past seven other clubs to ultimately win the pennant emphatically.

With Rabbit Maranville in his second year as the Braves' shortstop and the sage, savvy, and ultracompetitive Johnny Evers acquired from the Cubs before the start of the season to play second base, Stallings's infield was set and stable for the entire year. Butch Schmidt, in his first full major-league season, started all but 11 games at first base, and third base was held down first by Charlie Deal and then by Red Smith, obtained in a midseason trade from Brooklyn because he was a much better hitter than Deal. Hank Gowdy did most of the catching; his 115 games behind the plate were second in the league to the Giants' Chief Meyers. It was Evers's arrival that had some baseball writers perhaps overly optimistic about the Braves' outside chance of being a contender. They were right about that; Evers wound up the National League's Most Valuable Player. Maranville was the MVP runner-up.

Stallings had no such stability in his outfield, however, which was a mess. In previewing the upcoming 1914 season for *Baseball Magazine*, the great baseball writer Fred Lieb projected that fourth place was the best that could be expected of the Braves because "you can't do much with an outfield composed of Connolly, Mann, and Griffith." He was speaking of left-handed-batting left fielder Joe Connolly, right-handed-batting center fielder Les Mann, and the left-handed Tommy Griffith in right field. All three were rookies in 1913, with Connolly playing in 126 games; Mann in 120; and Griffith, who did not make his big-league debut until late August, in only 37. What Lieb didn't mention, but that might have figured in his assessment, was that Stallings had platooned all three at their positions in 1913. Although Mann and Griffith would have far longer careers, it was Connolly who showed the most promise in their shared rookie season—certainly in the batter's box, where he tied for the team lead in home runs with five, led the club in runs batted in, and whose .281 batting average was the highest among Stallings's regulars.

   With limited major-league experience among his corps of outfielders
and, with the possible exception of Connolly, holding a poor hand in
terms of talent, what Stallings did in 1914 was to rotate the seven to eight
outfielders he had on his roster at any one time among the three positions.
Stallings actually used a total of 11 different players in the outfield that
year. Connolly was the only Braves outfielder in 1914 who was a productive player. Playing in just 120 games, almost never against left-handed
pitching, Connolly was the Braves' most potent batsman, leading the
team with nine home runs and having the highest on-base and slugging
percentages on the club. The 10 other players Stallings used in the outfield had a collective player value of 1.1 wins *fewer* than a replacement-
level player. Stallings's brilliance was to have the insight to play them all
in a way to give his team comparative batter-pitcher advantages from
game to game, and even within games to take account of pitching
changes.
   The turning point for the Braves that made their 1914 miracle possible
was June 28. The team was mired in last place, the season already a major
disappointment based on preseason expectations. On that day, Stallings
traded Perdue to the Cardinals for Possum Whitted and outfielder Ted
Cather, both right-handed batters. Five days later, he traded with the

Joe Connolly, who was platooned in left field, and shortstop Rabbit Maranville of
the 1914 Miracle Braves. *George Grantham Bain Collection (Library of Congress).*

Phillies for the left-handed-batting Josh Devore, the Giants' left fielder when they won pennants in 1911 and 1912. And on August 23, when they were within a half-game of first place, the Braves acquired another left-handed-batting outfielder, Herbie Moran from Cincinnati, in a cash transaction. Although none of the four was better than a marginal big-league player in 1914 based on the WAR metric, each of those transactions proved instrumental in shoring up Stallings's outfield platoon.

The Braves played 158 games on their way to a 94–59 record. Platooning at all three outfield positions, Stallings's starting lineups had at least two of his three outfielders batting from the opposite side of the starting pitcher's throwing arm in all but 11 of the Braves' games, and 44 times during the season all three starting outfielders had the "platoon advantage" against the opposing pitcher. Of the players in Stallings's platoons, only Mann and Whitted—both right-handed batters—started a significant number of games against pitchers throwing from the same side they hit, even though neither did well against right-handers. Stallings, on the other hand, rarely saw fit to put one of his left-handed outfielders into the lineup when a southpaw started against Boston. It was conventional wisdom even a century ago, as it is today, that left-handed batters have more difficulty hitting lefties than right-handed batters do against righty pitchers.

Stallings's unwillingness to use the left-handed Joe Connolly against southpaws mystified some baseball writers because Connolly was the Braves' best hitter, certainly against right-handers. Connolly started only three games against southpaws and was removed from 16 games he started when a left-handed reliever came in. While one writer made sure to say that the left-handed Connolly "never had any trouble in hitting the southpaws in the minors," Stallings begged to differ, having decided in his very first year as Braves manager that Connolly, also in his first year with the Braves, however successful he may have been hitting southpaws in the minor leagues, was so fundamentally flawed as a hitter against left-handers that he was unlikely to improve. Stallings in fact had expected Connolly to be an everyday player in 1913, but after his batting prodigy got off to a rugged start and seemed particularly flummoxed by lefties, Stallings chose to start Connolly only against right-handers so he would always have a "platoon" advantage. Platooning was a strategy that worked to optimize the success of this major-league player.

Connolly's entire major-league career, 1913 to 1916, was as a platoon left fielder for Stallings, who never gave him the opportunity to play regularly against southpaws. Only 19 of his 322 career starts were against left-handers, and just five after his rookie year in 1913. Stallings, however, inserted him into 48 other games that a southpaw started against Boston, always to get his dangerous bat into the game after a righty was brought in as a reliever. Perhaps validating Stallings's apparent judgment that Connolly would not be successful against left-handed pitching, Connolly hit just .209 in the 67 games he played where the Braves faced a southpaw starter, compared to .298 in games with a right-handed starter.

* * *

By platooning his outfield, Stallings was able to maximize the offensive possibilities of his starting lineup regardless of whether the opposing starting pitcher was righty or lefty. What made his outfield rotation so effective, however, was quite likely Stallings's ability to take advantage of the fact that two of his infield regulars—first baseman Butch Schmidt and second baseman Johnny Evers—were both left-handed batters. Most other managers, with only one left-handed-batting infielder at most, and generally wedded to the same starting outfielders game in and game out, could count on no more than three left-handed batters against right-handed starting pitchers. Stallings, moreover, did not hesitate to replace his starting outfielders in games when the opposing team brought in a reliever who threw from the opposite side of the day's starting pitcher. The 87 defensive substitutions Stallings made in the outfield during the season, almost all because of pitching changes, were far more than the 1914 season average of 38 by the seven other National League teams; the eight American League clubs averaged 26.

With Evers and Schmidt playing every day unless hurt, Stallings's mixing and matching of his outfielders gave the Braves a platoon advantage in their starting lineup of at least four left-handed batters in 80 of the 102 games they faced a right-handed starter, and in 14 of those games he started five left-handed position players—three outfielders, Evers, and Schmidt. The payoff was that the Braves' 63–35 record in games started against them by right-handers was by far the best of any National League team. Only the American League champion Philadelphia Athletics had a better record against right-handed starters; Connie Mack had the advantage of five left-handed batters among his core regulars—infielders Eddie Collins and Home Run Baker, outfielders Amos Strunk and Eddie Murphy, and switch-hitting catcher Wally Schang—none of whom he made part of any platoon when writing out his starting lineups.

If there were any who might have wondered whether Stallings would rotate his outfielders in the crucible of the World Series, particularly with the Athletics being such a formidable opponent and heavily favored to win, Stallings stayed with what worked during the season. Connolly—Boston's most productive batter—and Moran, both left-handed, started only three games in the Braves' four-game sweep. As he had in all but three games all season, Stallings benched Connolly in Game Two when southpaw Eddie Plank took the mound for Philadelphia, giving the right-handed Ted Cather the start in left field instead. Stallings also benched Moran in favor of the right-handed-hitting Les Mann in right field. And in the fourth and final game of the Series, Connolly was pinch-hit for and replaced in left field by Mann as soon as Athletics right-handed starter Bob Shawkey was relieved by lefty Herb Pennock in the sixth inning. With the Braves in front when it came Moran's turn to bat for the first time against Pennock, Stallings elected to keep him in the game. The right-handed Possum Whitted, who finished the season as a regular in the Braves lineup, played every inning of all four games in center field, never mind that the Athletics started three righties.

Notwithstanding that Stallings's outfield rotation to gain a competitive platoon advantage against opposing pitchers was a key element under-writing the 1914 Braves' unexpected championship, there was surprising-ly little if any commentary at the time about his insightful strategy. None of the articles in *Baseball Magazine* in 1913, 1914, or 1915 mentioned it. The magazine's feature on the World Series praised Stallings for winning it all with "a club of green players and discards from other clubs" and "with one of the strangest assortments of misfit players we ever saw gathered together under one banner," and observed that Stallings had "performed the impossible" with a team that "had no license" to win either the pennant or the World Series, but did not say how exactly he did it. Stallings, in an extensive interview for that publication recounting his team's tribulations and ultimate triumphs in 1914, said nothing about platooning or how he used his outfielders. The closest he came to that point was to give what has become the now-standard trope about it being a team effort. "Ours is no one-man team," said Stallings.

* * *

The Braves nearly duplicated their 1914 miracle the next year. Once again, they were in last place in mid-July, 10 games below .500 at 32–42 on July 12, trailing the first-place Chicago Cubs by 8½ games. And once again, starting with 18 wins in their next 22 games, the Braves had the league's best record the rest of the way. The upstart 1915 Philadelphia Phillies, however, who moved into first place on July 13, were nearly as good, and the Braves' surge led them only as far as second place, where they ended seven games offpace. It was almost the same story in 1916. The Braves did not get over the .500 mark for good until June 24, then fought their way into a three-way tie for first place with Philadelphia and Brooklyn on September 4, but lost seven straight games—six of them to the Phillies and the Robins (as the Dodgers were then called)—to put an end to any hope of winning the pennant. They ended up third, four games behind Brooklyn. The 1916 Braves were not only the last competitive team Stallings managed—they failed to finish better than sixth in his four remaining years as their manager—but the last time the National League franchise in Boston was in a pennant race until after World War II. And the United States had yet to enter the *First* World War.

The 1914 Stallings outfield platoon was essential to the Braves' success because none of their outfielders were much good, except Connolly, who may or may not have been able to hit lefties had he been allowed to start routinely against them. But Boston's "miracle" season was really an anomaly, the confluence of exceptional years by Evers and Maranville up the middle, Connolly in his platoon role, Hank Gowdy's emergence as a steady hand behind the plate, first-rate pitching by Tyler and especially 26-game winners Rudolph and James, and of course, Stallings's brilliant insight to play all his outfielders in a way to give his team comparative batter-pitcher advantages from game to game and even within games to take account of pitching changes. This was a team for which the stars aligned perfectly, including the fact that McGraw's Giants could not hold on to the 6½-game lead they had as late as August 6, rather than a team with the quality core players that are the foundation for winning clubs to sustain success over multiple seasons.

Johnny Evers was near the end of the road in 1914—nonetheless, one of his best seasons—even though he was only in his early 30s. Officially listed as weighing only 125 pounds at 5-foot-9 (which was an average height for American males at the time), the scrawny Evers was worn down and beaten up by years of playing a middle-infield position, including takedowns by baserunners at second base and assorted on-the-field fisticuffs that were not unusual in the Deadball Era. The next season began with Evers sidelined by injury and ended with him on the field but bedeviled by personal demons. Indicative of his value, the Braves' 1915 surge into the pennant race began with his return to the lineup in July. He played in only 83 games in 1915 and 71 in 1916.

The 332⅓ innings Bill James pitched in 1914, during which his uncounted pitch count was certainly high because he surrendered 118 walks and fanned 156, effectively finished off his career, even though he was only 22. He pitched in only 13 games in 1915, and would make just one other appearance in the major leagues. Lefty Tyler remained a key figure on the Braves' pitching staff until traded in 1918 but was not one of baseball's top-tier pitchers. Dick Rudolph was 22–19 and 19–12 when the Braves competed in the 1915 and 1916 pennant races. Indisputably his team's best pitcher, and always a gamer—in 1915 he was 15–7 from the point in mid-July when the Braves were in last place until the end of the season—Rudolph also was not an elite pitcher.

Rabbit Maranville was the only Braves player during the Stallings years who was unquestionably one of the best players in baseball. Although a Hall of Fame shortstop, the WAR metric suggests Maranville was probably never the best all-around shortstop in the National League over any five-year stretch of his career; the Giants' Art Fletcher was probably the better shortstop during the years Maranville was at his best between 1914 and 1919. Best remembered as a terrific defensive short-stop and one of the game's most colorful personalities, not necessarily in that order, Maranville was not an impact offensive player.

Even with his success in platooning the entire Braves outfield in 1914, Stallings probably recognized that the surest road to winning, or even just being a competitive team, was to have as many position players as pos-sible he could feel comfortable writing into the starting lineup every game, regardless of the starting pitcher. Looking to defend the Braves' championship, Stallings did not stand pat with his reliance on platooning at all three outfield positions. He traded instead for right-handed-batting Phillies slugger Sherry Magee to be a daily presence in center field, giving up Possum Whitted and lots of cash in the exchange.

An 11-year veteran, the 30-year-old Magee had led the National League in hits, doubles, and RBIs in 1914 while crashing 15 home runs—the third most in baseball—and batting .314. Although he hit only two home runs for Boston in 1915 on account of his new team's home fields being far more expansive than Philadelphia's Baker Bowl—the Braves played in Fenway Park until their new ballpark, Braves Field, was ready for baseball in mid-August—Magee played every game but one in Stall-ings's outfield and was the Braves' best player and most potent hitter. None of his teammates hit more than two home runs either, and the Braves hit only three of their 17 home runs at home in 1915. Stallings continued to platoon at two outfield positions, with Connolly the left-handed fixture in his left-field rotation. Connolly hit .298 with nearly 300 fewer plate appearances in his platoon role than Magee.

After finishing third in 1916, the Braves were sold to a consortium of bankers who were less than willing to invest much in the way of precious dollars to keep the Braves competitive, let alone help them get better. Maranville was the Braves' only star player as they slipped from conten-tion, and he would be gone after 1920, dealt to Pittsburgh for players and cash. Money going to the Braves was also a key element in the deals that sent Tyler to the Cubs in 1918, promising young southpaw Art Nehf to the Giants in 1919, and versatile infielder Johnny Rawlings to the Phillies in 1920. Nehf had been the Braves' best pitcher in 1917, when he went 17–8 with a 2.16 earned run average for a sixth-place club with a losing record.

The Boston outfield, meanwhile, remained a mess. Magee had a mediocre 1916 season and left the Braves in August 1917 after being put on waivers, apparently not worth what he was being paid. Stallings cy-cled multiple outfielders through all three positions in his remaining years in Boston. Ironically, as his team became progressively worse, and generally lacking quality players, Stallings used less a deliberate platoon system than a more mix-and-match philosophy of trying different combinations of players in both his outfield and infield—with little success. By 1920, George Stallings had had enough. Even though he certainly understood the financial constraints, it was obvious to Stallings there was no ownership commitment to winning. But Stallings's historical legacy remained secure.

* * *

Because the narrative of the "Miracle" Braves is so compelling, 1914 historically is considered the baseline year for platooning. But had the Braves not made their miracle run, or perhaps even fallen just short, would Stallings's platoon stratagem have even been noticed? This is a fair question because six clubs tried platooning in 1913, and the payoff seemed to generate mostly a collective shrug.

There does not appear to have been any meaningful attention brought to that particular lineup strategy, even if baseball writers were aware it was happening. Moreover, most of the players platooned in 1913 were over the hill or just getting started. Among those platooned who were closest to being impactful players, Cubs veteran second baseman Johnny Evers and Braves rookie Joe Connolly were both left-handed batters who were in their teams' starting lineups most days anyway because most pitchers were right-handed. Moreover, Evers platooning himself may have been obscured by his also being the manager, by the fact that he didn't begin doing so until the end of July, and because he started at second base in more than two-thirds (39) of the 57 games his team faced a southpaw. McGraw's third-base platoon involving the right-handed-batting Buck Herzog, in his sixth big-league season, and the switch-hitting Tillie Shafer, in only his second year, went largely unnoticed because Herzog often played against right-handers when McGraw used the versatile Shafer to fill in for an injured player at another position. Herzog, however, was known to have been unhappy about his playing time.

While Stallings was far from alone in trying out platooning as a starting lineup strategy in 1913, he was the most perceptive and committed as to its efficacy. Without specifically mentioning platooning, Stallings when asked about his approach to managing is said to have often answered: "Play the percentages," which is of course what platooning is intended to do. Because managers were already "playing the percentages" to give their team the best possible comparative batter-pitcher advantages at key moments within games, the strategy of platooning can be seen on its merits alone as arguably less revolutionary than evolutionary. An argument can be made that platooning two players at the same position to take advantage of a right-handed/left-handed split became institutionalized by the collective wisdom of managers observing and learning from each other and becoming more strategic in their thinking. That more teams would pick up on the advantages of platooning was likely inevitable, a logical extension of position-player substitutions during games, especially for managers who, like Stallings, did not have eight players they felt comfortable starting every day. But had the Braves not won it all in 1914, the concept would probably have remained relatively obscure until some team *did* win using a platoon system.

What *was* revolutionary is how quickly other teams adopted the strategy once the Braves' "miracle" season ratified platooning as a winning strategy. While platooning seemed an obvious strategy for bad or mediocre teams to try to compensate for the weaknesses of individual players—and for the Braves, their entire outfield was a weakness—it was not intuitively obvious that managers of very good teams would find much merit in platooning, even if they—like McGraw, especially—nonetheless sought platoon advantages in the course of a ballgame. But taking notice of the Braves' championship year, managers with much stronger cohorts of players than Stallings had were quick to see the value of platooning at a position of relative weakness in their lineup—and every team had at least one. By the end of the Deadball Era and through most of the 1920s, platooning was widespread in the major leagues, and most teams had a tandem lefty-righty couple playing at least one position, almost always in the outfield, and also often the catcher. Platooning in the middle-infield positions was very rare, because most infielders were right-handed batters and because managers desired day-to-day stability at such premium defensive-skill positions.

Unlike Stallings, who used multiple players interchangeably in his outfield, most managers who platooned relied on a designated tandem pair to split the position between them. As with a set lineup, managers who platooned almost all wanted a semblance of stability in which players understood their roles in the scheme. Of course, players understanding their role is not the same as *agreeing* with such a division of their playing time. As Bill James—the baseball historian, not the 1914 Braves pitcher—has suggested, the fact that good players understandably resented the implication they lacked the ability to be everyday players helped to doom the widespread use of position platoons as a lineup strategy by the end of the 1920s. Although platooning did not die out, it did not make a comeback until after World War II, courtesy of a manager who was himself platooned as a player on three pennant-winning teams—Brooklyn in 1916 and McGraw's Giants in 1922 and 1923. The name? Stengel. Casey Stengel.

9

MANAGERIAL PARADIGM SHIFT AND THE TURNAROUND IN PHILLIES AND REDS FORTUNES

George Stallings was representative of an important paradigm shift in the development of Major League Baseball as a business enterprise in which the role of "major-league manager" developed as its own profession separate from past or present accomplishments on the field of play. It was not so much that the manager position was becoming more professional, but rather that its professionalism was evolving into greater complexity. Managers were always professionals. It's just that what team owners looked for in managers had changed at least twice since baseball became a "professional" sport in the late nineteenth century.

In the 1880s when Major League Baseball was establishing itself as a viable business enterprise, as well as America's national pastime, the men who were professional baseball managers had business-organizational skills that were arguably as important as managing the game on the field because they kept their teams viable and intact, which was necessary to sustain and grow the professionalism of the game itself. Managers were an integral part of small front office operations. It was a version of the industrial-business model, with an owner making the capital investment and expecting results, a floor manager making sure the operation was productive and profitable, and the players as skilled labor doing the job. The broad extent of a manager's responsibilities meant that some were not qualified to manage the game on the field, leaving that responsibility to a player who assumed the role of "captain" on the field.

A few managers—most notably Cap Anson and Charlie Comiskey—were themselves outstanding players and were in effect their own field captains, directing the action on the field while also attending to the many administrative and logistical tasks at hand. Anson managed the Chicago White Stockings to five National League pennants in seven years between 1880 and 1886, and Comiskey led the American Association St. Louis Browns to four straight pennants from 1885 to 1888. Their competitive success established the importance of managers being well versed in the nuances of the game and able to be effective leaders of players on the field, even if they sat on the bench. Moreover, beginning in the 1890s, managers no longer needed to bring entrepreneurial savvy and skills to the job. They could now concentrate on their responsibilities for the game on the field because baseball's owner-barons—the men with the money—were consolidating more of the responsibility for organizational matters into their own hands to protect their business investment.

Playing managers consequently became more prevalent in the 1890s, but they still had to perform other "managerial" responsibilities necessary for the business functioning of the ballclub, particularly when it came to wheeling and dealing with players, which remained a core responsibility of the managers' job even though the owner was ultimately writing their paychecks. Many in baseball's pioneering generation of *player*-managers were also quite talented entrepreneurial types who were masterful at organization, marketing, and recruiting and keeping players. A few, like Anson, Comiskey, and Connie Mack, were so good at those tasks that they became important powerbrokers in the game, and it was not unusual well into the twentieth century for managers to have a stake in ownership—as did Mack, Clark Griffith, John McGraw, and Wilbert Robinson.

Predictive of the future, neither of the two most successful and influential managers in the 1890s were player-managers. Frank Selee, named manager of the Boston Beaneaters in 1890—a year of significant upheaval because about three-quarters of National League players unilaterally left their teams to play in the Players' League—had no major-league experience of any kind. His professional playing career was limited to a single year playing minor-league baseball in New England in 1884. Recognizing his limitations on the field of play, Selee turned to managing the next year; he managed five years in the minor leagues, which included winning two pennants in the Northwestern League, and developed a reputation as a shrewd administrator of his team's operations, a keen observer of how the game was and could be played, and an astute judge of players' abilities and potential—characteristics that were instrumental to his leading the Beaneaters to five pennants in the last decade of the nineteenth century. Selee's rival in the pursuit of excellence, Baltimore manager Ned Hanlon, led the Orioles to three straight pennants from 1894 to 1896. Hanlon had been at best an average player as an outfielder in 12 big-league seasons and had not had winning success in his two prior years as a manager, which included a year in the Players' League and being removed as Pirates manager halfway through the 1891 season. Despite that less than august resume, his cleverness as a baseball strategist was enough for Baltimore owner Harry Von der Horst to take a chance on Hanlon.

Selee and Hanlon did much to make the job of "baseball manager" its own discipline precisely because of their ability to anticipate and think ahead in game situations and to come up with strategies and tactics to give their teams a game-deciding edge. Perhaps being fully engaged as bench managers, rather than player-managers, gave them a distance from actually playing in the game that allowed them to be more observant, take a broader perspective, and think more critically not only about ways to win, but what it took to win. They were innovators bringing the game into the modern era.

As the centuries turned, however, the future was put on hold as owners mostly favored either the best players on their teams, sometimes only in their midtwenties, or men who were stars in the 1890s at the end of their careers when it came to making a managerial change. Many of the new managers were chosen for the intensity with which they played, strong on-the-field leadership, and their insight into the game. Outfielder Fred Clarke was the prototype of the star-player-named-manager-of-his-team paradigm. Although only 24 years old, Clarke was in the midst of an exceptional season—his fourth in the big leagues—in which he would hit .390 when he was named player-manager of the Louisville Colonels in June 1897. After Louisville was downsized out of the National League in 1900, Clarke was transferred to Pittsburgh by Barney Dreyfuss, who owned both clubs, and immediately named player-manager of the Pirates.

From a base of 16 managers to start the 1901 season—which included active star players Jimmy Collins, Clark Griffith, and John McGraw in the newborn American League—there were 53 managerial changes in the first decade of the twentieth century, not including interim managers who managed only a handful of games. Twenty-three times a team's owners turned to an active player to take over as player-manager, most of whom were either stars or prominent players on the downside of their careers, and 12 other managerial changes went to former star players. White Sox outfielder Fielder Jones in 1904, and Cubs first baseman Frank Chance and Cleveland second baseman Napoleon Lajoie, both in 1905, were the most notable star players still in their prime to become managers of their teams that decade. A handful of the new managers had experience playing in the majors but were not "star" performers, and a few had played only in the minors. None of those stayed as manager of their team for very long.

As the first decade of the twentieth century drew to a close, the managerial landscape was once again changing. By now it was increasingly apparent that the most successful teams were those that were not only the most talented and skilled in execution, but also the most sophisticated in their use of strategy to win games. The skills and competitive fires of a star player or former star player to inspire and lead his team were no longer necessarily sufficient to make for a good manager. Managerial titans Mack and McGraw were prototypes of the "professional" manager because of their success in developing winning teams and mastery of strategy. So too were player-managers Chance and Clarke, who each won four pennants. And the same was true of Griffith, although his teams were much less successful.

Playing managers consequently were becoming more the exception than the rule, and only five teams had player-managers in 1910, including Chance with the Cubs and Clarke with the Pirates, both having been extraordinarily successful in their dual roles for many years. But if playing managers were no longer as prevalent, nine of the 11 other big-league teams were still managed by former *star* players trading on their baseball acumen. While player-managers were hardly an endangered species, their focus was understandably divided; they needed to devote time and energy to their playing careers as well as their managerial responsibilities. So it was that the teens saw a new trend of franchise owners hiring managers who had an astute knowledge of the game and its players, and of whom it was expected their complete focus would be given to the team's performance on the field.

The new model baseball manager was a "professional" who was older than all or most of his players, had strong organizational and leadership skills, was a student and master of the many nuances of the game, and who gave considerable thought, time, and energy to training regimens, learning the strengths and weaknesses of his players, and inculcating an inherent understanding of fundamentals and instinctive play among his ballplayers. The best managers, of course, already had these attributes—especially McGraw and Mack, the rock star and the distinguished gentleman—but now these qualities were being more deliberately sought in the men who would be managers. Rather than active players on the roster or former star players, many of the managers hired in the teens were former journeyman ballplayers of a certain age who were respected for their ability to handle players and their mastery of the many intricacies of game strategy.

This was particularly true in the National League. Of the 23 managerial changes in the National League between 1911 and 1920 (not including interim managers), eight were given to active players who began their managerial careers as playing managers and four to former star players.

Among them, only Wilbert Robinson, who took charge in Brooklyn in 1914, is remembered as a manager. The other 11 named as new managers by NL clubs in the teens had limited or undistinguished major-league careers, and one, Hugo Bezdek, a highly esteemed college football coach named to manage the Pirates in 1917, had no prior baseball career as a player. Of these 11 men, three—George Stallings, Pat Moran, and Fred Mitchell—would win pennants, and one, Branch Rickey, would become famous as a trailblazing front office executive. All four were selected more for their baseball acumen than for name recognition. Stallings and Moran probably best exemplified this new model of the "professional" baseball manager.

* * *

Six different National League teams won the pennant in six years from 1914 to 1919—Boston, Philadelphia, Brooklyn, New York, Chicago, and Cincinnati. Two of those clubs were managed by Pat Moran, a journeyman catcher in an 11-year playing career that ended in 1911 and widely respected for his deep knowledge of the game. Neither the Philadelphia Phillies nor the Cincinnati Reds had won a National League pennant before Moran took charge as manager. Both clubs won for the first time in his first year at the helm.

A National League franchise since 1883, the Phillies were less known for winning than they were for their history of top-flight outfielders. Sam Thompson, Billy Hamilton, and Ed Delahanty—three of the best outfielders in the first 50 years of Major League Baseball—played together in Philadelphia for five years between 1891 and 1895, and all three hit over .400 in 1894, which was arguably the best year ever to be a hitter. Delahanty batted .400 three times in the 1890s, all with the Phillies. Thompson's 165 runs batted in for the Phillies in 1895 were just one fewer than the record of 166 he had set eight years earlier with the Detroit Wolverines—a record that stood for 34 years until Babe Ruth drove home 168 runs in 1921. Hamilton's 914 career base swipes, 510 with Philadelphia, were the most by any player until Lou Brock in 1978 and Rickey Henderson in 1990 passed him.

Their outfield remained the Phillies' biggest strength in the first decade of the new century. Center fielder Roy Thomas, a rookie in 1899, was particularly adept at getting on base, drawing 100 walks in each of his first seven big-league seasons and leading the league in seven of his nine years with the Phillies before being sent across state to the Pirates in 1908. Left fielder Sherry Magee joined Thomas in the outfield in 1904 and soon became one of the league's best run-producers, leading the league in runs batted in three times in 11 years in Philadelphia and winning the batting crown in 1910 to break Honus Wagner's four-year stranglehold on the title. His 27.5 cumulative wins above replacement between 1906 and 1910 was highest of all National League outfielders since the turn of the century until exceeded by both Hack Wilson and Paul Waner from 1926 to 1930.

Other than finishing second in 1901, 7½ games behind Pittsburgh, and arguably not even that year, the Phillies had never in their history been a serious contender in a pennant race before Moran was given charge of the team. But having had a winning record in six of the 13 previous seasons, they hadn't been all that bad. In 1913, the Phillies were runners-up, although far behind the Giants. It is reasonable to say that the Phillies were already a good team on the cusp of being pennant competitive at the time Pat Moran took the reins in 1915. Although Magee was traded away just as Moran was arriving, right fielder Gavvy Cravath, who didn't make it to the major leagues to stay until 1912 at the age of 31, had emerged as one of the most feared power hitters in baseball. In 1913, his second year with the Phillies, Cravath led the league with 19 homers and 128 runs batted in and was five hits shy of winning the batting title and the Triple Crown. Fred Luderus, their first baseman since 1912, was also a danger-ous hitter; his 18 homers in 1913 were second to Cravath. (Full disclosure requires noting that the short right field in Philadelphia's Baker Bowl contributed to Magee, Cravath, and Luderus being as productive at the plate as they were.)

But the new manager's most important asset was right-hander Grover Cleveland Alexander, eventually better known as "Pete." Alexander was already one of the best pitchers in baseball, although perhaps not yet with the aura of Christy Mathewson and Walter Johnson. Having introduced himself to the National League in 1911 by going 28–13 in his rookie season, Alexander started the 1915 season with a career record of 96–53 in his first four years. Telling of his excellence on the mound, 25 of his 96 wins were shutouts. While the American League team in Philadelphia had featured such great pitchers as Rube Waddell and Eddie Plank, the Na-tional League team had none to call great until now.

Notwithstanding their talent, Pat Moran inherited a team in 1915 whose would-be competitive arc was still uncertain. If finishing second in 1913 raised expectations for a more competitive run the next year, 1914 proved a major disappointment when the Giants faltered and it was Bos-ton's "Miracle" Braves, not Philadelphia's Phillies, that took advantage. The Phillies finished sixth, costing manager Red Dooin his job and open-ing the door for Moran. Changes were made, beginning with Moran imposing greater discipline that included a more rigorous spring-training regimen. The Phillies opened the season with eight straight wins and won 11 of their first 12 to serve notice they would be a contender. They moved into first place for good in mid-July and won the pennant by seven games over the second-place Braves.

Alexander was the best pitcher in baseball in 1915 with a 31–10 record and a 1.22 earned run average. His 12 shutouts were the most by a National League pitcher since Pud Galvin of the Buffalo Bisons threw 12 in 1884 in an era where it was possible for him to start 72 of his team's 115 games because allowed pitching techniques were so different. Cravath led the league in home runs for the third straight year with 24—the most in the majors since Buck Freeman hit 25 back in 1899—and in runs batted in with 115, his third straight 100-RBI year. Luderus's .315 batting average was second in the league, and Cravath and Luderus were first and second in both on-base percentage and slugging average. It was the acquisition of Pacific Coast League star shortstop Dave Bancroft, however, that was probably the linchpin to Philadelphia's pennant. A terrific defensive shortstop, Bancroft solidified the Phillies' middle infield, and they went from the worst team in the league defensively in making outs on batted balls to the most proficient.

Philadelphia and Boston were World Series cities for the second year in a row, but this time instead of the Athletics and Braves, it was the Phillies and Red Sox. The Phillies got off to a promising start when Alexander shut down the Red Sox in the opening game. Boston won the next four as Red Sox pitchers completely stymied Phillies hitters. Alexander was a tough-luck 2–1 loser in the third game when a two-out single by Duffy Lewis in the bottom of the ninth at Fenway Park drove in the winning run. Nobody would have thought at the time that the Philadelphia Phillies would not be in another World Series until 35 years later, or that after Alexander's Game One victory they would not win another World Series game for 65 years.

The Phillies remained in the hunt each of the next two years, finishing second both times. In 1916, they were within a half-game of first-place Brooklyn with six games remaining, only to lose four and finish 2½ back. Alexander was 33–12, again leading the league in ERA (1.55), and established the record for most shutouts in a single season with 16. (Technically, Alexander only tied the record set by George Bradley in 1876, the National League's inaugural season, when pitching was such a fundamentally different profession that Bradley could start every one of his team's 64 games that year.) Southpaw Eppa Rixey, in his fifth big-league season, had a breakout year to complement Alexander's 33 wins with 22 of his own, and his 1.85 earned run average was third in the league. The Phillies finished second again in 1917, but that year the Giants had command of the pennant race by midsummer. Their cause was not helped by Rixey going from 22 wins to 21 losses. Alexander, however, with a 30–13 record, once again led the league in wins, earned run average, and

Phillies slugger Gavvy Cravath with Red Sox star center fielder Tris Speaker during the 1915 World Series. Cravath led the NL with 24 homers and 115 RBIs. *George Grantham Bain Collection (Library of Congress).*

shutouts. For the fourth consecutive year, he threw more innings, had more complete games, and sent more batters back to the dugout as strike-out victims than any other pitcher in the National League.

Americans today might know more about Alexander the twentieth-century baseball pitcher, who even had a movie made about him in 1952 starring Ronald Reagan, than the late nineteenth-century US president he was named after—Grover Cleveland, in the middle of whose first administration the future "Old Pete" was born. President Cleveland is best remembered, if remembered at all, for being the only US president to serve two nonconsecutive terms, having lost his first-administration re-election bid in 1888 in the electoral college despite winning the popular vote, before winning again in the next presidential election and not mounting another reelection bid in 1896 because his party deserted him in favor of William Jennings Bryan on account of his perceived failed stewardship of an economy in depression. Grover Cleveland Alexander, the pitcher, won 373 major-league games, which is tied with Christy Mathewson for the third most in history and for the most ever by a National League pitcher. His 90 career shutouts are the second most in history, after Walter Johnson, and 11 more than Mathewson for the most by a National League pitcher.

By 1918, with the country now fully engaged in World War I and Phillies owner William Baker beginning to shed his club's best players for financial reasons, Pat Moran recognized he no longer had a potential winning situation in Philadelphia. Most notably, Alexander was sent to the Cubs in primarily a cash transaction after the 1917 season ended, notwithstanding 190 victories in his seven years with the Phillies and having just had three consecutive 30-win seasons. Mathewson from 1903 to 1905 is the only other pitcher since the end of the nineteenth century to win 30 three years in a row. The Phillies were counting on Rixey, after his 16–21 performance in 1917, to revert to his 22–10 form of 1916 to make up for Alexander's departure. Cravath and Luderus were nearing the end of their careers, although Cravath would lead the league in homers again in 1918 and 1919, and Bancroft seemed stalled in his development.

After finishing sixth with an Alexander-less roster in 1918, and with his team further hurt by Rixey's absence owing to military service in World War I—Alexander also missed almost the entire year for the same reason and played virtually no role in the Cubs' winning the pennant—Moran was released from his contract and promptly signed on to manage in Cincinnati. Thus began more than three decades of losing season after losing season for the Philadelphia Phillies, while the Cincinnati Reds were the next long-suffering franchise that Pat Moran turned into an instant winner.

* * *

Cincinnati was baseball's cradle of civilization. It was there that Harry Wright, outfielder, pitcher, baseball promoter and entrepreneur, organized the first openly professional team in 1869 by recruiting and paying the best talent he could find, not just locally but far and wide. This was the team—the Cincinnati Red Stockings—whose winning 81 (or maybe 84 or 89) consecutive games against all comers before finally losing in June 1870 led directly to the birth of a professional "major" league in 1871. Cincinnati did not have a club in that league, but became a charter member of the National League in 1876 and lasted five seasons without a pennant before folding after the 1880 season. Cincinnati returned to Major League Baseball in 1882 in the new American Association, then transferred allegiance to the National League in 1890—a year of tremendous turmoil in the professional baseball world that unfolded with three major leagues in play, including the short-lived, one-year-only Players' League. Shortening their nickname from Red Stockings to simply Reds, Cincinnati has been a National League mainstay ever since.

But in all that time, until Pat Moran came to town, Cincinnati—the city where the professional game was born—had won just one "major-league" pennant, in the 1882 inaugural season of the American Association. The Reds had finished as high as third only three times since 1890 and had never seriously contended for a pennant. From 1906 to 1916 they had just one winning season. Perhaps the Reds' most notable player in historical context in the years since the turn of the century was Miller Huggins, best known for starting a dynasty as manager of the New York Yankees. Hardly a top-tier player—in fact, more of an average, everyday big-leaguer—Huggins was precisely the kind of underappreciated player whose will to succeed and do the little things to help his team win makes him especially valuable to teams that already have the talent to compete for championships. That kind of team, the Reds surely were not in the six years Huggins played second base for them from 1904 to 1909 before being traded to the Cardinals. Using his small stature to great effect for drawing walks—he was no more than 5-foot-6 and weighed barely 140 pounds—Huggins understood that it didn't matter how you got on base, just that you got on base.

It was not until the midteens that the Reds, who finished seventh or eighth four years in a row, began assembling the team that Pat Moran turned into a winner. The foundation for their success were the acquisitions of Heinie Groh, a young player McGraw inexplicably included in a May 1913 trade for an overrated right-hander named Art Fromme, and center fielder Edd Roush, another young player whom McGraw inexplicably included in a July 1916 trade for over-the-hill former Giants infielder Buck Herzog. The Roush trade was most prominent at the time for sending the great Christy Mathewson to Cincinnati for the express purpose of taking over as manager of the Reds. Matty's managerial stint lasted until he left in late August 1918 to serve his country in France during World War I.

Groh and Roush were probably Cincinnati's two best position players in the entire first half of the twentieth century. Perhaps most famous for his unusually shaped "bottle bat," which differed from ordinary bats by *not* being gradually tapered from the meat of the barrelhead to the handle, Heinie Groh was unquestionably the best third baseman in the National League since the late nineteenth-century days of John McGraw and Jimmy Collins. Groh's 28 wins above replacement from 1915 to 1919 were the most of any National League third baseman over any five-year period in the twentieth century until Eddie Mathews in the 1950s. Edd Roush led the league with a .341 batting average in 1917—his first full season in Cincinnati—and again with a .321 average in 1919. His .331 batting average in 12 years with the Reds proved to be his ticket to the Hall of Fame.

Partially on the strength of winning 13 of Mathewson's final 15 games before their manager went off to war, the Reds had finished third in the war-curtailed 1918 season—their best ending since third place in 1904—and had back-to-back winning seasons for the first time since 1902 to 1905. Signing Moran as manager and trades with Brooklyn for veteran first baseman Jake Daubert and with the Giants for veteran southpaw Slim Sallee before the start of the 1919 season were a significant boost to the Reds' prospects. Until mid-August, the Reds were in a tight race for the pennant with McGraw's Giants. By the end of August, their lead was seven games. They won the pennant by a convincing nine games. The 1919 Cincinnati Reds are remembered almost entirely because they were the winners in a World Series the Chicago White Sox conspired to lose. But Cincinnati, whose collective wins above replacement were higher than Chicago's, might really have had the better team that year, or at least the team that played fully to its potential.

The Reds, however—like Stallings's Braves in 1914, and Moran's Phillies in 1915, and Wilbert Robinson's Dodgers (then known as the Robins) in 1916, and Fred Mitchell's Cubs in 1918—were one-shot pennant winners whose roster of players was not up to the task of sustained success. Although Moran had his team in the thick of the pennant race for most of the 1920 season, including a game-and-a-half-lead in early September, Cincinnati could not keep pace with either Brooklyn or New York and had the worst record in the National League thereafter on their way to a third-place ending, 10½ games behind. Their September swoon perhaps predicted their struggles the next year, when they fell below .500

in the third game of the 1921 season, never to see a winning record again. They finished sixth. Unhappy in Cincinnati, Heinie Groh was traded to the Giants when the season ended in return for a significant amount of cash and veteran outfielder George Burns. Groh helped the Giants to pennants each of the next three years; Burns played three years for the Reds before his career ended in 1925 with the Phillies.

After his 1919 World Series triumph, however tainted it might have been, Pat Moran managed the Reds four more years before dying at the age of 48 during spring training in 1924 from kidney disease. By then, however, he had assembled one of the finest pitching staffs in the league. With Eppa Rixey, Dolf Luque, and Pete Donohue as their top three starters, the Reds were first or second in the league in fewest runs allowed every year from 1922 to 1927. Pitching was the foundation for consecutive second-place finishes in 1922 and 1923, although the Reds were not really competitive with McGraw's Giants either year, and again in 1926 under Jack Hendricks, who took over as manager after Moran's untimely death. Rixey, acquired from the Phillies in 1921, and Donohue each had three 20-win seasons. The right-handed Luque, the first and only prominent player from Cuba until after Jackie Robinson broke Major League Baseball's color barrier, was outstanding in 1923 with a 27–8 record and league-leading 1.93 ERA, and he led the league in earned run average again two years later.

Unfortunately for the pitchers, Cincinnati did not have a productive offense. They were seventh or eighth in the league in runs in all but two of those years. Edd Roush batted .341 between 1922 and 1926, but in the context of "lively ball" times was less of an impact offensive player than he had been in his first five "Deadball" years with the Reds. The most interesting offensive note for the Reds during these years was that in 1926 they claimed the National League's top two hitters in batting average—catcher Bubbles Hargrave at .353, and outfielder Cuckoo Christensen at .350. Neither, however, started more than 89 of their team's 157 games or had more than 385 plate appearances. Christensen, a left-handed batter, rarely started against southpaws, and Hargrave shared starting-catcher duties. Neither of the next two at the top of the NL batting average leaderboard in 1926 had more than 384 plate appearances, either. Pittsburgh rookie Paul Waner, whose .336 average was officially fifth in the league, would have been the National League batting champion by current rules. Playing in 144 of his team's games, Waner had 618 plate appearances.

* * *

There were also 23 managerial changes in the American League between 1911 and 1920, the same number as in the National League. Nine of the new managers were still mainstays in their team's lineup. Several others already had established resumes as managers, most notably Clark Griffith when he became Washington's manager in 1912, Frank Chance when he took over in New York in 1913, and Miller Huggins, selected by the Yankees to be their manager in 1918 after five seasons managing the perennial-loser St. Louis Cardinals.

As was the case in the senior circuit, many of the first-time managers chosen to skipper American League teams in the teens were men respected for their mastery of baseball strategy, knowledge of players, and organizational skills relating to training and preparation, as well as for their leadership abilities. Whether they had been star players themselves was beside the point. Branch Rickey, for example, named to manage the St. Louis Browns in 1914, had played in only 118 major-league games, and Pants Rowland, who managed the White Sox from 1915 to 1918 and led them to a World Series championship in 1917, did not have a major-league playing career.

Although his actual baseball savvy and leadership skills were open to question—he had a losing record in four of his six full seasons managing in the minor leagues—Rowland is said to have impressed White Sox owner Charles Comiskey with his baseball intellect and ability to judge and mold talent when managing in the Three-I League, at least according to Comiskey biographer Tim Hornbaker. After hiring a series of managers, beginning with Griffith, who were highly respected if not great players in their big-league careers, Comiskey's selection of Rowland was consistent with the new paradigm for selecting managers that surfaced in the teens. Similarly, Kid Gleason, Comiskey's choice to replace Rowland in 1919, earned his job as a well-respected baseball mind from years of coaching rather than for his distinguished major-league career in the 1880s and 1890s as a pitcher and second baseman. Having led a team regarded as one of the best baseball had yet to see to the pennant in his first year at the helm, Gleason was left to wonder what might have been were it not for the conspiracy of eight of his players—seven of whom were position regulars or starting pitchers—to throw the 1919 fall classic to Pat Moran's Cincinnati Reds.

10

THE FALL OF THE RED SOX DYNASTY

The year 1918 became infamous in Boston baseball lore for being the last championship won by the Red Sox in the entire twentieth century. It hardly would have seemed so at the time. The Boston Red Sox had six American League pennants to their credit and won all five of the World Series they had played; there was no World Series in 1904. With Connie Mack's Philadelphia Athletics, also with six pennants and winners of three of the five World Series they had played, lost in the wilderness, the Red Sox were the dominant franchise in the American League, although some in Chicago would have argued otherwise, the White Sox having dominated the league in 1917.

Then came "The Curse"—Boston selling Babe Ruth to the New York Yankees in December 1919, ostensibly so that Red Sox owner Harry Frazee, also a Broadway producer, could fund *No, No, Nanette*. The Yankees went on to become the most glorious franchise in major-league history, if not in the history of all sports anywhere in the world, while the Red Sox wallowed in envious misery, doomed for the next 84 years. But if Frazee brought on the Curse, was not the Pre-Cursor to the Curse the decision of the previous Red Sox owner, Joseph Lannin, to sell his outstanding center fielder, Tris Speaker, to the Cleveland Indians just before the start of the 1916 season despite his team about to embark on a defense of their 1915 championship? Like Ruth, Speaker continued to play at an extraordinarily high level for a full decade after leaving Boston. If he never had the satisfaction of claiming the mantle of undisputed best player in baseball, it was only because when Speaker finally eclipsed Ty Cobb beginning in 1920, there was Babe Ruth.

Both Boston superstars were dispatched because the franchise faced financial difficulties—the *No, No, Nanette* story was mostly for dramatic effect—and because both were demanding a bigger paycheck. The Red Sox, winners of two World Series with Speaker as their preeminent star, went on to win two more without him, in large part because they now had Ruth. But the precedent was set . . . and sometimes it takes time for curses to become apparent. The Pre-Cursor to the Curse came back to haunt Boston in 1948, when the Red Sox and Indians finished the 154-game schedule tied for first, necessitating the first ever playoff in American League history. Cleveland won the one-game playoff to go to the World Series, which they also won. Everything in the playoff game that could go wrong for Boston did, including the most fundamental pitching decision—who to start—by the most esteemed manager in the game, Joe McCarthy, which was controversial at the time and has been second-guessed ever since. One of Cleveland's spring-training coaches was none other than Tris Speaker.

* * *

Even had Connie Mack not begun breaking up his great team after being swept in the 1914 World Series, the Philadelphia Athletics might have had difficulty extending their dynasty—although they would have remained competitive—because the Red Sox were reaching their peak at precisely that moment. Their drive to dominance began in 1909—the same year the Athletics laid the foundation for their 1910–1914 dynasty—with Bill Carrigan settling in as their catcher, rookies Speaker and Harry Hooper becoming core regulars in the outfield, and Smoky Joe Wood, another rookie, joining a pitching staff that was a work in progress now that Cy Young had left after the 1908 season. They were joined the next year by two rookies who likewise became top-tier players, infielder Larry Gardner, who played second his rookie season before moving permanently to third base in 1911, and outfielder Duffy Lewis. Those six were the key to Boston's return to greatness after seven lost years following their 1904 pennant. Lewis in left, Speaker in center, and Hooper in right played together for six years, from 1910 to 1915, and are probably the most famous outfield in history (which doesn't mean they were the best).

The first two years those six played together were not successful ones for the Red Sox. They were not competitive either year, finishing fourth in 1910 and regressing to fifth place in 1911. It was not just because Philadelphia's Athletics overwhelmed the rest of the league. Wood, who threw very hard, had a breakout season in 1911 with a 23–11 record and a league-leading ratio of 7.5 strikeouts per nine innings, but was temperamental and considered somewhat of a clubhouse cancer. First baseman Jake Stahl's decision to quit baseball in 1911 removed a potent bat from the Boston lineup. Unusual for the Deadball Era, the power-hitting Stahl was a free swinger with a propensity to strike out. In addition to his leading the league in homers and his team in RBIs in 1910, he fanned in nearly one-quarter of his at-bats and more than a fifth of his plate appearances while setting a new record for strikeouts (128) that not even the slugging, swing-as-hard-as-he-could Babe Ruth ever approached. Stahl's unenviable record stood until Vince DiMaggio whiffed 134 times in 1938.

Representing a microcosm of American societal prejudices and tensions of the time, the Red Sox clubhouse was divided between Catholic and Protestant factions. In keeping with the country's republican form of government, there had been a strong anti-Catholic strain in American society since the founding colonies because of inherent suspicion of papal supremacy in matters of both faith and state. The mostly impoverished Irish and Italian immigrants who were then coming to the United States in seemingly endless waves for jobs and a better life was alarming to many Americans who feared that growing ethnic communities of Catholic immigrants would upend a recognizable American way of life, including largely rural cultural values and decentralized religiosity manifest in the many Christian faiths that populated the country. Many German immigrants, who were also coming in large numbers, likewise were Catholic. Nativist opposition to the perceived threat posed by immigration took on an often-ugly anti-papist cast. Speaker and Wood were leaders of the Protestant faction of the Red Sox, Carrigan and Lewis of the Catholic faction. Toward the end of Boston's disappointing 1911 season, Carrigan and Speaker were said to have had brutal fisticuffs provoked by the catcher taking exception to the star center fielder's anti-Catholic slurs. Despite clubhouse sectarian tensions that persisted at least until Speaker and Wood left Boston, most accounts do not suggest they carried over onto the ball field.

Whatever their divisions, the Red Sox soared to the pennant in 1912 by 14 games over the even more surprising Washington Senators and 15 over the heavily favored Athletics, who nonetheless probably had the best all-around team. No team in Boston's baseball history has matched the 105 victories of the 1912 Red Sox. Even if the principal players were mostly the same, the 1912 season began with a more optimistic outlook because of three fundamental changes—new owners, new manager, new ballpark. The change in ownership occurred at the end of the previous season and was brokered by league president Ban Johnson, who made sure that Jimmy McAleer took over as president of the Boston franchise. Managing the Senators at the time the league president came calling, McAleer was a longtime Johnson loyalist who had helped recruit National League players for the American League start-up enterprise in 1901. As the Red Sox' new top executive, McAleer persuaded Jake Stahl to return to Boston, not only as the first baseman, but also as manager. And the Red Sox opened the 1912 season in a brand-new home that over time would assume mystical importance in baseball lore. That would be Fenway Park.

Speaker's .383 batting average was third in the league, and he was the best position player in Major League Baseball, based on wins above replacement. Lewis played every game and drove in 109 runs—tied for second in the league—while mastering the outfield incline up to the left-field wall, not yet a "monster," to such an extent it became known as Duffy's Cliff. And the Red Sox had three 20-game winners led by Smoky Joe Wood with a 34–5 record, whose 35 complete games in 38 starts included 10 shutouts. The highlight of the season came on September 6 at Fenway Park, the pennant race all but over because Boston held a 14½-game lead with a month left, when Wood hooked up against Washington's great Walter Johnson, who would finish the season with 33 wins of his own. The stakes were high because Johnson's record-setting 16-game winning streak had come to an end less than two weeks before, and Wood was working on 13 in a row. They were two of baseball's fastest pitchers in a face-off. Back-to-back ground-rule doubles by Lewis and Speaker into an overflow crowd secured for Wood his 14th consecutive victory, 1–0. He went on to tie Johnson's 16 straight before he was finally beaten.

After defeating the favored Giants in the only seven-game World Series that required eight games (the second being called because of darkness after 11 innings with the score tied), the Red Sox showed they were not yet ready to compete with Connie Mack's superior ballclub. By any standard, 1913 was a failed season. The defending champions could not even break the .500 barrier for good until September, and they went on to finish fourth, 15½ games behind the Athletics. Their poor season exacerbated clubhouse tensions between the rival Speaker and Carrigan camps and, more damaging, also fueled political gamesmanship in the front office between the team president and the manager. Jake Stahl also held ownership shares and seemed inclined to want to move into an executive position; his sights were thought to be set on McAleer's team presidency. In mid-July, after a tough loss in Chicago that felled the team to 18½ games out of first, McAleer dismissed Stahl, a controversial move that did not go unnoticed in the offices of the American League president.

Angered by the move and convinced that McAleer was neither competent as team president nor (the graver sin) any longer sufficiently loyal to him personally, Ban Johnson engineered the sale of the Boston Red Sox to Joseph Lannin, a wealthy Canadian developer with extensive real estate holdings in New England. Lannin's deep pockets were especially valuable at the time because the nascent Federal League, which unilaterally declared itself a "major league" in 1914, was aggressively pitching star players, including Tris Speaker. Johnson would know; the Federal League's playbook was the same as Johnson's 14 years earlier to start up the American League. Catcher Bill Carrigan, highly regarded as a leader and for his knowledge of the game, even if not much liked by Speaker, replaced Stahl as manager. Under new management, Boston improved from 79 to 91 victories in 1914 and finished second to the Athletics.

By the end of the season, it was clear that the Red Sox were poised to challenge for the American League pennant in the years ahead even had Mack kept his outstanding team intact. Not only were Lewis, Speaker, Hooper, and Gardner in career prime time, but the Red Sox' pitching was bolstered by the additions of Dutch Leonard (first name Hubert, to distinguish him from a later Dutch Leonard, first name Emil) in 1913; Rube Foster and Ernie Shore, who was included in the same mid-July deal with the International League's Baltimore Orioles that brought one Babe Ruth to Boston—in 1914; and Ruth in 1915. (The Babe mostly sat on the bench to observe and learn after coming to Boston the previous summer.) Leonard's league-leading 0.96 earned run average in 1914, when he went 19–5, remains the only time a major-league pitcher throwing more than 200 innings had an ERA of less than one run a game. Those pitchers' integration into the Red Sox' starting corps proved indispensable to the three championships that followed because all three of Boston's 20-game winners in 1912 had flamed out. Two were gone, and Smoky Joe, though still there, had thrown almost exactly 1,000 innings by his 23rd birthday in October 1912; plagued by injury and illness, he averaged just 139 innings pitched the next three years, compared to the 344 he threw in 1912 alone. And by 1915, Smoky Joe was no longer throwing smoke. After averaging 7.2 strikeouts per nine innings the previous five years, Wood's strikeout ratio in 1915 dropped to exactly half that. He was finished as a pitcher, but because, like Ruth, he was a good hitter—except not nearly *that* good, and certainly not with *that* power—Joe Wood went on to have a second career as an outfielder. Ruth's 18–8 record as a rookie pitcher and Wood's 15–5 mark helped the Red Sox to the 1915 pennant, but neither pitched in the World Series as Boston made quick work of the Phillies in five games.

* * *

The year 1915, Babe Ruth's first full year in Boston, turned out to be Tris Speaker's last. The best offensive player in baseball at the time besides Ty Cobb, and arguably a better all-around player because of his defensive brilliance in center field, Speaker hit just .322 in 1915—his lowest batting average since his first full season in 1909. Now that the Federal League had financially failed and was no longer in competition for players' services, and using the fact that Speaker's average had declined each year since he batted .383 in 1912, Boston owner Lannin wanted to cut back his best player's salary from $17,500 to the $9,000 he was being paid before being given a big boost to stay away from the Feds.

Speaker's cause to keep at least most of what he had earned in 1915 was not helped by the fact that, in addition to being his team's best player, he was also a divisive figure in the clubhouse, particularly with Carrigan, his manager. Speaker held out; Lannin engaged in some character assassination about Speaker no longer being the great player he was; and Ban Johnson maneuvered as league president to engineer a deal that sent the great Tris Speaker to the Cleveland Indians just days before the 1916 season got under way. Boston got pitcher Sad Sam Jones as part of the deal, and Jones would go on to have a quite decent career, including being an important member of the pitching staff in 1918, but this deal really was about the money.

After Speaker was sent packing to Cleveland, the Red Sox lost a bit of their offensive edge, but none of their competitiveness. Without Speaker, who led the league with a .386 batting average for his new team, Boston won a second consecutive pennant and World Series in 1916 despite being sixth in the league in scoring. Pitching and defense were the key to Boston's success. The Red Sox gave up the fewest runs of any team in the league, and would do so each of the next two seasons as well. Ruth was 23–12 in 1916, led the league in earned run average (1.75) and fewest hits per nine innings (6.4), and appeared to be well on the way to maybe becoming one of the game's best pitchers of all time . . . had he not been such a productive slugger. He did not give up a single home run in his 323⅔ innings of work, but did hit three of his own, giving him a career total of seven. Ruth also surrendered a home run in Game Two of the World Series—the only game he would pitch, as Boston needed just five to dispense with Brooklyn—when Hi Myers circled the bases on an inside-the-park drive to Fenway's deepest part in right-center field in the first inning. He then held Brooklyn without a run for the next 13 innings until his team won in the bottom of the 14th.

Notwithstanding the challenge of trying for three championships in a row, manager Bill Carrigan decided to retire after the 1916 World Series and owner Joe Lannin sold his interest in the club to Harry Frazee, a New York theater owner and producer of plays, before the start of the 1917 season. Although Lannin had been Ban Johnson's selection to buy the Red Sox when the league president felt a change in the executive leadership of the Boston franchise was necessary for capitalization purposes, his sale of the team to Frazee was not vetted by Johnson. Jack Barry, the shortstop in Connie Mack's famed $100,000 infield for whom the Red Sox paid $10,000 in July 1915 to play second base, was named player-manager. The Red Sox' quest for three straight pennants in 1917 was upended by the White Sox, who won by nine games. Ruth won 24 and hit two homers to up his career total to nine after three seasons. Who knew he would hit 705 more?

The 1918 season, of course, became progressively more infamous the closer the twentieth century came to its end as the last World Series Boston won. The Red Sox won their fourth pennant in seven years with their third manager because Barry answered his country's call to duty as America became fully engaged in World War I. Frazee lured Ed Barrow from his tenuous position as president of the International League to take over as manager. Barrow never played at a professional level. His managerial experience consisted of eight years in the minor leagues and two in the majors as skipper of the Tigers in 1903 and 1904, both losing seasons. He had not managed even in the minors since 1906. Instead, Barrow's career was primarily as a baseball executive owning minor-league franchises, and he had been president of two minor leagues. With the defending champion White Sox particularly hard hit by key players serving in either the armed forces or defense industries during the war, Barrow's

Red Sox owner Joseph Lannin, AL president Ban Johnson, NL president John Tenner, and Garry Herrmann, chairman of the National Commission, before Game Three of the 1916 World Series. *George Grantham Bain Collection (Library of Congress).*

lack of any recent managerial experience did not prevent him from returning the Red Sox to the top of the American League.

Cleveland may have had former Red Sox star Tris Speaker still at the
top of his game, but Boston had Babe Ruth. Barrow's deciding that the
Babe's prodigious productivity merited converting him from star pitcher
to full-time home-run-slugging outfielder, while also relying on him as
the team's ace on the mound, might ultimately have been the difference in
the outcome of a pennant race prematurely terminated on the second day
of September because of the war. Ruth started 70 games in the outfield or
first base and 19 on the mound. His 11 homers tied Athletics outfielder
Tillie Walker for the major-league lead. Ruth spent the first month, mid-
April to mid-May, as a regular in the starting rotation starting seven
games and winning four, but made just one pitching start in June and
three in July while playing left field or first base and batting fourth on a
daily basis. With the Red Sox up by 4½ games at the end of July, Barrow
put Ruth back on the mound, in addition to starting him in the outfield
between starts. The pitcher Babe started eight games in what turned out to
be the final month, winning six on his way to a 13–7 pitching record,
proving that while his heart was into hitting, he was still one of the best
pitchers in baseball.

The Red Sox won the World Series in six games over the Chicago
Cubs, who would have their own postseason demons to deal with for the
rest of the century and beyond. Ruth hurled a 1–0 shutout to win the
opening game, shut out the Cubs for seven innings in Game Four before
surrendering a pair of runs on his way to a 3–2 victory, and played the last
two innings of the deciding Game Six in the outfield without coming to
bat. Going back to his Game Two victory in the 1916 Series, Ruth had
thrown 29⅔ consecutive World Series innings without giving up a run—a
record that stood until Whitey Ford broke it in 1961.

To this point in his career, with three wins, no losses, and a 0.87
earned run average in three starts, Ruth's World Series exceptionalism
was all on the mound. At the plate, he had only one hit—a triple—in 11
at-bats and had struck out four times. His future, however, was clearly not
in the center of the diamond. In 1919, Ruth did start 15 games and pitched
twice in relief, and he pitched well with a 9–5 record for a team that lost
more games than they won in defense of their championship. But it was
as the cleanup hitter in Barrow's lineup that Ruth established the identity
that would make him both the greatest player and the greatest celebrity in
baseball history. Starting 106 of Boston's 138 games in left field, he hit a
stunning 29 home runs to set a new record.

By now Babe Ruth was not just a superstar, he was an entitled superstar. He demanded to be paid at least twice the $10,000 he was earning.
And reflecting in his own glory, he was becoming disruptive to team

cohesion, basically acting however he wished. The Babe was often in conflict with both teammates and his manager, contributing to Frazee concluding, wrongly, that Ruth was more trouble than he was worth, and correctly, that Ruth was worth quite a lot. Facing financial difficulties as both the Red Sox' owner and in his New York theater businesses, Frazee made the decision that would have profound consequences for the future of two franchises—good for one, a curse on the other. He sold the Babe to the Yankees for $125,000, including interest, and a $350,000 loan on the mortgage for Fenway Park. When he left Boston, Ruth had a lifetime 89–46 record as one of the best pitchers in baseball, and had hit 49 home runs on his way to 714.

* * *

Had anyone said during the New Year's celebrations as 1919 turned to 1920 that Ruth would approach perhaps 200 home runs in his career, that might have met with some skepticism but would not have been outrageous. Had they said he would hit over 700, they would have been assumed to be quite inebriated and perhaps told, this is why we have Prohibition. The 18th Amendment to the Constitution was ratified in January 1919 and went into effect across the country a year later. The New Year's Eve parties just days after the Babe was sold by the Red Sox to the Yankees were the last where becoming intoxicated was legal until 1933 when the amendment that repealed the Prohibition amendment went into effect.

A familiar face awaiting Ruth in New York was that of his former Red Sox teammate Carl Mays, whose controversial trade to the Yankees at the end of July 1919 not only set the foundation for a host of Boston's best players being dealt to the Yankees over the next five years, but set the stage for American League president Ban Johnson's ultimate downfall. By his fifth year in 1919, Mays was established as one of the best pitchers in baseball. After going 22–9 in 1917, Mays became effectively the ace of the staff in 1918 as Ruth—still Boston's best pitcher—began his transition to full-time outfielder. Mays was 21–13 and pitched even better than Ruth in the World Series, beating the Cubs twice, including a 2–1 victory in the deciding Game Six. He allowed the Cubs just two runs on 10 hits and three walks in 18 innings. Ruth's numbers were two runs on 13 hits and seven walks in 17 innings; Barrow removed the Babe in the ninth inning of Game Four after he gave up the pair of runs that ended his string of consecutive shutout innings in World Series competition.

But Mays was a difficult, prickly personality, and his team's struggles in the summer of 1919 undermined both his pitching prowess and his frame of mind. His 5–11 record in 21 games for the Red Sox was belied by his strong 2.47 earned run average. The Red Sox had been shut out in five of his losses, and five of his losses were by a single run. The final straw came in mid-July when he walked off the team during a game he was pitching and announced he would not play for Boston any longer. Two weeks later, Frazee and Barrow traded him to the Yankees—a trade that Johnson immediately nullified on the grounds that he had already decided, as league president, to suspend Mays for the sin of abandoning his team, and also on the principle that no player should be able to force a trade. Despite Johnson's edict that there could be no deal regarding Mays until his suspension had been served, the Red Sox and Yankees went ahead anyway. The Yankees were in fourth place at the time, 6½ games behind the White Sox, but believing that with Carl Mays added to their staff they still had a shot at the pennant. Johnson immediately blocked the trade, the Yankees and Red Sox got a court order preventing him from doing so, Mays finished the season 9–3 with a superb 1.65 ERA for the Yankees, and New York ended up third.

While Mays would be the Yankees' ace when they came close in 1920 and won their first pennant in 1921, the most significant outcome of the Carl Mays affair was how it pulled the rug out from underneath Ban Johnson. White Sox owner Charles Comiskey, who had teamed with Johnson to organize the American League in 1901, was no longer in the league president's camp, having become increasingly critical since the midteens of Johnson's autocratic ways. Johnson's move to block the Mays trade now made sworn enemies of Harry Frazee, whom Johnson did not have a hand in choosing as Red Sox owner, and Yankees owners Jacob Ruppert and Til Huston, whose purchase of the New York franchise he did approve. With New York, Chicago, and Boston—the three most important cities in the American League, especially now that the Philadelphia Athletics were bottom-dwellers—opposing him at virtually every turn, Johnson lost the power and leverage to which he had been accustomed, and his position became increasingly untenable.

* * *

The 1920 season must have been hard for Red Sox loyalists to take. Finishing fifth with their worst record in 14 years, they got to watch Speaker, now player-manager, lead the Indians to the pennant and Ruth blast 54 homers and dominate offensively as no player ever had before in helping the Yankees emerge as a formidable American League contender. The Curse of the Bambino was not yet named, but the die had been cast. Boston was condemned to toil at the bottom of the American League through the years America celebrated the Roaring Twenties, and well into the Great Depression besides. While the Yankees were dynasty building, the Red Sox finished last nine times in 11 years between 1922 and 1932, including six years in a row from 1925 to 1930. Their roster was in a constant state of turnover. And as the devil would have it in such cursed transactions, the Red Sox became like a Yankees farm team in the 1920s, dealing numerous players to the Bronx, including Hall of Fame pitchers Waite Hoyt in 1921, Herb Pennock in 1923, and Red Ruffing in 1930. Having sold the franchise in July 1923, Harry Frazee cannot be blamed for the Red Sox trading Ruffing to the Yankees. Ruffing failed to win even 30 percent of his decisions with the Red Sox; in 189 games for Boston, Ruffing was 39–96, including 47 defeats in back-to-back 20-loss seasons in 1928 and 1929.

The Boston Red Sox won only four more pennants the rest of the century. Their last World Series in the twentieth century? Who could forget 1986, the Red Sox failing to get the last crucial out with a two-run lead in Game Six of the World Series and nobody on base . . . moments away from exorcising the Curse . . . when . . . three singles, a wild pitch . . . and then . . . Mookie Wilson's ground ball met . . . er . . . failed to meet Bill Buckner's glove at first base. No more need be said, except that it wasn't until the twenty-first century when, four years therein, the Red Sox shed that curse in most dramatic fashion at the Yankees' expense. Perhaps the Red Sox had to pay in blood to reverse the Curse—specifically, the blood seeping through Boston ace Curt Schilling's sock as he gamely pitched in the 2004 American League Championship Series in a must-win game against the Yankees with staples in his ankle to keep a frayed tendon in place. Then they won the World Series. The Curse was finally put to rest.

11

CLEVELAND'S INDIAN SUMMERS

Although many baseball prognosticators expected the Chicago White Sox to repeat as American League champions in 1920 despite their increasingly suspicious loss to Cincinnati in the 1919 World Series, there was also a strong bias that the Yankees' winter acquisition of Babe Ruth, on top of the deal that added Mays to their pitching staff, made them the favorite to win the pennant. Instead it was the Cleveland Indians, now managed by their star center fielder Tris Speaker, who finished first. The Indians also beat Brooklyn in the World Series to make Cleveland a championship city in baseball for the first time.

But it was not as though the city of Cleveland had a history of persistent, unrelenting failure in Major League Baseball. For most of the 1890s, the Cleveland Spiders were one of the best teams in the National League. Established as an American Association franchise in 1887, the Spiders switched allegiances to the National League two years later. From 1892 to 1898 the Spiders, featuring some of the best players the game had yet seen, had the third-best winning percentage of the 12 major-league teams. It was their misfortune, however, to be competitively eclipsed by two nineteenth-century dynasties—the Boston Beaneaters and the Baltimore Orioles—that won every pennant those seven years. Cleveland came close in 1895, finishing second, three games shy of the Orioles, and were a more distant second in 1896. With such outstanding players as Cy Young, Jesse Burkett, and Bobby Wallace all in their prime, there was no reason to believe Cleveland might not break the Boston-Baltimore stranglehold on first place. It all ended badly, however, with the excesses of syndicate ownership when Cleveland's owner bought out the owner of the financially distressed St. Louis franchise in 1899 and transferred all of the Spiders' best players to his new team. The Spiders' decimation was so

complete it was inevitable they would be one of the four franchises eliminated when the NL consolidated from 12 teams to eight in 1900.

As the seventh-largest American city at the time, with more residents
than either Cincinnati or Pittsburgh, and with a history of competitive
baseball when Young and Burkett were two of the game's most prominent stars, Cleveland was an attractive location for a franchise in Ban
Johnson's scheme to start a new "major" league—a project whose credibility depended on the size and stature of its cities as well as recruiting as
many star players as possible from National League teams. Charles Somers, a wealthy local businessman interested in the return of Major League
Baseball to his city, provided important financial backing for Johnson's
new enterprise and became principal owner of the new league's Cleveland franchise.

Just as the 1890s Spiders had some of the game's best players in
contemporary context and were solidly competitive but unable to win a
pennant, the same was true of Cleveland's new major-league team. Third
baseman Bill Bradley and outfielder Elmer Flick, both of whom are historically underappreciated because they had a relatively short peak to
their careers, were two of the best players of their generation. A strong
argument can be made based on their cumulative WAR that Bradley,
rather than Jimmy Collins, was the best third baseman in baseball between 1901 and 1905, and Flick the best outfielder between 1903 and
1907. Right-hander Addie Joss won 20 games four consecutive years
from 1905 to 1908, including 27 in 1907; his career 1.89 ERA is the
second best in history behind contemporary Ed Walsh; he is the only
pitcher to allow fewer than one runner on base per inning in his career;
and yet the tall spindly right-hander is perhaps best remembered for his
brilliant Hall of Fame career being tragically cut short by meningitis,
which killed him in April 1911 just two days after he turned 31.

Cleveland's best and most popular player, however, was Napoleon
Lajoie, an exceptional hitter for both average and power and considered a
first-rate defensive second baseman. Until 1909 when Ty Cobb first exceeded him in level of performance, at least as measured by wins above
replacement, Lajoie was to the AL in the first decade of the twentieth
century what Honus Wagner was to the NL—by far, his league's best
player. Winning back-to-back batting titles in 1903 and 1904, Lajoie was
so popular in Cleveland that the team became known as the "Naps" even
before he was named player-manager in 1905. Lajoie would likely have
led the league in batting in 1905, too, but missed more than half the
season because of blood poisoning resulting from a spike wound. Instead,
the batting crown went to Flick.

Both Lajoie and Flick were directed to Cleveland in April 1902 by
league president Ban Johnson and Connie Mack to counter a legal gambit

by Philadelphia's Phillies to keep them from playing for Mack's Philadelphia Athletics. The Phillies had obtained a court order in April 1902 prohibiting Lajoie from playing in Pennsylvania by claiming he was still under contract when he jumped leagues to play for the Athletics in 1901. Flick had just made the same jump from the Phillies to the Athletics, and he, Johnson, and Mack likely expected the Phillies would attempt a similar injunction against him. They did not, which allowed Flick to play in Philadelphia when Cleveland traveled there while Lajoie was still legally constrained from doing so. The issue became moot in 1903 once the two leagues settled their differences, but there was never any question that both Lajoie and Flick would remain in Cleveland.

None of the Naps' first four star players ever played in a World Series. Lost in the exciting pennant races of those years is the fact that Cleveland had the second-best overall record in the American League from 1904 to 1908 after Chicago's White Sox, who themselves won only one pennant. The closest they came was 1908, when Cleveland lost the pennant to Detroit by a mere half-game. The yearlong absence of Elmer Flick, who played in only nine games because of serious health problems, almost certainly cost the Naps the pennant that year. The Naps had the best record in the league in September and October—a 24–11 mark that was three games better than the Tigers and 1½ games better than the White Sox, who finished third, just one game behind Cleveland. One of those wins came in a pitching duel pitting Addie Joss against Ed Walsh with just five games left in the season. Walsh's superb performance, striking out 15 Naps and giving up a single unearned run, was outdone by Joss, who not only did not surrender a hit, but didn't allow a single White Sox batter to reach base. Joss's perfect game kept his club just a half-game behind Detroit and all but ended Chicago's hopes by dropping them 2½ games back, but the Naps were unable to close their own half-game gap with the Tigers. Ironically, the Naps at 14–8 against Chicago and 13–9 against Detroit crushed both their pennant-race rivals in their season series.

While the ailing Flick was surely missed in 1908, the Naps' pennant chances were probably also undermined by having Lajoie as their manager. Although he was one of the greatest players in baseball history, Lajoie was reputedly indifferent when it came to managing. He was not a master tactician and showed little interest in such elementary things as protecting his team's signs. Lajoie voluntarily stepped down as manager in late August the next year with his team mired in fourth place, but continued on as the star of the Cleveland franchise, who would remain known as the Naps until he moved on to the Athletics in 1915 for the final two years of his career. Napoleon Lajoie left town after 13 years in Cleveland with a career total of 3,001 hits, about two-thirds of them for the team nicknamed after him. He had just become only the third player in history after Cap Anson and Honus Wagner to accrue 3,000 hits. Wagner's 3,000th hit also came in 1914.

* * *

The 1911 Naps introduced a dynamic new batting star to complement Lajoie. Outfielder Shoeless Joe Jackson burst onto baseball's consciousness with a .408 batting average on 233 hits that was still not high enough to prevent Ty Cobb from winning yet another batting crown, and by a fairly comfortable margin; Jackson would have needed seven more hits just to match Cobb's .420 average. Quite possibly the best natural pure left-handed batter in history until Ted Williams came along, with a batting stroke Babe Ruth himself said he tried to emulate, Shoeless Joe had a phenomenal start to his career. He led the league in hits the next two years, batting .395 in 1912 and .373 in 1913. Both years he finished as the runner-up to Cobb. Jackson's 1914 season was marred by a significant leg injury that cost him nearly a month from mid-June to mid-July, contributing to his batting average slipping to .338—tied for third in the league with Tris Speaker. Cobb was again at the top of the heap.

Despite having batted .381 so far in his Cleveland career, Jackson had antagonized team owner Charles Somers with his offseason escapades as a vaudeville performer, demands for a more lucrative contract, and reluctance to shift to first base from right field, where the strength and accuracy of his throws was a significant advantage, to make room for rookie outfield prospect Elmer Smith. Now without the popular Lajoie for the first time since 1902 and his team—rechristened the Indians—looking hopeless, and knowing both that his star player was unhappy in Cleveland and that the Federal League team in Chicago was wooing Jackson with the promise of a substantial salary boost to jump leagues, Somers was shopping Shoeless Joe. The Yankees, perhaps the club initially most interested, backed off when the Indians asked for third baseman Fritz Maisel, who seemed on the cusp of stardom. The White Sox, on the other hand, likely enticed by Somers's success in signing Shoeless Joe in mid-season to a three-year extension of his current contract at $6,000—far below his actual worth as a ballplayer—offered three prospects and $31,500 in cash. Done deal.

With Lajoie and Jackson both gone, the franchise not having been competitive since 1908 and losing 65 percent of their games in 1914 and 1915, attendance in a downward spiral because of the team's poor performance and the recession that gripped the US economy, and Somers going broke, the Cleveland Indians were in need of a bailout and reinvigoration. As the 1916 season approached, the Indians were in a Ban Johnson–engineered recovery program that began with the league president

Ty Cobb and Shoeless Joe Jackson in 1913. Cobb hit .390 to lead the league in batting and Jackson .373 to finish second. It was the third straight year Jackson finished second to Cobb. *Louis Van Oeyen (Library of Congress collections).*

organizing a syndicate led by Chicago-based self-made millionaire James Dunn to buy the franchise. Taking an interest in helping Dunn build a competitive team in Cleveland, Johnson also facilitated the transaction that sent Tris Speaker from Boston to Cleveland, rather than New York, where the Yankees, having passed on Jackson, were reportedly very interested. If the Red Sox thought that perhaps Speaker had peaked, he proved otherwise in his very first year as an Indian in 1916 by leading the league in batting.

Although Cleveland finished sixth while now-Speakerless Boston won another pennant, 1916 was a pivotal year for the Indians in building toward their 1920 pennant, and not just because they now had Tris Speaker. The pitching staff improved dramatically with the arrivals of Stan Coveleski and Jim Bagby, both rookie right-handers who had pitched a smattering of innings for other teams in 1912. But Cleveland's biggest step forward came in 1918 with their emergence as a formidable offensive ballclub, leading the league in runs, extra-base hits, on-base percentage, batting average, and slugging percentage. Among Cleveland's hitting stars was Speaker's old pal from his Red Sox days, Smoky Joe Wood, whose career transition from top-tier pitcher to an offensive player was impressive, but still only a pale echo of Babe Ruth's. Cleveland had closed to within 2½ games of Boston when the 1918 season was ended prematurely at the beginning of September because of the war. The Indians might not ultimately have overtaken Boston had the schedule played out, but it was surely reasonable to suppose they were primed for another run at the pennant in 1919. As if to accentuate the point, the Indians traded with the Athletics for another former Red Sox star, Larry Gardner, to shore up their infield defense and the middle of their batting order.

* * *

The most significant development of the 1919 season was Tris Speaker being named player-manager in mid-July, the catalyst for which was Babe Ruth getting Lee Fohl fired as Cleveland's manager. Well, not exactly, but for all intents and purposes he did. The date was July 19. The place was Dunn Field in Cleveland, where the Indians were hosting the Red Sox in the third of a four-game series. The Indians had won the first two games and seemed on the verge of making it three straight toward a possible series sweep. They held a three-run 7–4 lead in the ninth inning. Cleveland was one out from securing the victory, but the Red Sox now had the bases loaded and Babe Ruth, having hit his 12th homer of the season earlier in the game, was coming to bat . . . against a right-handed pitcher.

Since Ruth could put the Red Sox in the lead with one mighty swing, Fohl played the percentages and called in left-hander Fritz Coumbe to pitch to the left-handed slugger. Coumbe was a 13-game winner the previous year but was used sparingly in 1919 because of arm trouble. The Babe promptly knocked out his second home run of the game—only the second time in his career he had done so, so far—and the 13th of his record-setting 29 homers that year, this a grand slam, to hand Cleveland an 8–7 loss. Needless to say, club owner James Dunn was most unhappy with this outcome. The price Fohl paid for his pitching change that backfired was a forced resignation, despite his having won four of the previous five games and seeming to right the team from a stretch in which they had lost 14 of 21 games. But if Fohl was going to play the percentages by bringing in a lefty to pitch to the Babe, he really had no choice other than Coumbe, who was one of only two southpaws who pitched for the Indians in 1919—and the other, Charlie Jamieson, already destined for the outfield, had worked just 13 innings and not at all since July 3. As for Fritz Coumbe, he pitched just once more for Cleveland—one-third of an inning to finish a game in late August—before being dispatched to the minor leagues.

The Indians rallied under their new manager, Tris Speaker, to finish a strong second to the White Sox, 3½ games out. The next year, Speaker presided over Cleveland's first pennant. The Indians had a 4½-game lead in early August, lost it by the end of the month, and closed the season with 14 wins in their final 18 games to edge out the White Sox by two games and the Yankees by three. Speaker astutely platooned in the outfield positions on either side of him in center field, using the left-handed-batting Charlie Jamieson and the right-handed Joe Evans as his left-field tandem, and the left-handed Elmer Smith and right-handed-batting Joe Wood in right field. Six of the Indians' eight players with more than 400 plate appearances batted over .300, including Speaker, whose .388 average was second in the league. Gardner drove in 118 runs. Coveleski had a 24–14 record and followed up with three complete-game victories over Brooklyn in the World Series, allowing just two runs in 27 innings. Bagby won 31 while losing just 12. Ray Caldwell, nearing the end of a career spent mostly with the Yankees, also won 20 for the '20 Indians.

The 1920 season was marked by baseball's supreme tragedy when Ray Chapman, Cleveland's popular shortstop, was hit on the side of the face by a pitch from Yankees ace Carl Mays on August 16 and died from swelling of the brain inside his fractured skull the next day. One of the best pitchers of his time, bridging the Deadball and Lively Ball Eras, Mays relished pitching high and tight to batters, one of many personality traits contributing to his being widely disliked around the league. His reputation for being a deliberate headhunter made Mays a most unsympathetic villain in this case, even though Chapman being hit by the pitch was almost surely an accident. Either way, because Carl Mays had a deceptive, almost corkscrew-like, virtually underhand delivery that made the ball seem to come out from the dirt on the mound, his pitches were difficult to track and were often picked up late by right-handed batters. Chapman, the Indians' starting shortstop since 1913, unlike Mays, was highly respected as a competitor and a teammate. For the record, Coveleski outpitched Mays on the day Chapman was mortally hit by that pitch, enabling the Indians to take a half-game lead over the White Sox and push the third-place Yankees 1½ games back.

* * *

It would be 28 years before Cleveland won another pennant. The Indians were no match for the powerhouse Yankees in the early 1920s. Bagby never recovered from the 339⅔ innings he pitched in 1920 to win his 31 games; he pitched just two more years for the Indians, with only 18 more victories. Coveleski won 23 games in 1921 and led the league in ERA in 1923 before being traded to Washington in 1925. Besides Speaker, the Indians' only impact position player in the 1920s was Joe Sewell, who took Chapman's place at shortstop in September 1920 and within a few years was the league's best at his position. Sewell is famous for being almost impossible to strike out. In his 11 years playing for Cleveland, Sewell ambled back to the dugout a strikeout victim just 99 times in 6,580 plate appearances—an average of once every 66 times he took his place in the batter's box. In 1925 when he hit .336, Sewell's strikeout rate was once every 174 plate appearances—four strikeouts in 699 plate appearances. Four years later, it was four strikeouts in 671 trips to the plate.

The Speaker era in Cleveland came to an end in 1926, but not without the excitement of participating in another push for the pennant, this time trying for a remarkable comeback from a deep midsummer deficit. Trailing the Yankees by 11 games in early August, Cleveland closed the season with a 28–18 rush, only to run out of time and fall three games short, while New York struggled to a 21–27 finish. Right-hander George Uhle, a mainstay on the Cleveland staff since 1921, won 27. Soon after the season ended, Speaker was caught up in allegations, along with Cobb, of having conspired to fix a game eight years earlier. Although Ban Johnson sought to banish both players from the game, Commissioner Kenesaw Mountain Landis, despite his reputation for fiercely defending the integrity of the game by imposing a lifetime exile from all of Organized Baseball on the 1919 Black Sox conspirators, cleared both Speaker and Cobb. Speaker was about to turn 39, Cobb was a year older, and both finished their careers with other clubs.

Tris Speaker hit .354 in his 11 years with Cleveland and had an on-base percentage of .444. A career-long rival of Ty Cobb's, Speaker might have had a case for being the better all-around player because of his unmatched defensive brilliance as a center fielder, even if Cobb's extraordinary offensive prowess, including on the base paths, made him the more valuable player. In terms of player value based on wins above replacement, Speaker got the better of Cobb as the Deadball Era gave way to Lively Ball Era, almost certainly, however, in part because the ferocity of Cobb's style of play had worn him down and diminished his skills. From 1920 to 1926, Speaker hit .363 in 965 games for Cleveland while Cobb batted .361 in 877 games for Detroit. Like Speaker, Cobb was also a player-manager, assuming command of the Tigers in 1921. In the six seasons they faced each other as player-managers, Speaker's Indians beat Detroit 66 times, and Cobb's Tigers beat Cleveland 66 times.

Part II

Baseball in Transition

12

BUT FOR BLACK SOX GREED, THE YANKEES DYNASTY MIGHT HAVE BEEN DELAYED

"What if" is never an entirely serious historical proposition, but *what if* the "Black Sox" had had personal and professional integrity and *not* conspired to fix the 1919 World Series for gambling interests? Even though history is as history was, this is a question of some interest because the abrupt end of Chicago's run as the American League's best team paved the way for the beginning of the Yankees dynasty.

The year 1920 was an inflection point for Major League Baseball, and not just because it marked the end of the Deadball Era and gave rise to the sanctity of the home run. Babe Ruth was already ensuring that would happen. As the country was turning its back on the traumas of having fought a bloody "war to end all wars" in Europe and getting beyond the "red scare" that culminated from the social, political, and labor dislocations caused by America shifting from an agrarian to an urban society, the empowerment of the Progressive movement, and the rise to power of Lenin and his Bolsheviks in Russia, so too did 1920 mark the end of corruption in the national pastime and the beginning of baseball as American and savory as apple pie, overseen by an all-powerful czar with the stern visage and morality of an Old Testament prophet. And it marked the rise of the greatest, most enduring dynasty in sports history—the New York Yankees. Both of those developments were a direct consequence of eight players on the Chicago White Sox, a team poised to assume its own mantle of a dynasty, conspiring to lose the 1919 World Series—or in one case, perhaps just knowing of the plot—so that high-stakes gamblers could make a windfall betting on the underdog Cincinnati Reds.

The White Sox had played the entire 1920 season dogged by rumors of the conspiracy, although there was nothing definitive. Fighting for a return trip to the World Series in a highly competitive pennant race with both the Indians and the Yankees, those rumors suddenly became more definitive in early September when Cook County, Illinois, convened a grand jury to investigate allegations that a game between the Cubs and Phillies in Chicago on the last day of August had been fixed. Testimony that included inside knowledge about the 1919 World Series upped the ante, and the grand jury investigation became much broader in scope.

Meanwhile, the American League pennant scramble continued. With just five games remaining, Chicago trailed Cleveland by a half-game. Having won nine of their last 11, momentum looked to be with the White Sox. Only then did their season come crashing down. While Shoeless Joe Jackson was driving in the winning run in a 2–0 victory on September 27, revelations of the World Series fix by an insider in the gambling world who was in on the conspiracy appeared in a Philadelphia newspaper. The next day the scandal was being trumpeted in the Chicago press. Although his team was just a half-game behind with only three games left on their schedule in St. Louis, White Sox owner Charles Comiskey immediately banished the players involved—four starting position players, two starting pitchers, and a marginal at best bench player—including Shoeless Joe and pitching ace Eddie Cicotte. There was grand jury testimony, indictments were handed down in the days that followed, and the White Sox— now tarred the "Black Sox"—traveled to St. Louis for the final weekend of the regular season without most of their best players. The undermanned remaining "clean" Sox lost two of three to the fourth-place Browns, while Cleveland split its final four games that weekend, and the season ended with the Indians on top and the White Sox two games behind in second, one game ahead of the third-place Yankees. Thus came the abrupt end of the team then considered the best in baseball, with perhaps a claim to a dynasty in its "alternate-history" destiny.

* * *

Much has been made of how good, or even great, that disgraced Chicago team was. This in fact was long a crucial element in the narrative of the Black Sox scandal. As if the damage to the integrity of the game was not enough, requiring the establishment of an all-powerful commissioner and—enter from stage right field—the transformational presence of the homerific Babe to repair, the cautionary tale this story tells is dramatically bolstered by the idea that the White Sox were a great team that squandered their historical legacy by the avarice of their "eight men out"— outfielders Jackson and Happy Felsch; pitchers Cicotte and Lefty Williams; first baseman Chick Gandil, the ringleader who ensured he profited the most from the fix and who chose to retire after the Series; third baseman Buck Weaver; shortstop Swede Risberg; and utility in-fielder Fred McMullin. Thus, the *mythology* that Chicago's 1919–20 White Sox were one of baseball's best teams ever, done in by greed.

The foundation for this assessment was based on their 1917 cham-pionship, when the White Sox won the pennant convincingly with 100 wins and a nine-game margin of victory over the defending two-in-a-row World Series champion Red Sox and followed up by taking out John McGraw's Giants in six games in the World Series; their cruising to another pennant in 1919—their disastrous sixth-place finish the previous year attributed mostly to many of the team's best players serving in war industries during World War I—only to fall prey in the World Series to gamblers (and the Reds, Cincinnati fans have every right to insist); their winning 96 games in 1920; and finally, a roster starring two of the great-est players in history—Eddie Collins and Shoeless Joe Jackson—Eddie Cicotte, one of the best pitchers of his era, and catcher Ray Schalk and pitcher Red Faber, both Hall of Famers, although 1919 was a lost season for Faber because of illness and injury. Playing into this great team my-thology, Ed Barrow, who presided over the Yankees dynasty for more than two decades as general manager, called the 1919 White Sox "the greatest team of all time," better even than his 110-win 1927 Ruth-and-Gehrig Yankees.

Various accounts of the time from players on other clubs and the press box, however, suggest that the White Sox were only as good as they wanted to be, able to ramp up their level of effort when it counted but often merely just going through the motions to stay in a competitive holding pattern. The irony of this assessment, of course, is that under-achievement is not typically thought to be a good thing. Irrespective of whether any players participated in fixing games beyond the 1919 World Series, there was a widespread perspective that the deep divisions be-tween those who would become the "Black Sox" and those who were the "Clean Sox" likely kept the White Sox from being better than they were. But when they had to win, they won. They didn't blow open the 1917 pennant race until an 18–1 surge in August and September; the 1919 race was never as competitive as Chicago's final 3½-game margin might sug-gest, like they were just toying with their lead; and in 1920, the White Sox did not challenge for first place until August, getting down to busi-ness with the league's best record the rest of the way after trailing in third place.

* * *

There then came, however, a revisionist sentiment whose story line was that, while conspiring with gamblers was indisputably wrong, 'twas tightwad owner Charles Comiskey's miserliness made them do it. More-over, Comiskey was accused of trying to cover up the scandal during the winter to keep his great team intact, a sin nearly as bad as what the Black Sox did. Perhaps. But until the operative details of the scandal broke—first from one of the gamblers involved, then from players' testimony—Comiskey had no proof to go on that would have justified his refusing to give contracts to star players dogged only by suspicions that something was amiss.

As to the owner being a cheapskate, White Sox players in general, with the notable exception of Jackson, were paid fair market value commensurate with the time for their talent and services. The White Sox, in fact, may have had the second-highest payroll in baseball after the New York Giants. Second baseman Eddie Collins, making $15,000 a year in a multiyear deal, was by far the best-paid player in Chicago, one of the best paid in all of baseball, and certainly the highest-paid player at his position. Catcher Ray Schalk and third baseman Buck Weaver were quite likely the best-paid players at their positions. Furthermore, none of the players who testified before the grand jury said anything about Comiskey being a cheapskate.

Eddie Cicotte was perhaps the most aggrieved of Comiskey's employee-players feeling their pay was insufficient for the value of their performance. A right-hander whose pitching arsenal included his substance-enhanced emery and shine balls, Cicotte was acquired from Boston in July 1912 in the first of Comiskey's moves to remake the White Sox, who had faded from contention following their just-missed-the-pennant run in 1908. Four years later, Cicotte was their pitching ace. He was 28–12 in 1917, leading the league in wins and ERA and won the opening game of the World Series to set the White Sox on their way to the baseball championship of the world —for which he was offered the same $5,000 salary in 1918, sweetened by a $2,000 bonus. Although Cicotte had a losing 12–19 record for a sixth-place club undermined by wartime player losses, Comiskey rewarded him with a significant salary boost to nearly $10,000 for 1919, putting him among the highest-paid pitchers in baseball. Cicotte likely earned even more that year than the great Grover Cleveland Alexander, pitching on the north side of Chicago for the Cubs.

Cicotte nonetheless did feel he was underpaid for being the White Sox ace. Eliot Asinof in his 1963 book on the scandal, *Eight Men Out*—a blend of fact and fiction for dramatic effect—surfaced a story that Cicotte believed Comiskey was stiffing him out of a promised $10,000 bonus on top of his salary if he won 30 games by ordering his manager not to pitch him in the closing weeks of either the 1917 season, according to Asinof's book, or the 1919 season, according to the 1988 movie dramatization. The 1917 version is dubious just by the facts. Although it's possible

Comiskey may have thought there was no way a pitcher who had never won more than 18 games in any season could possibly win 30 and so blithely made the offer, Cicotte started September with 21 wins, made six starts in the final month, and pitched twice in relief (winning both times) to finish with 28 wins. There were two occasions when he had five days of rest. Both times they included a day on which there was no game.

The facts of the allegation square more with the 1919 version. There were 19 games left to play when Cicotte won his 28th game in early September. He did not pitch again for 13 days, whereupon he won his 29th game. Of the seven games remaining, Cicotte started twice without earning a decision. He was pinch-hit for in the seventh inning, trailing 5–2, in the first of those games, and in the second was removed after two innings in the White Sox' final game of the season, just three days before he was to start the first game of the World Series. Eddie Cicotte finished with a 29–7 record and did not get his bonus. There is no evidence, however, that Comiskey ever promised such a bonus, and it seems unlikely that he would have, but the story fits well into the revisionist narrative Asinof and the movie spinoff were pushing about Comiskey the tightwad; it gave Cicotte a powerful motive to go all in on Gandil's scheme. The most likely explanation for Cicotte's 13 days of idleness was that the right-hander was laboring with a sore shoulder and may have needed the time off, especially with a World Series on the horizon. He had already thrown 288⅔ innings in 32 starts when he completed his 28th victory, and the White Sox enjoyed a seven-game lead.

The one player who *was* grossly underpaid relative to his contributions was Shoeless Joe Jackson. Comiskey almost certainly knew he was taking advantage of someone from rural South Carolina who was illiterate and unsophisticated in everything but his enormous talent to play baseball. Jackson came to Chicago in much the same way Eddie Collins had. With the Cleveland Indians, for whom Jackson had starred since 1911, in serious financial difficulties as a result of the recession that was undermining the US economy, Comiskey came to the rescue in August 1915—the same as he had in snapping up Collins from Connie Mack's Philadelphia Athletics the previous winter—by trading three unproven players and throwing in $31,500 in cash for Jackson and his $6,000 salary for the next three years, according to the contract he had just signed with Cleveland. Shoeless Joe was outstanding in his first full year in Chicago in 1916 with a .341 average and league-leading 21 triples. Although he hit only .301 when the White Sox won the 1917 pennant, he was nonetheless the team's best position player.

Advanced metrics to evaluate player performance being far in the future, all Comiskey appears to have focused on was the decline in Jackson's batting average in 1917, and Shoeless Joe's salary remained what it was in Cleveland. Despite serving in US defense industries to support the war effort, his missing virtually the entire 1918 season was certainly not an argument for a baseball-pay increase, particularly when his multiyear contract was still in effect. Moreover, Comiskey was irate that his star player abandoned the team to serve in the war industries, where his principal role was to play baseball as a morale boost for those doing the real work, rather than go off to fight the war in Europe. Jackson was paid the same mere $6,000 in 1919, far less than Ty Cobb, earning $20,000 in Detroit, and Tris Speaker, $18,000 in Cleveland—baseball's two best position players in the teens, with whom he was legitimately compared when it came to ability and accomplishments—and less on his own team than not only Collins and Cicotte, but also Weaver and Schalk, neither of whom could fill his shoes.

The revisionist-sentiment story line includes the conviction, pun intended, that, while the six other Black Sox were guilty as charged (although the seven tried were all acquitted), Jackson and Weaver both played to win. By this rendering, Shoeless Joe was a naive pawn who got caught up in the plot, and though he did receive an envelope with $5,000 in it for his role, he did not personally participate in the fix, and while Buck Weaver knew of the conspiracy, he took no money and also did not play to lose.

Of the others, there is no doubt they followed through on the fix. Cicotte and Lefty Williams were the pitchers responsible for all five of Chicago's losses—the first World Series since 1903 that scheduled nine games if it went the distance. Cicotte, whose 1.82 ERA was the second best in the American League during the year, and who gave up as many as six runs in only two of his 35 starts, surrendered six to the Reds in fewer than four innings in his Series opener meltdown. Williams, who ordinarily had good control and walked as many as four batters only once in 40 starts during the regular season, walked six in his Game Two loss. Happy Felsch hit less than .200 and made numerous questionable plays in the outfield. Swede Risberg batted less than .100 and made four errors at shortstop. Chick Gandil, the ringleader of the fix, also did not play well, batting .233. Fred McMullin barely played at all, being a backup, but was in on the conspiracy, either because he caught wind of the plotting, or because he could be counted on to keep the other plot participants in line.

Jackson and Weaver, by contrast, both had statistical lines their defenders say showed they played very well, especially compared to their clean-cut teammate Eddie Collins, lending credence to the sentiment that neither participated in any shenanigans to throw games. Jackson had 12 hits to tie a World Series record, batted .375, hit Chicago's only home run, and led his team with six runs batted in. Weaver had 11 hits, batted .324, and did not make any errors. Collins, the star of the 1917 World

Series when he batted over .400 for the third time in a fall classic, was stymied by Cincinnati pitching, hitting just .226, but there was never any question about his integrity on the field of play. As to their knowledge of their teammates deliberately losing ballgames, their defenders point out that Jackson before the first game in Cincinnati told his manager he wanted to be benched for the Series, and Weaver was either in denial, having supposedly told Black Sox conspirators that their plan was unlikely to succeed, or couldn't get himself to rat them out.

Statistics, however, can be misleading. Many subtle things can be done to affect the outcome of games—failing to advance runners or take the extra base, for example; overthrowing the cutoff man or cutting off throws when there was a chance for an out; misplaying groundballs or fly balls that should have been outs; failing to take an extra base, or stupidly trying for an extra base and being thrown out—precisely the sort of things that would drive the baseball-savvy Collins and Schalk to conniptions, and did. Such things, certainly done by their teammates, were observed at the time, though not understood in context, by scribes in the press box and "clean" players in both dugouts.

Even before Cicotte supposedly signaled to the heavyweight gamblers behind the scheme that the fix was on by hitting the first Cincinnati batter with a pitch in the opening game, Collins later claimed that in the top half of the inning, with him on first base, Weaver signaled the hit-and-run play was on and then did not swing at the pitch, resulting in Collins easily being thrown out at second. And although his word might be suspect, Jackson told reporters after his grand jury testimony that "the eight of us"—which had to include Weaver—"did our best to kick it" when Dickey Kerr pitched the Sox to a 3–0 victory in Game Three. Cicotte, in his testimony, also identified Weaver as in on the fix. As for Shoeless Joe, there were a few instances where observers noted when he failed to make catches that he might have and that his outfield positioning seemed misplaced for the batter at the plate.

Just as their defenders point to how well both Jackson and Weaver batted in the World Series to argue that neither participated in throwing games, a game-by-game breakdown of their at-bats could suggest otherwise—not necessarily that they played to lose, but that they did not play to win, at least not until the final three games of the Series. Perhaps coincidentally, or perhaps not, both players' most significant offensive contributions came *after* the Black Sox conspirators did not receive an expected payment from the high-stakes gamblers whose betting interests they were serving, concluded they had been double-crossed, and vowed before Game Six to play thereafter to win. With Chicago trailing in the Series four games to one, Weaver, Jackson, and Gandil all had key 10th-inning hits to win Game Six for Kerr; Felsch, who had only one hit in 13 at-bats in the first five games without an RBI, finished the Series with five hits, a .192 batting average, and three RBIs; and Cicotte, who had pitched horrifically in the opening game and sabotaged his own cause in his Game Four loss with two errors resulting in the only two runs he allowed, pitched as well as he had during the season to win the seventh game, 4–1. The Reds won the Series the next day, starting with four first-inning runs off Williams, who is said to have received death threats if he failed to pitch poorly.

Weaver did not get untracked offensively in the World Series until the fifth game, having gone just 4-for-16 in the first four games. In Chicago's 2–0 loss in Game Four, which put them in a three-games-to-one hole, Weaver came up twice with runners on base and failed to get a hit. His 89 runs scored during the regular season led the team and was fourth in the league, but he did not score a single run in the first five games. Of course, Jackson, Felsch, Gandil, and Risberg batted behind him, at least three of whom were in it to lose. Buck Weaver finished the Series with seven hits in his last 18 at-bats (.389), the first two in Game Five's 5–0 loss, and all four runs he scored in the Series came in the final three games, two of which the White Sox won. Those were precisely the games the Black Sox, with the likely exception of Williams, who may have started the eighth game thinking his life was in jeopardy, were motivated to win because of the gamblers' perfidy. The dichotomy in Weaver's performance may not prove anything, but it is suspiciously coincidental.

Similarly, Shoeless Joe Jackson's 12 hits and .375 batting average obscure the fact that his offensive contributions were marginal at best in the first five games of the Series, four of which his team lost. While he had six hits in 19 at-bats, Jackson scored just once—remember who was behind him in the batting order—and did not have a single run batted in. Four of those hits came when he led off an inning and one was with two out and none on, meaning he was not coming through with runners on base. Even great hitters, of course, cannot necessarily will themselves to come through in the clutch, if for no other reason than the opposing pitcher is trying just as hard to get him out. Jackson, however, came to bat seven times with runners on base in the first five games and got just one hit, and he was 0-for-6 with runners in scoring position. After one of his leadoff hits in the third game, with Kerr holding on to a slim 2–0 lead trying to pitch the White Sox to their first victory in the Series, Jackson was immediately thrown out attempting to steal second. Felsch followed with a walk, and he, too, was cut down trying to steal. Earlier in that game, with runners on first and second, nobody out, and a chance to break open the game and give Kerr some breathing room, Jackson attempted a bunt, which he popped up, failing to advance either runner, let alone drive in at least one run.

Shoeless Joe may have hit over .300 through the first five games, but he was hardly the same player whose .351 batting average (fourth in the American League), 96 runs batted in (third), and .923 on-base-plus-slugging percentage (third) made him the third-best offensive player in all of Major League Baseball, based on offensive wins above replacement, behind Ruth and, just barely, Cobb. Jackson was a more potent offensive threat in 1919 than Speaker, Rogers Hornsby, or George Sisler, and he would be even better in 1920 when he batted .382 and had a career-high 121 RBIs. But *that* Shoeless Joe Jackson was not apparent in the World Series until the last three games that the Black Sox, with the possible exception of the threatened Williams, played to win because they concluded the high rollers were reneging on their promises. All six of Jackson's RBIs were in the final three games. Whereas before he was unproductive with runners on base, five of his six hits in the final three were with runners on base. He was 5-for-7 with runners in scoring position, including 4-for-6 in Chicago's Game Six and Seven victories. *This* Shoeless Joe Jackson was not lying down on the job; the same seems difficult to say about his performance in the first five games, although it is possible Jackson was simply stymied by Cincinnati pitching in critical at-bats.

* * *

Following their embarrassing defeat to the Reds amid suspicions that something was not right, Comiskey was hoping the affair would just go away. He covered himself by offering a reward for anyone who could provide substantiation of the fix. Most accounts suggest that he learned about the plot in considerable generalized detail even before he sent out new contracts to all eight of the Black Sox thought to be involved, although he still lacked any proof. He offered each a raise, even utility infielder McMullin. Although he knew Cleveland was a bona fide threat to win the pennant and that the Yankees, especially now that they had Ruth, were a rising power whose time would surely come, perhaps sooner than later, Comiskey had the best team in baseball, and he wanted to keep it that way. How many pennants this team could win would be his defining legacy.

Still dogged by unsavory rumors, the White Sox got off to an indifferent start in 1920, spending most of the summer in third place. They made their move into pennant contention in August and spent virtually all of September within a game or two of first place. Yet the "Black Sox" members of the team may not have been playing every game to win even as the allegations of the World Series fix came to seem more credible and the grand jury investigation gained momentum as the month progressed. Collins and Dickey Kerr were both suspicious about the variable perfor-

mances of many of their "Black Sox" teammates—including Weaver—
and two bench players observed that their untrustworthy teammates were
paying attention to the scores in New York's and Cleveland's games and
playing to win, or not, based on whether or not the Yankees and Indians
were winning or losing.

Playing according to the scoreboard probably began no later than August 26 when the White Sox beat the Yankees in New York to take a 3½-
game lead in the standings—their biggest lead of a so-far mostly disappointing season. They were 17–6 for the month and seemed almost unstoppable. The betting money would have been on them, except for those
preferring a bigger payoff by betting on another of the contenders. Chicago proceeded to lose the next two in New York and three in a row to the
now-Ruthless fifth-place Red Sox to drop out of first place on the first of
September.

The White Sox had an excellent 18–8 record from September 1 until
the contemptible machinations of their gang of eight were publicly revealed, yet gained ground relative to first place on only five of the first 27
days of the month, including the one day they were tied. On one of those
five days, both Cleveland and New York were idle; on another, the Indians, then with a one-game lead in the standings, and the Yankees, a
game and a half out in third, played each other, with New York winning;
and on the three other days, the White Sox were playing either the Yankees, who came into Chicago on September 16 with a one-game lead and
left the Windy City having lost three straight, or the Indians, who held a
tenuous 1½-game lead when the White Sox came to town for a three-
game series. None of their three wins against the Yankees moved the
White Sox into first place because the Indians were also winning three
straight. The White Sox won two of three from the Indians, but their loss
was in the middle game, which ensured that regardless of the outcome of
the final game in the series—which Chicago did indeed win—they would
not leave Cleveland in first place. Two games later, both wins, the White
Sox were still a half-game behind the Indians and were about to play their
final three games in St. Louis against the fair-to-middling Browns when
the scandal hit the news.

Comiskey's hand was forced, especially since archenemy Ban Johnson was maneuvering behind the scenes for exposure of the scandal to
justify stripping the White Sox owner from his team. By banishing the
implicated players before Johnson could do so, Comiskey was now ahead
of the scandal he had hoped to keep under wraps. His club won 96 games.
Shoeless Joe had his best season since the first three years of his career in
Cleveland; Collins had his best year since 1915, and Felsch his best
season ever; Weaver hit for his highest average; Schalk caught the most
games in his career; and the White Sox had an unprecedented four 20-

game winners—Faber (23–13), Williams (22–14), Cicotte (21–10), and Kerr (21–9)—something that would be done just once more, by the 1970 Baltimore Orioles. They were an outstanding team.

But now Comiskey's legacy dream was ruined. Two-thirds of his starting outfield (Jackson in left and Felsch in center), three-fourths of his starting infield (first baseman Gandil, who had in any case not returned after the 1919 season, shortstop Risberg, and third baseman Weaver), and half of his four-man starting rotation (Cicotte and Williams) were gone, forever banished from Organized Baseball. In the next 30 years, 1921 through 1950, the White Sox would have a winning record only nine times. They would finish as high as third only three times. It would not be until the 1950s that the franchise became competitive again; not until 1959 that they were once again American League champions, for the last time in the twentieth century, as it turned out; and not until the twenty-first century, in 2005, would the White Sox win their first World Series since 1917.

* * *

As time went on, there emerged a more accurate but nonetheless revisionist history based largely on statistical analysis that, regardless of who played what role in the conspiracy, the Chicago White Sox who won the 1917 and 1919 American League pennants, and probably should have repeated in 1920, were a very good team, but hardly a great team, and certainly not one of the best teams in history, as their mythology would have.

Comiskey's deals for Cicotte in July 1912, Collins in December 1914, and Jackson in August 1915 were the underpinning of Chicago's would-be dynasty to replace that of the 1906–10 Cubs. From 1916, when they began their rise to prominence, to 1920, when the Black Sox' sins destroyed the team, Cicotte blossomed into a legitimately great pitcher, and Collins and Jackson were two of the top four position players in baseball, along with Cobb and Speaker (Ruth was a pitcher the first two of those years). With the exception, however, of Red Faber, who won three games in the 1917 World Series, none of their teammates was a standout player. While Felsch, Weaver, and Schalk were three of the better players in the league, none was the best at his position. First baseman Gandil and Risberg at shortstop were below-average players for their positions. Lacking a single player good enough to hold the position full-time, the White Sox platooned in right field when they won both their pennants.

Chicago's 1916–20 White Sox had a well-balanced and formidable offense that was hard for opposing pitchers to navigate but were not a dominant team offensively. The Indians in 1919 and both the Indians and Yankees in 1920 had a much higher percentage of their hits go for extra bases than the White Sox, resulting in a much better ratio of runs to runners on base. On the other side of the ledger, the White Sox were stingy in giving up runs and allowing baserunners, but their pitching staff was not notably better, if better at all, in any given year than their rivals for the pennant. Although they famously had four 20-game winners in 1920, the Indians and Yankees both had better pitching that year, based on modern metrics.

Nonetheless, had so many of their core players not been corrupt scoundrels, the White Sox almost certainly would have extended their run as a perennial pennant contender into the early to mid-1920s. Had they won another two pennants or so, they would surely have boosted their historical legacy as one of the American League's best ever teams, at least in the first half of the twentieth century. And that would likely have delayed the beginning of the Yankees dynasty. Adding Babe Ruth made the Yankees immediately competitive for the pennant in 1920, but they did not quite get there. Following that first taste of pennant fever, however, the Yankees won three consecutive pennants from 1921 to 1923—making them only the second team in American League history to do so, after the 1907–09 Tigers—before finishing a close second, two games back of Washington, in 1924.

But the Yankees were not yet a great team, only a very good team—and mostly because of the Babe. Even with Ruth having two of the best seasons ever by a position player in 1921 and 1923, the Yankees were not yet an offensive juggernaut. They did not dominate the rest of the league the way future Yankees teams made a habit of. They did not win their first trademark blowout pennant until 1923, and while they finished 16 games ahead of everybody else, the 1923 Yankees did not even need 100 victories to win by such a whopping margin; 98 were sufficient because second-place Detroit won only 83, and moreover, there were only three teams in the entire American League that had winning records that year.

Nor did the Yankees have to compete against a White Sox team in 1921, or in the years after, that had won two pennants the previous four years, might have won a third in 1920 but for the scandal breaking in the last days of the season, and which arguably was at its peak and poised to be competitive for at least the next several years. The average age of Chicago's position players in 1920 was 29 years, one year older than the Yankees' average age. Of their best players, only Collins at 33 and Jackson at 31 would have been over 30 in 1921 and likely on the downslope of their careers. Shoeless Joe, however, almost certainly would have had several more outstanding seasons had he not been exiled. According to the wins above replacement metric, only Ruth, Speaker, Sisler, and teammate Collins had a higher player value in 1920 than Jackson. Speaker and Cobb, both of whom were older, would remain outstanding ballplayers into the mid-1920s, and there is no reason to suppose Shoeless Joe would not have also, especially since the Ruth-inaugurated hitters' era had begun.

Eddie Collins did in fact remain a terrific player at least through the 1925 season, by which time he was 38 years old. Not only did he hit .343 for the five years after 1920, but Collins's aging legs carried him to league-leading totals of 48 and 42 stolen bases in '23 and '24. From 1909, when he displaced Napoleon Lajoie as the best second baseman in baseball, until 1927, when both the Yankees' Tony Lazzeri and Tigers' Charlie Gehringer eclipsed him, Collins had an unsurpassed run as the best at his position in the American League. Nobody else was close, and it wasn't until Rogers Hornsby won six straight National League batting titles between 1920 and 1925 that anyone could claim to be a better all-around second baseman than Eddie Collins. And even then, Collins was much better defensively and far more a team player than Hornsby. Lazzeri and Gehringer, both born in 1903, were barely even schoolboys when Collins first became a regular, and Hornsby was just beginning his teenage years.

Felsch, who was 28 in 1920, and Weaver at 29, were among the best—but not *the* best—in the league at their positions at the time they were terminated, and probably would have remained so for at least several years. Schalk did not turn 30 until the summer of 1922, and remained the White Sox' regular catcher until 1925. While his hitting prowess left something to be desired, Schalk's continued first-rate defensive skills and leadership behind the plate would have been a valuable asset for any team, particularly one with the strengths the extended 1917–20 White Sox would have had . . . had history been different.

Except for Ruth over everybody and Wally Schang as a better all-around catcher than Schalk, that same White Sox club would likely have had a clear advantage over the Yankees at second base (Collins over Aaron Ward), the two other outfield positions (Jackson and Felsch over Bob Meusel and several Yankees center fielders), and third base (Weaver over an aging Home Run Baker, followed by Joe Dugan). And some of the players who became White Sox in the early 1920s would have strengthened a team that already included Schalk, Collins, Weaver, Felsch, and Jackson and likely given Chicago an advantage at first base and shortstop as well.

Earl Sheely, taking over at first base in 1921, was a substantial improvement over the disgraced Gandil, and probably would have won the position even had Gandil not been corrupt and played beyond 1919. Although they were the same age, Sheely was probably the better first baseman than Yankees veteran Wally Pipp, whose career was fading when New York was winning three in a row. Disgraced shortstop Swede

Risberg, surely not in the same class as Yankees shortstops Roger Peckinpaugh in 1921 or Everett Scott the next three years, would probably have
been pushed out of his job by the arrival of third baseman Willie Kamm
in 1923, if not sooner. Weaver might have moved over to play shortstop—his original position—or perhaps Kamm would have taken over at
short. Either way, Kamm and Weaver together would have given the
White Sox an edge over the Yankees at both positions on the left side of
the infield.

And whether the White Sox would have still traded for veteran outfielder Harry Hooper in 1921, as they in fact did, had none of their stars
been blacklisted, platooned rookie outfielders Johnny Mostil (a right-
handed batter) and Bibb Falk (a lefty), or given the job outright to either
Mostil or Falk, they would have had a much better outfield in the early to
mid-1920s with any of them playing alongside Jackson and Felsch than
the platoon combination of Nemo Leibold and Shano Collins on the
1917–20 club. Instead, it was Falk taking over for the disgraced Jackson
in left, Mostil replacing the banished Felsch in center, and Hooper taking
over right field in a two-for-one swap, Comiskey having traded Leibold
and Shano Collins to get him from Boston. Newcomers Sheely, Mostil,
Falk, and Kamm were fixtures in the White Sox lineup through most of
the 1920s, and Hooper enjoyed four productive years in Chicago before
age took its inevitable toll on his career in 1925 when he was 37.

Pitching might have been more of a concern for the White Sox moving
forward even had the Black Sox not destroyed the team. Cicotte was 36
years old in 1920, and Faber was 31. For the Yankees, on the other hand,
while Ruth may have been their identity, pitching was the foundation of
their first three pennants. The Yankees had the league's lowest earned run
average three times between 1920 and 1923, and were just shy of the
Browns for the league-best ERA in 1922. Carl Mays, Bob Shawkey, and
Waite Hoyt were their three aces in 1921; Shawkey, Hoyt, and Bullet Joe
Bush in 1922; and those three plus Sad Sam Jones and Herb Pennock in
1923. While no team was likely to match New York's pitching in the first
half of the 1920s, Chicago's staff might have been good enough for the
White Sox to win the 1921, '22, and possibly 1924 pennants given the
likely core position-player advantages they would have had over the Yankees, the Babe notwithstanding.

Red Faber was the best pitcher in baseball in 1921 and 1922, perhaps
aided by his being one of just 17 major-league pitchers allowed to continue using the spitball after 1920, but Cicotte might have had two or three
more productive seasons had he not been banished for his very proactive
role in the 1919 Series fix. He had just won 20 games in 1920 for the third
time in four years and did not rely on throwing hard, which helps in
staving off the ravages of age. Lefty Williams was not one of baseball's

best at his craft and was likely overrated, but he had just had back-to-back 20-win seasons and might have continued to pitch with success had he not been barred from the game. Dickey Kerr, whose pitching in the 1919 World Series was nothing if not heroic given that half the team behind him was not in it to win, looked to have a relatively long and productive future ahead of him. After winning 19 games in 1921—he and Faber alone accounted for 44 of Chicago's 62 wins that year—Kerr held out for more money in 1922 and was himself blacklisted by Commissioner Landis the next two years for playing ball against, ironically, some of his former "Black Sox" teammates to keep in baseball shape during his holdout.

* * *

Whether the 1917–20 White Sox continuing on with their star players and being strengthened with the addition of players like Sheely, Hooper, Mostil, Falk, and eventually Kamm would have delayed the start of the Yankees dynasty, or at least prevented it from kick-starting with three straight pennants, is of course an unknowable and debatable proposition. History records that the Yankees won six pennants in eight years between 1921 and 1928 with Babe Ruth the centerpiece of all six of their American League championships. But the Yankees were a fundamentally different team when they won their first three in a row than what most people think about when they think "Babe Ruth's Yankees." Fellow Hall of Famers Lou Gehrig, Tony Lazzeri, and Earle Combs who teamed with Ruth in the fabled "Murderers' Row" of the iconic 1927 Yankees were not yet in pinstripes. When the Yankees won their first set of three straight pennants, Ruth was their only position player among the 10 best in the league, based on cumulative wins above replacement from 1921 to 1923. He was, of course, far and away the best in baseball. In fact, the rest of Ruth's position teammates at this point in their careers were just average major-league ballplayers.

13

HERE COME DA JUDGE

Landis, the Federal League Case, and the Commissioner Rules

Part of baseball's historical mythology is that Babe Ruth with his home-run swing and celebrity and Kenesaw Mountain Landis, properly addressed as "Judge" because he was a federal judge, in the new role of commissioner of baseball saved the game after its competitive integrity had been near-fatally compromised by the Black Sox scandal. "Saving the game," however, is an exaggeration. Baseball was America's game, its national pastime. It was played by kids all over the country. Schools had baseball teams. Factories had teams. Companies had teams. There were church teams and community teams.

The conspiracy of eight Chicago White Sox players—seven of them regulars—to throw the 1919 World Series for a big payoff was certainly a tremendous black stain, calling into question whether major-league games were played on the up-and-up. The Black Sox scandal sullied the major leagues. If Ruth and the creation of the Commissioner's Office had not come along, the major leagues as they then existed could well have faced an existential crisis. The two leagues, or perhaps just the American League whose White Sox were the offending team, might have folded in disrepute. But professional baseball had survived earlier crises, and would have survived this even without a Ruth or a Landis. With baseball so woven into the fabric of American life, it is inconceivable that professional baseball—the major leagues perhaps reorganized into new leagues—would not have soldiered on with an attendant press, new stars and heroes emerging, and a committed legion of hundreds of thousands of fans following the action.

Ruth nonetheless *did* reenergize the game and create a new level of interest in baseball because of his awesome displays of power hitting. And Judge Landis *did* impose the order and discipline on all of professional Organized Baseball that was necessary to restore the public's faith in the integrity of the games. They did not "save" the game as much as secure its virtually immediate recovery to the good graces of Americans in the aftermath of the Black Sox scandal's shock and betrayal of the public trust in Major League Baseball. Their contrasting visages became the two faces of baseball in the Roaring Twenties and beyond, worthy of being chiseled onto a baseball Mount Rushmore—Ruth's broad, soft, twinkling, facial features that warmly welcomed all Americans to watch the national pastime at the professional level and that said, hey this is fun, the way baseball is supposed to be; and Landis's stern sharp, angular features and deep lines that reassured fans and warned players, baseball is under adult supervision now, buddy, step out of line and you're done. That, of course, was exactly what Organized Baseball needed when the magnitude of the Black Sox scandal became known.

* * *

If Landis did "save" baseball, it was ironically not by his actions to clean up the Black Sox mess, but rather his inaction as a federal judge that contributed to the demise of the Federal League. Had he ruled on constitutional grounds in the case that found its way in January 1915 to his federal courtroom for the Northern District of Illinois in Chicago, the underpinnings that defined Major League Baseball might have changed dramatically.

Professional Organized Baseball had been governed since 1903 by the National Agreement that ended the open warfare between the established National League and the upstart American League characterized primarily by the AL enticing star players from the NL to its new "major" league. The National Agreement imposed order by ratifying the sanctity of player contracts through the notorious "reserve clause," which bound players to their existing clubs even once the term of their contract was up. The reserve clause also allowed teams to terminate player contracts or reassign them at will, even to the minor leagues. Players had no recourse, except perhaps to hold out in hopes of a better deal or to force a trade to a more favorable circumstance. Moreover, the National Agreement established a hierarchy under the rubric of Organized Baseball between the major leagues and the minor leagues that included rules affecting player transactions. Upstart leagues that tried to operate outside the strictures of Organized Baseball were considered outlaws. After the tumultuousness of the late nineteenth century, which included the rise and fall of three leagues in competition with the National League, the National Agreement provided the stability that the major leagues needed to thrive as an industry in early twentieth-century America.

The Federal League threatened to upend that stability.

Like the American League in 1901, whose origins were derived from the midwestern-based Western League, the Federal League began in 1913 as a six-club minor league based in the Midwest before presumptively asserting "major-league" status in 1914. Like the American League, which began with teams in three National League cities—Boston, Philadelphia, and Chicago—and added St. Louis in 1902 and New York in 1903, the Federal League targeted major-league cities for its inaugural season, placing teams in Chicago, St. Louis, Pittsburgh, and Brooklyn. Federal League teams were also established in Baltimore, the seventh-most-populous city in the United States with a proud baseball heritage, and Buffalo, the 10th-largest city in the 1910 US census. Kansas City and Indianapolis, which ranked twentieth and twenty-second among US cities in population, rounded out the eight-team Federal League. The cities of Baltimore and Buffalo both already had teams in the International League, and Kansas City and Indianapolis in the American Association.

Just like the AL in taking on the NL at its inception in 1901, the Federal League went after baseball men of gravitas to manage its teams—recruiting, for example, former Chicago Cubs stars Joe Tinker and Three Finger Brown to be player-managers—and went aggressively after established major-league players with enticements of much better pay. They did so, however, by honoring the sanctity of existing multiyear contracts, targeting only those players whose contracts technically expired with the end of the 1913 season, but who were, of course, still bound—not necessarily legally—by the reserve clause. It would indeed be the legality of the reserve clause that became the central issue as the Federal League tried to fight off a determined resistance by the major leagues to Federal raids on their players and players in the minor leagues.

Unlike the American League 14 years earlier, however, the Federal League was much less successful in stealing away established major leaguers. They weren't happy about being forced to do so—especially because the country was in the midst of a major economic recession—but major-league teams countered blandishments to their best players by offering them significant pay increases, sometimes as more lucrative counteroffers to star players the Federals had lobbied to join their new league. Perhaps most notably, the Red Sox nearly doubled Tris Speaker's $9,000 salary to keep him in Boston instead of playing for the Federal League's Brooklyn Tip-Tops. Players were also threatened with being

banished from the major leagues if they signed with the "outlaw" Federals.

The Federals had the most success attracting established players
whose teams paid them less than they were worth and were unwilling or
too slow off the mark to match their bids, going after veterans whose
salaries were declining as they aged, and recruiting journeyman players
who wanted to play a more important role than the ones they had on their
existing clubs. This last group included Giants reliever Doc Crandall,
who became a starting pitcher for the Federals' St. Louis Terriers, and
Bill McKechnie, with only 730 at-bats in parts of four big-league seasons,
who starred as the everyday third baseman for pennant-winning Indianapolis in 1914. Minor leaguers still looking for their break in the big leagues
were also a prime target for recruitment. The most notable among them
were Edd Roush and Benny Kauff, both with minimal prior major-league
exposure. Kauff led the Federal League in batting average and stolen
bases in both years the league was in business, earning plaudits as the
Federals' answer to Ty Cobb; he went on to have a productive, though
not stellar, five years with the Giants after the Federal League folded.
Roush did not burst onto the Federal scene with Kauff-like acclaim, but
later played his way into the Hall of Fame with Cincinnati.

Despite the lack of relative star power in its inaugural season as a
"major" league, the Federal League survived a full schedule. None of its
eight clubs folded, and the league and its franchises still had sufficient
finances to offer lucrative contracts to established major-league players.
Moreover, in a significant development that ultimately led to a seminal
Supreme Court decision upholding the reserve clause, the Federal League
team in Baltimore—a city that had seen two major-league franchises
uprooted since 1899—captured the fan base from the established minor
team in town, notwithstanding that the Orioles were the class of the
International League and had an exceptional and exciting young lefty
pitcher named George Herman Ruth, who could also hit with power. The
city's early acceptance of the Federal League's assertion that the Baltimore Terrapins were a legitimate "major-league" team, in contrast to the
minor-league Orioles, forced Orioles owner Jack Dunn to sell off his best
players to meet expenses—including budding star Ruth to the Boston Red
Sox. Unable to compete at the gate against the "major" league's rival
team in Baltimore, the Orioles packed up and moved to Richmond, Virginia, after the season; the Federal League would have Baltimore all to
itself in 1915.

The fact that the Federals went on a postseason blitz to try to attract
major-league stars threatened to both boost the rival league into a bona
fide major league and substantially increase the salary costs for American
and National League clubs to keep their best players. Although both were

at the end of their careers and had been placed on waivers by Connie Mack, pitchers Eddie Plank and Chief Bender of the powerful Philadelphia Athletics were prized recruits after the 1914 season. More seriously, the Federal League aimed for Mack's outstanding infielders Eddie Collins and Home Run Baker, resulting in White Sox owner Charles Comiskey spending an exorbitant amount to buy Collins from Mack and pay the second baseman double his 1914 salary, and Baker—who was tied to a multiyear contract that was clearly below market value, especially with the Federals interested in him—deciding to sit out the season. The Federal League's bombshell recruit, however, was the great Walter Johnson signing to play for the Chicago Whales. Although he did not get nearly as big a salary boost from Washington as Boston gave Speaker and Chicago gave Collins, Johnson decided that the Senators' counteroffer was good enough for him to renege on his Federals contract, mostly because manager Clark Griffith appealed to his personal integrity and loyalty.

* * *

The established major leagues' success in persuading players, most notably Walter Johnson, to forswear contracts they had already signed with Federal League teams was a primary impetus for the case that came before Judge Landis in 1915. The standard reserve clause was the basis for the American and National Leagues to feel they were on solid legal ground to persuade players to unilaterally break the contracts they signed with the Federals because their former teams still "owned" their rights. As the plaintiff in the case, the Federal League wanted the Judge to rule that the two major leagues were acting "in contravention of" US antitrust statutes "as part of a monopoly," including by preventing the Federals from signing players whose contracts with their existing teams had expired. The two established leagues argued that antitrust statutes did not apply in this case—first, because the players, as people, were neither a "commodity" nor an "article of commerce," and second, because baseball was entertainment, the same as theater performances, which earlier court rulings had established was not commerce.

In one sense, the case was in the hands of a federal judge whose judicial rulings had captured the populist zeitgeist at a time when there was significant sentiment against the very idea of rapacious monopolies. Landis, who had been appointed to his bench in 1905 by President Theodore Roosevelt, had a reputation for ruling decisively against the monopolistic practices of big businesses. Landis was a judge who—true to Roosevelt's leanings in this Progressive Era of American politics—was disposed to favor a level playing field for competitors in interstate commerce.

Kenesaw Mountain Landis, however, was also a big baseball fan. And like baseball fans through the ages, he was most comfortable with the game as it was—including the identification of players with their teams. That identification was a basic element of both the stability of Major League Baseball, now enshrined in the National Agreement, and the engagement and commitment of fans to the game of baseball, and Landis made clear on the opening day of the trial that he was not inclined to deliver a mortal blow to baseball, which he called a "national institution." Landis ended up asking whether he even had jurisdiction to decide the case, implying that the Federal League predicating its petition on antitrust statutes might not be correct. Earlier judicial rulings in 1914 cases brought by the Federals held that baseball was *not* interstate commerce, no matter how objectionable the reserve clause might seem. While having to grapple with the question of whether the established major leagues were operating as a monopoly, Judge Landis made clear that his sympathies were with baseball as a game beloved by Americans, saying that the decision he was being asked to make could "tear down the very foundation of this game."

Landis appears to have had a difficult time reconciling his antitrust inclinations with his love for the game. Had Landis decided he had jurisdiction, he would have had to address the merits of the Federal League case based on antitrust statutes. Had he then ruled in favor of the Federal League, there was a significant likelihood his decision would have been reversed on appeal based on precedent. Had he been forced to rule, therefore, Landis likely would have ruled against the Federal League. But the Judge did not rule on the case that came before him three months before the 1915 season got under way. He didn't rule during the season, either. By not giving the Federals any relief on their petition, Judge Landis virtually guaranteed the Federal League would not survive.

Without being able to improve by much the "star" quotient of their league before and during the season, the Federals could not compete with the established major leagues in attendance and profitability. With the possible exception of the dynamic Benny Kauff, because of the comparisons he drew to Cobb, the Federal League did not have players with the stature and excellence the likes of Jimmy Collins and Cy Young, or Napoleon Lajoie and George Davis, whom the American League was able to spirit away from National League teams in 1901 and 1902.

By the end of the 1915 season, the Federal League was suing for peace. The Federals agreed to shut down and drop their case before Judge Landis—sparing him from having to decide on its merits, including whether he even had jurisdiction—in exchange for Charles Weeghman, owner of the Federal League's Chicago franchise, being able to buy the up-for-sale Cubs and Philip DeCatesby Ball being given a similar opportunity in St. Louis (he bought the Browns); the owners of the Brooklyn and Pittsburgh franchises, located in National League cities, and the Newark franchise, across the Hudson River from two New York City teams, receiving some compensation for disbanding; and the Federal League maintaining contractual control of its players and allowed to sell them to major-league teams to recoup at least some of the league's financial losses. Federal League players did not have to worry about being blacklisted in Organized Baseball, including the majors. The owners of the franchises in Buffalo and Kansas City, having been taken over by the league because they were flat broke, were out of luck in the settlement.

The one Federal League holdout in accepting the terms of the settlement was Baltimore, whose owners wanted to buy into a major-league team that would play in the city. The American and National Leagues summarily rejected that proposition, making the point that Baltimore had twice failed as a major-league city—when it was downsized out of the NL in 1900, and when the AL abandoned the city in 1903 in favor of New York—while neglecting to mention that both times the relevant leagues had agendas that doomed the Orioles. The possible fallback position of allowing the Baltimore Terrapins' owners to have a franchise in the International League was unacceptable to International League president Ed Barrow, who supported Jack Dunn in his quest to bring Orioles minor-league baseball back to Baltimore from exile in Richmond.

More than a year after Judge Landis first heard arguments in the Federal League's case brought before him, the two sides returned to his courtroom asking that the case be dismissed. Landis was fine with that. Noting in his remarks the damage that the Federals' complaint could have inflicted on the national pastime had he ruled in their favor, Landis seemed to imply that there was merit to their complaint. The Federal League was now history.

The American and National Leagues never acknowledged the Federals' proposition that they had been a "major" league in their two years of operation. Yet all Federal League statistics count toward the major-league career totals of those who played in the league, although this was not officially the case until 1969 when the Special Baseball Records Committee formally declared the Federal League to have been a major league. That quite likely was a practical decision influenced in part by prominent Hall of Fame players at the end of their careers—Tinker and Brown, Plank and Bender—playing in the Federal League and a desire not to subtract their Federal statistics from their career records. Most baseball historians agree, however, that the level of competition in the Federal League was not up to that in the two established major leagues.

While the rest of the Federal League made its peace with succumbing to reality, its Baltimore franchise upped the ante on the case that had been before Judge Landis but was now dismissed as a result of the settlement. They filed a suit in the Washington, DC, District Court alleging antitrust violations based on the major leagues' using the reserve clause to prevent players whose contracts had expired from signing with Federal League teams. Unlike Judge Landis, the presiding judge was persuaded that baseball qualified as engaged in interstate commerce, making antitrust statutes applicable and resulting in a jury decision against the National Agreement that defined Organized Baseball. The case ultimately found its way before the US Supreme Court, which ruled in May 1922 that Organized Baseball's reserve clause did not meet antitrust standards because baseball was not interstate commerce as defined by statute.

The Supreme Court's unanimous decision was perhaps tortured reasoning in defense of the "national institution"—as Landis called it—that baseball had become. Coming less than two years after the grievous wounds inflicted by the Black Sox scandal, which broke in 1920, and based on a narrow interpretation of antitrust statutes, the decision was a triumph for baseball's special place and exceptional status in American culture and society. And the justices ruled on the case at a time when Americans were still spooked by the "red scare" in the wake of anarchist bombings in defense of labor rights and the mortal threat to the American way of life perceived in Lenin's Bolshevik Revolution in Russia. It allowed Organized Baseball to do pretty much what it pleased for another half century, becoming ever more sacred as the national pastime and immune to change even as events such as the Great Depression and a Second World War were causing profound changes in the country at large.

* * *

By putting off ruling on the merits of the Federal League case, and by making clear how he felt about baseball, Judge Landis was very much in the good graces of major-league owners. His was the name favored by National League owners to replace Cincinnati Reds owner Garry Herrmann as chairman of the National Commission to end a long impasse after he stepped down in early 1920. The three-member National Commission, composed of the two league presidents and a chairman, had been the governing superstructure for Organized Baseball since 1903, when the NL finally reconciled itself to the reality of the American League. While four men had served on the National Commission as president of the National League, Ban Johnson had been president of the American League and Herrmann served as chairman the entire time. The role of the National Commission was to adjudicate disputes that might arise between the two leagues and set common policies, such as standardized contracts and the length of the schedule, but the two leagues operated independently with little oversight by Organized Baseball's supposed governing body, and they operated quite differently. National League presidents generally did not interfere with team owners. Johnson, on the other hand, was an assertive league president who had a hand in everything important and manipulated the outcomes he wanted. He was down and dirty, forcing out team owners when he thought necessary, cobbling ownership groups to improve the financial position of franchises he wanted to be more competitive, even brokering the trading and selling of star players for the same purpose. What Ban Johnson wanted, Ban Johnson generally got.

Johnson's commanding presence and bullying in relentless pursuit of his objectives made him the dominant figure on the National Commission, reducing Herrmann to a virtually powerless figurehead chairman. Garry Herrmann may have owned a National League franchise, but his long-standing relationship with Johnson and the force of Johnson's personality meant he was not necessarily in the NL corner if the two leagues were in disagreement over any issue. In January 1920, National League owners refused to support Herrmann's reappointment as chairman, notwithstanding that his team in their league had just won the World Series. Meanwhile, Johnson's methods that were instrumental to the birth and early survival of the American League and helped it become the dominant league in the teens had alienated the owners of three of his league's four most important franchises. By the end of the decade Johnson was in all but open warfare with White Sox owner Charles Comiskey, a former ally who had been in on the ground floor when the American League was a start-up, and with the owners of both the Red Sox and Yankees. The AL was bitterly divided into Johnson and anti-Johnson factions. Philadelphia Athletics owner Connie Mack, one of the most respected men in the game, generally avoided the muck, but Johnson could count on his support.

A baseball power broker in his own right, Comiskey had become increasingly irritated by Johnson's autocratic ways. The last straw for Comiskey was Johnson's vote, along with Herrmann's, in awarding pitcher Jack Quinn to the Yankees in a contract dispute. Pitching in the Pacific Coast League when it shut down in July 1918 so that its players could be in compliance with the US government's able-bodied men must "work or fight" order for World War I, Quinn signed up to pitch for the White Sox the rest of the season, but during that time his contract was sold to the Yankees. Because the Yankees were an up-and-coming club in the most important city in America and were still without a pennant, there was more than a little reason to believe Johnson was interested in helping their cause. The next year, Johnson earned the undying enmity of both the Red Sox and Yankees owners when he tried to prevent Boston from sending Carl Mays to the Yankees in the midst of the 1919 pennant race in primarily a large cash transaction. This time the insinuation was that Johnson was more than a little interested in helping Cleveland's cause.

National League owners and the owners of the White Sox, Red Sox, and Yankees were not about to be railroaded by Johnson into accepting the candidate he supported for chairman of the National Commission. That individual happened to be the judge presiding over the grand jury that was investigating the Black Sox scandal, which Johnson may have imagined would allow him to settle scores with Comiskey and rid himself of the White Sox owner. The other five American League franchise owners continued to back the league president. Because of the impasse, a new commission chairman had still not been appointed when the Black Sox scandal exploded into the open in September 1920. Contrary to Johnson's expectations, the investigation did not buttress support for his candidate. Instead, public outrage over the revelations and Comiskey's tack that he wanted to get to the bottom of this betrayal by his players denied Johnson any opportunity to try to control the narrative in a way to influence the selection of the National Commission's next chairman.

In the midst of a crisis of this magnitude, it was unconscionable that there not be a chairman to lead the National Commission. Baseball needed a united front. The National League and the three AL franchises in opposition to Johnson advanced Judge Landis as their candidate and threatened to form a new 12-team league if necessary should Johnson and the five other American League club owners continue to obstruct the majority. They not only had the weight of numbers on their side as leverage—11 of the 16 major-league franchises—but also the fact that all five franchises in New York and Chicago, the two largest cities in America, and both in Boston were aligned against Johnson. The American League would not be a viable *major* league without those cities, and with at least two established teams in each city it was doubtful any new start-up franchises could compete. Johnson and his backers had no choice but to line up behind Landis.

Ban Johnson's maneuverings to try to ensure that the next chairman was *his* guy proved in the end to undermine his own power and influence in the governance of the game. Landis accepted the job as chairman of the National Commission, but soon made very clear that he did not envision his role to be the first among equals. The Judge demanded that his power to impose solutions to baseball's problems and make decisions in the "best interests of the national game of baseball" be absolute and not subject to override by the two league presidents acting in concert. Since the first order of business would be dealing with the fallout of the Black Sox scandal and restoring baseball's credibility, Landis knew he had the owners over a barrel. He was still a federal judge with a lifetime appointment; he could walk away. Baseball needed him more than he needed them, because baseball needed to show that someone with authority was in charge of fixing this terrible mess and ensuring it would never happen again. Johnson was holding out for the National Commission as it had been, where he would be a commanding voice, but Landis's ultimatum left him no choice but to concede.

By the end of the year, the National Commission had been replaced by a singular commissioner of baseball in the person of Judge Kenesaw Mountain Landis. The presidents of the two leagues had purview over the administration of their respective leagues, but the authority of the commissioner of baseball remained absolute. Landis continued to serve simultaneously as a federal judge until 1922, when he stepped aside to devote full-time to being commissioner in the face of mounting political pressure that federal judges must have no conflict of professional interests.

* * *

The Black Sox affair was the obvious first major issue Commissioner Landis had to contend with. It was the extreme inevitable result of baseball having failed to effectively grapple with the problem of corrupt players despite understanding that the public image of the game could not tolerate "dishonest" games, having rules specifically prohibiting players from conspiring to fix the outcome of games, and an awareness that there were players willfully associating with gamblers. Gambling, after all, and its subset of wagering on the outcome of any conceivable sporting event or contest, was perhaps even more of an American pastime than baseball. Of course, no one would dare say such a thing because gambling was decidedly less wholesome than baseball.

Placing bets on ballgames and the presence of big-time gamblers around baseball had been a problem from the beginning of baseball time, but the 1910s were probably the most corrupt era in the game's history. At a time of considerable social ferment because of the large economic inequities in American society aggravated by a major recession and uncertainty about whether the United States would be dragged into the war in Europe, baseball players were also feeling pinched by miserly owners. The collapse of the Federal League resulting in salaries being scaled back to previous levels, particularly those of nonelite players, was an eye-opening and embittering experience that widened the chasm between players and owners. Rumors of games being fixed became more commonplace, but specific allegations were virtually impossible to investigate because there was little if any hard evidence besides hearsay. Players who were approached by other players to participate in a fix were disinclined to snitch, and it was a dicey matter of whose word to believe without corroborating evidence in the cases where players did step forward against corrupt teammates.

The game's powerbrokers at the time were certainly not blind to at least the potential of players being bought off by gamblers to throw games. They did not necessarily turn a blind eye to the problem as much as try to keep whatever limited fixing of games there was hidden from view. It helped that most times players were probably acting on behalf of their own betting stakes rather than at the behest of big-time gamblers. The fact that baseball *was* the national pastime spared them from having to crack down on corrupt players because there were very few; everyone in the game—including the players, a significant number of whom engaged in all sorts of betting and some in high-stakes gambling—understood that their baseball livelihood would be threatened if there was a public perception that games were not honestly played and championships legitimately earned. Because nearly all players played "honest" ball, intensive efforts to root out corrupt players risked bringing unwanted public scrutiny to the problem. But halfhearted investigations and failing to root out corrupt players left baseball vulnerable to precisely what happened in the 1919 World Series. Until then, no player since the end of the nineteenth century was known to have been banished from baseball for fixing games on behalf of gambling interests.

If corruption in baseball had a face, its name was Hal Chase—and not just figuratively, but literally; a handsome man, Chase's face was corrupted by scars left from a bout with smallpox in the spring of 1909 when he was playing for the New York Highlanders. Chase was the best player on the Highlanders in the years between their competing for the 1906 pennant and the New York franchise deciding that "Yankees" would serve as a better nickname. He was also a charismatic personality who made many acquaintances, including with less savory elements of society, although even they would have been advised to check their wallet and count their fingers after being in his presence. Perpetually restless, often perturbed that his abilities as a ballplayer were not properly recognized, and always on the make, Chase was often suspected of "lying down" by his teammates. Nothing could be proven, however, and although insinuations of his corruption reached the level of the American League president in 1912, they came in the midst of a power play between the Highlanders' star first baseman and his manager, George Stallings. Ban Johnson not only took no action against Chase, he demanded Stallings's resignation.

Six years later, however, now playing for the Reds, Chase was in more serious trouble when his trying to entice a few teammates and opponents to participate in his schemes to fix the outcome of games caught the attention of his manager, Christy Mathewson, a paragon of virtue if ever

White Sox first baseman Hal Chase making a play against his former team, the Highlanders, at the Polo Grounds in 1913. *George Grantham Bain Collection (Library of Congress).*

there was one. It didn't matter that Chase had hit .339 to win the National League batting title wearing a Cincinnati uniform in 1916. Nor did it matter that Chase was the Reds' cleanup hitter and batting .301 at the time. Mathewson suspended Chase in early August for the remainder of what would be a war-shortened 1918 season, secured affidavits from several of the Reds' players concerning Chase's perfidy, and had the backing of the owner, Garry Herrmann, whose role as chairman of the National Commission was irrelevant to the case.

If ever there was a prime opportunity for baseball institutionally to take a stand against corruption and punish players who would compromise the integrity of games by accepting bribes or bribing others, this was it. The case went before National League president John Heydler, but not before Chase's principal and most credible accuser—Christy Mathewson—was off to war in Europe, making him unable to attend the hearing. Chase was well represented by lawyers who cast doubt on the motives of players testifying against the first baseman. John McGraw gave a glowing testimonial as to what a great fellow Chase was and offered that Chase was welcome to play for his ballclub if the Reds no longer wanted him. In the face of all that, with Mathewson absent, Heydler felt he had no choice but to let Chase off scot-free.

Sure enough, Chase was McGraw's first baseman the next year as the Giants competed against Cincinnati for the 1919 pennant. Notwithstanding McGraw's favorable character reference getting him off the hook before Heydler, Chase betrayed his manager's faith in him by reverting to old habits of trying to bribe his teammates to fix games. McGraw benched Chase for the final month of the season. During the offseason, while the Reds celebrated their improbable dominance of the ostensibly far better White Sox in the 1919 World Series, Heydler banned Chase from ever again playing in the National League based on evidence he was able to obtain of his perfidy from a Boston gambler.

Taking a chance on Chase also ultimately cost McGraw his third baseman, Heinie Zimmerman, likewise suspected over the years as being one of baseball's "dishonest" players. Like Chase, he was a star in his own right, having won the Triple Crown in 1912 and twice more leading the National League in runs batted in, including when the Giants won the 1917 pennant. Like Chase, there were occasions where Zimmerman's failure to make plays at pivotal moments seemed suspicious. And as with Chase, it was difficult to prove anything of the sort. Now together on the same team, Zimmerman and Chase proved a toxic combination. Since the Reds finished nine games in front, it cannot be said that their playing to lose games—and trying to entice teammates to help—cost their team the pennant. The end for both players came in the final month, after the pennant race was effectively over, when in relation to three separate games, Zimmerman told pitcher Fred Toney it would be worth his while to pitch poorly; Chase said the same to pitcher Rube Benton; and both offered a cash bribe to outfielder Benny Kauff to help them throw a game. Zimmerman was suspended for the rest of the year and, like Chase, never again played in Organized Baseball.

* * *

The inability or unwillingness of baseball's authority figures to crack down on players corrupting the game was the sordid background against which the new commissioner took charge of Major League Baseball. If *Judge* Landis patiently waited for the Federal League's inevitable collapse—which he might have precluded had he ruled before the 1915 season in their favor—to avoid having to decide on the merits of their case, *Commissioner* Landis acted quickly and decisively when it came to the eight Chicago players accused of conspiring with big-time gamblers to throw the 1919 World Series. None were convicted in their criminal trial on the charges against them, raising questions about whether Landis's decision to bar them for life from all of Organized Baseball—not just the major leagues—was justified, and indeed, whether the former judge was being excessively vindictive toward men who were found . . . "not guilty."

Even if the trial jury chose to ignore or dismiss the grand jury confessions of Shoeless Joe Jackson, Eddie Cicotte, and Lefty Williams, as well as evidence presented by prosecutors against the others, which was particularly weak concerning Buck Weaver, the new commissioner did not. And it mattered little to Landis whether they played to lose, which they all denied doing. In fact, that issue was ultimately irrelevant as far as the former federal judge was concerned. The confessions and the evidence spoke to the Black Sox players' *agreeing* to conspire with gamblers to lose World Series games, and that was all that mattered to Landis. Even if they did not compromise the outcome of the games on the field of play, their agreement to compromise the integrity of the games for a payout, whether given or not, defrauded Major League Baseball's interest, and fans' expectations, that games were honestly played and championships legitimately earned. And that was unacceptable.

The most controversial of the lifetime banishments was that of Buck Weaver, who claimed to have taken no money from gamblers (nor did anyone provide any evidence he did), batted .324 in the Series with 11 hits, and was the only starting infielder on the two World Series teams not to make an error. Weaver's irredeemable sin, as far as Landis was concerned, was having sat "in a conference with a bunch of crooked players and gamblers where the ways and means of throwing games are planned and discussed"—the commissioner's words—and not "promptly" telling his club about it. By making the point that no player who followed Weaver's example "will ever play professional baseball again," Landis effectively made it far more difficult for any player to hatch a plot with his teammates to fix the outcome of a game. No longer could players like Hal Chase and Heinie Zimmerman count on getting away with trying to bribe players to throw games because of the human tendency of teammates to look the other way and not snitch, even if they personally spurned such offers.

Indeed, although there had been rumors here and there of players on the take, the only known conspiracy to fix the outcome of a game on Landis's watch surfaced in 1924 when a player who was offered a bribe to throw a critical game in a pennant race not only said no but, after a brief interlude of soul searching, reported the approach to his manager. In search of an unprecedented fourth straight pennant, the Giants held a 1½-game lead going into the final weekend with three games left against the seventh-place Phillies. Apparently with the backing of Giants' first-base coach Cozy Dolan, if not at his direct behest, Jimmy O'Connell—the left-handed half of John McGraw's center-field platoon—offered Philadelphia shortstop Heinie Sand $500 to help the Giants win however many games were necessary to secure the pennant. Perhaps with the Weaver precedent in mind, Sand went to his manager, who went to the National League president, who informed the commissioner, who convened a hearing on the matter. O'Connell not only admitted his role, but implicated star teammates Frankie Frisch, George Kelly, and Ross Youngs—all of whom are now in the Hall of Fame—as being willing to chip in on the bribe.

The Giants, meanwhile, won the pennant fair and square. Landis concluded there was insufficient evidence to pursue any further investigation of McGraw's best players, much to the commissioner's relief because the involvement of such prominent players in fixing games would not only have been another major body blow to the integrity of Major League Baseball, but a significant wound to the commissioner himself by undermining the credibility of all he had done to ensure there was no corruption in baseball. Both O'Connell and Dolan were permanently barred from Organized Baseball. The O'Connell affair was the last time any commissioner of baseball had to deal with corruption on the field of play until, 65 years later, Pete Rose—one of the game's all-time great players—was placed on baseball's permanently ineligible list by Commissioner Bart Giamatti in 1989 for betting on games when he was manager of the Cincinnati Reds.

But Landis still had one more betting scandal to navigate. This one was particularly dicey because not only did it involve two icons of the game, Ty Cobb and Tris Speaker, but American League president Ban Johnson was the first to weigh in and had already decided both Cobb and Speaker were guilty and secured their agreement to retire immediately and never return to the game they loved and played so well. The allegations were that, in the closing days of the 1919 season, Cobb and Speaker agreed to place bets on Detroit winning a game between their two teams on the day *after* the Tigers had beaten the Indians to officially eliminate them from contention, ironically ensuring that the White Sox would be in the World Series. They were brought to Johnson's attention by disaffected former Tigers pitcher Dutch Leonard—Hubert, who starred for the Red Sox before going to Detroit in 1919, not Emil, then still a teenager—whose evidence included a supposedly damning letter from Cobb. None of the evidence provided by Leonard said anything about "fixing" the outcome of the game, only that their bets were on the Tigers.

Frustrated by having to continually fend off attacks on his authority by Johnson, and asserting that any case involving gambling and the fixing of games was necessarily a matter for the commissioner, Landis publicly repudiated the American League president's forcing Cobb and Speaker out of baseball by conducting his own investigation of an episode that happened before his watch and which could hardly be said to presage the World Series fix engineered by big-time gamblers and corrupt players just a week after the suspect Tigers-Indians game, which Detroit *did* in fact win. Although his alleged bet was against his own team, Speaker nonetheless went 3-for-5 for the losing Indians. After weighing the evidence, including interviewing Cobb and Speaker, Landis concluded that while they may have bet on the game, there was nothing to substantiate any attempt to "fix" the outcome. The commissioner exonerated both players and ordered that Cobb and Speaker be reinstated by the American League. Although their contracts were back with Detroit and Cleveland, it was understood neither would play again for his former team.

Both were at the tail end of their careers and both played just two more years, neither with the club that made them famous, before retiring on their own terms. Unlike attempts to "fix" the outcome of games, players and managers placing wagers on baseball games had up till now *not* been specifically prohibited, a fact that got Cobb and Speaker off the hook. Landis took action to close that loophole by decreeing that, henceforth, it was not just the fixing of games that was outlawed, but nobody involved in Organized Baseball was ever to bet on baseball games. And that included franchise owners. In 1943, Landis permanently banned Phillies owner William Cox for placing bets on his team.

The Cobb-Speaker affair proved to be the end of the line for Ban Johnson. Denied the power and influence to which he had been accustomed when major-league owners acquiesced to Landis's demand that he be given absolute authority—that Landis be, in effect, baseball's czar—Johnson had been trying his best to undermine the commissioner. Among other actions, Johnson demanded that either second-place Brooklyn represent the National League in the 1924 World Series on account of the O'Connell affair, or that the Series be canceled. In January 1925, obviously still smarting from Landis's refusal to even consider that the Giants' pennant might not have been legitimately won, Johnson publicly urged that the federal government establish a commission to supersede the commissioner's authority. By returning the two stars to the American League, Landis's decision on their case was a direct rebuke of Johnson, who had sought to banish them both. Johnson's immediate intemperate response was to criticize the commissioner's decision and add fuel to the fire by claiming that other Cleveland players besides Speaker were inveterate gamblers, including betting on baseball. He also implied that Landis had botched his investigation into allegations that Carl Mays, and perhaps others on the Yankees' pitching staff, conspired with gamblers to pitch poorly in the 1922 World Series.

Byron Bancroft Johnson, who had the audacity and drive to start up the American League and make a success of it, and who was the most powerful authority in Organized Baseball from the beginning of the century until Judge Landis became commissioner, overplayed his hand. Johnson had become an embarrassment. In addition to his insistent sniping at the commissioner, he had publicly delivered a cheap shot in blaming Washington Senators manager Bucky Harris for losing Game Seven of the 1925 World Series because of an undue "display of sentiment" by allowing the great Walter Johnson—a baseball icon and hero of the previous year's World Series—to continue pitching, though exhausted, in bad weather. Landis on several occasions made it clear to American League owners that their league needed a new president. In January 1927, AL owners publicly upbraided their league president for his criticisms of Landis's "handling of the several investigations concerning the integrity of players in the American League," praised "Judge Landis for his efforts in clearing baseball of any insinuations of dishonesty," and announced that Johnson would be taking "a much-needed rest" on the advice of his personal physician. Later that year, Ban Johnson's medical retreat turned into a resignation.

* * *

Kenesaw Mountain Landis, meanwhile, had been unanimously approved in December 1926 by major-league club owners for another seven-year term as commissioner of baseball. With still a year left on his existing contract, it was a vote of confidence for Landis in the midst of his having to deal with Johnson's decision in the Cobb-Speaker case. But it was also a vote that implicitly reaffirmed, despite some owners at various times being unhappy with the breadth of jurisdiction he claimed, that the commissioner had absolute authority in overseeing every aspect of the baseball business.

Seeing himself as not merely an enforcer to protect Major League Baseball from miscreants, Landis had not been shy in asserting his authority in any matter he felt warranted his attention. Among his first acts as commissioner, little noticed but quite important in the context of the Black Sox scandal, was ordering Giants owner Charles Stoneham and manager John McGraw to divest themselves of a casino and racetrack they owned in Havana, Cuba. Landis wanted to ensure that there was not even the appearance of impropriety in the affairs of baseball people when it came to big-time gambling. In a similar vein, he acted decisively his first year on the job, perhaps even unfairly, to prevent players from trying to leverage contract negotiations by banishing Ray Fisher for accepting a college coaching job after signing a contract to pitch for Cincinnati and preventing the Reds from trading their outstanding third baseman, Heinie Groh, to the Giants after Groh had signed a contract with the stipulation he be traded out of Cincinnati. And Landis made the point that no individual was greater than the game itself, no matter how idolized he was by the fans whose interest and attendance made Organized Baseball a viable business, when he suspended Babe Ruth and Bob Meusel for the first five and a half weeks of the 1922 season for violating the ban on postseason barnstorming by players on pennant-winning teams after Ruth had been personally warned not to go.

Having established his authority in cases that involved disciplinary actions, including the Ruth barnstorming affair, Landis turned his attention next to the competitive landscape—specifically the financial advantages that both New York teams were exploiting to gain the upper hand in close pennant races. Every year it seemed the Giants and Yankees were taking advantage of the August 1 trading deadline to make a late-season transaction (or two) for an impact player to help their cause, stoking resentment and criticism from competing clubs that they were effectively able to "buy" the pennant any year they were in a tight race. McGraw had a robust resume of late-season transactions that helped his Giants to four straight pennants between 1921 and 1924.

While the frustration of National League owners was palpable, it was the New York Yankees' deal sending three marginal players and $50,000 to the Red Sox for third baseman Joe Dugan on July 23, 1922, that forced the commissioner's hand, perhaps because American League president Ban Johnson chose to weigh in. Despite having Ruth back from his barnstorming suspension, the Yankees were in a dogfight for the pennant with the St. Louis Browns—a team with a woeful history that had never won before—whom they trailed at the time by 1½ games. Third base was the Yankees' one unsettled position; aging veteran Home Run Baker was unable to play because of injuries, and his would-be replacement, Mike McNally, had a miserable month of July. Dugan was not an impact player, but the Yankees' baseball hierarchy recognized that he was precisely the kind of complementary role-player who could be invaluable to their pennant prospects in 1922 and for years to come. Dugan was the new third baseman in the Yankees starting lineup every remaining game of the season, and the Dugan transaction may indeed have been the deciding factor that enabled the Yankees to ultimately prevail over the Browns by a single game for their second straight pennant.

The Dugan trade particularly outraged Johnson. Not only was it between two of the three American League franchises that had lined up against him, including in the battle over who should be commissioner, but it was at the expense of the franchise owner who was perhaps his most stalwart ally, Philip DeCatesby Ball, whose Browns were edged out by the Yankees. Johnson, who in 1919 had tried to prevent the deal that sent Carl Mays from the Red Sox to the contending Yankees, wanted no trades to be allowed during the season. Landis, having heard complaints from the Pirates in 1921 and the Cardinals in 1922 about late-season Giants acquisitions that helped short-circuit their pennant prospects, was sympathetic to the argument that the ability of teams to leverage superior financial resources to boost their chances late in a pennant race undermined the principles of fair competition. The former judge spurned Johnson's proposal and settled instead on Pittsburgh owner Barney Dreyfuss's recommendation that June 15 be the deadline for in-season trades. The June 15 date had the advantage of allowing teams to improve their rosters before the real pennant races took shape later in the summer. June 15 would remain Major League Baseball's trade deadline until 1986, when it was moved back to where it was before Landis changed it—well, actually, the last day of July instead of the first day of August.

* * *

Appreciating how the commissioner had restored the public's faith in the integrity of Major League Baseball, and with attendance booming during the Roaring Twenties, the owners' unanimous vote in favor of giving Landis another seven-year contract was virtually the same as assuring him he could be baseball's ruling power for as long as he wanted, the same as his presidential appointment to the federal bench had been until he voluntarily stepped down. Landis held the job for the remainder of his life, which came to an end in November 1944, just five days after his 78th birthday.

Few commissioners since—perhaps none, with the exception of Bud Selig—had the stature of Judge Landis. And none commanded such respect and stature from the very beginning of his tenure. Kenesaw Mountain Landis, along with Ruth and other star players in the two and a half decades he reigned supreme, was synonymous with baseball. Casual fans knew who he was. No commissioner since has measured up to him as identifiable with the integrity of the national pastime, including Selig, whose many achievements to ensure the game flourished at a time when many professional sports and other entertainments competed with baseball were sometimes buried by perceptions he was either blind to or even complicit in the early twenty-first-century steroid scandals. Landis was the opposite of Selig in dealing with performance-enhancing drugs. He acted quickly and decisively—sometimes perhaps intemperately—to crack down on any perceived threat to the integrity of the game.

Of course, the luster of Judge Landis as the commissioner who "saved baseball" from the Black Sox scandal has since been tarnished, the "face

Commissioner Landis flanked by Yankees owners Jacob Ruppert and Tillinghast Huston at the grand opening of Yankee Stadium on April 18, 1923. *George Grant-ham Bain Collection (Library of Congress).*

of God" features chiseled onto baseball's Mount Rushmore weathered, in large part because of his role in opposing the integration of black players into Organized Baseball.

14

GAME CHANGE

How the Babe Upended "Scientific" Baseball

Babe Ruth was baseball's greatest change agent in history. Before he opened eyes by demonstrating what a powerful weapon the home run could be, runs very often had to be earned the hard way with scoring opportunities set up by sacrifice bunts, stolen bases, and hit-and-run plays to advance baserunners. When Ruth shattered the single-season home-run record with 29 in 1919, it marked the divide between the Deadball Era of the first two decades of the new century and the Lively Ball Era of the 1920s and '30s. There were nearly three-quarters more home runs hit in the major leagues in 1919 than the previous year—a significant increase even considering that the final month of the 1918 season was canceled because of America's participation in World War I. Although the major-league schedule for 1919 was reduced to only 140 games despite the end of hostilities the previous November, the 447 home runs hit that year set a new record and were a third more than the 335 hit in 1917, the last time the majors had played a normal 154-game schedule. Ruth's 29 homers in his final year with the Red Sox accounted for all but four hit by his entire team and were 12 percent of the 240 total in the American League.

In 1920, when baseball's traditional 154-game schedule resumed, major-league batters hit 630 homers, nearly double the number in 1917. And Ruth, now with the Yankees, nearly doubled his record-setting 1919 total with a mind-boggling, not to mention eye-popping (because his clouts were so impressive), 54 four-base blasts. Notwithstanding that the closest anyone got to Ruth in long(ball)gevity that year was George Sisler with 19, and that all batters, the Babe included, benefited from new rules outlawing trick pitches and spitballs in all their various manifestations, except for two designated holdover pitchers allowed each team, baseball's new power era was officially under way.

There was speculation that the baseball itself had been "livened up" because baseball's powers-that-be saw that fans dug the long ball. They insisted nothing of the sort was true. The baseballs used in the 1920s were also said to be harder for pitchers to get a good grip on than before because of their gloss. Regardless of whether baseballs were deliberately manufactured to go farther when hit, which is unlikely, that was not the case when Ruth began his annual bombs-away campaign in 1919.

Ruth's revolutionizing the game with regard to an appreciation of the home run as the ultimate in offensive efficiency not surprisingly opened a contentious debate about whether such an unprecedented power surge was somehow robbing baseball of its purity. Home runs were perceived by traditionalists of the day as diminishing the refined "scientific" game of strategy and tactics that made the national pastime so appealing. Moreover, "scientific baseball" was conceptually in step with this distinctly American moment in the country's history where the "modern" cultural paradigm of brain over brawn prevailed in all manner of productivity—economic, military, even recreational—occasioned by the practical application of science to problem solving. America, however, was also on the imminent cusp of the Roaring Twenties, when flair, improvisation, good times, breaking hidebound rules (manifested especially with regard to Prohibition), and celebrity became all the rage. It was an era in American history perfectly matched for a man of the Babe's innate rebelliousness, showmanship, joyous spirit, and prodigious talent. And Babe Ruth, as much as anyone, embodied and defined the era.

It was not as though the four-base, clear-the-bases value of the home run was not understood in the Deadball Era, merely that—until Ruth proved otherwise—baseball generally dismissed the long ball as an unreliable offensive weapon. There were too many variables, starting with the baseball itself. Manufactured baseballs were in fact more "dead" than they would be in the 1920s because of production materials and processes. Moreover, baseballs were rarely removed from games until they became so dark or defaced that there was no alternative but to bring in a new ball. In the Deadball Era, balls were routinely doctored by infielders and pitchers during the course of a game, making it more difficult for batters to pick up spin and often even the ball itself from the background, not to mention the effect nicks, dings, and applied foreign substances might have on pitch trajectories.

And then there was a prevailing philosophy of hitting that was anything but homer-centric. Much of this was because the science of hitting at the time focused more on technique and tactics, such as bunting and place-hitting, rather than physical mechanics like working specifically on strength, balance, and extension. Outs were precious, and every batter was expected to put the ball in play. The deliberately home-run-focused Ruth, by contrast, was willing to strike out relatively frequently in his bid to hit the ball a long way, and perhaps because he was originally a pitcher, his managers in Boston were willing to put up with that. Once Ruth demonstrated that he could hit the ball out with unprecedented frequency and consistency, the rest was history. Ruth was moved to the outfield to get his bat in the lineup on a daily basis in 1919, and his managers were not bothered by the strikeouts, certainly not Ed Barrow in Boston or Miller Huggins in New York.

If home runs were rare before Ruth changed the equation, that did not mean extra-base hits did not power the best offenses. Extra-base hits are the surest and best way to produce runs because they not only immediately put runners in scoring position, but drive in more baserunners as well. In the deadball years, as throughout baseball history, teams that were at the top of their league in scoring typically had a higher percentage of extra-base hits than the league average. Power counts, whether defined by triples and doubles, as in the Deadball Era, or by home runs, once the Ruth revolution had been consolidated.

Although hastened by Ruth and dramatized by him in a way no other player was or could have been capable of, the home-run revolution was ultimately inevitable because the power game was always important. Even in the Deadball Era, whose death knell was sounded in 1919, baseball's best and most dangerous batters hit for power, although the power currency of the day was triples and long doubles rather than hitting the ball out of the park. Among the era's outstanding offensive players, 30 percent of Shoeless Joe Jackson's hits through 1919 were extra-base hits; Honus Wagner, Sam Crawford, and Tris Speaker had 29 percent of their hits go for extra bases; Napoleon Lajoie and Home Run Baker, 28 percent; and Ty Cobb, 26 percent. Except for Baker, they all hit at least two and a half times as many triples as homers, and notwithstanding his nickname, even Baker had more triples (98) than home runs (80) in the deadball years. Each of their extra-base-hit percentages was significantly higher than their league average for the seasons they played.

John McGraw, in particular, was not happy with the turn the sacred game of baseball had taken. But as much as he complained that Ruth's powerful example of the efficiency of one mighty blow scoring a run with nobody on base, or multiple runs with men on base, was killing intelligent "scientific" baseball, McGraw understood the importance of the power game even before the Babe burst on the scene. As a baseball strategist, McGraw was a practitioner of "big ball" himself to the extent it could be played in the Deadball Era. His teams were built on players who could drive the ball down the lines and into the gaps. In an era when extra-base hits accounted for about 20 percent of total hits in the first decade and around 23 percent in the teens, Roger Bresnahan, Red Murray, Larry Doyle, Fred Merkle, George Burns, and Benny Kauff all had more than 25 percent of their hits go for extra bases in the years they played for McGraw, and Dave Robertson had back-to-back seasons (1916 and 1917) with 12 homers to tie for the league lead. In McGraw's first 17 full seasons as manager from 1903 to 1919, the Giants led the league in scoring nine times, were second in runs three times, and no worse than third in any other year. In five of those years, the Giants led the NL in home runs.

McGraw would surely have appreciated the scoring implications of the Babe's raw power had he had Ruth on his team. Perhaps an argument could be made that his controlling insistence that baseball be played *his* way would have caused McGraw to tame Ruth's impulse to swing the bat with fierce aggressiveness, but that assumes he was set in his ways and those ways prioritized "manufacturing" runs the old-fashioned deadball way. McGraw may have been inflexible about how he thought the game *should* be played, but he was *always* flexible about the big picture. John McGraw would have welcomed the consistent over-the-fence dimension to the power game that Ruth brought to the batter's box, and he ensured that the Giants had a multifaceted offense that included a formidable power dimension in the 1920s. In his last 12 full seasons as manager, 1920 to 1931, McGraw's Giants topped the league in homers five times. George Kelly and Irish Meusel were the Giants' top power hitters when they won four consecutive pennants. By the end of his managerial career, McGraw was fully committed to the efficacy of the long ball as he nurtured one of the game's premier sluggers of the Lively Ball Era—Mel Ott.

* * *

Watching New York City become more and more Babe Ruth's town, however—his 59 homers in 1921 sealing that deal—McGraw looked askance at the notion of relying on home runs to score runs in big bunches. Such an approach offended his sensibilities. It was hardly the "scientific" approach to the game that the reputed master of "inside" baseball held to be sacrosanct. McGraw thought of the home run as somehow diminishing baseball the way it was supposed to be played— with speed, skill, daring, and, certainly important from his perspective, managerial savvy to outsmart the other team—rather than just rely on guys like Ruth to bludgeon the other team into submission. Much of his disdain might have been jealousy and resentment that his rock star status was usurped by the biggest act of them all, but McGraw did have a point.

In virtually an instant, the Deadball Era that McGraw had dominated as a strategist transitioned to the power game as other batters followed in the Babe's footsteps and offensive philosophies began revolving around the concept of the "big inning" instead of working to build small rallies a run at a time. The pace of scoring picked up. Although most teams continued to hit more triples than homers in the 1920s, and over-the-fence blasts would not forever eclipse three-baggers until the 1930s, the four-bagger became the new power currency in Major League Baseball. The old power currency, doubles and triples, did not have the same value as home runs in scoring impact and, unlike the home run, for which Ruth set the precedent of deliberately swinging for the fences, all other extra-base hits were more happenstance, even if the ability to hit the ball hard was a requisite for building a formidable offense. Deliberately swinging for the fences—the notion of the home run itself as an offensive strategy—resulted in a significant increase in the percentage of extra-base hits even when the ball stayed in the yard, which in turn led to greater success scoring runners on base.

Precisely because bases-clearing clouts were so rare prior to Ruth, and because the percentage of all extra-base hits was appreciably lower in the Deadball Era that McGraw dominated as a strategist, there was a premium on strategies to set up runs that emphasized speed and skillful handling of the bat to advance baserunners. Now that low-scoring games were much less the norm in this new era of power ball, run-creation strategies that either sacrificed outs to advance runners—whether by sacrifice bunts or hitting behind the runner for a "productive out"—or risked outs on stolen base attempts diminished in value. This was true even though about 30 percent of ballgames in the 1920s were decided by a single run, down from slightly more than a third of game outcomes in the last decade of the Deadball Era, but a significant number nonetheless. Granted that one-run games in the 1920s were generally higher scoring and that many ended up that way as a result of teams making up multirun deficits, there was still inherent importance to *every* run. The fact that classic pitchers' duels that might turn on a single run orchestrated by a walk, a stolen base or sacrifice bunt, and a single perhaps were far less frequent, and slugfests more so, does not obscure that playing for a single run, whether to score first, to start a rally in a close game, to score the tying run, or to break a tie game, still had merit.

The new manager's mind-set in the 1920s, however, was biased toward playing for multiple runs anytime there was a baserunner. Giving up an out to sacrifice bunt a runner to the next base, or having runners thrown out trying to steal the next base, was antithetical to the "big" inning. Stolen bases in particular dropped dramatically from Deadball Era levels. By 1930, the major-league steals total was less than half what it was in 1917, while the record-setting 1,565 homers hit that year were more than four and a half times the 1917 total. Managers, however, did not give up on the fine art of playing for a single run when they assessed that the game situation called for setting up a scoring opportunity, not even the Yankees with their Murderers' Row featuring Ruth and Gehrig. Miller Huggins didn't use such strategies often, but when he did it was with reason and for effect. The game-winning run in the bottom of the ninth of Game Four in the 1927 World Series that broke a 3–3 tie and secured the first Series sweep in Yankees history, for example, was set up by a sacrifice bunt attempt that was so perfectly executed it became a bunt single.

McGraw himself was very particular about what strategies he used to advance baserunners. Master strategist that he was, McGraw did not look favorably on sacrifice bunts as a means to set up runs because, like Earl Weaver some 60 years later, he didn't like wasting an out when there were other ways to create scoring opportunities. His first two years as the Giants' manager in 1903 and 1904 were the only times any of McGraw's clubs led the league in sacrifice hits. After that, the Giants were consistently below, and usually well below, the league average for as long as he was the manager. The Giants were last or next to last in the league in sacrifice hits every year but two between 1911 and 1920, and in the bottom tier throughout the 1920s.

Hit-and-run plays and stolen bases were always McGraw's preferred options for setting up runs. Having speed throughout his lineup, therefore, was always a priority. His Giants led both leagues in stolen bases by a wide margin when they won back-to-back pennants in 1904 and 1905, and again in 1911 and 1912; led the majors again when they won their third straight pennant in 1913, although with barely more than the Washington Senators; and led the National League when they won their next pennant in 1917. The Giants' 347 stolen bases in 1911 remain the most by a major-league team since the start of the twentieth century, and their 319 steals the next year were second most until eclipsed by the 1976 Oakland A's, who came within six of the Giants' 1911 record. Indicative of the speed McGraw had up and down his lineup, the 1911 Giants had seven players with at least 20 steals, four had more than 45, and both his 1912 and 1913 clubs had six players with at least 30 swiped bases.

As the Ruthian revolution gained momentum in the 1920s, McGraw began to view stolen bases as a riskier proposition than he had in the past, which was very much consistent with the trend now that the home run had emerged as such a potent weapon. Even though he still favored stolen bases as the best way to set up scoring opportunities, McGraw conceded that the new power reality significantly changed the equation in weighing the balance between the benefits of a stolen base and the possibility of short-circuiting a rally in a failed attempt. While caught-stealing data is not available for most years in the first quarter century, for those that it is, there was never a year, including in the Deadball Era, that even 60 percent of stolen-base attempts were successful. In his final decade as baseball's genius manager, McGraw's teams stole much less often than in the past in both actual and relative terms. After the Giants led the league in steals six times in seven years between 1911 and 1917, they did so only twice in the 1920s and otherwise never finished better than third in stolen bases.

* * *

Aside from its broad impact on deadball strategies, baseball's power surge also led to a shift in the offensive dynamic between the two leagues. For most of the last decade of the Deadball Era, the American League was more prolific in scoring runs, yet it was the National League that required fewer runners on base for each run scored. The reason was that, until Ruth's destiny was firmly settled in the outfield in 1919, the National League was *the* power league in Major League Baseball. Every year since 1906, NL batters had a higher percentage of their total hits go for extra bases and hit substantially more home runs—nearly two-thirds more in the teens—than AL batters. Even in 1918—the year Ruth was beginning his transition to full-time outfielder and daily devastating menace at bat, tying for the major-league lead in homers with 11—the National League hit nearly half again as many home runs as the American League.

In a seeming contradiction, however, the AL had a much better runs-to-hits ratio, which surely contributed to its scoring advantage. Part of the reason was that many more batters reached base in the American League because of a big edge in drawing walks, particularly in the second half of the 1910s. Not including errors because that data is unavailable, 28 percent of the batters reaching first base in the American League between 1915 and 1918 did so by way of ball four, compared to 23 percent in the National League. With more runners on base and a smaller percentage of extra-base hits to drive them in, AL teams put much greater emphasis on both stolen bases and sacrifice bunts to set up scoring opportunities than NL clubs. These strategies were clearly cost effective, allowing American League teams to be much more productive with their hits.

Coinciding with a dramatic increase in on-base percentage in the American League coupled with a significant decrease in the NL after 1914, the disparity between the two leagues in sacrificing outs to advance runners widened considerably in the second half of the teens. From 1915 to 1920, American League teams averaged 7 percent more baserunners and, incredibly, 18 percent more sacrifice hits per year (which, by definition, then included sacrifice flies) to advance runners, suggesting that AL managers were not using sacrifice bunts so much more often than their National League counterparts *only because* they now happened to have substantially more baserunners. It points instead to sacrifice bunting being used deliberately as a *preferred* strategy to advance runners and create scoring opportunities. And that trend did not change with the advent of the home-run era in the American League beginning with Ruth's 29 blasts in 1919. Notwithstanding their league's home-run surge, American League managers continued to emphasize the bunt to advance runners, averaging 205 sacrifice hits per team in 1920, much higher than the NL team average of 177.

That trend continued until near the end of the 1920s, which was consistent with the AL continuing to put more runners on base. Unlike in the teens, the percentage of extra-base hits was higher in the American League in every year of the '20s except 1925. The AL was the new power league in Major League Baseball. Carrying over from the last half decade of the Deadball Era, the much higher percentage difference in the American League between sacrifice hits and total baserunners suggests sacrificing remained a far more important strategy to advance runners for scoring opportunities than in the NL. The National League, conversely, far outpaced the AL in stolen bases until the mid-1920s. From then through the 1930s, it was the other way around.

The underlying dynamics for why National League managers relied less on run-creation strategies even in the 1920s was mostly the same as in the teens. Despite the American League—specifically the New York Yankees—having Ruth and, later in the decade, Ruth *and* Gehrig, it was the National League that maintained a persistent and, in most years, significant advantage in home runs. Although AL teams scored more runs in six of the 10 years between 1921 and 1930 and had a steady annual rise in extra-base hits from 25 percent in 1924 to 30 percent in 1930, the National League outdistanced the American League in home runs every year from 1922 to 1930. But of course, nobody could catch the Babe. Ruth topped 50 home runs four times in his career, beginning with 54 and 59 in 1920 and '21, and ending with his famous 60 in 1927 and 54 the year after.

* * *

The Roaring Twenties ended with an offensive outburst in 1929 and 1930 not seen since 1893 and 1894 when pitchers were adjusting with some difficulty to new rules that pushed them back to the current 60 feet, 6 inches and required them to keep their back foot on the pitcher's slab while delivering the baseball. In 1930, it seemed the whole season was one extended batting practice. Six of the 16 major-league teams averaged more than six runs a game. The Yankees scored nearly seven runs a game, and the Cardinals 6.5, as they became the first teams since the Boston Beaneaters in 1897 to score more than 1,000 runs in a season. Major-league hitters combined for a .296 average—the highest since 12 National League teams hit .296 in 1895—with nine teams alone batting over .300. With Bill Terry's .401 average leading the way, the top 10 hitters in baseball all batted .367 or better. The 1,565 home runs hit in the major leagues set a new record, eclipsing by more than 200 the 1,349 whacked in 1929. Hack Wilson set the major-league record—still standing as of 2018—for runs batted in with 191, and his 56 homers would stand as the National League record until 1998. In the AL, Ruth and Gehrig were first and second in home runs with 49 and 41, and together their 90 blasts exceeded the totals of six of the seven other American League clubs. Gehrig's 173 RBIs tied the American League record he set in 1927, one that he would break the very next year with 185.

But just as the American League at the end of the Deadball Era was clearly the dominant offensive league in every dimension, so it was the National League as the '20s turned into the '30s. In 1929 and 1930, the NL put more runners on base, scored more runs, and collected more hits and extra-base hits, especially home runs, although the AL kept its advantage, however slight, in percentage of hits that went for extra bases. NL batters clubbed 892 homers in 1930, up by 46 percent from 610 two years earlier and one-third more than the 673 fence-busters hit in the American League. The 1930 Cubs, for whom Wilson played, walloped 171 home runs, shattering the record of 158 set by the 1927 Yankees. Six of the NL's eight teams hit better than .300, and the league's collective .303 batting average was more than 20 points higher than the .280 to .282 range of the mid-1920s. The American League's share in the offensive surge of 1929 and '30 was much more modest. Although AL batters also set a new league record for homers, their collective .288 batting average was not the equal of the American League's three .290-plus seasons in the first half of the 1920s.

While the 1893–94 explosion in offense lasted for five years until 1897, the 1929–30 outburst ended in 1931, possibly because of the introduction of baseballs with raised seams giving pitchers a better grip on the ball. That did not mean, however, a return to anything approaching baseball's deadball days. The emphasis was now on generating rallies by hitting away. Home-run rates increased significantly in the 1930s. Sacrifice bunts would never recover the importance they had for setting up runs in the Deadball Era, or even in much of the 1920s after the Ruth revolution had taken hold. That there were many more stolen bases in the American League was probably more a reflection of much higher on-base percentages from both hits and walks than any greater preference for that strategy over sacrificing outs to advance runners. The power game ruled. John McGraw, who died in 1934, might have rolled over in his grave, but he also would have understood.

During the Depression years, the major leagues would not match the number of home runs hit in 1930 until 10 years later, when 1,571 went into the record books, but long-ball totals remained elevated throughout the decade, typically between 1,300 and 1,400. The National League had its share of sluggers in the 1930s with guys like Mel Ott, Wally Berger, Johnny Mize, and Dolph Camilli. It was the American League, however, with Ruth until 1934, Jimmie Foxx, Lou Gehrig, Hank Greenberg, Bob Johnson, Hal Trosky, Joe DiMaggio, Rudy York, and by the end of the decade, Ted Williams, that had more premium power hitters and was the dominant league offensively. Beginning in 1931, AL clubs outscored the NL, hit for higher averages, had more extra-base hits, and whacked more homers every year, usually by a considerable margin, until World War II temporarily changed the dynamic. The American League's reputation as the more offensively potent of the two major leagues was now firmly set.

15

KICK-STARTING THE YANKEES' FOREVER DYNASTY

The years between Jack Chesbro's wild pitch on the last day of the 1904 season that cost them the pennant and the 1920 arrival of the Babe were disappointing ones for the American League franchise in New York City. In putting a team in New York, Ban Johnson hoped for it to be the flagship franchise of his new league. Instead, the teams in Boston and Philadelphia were the ones that could lay claim to flagship franchise, each winning one-third of the first 18 pennants fought for since the league's inception in 1901. Entering the 1920 season, New York had endured 10 losing seasons in the 17 years since the Highlanders were born in 1903. But when those years of futility finally ended, they ended with the beginning of what should be called, not unreasonably, Major League Baseball's "forever" dynasty.

The franchise turnaround began in 1913 when the Yankees—the name to which the former Highlanders now answered—finally rid themselves of their ever-controversial first baseman, Hal Chase. By all accounts a superb defensive first baseman and a decent hitter, Chase was the cornerstone player and a fan favorite on a team of no-names as Willie Keeler, Jack Chesbro, and Kid Elberfeld succumbed to age or injury and the Highlanders wallowed mostly in the second division after their near miss in 1906. Known as Prince Hal for his dandy looks and charming ways, Chase may have been idolized by many, but his public charm obscured the corruption of his baseball soul. But in addition to having used his devilish wiles to charm his way into the hearts of Highlanders' fans, Chase was also close to the franchise owners, both of whom were themselves corrupt. Frank Farrell got away with running a notorious illegal casino and multiple other gambling dens because he was a crony of New

York City's corrupt Tammany politicians at the turn of the century, and his partner Bill Devery—known as "Big Bill"—was a corrupt senior police official whose protection-from-law-enforcement-crackdown racket for establishments like those owned by Farrell was abetted by his own connections to corrupt Tammany politicians. Prince Hal's influence with Farrell and Devery was such that he got the well-respected Stallings fired as manager with less than three weeks left in the 1910 season with the Highlanders in third place and was himself named player-manager, notwithstanding that Stallings had directed a dramatic turnaround of the Highlanders' fortunes since taking over a last-place club the year before.

After one year in charge—the Highlanders finished sixth—Chase decided he'd rather just be a player—albeit, a player without integrity. Farrell and Devery, probably knowing a loser when it came to leadership, were fine with that, and glad to keep Chase as their first baseman. Despite his popularity, or perhaps precisely because of his popularity, which many of his teammates undoubtedly felt he earned by subterfuge and disingenuousness, Chase's relentless greed and politicking in the clubhouse bred considerable resentment. This surely made it easier to trade him in June 1913 when the Yankees' new manager, the highly esteemed Frank Chance of Chicago Cubs–dynasty fame, demanded that Hal Chase be gotten rid of. Chance had no tolerance for Chase's defensive showboating in the field and absolutely zero tolerance for the errors Chase was making that were costing the Yankees games, which seemed more than suspiciously deliberate. With or without Chase, the Yankees got worse.

Ban Johnson surely erred in agreeing to two men of such questionable public morals as Farrell and Devery to take over the American League's new franchise in America's biggest city in 1903, especially since one of his marketing points for the new major league was to clean up baseball and the fan experience. Essentially, their ownership was bankrolled by the illicit funds of Farrell's gambling joints and Devery's police protection rackets that enabled such enterprises to function and profit handsomely. Owning the Highlanders, however, was itself a gamble—one both men were losing money on, which may or may not have contributed to growing tensions between the casino kingpin and the corrupt former cop. When Johnson began maneuvering to have the Yankees sold to more reputable businessmen so that the team might be built into a winner and finally allow New York to make the American League proud, both Farrell and Devery were willing by the end of the 1914 calendar year to give up their stake in Major League Baseball.

* * *

The second pivotal point in the Yankees' turn of fortunes—more important even than getting rid of the corrupt Chase—was the purchase of the club by Jacob Ruppert and Tillinghast L'Hommedieu Huston. Ruppert ran a very successful brewery in New York and had his own Tammany Hall connections that helped him get elected to Congress for three terms straddling the turn of the century, and Huston was an accomplished civil engineer who capitalized on infrastructure projects in Cuba after the Spanish-American War of 1898. By the time the Yankees made it big, both men were addressed as "Colonel"—Huston, because he really was one, commissioned when he was serving his country in France during the First World War, and Ruppert, because it was an honorary title bestowed on him as a very young man when, as a member of the New York National Guard in the 1880s, he was appointed aide-de-camp to the governor. At the beginning of their partnership, Huston was more visible, but it was Ruppert who became the real power on the Yankees' throne, beginning when Huston was overseas at war.

Of the players inherited when they bought the club, only shortstop Roger Peckinpaugh, probably the best all-around shortstop in the American League in the last half decade of the Deadball Era, would be consequential to the Yankees' future. Helped by some behind-the-scenes brokering and cajoling by Johnson, the new Ruppert-Huston regime began systematically building the Yankees into a contending club. Wally Pipp, acquired from the Tigers before the 1915 season, would be the Yankees' everyday first baseman for the next 10 years . . . until the coincidence of age (he was 32), a sudden drop in his offense, a badly timed persistent headache, and the obvious offensive talents of 22-year-old Lou Gehrig ultimately cost him his job. A charter member of the Yankees' original "Murderers' Row" before the arrival of Ruth, Pipp was one of baseball's premier power hitters in the last years of the Deadball Era. Home Run Baker, whom Johnson prodded Connie Mack to sell to New York in 1916 after the Athletics' star third baseman sat out the 1915 season in a contract dispute, was also in the original Murderers' Row. Now 30 years old and having not played for a year, Baker was no longer the impact player he was in his six years with the Athletics. He was still a formidable threat at the plate, however, and was among the league leaders in home runs each of his first four years with the Yankees.

The arrival of Baker to play third base opened up the possibility of preseason 1916 trades with either the White Sox for Shoeless Joe Jackson or the Red Sox for Tris Speaker in exchange for third baseman Fritz Maisel, one of baseball's most dynamic young players. He led the league with 74 stolen bases in 1914 and followed up with 51 in 1915, second to Ty Cobb's post-1900 record-setting 96. Maisel, however, was nowhere near the hitter that Speaker and Jackson were, and gave no indication he ever would be. Perhaps because both Speaker and Jackson were about two years older than their player, Ruppert and Huston decided to pass on both possible trades in the apparent belief that Jackson and Speaker, both of whose batting averages had declined three straight years, had peaked and Maisel's career was about to take off. The Yankees moved Maisel to center field in deference to Baker, where in mid-May, carrying a batting average of just .250, Maisel suffered a devastating collarbone injury trying to make a catch that kept him out of the starting lineup for over two months. His major-league career thereafter was short lived. Neither Jackson nor Speaker had peaked in their careers.

In the context of their later success, the Yankees' most significant pickup in the first years of the Ruppert-Huston ownership era was 24-year-old right-hander Bob Shawkey, in only his third big-league season, who turned out to be a steal for the modest $3,500 they paid to Mack for his contract in June 1915. Shawkey won 24 in 1916 to help the Yankees to their first winning season since 1910, the first of his four 20-win seasons in New York. He was the first acquisition in what proved an excellent pitching staff when the Yankees dynasty kicked off with three straight pennants from 1921 to 1923.

* * *

Ruppert's decision in October 1917 to hire Miller Huggins as manager was the third indispensable factor that got the Yankees started on their winning ways. His decision did not have the support of Huston, who preferred Brooklyn manager Wilbert Robinson, but he was with the US Expeditionary Force in Europe and powerless to influence the naming of the new manager. To the extent Ruppert and Huston were already having their differences, Huggins became a festering sore between them. Huston advocated Huggins be replaced after the Yankees fell just short in 1920 and again after they failed to win a game in the 1922 World Series against the Giants, their Polo Grounds landlords and bitter rivals for the affections of New Yorkers. Jacob Ruppert never soured on Miller Huggins. Huston, the real colonel, sold his share of the franchise to Ruppert in 1923.

By the metrics of final standings and won-lost records, Huggins had not been all that successful in his first five years as a manager. But that was because he was managing the St. Louis Cardinals, a bad team for almost the entirety of the first two decades of the twentieth century. Huggins, however, was well respected for his managerial acumen and his ability to get bad and mediocre teams to play above expectations; his Cardinals twice finished third, including in 1917. Alerted by John McGraw, one of Huggins's admirers, Ban Johnson noticed; when it became clear the Yankees owners were looking for a new manager, he encouraged them to look at Huggins. Meanwhile, in St. Louis, Branch Rickey had become team president, who Huggins knew would impose his direction on whoever was managing the Cardinals. But the Yankees were an intriguing proposition for Huggins not just because he felt his position to be untenable in St. Louis. The Yankees were committed to building a winning team and, unlike the Cardinals, had the financial resources to invest in doing so. If Huggins was going to win anywhere, it was going to be in New York.

After finishing fourth in 1918, a war-shortened season in which Shawkey spent the entire year working at a naval shipyard and Pipp left the team in August to train as an aviator, and rising to third in 1919 behind the dominating White Sox, the Huggins Yankees burst into pennant contention in 1920. They lost by three games that year, beat back the Indians in 1921, held off the Browns in 1922, secured dynastic momentum when they won the pennant by 16 games in 1923, and fell two games short of the Washington Senators in 1924. Their success, of course, was attributed to their now having Babe Ruth, whose acquisition is mythologized as the founding event of the Yankees dynasty while simultaneously being *the* signal event in the demise of another dynasty—the Red Sox—the echoes of which would reverberate for the rest of the century (and then some).

In his first five years with the Yankees, Ruth had four of the 10 best seasons ever by a position player. Ruth's 11.8 wins above replacement in 1920, when he introduced himself to New York with an incomprehensible 54 home runs that shattered the record 29 he hit for Boston the year before, is the eighth highest in history by a position player. He also walked 150 times to break Jimmy Sheckard's single-season record of 147 set in 1911. Ruth's .532 on-base percentage was the first time in the twentieth century that a player reached base in over 50 percent of his plate appearances, and was the highest since John McGraw reached base 55 percent of the time in 1899. And Ruth's 1.379 on-base-plus-slugging percentage shattered Hugh Duffy's 26-year record of 1.196 set in 1894 and would last 82 years before Barry Bonds barely topped him at 1.381 in 2002.

But as they say, baseball hadn't seen nuthin' yet.

It is fair to say that the 1921 Yankees would not have won their first pennant in franchise history without the Babe's 12.6 wins above replacement—still the second highest in history by a position player—since they beat out Cleveland by just 4½ games. Ruth was in fact at his best against the Indians, hitting .469 with a .642 on-base percentage against them. For the year, Ruth broke his own record with 59 home runs, scored 177 runs, and drove in 168—both career highs—and his 457 total bases are still the most by any player ever. The Yankees might have beaten the Giants in their first World Series had Ruth not opened a wound on his left arm while stealing a pair of bases in Game Two in the best-of-nine Series. Ruth soldiered on the next three games, but with the Yankees enjoying a three-games-to-two lead, he was unable to start any of the final three games because of the serious festering infection resulting from his abrasions. Having already hit the first of his 15 World Series home runs in Game Four in a Yankees loss, Ruth came to bat as a pinch-hitter representing the tying run in the bottom of the ninth in the eighth and final game, the Yankees trailing 1–0; he grounded out. Two outs later, the Giants were World Series champions.

Ruth hit only 35 homers and drove in just 96 runs when the Yankees repeated as American League champions in 1922, but might have walloped 50 with 130 RBIs had he not been suspended by Commissioner Landis until late May for violating baseball's rules against postseason barnstorming by players on pennant-winning teams. Apparently believing he could get away with flouting the commissioner's warnings not to do so, Ruth discovered that he was not bigger than the game—even if, arguably, he was. Despite Ruth's extended absence, the Yankees won the pennant, only to be humiliated by the Giants' sweeping them in the 1922 Series, although five games were required because one ended after 10 innings tied at 3–3. Ruth's humiliation was even greater than his team's as the Giants limited him to two hits and a .118 batting average—the lowest among Yankees regulars in Huggins's World Series lineup.

The best year ever by a position player was Babe Ruth's 14.1 wins above replacement in 1923, which he earned by leading the league in both homers (41) and runs batted in (130) for the fourth time in five years going back to 1919 when he was with the Red Sox. His .393 average was phenomenal by any standard, and the best of his career, but he failed to win the Triple Crown because Detroit's Harry Heilmann batted .403. Ruth powered the Yankees to their first blowout pennant and this time was a World Series star, torturing Giants pitchers for a .368 average and three home runs as the Yankees became baseball's world champions for the first time in their history. The Yankees failed to match the Giants with four consecutive pennants in 1924, but Ruth's 11.7 WAR that year is the 10th best in history. In addition to his league-leading 46 homers, Ruth won the only batting title of his career with a .378 mark. This time the Triple Crown eluded his grasp because his 124 RBIs were five fewer than Goose Goslin's 129.

To statistically summarize his first five years in pinstripes, Babe Ruth blasted 235 home runs, scored 723 runs, drove in 653, and batted .370. He alone was responsible for 27 percent of the Yankees' runs. Ruth's value to the Yankees was nearly 57 wins above what a replacement-level player would have contributed had he not been in their lineup. He alone accounted for 43 percent of the Yankees' collective offensive WAR for those five years; 47 percent if 1922 is excluded because he played in only 110 games. Ruth exceeded 10 wins above replacement five more times in

Babe Ruth's first homer of the 1924 season at Washington's Griffith Stadium was the 239th of his career. *National Photo Company Collection (Library of Congress).*

his career, but only his 12.4 WAR in 1927 was in the same atmosphere as his four best seasons in his first five years in New York. His 1927 player value, the year he hit 60 home runs, remains third best by a position player in baseball history, exceeded only by Ruth himself in 1923 and 1921.

Perhaps even more remarkable is that Ruth did all this without trusty sidekick Lou Gehrig, who did not take over at first base and bat behind the Babe in the lineup until 1925. The three highest walk totals of his career, and four of his five best, came during his first five years with the Yankees. None of the Yankees batting behind him—Del Pratt and Bob Meusel in 1920, Meusel and Baker in 1921, Pipp in 1922 and 1923, and Meusel in 1924—had a player value in any of those years meeting the five wins above replacement standard considered to be an all-star-quality season. Drawing an average of 152 walks in the four years he did not have to sit out more than a fifth of the schedule, plus his 84 bases on balls in the year he did, Ruth reached base on a four-ball count in 22 percent of his plate appearances from 1920 to 1924, got on base by a hit in 29 percent of his plate appearances, and circled the bases at a comfortable trot on 26 percent of his hits.

Gehrig may not yet have been his devastating sidekick to give a whole new meaning to the Yankees' Murderers' Row, but it is not as though Ruth did not have sidekicks in the clubhouse and for postgame evening reveries. Fueled not only by his on-the-field homerific heroics, but also by his off-the-field escapades, the Babe's legend took on a life of its own. Ruth thoroughly enjoyed his celebrity status, which inoculated him from the slings and arrows about his comportment, including with teammates in the clubhouse, that otherwise might have been the ruin of a baseball career. His gluttony, partying, and womanizing were sanitized by base-ball writers, who turned all that into the Babe being the fun-loving big kid in the heart and soul of all Americans who played the quintessentially American game of baseball with an exuberance and excellence no one had ever seen before. Heck, he had a special bond with kids, who did not merely idolize him as other baseball stars had been idolized, but adored him because he was a big kid himself.

Babe Ruth was outsized in every way, a perfect symbol of the times—the Roaring Twenties—with all its excesses. Some of his outrageous behavior was lionized—the Babe being fun-loving, not taking life too seriously but bashing a baseball very seriously, and ever-lovable—al-though anything that might sully his all-American image was usually suppressed. Some of what he did might even have been true, some of it not. Did Ruth really dangle his diminutive manager off the back of a moving train?

The Babe's general disregard for rules and discipline, his sometimes-obvious contempt for his manager, and his outsized clubhouse influence that often undermined Huggins's authority was a constant source of be-devilment for the Yankees manager. But notwithstanding Ruth's celeb-rity, not to mention the fact that even casual fans flocked to ballparks across the country, not just New York, in far greater numbers than other-wise would have come just to see him play, hoping to witness a prodig-ious Ruthian clout deep into the bleachers or out of the park altogether, Ruppert always backed his manager when Ruth got too out of hand. Most famously, in the lost-cause 1925 campaign Ruppert upheld a huge fine and suspension for the rest of the season that Huggins imposed on Ruth in late August for conduct detrimental to the team—specifically violating a curfew, but more a reflection of an accumulation of actions—despite the Babe's fury at such an affront. With Ruth suitably chastened and accept-ing being put in his place, Huggins lifted the suspension after six games.

Ruppert had three things going for him to act as he did on behalf of his beleaguered manager despite Ruth's undeniable leverage when it came to fan appeal and the Yankees' bottom line. The first was baseball's reserve clause, which tied him to the Yankees, and Ruth's almost-certain aware-ness that he could not match the earnings that came from being the star baseball attraction in New York doing anything else, or being anywhere else. The second was that the aftermath of the Black Sox scandal put an understood and accepted premium on the importance of discipline to ensure the integrity of the game, making it increasingly difficult for players to flout the authority of baseball's command structure, right down to the manager's spot in the dugout. Ruth had been taught the limitations of his outsized celebrity when he was suspended at the beginning of the 1922 season for flouting the commissioner, and Ruppert was not about to let Ruth undermine his manager's authority. And finally, most important-ly, Miller Huggins had proved himself to be an excellent manager on a team that was not yet dominant in the way that would become a Yankees tradition. Other than 1923, when the Yankees' third pennant was their first blowout, Huggins from 1920 to 1924 guided his team through four closely fought pennant races, with very near misses the first and last of those years.

* * *

If Jacob Ruppert and Til Huston taking over as the new owners in 1915, Miller Huggins taking command in the dugout in 1918, and Babe Ruth's dramatic entrance in 1920 were the indispensable foundations for kick-starting the Yankees dynasty, so, too, was the hiring of Ed Barrow to be the franchise's top "baseball" executive in the fall of 1920, after the Yankees just missed winning their first pennant. Like the Babe, Barrow came to New York directly from Boston, where he had been manager of the Red Sox since 1918, leading them to the pennant and a World Series championship that year. Having been in on the deal that sent Ruth to the Yankees, although he did warn Red Sox owner Harry Frazee it would be a big mistake, and following Ruth to New York, where he went on to greater fame and, indeed, the Hall of Fame as the Yankees' general man-ager, conspiracy-minded Bostonians—especially toward the end of the twentieth century—might be forgiven if they thought Barrow conspired with Ruppert to give them Ruth in return for his own subsequent employ-ment. But it was nothing like that. Knowing that the Red Sox' financial situation left them in no position to be competitive in a pennant race anytime in the near future, the Yankees were just too good an opportunity for him to turn down when it was offered.

An offense powered by Ruth was certainly not to be dismissed, but the foundation for the Yankees' first three pennants—and an important ele-ment for their next three from 1926 to 1928—was the best pitching staff in baseball. The Yankees had a pair of first-rate 20-game winners when Barrow took over the business side of the operation in Carl Mays (26–11 in 1920), whose trade from Boston to New York in 1919 he had helped facilitate, and Bob Shawkey (20–13). Both pitchers were still in their prime, but the Yankees' third-most-frequent starter was 36-year-old Jack Quinn. Hedging his bets, Barrow traded with the franchise he had just left for 21-year-old right-hander Waite Hoyt and established veteran catcher Wally Schang, for whom the Yankees gave up veteran second baseman Del Pratt and catching prospect Muddy Ruel. It was a great deal for the Yankees. Hoyt's 19 victories, on top of Mays's 27 and Shawkey's 18, probably made all the difference in the Yankees winning their first pennant in 1921, and Schang batted .403 and had a .565 on-base percentage in the final month as the Yankees held off the Indians.

The next year, Barrow fortified the Yankees' pitching and defense still more by trading once again with the Red Sox. The two teams exchanged veteran shortstops, with Roger Peckinpaugh going to Boston and Everett Scott coming to New York. Scott played every game for the Yankees at shortstop for the next three years before a slow start to the 1925 season ended his record consecutive-games streak, which started in 1916, at 1,307 games. He played just 83 more major-league games. The key acquisitions for the Yankees in that trade, however, were right-handers Sad Sam Jones and Bullet Joe Bush. Although Shawkey won 20 and Hoyt once again had 19 wins, it was Bush who led Yankees pitchers with a superb 26–7 record, including winning six of his last eight starts as the Yankees barely edged out the Browns for the 1922 pennant. Bush also beat St. Louis six times. Barrow dealt with the Red Sox again in late July, exchanging a handful of marginal players for Joe Dugan to shore up third base for their pennant push.

Still not done tapping into the Red Sox pipeline, Barrow dealt three rookies and $50,000 in cash to acquire southpaw Herb Pennock in advance of the 1923 season. In 11 big-league seasons and 241 games on the mound for the Athletics and Red Sox, Pennock had a modest 77–72 career record when he came to New York. Pennock, at 19–6, teamed with Jones (21–8), Bush (19–15), Hoyt (17–9), and Shawkey (16–11) in the Yankees' first blowout pennant to give Huggins the most formidable front-line pitching he would ever have as a manager. The five started 143 of the Yankees' 152 games and accounted for all but six of their 98 victories. Mays, who had struggled to a 13–14 record in 1922, had five of the other six victories in what was his last year in New York. Pennock led the team with a 21–9 record in 1924, when the Yankees missed making it four in a row by two games.

* * *

The grand opening of Yankee Stadium in 1923 was the capstone to the phenomenon the Babe Ruth New York Yankees had become. The Yankees had played in the Polo Grounds since 1913. That was the year they officially became the "Yankees," surely a more appropriate moniker for a team—the Highlanders—that had called Hilltop Park home since 1903 but now played in a ballpark at the base of Coogan's Bluff. They were no longer on high ground literally, nor were they figuratively, as they were now tenants in the Giants' ballpark. The shared arrangement at the Polo Grounds was always fraught with uncertainty for the Yankees. John McGraw wanted them out of his ballpark. But the Giants were also using their political connections to try to prevent the Yankees from acquiring any prime real estate that would attract a huge competing fan base. From the beginning of their partnership, Ruppert and Huston wanted to build a ballpark to call the Yankees' own.

By the end of the 1921 season, the spectacle of Ruth's home runs and the resulting competitive success of the Yankees made their continuing presence at the Polo Grounds untenable. Not only was McGraw competitively jealous, even if his team did beat the Yankees in successive World Series, but with the Babe as the attraction, the Yankees had been drawing more fans to the Polo Grounds than the Giants. In Ruth's first year in New York, the 1920 Yankees became the first team in history to draw more than a million fans with nearly 1.3 million attending their home games—360,000 more than went to watch the Giants. The difference was narrower in 1921, but it was still the Yankees with 1.2 million compared to 973,000 paying to see the Giants. Unwilling to renew their lease, McGraw and the Giants consented to one more year in 1922. The Yankees, meanwhile, had secured land across the Harlem River in the Bronx, within sight of the Polo Grounds. The Bronx was no longer a New York City backwater, but in the midst of a population and business growth spurt, and the city was expanding its state-of-the-art public transportation system—a combination of subway and elevated commuter rail—from Manhattan into the Bronx.

For the Colonels, it was not simply "Build It, and They Will Come." They were determined that their team, with its prized possession in Babe Ruth, play in a home worthy of their aspiration that the Yankees would be competing in the World Series, against any comer, year after year after year.

And not just a ballpark. Or a ball field.

But a stadium.

And not just a stadium.

But an imposing edifice—a coliseum for gladiatorial combat.

Indeed, if the Yankees were set to build a dynastic empire, they would build their own "coliseum," an arena worthy of an empire, like the Roman Colosseum. That coliseum, built late in the first century, was a massive architectural and engineering undertaking for the time. Unprecedented in scale, reflecting the grandiosity of the Roman Empire, and seating as many as 50,000 Roman citizens, the Colosseum has endured in our collective imagination for centuries because of spectacles such as gladiators fighting to the death and Christians being thrown to the lions. The construction of Yankee Stadium became trained-engineer Huston's pet project, while Ruppert and Barrow concerned themselves with running the team.

By now, nearly all of the first-generation modern "classic" ballparks that would serve as baseball's sacred arenas into the second half of the twentieth century had been built. But Yankee Stadium was something much different. Completed in time for the start of the 1923 season, the original Yankee Stadium, with its distinctive design features—including a soaring main entrance, three grandstand tiers, and the iconic façade that provides a dignified, even classical, background to the play on the field—was without question the architectural First Wonder of the Baseball World. Outdoing all other baseball parks and even the Roman Colosseum itself in grandiosity, the stadium seemed destined to confer greatness on those who would play for the New York Yankees. How could Yankees players not be inspired being able to call such a monument to *them* home—it being named for the team, after all, not for an owner, some other person of stature, or the surrounding neighborhood? And how could opposing teams not feel intimidated by their surroundings, especially at a time when smoking in public was normative and the haze of cigar and cigarette smoke would hang bluish in the air, under the façade, giving the stadium an almost otherworldly feel?

It didn't have to turn out that way, of course, but it did. Yankee Stadium was to become hallowed ground where the gods walked, not merely sacred ground where baseball was played, as is more the case with both Fenway Park and Wrigley Field. Officially, there were more than 74,000 people jammed into Yankee Stadium for the first game of the 1923 season on April 18, although the true number was likely 10,000–15,000 fewer. Babe Ruth hit the first home run, off Howard Ehmke, and Bob Shawkey pitched a three-hitter. The Yankees won the first game, against the Red Sox. They won the pennant. They won the World Series. Although the Yankees did not go to the World Series in either of the next two years, winning became contagious as a legion of outstanding players, or perhaps players inspired to be great by the magnificence of the place, took the field in pinstripes, one generation succeeding the next, seemingly in perpetuity. Year after year opposing teams would march into the Yankees' imposing coliseum and fall prey to pinstriped gladiators. The Yankees became a "forever" dynasty, making the "mystique and aura" of Yankee Stadium something real and tangible that Yankees opponents—especially their World Series opponents—had to contend with.

16

THE END OF THE NAPOLEONIC WARS

The Giants' Last Decade under McGraw

The appellation "Little Napoleon" fit John McGraw. He and the French emperor, born a century before (well, 104 years before McGraw came into the world in 1873, to be exact), were colossally ambitious—the real Napoleon on a global scale, the Little Napoleon wanting to conquer the baseball world. Both were dictatorial, and both built reputations based on their brilliant maneuvering, the one of the battlefield, the other on the ball field.

The 1920s were the twilight of McGraw's career as manager of the New York Giants. He was overweight, was ill much of the time, looked decidedly older than his years, and did not take well to being eclipsed in *his* town (New York City) by a certain Babe Ruth. But John McGraw was still brilliant when it came to managing a baseball team. In some respects, McGraw may have done his best managing under the pressure of pennant races in the 1920s. His 1921–24 Giants became the first team since Charlie Comiskey's 1885–88 American Association St. Louis Browns to win four consecutive pennants. The 1923 National League pennant race was the only one of the four where the Giants were in command the entire year, and that command was not as imposing as it might seem. While it's true that the Giants were in first place every day of that season and had an 8½-game lead in mid-August, they had to fend off the Reds down the stretch before finally securing the pennant in their 150th game. Coasting to the pennant since midsummer might have cost the 1923 Giants some of their edge because they were only 15–11 in the final month and, after beating them each of the two previous years, became the first World Series victim of the emerging Yankees dynasty.

Their three other pennants were not so easily won. The 1921 Giants had to overcome a 7½-game lead Pittsburgh held in late August to ultimately win the pennant by four games. The next year, the Giants had to contend with the unexpectedly competitive Cardinals before breaking away in late August to win in the end by seven games. After never once relinquishing first place in 1923, the 1924 Giants blew the nine-game lead they had on August 8 and had to fight off Brooklyn and Pittsburgh, both late to the chase, in September. The Giants won 17 of the 21 games they played in the final month with first place directly at stake. Their final margin of victory was 1½ games. Debilitating illness forced McGraw in late May to turn the managerial reins over to Hughie Jennings, his primary coach and blood-bonded teammate from their old Baltimore Orioles days. He didn't return from his health sabbatical until early July. But for catcher Hank Gowdy tripping over his mask and failing to catch a pop foul in the 12th inning of Game Seven, and a pebble or divot causing a bad hop over rookie teenage third baseman Freddie Lindstrom, the Giants might have won the 1924 World Series to give them three championships in four years.

* * *

McGraw's last great Giants team was built around infielder Frankie Frisch, right fielder Ross Youngs, and first baseman George Kelly. None of the three played more than a bit role on his 1917 pennant winner, but all were in place as core regulars in 1920 when the Giants finished second. Frisch and Youngs both batted .337 the next four years, with Frisch leading the league with 49 stolen bases in 1921, 223 hits in 1923, and 121 runs in 1924. Kelly hit .317 in the four pennant-winning years with 77 home runs and 468 runs batted in; his 23 homers in 1921 and 136 RBIs in 1924 led the league.

While all three are in the Hall of Fame, the 1970s selections of Youngs and Kelly remain controversial. Both were very good players. Neither was a historically great player. Both benefited from having played for a team that won four straight pennants, as did arguably Dave Bancroft, the Giants' shortstop from 1920 to 1923. And both benefited from Frisch, as well as the few surviving baseball writers who covered the Giants in the 1920s, lobbying on their behalf. It should not go without mention that until Bancroft in 1971, Youngs in 1972, and Kelly in 1973 were voted into the Hall by the Veterans Committee, the 1921–24 New York Giants—still the only National League team to win four consecutive pennants—had only one of their core regulars enshrined in Cooperstown.

That would be the switch-hitting Frankie Frisch, who was indisputably deserving of the honor. After having helped his team to four straight pennants in 1924, Frisch had six years in the majors and was probably the second-best position player in the National League, after Rogers Hornsby. Indeed, only Hornsby—whose 55.9 cumulative wins above replacement far outpaced Frisch's 29.2—had a higher player value in the National League than Frisch since his rookie year in 1919. Like McGraw-favorite Mathewson, who went to Bucknell, Frisch had a college pedigree, his from Fordham University in New York City. McGraw also liked Frisch's brashness, his win-at-all-costs attitude, his attention to mastering the fundamentals and nuances of the game, and his baseball IQ. Knowing he was approaching the twilight of his career, and planning for the Giants' future without him, McGraw began grooming his star pupil to eventually take over the team.

Frisch's versatility was a considerable asset as McGraw guided the Giants to four straight World Series. Although remembered as a second baseman, the Fordham Flash in his New York Giant years was really an exceptional multiposition regular. He was McGraw's third baseman in 1920, played almost an equal number of games at second and third the next two years, was the Giants' second baseman in 1923 and 1924, played almost an equal number of games at second, third, and shortstop in 1925, and was back at second base full-time in 1926—his last year in New York. Second base was the position Frankie Frisch would play for the rest of his career, which totaled 311 more games in a Cardinals uniform than he played in his eight years with the Giants.

While Frisch, Youngs, and Kelly were McGraw's guys from the beginning of their careers, it was a series of astute trades that proved the key to the Giants' success. During the 1919 season, with the Giants still in contention against the Reds, McGraw acquired catcher Frank Snyder from the Cardinals in mid-July and two weeks later traded with the Braves for right-hander Art Nehf. While the Giants could not ultimately keep pace with Cincinnati, who put the pennant away with a red-hot month of August, Nehf went 9–2 after his acquisition, and both players were part of the Giants' core when they won four in a row.

In early June 1920, with the Giants off to a terrible start, McGraw traded his star shortstop in the teens, Art Fletcher, to Philadelphia for Dave Bancroft, who was six years younger and by now the best shortstop in the game. Bancroft was instrumental in helping the Giants to three straight pennants before being traded after the 1923 World Series, in part for the opportunity to become a player-manager. More importantly, McGraw had 20-year-old Travis Jackson ready to take over at shortstop. Still a teenager in 1923, Jackson had filled in ably at shortstop in July and August when Bancroft was sidelined by pneumonia and its attendant complications. Beginning his career path to the Hall of Fame, Jackson batted .302 as the Giants' full-time shortstop in 1924.

McGraw made two noteworthy trades with the Phillies during the 1921 pennant race —the first for second baseman Johnny Rawlings and outfielder Casey Stengel, and the second for outfielder Irish Meusel, brother of Bob, the Yankees' left fielder. With the Giants playing catch-up all summer, both trades proved significant to winning the pennant. Rawlings allowed McGraw to shift Frisch from second to third, where rookie Goldie Rapp was failing to meet expectations, and Meusel shored up the outfield alongside Youngs and veteran George Burns. Stengel played hardly at all in 1921 after his trade to the Giants, but excelled the next two years as the left-handed-batting half of McGraw's center-field platoon, batting .368 in 84 games in 1922 and .339 in 75 games in 1923 while never once getting a start against a southpaw. His stumbling, bumbling run around the bases ending on what seemed like a comedic pratfall slide (he was Casey Stengel, after all) for a game-winning inside-the-park home run in the ninth inning of Game One in the 1923 World Series—the first World Series homer ever hit in Yankee Stadium—was Stengel's single greatest baseball moment, at least as a player.

McGraw went to a center-field platoon in 1922 because he traded the popular Burns to Cincinnati to get Heinie Groh, still the best third baseman in the National League. Frisch moved back to second base and Rawlings became a valuable off-the-bench player. A severe knee injury late in the 1924 season kept Groh out of the World Series (and effectively ended his career), forcing McGraw to use 19-year-old Freddie Lindstrom at third. Although Lindstrom had 10 hits in the Series, his inability to handle that 12th-inning bad hop allowed the World Series–winning run to score. It might have been a play the more experienced Groh would have made.

Unlike his 1904 to 1908 club, whose pretensions to dynasty after back-to-back pennants the first two of those years were shortchanged by the Cubs dynasty, and his team that won three straight pennants from 1911 to 1913, McGraw's 1921–24 Giants were more an annual work in progress, particularly the pitching staff. It seemed that every year McGraw had to find a different combination to be his top four starters, with Art Nehf the one constant, and even he had a much-diminished workload in 1923 and '24. Nehf won 87 games for the Giants between 1920 and 1924 but was not once among the National League's top ten pitchers based on pitching wins above replacement. The Giants, in fact, had only one pitcher make the top ten those five years—Virgil Barnes, with a 16–10 record and 3.06 earned run average in 1924, whose WAR was just eighth best among NL pitchers. In earlier five-year periods, by contrast—both 1904–08 and 1910–14—the Giants had six pitchers in the top *five* in pitching WAR. Of course, Christy Mathewson was their ace all those years. Unusual for pennant-winning teams, indeed for almost any competitive team at the time, only two of McGraw's pitchers worked as many as 200 innings in 1922 and '23, and only one did so in 1924. Nehf's 20–10 record in 1921 was the only one of their four pennant-winning seasons that any Giants pitcher won 20 games. Prior to 1922, the only World Series team that did not have at least one 20-game winner was Connie Mack's 1914 Athletics. Moreover, the Giants had only one pitcher make as many as 30 starts in 1923, and none in 1924. Until then, no first-place club in either league had failed to have at least one pitcher make 30 starts.

Hearkening back to his first years as Giants manager, when he was ahead of the curve in upending the orthodoxy of complete-game victories, McGraw used his bullpen wisely and well. Even though going to the bullpen had become commonplace in Major League Baseball, McGraw was more assertive in using relievers for effect than other managers. The Giants led the league in saves every year they won the pennant except 1922, used more relievers in noncomplete games than other teams, and pitched complete games in substantially fewer victories than the league average. Notwithstanding his past success with Doc Crandall, McGraw did not rely on a single pitcher as his relief ace. After Crandall left the Giants in 1914 to be a starting pitcher in the Federal League, McGraw— like virtually all other managers—got most of his saves from one of his starting pitchers playing the role of relief ace when needed. This was true through the 1921 pennant, when starter Jesse Barnes earned six saves in 11 relief appearances to go with his 18 wins in 31 starts. For the next three pennants, however, McGraw used two pitchers primarily as relief specialists—Claude Jonnard and Rosy Ryan—both right-handers. As relievers, the two combined for 33 wins and saved 17 of the Giants' 281 wins from 1922 to 1924. Giants pitchers who otherwise started at least 20 games won 13 and saved 14 others as relievers. Similar to Crandall in his first five years working for McGraw, Ryan was often used as a spot starter, including making 22 starts in 1922. Like Crandall in his last season with the Giants in 1913, Jonnard pitched almost exclusively out of the bullpen all three of his years in New York, starting only four of the 112 games he pitched for McGraw.

* * *

John McGraw was 51 when he won his 10th pennant in 1924. He might have suspected it would be his last the next year when the Giants could not sustain a 6½-game lead they had built by early June and wound up second, 8½ games behind. The Giants failed to get any traction in 1926, ending up fifth. That year proved the end of McGraw's preparing Frankie Frisch to be his successor. As team captain and best player, Frisch came under relentless pressure from McGraw holding him accountable for the Giants' lackluster performance when their fortunes shifted after 1924, even though the Fordham Flash continued to be an elite player. As much as he learned from McGraw, and as much as he admired his manager's baseball knowledge, Frisch was unwilling to put up with McGraw's increasing verbal abuse, made that quite clear to the Little Napoleon, and was traded at the end of the season to the Cardinals for their star second baseman and player-manager, Rogers Hornsby. While that trade proved to be the beginning of the end of Hornsby's great career, it was the beginning of a productive new chapter for Frisch. After playing in four World Series with the Giants, Frisch played in four more with the Cardinals, including 1934 when he was player-manager of the team that became known as the Gashouse Gang.

McGraw, however, still had two more pennant races to fight before calling it a career. In 1927, he rallied the Giants from a 10-game deficit in mid-July to put them in the hunt with three other teams. At the end of August, with his team trailing by 2½ games, illness once again forced McGraw into a leave of absence. Rogers Hornsby was given charge of the Giants for the rest of the season. Hornsby had led the Cardinals to their first ever World Series (which they won) the previous year as player-manager, only to be told good riddance because of his difficult personality, and nearly led McGraw's Giants to victory in September. The Giants finished third, two games behind Pittsburgh. Hornsby turned out to be too much for the Giants to bear as well; he was not much liked in the clubhouse and was probably perceived by McGraw as a threat to his leadership because of his divisiveness. Historically great batter though he was, and despite his .361 batting average, 26 homers, and 125 RBIs making him the National League's best player in 1927, Hornsby was traded to the Boston Braves in January.

The Giants were in another tough multiteam race to the finish the next year. Although 10 losses in 11 games left the Giants in third place, 6½ games out of first going into September, McGraw directed his team to the league's best record (25–8) in the final month in a furious bid to overtake the Cardinals. The Giants closed the gap to one game with three left on the schedule, including St. Louis due into the Polo Grounds for the final game of the season when the pennant might still be up for grabs. In McGraw's last serious bid for an 11th National League pennant, it never came down to that final game as consecutive losses to the third-place Cubs eliminated the Giants from contention before their now-meaningless game with St. Louis. That was as close as McGraw would come to another pennant in the few years that remained of his career. The Giants finished third the next two years, a very distant second in 1931, and were off to a bad start in last place when McGraw finally called it quits on June 1, 1932.

* * *

While they did not win a pennant, the Giants team McGraw managed the last four full seasons of his career may have been one of his best, at least as far as his core players were concerned. First baseman Bill Terry, shortstop Travis Jackson, third baseman Freddie Lindstrom, and right-hander Freddie Fitzsimmons were entering their prime in 1928. Mel Ott and Carl Hubbell were just beginning careers that would place them among baseball's all-time greatest players. All six, tutored and nurtured by McGraw, would be instrumental to the Giants' coming success in the 1930s . . . but that would be under Terry, whom McGraw named to succeed him as a player-manager when he finally stepped down and out of the Polo Grounds dugout.

By then, Bill Terry was the premier first baseman in the National League. Hardly missing a game, Terry had seven straight 100-RBI seasons and batted .355 between 1927 and 1932, including .401 in 1930—the last time any National League player won the batting title with a .400 average. His 254 hits in 1930 matched Lefty O'Doul's total the previous year, which (as of 2018) remain the most ever by a National Leaguer. And by the time McGraw stepped down, Mel Ott was the National League's premier outfielder. After playing sparingly for McGraw in 1926 and '27, Ott became a regular in 1928 having just turned 19. For much of the year the left-handed slugger was platooned in right field, starting only against right-handers. Promoted to playing every day in 1929, the now-20-year-old had his breakout season belting 42 homers, driving in 151 runs, batting .328, and reaching base in 45 percent of his plate appearances. He would remain the National League's best player through the 1930s and end his career in 1946 with 511 home runs. Both Terry and Ott are legitimate Hall of Fame players.

More problematic are the Hall of Fame credentials of the other two star position players in McGraw's last years as manager—Freddie Lindstrom and Travis Jackson, both elected by the Veterans Committee (in 1976 and 1982). Nobody says they were not very good players, but Hall of Fame great? Jackson, the Giants' shortstop from 1924 until crippling knee injuries limited him to only 105 games combined in 1932 and 1933, played three more years as a regular for Terry, mostly at third base, ending his playing career after the Giants lost to the Yankees in the 1936 World Series. He was at his best playing for McGraw from 1927 to 1931, averaging better than five wins above replacement, the standard for an "All-Star" level of performance. Lindstrom was the Giants' regular third baseman from 1926 until McGraw shifted him to center field in 1931, whereupon he broke his ankle in June and was never the same. He played more than 100 games in only eight of his 12 major-league seasons, and his .311 lifetime batting average came in a hitters' era. Aside from two exceptional years—1928, when his .358 batting average was third in the league, and 1930, when he batted .379—Lindstrom's player value as measured by WAR was mostly that of a typical big-league regular rather than an elite player.

Unlike when they won their four straight pennants, but very much like McGraw's earlier pitching staffs with guys named Mathewson, McGinnity, Marquard, and Tesreau, the Giants in the last five years of their Napoleonic era once again featured some of the best pitchers in the league. The enduring pitcher legacies of McGraw's last years with the Giants were Carl Hubbell and Freddie Fitzsimmons. Both pitchers were outstanding in McGraw's last run for the pennant in 1928. The right-handed Fitzsimmons was in his fourth year; rookie southpaw Hubbell pitched his first game in July. Fitzsimmons, at 20–9, had the only 20-win season of his 18-year career, including a stellar 5–1 record in eight September starts in the Giants' desperate bid to overtake St. Louis. His one loss was in his last start to the Cubs, which eliminated the Giants from contention. Hubbell established himself as an ace arising by winning seven of eight decisions in September. He beat the Cardinals in consecutive games—one a complete-game start, the other five innings in relief—in late September to bring the Giants to within one game of St. Louis, a position they could not ultimately capitalize on because the Cardinals matched subsequent Giants victories with their own. While Hubbell's best years on his way to 253 career victories were yet to come, he was already one of the best pitchers in baseball by the time McGraw called it quits.

* * *

In ill health, John McGraw finally retired 40 games into the 1932 season at the age of 59. His record as manager of the New York Giants since mid-1902, when he jumped ship from the American League, was 2,583 wins against 1,790 losses for a .591 winning percentage. He led the Giants to 10 pennants, the last in 1924, and three World Series championships in less than a quarter of a century. From 1903 to 1931—their 29 full seasons under McGraw—the Giants had a losing record only twice, in 1915 and 1926. Those were the only two years they finished in the bottom half of the standings. McGraw's teams were successful not only because of his preparation and capabilities as a manager, but because of the stability he brought to his roster.

Of course, McGraw had the advantage of greater financial resources at his disposal to build and maintain his team than most other ballclubs in Major League Baseball. A good judge of both talent and desire, and a good teacher of fundamentals, skills, and strategy, McGraw was not inclined to want frequent turnover. He built teams. McGraw developed and nurtured players, transitioned them to become regulars, expecting them to hold down a position for a baseball generation (five to seven years), and seemed to know when it was time to begin preparing for the transition of successors. Roster stability meant McGraw did not rely on trades to build his teams, but when he made trades they often brought players who provided both impact and leadership.

If Babe Ruth is the greatest player in baseball history, a powerful case can be made for John McGraw as the greatest manager. It may be just semantics, but there is a distinction between being the "greatest" and being the "best," despite those words being frequently conflated. Even at the time Ruth retired, pundits were debating whether Ty Cobb was the better player; Cobb in fact got more votes than Ruth in the election for the first five inductees to the Baseball Hall of Fame. Willie Mays has sometimes been said to be the best player ever; Barry Bonds was in that discussion until his reputation was besmirched by dabbling in performance-enhancing drugs; Honus Wagner legitimately deserves to be in the debate. But Babe Ruth is indisputably the greatest player in history. Few would question that judgment because he was a transcendent figure who had an enormous impact on the game as an institution, how it was played, and even as entertainment. The "best" are bounded by time—specifically the years they played—even if their legacies long outlive them. The "greatest" transcend time and had a transformational impact on the game itself.

As a manager, John McGraw had such an impact. His record of achievement speaks for itself, notwithstanding having lost six of the nine World Series he managed. With the possible exception of their 1924 Series loss to Washington, however, none of McGraw's teams that failed in the World Series were as good a club as the American League champion that beat them. His Giants may not have had a team in any five-year period that carries weight in any discussion about dynasties up till now—the first third of the twentieth century—at least not in comparison to the 1906–10 Cubs, or the 1910–14 Athletics, or the 1920s Yankees, but under McGraw's "Napoleonic" leadership, they were consistently competitive.

His New York Giants were the model of a *franchise* dynasty. The Chicago Cubs did not sustain their short-lived dynasty after 1910, and were often not even competitive thereafter. The Philadelphia Athletics endured a decade as one of the worst teams in history between 1914, when Connie Mack broke up his first great team, and 1926, when his second great team began taking shape. The New York Yankees were clearly now a dynasty, but only since 1921, and while their financial resources and management philosophy surely predicted they would be perennially successful, they were still a long way from matching the Giants' record of sustained success as a franchise.

What set McGraw apart was his intelligence and foresight at a time when the game was still discovering itself. While some of his insights were likely inevitable, such as using relief pitchers to "win" and "save" games and bench players for effect in key game circumstances, McGraw was quicker to see the possibilities and willing to break paradigms. He was ahead of his time, but that time was coming. There were other outstanding managers whose careers intersected with McGraw who built great teams and were outstanding in instruction and preparation and engagement with game situations. But none, not even Connie Mack, his contemporary rival for managerial greatness, impacted the way the game was played the way McGraw did. Managers who came after McGraw, and even most who were contemporaneous with him, could at best have only limited impact on the game because the baseball world was basically mapped out by the time John McGraw's health prevented him from carrying on. By then, one-third of the way through the twentieth century, basic game strategies were in place and the days of major new discoveries—including those like Ruth's home runs that were dramatically thrust upon the baseball universe—were, for the most part, over.

17

UNCLE ROBBIE'S BROOKLYN BURDEN

The official US census of 1890 showed Brooklyn, with a population over 800,000, to be the fourth-largest city in the country, behind New York, Chicago, and Philadelphia. No other city had even as many as 500,000 citizens. The beginning of the last decade of the nineteenth century was also the first year that Brooklyn had a franchise in the National League; in 1890, the American Association pennant-winning Bridegrooms, as the team was then called, switched league allegiances. The Bridegrooms picked up in the NL where they left off in the AA, winning the pennant and then splitting a seven-game unofficial "world series" (one game ended in a tie) against the American Association champion Louisville Colonels.

It is perhaps surprising that Brooklyn was not a charter member of either the National League, which started up in 1876, or the American Association, whose first season was 1882, because the city was at the center of things when baseball first took shape as a game that would be recognizable today. There were numerous amateur club teams playing ball in competitive matchups before crowds of spectators in the 1850s and 1860s. America's first fenced-in ballpark was built in Brooklyn in 1864, and it was there that the first upset in baseball history occurred. In June 1870, the Cincinnati Red Stockings—the first and, at the time, only professed-professional baseball team in America who had more than demonstrated their play-for-pay excellence by beating all amateur challengers dating back to the previous year—came to town to face the Atlantics and saw their 81-game (at least) winning streak come to an end in a come-from-behind 11th-inning rally by the Brooklyn amateur club.

Baseball remained enormously popular and well played by club teams in Brooklyn and New York, but that did not mean either city was in the

constellation of major-league cities in the first years of the game's professional growth. A Manhattan-based team called the New York Mutuals
that played in the inaugural year of the National League did not make it to
a second season. It was not until 1883 that New York City was again
represented in Major League Baseball, with teams in both the National
League and the American Association, and not until 1884 that Brooklyn
had a major-league team in the American Association.

After six years in the American Association and a pennant won in
their first year in the National League, the Brooklyn franchise endured a
decade of lost-cause seasons that ended in 1899 only because team president Charlie Ebbets invited Harry Von der Horst, owner of the Baltimore
Orioles, to buy a significant stake and become a co-owner of the Bridegrooms. Von der Horst immediately transferred most of Baltimore's best
players to Brooklyn, including longtime Orioles stars Willie Keeler, Joe
Kelley, and Hughie Jennings, as well as manager Ned Hanlon. Coming
along for the ride were the Orioles' three best pitchers and eight-year
veteran shortstop Bill Dahlen, recently acquired by Von der Horst for
Baltimore from Chicago, but who never played an inning for the Orioles.
Joining with veteran right-hander Brickyard Kennedy, who had won 132
games for the Bridegrooms since his rookie year in 1892, the Baltimore
infusion turned Brooklyn into a suddenly formidable team.

The new and much-improved "Superbas"—as they were now called, a
humorous reference to the coincidence of their manager's name matching
a popular vaudeville-circus act run by the famed Hanlon brothers—rose
from 91 losses and 10th place as the Bridegrooms in 1898 to 100 wins
and the National League pennant in 1899. Brooklyn beat out the Boston
Beaneaters, going for a third straight pennant, probably giving much
satisfaction to the Superbas' Orioles contingent that had seen Boston end
Baltimore's string of three straight pennants in 1897. Upon the demise of
his team in Baltimore, one of four franchises purged from the National
League in 1900, Von der Horst ensured that Joe McGinnity, a hard-
throwing right-hander who was 28–16 for the Orioles in his 1899 rookie
season, was brought to Brooklyn. McGinnity's 28–8 record was the best
in the league as the Superbas won again in 1900.

Von der Horst's decision to buy into the Brooklyn franchise probably
reflected a desire to cash in on the fast-growing vibrancy of Manhattan's
neighbor across the East River. Brooklyn was expanding geographically,
its population growing rapidly, its infrastructure improving dramatically—including a comprehensive trolley network that led to fans of the
baseball team being called "trolley dodgers"—and its economy was
booming. Most significantly, the opening of the Brooklyn Bridge in 1883
connected the city to finance, manufacturing, and jobs in Manhattan.
Baltimore must have seemed stagnant to Von der Horst by comparison.

Indeed, Brooklyn's growth was so fast paced that the city's revenue base could not keep up with the demands for continued improvement of public services, so in 1898 Brooklyn was itself incorporated into the new five-borough structure of New York City. (Of no small significance for the future of Major League Baseball, another of those boroughs was the Bronx.)

Being part of New York City was something many Brooklynites felt conflicted about. After all, with now more than 1 million inhabitants recorded in the 1900 census, Brooklyn would still have been the fourth-largest city in the United States had it remained separate from New York. Brooklyn's stature was diminished in the glare of the bright lights of Manhattan, the shining star of the great city called New York. As a borough, Brooklyn became a bit of a punch line—a quaint, sometimes eccentric community on the other side of the East River. It was not long before many "trolley dodgers" would come to see their baseball team treated with a similar lack of gravitas, certainly in relation to the Manhattan-based New York Giants and, in the not too distant future, the Bronx-based New York Yankees.

The good times in Brooklyn were short lived, however. Hanlon's Superbas—the baseball team, not the vaudeville act—were one of the National League clubs hardest hit by the upstart American League's raids on National League players. The most significant of their many player losses were McGinnity, an elite pitcher who defected to the new AL club in Baltimore in 1901, and Keeler, enticed to the new AL club in New York in 1903, just one year after he had collected 200-plus hits for the eighth consecutive year—a feat that would not be matched for more than a century when Ichiro Suzuki had 10 such years from 2001 to 2010. Keeler's accomplishment, however, began when the major-league schedule was 132 games and concluded in a 140-game season; Ichiro's—Suzuki is universally known by his first name—came in 162-game seasons. As Brooklyn plummeted in the standings, Von der Horst decided to get out of the baseball business and sold his ownership stake in the Superbas to Ebbets in 1903. He did like Brooklyn, however, and stayed there till his dying day, less than two years later. It was Charlie Ebbets's team now to do with what he pleased. Hanlon left his no-longer Superb(as) following their worst season in franchise history to this day in 1905.

During the 10 straight losing seasons Brooklyn suffered through from 1904 to 1913, their only star player was hard-throwing southpaw Nap Rucker. From his rookie season in 1907 through 1913, Rucker's last good year before arm problems took away his speed and limited his effectiveness, the Dodgers—as the team was now sometimes called—did not once have a winning year. Making more than 30 starts every year and pitching more than 300 innings four years in a row in one stretch, Rucker himself had only two seasons on the sunny side of .500, including 22 wins in 1911 for a seventh-place 64-win team, and in fact had a losing 116–123 record to that point in his career. Lack of run support was a significant problem for Rucker and all Brooklyn pitchers. As a testimony to Rucker's excellence, his .485 winning percentage in the first seven years of his career would have equated to 13 more victories than his team over a standard 154-game schedule.

Nap Rucker was probably the best left-handed pitcher in baseball from the mid-1900s to the midteens even though his career record of 134–134 is hardly a mark of distinction. In fact, advanced metrics suggest he has a strong claim to having been baseball's best lefty hurler between Eddie Plank and Rube Waddell, baseball's most accomplished southpaws in the first decade of the twentieth century, and Lefty Grove in the late 1920s. Rucker's 45.9 pitching wins above replacement from 1907 to 1913 were more than Plank and second only to Waddell over any seven-year period. Waddell's career was effectively over by the time Rucker was getting started, and while Plank outlasted Rucker in effective years, his best seasons were also almost all *before* Rucker broke in. And the Philadelphia Athletics for whom both Waddell and Plank pitched were, for the most part, consistently competitive. Brooklyn was not. Had they been competitive instead of finishing an average of 42 games out of first place in the seven years he was at his best, Nap Rucker would likely have had a Hall of Fame career. By 1914, with more than 2,100 innings pitched in seven years under his belt, Rucker's star began fading fast because of arm problems—just as his team's fortunes were rising.

* * *

Brooklyn's new look began taking shape in 1913 when the Dodgers opened Ebbets Field, the latest in a series of new concrete and steel ballparks that began with Forbes Field in Pittsburgh and Shibe Park in Philadelphia in 1909 and included Comiskey Park in Chicago (1910) and Fenway Park in Boston (1912). Proving that results matter more than an impressive new venue to play baseball, the sixth-place Dodgers, finishing 34½ games behind the Giants, did get a big boost in hometown attendance but still were just fourth in the league in paid customers.

The Giants were increasingly resented and hated by the Brooklyn faithful, both for their success and arrogance. It was perhaps with no small satisfaction, therefore, that the Dodgers welcomed Wilbert Robinson as their new manager in 1914 despite his having spent the last three years as John McGraw's right-hand man in the Giants' dugout and on the coaching lines. Robinson, after all, had an ugly breakup with his longtime bosom buddy from their Baltimore Orioles playing days when he loudly

criticized baseball's self-proclaimed top strategist for managerial decisions that cost the Giants the 1913 World Series. Less than a month later,
Ebbets hired Robinson to manage in Brooklyn.

Wilbert Robinson was 49 when he took charge of the Giants' rivals in
Brooklyn. He remained in command for 18 years. With a sharp baseball
mind of his own but a much more personable approach to life than his
former good friend McGraw, especially in his relationships with people,
Robinson's lighter touch quickly won over the clubhouse and endeared
him to the Brooklyn faithful—to the point where he became Brooklyn's
avuncular "Uncle Robbie" and the Dodgers, sometimes still called the
Superbas (although long since without Hanlon), soon became affectionately known as the Robins in honor of their manager.

The Uncle Robbie era began with another losing season in 1914—the
11th in a row for Brooklyn—but the Superba-Dodger-Robins improved
by 10 wins and reached as high as fifth place for the first time in seven
years. And for the first time since 1902, Brooklyn scored more runs than
its opponents. First baseman Jake Daubert won his second straight batting
crown; left fielder Zack Wheat, in his fifth year, had his first impactful
season; and rookie right-hander Jeff Pfeffer, with 23 wins, displaced the
sore-armed Rucker as Brooklyn's new ace. The club moved up to third in
1915 with its first winning season in 12 years and was in the pennant race
until a win-a-game, lose-a-game pattern in the final month condemned
them to wait for "next year." In late August, running a close second to the
Phillies, Robinson bolstered the pitching by trading with the Cubs for
Larry Cheney, a 20-game winner each of the three previous years, and
with the Giants for Rube Marquard, also with three straight 20-win seasons.

The next year was indeed *their* year as Brooklyn celebrated its first
pennant since 1900 as the borough's team outlasted both the Phillies and
Braves. The pennant race was effectively decided in the final matchup
between Brooklyn and Philadelphia—the Robins' 150th game—when
Marquard outpitched Phillies ace Grover Alexander to move into first
place for good. Pfeffer (25–11), Cheney (18–12), and Marquard (13–6)
all had earned run averages under 2.00; Wheat had his first superstar
season; and Uncle Robbie skillfully paired left-handed-batting Casey
Stengel with right-handed-batting Hi Myers and Jimmy Johnston in a
center-field/right-field platoon arrangement. Perhaps Brooklyn's most
consequential player, however, was 36-year-old Chief Meyers, picked up
by Robinson in the offseason after McGraw let the aging catcher go.
Meyers may have started fewer than half the Robins' games in 1916 and
batted just .247—compared to his .301 average in seven years playing for
the Giants—but his veteran experience and skills as a catcher, particularly

handling pitchers, may well have been the difference for Brooklyn in a pennant race decided by 2½ games.

Brooklyn's first exposure to the modern World Series was over in five games as the Red Sox dominated Robinson's Robins. Babe Ruth pitched a 14-inning gem in Game Two, shutting out the Robins over the final 13 innings; Ebbets provoked controversy by banishing Boston's band of Royal Rooters (a real band) to the far reaches of his ballpark when the Series moved to Brooklyn, the Red Sox leading two games to none, which may or may not have helped his team win Game Three; Boston third baseman Larry Gardner just did slide in safely under the catcher's tag on an inside-the-park three-run homer that wiped out a Brooklyn lead to win Game Four; and the Red Sox won Game Five when the teams returned to Boston, where the Royal Rooters put up a celebratory hoot. Nap Rucker's only appearance in the World Series, and the last game he ever pitched, was the final two innings of the Robins' 6–2 loss in Game Four. He surrendered one hit and struck out three without giving up a run.

It would not be until 1920 that Brooklyn was back in the World Series. Between their two pennants, the Robins endured three successive losing seasons, including a disastrous 1917 (the year after winning the pennant) when they dropped to one notch above the basement. Back to being competitive in 1920, the Robins broke open a tight three-team race between the defending World Series champion Cincinnati Reds and McGraw's resurgent Giants by winning 16 of 18 games in mid-September. Burleigh Grimes, acquired from Pittsburgh in 1918, emerged as the undisputed ace of the Brooklyn staff in his fourth big-league season with 23 wins.

Once again, the Robins were World Series losers, falling to the Cleveland Indians, five games to two. It was in 1920 that the Dodgers began their history of being snakebit by strange happenings on the ball field in the fall classic. Including 1916, Brooklyn lost all seven World Series they played before finally winning in 1955, and their Series losses always seemed to turn on some bizarre or heartbreaking play. In the 1920 Series, it was two unique events in Game Five that did them in. Grimes took the mound in Cleveland with the Series tied at two games apiece, having already pitched a shutout in Game Two. In this game, however, the first three batters to face him singled, loading the bases for cleanup hitter Elmer Smith, who promptly tagged Grimes for the first grand slam in World Series history. Cleveland led 4–0 and still had all 27 outs to play with.

As if that World Series first was not enough, in the fifth inning the Robins hit into the first and only unassisted triple play in World Series history. Trailing now by 7–0, the Robins had runners on first and second with nobody out when Clarence Mitchell, a good-hitting pitcher who had relieved the ineffective Grimes, hit a line drive that seemed destined to land safely in center field—except that second baseman Bill Wambsganss leaped to his right and snared the drive for the first out. Both Robins had taken flight for the next base when the ball was hit, certain it would land safely, allowing Wambsganss, whose momentum was carrying him toward second base, to double off the lead runner for the second out. When he turned to check on the runner from first—there he was, standing just off second in a what-the-heck-just-happened moment, and Wambsganss calmly tagged him for the third out on one play, handled only by him. Brooklyn did get a run in the ninth, but failed to score even once in the next two games. They were now 0–2 in World Series play.

* * *

Neither of Wilbert Robinson's two pennant-winning teams were necessarily worthy of the honor. Both years, the Robins were able to take advantage of better teams failing to play up to their potential—the Phillies in 1916 and the Giants in 1920. The Robins were successful largely on the strength of their pitching. Zack Wheat was their best position player, and he was hardly a superstar. After both pennants, the Robins were nonfactors the next three years. Uncle Robbie continued as Brooklyn manager for 11 more years before retiring at age 67 after the 1931 season, coming close to a pennant only once more—in 1924. Trailing by 13 games as late as August 9, Brooklyn nearly did to the Giants in 1924 what the Giants and Bobby Thomson did to the Dodgers 27 years later when New York famously trailed by 13½ games on August 11. While the 1924 Giants sleep-walked to the finish with a record just one game above .500 after August 9, the Robins won 75 percent of their remaining games, including 15 in a row straddling the end of August and the beginning of September, to pull within half a game of New York. Then it was Brooklyn that went into sleepwalk mode, with a 10–8 record to close out the schedule, while the Giants woke up and won 13 of their last 20.

Although he was 36 years old, Zack Wheat had the best year of his career in 1924. His .375 batting average was second in the league. In September, when the Robins were fighting valiantly to overtake the Giants, Wheat hit six of his 14 homers, drove in 28 of his 97 RBIs—by far his most in any month—and batted .392. Having already won the National League batting title in 1918, and with a .299 career average going into Brooklyn's pennant-winning 1920 season, Wheat was one of the veteran players still in their prime who seemed to get better when the Deadball Era gave way to Babe Ruth–instigated Lively Ball Era, batting a robust .339 between 1920 and 1927. While the big boost in his batting average was certainly an effect of baseball having entered a hitters' era, advanced metrics indicate he did ramp up his game in the 1920s; 45

percent of his career wins above replacement came in the eight years he played *after* he turned 32.

The pitching excellence of Dazzy Vance and Burleigh Grimes, however, was the most critical factor in the Robins nearly preventing the Giants from becoming the first team to win four straight pennants. They started 70 of their team's 154 games, threw 60 complete games (both had 30), and combined for 50 of Brooklyn's 92 victories. At 22–13, Grimes had his fourth 20-win season in five years. At 28–6, Vance led the league in wins, his 2.16 ERA was the league's best, and his 262 strikeouts were not only the most in the majors since Walter Johnson fanned 303 in 1912 but the most in the National League since way back in 1892.

Vance was a revelation because he was a late bloomer. His true name was Charles Arthur, but he earned the nom de guerre "Dazzy" because of the "dazzling" fastball he showcased early in his minor-league days. Until breaking in with Brooklyn as a 31-year-old rookie in 1922, however, Vance's career had been stalled almost entirely in the minor leagues because of chronic arm problems that contributed to an unacceptable lack of control, causing both the Pirates and Yankees to give up on him. Vance was supposedly cured of his sore arm in 1920, when he was pitching in New Orleans, by a doctor who operated on his shoulder following an injury sustained when a hand of poker got out of hand. Not only did he have a terrific fastball and a wicked curve that broke sharply downward, not only did he throw every pitch hard even as he paced himself to throw four or five pitches even harder when he most needed to, but Vance also was very deceptive in his windup and delivery—all of which made him a batter's worst nightmare. Dazzling Dazzy threw both his pitches with exactly the same motion, and famously wore a tattered long-sleeve white undershirt whose flapping as his right arm came around on the pitch made it even more difficult for the batter to pick up the ball.

Brooklyn's late-season surge was powered by Dazzy Vance. From the beginning of August till the end of the season, Vance made 14 starts, completed 12, won 11, and fanned 120 batters in 120⅔ innings. He also struck out six in a single four-inning relief appearance—his only time out of the bullpen that year—in which he was the winning pitcher. In all, Vance struck out 26 percent of the batters he faced the final two months of the season. More significantly, strikeouts accounted for more than a third of his outs. Including his victory in relief, Vance reeled off 15 consecutive wins from July 6 until September 20 before losing back-to-back starts in the Robins' 148th and 151st games of the season. The second of those losses, on a day that began with the Robins and Giants tied for first, dropped Brooklyn a game behind New York, winners of their game, and the three games remaining proved not enough time to catch up. Nonetheless, Vance's pitching was so exceptional that he was voted the National League's 1924 Most Valuable Player ahead of Rogers Hornsby, who hit a staggering .424 that year. Hornsby was only 2-for-14 in the three starts—all complete-game victories—that Dazzy had against the Cardinals.

* * *

The last seven years of Uncle Robbie's reign were mostly unsuccessful ones, beginning with five consecutive sixth-place finishes, although they were a bit player in the 1930 pennant race. Both Grimes and Wheat were gone after 1926, one traded and the other released. While Burleigh Grimes, who already had 182 victories in his career, went on to win 88 more, Zack Wheat played another year before retiring in 1927 just 116 hits shy of 3,000. At the time, his 2,884 hits were 10th on the all-time list, including nineteenth-century players. Dazzy Vance led the league in both total strikeouts and strikeouts per nine innings for seven consecutive years between 1922, his rookie season, and 1928. Only Walter Johnson had more consecutive years with the most strikeouts in his league.

The Robins, also now being referred to as the Dodgers, were a bad team, but a bad team with a few standout players. Besides Vance, who was traded to the Cardinals in 1933 and finally made it to the World Series with them in 1934 at the age of 43—he fanned three of the seven batters he faced in one relief appearance—the only other significant players for Brooklyn in Wilbert Robinson's remaining years as its manager were the talented, often star crossed, outfielder Babe Herman and southpaw Watty Clark. Aside from playing problematic defense in right field, Herman was not the elite player his impressive hitting statistics might suggest, including batting .381 in 1929 and .393 in 1930, when he also smacked a career-high 35 homers and drove in a career-high 130 runs. Those were the two most hitter-friendly years of the Lively Ball Era, and they were the only two years Herman hit more than 20 homers or had more than 100 RBIs. Clark picked up as Brooklyn's ace when age began catching up with Vance in the late 1920s.

Brooklyn had had notable characters before—Casey Stengel, for one—but it was during these years that the baseball team acquired the "daffy" identity that would follow them through much of the Great Depression. The "Daffy Dodgers" moniker was less a comment on player personalities than on their frequent failure to play heads-up baseball. Indeed, Babe Herman keeping his head down instead of up is what led to the embarrassing three-men-on-third episode that defined the Brooklyn brand of "daffiness"—that and stories like the one about how he got conked on the head by a fly ball he misjudged. In the three-men-on-third play in question, Herman charged around second base after hitting a double, apparently assuming there would be a play at the plate on Jake

Flowers, who had been on first. Flowers, however, held up at third when he saw that Vance, the runner who had been on second, was coming back to third after getting halfway home, apparently concluding he could not score. Vance had delayed his departure from second base too long because he thought Herman's double might be caught. Anyway, that's the best possible face to put on a play that ended with Vance and Herman sliding into third at right angles to each other, with Flowers standing on the bag caught in the middle. All three were tagged. Only Vance had legitimate claim to the base and was safe.

However, it's not like the zaniness on the ball field that came to characterize the Dodgers was unique in baseball. Many of the same mishaps that caused people to make fun of the Dodgers—even players getting hit on the head by fly balls, though perhaps not winding up with three men on one base—had happened before and would happen again to other teams, including good ones. Of course, the Dodgers certainly had their share of eccentric goofballs on the ball field. But they weren't alone, certainly not in the teens and '20s. If Stengel doffed his cap to release a captive pigeon, Rabbit Maranville, one of the best shortstops in the game, also made a name for himself by clowning around on the field. But the seemingly never-ending miscues became emblematic of a team that was struggling to be relevant in the greatest city in the world, where the Yankees and Giants ruled the roost. And that seemed somehow symbolic of Brooklyn's second-tier status relative to Manhattan as a part of New York City.

18

CAPITAL TIME

When the Senators Mattered

For much of the twentieth century, the nation's capital was often the back end of the old joke about being first in war, first in peace, and last in the American League. In their first 23 years as an original American League franchise, the Washington Senators had mostly been either dead-enders or the very definition of mediocrity, with only six winning seasons to their record. In the 10 years between 1924 and 1933, however, the Senators, with three pennants, 874 wins, and a .574 winning percentage, were the third-most-successful team in Major League Baseball, behind the Yankees (four pennants, 926 wins, and a .604 winning percentage) and Philadelphia Athletics (three pennants, 917 wins, and .602).

In the nineteenth century, Washington was a National League city, twice over. First there were the Nationals, who introduced themselves to the league in 1886 with a 28–92 record. They lasted just four years, finishing last three times, until they were eliminated in 1890 in favor of Brooklyn, which had just won the American Association pennant. Then came the Senators, added in 1892 when the NL expanded to 12 teams. They were cast off after eight years when the league downsized to a more manageable eight clubs in 1900. Neither franchise ever had a team with a winning record. The city's notable lack of success in the Major League Baseball world of the late nineteenth century, however, did not preclude Ban Johnson from believing that having a team in Washington would be a very good idea. What could be more American than an American League team in the nation's capital, after all? And there was of course the calculation that having a team in Washington, DC, was good politics, especially for an upstart self-proclaimed new major league.

Washington's new start in Major League Baseball did not mean a turn to winning ways. The new Senators, who throughout their history would interchangeably be called the Nationals, did not fare well in attracting quality players from the National League—with one exception, and not until their second year in existence. Outfielder Ed Delahanty, one of baseball's best players in the 1890s, had seen his salary barely increase from his first years in baseball and decided enough was enough after 13 outstanding seasons with the Phillies and a .354 batting average in 1901 that was second best in the established league. Defecting to the new league, Delahanty landed in Washington, giving the Senators their first star player. He did not disappoint, leading the AL in batting with a .376 average in 1902. At 35, however, he was deep in debt, a heavy drinker, and having difficulty coping with life. On July 3, 1903, carrying a .333 batting average in 42 of the Senators' first 59 games, Delahanty died in somewhat mysterious circumstances, exiting a train after an incident with another passenger on board, walking along the rails on a bridge crossing the Niagara River, and jumping or stumbling off, his body being found on the Canadian side of Niagara Falls.

After enduring an endless succession of sixth-, seventh-, and eighth-place finishes, a turning point for their fortunes came in 1912 when the well-respected Clark Griffith was enticed to Washington to take over as manager in an arrangement that included stock in the franchise. With the exception of Washington's pitching staff, led by the incomparable Walter Johnson, center fielder Clyde Milan, and veteran no-hit shortstop George McBride, Griffith remade the team as soon as he took over. Milan and McBride were the only position regulars held over from the previous year. Few of the new guys had any appreciable major-league experience, and none were or would become top-tier or even top-middle-tier players. That did not prevent Griffith, however, from proving well worth the price of his ownership shares. The Senators not only had their first ever winning season in 1912 (and Washington, DC, too, for that matter), but finished second with 91 victories—a 27-win improvement—and did virtually the same (90 wins and second place) the next year. Unfortunately for Washington, however, Boston's Red Sox were far superior in 1912 and Philadelphia's Athletics much better in 1913, and the Senators did not really compete for the pennant either year.

Even if the Senators overachieved for the roster they had in 1912, 1913, and 1914 when they finished third, a big credit to Clark Griffith's managerial legacy, they did give long-suffering Washington fans something to finally cheer about. The major reason was that the best pitcher in baseball, and probably in all of baseball history, pitched for the Senators. He was Walter Johnson. The strapping right-hander first came to Washington in August 1907. Even though he had been pitching in an obscure semipro league in Idaho, Johnson's overpowering stuff and dominance on the mound came to the attention of Washington manager Joe Cantillon, who sent one of his catchers to investigate, who in turn wasted no time in signing him up. Johnson had a losing 32–48 record to show for his first three years in the big time, including 13–25 in 1909 when the Senators lost 110 games and not only finished last in the American League by 56 games, but were 20 games behind the seventh-place team.

Beginning in 1910, however, Walter Johnson went on a 10-year run of excellence as good as any pitcher ever, even taking into account that this was the Deadball Era when pitchers dominated the game. Johnson put together 10 straight 20-win seasons; he had back-to-back 30-win seasons in 1912 (33–12) and 1913 (36–7); he led the league in earned run average both years, and did so again in 1918 and 1919; his ERA was 1.59 in the 3,427⅔ innings he pitched between 1910 and 1919, and below 2.00 in nine of those 10 years, including seven in a row from 1910 to 1916; he led the league in shutouts six times, including 11 of his 36 wins in 1913; and he won 265 games those 10 years with 74 shutouts, while losing just 143—a .650 winning percentage for a club that won just 51 percent of its games. Walter Johnson was the winning pitcher in 35 percent of the Senators' victories.

With Walter Johnson baseball's ace of aces, the Senators were generally one of the tougher teams to score against in the American League during the teens. Their lack of offense was a problem, however; Washington was usually in the bottom half of the league in scoring, and never better than fourth. Clyde Milan was Washington's only position player in the Deadball Era who could be counted among the better players in the league—which is not to say, among the best. Among major-league outfielders, he was not remotely in the conversation with Ty Cobb, Tris Speaker, Shoeless Joe Jackson, and Sam Crawford. Milan's 88 stolen bases in 1912 broke Cobb's American League record of 83 set the year before, and would be eclipsed by Cobb's 96 just three years later.

Clark Griffith stepped down as manager when he assumed complete control of the franchise after the 1920 season. As owner, Griffith's name became synonymous with the Washington Senators, or Nationals (whichever name the team happened to go by at the time), until they moved to Minnesota to become the Twins in 1961. The ballpark that carried his name since 1920, however—Griffith Stadium—was still around to become the home park (for one year only) of the 1961 expansion Washington Senators (who are now the Texas Rangers). Of particular historical interest is Griffith's loyalty to Washington players in his managerial selections as owner. Beginning with the man he chose to replace himself, George McBride, all 10 of the managerial changes Griffith made between 1921 and 1955 were from within the organization or men who had spent

Washington's Walter Johnson warming up in 1913, when he went 36–7 with a 1.14 earned run average. *Harris & Ewing Collection (Library of Congress).*

most of their playing careers with the Senators. Not until Charley Dressen in 1955 did the Senators name a manager who had no previous ties to the franchise, and by then Griffith's control of the club was more in name only because he was an ailing 85-year-old man in the last year of his life.

* * *

As the 1924 season approached, there was little reason to expect the Washington Senators to compete for the American League pennant. The Yankees had won three in a row, including a dominating performance in 1923, while the Senators had finished fourth, sixth, and fourth under three different managers since 1921. But Washington had a nucleus of accomplished veterans 30 years or older in Walter Johnson; southpaw George Mogridge; shortstop Roger Peckinpaugh, who was traded to the Senators in 1922 after nine years with the Yankees; and right fielder Sam Rice, whose career batting average going into 1924 since becoming a regular eight years earlier was .316. First baseman Joe Judge was an accomplished eight-year veteran just under 30, and 28-year-old left-hander Tom Zachary was a dependable mainstay in the starting rotation alongside Johnson and Mogridge, although not nearly as good. Importantly, the Senators also had some young hustlers in catcher Muddy Ruel, second baseman Bucky Harris, third baseman Ossie Bluege, and left fielder Goose Goslin.

For the fourth time in the four years since he stepped out of the dugout, Griffith decided to change managers. After first considering trading Harris to the White Sox for Eddie Collins so that Collins—one of the most esteemed players in baseball, as well as still one of the best—could be manager, Griffith turned the team over to the second baseman he had in hand. Because the 27-year-old Harris had only four major-league seasons behind him as a player and was younger than all but two of Washington's position regulars—Goslin and Bluege were both 23—Griffith was careful to secure support for his decision from Johnson and Rice, the Senators' two biggest stars. Bucky Harris more than validated Griffith's faith in him by proving to be a dynamic and innovative leader, guiding the Senators to the World Series, where they had never before been, in each of his first two years on the job. Washington surprised the baseball world in 1924 by beating out the Yankees by two games to grab the American League pennant and winning the World Series, and repeating in 1925 (except for the World Series part), taking the pennant by 8½ games over second-place Philadelphia.

The 1924 pennant race turned on Washington taking three of four from the Yankees in New York in their final series against each other in the last days of August to take a 1½-game lead into September. But with still more than a month of baseball to be played, the Senators had virtually no margin for error against the powerful, Ruth-driven New Yorkers; their strong 18–7 finish in September proved absolutely necessary because the Yankees kept the pressure on with an 18–8 record of their own. Having vanquished the Yankees, the 1924 Senators went on to win a thrilling seven-game World Series against the New York Giants. Goslin was the batting star, with three home runs, seven RBIs, and a .344 batting average, and Johnson—everybody's sentimental favorite— pitched four epic innings in relief to get the victory after being called into Game Seven in the ninth inning with the score tied just two days after he had lost a complete game in which he surrendered six runs on 13 hits. Washington for the first and, so far, only time in history was first in war, first in peace, and first in Major League Baseball.

Although Washington ended up winning the 1925 pennant decisively, it was close for most of the summer. The race finally broke open when the Senators won nine of 10 in late August–early September, while the Athletics were mired in a 12-game losing streak. This time against the Pittsburgh Pirates, the Senators lost a seven-game World Series thriller. Goslin once again hit three homers (with six RBIs) and Johnson, pitching in sometimes-heavy rain, was the losing pitcher in a heartbreaking complete-game finale after having surrendered only one run in two complete-game victories earlier in the Series. Commissioner Landis decided that, rainstorm or not, Game Seven was going to be played, and played to its nine-inning conclusion. There would be no postponement, calling it an official game when the Senators had the lead after five innings, or calling the game a 6–6 tie after seven innings and playing an eighth game the next fair-weather day. Peckinpaugh made an unfathomable eight errors in the seven games, including two in the late innings of Game Seven—a dropped popup that led to two unearned runs, allowing the Pirates to tie the score at 6–6 in the seventh, and an errant throw in the last of the eighth that led to Pittsburgh scoring the final two runs, breaking a 7–7 tie to decide the game and the Series.

* * *

Cleanup hitter Goose Goslin, the 1924 league leader in runs batted in, was Washington's only player in the American League's top 10 for offensive wins above replacement in the two years they won the pennant. The Senators did not have any player either year in the American League's top five in batting average, on-base percentage, slugging percentage, or home runs. To be fair, Griffith Stadium was definitely not a good ballpark for hitters to go deep. They were outscored in their league by five other clubs in 1924 and by three in 1925.

Instead, 'twas pitching and defense that were the foundation for the Senators' capital success. With Johnson, Mogridge, and Zachary combining for a 54–27 record in 1924, and Johnson, Stan Coveleski, and Dutch Ruether going 58–19 in 1925, Washington's pitching staff, backed by excellent defense, had the league-best earned run average both years. Coveleski and Ruether came to Washington in 1925 in preseason trades as 30-something veterans, each having already pitched in a World Series. Those moves to bolster the pitching staff proved critical for the Senators because Zachary was not nearly as effective in 1925—he had a losing record—and Mogridge was traded away in June after getting off to a sluggish start. As good as their front-line pitching was, however, the Senators almost certainly would not have won the 1924 pennant, and might not have repeated in 1925, had they not introduced the concept of a dedicated relief ace to Major League Baseball.

Fred "Firpo" Marberry, still officially a rookie in 1924 notwithstanding the 11 games he pitched as a late-season call-up the previous year, was the trailblazer for relief pitching as its own discipline. Marberry not only threw hard—very hard—but, much in the manner of today's closers, displayed a fearsome, stalking, intimidating presence on the mound. It had not been unusual since at least the mid-1910s for promising rookie pitchers to begin their careers working out of the bullpen, but ordinarily a pitcher of Marberry's talent, especially with his fastball, was destined soon for the starting rotation. Instead, he began the season as a part-time starter before Harris shifted him full-time to the bullpen in August as the pennant race heated up. In 1924, Marberry won six and saved 15 in 36 relief appearances, including two saves and a victory without allowing a run in 6⅓ innings in the Senators' pivotal late-August series against the Yankees that put them in first place to stay. Marberry pitched 55 times in 1925, all in relief, with 16 saves as his team again won the pennant. Bucky Harris called on Marberry for 91 of the 273 pitching changes he made in managing back-to-back pennant winners. In just over half of those games, Marberry got either the win (15) or the save (31). He also was the losing pitcher 11 times. Including five wins as a starter, Marberry accounted for 27 percent of Washington's 188 victories in 1924 and '25.

The Senators were the first team to dedicate a young pitcher with the potential to be a first-rate starter almost exclusively to the role of relief ace, rely on him to win and "save" close games in relief and not take a step back. At least they didn't until after Harris left Washington in 1929. The decision to employ Marberry's prodigious talent in the bullpen was critical to Washington's success because Harris inherited a pitching staff whose two best pitchers—Walter Johnson and George Mogridge—were both 35 years or older, and in 1925 Mogridge was replaced by 35-year-old Stan Coveleski. Having a pitcher as fine as Marberry to rely on in the bullpen allowed Harris to better pace his aging staff aces. With the reliable Marberry as Washington's (relief) ace in the hole, the Senators' old-guy starters benefited by not necessarily having to complete their own victories. Marberry saved 11 of Johnson's 43 wins in '24 and '25, four of Mogridge's 16 wins in 1924, and four of Coveleski's 20 victories in 1925.

Marberry's role helped rejuvenate the twilight of Walter Johnson's career. The Big Train had not won 20 games since 1919, but had nonetheless completed 70 percent of his starts and had also appeared 27 times in relief between 1920 and 1923. With a pitcher of Marberry's excellence in the bullpen, Johnson no longer needed to make relief appearances to save wins for Washington and could be bailed out by Marberry in games he started. The 36-year-old Johnson was 23–7 in 1924, leading the league in wins, winning percentage, earned run average, and strikeouts, and he was voted the American League's Most Valuable Player. And in 1925, he went 20–7. Johnson appeared only once in relief those two years, and completed 36 of his 67 starts—given his age, a more reasonable 54 percent.

Ironically, despite having relied on Marberry many times in precisely such circumstances during the season, Bucky Harris did not call on his relief ace to save the seventh game of the 1925 World Series for the Big Train as the Pirates scored three times in that fateful eighth inning to overcome a 7–6 deficit after Johnson retired the first two batters. The weather was messy and Peckinpaugh was sloppy defensively, but Johnson was pitching on fumes. Questions were raised about whether Harris let sentiment overcome judgment in his failure or unwillingness to relieve the beloved Walter Johnson, who was clearly struggling. Among those critics was American League president Ban Johnson.

Thirty-five-year-old George Mogridge went 16–11 in 1924, completing 13 of his 30 starts, after having completed 57 percent of his starts his three previous years in Washington. And Stan Coveleski, after a relatively mediocre 15–16 record with Cleveland in 1924 that might have marked the beginning of the end of his great career, was 20–5 with the Senators in 1925, leading the league in both winning percentage and ERA, just as Johnson did the previous year, but completed only 15 of his 32 starts. It was the first time since his 1916 rookie year that Coveleski completed fewer than half of his starting assignments.

* * *

The Senators were not in the pennant hunt the remaining three years of Harris's first of three extended tours as their manager. While Washington's core of position regulars from 1924 and 1925 remained largely intact, the pitching staff transitioned from aging veterans Johnson, Mogridge, and Coveleski anchoring the starting rotation to less formidable arms, not all of them youthful. Their best pitcher was baseball's first sustained relief ace, Firpo Marberry. By 1928, when their pitching was beginning to get better, the Senators' offense had become even less imposing. Goslin was the Senators' only position player among the top 10 in the American League.

By the end of the 1928 season, Bucky Harris had worn out his welcome in Washington. Griffith negotiated a trade with Detroit that allowed him to become manager of the Tigers and chose Walter Johnson, an icon in Washington who had retired as a pitcher after the 1927 season, to take charge of his team. The Big Train's first season at the helm in 1929 was less than successful, at least by measure of the final standings—fifth place, 34 games out of first, with a losing record of 10 games below .500. As a teaser for what was to come, however, Johnson managed Washington to the second-best record in the league, by just a half-game, in the final two months of the season. The Washington Senators ordinarily would have been legitimate contenders the next three years—winning 94 (finishing second), 92 (third), and 93 games (third again)—except they weren't because the Philadelphia Athletics in 1930 and 1931 and the Yankees in 1932 were so dominant they ran away with those pennants.

Perhaps the most interesting aspect of Walter Johnson's tenure as manager is that, despite his observing and personally benefiting as an aging workhorse starting pitcher from Bucky Harris's possibly Griffith-inspired epiphany about the value of a dedicated relief ace, the Big Train was more of a traditionalist when it came to how he employed his own pitching staff. Having a starting pitcher's mind-set, Johnson moved Marberry from the nearly exclusive relief-ace role he had when Harris was manager into the starting rotation in early June 1929, almost certainly because Washington's starting pitchers had given up just shy of five earned runs a game. Marberry almost certainly wanted to start, notwithstanding his success as an ace reliever, because therein was the glory, not to mention the money, for a pitcher. In 26 games as a starting pitcher in 1929, Marberry completed 16, was 16–8, and had an excellent 2.78 earned run average to validate Johnson's faith in him in that role. But Washington's bullpen, with a 5.17 ERA, was hardly a relief for Johnson when he needed relief. Like most other managers, and as he had been worked in his pitching prime, Johnson used his starting pitchers to finish close games for the win or a save, and that is how he used Marberry.

* * *

Despite his team coming off three consecutive 90-win seasons and having the American League's best record in the final month of the 1932 season, Griffith decided to replace Walter Johnson as manager in 1933 with his shortstop, Joe Cronin. Clark Griffith was in love with Joe Cronin. Well, his niece was, anyway; the boss's niece, who was like a daughter, married the star shortstop, although that did not necessarily have anything to do with the managerial change. Griffith, remembering the instant success his team had with consecutive pennants immediately after naming young second baseman Bucky Harris as manager, was captivated by the possibility of another inspiring young on-the-field team leader doing the same. And the same he did do, leading Washington back to the promised land of the World Series in 1933.

It does not seem to have been a necessary move, replacing a Washington icon as manager with the team's star shortstop, especially when it would have been dubious to argue that the Senators could have done any better than they did under Johnson. Philadelphia in 1930 and '31 (after also winning the pennant in 1929), and New York in 1932, were just too powerful. They were two of the best teams in history, against which the Senators were no match, player for player. Philadelphia's 1929 to 1931 championship teams featured Jimmie Foxx, Al Simmons, Mickey Cochrane, and Lefty Grove—Hall of Famers all, and at the peak of their careers. The Yankees had Lou Gehrig, Tony Lazzeri, Babe Ruth, Earle Combs, Bill Dickey, Joe Sewell, Red Ruffing, and Lefty Gomez—Hall of Famers all, most at the top of their careers. Washington's Hall of Fame players included Sam Rice, who was at the end of his career; Heinie Manush, in his third year in Washington, approaching the twilight of a career that began in 1923; and Cronin, the team's brightest star and the best all-around shortstop in the American League.

The team Cronin inherited from Johnson was solid and mature but by no means great. Cronin, Manush, second baseman Buddy Myer, and third baseman Ossie Bluege were Washington's cornerstone position players. With outfielder Sam Rice, at 42, by now reduced to a backup role, Griffith shored up the offense by dealing with the Browns to bring back Goose Goslin, who had been sent to St. Louis in 1930 to get Manush. Washington's pitching staff was a core strength during Johnson's tenure as manager, solidified by the acquisition of Alvin "General" Crowder in the same trade that brought Manush to Washington in exchange for Goslin. (Crowder was nicknamed "General" after a real US Army general, Enoch Crowder, who commanded cavalry troops in the last of the Old West "Indian Wars" and later was the brains behind the Selective Service System to draft Americans to fight in World War I.) Crowder was in the midst of a six-year stretch from 1928 to 1933 when he was one of the American League's elite pitchers, including leading the league with 26 wins in 1932. The Senators were the league's stingiest club in surrendering runs in 1932, but still Griffith thought to further improve the pitching for Cronin's first year in charge by making trades for southpaw pitchers Earl Whitehill and Lefty Stewart to join Crowder in the starting rotation, and Jack Russell to be the new relief ace in place of Marberry, who was traded to Detroit to get him.

And fortuitously for young 26-year-old first-time manager Cronin, the Yankees team that was so dominant in 1932 was vulnerable in 1933, mostly because age was catching up with key core players, most notably Ruth, Combs, and Sewell. The Great Depression, meanwhile, was forcing Connie Mack to once again break up the core of a great Philadelphia team. Washington rode a stretch of 23 wins in 26 games to take a four-game lead over the Yankees soon after Independence Day and were fully in command by September. The Senators ended up winning their third pennant in 10 years by seven games over the Yankees, but lost the World Series to the Giants in five games. Crowder won 24, Whitehill 22, and Stewart 15. Russell led the league in saves with 13. The 1933 Senators' 99 victories are still the most by any team that has ever played in the nation's capital. For the record, there is no reason to suppose, based on *his* record, that Walter Johnson could not have won the pennant with this team had he remained as manager, especially with the Yankees in decline and the Athletics splitting up.

By 1934, however, the mature pennant-winning Senators of 1933 were decidedly older, as the Yankees had been the year before. They were also beset by injuries to key players. Unlike the 1933 Yankees, who were the only other team making any play for the pennant that year and finished second, Washington did not have the depth of talent to fall back on to prevent a catastrophic plunge from first to seventh. The franchise would forever more be the back end of that old joke about Washington baseball until moving to Minnesota in 1961 ended the pain, after which another American League team in Washington took up that particular mantle (until they moved to Texas).

19

MOUND TRANSITIONS

On Strikeouts and Relief Pitching

Baseball has always had to grapple with the balance between pitching and offense. Moving the pitcher's rubber from 55 feet, 6 inches from the center of home plate to the current 60 feet, 6 inches from the pointy end of the plate in 1893 inaugurated a relatively short-lived hitters' era that lasted till the turn of the century. Five players batted better than .400 the next year, and 11 between then and 1900. Team scoring increased overnight from five runs per game to 6.6 in 1893 and stayed over six runs until late in the decade. Strikeouts decreased dramatically as hitters had more time, albeit measured in fractions of seconds, to react to the pitched ball.

At the dawn of the new century, and of the two-league structure that has since defined Major League Baseball, batters lost a bit of their new edge as foul balls, which had not counted as strikes, now did until there were two strikes in an at-bat. This rule, which went into effect in 1901 in the National League and 1903 in the American League, dropped team batting averages by about 20 points and scoring to about four runs a game and ushered in two decades of the Deadball Era where pitchers ruled. Every year from 1904 to 1910 there were at least eight major-league pitchers whose earned run average was under 2.00.

Of the many impressive pitchers who defined the Deadball Era, the two most dominant power pitchers were the Philadelphia Athletics' eccentric southpaw Rube Waddell and the Washington Senators' statesman-like right-hander Walter Johnson. There were others, of course. White Sox right-hander Big Ed Walsh fanned more than 200 batters five times in six years between 1907 and 1912. Red Sox right-hander Smoky Joe

Wood's fastball was considered the near equal of Johnson's before he threw out his shoulder at the tender age of only 23; Wood averaged 7.1 strikeouts per nine innings from 1910 to 1913, higher than the Big Train's 6.8 ratio, although Johnson logged nearly 10 percent more innings. The Giants' Christy Mathewson led the National League in strikeouts five of six years between 1903 and 1908, but only once in strikeouts per nine innings. The Phillies' Grover Cleveland Alexander (not yet "Old Pete") also led the NL in Ks in five of six years (between 1912 and 1917) and twice in strikeout ratio. But neither National League ace was as feared with the fastball as the Rube, the Big Train, Smoky Joe, or even Big Ed.

Waddell led the American League in strikeouts six consecutive years from 1902 to 1907 and in strikeouts per nine innings seven straight years extending to 1908. In 1904 Waddell established a modern major-league record that would last for 61 years when he kayoed 349 batters in 383 innings, 46 percent more than runner-up Jack Chesbro's 239 strikeouts. (The all-time record of 441 was set by Old Hoss Radbourn in 1884, when baseball was such a fundamentally different game that Old Hoss started 73 of his team's 114 games, finished them all, and pitched nearly 680 innings.) Waddell was so overpowering in 1904 that his ratio of 8.2 strikeouts per nine innings was exactly double the 4.1 Ks per nine innings by American League pitchers collectively and more than double the major-league average of 3.8. Waddell's strikeout ratio was even higher the previous year when his 302 Ks in 324 innings came to 8.4 per nine innings.

Walter Johnson, however, was the preeminent strikeout pitcher of the Deadball Era. Employing a deceptively easy, almost casual, side-armed delivery, Johnson's fastball was considered by many, at least until Sandy Koufax in the 1960s and Nolan Ryan in the '70s, to be the best of any pitcher in history, with all due respect to Lefty Grove and Bob Feller. No pitcher in history has matched the 12 times Johnson—the "Big Train"— led his league in strikeouts, although Ryan came close with 11. Nor has any pitcher matched the eight consecutive years, 1912 to 1919, Johnson led his league in strikeouts—a record Feller might have broken were it not for World War II, when "Rapid Robert" had priorities other than throwing a baseball at blazing speed, because he led the league in Ks each of the four years before he went off to war at 23 years old and the first three years after the war was over despite missing nearly four full seasons in the navy. In his prime, Johnson had strikeout ratios of 7.6 and 7.4 per nine innings in the only two seasons he fanned 300 batters (1910 and 1912); the major-league average both years was about four Ks per nine innings. And leading the league in Ks three times between 1921 and 1924, Walter Johnson was the one Deadball Era pitcher who remained among the most proficient strikeout pitchers in the beginning years of the Lively Ball Era.

* * *

Pitchers no longer had the upper hand in baseball's post–World War I landscape. Beginning in 1920, major-league owners agreed to enforce rules predating the twentieth century that prohibited players from "damaging" the baseball, defining the prohibition to include not only deliberately scuffing the ball, but putting saliva on it. The move was almost certainly intended to eliminate an unfair advantage for pitchers over batters at a time when baseball's lifeblood—the fans—were growing ever more excited by higher-scoring games, and owners were intent on picking up attendance after a decade that featured both a deep recession and a world war. While damaging the surface of the ball was outlawed outright, each team in 1920 was allowed a maximum of two pitchers permitted to throw a "spitball." Following the 1920 season, any doctoring of the ball—including with saliva—was banned, except for a select handful of veteran Deadball Era pitchers whose career success depended on the spitball, a group that included historically outstanding pitchers such as Stan Coveleski, Red Faber, Burleigh Grimes, and Urban Shocker.

In dramatic contrast to the twenty-first century, when strikeouts have never been higher, strikeouts during the Roaring Twenties were at their lowest sustained level since current strike rules were adopted by both leagues in 1903. Even though this was the decade Babe Ruth busted loose, giving swinging for the fences—and the attendant risk of going down swinging instead—the good-baseball seal approval (although John McGraw, Ty Cobb, and a host of other "traditionalists" who favored the practice of "scientific" baseball surely did not approve), there was no year in the 1920s in which the strikeout rate was as high as even three per nine innings. The only pitcher to strike out as many as 200 batters in a season was Brooklyn's Dazzy Vance, who did so three times. Until the war-shortened seasons of 1918 and 1919, by contrast, there was at least one pitcher every year in the Deadball Era with 200 strikeouts, except for 1906 when Waddell just missed with 196.

The decline in strikeouts to 2.8 per game for each team from an average of 3.9 in the last decade of the Deadball Era (not including the war-shortened 1918 and 1919 seasons) can be attributed to several factors. Besides baseball's institutional banishing of the spitball and other deviously treacherous pitches in 1920, the tragic hit-by-pitch death of Ray Chapman in August that year led to replacing baseballs whenever grass and dirt stains made them too difficult to see. Meanwhile, the higher-quality wool available after World War I and enhanced manufacturing processes allowed baseballs to be more tightly wound. Finally, even though more batters took pleasure in adopting Ruth's slugger mind-set, except for the Babe, most were still embarrassed about striking out too often, and once they had two strikes on them, they were more concerned with putting the ball in play than swinging for the fences.

No year in which a full 154-game schedule was played had as few Ks in the official scorebooks as the 6,643 batters who went down on strikes in 1924. Ruth led the major leagues with 46 home runs and 391 total bases. Brooklyn first baseman Jack Fournier led the National League with 27 round-trippers. In all, there were four players in the NL and two in the AL who hit more than 20 homers, and there were an additional eight players with 15 or more triples—still the long-ball currency in the big leagues. In the midst of the Ruth-instigated Lively Ball Era, the power numbers in 1924—896 home runs, 1,175 triples, and 25 percent of all hits going for extra bases—although down somewhat from the previous three years, suggested that big-league hitters were swinging away at the plate. Yet pitchers averaged a record-low 2.7 batters rung up for every nine innings of work. Only 7 percent of the 95,391 plate appearances in the major leagues in 1924 resulted in a walk back to the dugout by a strikeout victim. Ruth's 81 strikeouts were by far the most in baseball. The Cubs' George Grantham came closest to the Babe's mark, striking out 63 times, and just five players overall struck out as many as 60 times.

Only six pitchers struck out more than 100 batters in 1924, four of them in the American League. The leading K practitioner in the junior circuit was Washington's 36-year-old Walter Johnson, whose 158 strike-outs in 277⅔ innings gave him an average of 5.1 Ks per nine innings. Finishing a distant second in strikeouts was Boston's Howard Ehmke with 119, and the Yankees' Bob Shawkey (114) and Herb Pennock (101) were third and fourth. Shawkey was the only qualifying pitcher in the league to approach Johnson in strikeout ratio that season, with 4.9 Ks per nine innings; Ehmke averaged 3.4, and the lefty Pennock averaged 3.2 per nine innings in the only year of his Hall of Fame career that he fanned as many as 100 batters.

While Johnson's 158 Ks came in the twilight of his career, baseball's premier strikeout pitcher in 1924 was Dazzy Vance in his breakout season. Not much younger than Johnson at 33 years old, and long beset by arm problems, Vance had resurrected his going-nowhere career the two previous years with back-to-back 18-win seasons, leading the National League in strikeouts both times with 134 and 197. But in 1924, he went 28–6 and led the league in strikeouts with a phenomenal—for the time— 262 in 308⅓ innings pitched. His strikeout ratio of 7.6 per nine innings approached nearly three times the major-league average that year, and exceeded Johnson's by almost 50 percent.

Vance by himself accounted for nearly 8 percent of all punchouts by National League pitchers, and he struck out 104 more batters—the equivalent of three complete games and 7⅔ innings of a fourth—than Walter Johnson, second in the majors in strikeouts. Second in the league with just over half as many Ks as Vance was teammate Burleigh Grimes with 135, and third was Cincinnati's Dolf Luque with all of 86 strikeouts. A grizzled eight-year veteran in the major leagues, but actually, at 30, two and a half years younger than Vance, Grimes had the advantage of being grandfathered in as a practitioner of the spitball when the pitch was outlawed, which probably helped him get batters to swing and miss.

The fact that the Dodgers, then known as the Robins, had the National League's top two strikeout pitchers goes a long way to explaining how Brooklyn was suddenly competitive in 1924, finishing second with a 92–62 record, 1½ games behind the Giants, after coming home sixth with a 76–78 record each of the two previous years. Paced by the 397 Ks courtesy of Vance and Grimes, Brooklyn's 638 strikeouts in 1924 accounted for 19 percent of the National League total. The fourth-place Reds were a distant second with 451 strikeouts. Getting 15 percent of their outs by way of the strikeout, compared to less than 10 percent for the seven other NL teams, meant needing fewer outs in the field—about two per game, on average—reducing the opportunities for hits to sneak through, to fall between fielders, and for defensive miscues. This was important for Brooklyn because the Robins were a poor defensive team and had limited range; their 197 errors were third most in the league, consistent with their fielding percentage being the third worst, and their defensive efficiency in making outs on only 68.4 percent of balls put into play was below the league average.

Dazzling Dazzy's dominance in the strike zone in 1924 has no equal in two respects. First, his 262 strikeouts being nearly two-thirds more than the 158 racked up by Walter Johnson is the largest difference ever between baseball's strikeout leader and the runner-up. Within his own league, Vance had nearly double the 135 strikeouts recorded for second best by Grimes. Furthermore, no pitcher other than Vance has ever approached being 50 percent better than his closest rival for strikeouts per nine innings; Dazzy fanned 49 percent more batters per nine innings than the Big Train in 1924. Johnson would have needed 78 more Ks for the 277⅔ innings he pitched, or approximately two additional strikeouts per start, to match Vance in strikeout proficiency. For the 310⅔ innings he pitched, Grimes would have needed to fan 127 more batters, approximately 3.5 per start, to keep pace with Dazzy's strikeout ratio. The next year, Vance's strikeout ratio was 41 percent better than major-league runner-up Lefty Grove, giving him three consecutive seasons in which his was at least one-third higher than the pitcher with the second-best mark; he had been 33 percent better than Johnson in 1923.

The pitcher who came closest to Vance's 1924 record for outdistancing the runner-up in strikeout ratio was the California Angels' Nolan Ryan in 1973. The 1973 "Ryan Express" topped Sandy Koufax's single-season strikeout record, set just eight years before, by one with 383, and Ryan might well have fanned more than 400 had this not been the first year in the American League that pitchers did not have to bat for themselves because of the new designated-hitter rule. Ryan's ratio of 10.6 Ks per nine innings that year was exactly double the major-league average, but only 36 percent better than runner-up Tom Seaver's 7.8 strikeout ratio in the National League, still far short of Dazzy's 1924 standard for K dominance.

Lefty Grove displaced Vance as the premier power pitcher in the game in the late 1920s, and historically his fastball's fame has eclipsed that of Vance. But for all his acclaim in blowing batters away with a fastball some said was better than Walter Johnson's in his prime, and notwithstanding his leading the American League in strikeouts in each of his first seven years in the big time, Grove never struck out more than 32 percent more batters than the league's runner-up—in 1928, with 183 to 139 by the Yankees' George Pipgras. Grove led the majors in strikeouts only three times, never had the best strikeout ratio in the major leagues (although he did in the American League five times), and only three times averaged as many as six strikeouts per nine innings. Despite completing two-thirds of his starts when he was in his prime with the Philadelphia Athletics, only once in his career did Grove reach 200 strikeouts in a season. Vance cracked the 200-K barrier in three different years, all when strikeouts were hard to come by for pitchers.

Waddell. Johnson. Grove. And still to come—Bob Feller, Koufax, Sam McDowell, Ryan, Dwight "Doctor K" Gooden, Roger Clemens, Pedro Martinez, Randy Johnson, Clayton Kershaw, Max Scherzer. Their names are synonymous with "overpowering strikeout pitcher." (There are others, of course.) Even as time marches on, their names are not forgotten because each has been a standard against which subsequent generations of strikeout pitchers are measured. Relative to their peers, however, none of them, nor any other pitcher, was as dominant striking out batters in any single season as Dazzy Vance in 1924. And he pitched in the toughest year to strike out batters.

* * *

While certainly not heralded at the time and probably not even realized for many years thereafter, 1924 was also a pivotal year in the history of relief pitching. It was the year the Washington Senators introduced hard-throwing right-hander Firpo Marberry as their relief ace and kept him in that role in the years ahead despite his clearly having the ability to succeed as a top-flight starting pitcher. Using Marberry in this way had just one somewhat inexact precedent. The only pitcher prior to Marberry to have been used primarily as a relief pitcher for an extended number of years was Doc Crandall by John McGraw from 1909 to 1913, and he was not nearly as good a pitcher as Marberry and, moreover, started nearly 30 percent of the games he pitched. From 1924 to 1928, Marberry started only 15 percent of his games.

By the 1920s, the importance of relief pitching was accepted baseball wisdom. What was not was the concept of developing pitchers exclusively for a role as a game savior in the bullpen. Since the beginning of baseball time, pitchers were groomed and expected to be starting pitchers. Except possibly by McGraw with Crandall, no thought was given to the idea of relief pitching being its own discipline. With the percentage of complete games having only gradually declined from about 60 percent in the early teens to about 50 percent in the early 1920s, and with 70 to 75 percent of all victories being complete games, there was not a significant requirement to have a stable of relievers in an established bullpen. Many of the new generation of starting pitchers apprenticed as relievers in their first one or two big-league seasons and sometimes pitched several more years both starting and relieving before either becoming full-time starters who might occasionally be used in relief between starts to win or save ballgames (typically mediocre journeymen pitchers in both roles) or failing to make the major-league grade. Up to now, those who pitched primarily out of the bullpen were, with all due respect to Crandall, no-names who did not last long at the big-league level.

All that changed with Firpo Marberry, although the seed for a dedicated relief ace in Washington was planted the previous year, probably under team owner Clark Griffith's direction. As manager of the Highlanders in the first decade of the century, Griffith was one of baseball's pioneers in the use of relief pitchers, although not so much to "save" victories as his contemporary McGraw was doing, as to replace starters who were having a bad day. Just before spring training in 1923, Griffith acquired right-hander Allen Russell from the Red Sox. An eight-year veteran with 119 relief appearances to go along with 105 starts, Russell was turned into a full-time reliever in Washington, not just to mop up, but to win and save games. He appeared in 52 games, five of which were starts spaced out approximately a month apart. His 47 relief appearances were the most ever by a pitcher coming in from the bullpen. In that role, Russell went 9–3, led the league with 9 saves, and had the best year of his career based on pitching wins above replacement.

Positioned to play the same role in 1924, Russell proved not nearly as effective as the previous year, causing the Senators to quickly turn to hard-throwing rookie right-hander Marberry as their ace in the bullpen. Beginning the season as a spot starter otherwise resident in the bullpen, Marberry probably assumed he was auditioning for a role ultimately as a front-line starter by first proving himself as a reliever. There was, after all, little future for a pitcher perceived to be *only* a reliever, but there was one for Marberry in Washington. Marberry pitched well in a starting role; in 14 starts he threw six complete games and had a 5–6 record and 3.66 earned run average. But as Washington's ace reliever, he was even better, averaging nearly three innings in his 36 relief appearances with a 6–6 record, 15 saves, and 2.82 ERA. Unknown at the time because the "save" was not an official statistic—and would not become one until 1969—his 15 saves set a new major-league record. Most tellingly, Marberry got 20 percent of his outs as a reliever by strikeout, compared to less than 10 percent in his starts. His performance as their relief ace was indispensable to the Senators winning their first pennant in a tight race to the end with the Yankees. And the powerful right-hander's reward was . . . to stay on in the role of master in the bullpen . . . all the way until 1929, a year he started 26 games but relieved in 23 others, leading the league with nine saves.

Although he did not get a single start in 1925, Marberry relieved in 55 of the Senators' 152 games, going 9–5 with 16 saves. Indicative of his value in the bullpen, Marberry had a ratio of 5.1 strikeouts per nine innings—19 percent of his total outs—which was nearly double the 2.7 strikeout ratio for American League pitchers as a whole. The next year he saved 22 in 59 relief appearances. Those 22 saves would stand as the record for 23 years until the Yankees' Joe Page saved 27 in 1949. By the end of the 1928 season, Marberry had pitched in 284 major-league games, 240 of them in relief. Five consecutive years pitching primarily in relief, averaging 47 games coming out of the bullpen, was unprecedented, especially for a pitcher with Marberry's talent and success. No other team had ever invested as many years on a single high-quality pitcher to be primarily a reliever.

Had he not spent his formative years almost exclusively as a reliever, Firpo Marberry would likely have been hailed as one of the best pitchers in baseball from the mid-1920s to early 1930s. When he became primarily a starting pitcher in 1929, Marberry immediately showed he could excel in *that* role, not just out of the pen, although his strikeout ratio of 6.5 per nine innings was far higher in the 23 games he pitched in relief compared to 3.9 in his 26 starts. For the rest of his career, Marberry excelled in the dual role of mostly starting, but also frequently being called upon to save the day in relief when necessary. He won 70 percent

Fred Marberry pitcher
"Firpo"

F. Marberry

Washington relief ace Firpo Marberry in 1925. Marberry was the first high-quality pitcher to be used as a dedicated relief ace for multiple seasons. *National Photo Company Collection (Library of Congress).*

of his decisions as a starter between 1929 and 1933 and saved 33 as a reliever, leading the league three times in saves. This was in fact the paradigm that began with the likes of Three Finger Brown and Ed Walsh, although Marberry was never such an elite pitcher. And it was the paradigm that still prevailed in the major leagues despite Marberry having shown the value of having a high-quality pitcher as ace reliever.

After the Senators with Marberry, it wasn't until the Yankees did so with Johnny Murphy in 1935 that another team specifically developed a young talented pitcher to be their relief ace and kept him in that role for many years to come. Although managers by now recognized the value of having a relief corps, they continued to rely on starting pitchers to close out victories rather than use their designated relief pitchers for such an important task. The pitchers who worked primarily out of the bullpen as designated relievers spent much if not most of their time replacing starting pitchers who were knocked out early or working in games that were lost causes.

If teams were not receptive to the idea of using talented young pitchers like Marberry in relief roles for very long before making them starters, they increasingly did see value in extending the careers of proven, reliable veteran pitchers by making them primarily relievers—which did not necessarily mean relief "ace" to win or save close games. While no longer having the speed on their pitches or the physical stamina to be effective as starters, older pitchers could draw on their experience and veteran savvy from good work in their younger years to be productive in the bullpen. In his 48th and 49th year on planet Earth, for example, grizzled veteran Jack Quinn, whose rookie season was 1909, extended his major-league career as Brooklyn's relief ace in 1931 and '32, leading the National League in saves both years; Red Faber closed out his great career with the White Sox as a reliever in 1932 and '33 when he was 43 and 44; and the no-longer-quite-so-dazzling Vance spent the last three years of his august career, beginning when he was 42, pitching mostly out of the bullpen for the Cardinals in '33 and '34 and the Dodgers in 1935.

* * *

While the economy of the United States of America was in a devastating depression in 1930, hitting in Major League Baseball surely was not. Since the turn of the century, baseball had not seen anything like the offensive explosion in 1930. Major-league pitchers had a collective earned run average of 4.81, with Washington's 3.96 the only team ERA below 4.00. Four teams had an ERA over 5.00. Grove and Vance were the only qualifying pitchers with an earned run average under 3.00. Even for the time, the hitting assault on pitchers that year was an anomaly. It turned out to be the peak of the Lively Ball Era.

Probably without deliberate intent to help pitchers, a new baseball was introduced in 1931 with raised stitches that made the ball easier to grip and manipulate on release. Whatever the reason, batting averages quickly dropped to the levels that prevailed through most of the 1920s, but it was in fact still a hitters' era, in some ways—specifically home runs—more pronounced than during the Roaring Twenties. The game settled on a relative balance between batters and pitchers where the major-league batting average was typically between .275 and .279—only once going above .280, in 1936—and collective earned run averages were around 4.25—only once going below 4.00, in 1933. There would be no return to Deadball Era–like pitching dominance to offset the Ruth revolution, at least not until a few years in the mid-1960s.

Part III

Empire Building in the Lively Ball Era

20

ST. LOUIS—GATEWAY CITY TO THE BOTTOM OF BOTH LEAGUES

They call St. Louis the "Gateway City." Just beyond the Cardinals' new stadium, which opened in 2006, is the Gateway Arch, built to commemorate the trail west for pioneer settlers in the mid-1800s as the United States fulfilled its manifest destiny of westward expansion. In 1925 there was no Arch, and St. Louis was both the westernmost and southernmost geographic scope of Major League Baseball, and that only because it was well served by rail. The closest other big-league city was Chicago, 300 miles to the north; Cincinnati was about 350 miles to the east. After Cincinnati in 1919, Cleveland in 1920, and Washington, DC, just the previous year, St. Louis was also the only major-league city since the advent of the World Series in 1903, 22 years before, that had not yet been privileged to host baseball's premier event, and its two major-league teams were the only franchises in their respective leagues not to have participated in the fall classic. All 14 other major-league teams had been to the World Series at least once. Even worse, only once had either St. Louis team even come close.

The National League St. Louis Cardinals and the American League St. Louis Browns were, at this point, arguably the two worst teams in the history of the game since 1901. In the quarter century from 1901 to 1925, the Cardinals finished fourth or higher in the National League only six times, and never better than third; they had a winning record just eight times. As for the Browns, in 24 years since 1902, when they replaced Milwaukee in the American League, St. Louis finished fourth or better in the American League seven times and had a winning record in seven seasons. That's 15 St. Louis teams that ended their schedule with a winning record in 49 baseball seasons between them.

* * *

The Cardinals trace their lineage back to 1882 when they were the "Browns" in the American Association during the 10 years that league competed with the NL as a major league. The *original* Browns had a distinguished history. Unless one counts the Boston Red Stockings in the pre–National League era, the 1885–88 Browns, managed by their star first baseman Charlie Comiskey, were the first major-league team to win four consecutive pennants, all but the last by robust double-digit margins. When the eight-team American Association folded after the 1891 season, St. Louis was one of four franchises picked up by the National League, which expanded to 12 clubs as part of the settlement to consolidate a single "major" league. The Browns were dismal their first seven years in the National League. The best they did in the standings was ninth, in 1894. The four years after that, the Browns won just slightly over a quarter of their games with a cumulative winning percentage of .271.

The franchise-saving turning point came in 1899 when Cleveland Spiders owners Frank and Stanley Robison were allowed, even encouraged, by the league's tolerance for syndicate ownership to rescue the Browns from financial insolvency. With two franchises to call their own, the Robison brothers wasted no time in denuding their relatively competitive team in Cleveland of all its best players—most notably pitching great Cy Young, outfielder Jesse Burkett, and shortstop Bobby Wallace, not to mention a host of others, including player-manager Patsy Tebeau. Fortified by Cleveland's regulars, St. Louis went from last place and just 39 wins in 1898 to fifth place and 84 wins in 1899. With the Spiders' star players now safely in St. Louis, the Cleveland franchise was disbanded in the NL's 1900 contraction to a more economically viable eight teams. St. Louis survived the downsizing, took on the name "Cardinals," and even had John McGraw and Wilbert Robinson—refugees from Baltimore, where the Orioles were also eliminated—at third base and as backup catcher in 1900.

But the Cardinals' good fortune in quality players was short lived. St. Louis was hit hard by the upstart American League's raids on National League teams to give the infant league "major" credibility. Most notably in 1901, Cy Young defected to the new AL team in Boston, and McGraw and Robinson went to Baltimore. Then it got much worse. The American League's abandonment of Milwaukee in favor of St. Louis in 1902 to compete in yet a fourth National League city—Boston, Philadelphia, and Chicago were the first three—spelled competitive doom for the Cardinals. Peace was yet to be negotiated between the two leagues, and the AL still considered it open season on NL players, especially the good ones.

The new American League franchise in St. Louis picked up the nickname "Browns" to remind St. Louis fans of the Charlie Comiskey championship era. In addition, league president Ban Johnson made the strategic choice that former Spiders star outfielder Jimmy McAleer should manage the Browns, notwithstanding that he was already managing the AL entry in Cleveland. McAleer had retired as a player in 1898 when it became clear the Spiders were on the chopping block and the Robisons were sending their best players to their *other* team in St. Louis and was quickly recruited by Johnson for his new, still "minor" league the next year. Johnson wanted McAleer for the manager's job in St. Louis precisely because, as Cleveland's manager both before and after the American League proclaimed itself a "major" league, he was so good at luring established National League players to the new league.

McAleer did not disappoint Johnson's expectations in St. Louis. He went after the Cardinals' best players with a vengeance, many of whom he knew from their days together on the Spiders. No fewer than seven core regulars were robbed from the Cardinals to play for the Browns. Getting Burkett and Wallace to jump leagues but stay in St. Louis was a particular coup for McAleer. Although he was nearing the end of his career and had already made his case for the future Hall of Fame, Burkett was still an outstanding player and had just won his third batting title in 1901. Wallace, on the other hand, was just beginning what would also be a Hall of Fame career. The roster makeover of the AL team that had been in Milwaukee with players from the Cardinals was so comprehensive it is arguable whether it was even a franchise "move," as opposed to the termination of one franchise and the beginning of another. Only two players of consequence from Milwaukee's Brewers—first baseman John Anderson and reserve Bill Friel—played for the Browns in their inaugural season.

* * *

The effect was immediate for both St. Louis franchises. Thanks to the infusion of former Cardinals players, the American League Browns finished second to Philadelphia's Athletics in 1902, their first year in St. Louis. The very next year, however, the Browns began their historical pattern of lost-cause seasons on their way to becoming one of the worst franchises in the twentieth century before moving to Baltimore in 1954. The National League Cardinals, meanwhile, who had finished fourth with a winning record in 1901, plunged to sixth in 1902 after being plundered by McAleer and the Browns, and finished last in 1903. They would not have a winning record again until 1911, finishing an average of 48 games out of first place during that time. They were outscored every year until

1914, scoring the fewest runs four times and giving up the most runs eight times.

With their best players working for the other team in St. Louis, the Cardinals were hamstrung the rest of the decade by their pitching staff being in a constant state of flux and persistent turnover of their starting position players. The Cardinals did have a promising rookie named Mordecai Brown in 1903, but the pitcher known as "Three Finger" was traded to the Cubs after going 9–13 for veteran righty Jack Taylor, who was dogged by allegations he was "not an honest player." And until first baseman Ed Konetchy reached that total in 1910, the only Cardinal to play as many as 500 games that decade was Homer Smoot, their center fielder from 1902 to July 1906. Making his debut in June 1907, Konetchy was the first legitimate star to play for the Cardinals since the Spiders' stars were sent to St. Louis, and none of *them* had stayed very long. A potent hitter in the Deadball Era, "Big Ed" rarely missed a game and by 1909 had displaced Frank Chance as the best all-around first baseman in the National League, if not all of baseball.

In 1907, with Frank Robison in ill health and frustrated by the Cardinals' inability to get better, Stan Robison secured most of his brother's shares in the franchise. Two years later, he tried importing some of that old McGraw magic by making a deal for Giants catcher Roger Bresnahan to become his club's player-manager. While never competitive, the Cardinals under Bresnahan began showing improvement, increasing their win total each of his first three years as manager from 1909 to 1911. There was now also more continuity among both pitchers and core position regulars from one year to the next. The acquisition of second baseman Miller Huggins from Cincinnati in 1910, all 5-foot-6 of him, proved to be by far the Cardinals' most consequential move in the Bresnahan years, and not just because he got on base in more than 40 percent of his plate appearances with St. Louis. After the Cardinals regressed from a winning record to 90 losses in 1912 and the fiery, impolitic Bresnahan ran afoul of Helene Robison Britton—Frank Robison's daughter, who had inherited the franchise when Uncle Stanley died the previous year—it was Huggins she named the new manager.

The Cardinals slid further back in Huggins's first year in charge, losing 99 games and finishing last, before becoming unexpectedly competitive in 1914 to finish third. They led the league with an earned run average nearly two full runs lower than in 1913, but reverted back to being a much-scored upon team in 1915, giving up more runs than they scored even though they were first in scoring. Ending up fifth, St. Louis was back in the second tier of National League teams. It got even worse in 1916 when they finished seventh. The one bright spot was the debut of Rogers Hornsby at shortstop. By his second year in 1917, Hornsby was a bona fide star. His .327 batting average was second in the league, his 9.9 wins above replacement was the best of any National League player since Honus Wagner in 1908, and the Cardinals improved by 22 wins to have just their third winning season since 1901.

Despite leading the Cardinals into third place with their most victories since 1899, Huggins left St. Louis after the 1917 season in disagreement with the philosophy and methods of the Cardinals' new president, Branch Rickey. Notwithstanding his differences with Rickey, Huggins was considered to be one of baseball's best managers. His success in turning around the competitive fortunes of the National League's most dismal franchise sufficiently raised his profile such that when the New York Yankees were looking for a new manager to take over in 1918 . . . well, the rest of the Miller Huggins story is the beginning of the Yankees dynasty.

* * *

After registering as nothing more than an afterthought following their relatively successful 1902 first year in St. Louis, the Browns were a surprising player in the *other* Great Race in '08—the one in the American League. McAleer had them in first place as late as mid-July and the Browns were still in the thick of the pennant race, trailing the Tigers by a half-game, on September 7. But losing nine of their next 12 games, all against pennant-race rivals, dropped the Browns to fourth, which would be their final resting place for the 1908 season, 6½ games off the pace. Their 83–69 record was the complete opposite of 1907, when they were 69–83 and finished sixth. For whatever it's worth, the Browns played well against the *real* competitors for the 1908 American League pennant, finishing 10–12 against first-place Detroit, 11–11 against second-place Cleveland, and 10–11 against third-place Chicago. The cornerstone players on the 1908 Browns were shortstop Bobby Wallace, indisputably their best player, and left fielder George Stone. Having already won a batting title by beating out Napoleon Lajoie, .358 to .355, in 1906, his second year in the majors, Stone led the Browns in virtually every batting category in 1908. With George Davis by now at the end of his career, there was no question Wallace was the best all-around shortstop in the American League; he was one of the first to master the quickness and efficiency of fielding and throwing in a single, fluid motion—the speed of which greatly facilitated executing double plays and throwing batter-runners out at first on slow infield rollers.

Age, however, compromised the Browns' immediate future. With six of their eight core position players and their top two pitchers 32 or older, the Browns plummeted to seventh place in 1909. Wallace, now 35 years old, had one of the worst seasons of his career, plagued by nagging injuries that caused him to miss 38 games. Done in by a severe ankle turn, the 32-year-old Stone played just 83 games in 1909 and was never again the same. The ankle injury and persistent arm problems that allowed baserunners to take liberties on hits to his section of the outfield derailed his promising career, which came to an end in 1910. Ironically, as often happens, however weak and inaccurate his pained throwing arm may have been in his final big-league season, Stone in 145 games had the most assists and fewest errors in his career as baserunners were perhaps too reckless in trying to exploit his debilities for an extra base.

Jimmy McAleer stepping down as manager after his team's 1909 implosion sent the Browns into an extended period of managerial instability hardly helped by the fact that they were not a very good team. Not once did the Browns escape the second division in the teens, and 1916 was their only winning season between 1908 and 1920. The team went through six different managers in that time, including a baseball egghead named Branch Rickey for two years. After McAleer, the St. Louis Browns did not have another manager survive for even as many as four complete seasons until Luke Sewell from 1940 to 1946. On two different occasions, third baseman Jimmy Austin, known for his leadership on the field, served as interim manager to give the Browns the week or two they needed to find a suitable replacement for the guy they had just fired. A late bloomer—he was 29 when he broke into the majors in 1909—Austin epitomizes the many players over the years with modest ability who had a decade-or-longer career because of their work ethic, unwavering hustle, and incessant observation of the game to grow their baseball IQ.

The Browns may have broken the .500 plateau only once in the teens, but they did have some quality players even after Wallace was relegated to a supporting role in 1913. Del Pratt, their second baseman from 1912 to 1917, was probably the best player at his position in the American League after Eddie Collins; Burt Shotton, their center fielder from 1911 to 1917, was a skillful leadoff batter with good plate discipline and base-stealing speed; and then, of course, there was . . . George Sisler.

If Bobby Wallace was the Browns' first great player, George Sisler was their first superstar. Brought up by Rickey in June 1915, Sisler quickly became baseball's premier first baseman. Having already hit .341 in his first five years, Sisler got into the spirit of the new era Babe Ruth inaugurated in 1920 by not only winning the batting title with a .407 mark while setting the new major-league record for hits in a single season with 257—which was more shades of Ty Cobb's style of play—but ramped up his power game with 19 homers, second to the Babe's 54, and 122 RBIs, second to Ruth's 137. He also gained a reputation for defensive excellence at first base that has carried forth to this day. None of the advanced modern metrics, however, support such a reputation; Bill James gives George Sisler a grade of C− for defense.

* * *

The beginning of the Babe Ruth era turned out to be the best of times for the St. Louis Browns, notwithstanding they did not win a single pennant. From 1921 to 1925, the Browns won 404 games and lost 361 for a not particularly impressive .528 winning percentage, and they had back-to-back losing seasons with identical 74–78 records in 1923 and '24, but those proved ultimately to be the five best years in franchise history before they moved to Baltimore in 1954 to become the Orioles, even taking into account the pennant the Browns won in 1944 when major-league rosters were decimated by players serving in World War II. The 1921–25 Browns finished third twice and in 1922 came close to winning the American League pennant, losing out to the Yankees by a single game. Their 93 wins that year was a franchise record, unmatched by the 1944 pennant-winning Browns, until the Orioles won 95 in 1961.

Their 1922 pennant run was presaged by a strong finish the previous year, when the Browns surged from a game out of last place in mid-July to finish third—their highest standing since second place in their first St. Louis season 19 years before—with 81 wins, just two short of the 83 games they won in 1908. Right-hander Urban Shocker, in his sixth big-league season, was the player most responsible for the Browns' dramatic turn of fortune in 1921. After being shell-shocked by the Yankees on July 13 left him with a middling 10–9 record and the Browns seemingly doomed to another losing season, Shocker became virtually unbeatable, winning 17 of his last 20 decisions to finish with a 27–12 record, confirming his status as one of baseball's elite pitchers.

Still, nobody expected the Browns to challenge the Yankees, or even second-place Cleveland, for the pennant in 1922. But they did. The Browns certainly benefited from the Yankees having to endure the simultaneous suspensions of Babe Ruth and Bob Meusel for the first five weeks of the season, the penalty imposed by Commissioner Landis for their unauthorized barnstorming following the 1921 World Series. To whatever extent the Browns were able to capitalize on their unavailability to the Yankees, it wasn't enough to put them in first place; they were second to New York, trailing by two games when Ruth and Meusel returned to action. Quite surprisingly, from the Babe's return on May 20 till the end of the season, St. Louis actually had a better record than New York—alas, by just one game, which was one too few to have forced a playoff for the pennant, and two short of winning the pennant outright.

The Browns were able to compete with the Yankees all summer because they led the league in virtually every offensive category—runs, hits, extra-base hits, on-base percentage, batting average, slugging percentage, even stolen bases. Only five American League batters drove in more than 100 runs in 1922, and four of them were St. Louis Browns. Not even the Yankees had a 100-RBI guy. The Browns also hit more home runs than the Yankees, 98 to 95, although it was next-to-last Philadelphia that led the league. Sisler hit .420 to win his second batting crown in three years. He also topped the league with 134 runs, 246 hits, 18 triples, and 51 stolen bases. Left fielder Ken Williams, part of an outfield including William "Baby Doll" Jacobson in center and Jack Tobin in right that had been together since 1919 and would be until 1926, was first in homers with 39—Ruth, playing in only 110 games, hit 35—total bases with 367, and runs batted in with 155. As a left-handed hitter, Williams batted cleanup against right-handers but sixth in manager Lee Fohl's batting order whenever a southpaw started against the Browns; his home-run percentage was about the same against both lefties and righties. Jacobson, who otherwise hit fifth in the lineup, usually batted fourth instead of Williams when a lefty started and was one of the four Browns to drive in 100 runs. Tobin, the Browns' leadoff batter, had his third of four straight 200-hit seasons.

The 1922 Browns, however, just could not beat the 1922 Yankees. Losing 14 of their 22 games to the Yankees is the reason why the St. Louis Browns had to wait another 22 years before finally playing in a World Series. In the second half of the season, every time the Browns had a chance to boost their slim lead over the Yankees, they failed to do so. They had a 1½-game lead on July 11 going into New York, but lost two of three to see their lead reduced to a half-game. The next time the two teams met in St. Louis at the end of July, the Browns still in first place, again by 1½ games, Shocker pitched a shutout in the opener of the four-game series to extend their lead, but the Yankees won the next three to leave Sportsman's Park with a half-game lead. It was the same story when the two clubs next met in a four-game series at the Polo Grounds in late August, the Browns once again on top, this time by a half-game. Shocker once again won the first game and the Yankees once again took the next three, leaving the Browns 1½ games behind in a squandered opportunity. The Yankees paid a final visit to St. Louis for three games in mid-September, coming in with a half-game lead, won two of three, and left the Gateway City with a 1½-game edge that effectively sealed the Browns' fate.

The decisive factor in the pennant race was that the Yankees had all-around better pitching and defense. The Yankees had a pair of 20-game winners in Bullet Joe Bush (26–7) and Bob Shawkey (20–12), as well as Waite Hoyt with a 19–12 record. The Browns' top-tier ace Urban Shocker, with a 24–17 record, was as good as, perhaps even better than, any of the Yankees' starters, but the St. Louis staff behind him was far less imposing. Elam Vangilder, a righty with a 19–13 record, was the only other Browns pitcher to win more than 14 games or throw more than 200 innings. Shocker himself struggled in the final month. After beating the Yankees for his 21st win on August 25, Shocker won only three of his last eight starts, losing twice to New York. The Browns outscored the Yankees 300 runs to 239 in the final month, but failed to score more than three runs in any of Shocker's five losses. In two games that he lost, Shocker did not give up a single earned run, and in two other losses he gave up just two.

The Browns were unable to replicate any of their 1922 success the following year, the major reason being the absence of George Sisler for the entire season with a lack of visual acuity said at the time to have been caused by a sinus infection. Although Shocker had a fourth straight 20-win season, the Browns without Sisler were out of the running by the end of May. They finished fifth. It would take a second world war and the disruption that that caused to major-league rosters before the St. Louis Browns again competed for the pennant.

* * *

While the Browns were returning to the nether regions of the American League after their one best shot for a pennant fell just short in 1922, the other St. Louis team—the Cardinals—were on an upslope, although it wouldn't have appeared so looking at their seeming regression from finishing third in both 1921 and 1922 to out-of-the-running fifth, sixth, and fourth the next three years.

But the Redbirds, they were arising.

Branch Rickey was the architect, Sam Breadon the enabler, and Rogers Hornsby, now playing second base, the cornerstone player.

It didn't take much persuading by a civic group of St. Louis businessmen to entice Rickey, the Browns' former manager who was then in the front office with little in the way of influence with their new owner, to go in with them in buying the financially struggling Cardinals when Helene Britton put the franchise up for sale in 1917. He being the one baseball professional in the group, Rickey was named team president and took responsibility for all baseball operations. After two years in charge of the front office and a short stint in Europe during World War I, Rickey returned in 1919 to find that Breadon had upped his financial stake in the Cardinals to become the principal owner and named himself team president, displacing Rickey. Breadon knew what he didn't know about baseball, however, and gave Rickey free rein to continue running the team as he had been, both in the front office with the title of vice president and in the dugout as the Cardinals' new manager following their 1918 last-place debacle.

With Breadon's full backing, including the needed monetary support, Rickey set about transforming the makeup and culture of the St. Louis Cardinals from losers who had never won anything to a franchise that would win nine National League pennants and six World Series in 21 years between 1926 and 1946. As the principal baseball executive, Branch Rickey was the mastermind of the farm system that revolutionized the business of evaluating and developing players as a self-sustaining investment by the parent major-league club. As both manager and executive, Rickey emphasized teaching and developing skills at every level of the Cardinals' system, so that his players were well schooled in fundamentals. Beginning with their first pennant in 1926, the Cardinals fashioned a legacy that remains to this day of teams that play fundamentally sound baseball and know how to win by being pesky and gritty even when they do not dominate the league.

And as the manager, Rickey brought the Cardinals a newfound respectability. Finishing third behind McGraw's Giants in both 1921 and 1922, the Rickey Cardinals probably overachieved for the quality players they had. They finished fifth in 1923, barely over .500, plummeted to sixth the next year with 89 losses, and were buried in last place on May 30, 1925, with a terrible 13–25 record when Sam Breadon told Branch Rickey that he was changing managers so that Rickey could focus on doing what he was best at—setting the strategic direction of the franchise, including player development through the minor-league clubs he had begun to acquire in 1920. Rickey was sufficiently miffed that he sold his shares in the franchise to Breadon and his replacement as manager, second baseman Rogers Hornsby. Rather than leave St. Louis, however, Rickey settled down to secure the first part of his enduring baseball legacy as the founding father of minor-league farm systems.

Rogers Hornsby was baseball's greatest player in the 1920s, excepting of course the one and only Babe Ruth. From 1920 to 1925, Hornsby hit .397 with 153 homers and 692 runs batted in. Granted that it was the beginning years of the Lively Ball Era, but no player in history before or since has ever hit for a higher average over a similar stretch; Ty Cobb, who hit .393 from 1909 to 1914, comes the closest. Hornsby led the league in batting all six years, including three .400 seasons, with a career high of .424 in 1924—the highest single-season average since Napoleon Lajoie hit .426 in 1901, a year that foul balls didn't count as strikes. Hornsby also led the league in on-base percentage and slugging percentage all six years. He was first in hits four times and likely would have had six consecutive years with more than 200 hits had he not been limited to only 107 games in 1923 because of injury. He led the National League in

Branch Rickey as a first-year manager with the St. Louis Browns—before he moved to the Cardinals and secured his fame by developing a comprehensive minor-league farm system for the big-league club. *George Grantham Bain Collection (Library of Congress).*

doubles four times, homers twice, and RBIs four times. The Triple Crown was his in both 1922 and 1925. Not without merit is Rogers Hornsby considered the greatest right-handed batter in baseball history. He ultimately retired with a career .358 batting average, second only to Cobb's .366.

Led by the batting of Hornsby, the Cardinals during Rickey's tenure as manager were consistently one of the top-scoring teams in the National League. The Texas-born Hornsby, however, was virtually the lone star. First base was the Cardinals' only other position of strength during those years, first with Jack Fournier and then Jim Bottomley. Fournier batted .343 in 1921, but at 33 years old in 1923 was traded to Brooklyn to make room for Bottomley, a mid-August call-up the previous year who was 10 years younger. Bottomley's .371 average in 1923 in his first full year as the Cardinals' first baseman was second in the league to his teammate Hornsby, and in 1925 he led the league with 227 hits and drove in 128 runs while batting .367, once again second in the league to Hornsby.

The outfield was the Cardinals' biggest weakness when Rickey was manager. At the beginning of the 1920s it seemed likely that left fielder Austin McHenry would be a cornerstone in the outfield and a complement to Hornsby in the middle of the batting order for many years to come. In June 1922, a year after he was third in the National League in batting and fourth in both homers and RBIs, he suddenly developed vision problems that put him in a bad batting slump. A medical checkup revealed that McHenry's visual impairment was caused by a brain tumor, ending his career on the spot and, just two months after he turned 27 in September, his life. With no other high-caliber outfielders, Rickey used a lefty/right platoon at two outfield positions nearly every year he was manager and routinely substituted for them in games for the "platoon advantage" to take account of pitching changes. The Cardinals' pitching was decidedly pedestrian, although right-hander Jesse Haines, a 20-game winner in 1923, seemed perpetually on the threshold of greatness.

Breadon's decision to replace Rickey as manager proved a shot in the arm for the Cardinals. Rickey's intensity in the dugout and academic approach to the game—including pregame meetings with a chalkboard, not to mention some unorthodox training methods—had worn thin with his players. Hornsby did away with all that, and the Cardinals had the second-best record in the National League the rest of the way to finish the 1925 season in fourth place with a winning 77–76 record that seemed highly improbable at the time Rickey stepped out of the dugout to sit full-time in the Cardinals' executive offices. The additional responsibilities as manager didn't slow Hornsby as a player. He was hitting .368 with 12 homers and 39 RBIs at the time he took charge of the team and finished the season with his second Triple Crown—a .403 average, 39 home runs, and 143 runs batted in. Hornsby hit .415 after he became a playing manager.

The Gateway City finally had a pennant winner and World Series champion in 1926. The Cardinals won a tight race decided by two games over Cincinnati and 4½ over defending champion Pittsburgh. Unlike Rickey, Hornsby as manager had a stable lineup and did not platoon at any position. He also made very few in-game position-player substitutions, allowing players in the starting lineup to finish most games. As his club's second baseman, Hornsby had the worst year of his career, batting only .317 with just 11 homers and 93 runs batted in. Bottomley, however, led the league with 120 RBIs and the club with 19 homers.

While second-year pitcher Flint Rhem led the league with 20 wins, Bill Sherdel won 16, and Haines, hobbled by an ankle injury, was 13–4, the Cardinals' best pitcher in 1926, based on pitching wins above replacement, was not even there when the season began. That was 39-year-old Grover Cleveland Alexander, by now affectionately known as Old Pete. The former Phillies and Cubs great, Alexander was picked up by Rickey on waivers after Joe McCarthy, the Cubs' new manager, decided Old Pete was a cancer he'd rather not have in his clubhouse, in part because of his drinking. Alexander's regular-season record may have been only 9–7 for the Cardinals, but he became the World Series hero for St. Louis in such dramatic fashion that Hollywood made a movie about it 26 years later, starring Ronald Reagan as Old Pete in *The Winning Team*.

The pivotal World Series moment came in Game Seven of the World Series against the powerhouse Yankees, the first Series in which Ruth and Gehrig were teammates. Pete Alexander was sitting in the bullpen at Yankee Stadium, soaking up the sun and probably thinking his season was over after having pitched a complete-game victory the day before to tie the Series at three games apiece. He had also pitched a complete game to win Game Two at Yankee Stadium. Jesse Haines, who threw a shutout in Game Three in St. Louis, was protecting a tenuous 3–2 lead in the bottom of the seventh when a single and walks to Ruth (intentional) and Gehrig (not intentional) loaded the bases. There were two outs. Hornsby chose this moment to call Alexander in to pitch to the dangerous Tony Lazzeri, whose 117 runs batted in were second to Ruth in the American League. While it is true that Old Pete was being asked to escape a bases-loaded, two-out situation with no margin for error in the final game of the World Series without a day of rest following his victory that denied the Yankees a championship the previous day, Hornsby probably preferred that the savvy veteran Alexander pitch to Lazzeri, who was still a rookie and only 22 years old, likely calculating that age and experience would outwit youth and power.

   Accounts differ as to whether Old Pete was hung over when he stumbled and then sauntered into the game to face Lazzeri. After Lazzeri blasted a heart-stopping long foul down the left-field line, Alexander struck him out to secure a storied place in World Series lore. Alexander retired the Yankees in order in the eighth and the first two batters in the ninth before pitching carefully to the Babe and walking him. In the movie, Ronald Reagan—I mean, Old Pete—retired the side in order in the ninth and struck out the final unnamed Yankees batter to end the game and the Series. In reality, the World Series ended when Ruth was thrown out inexplicably trying to steal second base with the dangerous Bob Meusel at bat against Alexander, and Lou Gehrig on deck.

   Good feelings dissipated quickly, however. The opinionated Hornsby had an adversarial relationship with Breadon over matters large and small that boiled over into the public realm, including Hornsby accusing Breadon of being a skinflint and Rickey of meddling with his team. The final straw for the franchise owner came in September when Hornsby yelled at him to "get the hell out of my clubhouse." But Breadon also recognized that getting rid of Hornsby would be a very unpopular move with St. Louis fans. Hornsby's demand for a new three-year contract and, back east in New York, an increasingly fraught relationship between McGraw and Frankie Frisch opened the door for the only kind of deal that could be justified to both cities' team loyalists, one great second baseman for another. Nonetheless, St. Louis, for the first time in history, was a World Series championship city.

21

DUELING DYNASTIES

Mack's New Powerhouse Battles
the Ruth-Gehrig Yankees

As soon as New York's Yankees clinched their third straight pennant on the final weekend of the 1928 season, they tied Boston's Red Sox and Philadelphia's Athletics as the most successful franchises in the American League. All three clubs had won six pennants. The Athletics, however, broke that tie with a string of three in a row from 1929 to 1931, after which the Yankees won again in 1932.

In the annals of baseball history, the New York Yankees are often remembered as being most formidable when they had Babe Ruth batting third and Lou Gehrig right behind him in the cleanup slot. They were the heart of the 1927 Yankees—still mythologized by many as the greatest team ever there was. The 1927 Yankees finished every day of the season in first place, won 110 games, took the pennant by 19 games, outscored their opposition by 376 runs (2.4 runs a game), and were said to so intimidate the Pirates during batting practice before Game One in Pittsburgh that their quick sweep in the World Series was a foregone conclusion, or any other words you might choose to connote inevitability. Ruth and Gehrig teamed together for 10 years, 1925 to 1934, but despite power production unmatched in history by any other dynamic duo, they led the Yankees to only four pennants. The Ruth-and-Gehrig Yankees won three consecutive pennants from 1926 to 1928, and a fourth in seven years in 1932.

The team that interrupted and shortchanged the Ruth-Gehrig Yankees dynasty was the Philadelphia Athletics, whose three consecutive pennants were all won in convincing fashion. One would be misguided to think that Ruth and Gehrig should have won more than the four pennants they did together, so great was their team, because the rival Philadelphians had their own luminescent stars in baseball's historical firmament—muscular first baseman Jimmie Foxx, left fielder Al Simmons, catcher Mickey Cochrane, and pitching ace Lefty Grove. It was no disgrace for the Ruth-Gehrig Yankees not to win more often when those guys were their contemporaries on the Athletics. In fact, it is quite possible that the Foxx-Simmons-Cochrane-Grove Athletics were actually a better team than the Ruth-Gehrig Yankees. Yet, while the Athletics were the first team in baseball history to have three consecutive 100-win seasons—the Ruth-and-Gehrig Yankees managed two in 1927 and 1928—their three straight blowout pennants are largely forgotten in the broad arc of popularized baseball history, except perhaps in the collective historical memory of the City of Brotherly Love.

* * *

For both franchises, 1925 was a pivotal year. For the Yankees, who overnight went from being a perennial contender to an early-out also-ran, it was a year of reassessment and transition. For the Athletics, it was the year Connie Mack finally had in place the foundation of his second dynasty, following a decade of losing seasons after he began breaking up his first great dynasty—the 1910–14 Athletics—which he did for economic reasons rather than embarrassment and pique at being swept four straight by the underdog Boston Braves in the 1914 fall classic, another long-popularized narrative.

The momentum the 1921–23 Yankees had built toward becoming a dynasty was stunted in 1924 when they narrowly missed winning a fourth straight pennant by two games, and especially by their near-total collapse in 1925—their worst season since 1913, the year they officially became "the Yankees." They finished seventh, 28½ games behind first-place Washington. They won only 69 games. It certainly did not help that the Babe, who won his only batting title the previous year with a .378 average, played in just 98 games. He missed his team's first 41 games recovering from abdominal surgery—the "bellyache heard 'round the world," although overindulging in hot dogs and Cokes had nothing to do with his stomach abscess—and was suspended by his manager for 10 days in August–September for insubordination. He did not return until apologizing to Miller Huggins for his behavior. Ruth ended up with just 25 homers and a .290 batting average, which raised incidental questions about whether the hard-living (he drank more than Cokes, for example, despite these being Prohibition times) now 30-old could return to the glories of his first five years in New York.

But even had Ruth been healthy and productive, the 1925 Yankees were a team in transition, particularly among their core position players. Besides Ruth, only third baseman Joe Dugan, outfielder Bob Meusel, and pitchers Herb Pennock and Waite Hoyt bridged the Yankees' first three pennants (1921 to 1923) with their next three (1926 to 1928). The foundation for the Yankees' second set of three-peats was fortified in 1925 when right-hander Urban Shocker, an elite pitcher, was acquired from the St. Louis Browns; center fielder Earle Combs joined Ruth and Meusel in the outfield; and Gehrig replaced Wally Pipp at first base. Putting aside the story about how a headache cost him his job, the veteran 32-year-old Pipp was in a seemingly interminable slump, batting .174 in the last 21 games he was in the starting lineup before being sat down on June 2.

While the 1925 Yankees were on an express down elevator to seventh place, the Athletics, bolstered by the arrivals of Mickey Cochrane, Lefty Grove, and Rube Walberg, continued on the up escalator following a decade of losing seasons. Connie Mack's second great dynasty was the work of patient reconstruction. The first foundation stones were set in 1920 with the arrivals of infielder Jimmy Dykes and rookie right-hander Eddie Rommel. Dykes proved to be not only a quintessential multiposition regular, alternating mostly between second and third, depending on where his manager had the greatest need, but an astute observer of the game. Rommel became one of baseball's best pitchers in the first half of the 1920s. Even though the knuckler was his signature pitch, Rommel was every bit as good, if not arguably better, in his five best years as Pennock and Hoyt, the Yankees' Hall of Fame pitchers in the 1920s. Unlike them, however, Rommel was at his best in the years before the Athletics returned to prominence.

As the good times rolled for America in the Roaring Twenties, money became less of a constraint for the Athletics' frugal owner. In 1924, Mack paid $40,000 to Milwaukee in the American Association for outfielder Al Simmons and $20,000 to Baltimore in the International League for second baseman Max Bishop. As rookies, Simmons had the first of 11 consecutive years in which he hit over .300 and drove in more than 100 runs, while Bishop showed his talent for getting on base in 38 percent of his plate appearances. The Athletics moved up to fifth place. In the 10 years since 1914, the Athletics had an abysmal .354 winning percentage (528–963), but with 71 victories in 1924 putting them within six wins of a .500 record, their future was looking bright.

Cochrane, Grove, and Walberg weren't the final pieces to Mack's second great dynasty, but their addition in 1925 not only propelled the Athletics to their first winning season since 1914, they landed Philadelphia in second place (second place!), 8½ games behind Washington. The 1925 Athletics even held first place for nearly two full months in May and June, and for nearly another month between late July and mid-August. A left-handed batter often platooned when a southpaw took the mound against Philadelphia, Mickey Cochrane was soon the best-hitting catcher the game had yet seen. At 25, Lefty Grove got a later start in the majors than he should have because the minor-league Baltimore Orioles, for whom he had pitched since 1920, were not about to give up their star pitcher without sizable compensation—over $100,000 of Mr. Mack's money. Perhaps as a public justification for spending so much on Lefty, Mack started him on Opening Day in 1925 even though Rommel was the proven ace on his staff. By the end of the month, however, overmatched by big-league hitting, Grove was out of the starting rotation and pitched mostly in relief the rest of the year. Rather than the brilliant Grove, who arrived with such high expectations, it was Rube Walberg who pitched more effectively, even if not as impressively, in 1925. Notwithstanding second place and staying in contention until late August, Mack's budding great team was still not ready.

* * *

Notwithstanding seventh place and never being in contention in 1925, the Yankees were a much better ballclub when they broke spring training in 1926, perhaps the best in the league before having played a single regular-season game. With Pennock, Hoyt, and Shocker in the lead, the Yankees had one of the strongest pitching staffs in baseball. The Babe was fully recovered and much better behaved, having learned the previous September that owner Jacob Ruppert was fully behind Huggins in any contest of supremacy between superstar player and manager. The final pieces essential to the Yankees' resurgence that year were a pair of rookies to stabilize the middle of the infield—Tony Lazzeri playing second base and Mark Koenig at shortstop. The fact that Koenig, like Dugan, was an average player with a relatively short career as a regular belied his importance to the Yankees' success. Lazzeri, by contrast, was a dangerous hitter whose 12 years in pinstripes earned him the Hall of Fame. He was also the first in a line of players of Italian American heritage important in the making of New York Yankees history that included Frankie Crosetti, Joe DiMaggio, Phil Rizzuto, Yogi Berra, and Billy Martin. Lazzeri, Crosetti, and DiMaggio were all from San Francisco, and Martin was from Berkeley, also in the Bay Area. Nearly blowing their seemingly safe 10-game lead on August 23 to win the pennant by 3½ games, and then losing the World Series, the Yankees gave no evidence of the juggernaut they would be in 1927.

Lou Gehrig's breakout, particularly as a home-run threat nearly on par with the Babe, was the catalyst to their epic 110-win season. Now opposing teams were forced to pick their poison, because pitching around Ruth

Right-hander Waite Hoyt had the best season of his Hall of Fame career with the 1927 Yankees when he went 22–7. *George Grantham Bain Collection (Library of Congress).*

meant having to deal with Gehrig. The two Yankees sluggers vied with each other for the league lead in home runs all summer before Ruth finally pulled away with 17 big blasts in September to reach 60, leaving Gehrig far behind. Gehrig, who had 41 compared to Ruth's 43 going into the final month, finished with 47 homers, but led the league with 52 doubles and 173 RBIs while batting .373. He was the American League MVP—a completely legitimate selection even though Ruth was not eligible because the rules at the time precluded any player who had previously won the award, which the Babe had in 1923. Although the Yankees won 101 games in 1928 to win a third straight pennant, their margin of victory was only 2½ games over Philadelphia.

Connie Mack completed his dynasty-rebuilding project in 1928 by bringing back Bing Miller, who he had traded away two years before, and adding Mule Haas to complement Simmons in the outfield, acquiring hard-throwing right-hander George Earnshaw in another deal with the International League Orioles to join Grove and Walberg in the starting rotation, and introducing the baseball world to right-handed-slugger Jimmie Foxx, whose rookie season was spent mostly playing third base on his way to becoming one of the greatest first basemen ever. While the 1928 Athletics did not win the pennant, they did put a deep scare into the Yankees with a surge of 40 wins in 52 games to not only overcome a 12½-game deficit as late as July 18, but bring a half-game lead into Yankee Stadium for a doubleheader showdown with the Bronx Bombers on September 9. Hardly willing to hand over their crown, the Yankees swept the twin bill, beat Grove for good measure the next day, and the Athletics never saw the sunny side of first place again in 1928.

Philadelphia, however, had sent a clear message to New York that the Athletics were poised to challenge the formidable Yankees, and the next three years belonged to the Athletics. Their stretch as the best team in baseball arguably began on July 20, 1928, when Foxx, who so far had occasionally platooned behind the plate with the left-handed-batting Cochrane against southpaw starting pitchers and also filled in at first and third when needed, moved into the starting lineup at third base on a daily basis after Philadelphia's regular third baseman was injured. Twelve games behind the runaway Yankees at the time, Philadelphia was 45–20 the rest of the way—a pace that would equate to 106 wins over a full 154-game season, which was nearly the number of wins the Athletics would average the next three years. Moved over to first base in 1929, Foxx had his breakout season, batting .354 with 33 homers and 118 runs batted in. It was the first of 12 consecutive years in which he hit 30 or more home runs, something not even Babe Ruth accomplished, although the Babe likely would have if not for his various travails in 1925 that cost him 56 games. Foxx's record stood until the next century when Barry Bonds and

Alex Rodriguez both had 13 straight 30-homer seasons. It was also the first of 13 consecutive years in which Foxx drove in 100 runs, a career record he shares with Lou Gehrig.

The Athletics won more than 100 games in all three of their consecutive pennants and were never challenged after midsummer, winning decisively each year. Mack's 1929 club won 39 of their first 50 games without back-to-back losses until mid-June to put a quick end to the pennant race. They finished with 104 wins and an 18-game advantage that was nearly the equal of the 1927 Yankees' 19-game romp. The 1930 Athletics actually trailed the unsuspected Washington Senators by a half-game on July 9 and 10, but were eight games in front by the end of the month and never looked back on their way to 102 victories and an eight-game final margin of victory. And 1931 was 1929 all over again in Philadelphia's complete dominance of the league—12 games up by the end of July and 15½ by the end of August. They wound up taking the pennant by only 13½ games, but their 107 wins were more than any other of Connie Mack's 50 Philadelphia teams, including his great 1910–14 Athletics. Indeed, no team in the franchise's history—including after the A's moved to Oakland, via Kansas City—won more games than the 1931 Philadelphia Athletics.

The great expectations the Yankees had to extend their streak to four pennants in a row in 1929 had been crushed by the reality of how good the Athletics had become. Once again in transition—Joe Dugan was gone after 1928, Bob Meusel was let go after the 1929 season, and the pitching staff needed to be overhauled as both Waite Hoyt and Herb Pennock were worn down from having each thrown more than 2,400 innings the previous 10 years—the most significant change at Yankee Stadium was brought about by tragedy. Miller Huggins died of blood poisoning at the age of 50 just days before the end of the 1929 season. Although his team was never in contention, already 11½ games behind the Athletics before June turned to July, Huggins had managed the Yankees to six pennants and three World Series championships since becoming manager in 1918. After a year of Bob Shawkey in charge—the Yankees finished third—Ruppert seized upon the sudden availability of fired Chicago Cubs manager Joe McCarthy, bringing him to the Bronx in 1931. That proved to be a move of inspired genius, even though the Yankees were unable to keep up with the Athletics in McCarthy's first year.

In 1932, however, the Yankees did their best imitation of 1927, winning the pennant by 13 games over the still-formidable 94-win Athletics. Their 107 wins in 1932 would remain the second-highest total in the Yankees' storied history until 1961. Ruth, Gehrig, Combs, and Lazzeri were still the heart of the batting order, and the other core position regulars were actually an upgrade, with rookie Frankie Crosetti and veteran

Joe Sewell now at shortstop and third base instead of Koenig and Dugan; the dynamic Ben Chapman replacing Meusel in the outfield; and Bill Dickey was emerging rapidly as an elite catcher. After five years of catchers sharing the position, Dickey began a record-setting stretch of 13 consecutive years catching at least 100 games in his 1929 rookie season that Johnny Bench would tie in 1980. And Red Ruffing and Lefty Gomez, both picked up in 1930, gave the Yankees a new pair of pitching aces to replace the departed Hoyt and the winding-down Pennock.

* * *

It perhaps comes as a surprise, given Ruth and Gehrig were the Bronx Bombers' headliners, that between 1926 and 1932 the Philadelphia Athletics' achievements were comparable to those of the New York Yankees. Each club won three consecutive pennants, although the Yankees won four American League titles in all. The Athletics' three straight were each won decisively; the Yankees' three in a row included their 1927 "greatest team ever," but also two pennants won despite dissipating big midsummer leads that seemed destined for blowouts. Philadelphia won two World Series; New York won three. The Yankees won 677 games and lost 400 for a .629 winning percentage. The Athletics, even though playing 10 fewer games resulting in a decision, had two more victories than the Yankees and, with 679 wins against 388 losses, a slightly higher .636 winning percentage. Taking the narrower slice of 1928 to 1932—three pennants sandwiched by runner-up status to New York—Philadelphia's .662 winning percentage (505–258) is exceeded only by the 530–235 record (.693) compiled by the 1906–10 Cubs for the highest by any team over any five-year period in the major leagues since 1900. No New York Yankees team over any five-year period—not with Ruth, not with Gehrig, not with DiMaggio, not with Mantle, not with Jeter—ever had as high a winning percentage as the 1928–32 Philadelphia Athletics.

Led by Cochrane, Simmons, and Foxx batting third, fourth, and fifth, the Philadelphia Athletics were a formidable offensive ballclub. Mickey Cochrane hit a robust .345 and drove in 269 runs the three years the Athletics dominated the American League. Al Simmons was at his best those same three years; he led the league with 157 RBIs in 1929, was second with 165 in 1930, and won back-to-back batting titles with .381 and .390 averages in 1930 and '31. Simmons also hit .333 in the three World Series with six home runs, two in each Series. And Jimmie Foxx hit exactly 100 homers, had 394 RBIs, and batted .327, which he followed up by batting .344 with four homers and 11 RBIs in the three World Series.

Jimmie Foxx was a "beast," and that was indeed his nickname. If Gehrig and Ruth are linked in history as the most potent pair a manager ever had the privilege of writing into his lineup, Gehrig and Foxx are linked as contemporary first basemen who were two of the greatest in the history of the game. The Beast's two greatest years came just after his team's three straight pennants. In 1932 he mounted an assault on Ruth's single-season record of 60 home runs, falling just short with 58. He went into the final game of the season with 57—three shy of Ruth's record—against Washington's Alvin Crowder, who might have been the second-best pitcher in the league that year after Grove. Foxx went 3-for-3 against the tough right-hander, but only one of his three hits went the distance. Foxx also led the league with 169 RBIs, and his .364 batting average fell two hits short of Dale Alexander's .367. In 1933, however, Jimmie Foxx did win the Triple Crown with 48 homers, 163 RBIs, and a .356 average.

Leading off for the Athletics was Max Bishop, who excelled in getting on base for the big bats that followed, although less by his hitting prowess than his willingness to draw walks. Taking advantage of his diminutive 5-foot-8 stature and Ted Williams–like refusal to swing at pitches outside the strike zone—his nicknames included "The Human Eyeball" and "Camera Eye"—Bishop had a .420 on-base percentage while batting just .270 in the five years between 1928 and 1932. For his entire 12-year career, Bishop's 1,156 walks were only 60 fewer than his 1,216 total hits. Taking into account the 31 times he was hit by a pitch, base hits accounted for barely 51 percent of the total times he reached base without benefit of an error or a force play. Bishop set a record with at least 100 walks in eight consecutive seasons from 1926 to 1933 that has yet to be surpassed—not by Ruth (although only because of injury or suspension-shortened seasons), not by Gehrig, not even by Ted Williams (perhaps only because he lost three years serving in World War II), despite them being far more dangerous power hitters who were often put on base, either intentionally or from being pitched around, by cautious managers and fearful pitchers. Barry Bonds never walked 100 times eight years in a row, although he might have done so 17 years straight if not for three interrupting years in which he missed at least 50 games on the disabled list.

As imposing as Philadelphia's Athletics were offensively, they did not once lead the league in scoring because, well, because they were *not* the Bronx Bombers with their fabled Murderers' Row. With Ruth and Gehrig being, well, Ruth and Gehrig, the Yankees dominated all of baseball offensively between 1926 and 1932, leading both major leagues in scoring six of the seven years. In 1930 the Yankees became the first team since the Boston Beaneaters in 1897 to score more than 1,000 runs, touching the plate 1,062 times—the first of three consecutive 1,000-run seasons. (The 1930 Cardinals also scored more than 1,000 runs, but did not reach that plateau until their next-to-last game of the season, nine days after the Yankees.)

The Yankees' imposing offense began with Earle Combs, whose hitting proficiency at the top of the order routinely set up the power bats that followed. Combs hit .328 leading off for the Yankees from 1926 to 1932 and was capable of driving the ball for extra bases, leading the league three times with more than 20 triples. If Combs was a hard guy to get out, however, it was the sluggers at the heart of the Murderers' Row that were most feared. There was little respite for opposing pitchers after Ruth and Gehrig, batting third and fourth, because Bob Meusel (through 1929) and Tony Lazzeri, next up, were also dangerous power hitters. Both were right-handed batters whose home-run totals were suppressed by the expanse of Yankee Stadium's left field.

Ruth quickly disabused anyone of the notion his 1925 performance was the beginning of the end of his extraordinary career by going on an unprecedented power binge. The Babe, who blasted 235 homers in his first five Yankees years, walloped 256 in the five years after his tumultuous and unhappy 1925 season, including his historic 60 in 1927 and 54 the following year. He led the American League in homers each year, and only the Cubs' Hack Wilson, with 56, hit more home runs than Ruth's 49 in 1930. The next year, at 36, when most players of his era were on their last legs, Ruth really was on his last legs—he was in at the finish of only 88 of the 141 games he started, in deference to his weary legs—but nonetheless had 46 homers to lead the league for a sixth straight year, and his 41 home runs in 1932 gave him seven straight years with 40 or more shots going the distance. Neither Barry Bonds nor Alex Rodriguez ever matched that, and it probably would have been 13 years in a row had Ruth not missed 44 games in 1922 (when he hit 35 home runs) and 58 in 1925 (when he had 25). In the seven years after his 1925 fall from grace, Ruth batted .353 and averaged 49 homers and 153 RBIs. His .372 and .371 batting averages in 1926 and 1931 were second in the league.

For Gehrig, there was no turning back from greatness following his breakout year and home-run duel with Ruth in 1927. Nor was there taking a day off despite criticism that he would benefit from rest, similar to what Everett Scott heard when he set the consecutive-games record. While his home-run count dropped to 27 in 1928, Gehrig again led the league with 147 RBIs. He batted .374. In 1930, Gehrig hit .379—his career high—and led the league in runs batted in for the third time with 173; the next year, Gehrig's 163 runs, 211 hits, 46 homers, and 185 RBIs were tops in the league; and in 1934, the last year he and Ruth played together, Gehrig won the Triple Crown, batting .363 with 49 home runs and 161 RBIs. Ruth batted .338 with 424 home runs among 713 extra-base hits in the time they played together, and Gehrig hit .344 with 881 extra-base hits, 348 of them homers.

The tandem was just as lethal in the four World Series they played in together. Ruth hit four home runs against the Cardinals in a seven-game losing cause in 1926, although he was ignominiously thrown out on an attempted steal of second in a one-run game to end both Game Seven and the World Series with Meusel batting and Gehrig, who hit .348 in the Series, waiting on deck. Ruth batted .400 with two homers in the Yankees' four-game sweep of the Pirates in 1927, while Gehrig hit only .308 without going deep. The two were unstoppable in the Yankees' four-game revenge against the Cardinals in 1928; Gehrig hit four home runs and Ruth three, and Ruth batted .625 and Gehrig .545. Ruth had his "called shot" in the 1932 Series sweep, but Gehrig had three homers of his own and batted .529.

Appropriately for being the "Bronx Bombers," the 1926–32 Yankees led the league in homers every year except 1932, when the Athletics hit 172 to their 160. Indicative of their clout, 38 percent of the Yankees' victories were by blowout margins of five runs or more—including an astonishing 44 of their 94 wins in 1931, a year in which they finished 13½ games behind the Athletics *despite* outscoring Philadelphia for the season by 209 runs. And why would that be? Because the Athletics had superior pitching and defense. Philadelphia led the league in fewest runs allowed four times those seven years even though the park effects at Shibe Park were not favorable for pitchers. With Grove and Earnshaw on the mound, the Athletics were also the premier power-pitching team in baseball, leading the league in strikeouts six straight years beginning in 1925, before finishing second to the Yankees in 1931 and 1932. George Earnshaw's emergence as an elite pitcher in 1929 may have been the decisive breakthrough enabling the Athletics to win three straight pennants, when he went 24–8, 22–13, and 21–7. But it was Grove who was otherworldly.

From 1928 to 1932, Lefty Grove made a strong case for having the best five-year stretch of any pitcher ever by winning 128 games while losing only 33 for a .795 winning percentage; leading the league in earned run average the last four of those years; and leading the league in strikeouts the first four of those years—and all this in the peak years of a hitters' era. Grove was 20–6 in 1929, 28–5 in 1930, and his phenomenal 31–4 record in 1931 made him the first American League MVP selected by the Baseball Writers' Association of America. He led the league in winning percentage all three years, and his 2.46 ERA for the three years was nearly two full runs lower than the 4.42 earned run average compiled by all the league's pitchers. In 1932, Grove finished at 25–10 as the Athletics' bid for four straight pennants fell far short of the Yankees, but for the third time in four years, he was the only American League pitcher with an ERA under 3.00; another Lefty, Gomez of the Yankees, had a 2.67 ERA in 1931, when Grove's 2.06 was by far the lowest since the Deadball Era ended in 1920.

At a time when top-tier pitchers were not developed as relievers—Washington's Firpo Marberry being the only exception to this point in the game's history—Grove's value extended beyond being the ace of the staff to also being called upon to win or save games in the late innings, much in the mold of Three Finger Brown and Ed Walsh a generation earlier. In addition to his 99 starts between 1929 and 1931, Grove pitched 34 times in relief with a 9–3 record and 18 saves; in 1930 his nine saves were the most in the majors. Eddie Rommel pitched nearly twice as often in relief—67 times those three years—but like modern managers, Mack clearly preferred Grove's hard stuff and ornery competitiveness if he needed a relief pitcher with the game still in play. Like modern closers, Lefty Grove was overpowering, averaging more than a strikeout an inning with 77 Ks in 75⅓ innings pitched in relief. For those three years, Grove's overall strikeout ratio was 5.8 per nine innings.

Lefty Grove, with catcher Mickey Cochrane, was 79–15 for an .840 winning percentage with an outstanding 2.46 ERA when the Athletics won three straight pennants between 1929 and 1931. *National Baseball Hall of Fame and Museum.*

Despite leading the league in starts, pitching the most innings in his club, and a 20–6 record in 1929, Grove did not start any of the World Series games against the Cubs that year. Instead, Mack used him twice in relief, including pitching the last two innings of Game Four for the save after the Athletics overcame an eight-run deficit by scoring 10 runs in the home seventh. In 6⅓ innings in his two World Series appearances, Grove struck out 10 Cubs. Grove was 2–1 in each of the next two World Series, both against the Cardinals, making five starts and pitching once in relief. His strikeout ratios in both Series were much lower because, as a starting pitcher, he had to moderate his effort in the interest of pitching nine innings. Throwing 45 innings in the 1930 and '31 World Series, including four complete games in his five starts, eight innings in the start he failed to complete, and two innings to win a game in relief, Grove struck out just 26 batters.

While the Athletics' pitching staff had a stable core of Grove, Earnshaw, and Rube Walberg, the Yankees' was in transition from Waite Hoyt and Herb Pennock, their top duo for three consecutive pennants from 1926 to 1928, to Red Ruffing and Lefty Gomez, who emerged by the pennant-winning year of 1932 as the foundation for what proved to be an excellent staff later in the 1930s. In the between years when the Athletics were winning *their* three straight, the Yankees had one of the worst pitching staffs in the league, based on their collective pitching WAR. Unlike their Philadelphia counterparts, Yankees pitchers worked with a much less solid defense behind them. Coincidentally, neither the Yankees nor the Athletics had a particularly strong left side of the infield defensively.

* * *

The Roaring Twenties were riding high when the Yankees had their iconic 1927 season, and perhaps their 110 wins and Ruth's 60 clouts might be considered an excess in keeping with the tenor of the times in American history. The country's booming economy had doubled the national wealth since the end of World War I, fueling an age of unprecedented consumerism that gave rise to the birth of "mass culture"—including, in the wake of the 19th Amendment guaranteeing women the right to vote, free-spirited flappers and popular music, specifically jazz. Prohibition was being honored more in its breach in big-city speakeasies. Life in America was great, and Babe Ruth was as appropriate a symbol of this age as any. Two years later, the Athletics finished wiping out the Cubs in the 1929 World Series just 15 days before the stock market crash on "Black Tuesday" plunged the country into its worst domestic crisis since the Civil War. Herbert Hoover had been sworn in as president just seven months before. Life in America was now not so great.

When the Yankees returned to the top of the baseball world by crushing the Cubs four straight to take the 1932 World Series, Hoover was still president, presiding over a country whose GDP was less than 60 percent of what it had been in 1929 before the crash, and unemployment had surged from about 4 percent when he was elected to nearly a quarter of the American working-age population. Life in America was definitely not good, and Franklin D. Roosevelt was elected president six weeks after the Yankees completed their "we came, we saw, we conquered" campaign in Chicago.

The New York Yankees, with far greater resources to fall back on, were much better positioned than the Philadelphia Athletics to fare well during the Great Depression, and the two franchises took radically different directions after 1932. The New York team also benefited from a command structure that was a triumvirate, having an owner (Jacob Ruppert), a general manager (Ed Barrow), and a manager (Joe McCarthy) with defined roles who accepted their boundaries and worked collaboratively toward keeping the Yankees the best team they could possibly be. The team in Philadelphia had an owner, general manager, and manager who was one and the same in the sole person of Connie Mack—a trinity rather than a triumvirate. Operating in this way, Mack's financial responsibilities of ownership were not leavened by advice from a GM and manager whose principal concerns were competitiveness. His personal savings wiped out in the crash, Mack did not invest again in trying to rebuild a championship-caliber team, as he eventually did after dismantling his first great team.

Just as two decades before, the country's economic travails had a profound effect on the Athletics' attendance, despite their winning ways. As Mack steadily improved his club during the 1920s, coincident with the booming economy, average per-game attendance at Shibe Park soared from among the worst in baseball to consistently second behind the Yankees beginning in 1925, when the Athletics actually drew more fans than anyone else. While winning the 1929 pennant resulted in a 22 percent increase in home attendance for the Athletics, the beginning years of the Depression resulted in a 14 percent decline when Philadelphia repeated as champions in 1930, another 13 percent drop when Mack's men won their three-peat in 1931, and a far more precipitate 35 percent decline in 1932 (third-best in the league), when the Athletics were still a baseball power but could not keep pace with the Ruth-Gehrig Yankees.

Perhaps more to the point, per-game home attendance decreased from about 38 percent of Shibe Park's capacity in 1929 to only 16 percent of capacity in 1932—the Athletics' lowest level since 1919, when Mack's last-place team with its atrocious 36–104 record was the worst draw in the American League. Mack leveraged his club's poor attendance to influence the good citizens of Philadelphia to vote favorably on lifting the prohibition on Sunday baseball in 1934 and to beat back a lawsuit by irate neighbors when he increased the height of Shibe Park's right-field wall from 12 to 50 feet to deny free rooftop viewing from apartments across the street.

The financial responsibilities that ownership entails necessarily took precedence over Mack's presumed managerial interests. Just as he dismantled the 1910–14 Athletics for economic reasons in the midst of a grave recession, so did the Great Depression compel Mack to break up his even better 1929–31 team in what would be the beginning of a very long end—more than two decades—for American League baseball in the City of Brotherly Love. As before, Mack traded his stars for bit players and (primarily) big money. This time, however, the breakup was less precipitous, and also less immediately calamitous. Of the four Hall of Famers who were the centerpiece of this team, Simmons was gone in 1933, Cochrane and Grove left in 1934, and Foxx remained two more years before leaving after the 1935 season. Of the other core regulars, Jimmy Dykes and Mule Haas were gone in 1933; Bishop, Earnshaw, and Walberg in 1934; and Bing Miller in 1935. The Athletics dropped to third in 1933 and fifth in 1934 before finding a home in the American League basement for seven of the next nine years.

Connie Mack had a willing partner in Tom Yawkey, a "rich kid" who bought the Boston Red Sox in 1933 and was enthused to spend lots of money even in the middle of the Depression in hopes of building a pennant-winning ballclub. Grove, Bishop, and Walberg were part of a package deal in December 1933 that returned two unsung players and $125,000 to Mr. Mack. While Bishop and Walberg were near the end of their careers, Lefty Grove was in the middle of his. He went to Boston as the best pitcher in baseball with a lifetime record of 195–79, having won 71 percent of his decisions in nine years pitching for Philadelphia. Two Decembers later in 1935, Mr. Mack sold "The Beast" to Mr. Yawkey for $150,000. Jimmie Foxx, only 28 at the time, had just led the league in homers with 36 and had hit 302 playing for the Athletics. Less than a month after the Foxx deal, Mack got $175,000 of Yawkey's money in exchange for pedestrian shortstop Eric McNair and outfielder Doc Cramer, whose back-to-back 200-hit seasons in '34 and '35 made him attractive to the young Red Sox owner.

Right-handed-batting Bob Johnson, a formidable power hitter who replaced Simmons in left field as a rookie in 1933 and quickly became one of the best all-around outfielders in the American League, was the one high-performing player Mack could have gotten good money for but kept instead. Great Depression or not, Mack understood he needed more than just the pretense of a major-league team to attract fans to Shibe Park;

he needed at least some quality players Philadelphians would pay to see. Johnson's time in Philadelphia did not come to an end until 1943—the first year the war had a dramatic impact on major-league rosters—when Mack sent him to Washington for two players and cash. Approaching 40, Johnson played through the war years before retiring in 1946 when baseball's best players who had gone off to war returned. The only outfielder better than Bob Johnson to play for the Athletics in their 54-year history in Philadelphia was Al Simmons. Frankie Hayes, Cochrane's replacement behind the plate in 1934, and Wally Moses, who took over right field in 1935 and became a perennial .300 hitter, were the two other quality players Mack kept through the Depression years.

An easing of the worst of the Depression in the mid-1930s resulting in more people back at work and more disposable income helped boost the Athletics' attendance, but never to better than sixth best in the league. It certainly didn't help that competitively Mack's men never rose above seventh place, and did so just once. With the Athletics not moving up in the standings, and the United States now involved in World War II, Mack traded Moses after the 1941 season and Hayes early in the 1942 season for replacements less costly to have on his roster. Hayes returned to Philadelphia in 1944 and started every one of the Athletics' 155 games—including 34 doubleheaders, in which he caught the entirety of both games 18 times.

As for the burgeoning Yankees dynasty, whose string of successes was interrupted by Mack's 1929–31 Athletics, Depression or not, they shed only those players they no longer needed or wanted. By 1935, that included the Babe himself, despite his iconic status in New York City. It would be inaccurate to say, you ain't seen nuthin' yet, if for no other reason than the excellence of Ruth and Gehrig, but with Yankees dynastic aspirations now in the hands of Joe McCarthy, with excellent scouts, one of baseball's premier minor-league systems, and a trademark commitment to excellence, well, in fact . . . you ain't seen nuthin' yet.

* * *

Connie Mack was 68 when the Athletics ran away with the American League pennant in 1931. Had he stepped aside as manager after the 1932 season, when 94 victories were not nearly enough to overtake the Yankees' resurgence, and let Jimmy Dykes, whom he had been grooming as a successor, take over, Mack would have gone out having just managed a second dynasty. And the timing would have been nothing if not appropriate, since John McGraw, his National League rival for greatest manager of all time (at least up till then), had himself retired from the fray in June. In baseball's first midsummer All-Star showcase in 1933, conceived by the *Chicago Tribune* to not only complement the Chicago World's Fair but also to burnish baseball's standing and popularity in the depths of the Depression, the retired McGraw and the still-active Mack were named the managers of their respective league's All-Stars in recognition of their historical greatness. Had he also been retired, Mack would still have managed the American League team, a managerial god come down from baseball's Mount Olympus just like McGraw.

By hanging on for what turned out to be another 18 years, until he was approaching his 88th birthday in December 1950, Mack's historical legacy lost some of its luster. Had he chosen to wait until after the 1933 season to retire, Mack would have managed the Philadelphia Athletics for exactly one-third of a century. He would have stepped down having won nine pennants, more than any other American League manager. Moreover, including when he managed the Pirates from 1894 to 1896, he would have had a 2,745–2,459 record as a major-league manager—and that takes into account the Athletics' 10 consecutive losing seasons between dynasties in which they were not only bad, but mostly very bad. Instead of having managed 286 more victories than losses had he retired then, his career record of 3,731–3,948 shows a deficit of 217 losses.

Connie Mack arguably developed and managed more great players than any other manager in history, including McGraw. In managing the game, he was generally conservative in his approach. Historically credited with being a trailblazer in positioning his players according to the game situation, such as guarding the lines in the late innings to prevent extra-base hits or taking account of what kind of stuff his pitcher had compared to the strengths, weaknesses, and hitting disposition of the batter, Mack on the bench, dressed in a business suit (sometimes without his jacket) and waving a scorecard to properly position his defense, is a part of baseball lore.

22

FROM RICKEY'S FARMS TO REDBIRDS' TABLE

The Cardinals' Model for Sustained Success

In his 1963 thriller *The Birds*, the director Alfred Hitchcock, the cinematic master of suspense, set up the foreboding menace of the horror to come in the famous scene where blackbirds—crows, actually—fly into a playground and begin perching on a jungle gym, commonly referred to at the time as monkey bars, one at a time in silence at first, not obviously threatening, quickly joined by others, and then more and more until a crow assault team has taken shape, soon to go on a killer rampage against the good citizens of a bucolic coastal town in Northern California.

Decades earlier, a similar scene might be said to have played out involving redbirds of an entirely different feather—the baseball Cardinals, actually—under the direction of Branch Rickey, another creative master of his trade, and not over the course of a few moments in a single day, but over many years. And they were just as relentless as Hitchcock's birds. Through the extensive system of minor-league "farm" teams he constructed for the St. Louis Cardinals franchise, there were always major-league-ready Redbirds perched on the monkey bars ready to carry on what had become a new Cardinal tradition—consistently competitive teams that seemed inured to the ravages of time.

* * *

A catcher who played a grand total of 117 big-league games in 1906 and 1907, Branch Rickey was forced to discover that his baseball talent was infinitely more cerebral than physical. His playing career a bust, Rickey was coaching baseball at the University of Michigan in 1913 when he was approached by the Browns' owner about working for him as a personal assistant. In their quest to engineer a turnaround of the hapless Browns, Rickey's focus was on scouting minor-league players. He impressed his boss, and outside observers, by his rigorous systematic approach to evaluating talent. In September's last days of a dismal last-place season, his boss made Rickey manager of the Browns.

As their manager, Rickey expanded his focus beyond evaluating players to developing their skills. His methods were controversial because they went well beyond a practice-makes-perfect approach to game situations. Rickey's approach was instead highly theoretical—as in, teaching the proper physical mechanics for doing things, not just practicing plays and proper positioning. He incorporated the use of dirt pits to practice the correct way of sliding into a base, had pitchers work on their control by throwing through a strike zone outlined by cords stretched across the front of the plate at the knee and chest levels of a typical batter, and even organized handball games to work on eye-hand coordination. Critics, including the other manager in St. Louis—the Cardinals' Miller Huggins—believed these were gimmicks too divorced from the reality of the game as it is played and that the emphasis should be on developing instinctual anticipation, reaction, and coordinated teamwork to the specific action of each baseball event. Rickey believed that the application of theory to practice—specifically *his* theories on the proper way of doing physical things—was necessary to master any and all game situations. But however innovative and "scientific" Rickey's practices and preparations may have been, there is little evidence to suggest he was either insightful or even savvy about strategies and tactics to win games; it was McGraw's strategy-focused definition of "scientific" baseball that counted.

Rickey's days managing the Browns were over as soon as Philip DeCatesby Ball, one of the two Federal League owners allowed to buy a major-league franchise as part of the settlement to tidy up that league's demise, bought the club in December 1915. Marginalized and frustrated by the new regime, Rickey did not hesitate to keep the same St. Louis address but switch over to the National League club in town when offered the chance to join with local businessmen to buy into the Cardinals in 1917. When Sam Breadon, one of those St. Louis businessmen, became principal owner two years later, he relied on Rickey to run the ballclub both not only in the Cardinals' executive suite but in the dugout as well. Together they set out to make the St. Louis Cardinals a winning team and a long-term success. Rickey knew, however, that the Cardinals not only did not have the players to compete with the top teams in the National League—the same was true of the Browns in the AL—but could not even hope to because of the economics underlying player transactions in Organized Baseball. The Cardinals labored under the handicap of tight bud-gets. Perennial contenders in big cities—most notably the New York Giants—did not. They could afford to go get whatever they needed. As if he needed reminding, Rickey found himself in the position of having to consider a very lucrative offer from the Giants for Rogers Hornsby, the only top-flight player the Cardinals could call their own. Rickey realized with great clarity that trading his star infielder for lots of money was counterproductive to his club's competitive future, even if New York's offer would have enabled the St. Louis franchise to pay off its debts; that indeed, the Cardinals would always be vulnerable to having to sell their best players to help make ends meet, which would leave them always in the position of "also-ran."

But it was not just about the trading or buying and selling of major-league players. Nearly all big-leaguers apprenticed in the minor leagues, and financially strapped teams like the Cardinals were at a disadvantage competing for players whose contracts were owned by the minor-league clubs they played for. Major-league franchises were prohibited by the National Commission from having an ownership stake in minor-league teams. Nor were they allowed to have exclusive relationships with any minor-league club to have dibs on that team's best players. Many fran-chises nonetheless did have ad hoc arrangements, often based on personal relationships with minor-league club owners, to buy or trade for players, but these were gentlemen's agreements to circumvent the rules—non-binding and not enforceable—which, at best, gave them the right of first refusal if a rival major-league club was interested in a particular player.

Baseball was every bit as much a business for minor-league team owners as it was in the majors. They depended on player transactions—principally money for prospects ready for the next level—to make ends meet. Bristling at the major leagues' right under the rubric of Organized Baseball to draft players from their rosters, as well as rules that allowed major-league teams to "option" players under contract to minor-league clubs so they could develop their skills, the minor leagues collectively opted out of the National Agreement that governed all of Organized Baseball in 1919 because the majors refused to compromise on their demands for a more equitable relationship. Both sides, however, had a compelling interest to respect each other's player contracts and continued to do business. Most of the lower-classification leagues continued to submit to an annual major-league player draft because they needed the money they got in compensation. All three leagues at the highest Double-A classification level, however, no longer allowed their players to be subject to the draft; they could set a higher "fair market" price for the best major league–ready players that only financially well-heeled major-league teams could afford.

The St. Louis Cardinals were not a financially well-heeled franchise and could not afford to compete for top minor-league talent. They were also vulnerable to being outbid for players at lower levels, where minor-league owners would often leverage an offer for a player from one major-league club to get a better offer from another; if the Cardinals, for example, given Rickey's reputation for being an astute judge of player potential, was interested in someone, maybe other teams should be, too—even if they weren't before.

The Cardinals' only salvation, Rickey was convinced, was to find a way to develop players in the minors while maintaining control of their contracts to prevent the best among them from being sold by the minor-league club they played for to the highest major-league bidder. His ambition was to build an extensive system of minor-league affiliates, with players in the pipeline at every level of the game under franchise control, so there would be a steady stream of players coming to St. Louis to continually refresh the major-league roster. Rickey once described his vision in terms of an educational system, with a large number of prospects starting in kindergarten and progressing through grade school, many making it to prep school, some to college, with a select few going to university for the privilege of ultimately graduating with a PhD in baseball that brought them to the St. Louis Cardinals.

Surveying the postwar competitive landscape, Rickey took advantage of the minor leagues having unilaterally abrogated their traditional relationship with the majors by backing out of the National Agreement. Since the concept of major-league "farm teams" was frowned upon and still technically prohibited, Rickey proceeded with caution. Financed in large part by Breadon's sale of their dilapidated ballpark and the more valuable land it sat on, made possible only because the Browns offered a below-market-value lease in 1920 to play in their home—Sportsman's Park— the Cardinals soon had an ownership stake in two minor-league franchises. With one in the Class D Western Association and the other, Houston, in the highly regarded Class A Texas League, the Cardinals now had a bottom-tier farm team to assess prospects, and a next-to-top-tier farm club to send those showing big-league potential. Any opposition to their move by other major-league clubs was mitigated by the distraction of the National Commission having collapsed, followed by the fallout from the Black Sox scandal, and the minor leagues' asserting their independence such that the former rules could be said to no longer apply. Although the new commissioner, Judge Landis, was opposed to the concept of farm teams because he believed—correctly, as it turned out, certainly in the case of the Cardinals—that they allowed the parent major-league club too much control over players' careers, he was presented in effect with a fait accompli as he grappled with more urgent issues of restoring the integrity of the game.

While the Cardinals' first two affiliates were almost certainly acquired in violation of league rules, a new agreement negotiated with the minor leagues in 1921 did not explicitly say no to major-league clubs owning minor-league teams, but it didn't say yes, either. It was game on for Branch Rickey. As the 1920s progressed, Rickey incrementally added minor-league clubs at lower classifications to the Cardinals' system by securing a significant minority share of their ownership or establishing year-to-year working arrangements wherein Breadon provided important monetary support that could be terminated at will, depending on how he and Rickey assessed the financial burden and the quality of their player development. By the end of the decade the Cardinals' farm system had eight affiliates, including one in both Class A and, beginning in 1927, Double-A in the International League.

Though still few in number, Cardinals' affiliates quickly became the breeding ground for players that helped the major-league team rise from the ranks of the noncompetitive to persistent contender and frequent pennant winner. Seven of the core players that finally gave the Cardinals their first pennant and World Series championship in 1926, including first baseman Jim Bottomley, outfielders Taylor Douthit and Chick Hafey, and 20-game winner Flint Rhem all came to St. Louis after making the grade in the Cardinals' farm system. Some got their start in the Class D affiliate and most played in Houston as their last stop before St. Louis. Those four were also core regulars when the Cardinals won their second pennant in 1928.

* * *

The Cardinals were a team in transition when they won their third and fourth pennants in 1930 and '31, but benefited from the continuing pipeline of players from Rickey's farm. The most consequential were right-handed pitchers Bill Hallahan, 15–9 and 19–9 those two years, and Paul Derringer, an 18-game winner in his 1931 rookie season; first baseman Ripper Collins; shortstop Charlie Gelbert; and outfielder Pepper Martin. The Cardinals' seven-game triumph over the Athletics in the 1931 World Series was in no small measure due to Martin batting .500, tying a Series record with 12 hits, and stealing five bases. All 12 of his hits came in the first five games, in which he made outs in only six of his 18 at-bats.

While St. Louis was not competitive either of the next two years, in 1932 they welcomed to the majors a pair of right-handers who had been pitching for their Houston affiliate—Tex Carleton and the enigmatic, colorful, pitching sensation Dizzy Dean—and in 1933 Joe Medwick took his place in left field. Meanwhile, in 1933, Dizzy's younger brother Paul was winning 22 games for the Cardinals' Double-A American Association affiliate in Columbus, Ohio, earning himself a promotion to St. Louis the next year. The Dean brothers, Carleton, Hallahan, Martin, Collins, and Medwick, all reached St. Louis by progressing through Rickey's minor-league farm system. They would be the foundation of the 1934 Cardinals who won for St. Louis a fifth pennant in nine years since 1926, and a third World Series. They were the famous Gashouse Gang. But not all of the Gashouse Gang got to St. Louis as Cardinals farmhands.

In addition to the long-term horizon that underpinned his conceptualizing and organizing a network of minor-league affiliates to develop future Cardinals players, Branch Rickey was an astute wheeler-dealer to get the players he wanted from other major-league clubs to fill holes where experience was needed. Rickey would become famous for his dictum about trading good players at their peak, just before he suspected they were about to start the downslide of their careers, in order to get the best

The St. Louis Cardinals' starting lineup for both Games One and Seven of the 1934 World Series included third baseman Pepper Martin leading off (far right), outfielder Joe Medwick (fourth from right), and pitching ace Dizzy Dean (far left). Second baseman and manager Frankie Frisch is third from right, and shortstop Leo Durocher stands next to Dean. *National Baseball Hall of Fame and Museum.*

possible return, but he was also savvy at picking similar such players to meet his team's needs, even if that seems contradictory to his basic premise. Because he had a burgeoning farm system with so many young prospects vying to make it to the major leagues, Rickey's horizon for players he wanted from other clubs for their experience was the short-term gain they would give the Cardinals.

St. Louis would not have won its first pennant in 1926 without his trading with the Cubs for veteran catcher Bob O'Farrell in May 1925 and picking the once-great Grover Cleveland Alexander off waivers from the Cubs in June 1926. O'Farrell had hit .324 and .319 as the Cubs' starting catcher in 1922 and 1923, but was now a backup to Gabby Hartnett. In 1926, he caught 146 games for the Cardinals and hit .293. The 39-year-old Alexander had seemed at the end of the road when Rickey picked him up. He not only was instrumental in pitching them to the pennant and beating the Yankees in the World Series, but his 16–9 record at the age of 41 in 1928 helped them to another pennant. Alexander won 55 games for the Cardinals against only 34 losses from 1926 to 1929. By then, it really was the end of his career.

In May 1928, Rickey traded with the Phillies to acquire veteran catcher Jimmie Wilson, who would be a mainstay on three pennant-winning Cardinals teams before he was traded back to the Phillies for another catcher, Spud Davis, who played for the 1934 Gashouse Gang. In June 1930, Rickey was able to acquire the grizzled 36-year-old veteran Burleigh Grimes to bolster the Cardinals' pitching staff. Having already won 243 major-league games with five 20-win seasons, Grimes finished the year 13–6 to help St. Louis win a close pennant race, and he was 17–9 for the runaway 1931 Cardinals. Grimes won two games, including the decisive Game Seven, in the 1931 World Series.

Perhaps the most consequential trade Rickey made where the Gashouse Gang was concerned was the deal that sent Paul Derringer to the Cincinnati Reds for brash shortstop (and fashion dandy) Leo Durocher in May 1933. That trade became necessary from Rickey's perspective only because Charlie Gelbert nearly shot off his foot in a hunting accident over the winter, leaving the Cardinals without a shortstop. At his best, Durocher was a marginal major-league ballplayer. In his two brief years with the Yankees in 1928 and '29, Babe Ruth famously called him the "All-American Out." He hit only .217 for the Reds as their everyday shortstop in 1932. His fielding skills were what kept him in the big leagues—that, and his ego and cockiness, his scrappiness and insatiable desire to win, his instinctual feel for the game. Those were the intangible qualities that caused Yankees manager Miller Huggins to keep Durocher on the roster—although, unlike most managers, with the lineup he had, Huggins could afford to carry an "all-American out." Now Rickey wanted him for the Cardinals for precisely those reasons, and with Derringer chafing at Rickey's stinginess in contract negotiations, he had a very capable pitcher to offer in return. Indeed, Reds general manager Larry MacPhail probably thought he was getting the better of the deal, and in the long term Derringer was a far better player for Cincinnati than Durocher was for St. Louis. From the perspective of Rickey's short-term horizon, however, Durocher was every bit as valuable to the Cardinals as Derringer would later be for the Reds, whom he helped to pitch to consecutive pennants at the end of the decade. Leo Durocher was a Cardinal catalyst in both spirit and performance on the field for the 1934 Gashouse Gang.

* * *

Only a handful of major-league clubs followed the Cardinals' lead in acquiring farm teams in the 1920s. Notwithstanding the advantages of minor-league affiliates, most owners were unwilling to pay for them, and some almost certainly could not. Making deals for the minor-league players they wanted remained baseball's business model, even if—as Yankees owner Jacob Ruppert, in particular, finally concluded—financially well-off clubs were sometimes paying exorbitant sums for players who didn't pan out in the major leagues, and poorer clubs were often priced out of the market. Moreover, Commissioner Landis's view that the Cardinals' growing farm system was detrimental to minor-league baseball because local ownership was critical to the relationship between minor-league clubs and the community was the accepted wisdom. Rickey's counterpoint that many minor-league clubs could use the financial help that a major-league benefactor could provide, especially at the lower classification levels in small cities, was generally dismissed as self-serving (which it was) or irrelevant (which it was not).

That changed with the Great Depression.

Sam Breadon's fellow owners certainly noticed his franchise's success in developing and controlling future-productive major-league players in the minor leagues, particularly at the level just below the majors, where they, unlike St. Louis, were still forced to pay market prices for top major league–ready talent. The turning point for the realization that investing in a minor-league farm system was an investment for the future was quite likely the economic impact that the Depression was having on the solvency of minor-league teams. There were 182 minor-league clubs playing ball in 1929 before the October stock market crash, according to baseball-reference.com. By 1932 that number was down to 134. Several clubs in hard-hit small towns couldn't make ends meet in the preceding years and were moved elsewhere in midseason so their league's schedule could be completed. Several leagues had folded. Many, if not most, minor-league clubs were barely holding on. The financial failure of minor-league teams, particularly at lower levels of competition, ultimately meant there would be many fewer players in the pipeline getting the experience needed to play in the major leagues. That of course could theoretically be accommodated, but the result would be many more players making it to the majors who did not really belong there.

The major leagues needed robust minor leagues, or at least as robust as the economic times would allow, and to the extent they could afford to, major-league owners began spending on minor-league teams to help keep them afloat. While that also gave them exclusive access to the players on those clubs, because they did not start when Rickey did, and so did not have a network that helped pay for itself, few franchises had the resources to do what the Cardinals were doing—building a network of teams at all minor-league levels to ensure they maintained continuous control of their players as they became more experienced and proficient in their skills. Their networks also included exclusive working agreements with minor-league clubs where the major-league team did not control their players, but had their pick of purchasing a player or two from their roster every year in exchange for some financial assistance along the way. Rickey had pioneered that approach as well, to add even more depth to the Cardinals' system.

The year 1932 was pivotal in the rest of the major leagues following the road map laid out by Rickey. In 1931, just three major-league teams had fully owned minor-league affiliates, according to baseball-reference.com, and only the Cardinals with three—in Rochester, Houston, and Keokuk in a Class D league—had more than one farm club. Just five of 136 minor-league clubs in 1931 were officially affiliated with a major-league team. As the Depression economy took a turn for the worse in 1932 with 12 million out of 51¼ million Americans in the labor force unemployed, that jumped to 41 of 134 minor-league clubs having a major-league affiliation. Every big-league franchise except for the impoverished Philadelphia Phillies had at least one farm club. The Cardinals now had 11, including two at the highest Double-A level—Rochester in the International League and Columbus in the American Association—and three Class A clubs. As far as the minor leagues themselves, the Class D Mississippi Valley League might have folded entirely in 1932 were it not for major-league investments in six of its eight teams.

Once Roosevelt's New Deal began having a positive impact on the economy and unemployment dropped below 15 percent in 1937, the minor leagues expanded significantly from 178 teams the previous year, of which 60 percent were affiliated with a major-league club, to 254 teams, 55 percent of which were major-league affiliates. By 1939, big-league franchises owned 170 of the 278 minor-league clubs; Rickey controlled 28. The number of minor-league clubs any big-league franchise controlled from year to year during the Depression was variable. Continuity in affiliate relationships was most consistent at the highest Double-A and Class A levels. At lower classifications, particularly Class D leagues, relationships were more fluid; major-league franchises often sold affiliates to local investors so they could put their farm system money in a minor-league club elsewhere, or because their own economic constraints forced them to cut back on minor-league spending.

Nobody's farm system could match the breadth of teams or depth of talent that the Cardinals had. From the mid-1930s until large numbers of able-bodied minor leaguers began being drafted for World War II, the Cardinals maintained a stable of at least two dozen affiliates in their farm system—the Rickey "chain gang"—with the towns represented by their numerous Class D clubs in constant flux. By 1940, Rickey's vertically integrated operation had more than 30 minor-league affiliates, including one in every Class D league, and controlled as many as 700 players. The future careers of a significant percentage of minor-league players, whether with their parent club or elsewhere, depended on what one franchise—the St. Louis Cardinals—intended to do with them. Major League Baseball had seen this before. At the end of the first decade of the twentieth century, half the franchises owned minor-league clubs that allowed them to control a large stable of players. Unlike then, however, when the National Commission put an end to the practice in the midteens on the grounds that it both blocked players' paths to the major leagues and disadvantaged big-league clubs that could not afford to own minor-league clubs, Commissioner Landis, despite his sympathy for both arguments, had lost his window of opportunity to reinstitute a ban on owning minor-league teams.

It wasn't until the United States was officially at war with Germany and Japan in 1942 that the minor leagues began to scale back teams as the country fully mobilized for war. While the military draft had a big impact on major-league rosters for three years beginning in 1943, its effect on the minor leagues was devastating with so many minor leaguers in their late teens and early 20s being called into service. Flush with nearly 300 teams in 1941, down to 212 in 1942 as the United States went to war, the minor leagues were reduced to just 66 teams in 1943. The reason was primarily that most players were off to war, or soon would be, rather than financial constraints, although the expense of operating a club in a wartime economy without big-league financial assistance was beyond the means of many minor-league owners. Whole leagues disbanded for the duration of the Second World War. Major-league clubs controlled 70 percent of the existing minor-league teams in 1943.

* * *

In the beginning, the commissioner's opposition to Rickey's farm system concept was more philosophical and argumentative than juridical. Landis was concerned, first, about the impact on the relationship between minor-league teams and the local communities that supported them and called them their "home" team. This was, after all, still an era before mass media was able to bring major-league games into the living rooms of American homes wherever they lived, including in small towns and cities far from any major-league team. Populations in minor-league towns had as much of a vested "fanatical" rooting interest in their home team as big-league cities had in theirs.

The Cardinals' decision after the 1927 season to uproot their Double-A affiliate in Syracuse—population 209,000, according to the 1930 census—to bigger-market Rochester—with 328,000 people, the 22nd-largest city in the United States—was precisely the sort of move that troubled Landis, because a remote parent major-league franchise broke a long-standing connection between a city and its minor-league club. The Syracuse Stars had been a franchise in the prestigious International League since 1918. There would be another team in Syracuse the next two years, but in the much-lower-profile Class B New York–Pennsylvania League, then none for four years until the Boston Red Sox established an affiliate there in 1934, back at the Double-A level in the International League.

But it was the Rickey "chain gang" and the potential that minor-league players could be trapped in the farm system of their parent major-league club and not get the major-league opportunity that might otherwise be available that most bothered Landis. From the commissioner's perspective, born of the Progressive Era politics he embraced, farm systems were fundamentally morally unjust to minor-league players, particularly in a system as expansive as the Cardinals' became, where the future of so many players was controlled by a single major-league franchise. He held this view in seeming contradiction to his adamant opposition to any such thing as a players labor union that could put at risk the reserve clause, which he and all franchise owners, including in the minor leagues, considered integral to the efficient functioning of Organized Baseball.

But it was not a contradiction, really. While he did not believe players should be free at the expiration of their contracts to pursue the best possible deal with any ballclub other than the one to which they were bound by the reserve clause, Landis also thought no minor-league player should be denied the opportunity to advance his career—including making it to the major leagues as soon as his talented merited—because Mr. Rickey and the Cardinals owned his contract, controlled his future, and could keep him down on the farm for as long as they wanted, even if another big-league team was interested in acquiring him. Consistent with that was a firm belief that any and all major-league clubs should be able to compete in a free market for minor-league players they were interested in, rather than have players off limits because they belonged to somebody's farm system. And finally, such control by the parent club was contrary to Landis's conviction that minor-league clubs should be able to benefit from making their own deals for players.

Landis had a point on all three counts, but his concern was overstated to the extent that any minor leaguer on the threshold of being major-league ready was a valuable asset. Such a player, if there was no room for him at his position on the parent major-league club, was likely sooner or later to be sold or traded for other prospects or players to fill immediate needs at the big-league level, which in fact is what the Cardinals often did. He might not have made it to the big leagues as quickly as he deserved, but he quite likely was going to have an opportunity to get there.

On the issue of minor-league franchises having the right to make their own deals, that, too, could cut against players' interests. This was particularly the case with the Double-A leagues in the 1920s that no longer allowed major-league clubs to draft any of their players. They could profit handsomely from selling their best players for the highest possible price, but that also meant minor-league players could be stuck in place until their club got what they considered to be fair market value. Many star players on the International League's Baltimore Orioles in the mid-1920s, including Lefty Grove, might have made it to the majors much sooner had owner Jack Dunn not demanded compensation commensurate with their prodigious talents.

Notwithstanding his misgivings, Landis could not roll back the concept of vertically integrated minor-league systems intended for the development of players under parent-club control. His chance to have done so was in the 1920s when Breadon and Rickey first embarked on their farm system endeavor, especially since most other major-league owners at that time were not inclined to follow suit. Because he was preoccupied with both more high-profile matters and consolidating his authority over the owners, that was a battle Landis was unwilling to fight. Furthermore, reassurances by Pittsburgh owner Barney Dreyfuss and Detroit owner Frank Navin that franchises could not financially afford to maintain a farm system of multiple minor-league affiliates may have convinced Landis that Rickey's ambition would either collapse of its own weight by threatening to bankrupt the Cardinals, or be very limited in scope. Dreyfuss and Navin could speak from experience; the Pirates had controlling interest in a Texas League club in 1920 and 1921 that they sold to the Cubs in a cost-cutting move, and the Tigers did not expand to more than their one affiliate, also in the Texas League, until 1932.

Since the Cardinals' system started out relatively small and added affiliates incrementally, and since the few other clubs that followed their lead in the 1920s had far more limited stakes in the minor leagues, Landis probably saw no urgency in trying to head off the ultimate logic of Rickey's minor-league farms-to-big-league-table concept. What was perhaps not anticipated was that the Cardinals' investment in minor-league affiliates, however few at first, was in fact profitable not just in terms of player control and development. Rickey ensured the Cardinals had a first-rate cadre of scouts to recruit talented young players for their lowest-level farm teams, maintained coherent guidelines for evaluating players, and had a systematic approach to player development that made players in their system attractive to other clubs. Selling prospects to other clubs, particularly from their Class D teams, was a way to keep the system self-funding with minimal cash infusions from St. Louis. Indeed, some higher-profile affiliates were making money for the Cardinals. Rickey's astute management of the whole enterprise proved the value of a farm system not only to institutionalize a developmental pipeline of players under team control through the minors until they made the majors, but in being self-sustaining and sometimes even turning a profit.

By the 1930s, there was nothing the commissioner could do because all major-league clubs, with the arguable exception of both very cash-strapped franchises in Philadelphia, were fully invested in having their own minor-league affiliates. Major league–supported farms clubs were also a necessity for the survival of minor-league clubs during the Depression years. Some of Landis's specific concerns, even if not his philosophical opposition in principle to the farm system concept, were alleviated by new rules agreed to with the minor leagues in which all classifications became subject to a major-league draft—including the Double-A leagues that had refused to be so in the 1920s—with the proviso that no players on any of their clubs not affiliated with a big-league franchise would be subject to a draft unless they had at least four years of minor-league experience. The new rules also stipulated that the longest any player could be held in a single club's farm system was seven years, after which he was a free agent on the open market.

As the Cardinals' system grew exponentially in the 1930s—Rickey controlled 13 percent of the minor-league teams in 1936—Landis had another concern. He worried that any franchise controlling so many players on such a large number of affiliated clubs at all levels of the minor leagues could compromise the integrity of *their* pennant races, breaching faith with *their* fans. Those clubs, after all, answered to the parent major-league franchise that could dictate player moves, or moves not made, in ways that were not necessarily in the best competitive interests of their minor-league teams. If that was the case, the relationship between the minor-league club and the local community that rooted for their "home" team to be successful was further frayed. Even more disturbing to critics of Rickey's growing empire, the Cardinals' far-flung minor-league system was less than transparent; in addition to the farm teams St. Louis owned outright, there were working agreements with many other minor-league clubs that included claims on their players and influence over their player transactions. St. Louis had working agreements with the Arkansas State and Nebraska State Class D leagues to have the right of first refusal to all of their players in exchange for financial support to keep both leagues solvent.

If farm systems were now a fait accompli, what Landis could do was try to impose greater transparency on major-league operations in the minors. In the most consequential of Landis's skirmishes with Branch Rickey over his farm system, the commissioner in 1938 declared 74 Cardinals' farmhands free agents—by some accounts, 91—on the grounds that they were part of an illegitimate system run by St. Louis that masked the extent of one of their Class A affiliate team's connections to clubs in four different Class D leagues, and that many player transactions involving those clubs were not properly registered. The Cardinals were also castigated for that particular Class A team making player transactions ostensibly on its own behalf that were actually dictated from St. Louis and did not benefit the minor-league affiliate. An additional grievous sin of Rickey's operation was that controlling multiple clubs in some Class D leagues, either by direct ownership or a working arrangement, could result in player transfers from one or the other club—including promotions to a higher classification level—affecting the competitive balance between two clubs in the same league.

The most noteworthy of the 74 Cardinals players granted free agency was Pete Reiser, then 19 years old in only his second year of professional baseball, who had played for two of their Class D affiliates in 1937. The Brooklyn Dodgers moved quickly to sign Reiser, who made it to Ebbets Field less than two years later in July 1940. Without Reiser's league-leading .343 batting average in 1941 the Dodgers would not have held off Rickey's Cardinals to win the National League pennant. This episode is also said to have been the undoing of Rickey's relationship with Breadon, who was greatly embarrassed by his franchise being called out by the commissioner for unethical conduct.

Two years after slapping down the Cardinals, Landis declared 91 players in Detroit's much smaller farm system to be free agents because the Tigers tried to hide their rights from other clubs and, in some cases, from the players themselves. Although Landis's decision stripped away more than half of Detroit's minor-league prospects, it did not ruin the club's future, as the Tigers thought it might. The Tigers won the

American League pennant in 1940 with a mostly veteran club that had no need for an infusion of minor-league talent, and they won again in 1945, once more with a mostly veteran club—this time because so many younger players, including thousands of minor leaguers, were still serving in the Second World War.

The commissioner's punishment did not prevent St. Louis from dominating the National League in the first half of the 1940s, winning four pennants and three World Series in five years from 1942 to 1946, after also nearly winning in 1941. Their core regulars during those years were all homegrown Redbirds promoted to the Cardinals from one of their top minor-league affiliates, foremost among them Enos "Country" Slaughter, Terry Moore, Marty Marion, the brothers Mort and Walker Cooper, Harry Brecheen, and Stan Musial. Only a handful began their careers in other organizations, but even they had to prove themselves within the Cardinals' system before earning their chance to play in St. Louis. Of no small significance, so, too, did their managers have to prove themselves in the Cardinals' minor-league system.

Just as the farm system was valuable for grooming minor-league players under franchise control for a future with the parent major-league club, it also had the advantage of allowing Rickey and Breadon to develop, evaluate, and ultimately promote managers. Rickey's systematic approach to player development, including specific-skills training and metrics for evaluating players' progress through the farm system, lent itself to the logic of having players and their manager at the big-league level share a common base of experience and knowledge in how to play Cardinals baseball. Billy Southworth, whose first stint as St. Louis manager in 1929 had been a failure, got another shot at managing the Cardinals in 1940 after spending most of the 1930s managing in their minor-league system. He led the Cardinals to three straight pennants from 1942 to 1944. After Southworth left following the 1945 season, Breadon turned to Eddie Dyer, who had managed St. Louis affiliates at every level since the early 1930s before he took over in 1946 and immediately led the Cardinals to another pennant.

* * *

Branch Rickey, his relationship with Sam Breadon by now very strained, left St. Louis for new challenges in Brooklyn after the Cardinals' championship in 1942. He did not directly witness their next three pennants, but they were a legacy of his genius and unblinking determination and brazenness to press ahead in establishing an extensive network of affiliates at every classification level for the purpose of developing major league–ready players for the St. Louis Cardinals despite knowing the commissioner was opposed to the very idea. Rickey's ruthless strategy of holding on to promising talent in the Cardinals' system as an investment in the future allowed him to simultaneously be equally ruthless in discarding veteran players abruptly when he felt their skills were on the precipice of decline, all of which contributed to St. Louis being able to field a competitive team for the better part of three decades.

Every other major-league club eventually followed suit. They really had no other choice. None did it better than the Cardinals, who had extraordinary depth of players in their system, although the New York Yankees came close. Most of the Cardinals' prospects washed out before reaching the top classification levels in the minor leagues. Fewer still made it to the majors. Those who did—not all with the Cardinals, because Rickey was more than willing to trade or sell minor-league prospects to other clubs while keeping the best for St. Louis—earned their promotions. Of the 400 players on the opening day rosters of the 16 major-league clubs in 1946—the first year when nearly all of the players who served during World War II were back playing baseball—*The Sporting News* reported that 90 had played for Cardinals farm teams.

It might perhaps be more accurate to say that none did it better than Branch Rickey, because after he left St. Louis, the quality of players in the Cardinals' system was soon no longer exceptional relative to other clubs, certainly not compared to the Brooklyn Dodgers' minor-league system, which Rickey soon made the best in baseball.

23

STAR TURNS AS MANAGERS

While still in the prime of his career, but with the end horizon in view, the Babe aspired to replace Yankees manager Miller Huggins as a player-manager, both well before as well as immediately after chronic ill health cost Huggins his life as the 1929 season came to a close. The defining celebrity of the Roaring Twenties, a star of unprecedented magnitude, Ruth had few inhibitions about doing whatever he wanted, team discipline be damned, and was a constant challenge to manage. At least until he was reined in for insubordination in 1925 by Yankees owner Jacob Ruppert siding with his manager instead of him, the Babe also persistently subverted Huggins's authority in the clubhouse, either deliberately, or by the example of his actions. Ruth's behavioral history undermined any prospect of his managing the Yankees in the Jacob Ruppert regime, although Ruppert was not prepared to part with the Babe's Ruthian clouts. First, he was spurned in favor of former Yankees pitching star Bob Shawkey. Disappointed with the Yankees finishing third under Shawkey in 1930, Ruppert once again gave no thought to Ruth and turned instead to Joe McCarthy as manager, and it was McCarthy whose teams consolidated the greatness of the Yankees' forever dynasty. Ruth remained with the Bronx Bombers through the 1934 season, making little effort to hide his disdain for Marse Joe, the man who became, many baseball historians say, the greatest manager in history. He certainly believed he would have been a successful manager, perhaps even a great manager—especially if he got to manage a team as loaded with talent as the Yankees. Ironically, 1930 would have been a less than auspicious year for Ruth to break in as a manager, let alone a player-manager, because Philadelphia's Athletics were a much better team than the Yankees and in the midst of three straight pennants. Some 80 years later, on March 10, 2014, the *New York*

Times quoted his daughter as saying, "He really thought he deserved to manage. . . . He always felt he would be a better manager than Joe McCarthy. He always talked about that."

Babe Ruth would have regarded being named manager as a validation of his own greatness. To not be named manager when the opening presented itself—as it did with Huggins's death—might well have been perceived by the Babe as disrespectful of his place in the baseball pantheon. Having seen most of the biggest big-name players who were his contemporaries, like Speaker, Cobb, Sisler, Collins, Bancroft, and Hornsby, become player-managers, the Babe's aspirations to manage at the same time he was bashing home runs was not an unrealistic expectation. And Ruth surely noted that Bucky Harris, a good but hardly standout player compared to those esteemed names, led the Washington Senators to back-to-back pennants in his first two years as an under-30 player-manager in 1924 and 1925, interrupting Yankees strings of three straight pennants.

Tris Speaker, Cleveland's outstanding center fielder, was 31 and probably the best player in the game when he was named their manager in July 1919. The next year he guided the Indians to their first American League pennant, and won the World Series to boot. Ty Cobb, the Babe's rival at the time for the sobriquet "best player in baseball history," and who stoked the fires of their "rivalry" by his disdain for the power game, became player-manager of the Tigers in 1921 at the age of 34. The Browns named their star first baseman, 31-year-old George Sisler, player-manager in 1924, and later that season the White Sox did the same with Eddie Collins—still one of the best players in baseball, even at 37. All four were replaced as manager of their teams after the 1926 season—Speaker and Cobb because they were accused of betting on the outcome of a baseball game seven years earlier, and Collins and Sisler because their teams were not competitive. Over in the National League, longtime star shortstop Dave Bancroft became manager of Boston's Braves in 1924 after being traded by the Giants, in part to afford him that opportunity. Stuck managing a bad team, Bancroft was axed after four years. The latest date in any season his Braves had a winning record was on May 17 in 1924, only 23 games into the schedule.

And then there was Rogers Hornsby, whose managerial career might best be described as "Rajah Antagonistes." Hornsby was 29 and in the midst of his second Triple Crown season in four years when the Cardinals made him player-manager early in the 1925 season. The next year, Hornsby managed the Cardinals to their first pennant and a World Series triumph over the Yankees in which "Rajah" got to tag out the Babe himself on an attempted steal for the final out of the fall classic. It didn't matter that Hornsby had managed the Cardinals to the top of the baseball world, their owner disliked him, wanted him gone, and traded him to the

Giants. After a year playing for McGraw, Hornsby's next stop was Boston, home of the woebegone Braves, for whom he won another batting title, became player-manager in May 1928, and presided over a horrific 39–83 record the rest of the way. The Cubs paid $200,000 for Hornsby to play for them in 1929. Hornsby became a player-manager for the third time in the closing days of the 1930 season when Cubs owner William Wrigley and team president William Veeck decided to fire manager Joe McCarthy. They should have been alert to Hornsby's leadership shortcomings, however, if for no other reason than because he had done his deliberate best all year to undermine McCarthy. Less than two years later, Hornsby was forced out amid not only frayed relations in the clubhouse and with the executive suite, but also under investigation by the commissioner for gambling debts and perhaps even leveraging his role as manager to get some of his players to lend him money.

Undeniably a great player, Hornsby was an antagonistic man—definitely *not* a people person—who alienated both players and bosses everywhere he managed. Hornsby managed by intimidation. McGraw was himself an intimidating personality, but the difference was that John McGraw understood leadership and Rogers Hornsby did not. McGraw was a tough taskmaster, but ultimately respectful of his players. They, or most anyway, understood that the often-tyrannical McGraw—he wasn't the "Little Napoleon" only because he was short—was making them better ballplayers. Hornsby was just a jackass. Easily frustrated and quick to anger when players didn't meet his expectations, Hornsby was unable to get players to buy into his leadership because he displayed no particular wisdom. He was insulting, crude, and disrespectful. He put the Cubs' popular slugger Hack Wilson in the doghouse and had him traded away after the 1931 season. It was all about him. For John McGraw, it was about team, although he certainly didn't mind the personal fame that came his way.

* * *

To a significant extent, Ruth was the antithesis of Speaker, Cobb, Collins, Bancroft, and Hornsby as great players becoming player-managers. It wasn't so much that he lacked the baseball acumen for the job. It wasn't even so much that he lacked the personal discipline to be a manager or questions about whether he could command the respect of players who were his teammates and, in some cases, his running mates in extracurricular activities. Those were both legitimately debatable propositions about the Babe, but others named to be managers faced similar doubts. His being the antithesis of the great contemporary players whose company he hoped to join as a player-manager was more along the lines of them being totally committed to the game; baseball was the totality of their public life, while Ruth actually *had* a public life that was the stuff of later-in-the-twentieth-century tabloid fare.

Ruth's unrealistic best hope of becoming the Yankees' manager came when Huggins died near the end of the 1929 season. His hopes were not only unrealistic because of doubts raised by his earlier hell-raising and insubordination, which were not forgotten even though his lifestyle and clubhouse behavior had moderated in more recent years, but also because playing managers in Major League Baseball were less prevalent than before. Since the first decade of the twentieth century, owners had turned more to baseball professionals—men like George Stallings and Pat Moran in the teens, Bill McKechnie and McCarthy in the twenties—who had long experience in the game, not necessarily as former star players, than to active players on their rosters when they made managerial changes. Only about a quarter of the managers named since 1910 were players on their teams, not including a handful who served in an interim role while the new manager was being found. There was a distinct difference in philosophy about player-managers between the two leagues.

National League owners, on the rare occasions they turned to an active player to become manager, selected mostly aging veterans near the end of their careers who were no longer invested in much playing time rather than star players still in their prime. Bancroft and Hornsby, on three occasions, were the exceptions. American League clubs, by contrast, bought into the star-player-as-manager paradigm to the extent they employed player-managers, which contributed to a 24-to-7 advantage over the National League in player-manager years from 1919 to 1929 where the manager was a regular on his team. That included Speaker for eight years in Cleveland, Cobb for six in Detroit, and Harris for five in Washington, all exceeding Bancroft's four years in the dual roles that was the most for any National League player-manager. Of the American League's five core-regular playing managers in the 1920s—who also included Sisler and Collins—Bucky Harris alone was not a star player, although he was an acknowledged leader on the field and a popular player with the Senators. Leading his club to two pennants in his first two years in charge, Harris was certainly the most successful of baseball's player-managers in the 1920s. Speaker and Cobb, however, were the most compelling because they still were such great ballplayers. The same was true of Hornsby in the National League. It was in their footsteps that Ruth thought he deserved to travel, except he'd be not just a great player, but also a great player-manager because the Yankees were a great team.

If Ruth's last best hope to manage the Yankees while still starring in the batting order was when Huggins died, he had *no* chance, at least not with Ruppert in charge, and not just because of behavioral or maturity issues. The Yankees' success under Huggins almost certainly reinforced to Ruppert that a baseball professional devoted exclusively to the role of manager was the necessary foundation to continue dynastic momentum. Ruppert greatly appreciated Huggins's skills in preparation, player development, and player assessments—including players on other teams to fill a Yankees need that might not even seem obvious—as well as his abilities as a game strategist. Those were not job requirements that could be easily handled by any player who also had to attend to his playing career, no matter how much of a star or baseball genius he might be. A player-manager might work for other clubs, especially those with more limited ambitions, but not for Ruppert's Yankees.

*** * ***

Playing managers had in fact all but disappeared from Major League Baseball. In 1930, when Ruth was expecting at least strong consideration for the job, none of the 16 major-league teams was being managed by one of their players. Unless one counts Bucky Harris in 1929, now managing Detroit but having for all intents and purposes retired as an active player—he played himself in just seven games and had only 11 at-bats all season—baseball was entering its second year with no playing managers. The year before that, the only player-managers who were also regulars in their starting lineups were Harris in Washington and Hornsby with the Braves. In 1927, there had been just three player-managers—Harris, Bancroft in his fourth and final year with the Braves, and veteran catcher Bob O'Farrell of the Cardinals, who was unable to play for much of the season because of injury.

The Cubs naming Hornsby as their manager at the very end of the 1930 season gave the major leagues a single player-manager in 1931. Ruppert and Barrow, meanwhile, unhappy with Bob Shawkey as their manager in 1930, once again were looking for a replacement for Huggins. Once again, they had to both say no to the Babe's aspirations and massage his resentful ego. The man they chose, Joe McCarthy, may have been disdained by Ruth and others for never having played in the major leagues, but even when the Yankees' dynastic momentum appeared stalled with only one pennant to show in the first five years of the McCarthy era, Ruppert and Barrow never thought twice about looking for another manager, and certainly not in the direction of Ruth, even if the Babe genuinely believed he would have been a better manager than McCarthy.

The major leagues began the 1932 season without any team being managed by a core regular. It did not end that way. While there were two ostensible player-managers in charge of their teams at the beginning of the season, both played themselves very sparingly; the Cubs' Rogers Hornsby had all but officially retired as a player, physically battered after

16 years as one of baseball's biggest stars, a decision made easier by the excellent spring-training performance of rookie second baseman Billy Herman. By the end of the year, however, two National League clubs were being managed by an active everyday player—the Giants by their star first baseman, Bill Terry, who took over when the ailing McGraw stepped down at the beginning of June, and the Cubs by their first baseman, Charlie Grimm, who replaced the fired Hornsby in August. Over in the American League, the Red Sox named veteran infielder Marty McManus to be their manager in mid-June. McManus had started in 46 of the Red Sox' first 55 games, but was batting only .253 at the time and put himself into the starting lineup in only 29 of the 99 games that remained on Boston's schedule.

Player-managers were making a comeback. The Senators named their outstanding shortstop Joe Cronin player-manager in 1933. By midseason that year, star second baseman Frankie Frisch was managing the Cardinals. Including Terry, Grimm, and McManus, five major-league clubs were now managed by a core player on their roster. McManus did not survive as Red Sox manager beyond that season, but in 1934 the Phillies opened the season with catcher Jimmie Wilson as their manager; the Tigers began the year with outstanding catcher Mickey Cochrane as their manager; and before the season was over, Pie Traynor, in his 13th year as the Pirates' third baseman, and Jimmy Dykes, the White Sox' third baseman, became player-managers. Seven of the 16 major-league teams ended the 1934 season with playing managers, the most since 1926. The next year, Cronin went from two years as player-manager in Washington to having the same dual roles for the Red Sox, and in the middle of the 1938 season, the Cubs named Gabby Hartnett, their outstanding catcher since 1923, to replace Grimm.

The 1930s were both a revival and the last hurrah for player-managers in Major League Baseball. The duration of the Great Depression had changed the dynamic, breaking the bias against player-managers that seemed to have settled by the time the stock market crashed. It made more financial sense for many clubs, including those with higher payrolls like the Giants, Cubs, and Tigers, to pay an established player something extra to manage than to hire someone else as a manager who would demand a competitive wage. In the 13 baseball seasons between the crash of October 1929 and the first year that major-league rosters were hit hard by World War II in 1943, about one-third of the managerial changes in the National League and 20 percent in the American League went to active players on the roster, mostly to core regulars. The American League figure probably would have been higher but for the fact that Connie Mack owned the club he managed and saw no need to replace himself, and the Yankees were perfectly happy with McCarthy for the long term.

From 1932 to 1938, every National League pennant winner and three of the seven American League pennant-winning teams were managed by a player-manager, or a manager who until recently had been a playing manager on his club. All four of the teams that were not so led were the McCarthy-managed New York Yankees. In the 22 years following first baseman Frank Chance leading the Cubs to the 1910 pennant, by contrast, only five of the 44 teams that played in a World Series were led by a core-regular player-manager—the 1912 Red Sox, by first baseman Jake Stahl; the 1920 Indians (outfielder Tris Speaker); the 1924 and '25 Senators (second baseman Bucky Harris); and the 1926 Cardinals (second baseman Rogers Hornsby).

Financial considerations during the Depression years also resulted in less managerial turnover than had been the norm. Most of the player-managers named in the 1930s stayed on as manager for the teams that gave them the opportunity even after their playing careers wound down. Indeed, few continued as core regulars after they were named player-manager for more than four or five years. Until assuming a more modest off-the-bench role in 1942, Cronin had the longest tenure as a player-manager—nine years as his teams' regular shortstop—since Fred Clarke. As the Depression wound down, so, too, did the hiring of players as managers. After Hartnett in 1938, only three players of consequence were made managers of their teams—veteran shortstop Leo Durocher of the Dodgers in 1939 and veteran outfielder Mel Ott of the Giants and young shortstop Lou Boudreau—only 24 at the time—of the Indians in 1942.

In 1948, Lou Boudreau became the major leagues' last player-manager to lead his team to a pennant. Whatever his managerial prowess—and the Indians' new owner, Bill Veeck, having doubts, considered trading him before fiercely negative fan reaction caused him to think better of it—it was Boudreau's superb season as a player that was critical to Cleveland finishing the 154-game schedule in a tie for first with Boston, winning a one-game playoff for the pennant, and then winning the World Series. Boudreau's player value of 10.4 wins above replacement in 1948 was the best ever by a playing manager, including any single season by Speaker, Cobb, and Hornsby, all of whom were still great hitters when they were player-managers.

After Ott and Boudreau, very few players were named managers and none were still regulars on their teams, let alone star players. By the 1960s, player-managers had all but vanished from the scene as managing a major-league club became an increasingly complex undertaking.

24

TRADING PLACES IN NL RACES

None of the American League pennant races in the 1930s went into the final weeks with the outcome still uncertain. Not so in the National League. After the St. Louis Cardinals won the 1931 pennant by 13 games, NL fans were witness to pennant races with furious finishes involving the Cardinals, Cubs, Giants, and Pirates in six of the next seven years.

'Twas 1932, and while their former manager Joe McCarthy had the Yankees waltzing to the American League pennant, the Chicago Cubs decided on August 2 they had had enough of Rogers Hornsby. The Cubs were second with a 53–46 record at the time, trailing Pittsburgh by five games, when 34-year-old first baseman Charlie Grimm, in the waning days of a modest playing career dating back to 1920, took charge as manager. Under new leadership, the Cubs won 26 of their next 32 games, including a 14-game winning streak, to take a commanding lead on their way to a pennant and a fateful encounter with McCarthy's Yankees, the outcome of which is best left unsaid to past generations of long-suffering Cubs fans.

Their 1932 pennant represented the end of Chicago's McCarthy era, even though McCarthy had been fired two years before. Grimm, third baseman Woody English, outfielders Riggs Stephenson and Kiki Cuyler, catcher Gabby Hartnett, and pitchers Charlie Root, Guy Bush, and Pat Malone remained as core players from McCarthy's team that ran away with the 1929 pennant, although Hartnett was hurt that entire year and hardly played. No longer there were the two biggest stars on McCarthy's 1929 club—center fielder Hack Wilson and second baseman Hornsby; Wilson because he got on the wrong side of Hornsby and was traded before the 1932 campaign began, and Hornsby because he got on the wrong side of many of his players and the front office and was fired. The

1932 Cubs also featured in their first or second year in the majors second baseman Billy Herman, shortstop Billy Jurges, third baseman Stan Hack, and the exceptional right-handed pitching talent Lon Warneke. Along with Hartnett, these players would be the foundation for the Chicago Cubs moving forward in the 1930s.

Joe McCarthy had begun his major-league managerial career in 1926 by resurrecting Chicago's Cubs from the noncompetitive funk they had been in since their 1918 pennant, and he did so dramatically. The Cubs had been in the second division every year since 1920 and finished last in 1925. Undeterred by those who doubted he would be accepted as manager because he had not played a single inning in the major leagues, McCarthy wasted no time making clear he was the boss and setting the foundation for a formidable club that, by the late 1920s, was strong in all facets of the game. He quickly lost patience with the aging and mercurial Grover Cleveland Alexander, whose sins included alcoholism and total disregard for his new manager, and suspended the Cubs' most prominent and still arguably best pitcher in May. Alexander had won 125 and lost 80 for the Cubs going into the 1926 season since arriving in Chicago in 1918—a year he spent fighting for his country in World War I. Placed on waivers in June, Alexander was picked up by St. Louis, and came back to shut out the Cubs in Chicago at the beginning of September to help give the Cardinals momentum on their way to the 1926 pennant. McCarthy not only subtracted a distraction, at least as far as he was concerned, he gave prominent roles to right-hander Charlie Root and outfielders Wilson and Stevenson, the new cornerstones of the Cubs' offense. All three were found wanting by their initial major-league clubs and sent packing to the minors, from where they were shoplifted by Chicago. From last place and 86 losses the year before McCarthy arrived, the 1926 Cubs finished fourth with 82 wins. Wilson led the league in homers and was second in runs batted in.

By 1927 the Cubs had arrived as a legitimate contender. Root won 26 to lead both leagues, and Wilson once again led the league in homers and was second in RBIs. The Cubs were nurturing a lead of six games as late as mid-August before 14 losses in 18 games destined them to another fourth-place outcome. In 1928 they did even better, finishing third, just four games behind the pennant-winning Cardinals, a result of McCarthy strengthening the Cubs' firepower by trading with Pittsburgh for Cuyler and bolstering the pitching by purchasing the minor-league contract of hard-throwing right-hander Malone. Cuyler, the batting star of the 1925 Pirates when they won the World Series, had worked his way into the front office's bad graces by holding out in the spring of 1926 and into the manager's doghouse on the 1927 pennant-winning Pirates for general disgruntlement about how he was being treated, including insinuations of not giving his all when he was playing on a bum leg. Wilson led the league in home runs for the third straight year; Malone led the club with 18 wins.

After three straight pennant races decided by two games or less, the National League watched helplessly as McCarthy's Cubs put an early end to the contest in 1929. Their lead was never less than 10½ games the final six weeks of the season. The Cubs hit .303 as a team and scored 982 runs, seven more than the powerful Ruth-and-Gehrig Yankees in 1927 and the most in the majors since 1897. And they did all this without Gabby Hartnett, whose eighth season with the Cubs was spent entirely on the bench as a pinch-hitter because a "dead" arm kept him out of the lineup. Hartnett had already established himself as one of the best all-around catchers in baseball's now-half-century history, and he was a catcher who could hit for both average and power. It helped to have Rogers Hornsby, by now a nomad because of his difficult personality; playing for his fourth team in four years, Hornsby had a typically sensational year—the last of his great career—with 39 homers, 149 runs batted in, and a .380 batting average. Wilson also hit 39 homers, led the league with 159 RBIs, and batted .345. Cuyler hit .360 with 102 RBIs, and Stephenson batted .362 with career highs in home runs and RBIs. On the mound, Malone's 22 wins and Root's 19 were first and second in the league.

As imposing as the 1929 Cubs' juggernaut was, they proved no match for Connie Mack's equally imposing Philadelphia Athletics in the World Series. Both clubs had high-powered offenses—the Athletics matching Hornsby, Wilson, Cuyler, and Stevenson with Mickey Cochrane, Al Simmons, and Jimmie Foxx—but the Athletics had far superior pitching led by Lefty Grove, George Earnshaw, and Rube Walberg. And yet it was over-the-hill, barely used veteran Howard Ehmke who set the tone of the World Series as Philadelphia's surprise starter in the opening game, in which he not only limited the Cubs to one run but set a new World Series record by striking out 13 batters. The ending to the Series was a nightmare for Cubs fans. First, the Cubs were on the verge of evening the Series at two games apiece when they blew an 8–0 lead in the seventh inning of Game Four by becoming the first team in fall classic history to be battered for 10 runs in one inning. Then in Game Five, the Cubs could not hold on to the 2–0 lead they took into the bottom of the ninth. A two-run home run by Mule Haas off Malone tied the score, and a two-out walk-off double by Bing Miller ended the game and the World Series. Not that anyone was counting yet—except perhaps Cubs owner William Wrigley, who blamed McCarthy for the loss—but the Cubs had now gone 21 years since they were last World Series champions. There was a general sense that McCarthy was completely outmaneuvered by Connie Mack.

As successful as he had been in turning around the Cubs' fortunes, McCarthy was now living in Chicago on borrowed time.

Hartnett was back in 1930 and better than ever, knocking out 37 homers, driving in 122 runs, and batting .339 while catching 132 games—the most so far in his career. Wilson not only hit .356, but his 56 home runs would stand as the National League record until Mark McGwire hit 70 and Sammy Sosa, a Chicago Cub, hit 66 in 1998, and his 191 runs batted in remains the most in a single season by anyone in major-league history. Malone was once again a 20-game winner. Hornsby, however, missed most of the year with a fractured ankle, an injury that proved to be the beginning of the end of his fabulous playing career. Notwithstanding the nearly season-long absence of Hornsby, McCarthy had the Cubs in front by 5½ games going into September. Losing 10 of the next 14, however, dropped them out of first place and sealed their manager's fate with the owner. The Cubs finished two games behind the Cardinals. McCarthy was fired. Rogers Hornsby was now in charge.

Hornsby's first year as manager ended with the Cubs in third place, 17 games behind the runaway Cardinals, and with his arousing the ire of Wrigley Field fans by his contempt for Hack Wilson, the most popular player in Chicago. Trading Wilson for 38-year-old Burleigh Grimes over the winter did not help Hornsby's cause. His position became untenable in the summer of 1932 when he began feuding with Hartnett and Cuyler, both far more popular than he, while his team was losing ground to first-place Pittsburgh. No sooner was he fired and first baseman Grimm put in place as the new manager than the Cubs became nearly unbeatable. Most notable to the Cubs' success were rookie second baseman Billy Herman hitting .408 during their August surge, and second-year pitcher Lon Warneke winning 15 of his last 18 decisions.

* * *

'Twas 1933, and first baseman Bill Terry, 33 years old when he replaced McGraw in June the previous season, led the New York Giants to their first pennant in eight years in the one National League race between 1932 and 1938 that was decided without a summer-long fight. The Giants secured first place in early June and were in command the rest of the season. Terry hit .322 and Mel Ott knocked out 23 homers and drove in 103 runs. Left-handed screwball artist Carl Hubbell, probably the best pitcher in the National League now that Dazzy Vance had faded with age and with Warneke and Dizzy Dean still very early in their careers, led the league with 23 wins; his 1.66 earned run average was the first under 2.00 in the majors since Alexander in 1920; and his 10 shutouts the most since Alexander's 16 in 1916. Hubbell's exploits included shutouts in three consecutive starts in July, in the midst of which he also threw 8⅓ shutout innings in one game in relief. Two of those starts and the relief appearance came on just two days of rest.

Unlike the '32 Cubs, the '33 Giants did not have to play the Yankees in the World Series. Instead, they were up against the Washington Senators. Giants pitchers dominated the Series, holding the Senators to a .214 batting average and 11 runs in five games. Hubbell had two complete-game victories totaling 20 innings in which he did not allow an earned run. Ott's top-of-the-10th-inning home run in Game Five to break a 3–3 tie was the deciding run in the Series. The Polo Grounds faithful surely did not expect that their Giants would not win another World Series until 21 years later in 1954.

* * *

'Twas 1934, and the Cardinals' turn as they rallied to a dramatic come-from-behind pennant, edging out the Giants by two games. Like the '32 Cubs and '33 Giants, the '34 Cardinals were led by a playing manager, second baseman Frankie Frisch having been given the reins at the age of 34 in July the previous year. The Cardinals had fallen to sixth and improved only to fifth in the two years since their 1931 championship. There was reason to believe, however, that the Cardinals were better than that. For one thing, they led the league in scoring in 1933. Third baseman Pepper Martin had an outstanding season as the catalyst for the Cardinals' offense; outfielder Joe Medwick had an impressive rookie year; and Frisch was still a top-rated player.

For another, the Cardinals' pitching was intriguing. Dizzy Dean, in only his second year, emerged as the undisputed ace of the staff in 1933 with his first 20-win season. Leading the league in strikeouts in both his first two seasons, Dean cut down substantially on his walks, from 3.2 per nine innings as a rookie to just two per nine in his second year. When he was good, he was great—or nearly so. When he was not, however, he really was not—Dean's ERA in his 18 losses in 1933 was 5.62, compared to a superb 1.64 in his 20 victories. And as if that was not enough, Paul Dean made it to St. Louis as a rookie in 1934, and if he was anywhere near as good as his brother, well that would be something. Indeed, Dizzy predicted that "me 'n Paul" were "sure to win 45 games between us." Older brother Dean underestimated their combined success. Turned out they won 49 games between them, Dizzy with a 30–7 record and Paul with a 19–11 mark. They were just two of the great characters on the team that has gone down in history as the Gashouse Gang.

The 1934 Cardinals were scrappy and dirty in a good way, as in their uniforms needing a thorough wash after every game, not that that necessarily happened. For most of the summer, it was the Giants on top and the Cubs close behind in second. Leading the Cardinals by seven games with just three weeks and 22 games left on the schedule, the Giants' quest to return to the World Series seemed all but certain. The Cardinals got hot, going 18–5 the rest of the way, and the Giants were not at 8–13. The two clubs were tied entering the final weekend of the season, each with two games remaining. The Cardinals won both of theirs against last-place Cincinnati, while the Giants lost both of theirs against the sixth-place Dodgers as Bill Terry's smart-ass rhetorical sound bite back in spring-training questioning whether Brooklyn was still in the league came back to bite him hard. Dodgers manager Casey Stengel had the last laugh in an otherwise unsuccessful season.

Carl Hubbell, who was 21–12 and led the league with a 2.30 ERA, made his last start exactly one week before the season ended, almost certainly because his workload down the stretch had him near exhaustion. Beginning on September 4, when his 19th win of the year gave the Giants their seven-game lead, Hubbell made six starts in 20 days, winning three and losing two, which brought his innings total to 310. After that, in the last seven days of the season, he pitched just twice in relief, totaling three innings. In the final game of the year against the Dodgers, with the Giants trailing the Cardinals by a single game and the outcome of the game in St. Louis still to be settled, Hubbell came into a tie game in the 10th inning with two runners on, allowed both to score, and gave up a run of his own. His un-Hubbell-like performance, however, did not cost the Giants the pennant since the Cardinals won their game.

On the Cardinals' side, the Dean boys were both also overworked down the September stretch. Dizzy started seven games, relieved in five, and was 7–1 for the month with two saves. Paul also made seven starts, relieved once, and was 5–3 in September. In a crucial four-game series against the Giants at the Polo Grounds in the middle of the month, which started with the Cardinals still 5½ games behind, Paul beat the Giants twice, including outlasting Hubbell in 11 innings to close out the series, and Dizzy beat them once. Dizzy pitched St. Louis into a first-place tie with New York when he blanked the Reds on the final Friday of the season; Paul pitched them into first place the next day while the Dodgers beat the Giants; Dizzy finished up with a Sunday shutout on one day of rest to clinch the pennant while the Dodgers once again showed the Giants they were indeed still in the league; and then the Dean brothers accounted for all four of the Cardinals' wins in the World Series, each winning twice, as St. Louis outlasted Detroit in seven games.

* * *

After winning the '32 pennant, the Chicago Cubs finished third the next two years without really being a serious contender. But now 'twas 1935, and another dramatic finish to a pennant race that once again had seemed well in hand for the Giants. An Independence Day doubleheader sweep of the hapless Braves, who won only 35 games that year, gave New York a nine-game edge over second-place St. Louis, and Chicago was buried in fourth place, 10½ games behind. Only 18 days later, which included losing four straight in Chicago, the Giants' lead was down to a half-game, and they were now in a heated battle for the pennant with both the Cubs and Cardinals. On August 25, the Cardinals took over first place.

When they awoke on September 4, the Cubs were in third place. They trailed the Cardinals by 2½ games, and the Giants by a half-game. They then did not lose another game for more than three weeks. In fact, not until clinching the pennant did Chicago lose again. They won 21 straight, including the first three of their final five games in St. Louis to end the season. Warneke outpitched Paul Dean to win the opener of that series, 1–0, and ensure the Cubs at least a tie for first place. When they beat Dizzy Dean in the next game, the National League pennant was returned to Chicago. The pennant secured, the Cubs allowed themselves the luxury of letting up, losing the last two meaningless games of the season to conclude the month of September with a 23–3 record. The Cubs went 2–4 in October, however, meaning they lost the World Series to the American League champion Tigers.

Manager Charlie Grimm had by this time effectively called it quits as a player, although he did return for a minor encore of 39 games the next season. Gabby Hartnett batted .344 with 91 runs batted in; Billy Herman was just a few points behind at .341. Stan Hack hit .311 and was now the best third baseman in the league. Warneke, second-year right-hander Bill Lee, old-timer Charlie Root, and the offseason acquisitions of veteran southpaw Larry French from the Pirates and righty Tex Carleton from the Cardinals gave the 1935 Cubs the best pitching staff in baseball. Lee's 20–6 record counted for the best winning percentage in the majors. Warneke had his third 20-win season in four years and was by now acknowledged as one of the three best pitchers in the National League. The only two better were Carl Hubbell, a 20-game winner for the third straight year, and Dizzy Dean, whose 28 wins nearly repeated his 30-win season the year before and who led the league in strikeouts for the fourth straight year.

For the Giants, the 1935 season had been a catastrophe. From their doubleheader sweep on July 4 to the end of the season, they suffered a 19-game swing in the standings against Chicago, going from 10½ games ahead of the fourth-place Cubs to finishing 8½ games behind them. Hubbell had 14 of his 23 victories after July 4, including four in September, but their right-handed ace, Hal Schumacher, 19–9 for the season, won none after September 6.

* * *

The same three teams battled it out for the 1936 pennant, sequentially succeeding each other at the top of the standings. First, it was the Cubs on top from mid-July to early in August. Then the attention shifted to St. Louis, where the Cardinals held first for most of August. While first the Cubs and then the Cardinals couldn't hold on to first place, Bill Terry drove the Giants from fifth, 10½ games behind in mid-July, to a 3½-game lead at the beginning of September, winning 24 of the 27 games they played in August. They maintained their lead the rest of the season, finishing five games ahead of both Chicago and St. Louis, only to encounter Joe McCarthy's Yankees. They never had a chance, even with Hubbell and Ott. Back in the World Series for the first time in four years, the Yankees had retooled with a gentleman named Joe DiMaggio in center field. The Series was over in six games.

Now it's 1937. Terry decided his aching knees made it too difficult to play any longer and retired as a player to focus entirely on being manager. The Cubs held first place for most of July and all of August. They led the league by 6½ games on August 13, then lost 15 of their next 23 games to find themselves three behind the Giants on September 6. The Giants finished with a 24–10 record down the September stretch to win the pennant by three games. As in 1934, the Giants concluded the season with three games against the Dodgers, sporting a three-game lead over the Cubs. This time the Giants beat the Dodgers to finish the season with their second consecutive pennant and third in five years, three games out in front. Once again, they had the dubious honor of playing their cross-river rivals. McCarthy. DiMaggio. Gehrig. Gomez. Ruffing. Dickey. No more need be said. It took the Yankees just five games to dispatch the Giants this time.

Mel Ott and Carl Hubbell were the indispensable Giants. Ott led the league in home runs both years and would again in 1938. Still only 28, Ott hit his 300th career round-tripper in August 1937 to become the first National League player to reach that milestone, breaking Rogers Hornsby's record of 298 (Hornsby's career total of 301 homers included three in the AL). While 323 of Ott's 511 career homers, nearly two-thirds of his total, were hit at home, the Polo Grounds might have been a mixed blessing for Ott, a left-handed pull hitter known for an extreme front leg lift in his stride. Ott was able to take great advantage of the mere 257 feet to the right-field foul pole whenever he pulled the ball tight down the line. On the other hand, the grandstand angled sharply away from the foul line to create a vast expanse in right field that probably resulted in many long fly outs for Ott that might have been home runs in most other parks.

Hubbell extended his 20-wins-a-year streak to five seasons with a 26–6 record in 1936 and 22–8 in 1937, leading the league in winning percentage both years. He finished the 1936 season with 16 consecutive wins and began 1937 with eight straight. In between, he won the opening game of the 1936 World Series, then suffered his first loss since July 13, 1936, on October 4 in Game Four, with Gehrig belting a two-run homer off him. Notwithstanding that postseason loss, Hubbell's 24-game winning streak remains the longest in major-league history. Hubbell was the only Giants pitcher to win more than 14 games in 1936; in 1937, rookie Cliff Melton, also a southpaw, joined him in the 20-win club with exactly 20.

The Giants were poised to make it three pennants in a row on July 4, 1938. They were up by 3½ games in the standings, and their 45–25 record was better even than the first-place Yankees in the other league. Hubbell already had nine wins. Ott had 19 home runs. The run for the 1938 National League pennant would once again be a nailbiter, but the Giants wound up not in the mix. They did not blow a big lead. Instead, they played badly. The Giants had a losing 38–42 record after Independence Day—second worst in the league—and finished third, five games out. Hubbell was bothered by bone chips in his elbow and won only four more games before being sidelined for the rest of the year in mid-August. Ott finished with 36 homers, the third year in a row and the fifth time in his career he led the league.

Five losses in six games against the Cubs in a two-week span at the end of July and the beginning of August sounded the death knell for the '38 Giants and helped spur Chicago to the pennant. The major change on the Cubs since their 1935 pennant was that Lon Warneke had been traded after the 1936 season to the rival Cardinals for first baseman Ripper Collins after having won exactly 100 games for Chicago. The day before the 1938 season got started, Chicago traded again with St. Louis to bring on board one of the only two National League pitchers with a legitimate claim to being better than Warneke between 1932 and 1936. His name? Dizzy Dean.

* * *

The arc of Dizzy Dean's career was emblematic of the rise and fall of the Gashouse Gang. After winning it all in 1934, the St. Louis Cardinals seemed poised for an extended run as the best team in the National League. They had a dynamic offense that led the league in scoring, extra-base hits, batting average, slugging percentage, and stolen bases when they won the pennant. The right-handed-batting Joe Medwick was just 22 in 1934, already the cleanup hitter, and getting better. And the Cardinals appeared to have the nucleus of a strong starting rotation for years to come with Dizzy and Paul Dean, both under 25, and 27-year-old Tex Carleton.

If Branch Rickey had any concerns in the St. Louis executive suite, it was that three of the Cardinals' core position regulars were already 30 years old, and two others were 29. Foremost among them was 36-year-old Frankie Frisch, in his 16th big-league season in 1934 and slowing down. He started just 89 games the next year and 80 in 1936 before conceding that the Fordham Flash was no longer a flash and retiring as a player. Frisch hit .312 in the St. Louis portion of his career to retire with a .316 lifetime average, just 120 hits short of 3,000. Pepper Martin was also soon no longer living up to his peppery nickname. Ripper Collins followed up his league-leading 35 homers in 1934 with 23 the next year, but the year after that, 1936, he lost his starting job to 23-year-old slugger Johnny Mize and became expendable to be used as trade bait to get Warneke from the Cubs.

St. Louis won 96 games in 1935—one more than when they won the pennant the previous year—but got off to a sluggish start that had them lagging by nine games on the Fourth of July. While recovering to move into first from August 25 through September 13, the Cardinals played badly in the final month and finished second to the Cubs, four games out. In 1936 the Cardinals spent most of the first half of the season and much of August in first place only to wind up second again, this time by five games to the Giants. An exactly .500 record in the final two months proved their undoing. Then the bottom fell out. Finishing fourth in 1937, the Cardinals were out of the running by the end of July, and in 1938 they ended up sixth with a losing record.

The Gashouse Gang was now history, never to be forgotten, but with only one pennant and World Series championship to show for their efforts. Why did the Cardinals fail to win another pennant after 1934?

Scoring was not the problem. The Cardinals led the league or were second in runs every year between 1934 and 1938; indeed, St. Louis outscored every other National League team even in 1938, when they had a 71–80 record. Other than Ott, Medwick was the best outfielder in the league between 1934 and 1939, batting .342 with four 200-hit seasons, 125 homers, and 763 runs batted in. He led the league twice in hits, three times in doubles, and three times in RBIs—consecutively in each of those categories—and won the Triple Crown in 1937. Medwick was the ninth player since 1900 to win the Triple Crown, and only six have accomplished the feat since—none in the National League. His 154 RBIs that year would not be eclipsed in the senior circuit until Sammy Sosa drove in 158 runs in 1998, when the schedule was eight games longer; Sosa had 154, matching Medwick, after 154 games—the length of the baseball season back in 1937. Mize was first or second in offensive wins above replacement every year between 1937—his second year in the majors—and 1940.

Manager Frankie Frisch was the problem.

Notwithstanding the brothers Dean, Frisch managed his pitching staff badly. Or perhaps it was *because* of the Dean boys that Frisch badly managed his pitching staff. Either way, Frisch wore out his two aces by using them too often in relief. Frisch allowed the brilliant Dizzy Dean to pitch 50 games in both 1934 and 1935, and 51 games in 1936. Forty-eight of those 151 appearances, nearly a third of the time he took the mound, were in relief, during which Dizzy saved 23 games (leading the league with 11 in 1936) to go along with his 82 victories. Frisch started Dizzy on 34 different occasions with only one or two days of rest from his previous appearance, and Dizzy relieved in another 44 games with two or fewer days of rest for the weary. Remarkably, his record in starts on less than three days' rest was 23–9, and in relief appearances with fewer than three days off, he was 9–8 with 22 saves. And Frisch used Paul Dean 85 times—59 starts and 26 games in relief—in 1934 and 1935, including 17 starts and 20 relief appearances on less than three days' rest.

By 1936 the Cardinals' staff was breaking down. Paul hurt his arm in the spring and never recovered, and Dizzy suffered a broken toe in the 1937 All-Star Game, then injured his much-overworked arm trying to compensate. He, too, was never the same. In 1937 the Cardinals' staff recorded only four saves all year (in 81 wins) and had 81 complete games, indicative of Frisch not trusting his bullpen with the game on the line—especially with the injured, overworked Dizzy not available to be his relief ace as well as his top starting pitcher. Dizzy Dean was now damaged goods, and in 1938 he was no longer a Cardinal. He was a Cub.

* * *

The Pittsburgh Pirates, meanwhile, had been skulking in the background since winning pennants in 1925 and 1927. Returning to the World Series for the first time since 1909, the 1925 Pirates became the first team to recover from a three-games-to-one deficit to win three in a row for the championship of the baseball world. Poised to repeat in 1926, the Pirates were derailed by factionalism occasioned by the role of Fred Clarke, the outstanding former player-manager who led Pittsburgh to four pennants between 1901 and 1909. Now part owner of the club, Clarke sat in the dugout during games and voiced strong opinions about how the team should be managed and about the performance of Pirates players. Tensions reached the boiling point in early August when, with the Pirates clinging to a slim lead, a cadre of players demanded that Bill McKechnie, the impresario of their 1925 championship, be allowed to manage on his own and that Clarke be banished to the box seats. The Pittsburgh front office stood behind Clarke as one of their own, and McKechnie was fired once the season ended. Under a new manager, and with Paul and Lloyd Waner new to the outfield, the 1927 Pirates survived a taut three-team race to the finish line, only to run into the iconic '27 Ruth-and-Gehrig Yankees and be swept in four games. Ironically, notwithstanding their impressive firepower, the Yankees literally ran off with the World Championship on a wild pitch. In the Game Four finale, the score tied, Pirates reliever Johnny Miljus loaded the bases with nobody out in the bottom of the ninth and nearly pitched his way out of trouble by striking out both Gehrig and Bob Meusel, only to uncork his wild pitch with Tony Lazzeri at bat.

Not until 1932 were the Pirates again in a pennant race. They held first from July 3 until August 11 when the Cubs, just nine days after Charlie Grimm had replaced Hornsby as manager, beat them to move into first place for good in their surge to the pennant. The Pirates finished second in 1933, too, but did not give the pennant-winning Giants much trouble after midsummer. In June 1934, with the club in fourth place and fast slipping from contention, the Pirates turned to Pie Traynor, their star third baseman since 1922, to take over as manager and try to reverse course. It didn't get any better for the Pirates. They ended up fifth. Nearing the end of his Hall of Fame career, the highlight of Traynor's year was becoming the first—and, so far, only—player to steal home in an All-Star Game, the same game made famous by Carl Hubbell striking out Ruth, Gehrig, Jimmie Foxx, Al Simmons, and Joe Cronin in succession. Pie Traynor retired as a player after the 1935 season, bothered by an arm injury that severely limited his ability to make strong throws across the diamond. He was widely regarded as the best defensive third baseman in history until Brooks Robinson came along in the 1960s. Staying on as manager, Traynor guided the Pirates to fourth place in 1935 and 1936, and third in 1937. In none of those years did they compete for the pennant, but the '37 Pirates won 24 of their final 34 games to set the stage for competing in 1938.

Traynor had a mostly veteran club take the field in 1938. The brothers Waner—Paul and Lloyd—while no longer in their prime, were still foundation players in the top third of the order, even if their skills were diminishing with age. Nicknamed "Little Poison" by Brooklyn fans— "poison" being a Brooklynese pronunciation of "person"—Lloyd was actually slightly taller than his brother, "Big Poison" Paul. The point of the nicknames, however, was that Lloyd was an irritating poison because of his ability to get hits to start rallies, and Paul was a more lethal poison because of his ability to keep rallies going and drive in runs. Batting mostly third in the lineup since breaking in with a phenomenal rookie season in 1926, Paul Waner had three batting titles to his credit, most recently .373 in 1936, and his eight 200-hit seasons tied Willie Keeler for the most in National League history; Keeler's eight 200-hit seasons were all in a row (1894–1901) and in mostly much shorter seasons. At the time, only Ty Cobb with nine had more 200-hit years than Keeler and Waner. Lloyd began his big-league odyssey in 1927 with three straight 200-hit seasons totaling 678 hits—still the record for the beginning of a career—and would likely have had five straight had he not missed the first half of the 1930 schedule recovering from an appendectomy, but he had not been an elite player since then.

The infield included veterans Gus Suhr at first base and Arky Vaughan at shortstop. Suhr's 822 consecutive games played from September 1931 to June 1937—hardly comparable to fellow first baseman Gehrig's ongoing streak with the Yankees, up to 1,846 at the time Suhr's came to an end—remained the National League record until Stan Musial broke his mark in 1957 on his way to playing in 895 straight games. Vaughan was by now the Pirates' best player, mostly batting fourth since 1934. As a 20-year-old rookie in 1932, the left-handed-batting shortstop secured his future by hitting .402 in June and .331 in July as the Pirates made their move into first place, and .429 in the final month as Pittsburgh tried to catch Chicago. Entering the 1938 season with a .334 batting average in his first six years, Vaughan had an on-base percentage of .424 and walked three times as often as he struck out. Honus Wagner, Pittsburgh's outstanding shortstop from the first decade of the century and now a coach for the Pirates, was undoubtedly impressed by the current shortstop. Arky Vaughan certainly was not the second coming of Wagner—no other shortstop has come close to the Flying Dutchman's all-around excellence—but baseball historian Bill James, a founding father of advanced metrics to assess player performance, has made a compelling case for him being the second-best shortstop in history as of the start of the twenty-first century.

The Pirates began the 1938 season with significant questions about their pitching. Since trading Larry French to the Cubs in 1935—he had averaged 34 starts, 20 complete games, and 16 wins in the five years before he was sent to Chicago—the Pirates lacked an ace. None of their pitchers in 1938 would win more than 12 games as a starter. Pittsburgh's most valuable pitcher in 1938 turned out to be their relief ace—Mace Brown. Pitching 49 games in relief, Brown figured directly in the outcome of 28 of them with a 15–8 record and five saves; his 15 wins were the most of any Pirates pitcher. One of Brown's eight relief losses, however, cost Pittsburgh the pennant. It came on September 28 against the Cubs at Wrigley Field. The Pirates had been in first place every day since July 18, were as far as seven games in front on September 1, but now their advantage was down to just a half-game following a tough 2–1 loss to Dizzy Dean and the Cubs in the first of a three-game series at Wrigley.

* * *

The '38 Cubs were trying to replicate what they did in 1932 when first baseman Grimm replaced Hornsby as manager with the team struggling in midsummer and drove them to an unexpected pennant. Grimm was still the manager on July 19, 1938, his club in third place struggling to be consistent, when Cubs owner Phil Wrigley—son of William, who died in 1932—decided to replace him with Gabby Hartnett, the most popular player in Chicago, now in his 17th year as the Cubs' catcher.

At first, the change in managers made little difference to the Cubs' propensity for streaky play. They won just half of their first 32 games in Hartnett's first month as player-manager. On September 3 they were still third, trailing the first-place Pirates by seven games. But when Pittsburgh came to Chicago for three games beginning on September 27, 'twas the Cubs who were surging. They had won 17 of their last 20. They now trailed by just 1½ games. Dean's victory over the Pirates in the series opener was the Cubs' eighth win in a row. They were poised to take over first place . . . but only if they could complete a sweep of the Pirates in this, their last homestand of the season.

Hartnett had been sidelined as the Cubs' catcher since mid-August because he was hurt. As the Cubs' September surge put them back into contention, however, manager Hartnett wanted catcher Hartnett's extensive experience out on the ball field, and he wrote himself back into the starting lineup. He was catching and batting sixth for the Cubs on September 28. His team had just tied the score and had runners on first and second with one out in the eighth when Mace Brown was called in to end the threat. He did, getting an inning-ending double play. The Pirates failed to score in their half of the ninth, daylight was failing, and Brown had retired Chicago's first two batters in the bottom of the ninth when Hartnett came to bat. The umpires had already told both managers the game would be called because of darkness if there was no outcome by the end of the inning. After Brown got two quick strikes on him, Hartnett lashed the next pitch over the wall in left-center field for his ninth home run of the year. Gabby Hartnett had hit just .179 since inserting himself back as the starting catcher on a daily basis in mid-September, but his "homer in the gloamin'" gave the Cubs the victory and put them into first place by a half-game. The next day, the Cubs crushed the Pirates, 10–1, to extend their lead to 1½ games with four left to play. They won the pennant by two games.

It was quite the stirring comeback for the Chicago Cubs. Three years after virtually sweeping the month of September to win the 1935 pennant, the Cubs had done almost the same by winning twenty of their last 25 games. And for the second time in seven years they had come from behind to finish first after a managerial change to a popular player. Unfortunately, just as in 1932, the comeback Cubs faced off against McCarthy's powerful Yankees, with the same result—four and out.

The Chicago Cubs had now won four pennants in 10 years, once every three years since 1929, giving them nine since the turn of the century. Only the Giants and Yankees, each 10 times, had finished first more often. It had now been an interminably long—so it seemed at the time— 30 years since they last won the World Series, back in 1908.

* * *

Pittsburgh fans would soon join Cubs fans in pining for some glory days. While the Cubs made it back to the World Series seven years later, only to lose . . . again, Pirates fans had to wait two decades after 1938 before they had a truly competitive team again. The 1944 Pirates did win 90 games to finish second, but that was a war year, they did not spend a single day in first place, were 10½ games out as early as the Fourth of July, and 19½ behind at the end of August. Paul Waner was released after the 1940 season with 2,868 hits. In June 1942, playing for the Boston Braves, he became the seventh player in history to collect 3,000 hits in a game against, of all teams, the Pittsburgh Pirates. His brother Lloyd was sent away just before the June 1941 trade deadline and Mace Brown in August 1941. Arky Vaughan was traded to the Dodgers in 1942. In their stead, Elbie Fletcher, Bob Elliott, and Rip Sewell were the new star Pirates. Fletcher came to Pittsburgh from the Boston Bees (as the Braves were then called) in 1939 and had five solid seasons as the Pirates' first baseman before being drafted into World War II in 1944. Elliott played seven years for the Pirates, first in the outfield, then at third base, and finally alternating between both positions; a concussion kept Elliott out of the war. Protected from the draft by being in his mid-30s. Sewell had back-to-back 21-win seasons in '43 and '44.

A final player of note on the wartime Pirates was their center fielder— a San Francisco native by the name of DiMaggio. Vince DiMaggio, older (and less accomplished) brother of Joe and Dominic. In contrast to Joe's renown for being the rare power hitter who hardly ever struck out, famously striking out just 369 times in 7,673 plate appearances to go with 361 home runs during his 13-year career, Vince was a power hitter who whiffed a lot. In five years with the Pirates from 1940 to 1944, Vince DiMaggio struck out 479 times in 2,597 plate appearances while hitting 79 homers. He led National League batters in strikeouts in three of his five Pittsburgh years, including 126 in 1943, just six short of the record he had set five years earlier when he played for the Bees. Hardly the .325

lifetime batter that Joe DiMaggio was, or the .298 hitter that youngest brother Dom DiMaggio was in his 11-year career with the Red Sox, Vince batted just .255 with the Pirates and retired with a lifetime average of .249 in 10 big-league seasons. By modern metrics, however, it appears that Vince DiMaggio was a much better defensive center fielder than his brother Joe. Dom was better than both his brothers.

25

MISSION IMPOSSIBLE

Pitching in Baker Bowl

On June 30, 1938, the Philadelphia Phillies played their last game at Baker Bowl before moving to share Shibe Park with the resident Philadelphia Athletics. Playing the defending NL champion Giants, they lost 14–1. So what else was new? The Giants swept the three-game series, scoring 29 runs while limiting the Phillies to just four. The loss was the Phillies' 11th in their 15-game homestand. So what else was new? The Phillies lost 20 of the 25 games they played in June. In their 14-run beat-down of the Phillies, the Giants banged out 19 hits. Seven were doubles, one was a home run. Three of the Phillies' seven hits were doubles. In the doubleheader between the same two teams the day before, there were nine doubles and Mel Ott's 19th home run among 37 total hits. So what else was new? This was Baker Bowl, after all.

Baker Bowl, the Phillies' home park from 1895 to 1938 and bearing William Baker's name since 1913 when he bought the team, was built to fit into the surrounding urban area, as was true of most big-league ballparks at the time. One important exception was Yankee Stadium, built on an expanse of land in the Bronx used as a lumberyard and, hence, not hemmed in by existing streets, residences, and businesses. Constructing ballparks in urban environments by necessity precluded dimensions that were uniform around the majors because the playing field, arrayed as a diamond fanning out 90 degrees up the left-field and right-field lines, required a vast amount of land—far more than football fields, for example, whose set yardage in length and width were easier to accommodate because they were relatively contained rectangles. Far more expansive, baseball fields could be accommodated in urban locations only if there was allowance for variability in their outfield dimensions in order to be shoehorned within the geometry of the local neighborhood. This, of course, meant that the configuration and dimensions of no two ballparks were necessarily alike; that not all home runs, therefore, would be equal as to how far they had to go to clear the fences; and that franchises could, and indeed should, if they were smart about it, tailor their teams to fit their ballpark. This uniqueness of ballparks is an important part of baseball's appeal. And it is the reason why "park effects" are factored into all advanced statistics to normalize the advantages and disadvantages that teams might have based on their ballparks.

Not including some of the primitive nineteenth-century ballparks, Baker Bowl was probably the most hitter-friendly park in baseball history and an absolute nightmare for pitchers, especially after the Deadball Era gave way to the Lively Ball Era in the 1920s. While its dimensions in left, left-center, and straightaway center field were within the ballpark, so to speak, of contemporary major-league ballparks of that era, adjacent train tracks and a railyard left precious little space for right field. It was only 280 feet down the right-field line and a mere 300 feet to right-center. Before 1925, the dimensions were an even shorter 272 feet down the line and a slightly more roomy 325 to right-center.

Other parks were short down the right-field line—in the National League, New York's Polo Grounds, Brooklyn's Ebbets Field, and Forbes Field in Pittsburgh were all 300 feet or less, as was Yankee Stadium and Cleveland's League Park in the American League (and Boston's Fenway Park was barely over 300 feet)—but the fences in all those playing fields pulled away sharply to right-center to create open space, and often lots of it. The Polo Grounds, for example, with the shortest distance down the lines, had a vast expanse of outfield because of how dramatically the grandstand turned outward, with right- and left-center fields more than 440 feet away.

With a 40-foot-high tin-covered brick wall in right field topped by an additional 20 feet of fence looming menacingly behind their left shoulders, probably seeming so close they could reach back and touch it, even good pitchers simply weren't going to be very successful pitching for the Philadelphia Phillies. It was worse than Fenway Park because the Baker Bowl wall was much closer and more than a third taller, including the fence atop the wall, than the famed Green Monster in Boston. Playing half their games at Baker Bowl, the resounding boom of batted balls banged off the tin-plated wall no doubt left pitchers shell-shocked, perhaps even just listening to batting practice, let alone what occurred in the game.

* * *

Nobody liked pitching at Baker Bowl. Among the best pitchers of the era, Carl Hubbell and Lon Warneke had higher earned run averages at Baker Bowl than in any other National League ballpark. Baker Bowl was also a nemesis for Dazzy Vance and Dizzy Dean, both of whom had a worse ERA at only one other NL stadium—St. Louis's Sportsman's Park for Vance, and Pittsburgh's Forbes Field for Dean. That they all had winning records at Baker Bowl is beside the point because Philadelphia's Phillies were not only consistently bad during those years, but their pitching was about the worst in baseball, meaning other teams feasted on them whether at Baker Bowl or in their own parks.

But could that have been any different?

It is a true truism (as opposed to an anecdotal truism) that good pitching is an essential component of winning teams. The only Phillies teams to have any success at Baker Bowl were from 1915 to 1917, winning the pennant the first year and finishing second the next two. But this was the Deadball Era, and the Phillies' pitching staff included Hall of Famers Grover Cleveland Alexander—a 30-game winner all three years—and Eppa Rixey, still finding his footing but 22–10 in 1916 with a 1.85 earned run average. In 1915, when they won the pennant, the Phillies led the league in ERA, and they were third, then second in earned run average the next two years. Their home ERA was the best in the league in 1915, second best in 1916, and fourth best in 1917. Alexander had a better won-lost record and earned run average pitching at home each of those years than when the Phillies were on the road, with a comparable number of starts at Baker Bowl and in other teams' ballparks. Even so, Baker Bowl was a park that was distinctly more favorable to hitters than pitchers. More runs were scored in Baker Bowl in 1915 than in all but two other National League parks—Chicago's West Side Park and St. Louis's Robison Field—and in 1917 only fans in Weeghman Park in Chicago (later renamed Wrigley Field after chewing gum magnate William Wrigley bought the Cubs) saw more total runs scored than those who attended Phillies home games.

Once the Deadball Era passed into history, Baker Bowl's claustrophobic dimensions made it impossible for the Phillies to put together a good pitching staff. From 1919 until they moved out of the place in June 1938, the Phillies allowed the *most* runs in the National League every single season except 1934, when they allowed the second-most runs. More runs were scored by both teams at Baker Bowl than in any other NL park every one of those years except 1927, when the Phillies played 12 of their home games in Shibe Park, and 1934, when they played only 71 of their 77 scheduled home games in Philadelphia, and in both those years there were more runs averaged per game at Baker Bowl than in any other NL park. Having to labor in Baker Bowl for half the season, no pitcher was going to have a great career with the Phillies. And none did after Alexander and Rixey, both of whose years in Philadelphia were deadball days.

The advantage for hitters at Baker Bowl was so absurd there was no competition from contemporary ballparks, particularly in the 1920s and '30s—the most dominant hitters' era since the 1890s. Handicapped by Baker Bowl as their home, the Phillies had little incentive to try to build a quality pitching staff once it became clear the deadball days were over. How bad was it for Phillies pitchers during the offensive explosion in 1929 and 1930? The Phillies' team earned run average was 6.13 in 1929, a full run higher than the team with the next-worst ERA, and 6.71 in 1930, more than a run and a half higher than the second-worst team. Both years, the Phillies' ERA was predictably much worse at Baker Bowl—6.74 compared to 5.51 on the road in 1929, and 7.18 at home in 1930 compared to 6.41 in other teams' ballparks. Phil Collins, who had a very respectable 72–79 record as a starter and reliever for the Phillies from 1929 to early 1935, could be excused for being one among many who might have wanted a big-league-career do-over with another team. More than 90 percent of the games Collins pitched in his career were with Philadelphia, for whom he had a 4.67 ERA, and 47 percent were at Baker Bowl, where his earned run average was 5.27 compared to 4.12 in other National League parks.

After World War I, the best pitchers to have pitched for the Phillies at Baker Bowl made their mark *after* they left Philadelphia—Bucky Walters with the Reds, and Claude Passeau with the Cubs. Both were right-handers. From 1935 until traded to Cincinnati in June 1938, Walters had a 38–53 record with a 4.48 earned run average. At Baker Bowl, his ERA was 5.39. Once with the Reds, Walters had a near Hall of Fame career, helping pitch Cincinnati to back-to-back pennants in 1939 and 1940 with 27–11 and 22–10 records and a league-leading ERA both years. Although Passeau was 38–55 for the Phillies from 1936 until he was traded to the Cubs in May 1939, he was one of the relatively few pitchers who seemed able to handle pitching in Baker Bowl; batters hit *only* .300 against him there, and his ERA was *just* 4.14. Once he moved to Chicago, Passeau was one of the best pitchers in the National League through the war years, including a 17–9 record in 1945 that helped the Cubs to their last World Series appearance in the twentieth century. Had Bucky Walters and Claude Passeau been condemned to pitch their entire careers with Baker Bowl as their home park, it is likely neither would be remembered today.

* * *

On the other hand, the dimensions of Baker Bowl were clearly a significant asset for a succession of Phillies hitters who were among the National League's power elite of their times, beginning in the Deadball

Era. Gavvy Cravath led the league in home runs six times in seven years between 1913 and 1919 and retired in 1920 with 119 homers—the record until Babe Ruth surpassed him with his 17th home run in the 1921 season. Although a right-handed batter, Cravath took advantage of his home park's short right field; 92 of his career home runs, more than three-quarters of them, were hit in Baker Bowl.

Cravath was succeeded, and exceeded, in the pantheon of Phillies sluggers in the 1920s by Cy Williams, who hit 185 of his 251 career homers from 1920 to 1927, of which more than two-thirds came at home in Baker Bowl. Batting left-handed, Williams took such lethal aim at the short dimensions in right field that what famously became known as the "Williams shift" was originally used against him, not Ted Williams, although the name for overloading the defense to the right side was in honor of the Boston slugger, not the one from Philadelphia. Cy Williams led the league in homers three times, including 41 in 1923 to tie Ruth for the major-league lead and come within one of Rogers Hornsby's National League record set the previous year. Tying the Cubs' Hack Wilson for the league lead with 30 in 1927, Williams joined Hornsby as the only two National League hitters up to that time to have had two 30-homer seasons.

As the sands of time wound down on Williams's career, Chuck Klein emerged as the National League's preeminent power hitter. A left-handed slugger like Williams, Klein made a Hall of Fame career by pounding out 246 doubles (leading the league twice) and 191 homers (leading the league four times) while batting .359 in his first six seasons from 1928 to 1933 before being dealt after winning the Triple Crown in 1933. But 53 percent of his doubles (131) and 68 percent of his going-going-goners (130) were at Baker Bowl, where he also batted .413, compared to only .305 on the road. In his Triple Crown season, 20 of Klein's 28 homers were hit in the friendly confines of Baker Bowl, and his league-leading batting average of .368 was built on his hitting .467 in 72 games at home rather than his very ordinary .280 average in 80 games on the road. Those first six years aside, Chuck Klein was no better than an average major-league player based on wins above replacement in the seven other seasons he played on a regular basis, making it fair to question whether he would be in the Hall of Fame were it not for the Baker Bowl advantage.

The Baker Bowl effect was indeed highly beneficial to Klein's teammates. Lefty O'Doul's .453 batting average at home, compared to .344 elsewhere, enabled him to set the National League record for hits with 254 and lead the league with a .398 batting average in 1929; a 255th hit would have given him a .400 average. Batting .309 as a team in 1929 and .315 in 1930—despite which they finished last, seven games behind the seventh-place team—and leading the league in scoring by nearly 100 runs thanks to a .292 league-best team batting average in 1932, the Phillies had an ostensibly imposing offense during the Chuck Klein years. In fact, however, Baker Bowl was so extreme in favoring batters that it distorted the home-team offense, making the Phillies less competitive in more normalized ballparks on the road. The Phillies' lineup was well suited to banging the ball in Baker Bowl; they led the league in runs at their home grounds in four of Klein's six years in Philadelphia. Playing away from home, however, was a different matter; they were never better than the fifth-best NL team, just twice, in scoring on the road. The Phillies scored an average of 34 percent more runs at home than on the road, showing that their offensive numbers were heavily skewed by Baker Bowl and that their lineup actually tended more toward the mediocre than the imposing. And indeed, the Phillies led the league in scoring only once when Klein wore their uniform.

The move to Shibe Park, a far more spacious ballpark that would be renamed for Connie Mack in 1953 and be the Phillies' home until Veterans Stadium opened in 1971, did little to change the team's fortunes. The 1938 Phillies finished so far back in last place that there was less distance in the standings between first place and seventh place—18½ games— than between seventh-place Brooklyn and Philadelphia, 43 games behind the pennant-winning Cubs. And their landlords, the Athletics, were no better in the American League, a last-place team by 46 games.

* * *

If Baker Bowl conspired against the Phillies' competitive prospects after the Deadball Era, so, too, did serious financial constraints, a situation that the Great Depression made more acute. William Baker, who bought into the Phillies in 1913, was not independently wealthy and became known as a skinflint, which was one of the reasons why his team had little continuity among its core regulars in the 1920s. Cy Williams, shortstop Heinie Sand from 1923 to 1928, and second baseman Fresco Thompson from 1927 to 1930 were the only Phillies to start at least 100 games more than three consecutive years in the decade. Gerald Nugent, a retail entrepreneur who became owner after Baker died in 1930, did not generate sufficient income from his outside business interests to invest in improving the Phillies or, for that matter, keeping up the condition of Baker Bowl. Depression-era consumer spending certainly did not help the profitability of Nugent's nonbaseball businesses. Consequently, the Phillies had even less continuity of core players during the Depression years.

Player salaries and cash infusions were the primary consideration in a series of trades the Phillies made in the 1930s that sent away most of their best players. O'Doul was gone to Brooklyn soon after the 1930 season and won a second batting title two years later. Despite his Triple Crown in 1933—or actually because of it, since his value was at a peak—the Phillies wasted little time once the season was over in sending Klein to the Cubs for some bit players and a handsome cash transfusion. His glory years were left behind in Baker Bowl. Other notables the Phillies sent away for their value were third baseman Pinky Whitney (in 1933), first baseman Don Hurst (in 1934), shortstop Dick Bartell (in 1935), first baseman Dolph Camilli (in 1938), and, of course, Walters and Passeau. Bartell became one of the Giants' cornerstone players when they won the 1936 and '37 pennants, and went to the World Series again in 1940 playing for Detroit. Hurst, one year removed from 24 homers, 143 RBIs, and a .339 average in 1932, was traded to the Cubs for Camilli, then a rookie, after holding out in spring training 1934 at the height of the Depression. The left-handed-batting Hurst, whose hitting abilities played best at Baker Bowl, saw his career come to an end soon thereafter, while Camilli, also a left-handed batter, blossomed into a great player. In 540 games for the Phillies between 1934 and 1937, Camilli hit 92 home runs. Like Hurst, however, Camilli was perpetually unhappy with his contract—particularly after he hit .315 with 28 homers in 1936 and .339 with 27 home runs in 1937—a problem the Phillies resolved by trading him to Brooklyn, once again primarily for cash considerations. Unlike Hurst, who was very soon out of the game, Camilli became an even bigger star with the Dodgers.

By the early 1940s, the Philadelphia Phillies were a dysfunctional organization in serious financial stress. They had a bare-bones minor-league system. They finished last every year from 1938 to 1942, had the league's worst offense, had the league's worst pitching, and third base-man Pinky May—best remembered today, if at all, for being mentioned in the alliterative "Van Lingle Mungo" song—was their only player of consequence during those years. The situation was so dire that the National League felt compelled to buy out Nugent in 1943 to look for an owner who had the resources and the imagination to keep the franchise viable. William Cox took over, but he was soon ousted by the commissioner for betting on Phillies games. The next owner eventually settled on was an heir to the Du Pont fortune—a fortuitous development that led ultimately to the Whiz Kids of 1950 and the Phillies' first World Series appearance since 1915.

26

MASTERS OF THE UNIVERSE

The DiMaggio Yankees

Even though they had just won 107 games, finished 13 games ahead of Connie Mack's three-time-defending American League champion Phila-delphia Athletics, and gone on to crush the Chicago Cubs in the 1932 World Series, the 1933 Yankees were beginning their transition from the Babe Ruth era. In many respects, the Ruth-Gehrig addition of the Yan-kees dynasty might be considered a disappointment, given that they won only four pennants in the 10 years they were both at the heart of the Yankees batting order, but the Athletics were a genuinely great club with their own impressive cast of Hall of Fame players in their prime from 1929 to 1931. But now, many of the Yankees' core players, especially the 38-year-old Babe, were aging. Herb Pennock, a year older than Ruth, had nothing much left. Center fielder Earle Combs and third baseman Joe Sewell, both 34, were nearing the end of their Hall of Fame careers. The Yankees finished second that year, with 16 fewer wins, seven games behind Washington. They were all but officially out of the running by the beginning of September.

Ruth was still with the Yankees in 1934, but another year older. His 22 homers were the fewest he had hit since 1918, when he was still pitching for the Red Sox, and his .288 average was the lowest of his career since he had been a full-time pitcher back in 1916. Starting in 61 of the Yan-kees' 77 home games, and just 48 of their 77 road games, Ruth was in at the finish in only 34 of his 109 starts in the outfield. Sewell had retired and Combs was hobbled by injuries even before he was nearly killed in July when he fractured his skull running into the outfield wall in St. Louis. They finished second for a second straight year, to Detroit, again seven games back. The last time the 1934 Yankees were in first place was on the last day of July.

The Yankees were second once again to Detroit in 1935. Their final margin of defeat was only three games, but that was after having fallen 10 games behind in early September with too little time to make that up. The Tigers were six games below .500 the rest of the way, not that it mattered; they could afford to coast. Ruth was no longer a Yankee, and Combs was unable to return to form after his devastating injury the year before. He retired at the end of the year. Lou Gehrig and Tony Lazzeri were the last links to the Yankees' three pennants in a row from 1926 to 1928, and none remained from their first World Series championship in 1923. As for manager Joe McCarthy, he had now managed 10 years in the major leagues—five with the Cubs and five with the Yankees—and had just two pennants to show for his efforts, one in Chicago in 1929 and 1932 in New York.

That all changed in 1936 when Joe DiMaggio came to the Bronx. With "The Great DiMaggio" in Yankees pinstripes, McCarthy had the privilege of managing the most dominant team in history—the 1936 to 1942 New York Yankees—from DiMaggio's sensational rookie year until his departure for three years of military service during World War II. McCarthy's "DiMaggio" Yankees won six pennants and five World Series in seven years—four American League and World Series in a row from 1936 to 1939, and back-to-back pennants in '41 and '42, although they lost the 1942 Series. The four-(pennants)-and-four-(World Championships)-in-four-(years) 1936–39 Yankees were the first team to win more than back-to-back World Series. They doubled that.

Their World Series triumphs were truly decisive, with the Yankees requiring as many as six games to win a World Series only once, in 1936 against their rivals just across the Harlem River in Manhattan, the New York Giants. They swept the 1938 and 1939 World Series in four straight and needed only five games to win the 1937 and 1941 Series. The only World Series they lost was also a short affair, five games to the St. Louis Cardinals in 1942. The Yankees had a 21–8 record and .724 winning percentage in those six World Series. They won a seventh pennant and sixth World Series in 1943, but this was a different Yankees club because Joltin' Joe and other core Yankees were off to war.

How Dominant Were McCarthy's DiMaggio Yankees?

In winning their six pennants, the 1936–42 Yankees did so with 100 or more victories five times and the one pennant without 100 wins in 1938, they just missed with 99 in 152 decisions. They won two of every three games they played in their six pennant-winning seasons. All six of their pennants were won by decisive margins—by 19½ games in 1936, 13 in 1937, 9½ games in 1938, 17 in both '39 and '41, and nine games in 1942. A uniform characteristic of this iteration of the Yankees dynasty was their taking over first place early in the season and relentlessly building an insurmountable lead. In 1938, for example, the Yankees won 50 of 63 games from June 24 to the end of August to open up a 13-game lead going into the final month, never once losing more than one game at a time. In case the significance of that is missed, for more than two months the longest Yankees losing streak was one game, 13 times.

And in 1940, the only year in seven they did *not* win the pennant, the Yankees still dominated the last two months and almost stole off with what would have been a fifth straight American League title. Their 38–15 run to the finish after August 8, when they were in fifth place a game below .500, was 9½ games better than the Tigers (the ultimate pennant winner), and 10 better than the Indians (who ended the season in second place). While New York's late surge did not carry them to the top yet again, it surely gave a fright to Detroit and Cleveland fans, who by August must be forgiven for having thought the American League pennant race was all about them and blessedly, for once, not about the Yankees.

The DiMaggio Yankees led the American League, indeed both major leagues, in scoring five times in seven years, including each of their four straight pennants. No other team in baseball history was as efficient as the 1936–39 Yankees in runs-to-hits ratio or in scoring total baserunners, and that includes teams from the "steroid era" in the 1990s and early 2000s when offensive productivity was even greater than during the Lively Ball Era. No other team is even close. Having a power-laden lineup is what made the Yankees so offensively efficient. They solidified the franchise's "Bronx Bombers" reputation by leading the American League in home runs in each of the DiMaggio era's first seven years, and then led the league in all three of Major League Baseball's World War II years, too. In fact, the Yankees had more home runs than every other American League club each year from 1936 to 1947, and the only major-league team to hit more homers than the DiMaggio Yankees in any year before the war were the Giants, whose 109 round-trippers in 1942 were just one more than the Yankees. Indicative of the Yankees' power up and down the lineup, only twice between 1936 and 1942 did a Yankees slugger lead the league in home runs—Gehrig in 1936 and DiMaggio in 1937—but they always had at least one player in the top five in homers, and most years they had two. The Yankees' offense, however, did not live by the long ball alone. The Yankees were below the league average in steals just once, and in 1938, when their 174 homers were 37 more than any other club in the majors, they led both leagues in stolen bases with 91.

And their offensive productivity was matched by their stinginess. The Yankees surrendered the fewest runs in the American League in all six of their pennant-winning seasons, and in 1940 they gave up the second-fewest runs, even though Lefty Gomez, one of their two aces, was hurt nearly the entire year. Characteristic of an era when striking out was close to a cardinal sin, however, Yankees pitchers struck out only 3.8 batters per game. Since they retired only 14 percent of opposing batters by strike-out, they relied on their teammates in the field for the other 86 percent of their outs. The Yankees played better defense than any other team in baseball.

No other team in history was as dominant year after year as the 1936–42 New York Yankees in both scoring the most runs and giving up the fewest in their league. In 1939, most notably, the Yankees allowed 144 runs fewer than the American League's next-stingiest team (the Indians), scored 77 runs more than the next-most-prolific team (the Red Sox), and outscored their game opponents by a phenomenal 411 runs. No wonder there are many baseball historians who consider the 1939 Yankees, and not the Yankees of 1927 (or 1998), as having had the greatest single year of any team in major-league history. And 1939 was the year Lou Gehrig was forced out of the lineup by amyotrophic lateral sclerosis. The four-and-four-in-four Yankees outscored their opponents by an average of 328 runs a year—a little more than two runs a game.

Who Were These Guys—the Core Players on the 1936–42 New York Yankees?

Lou Gehrig was the first baseman in only the first three years of the DiMaggio era because the disease that would bear his name so tragically ended his career in 1939 and his life soon thereafter. Gehrig was by far baseball's best position player in 1936 when he batted .354, had 152 runs batted in, and his 49 homers led both leagues. The next year he hit 37 homers, drove in 158 runs, batted .351—second in the league—and was the American League's second-best position player after his teammate Joe DiMaggio. The beginning effects of the insidious disease that claimed his life took a toll on his performance in 1938; his home runs dropped to 29, his RBIs to 114, and his .295 batting average was the lowest of his career since he hit .295 in his 1925 rookie year.

The progression of ALS forced Gehrig out of the lineup after 2,130 consecutive games just eight games into the 1939 season. At just 35, soon to turn 36, the strength of his performance through even the 1938 season suggested he could have remained an elite player for at least several more years. Gehrig's 493 home runs when he took himself out of the lineup were the second most in history after Ruth, and there was a very good chance he would have reached 600 had he not had what he called "a bad break" in his memorable "I consider myself the luckiest man on the face of the earth" speech at Yankee Stadium on July 4, 1939, when his number 4 was retired. His 1,995 runs batted in were just 80 shy of Cap Anson's career total and 219 behind the Babe. Had he stayed healthy, Gehrig would likely have surpassed Ruth in RBIs. It would not be unreasonable to suppose he would also have caught up with Ty Cobb for the most runs scored; Cobb scored 2,244, Gehrig was 356 behind and had averaged 134 runs a year since beginning his extraordinary consecutive-games streak. With 2,721 hits, a strong and healthy Gehrig would have been two years away from 3,000. Gehrig's .340 career average was tied with George Sisler for 15th best in major-league history at the time he sat down. Only Ted Williams (.344) has hit for a higher career average since then.

No Yankees manager had had to worry about first base since 1925. Now McCarthy was forced to find a new first baseman. Babe Dahlgren was the Yankees' first baseman in 1939 and 1940, Johnny Sturm in 1941, and after Sturm became one of Major League Baseball's earliest draft picks for the war, Buddy Hassett played there in 1942. Not only were none of them anywhere close to being a Gehrig, which was not expected anyway, none proved to be anything more than a marginal major leaguer.

Tony Lazzeri was the second baseman when fellow San Francisco native DiMaggio came to New York in 1936. Although his 109 RBIs in 1936 were third on the club behind Gehrig and DiMaggio, Lazzeri had become more an average major leaguer than the elite player he had been in the heyday of the Ruth and Gehrig Yankees. With a much younger Joe Gordon waiting in the wings, starring for the Yankees' top farm team in nearby Newark, Lazzeri was unceremoniously released after the 1937 season. Gordon arrived in the big leagues at the very time that Detroit's 35-year-old Charlie Gehringer was entering the twilight of his career. Although he struggled at first, Gordon quickly became the best all-around second baseman in the game until he was drafted into the war after the 1943 season. Gordon was voted the American League's Most Valuable Player in 1942, even though he did not lead the league in any offensive category (unless you want to count his 95 strikeouts and the 22 times he hit into a double play). Still, his 8.2 WAR was second best in the league after Ted Williams, who, by all accounts and by virtue of winning the Triple Crown, was actually far more deserving of the award. Although it was not until 2009 that he finally made the Hall of Fame, a generous explanation being that he played only 11 years in the majors and was interrupted in his prime by two years in World War II, Joe Gordon averaged nearly six wins above replacement over eight consecutive baseball-playing years beginning in 1939.

Frankie Crosetti, another San Francisco–born Italian American, was the Yankees' regular shortstop from 1932 to 1940. Although his overall player value as measured by WAR was at the bottom range of performance for a regular, Crosetti was a superb defensive shortstop. After hitting only .194 in 1940, however, with an on-base percentage a shade under .300—horrible numbers for a leadoff batter, and certainly not helping the Yankees' losing cause that year—Crosetti was sent to the bench in 1941 in favor of Phil Rizzuto. Generously listed at 5-foot-6 and 150 pounds (he had been dismissed at a Dodgers tryout by Casey Stengel saying something about him being a shoeshine boy), Rizzuto was not only superb defensively, but a far better offensive player than Crosetti because of his speed and ability to make contact. Rizzuto hit .307 in his rookie year and .284 in 1942 before being drafted into the navy, where he spent the duration of World War II, mostly, it might have seemed, playing baseball. Crosetti partially reclaimed the shortstop position when Rizzuto was off to war.

Playing third base for the 1936–42 Yankees and usually batting second in the order was Red Rolfe, considered by many at the time to have been the best in the league at his position—although that nod more deservedly goes to the St. Louis Browns' Harlond Clift, by far the more formidable offensive player. From 1935 until 1942, when he missed nearly the entire first half of the season because of illness, Rolfe was written into McCarthy's starting lineup for virtually every game. Rolfe called it quits after playing just 69 games in 1942 and batting only .219—hardly reflective of his .293 batting average, including four .300 seasons, before that, but he ended his career on a high note by hitting .353 in the 1942 World Series—the only one of the six he played that the Yankees did not win.

Bill Dickey, the Yankees' catcher since 1929, had the four best years of his career coincide exactly with the four championships they won from 1936 to 1939. They also coincided with McCarthy moving him from the bottom third of the lineup to batting fifth in the order. After averaging 77 RBIs his first seven years, Dickey became the first catcher in history to have back-to-back seasons driving in 100 or more runs—he had four in a row—and also put together four straight years with at least 20 homers. And he batted .326 for the four-and-four-in-four Yankees. Because he was a left-handed batter, his manager could have chosen the days the opposing starter was a left-hander to rest Dickey, but McCarthy didn't really do that until 1940. When the Yankees were winning their four straight pennants, Dickey started nearly 70 percent of the time a lefty took the mound against them, and hit .299 in those games. Dickey turned 33 in

1940, however, and McCarthy for the first time began giving him a day off on a regular basis when the opposing starting pitcher was a southpaw. The next four years before he went off to war in 1944, Dickey was platooned behind the plate, starting in only 36 of the 190 games the Yankees faced a southpaw.

* * *

Joe McCarthy's outfield was less stable than his infield from year to year, mostly because of injuries to regulars, but that was hardly a weakness. The one constant, of course, was DiMaggio.

Joe DiMaggio was the best player in baseball his first seven years in the majors before he became a Selective Service draft pick for the war in 1943. The young man of whom great things were expected was already being regarded with wariness about his potential to be injury prone when the Yankees purchased his contract from the San Francisco Seals in November 1934. His 61-game hitting streak as an 18-year-old in his 1933 Pacific Coast League rookie season began talk that the Seals might be

Hall of Famers Lou Gehrig, Joe Cronin, Bill Dickey, Joe DiMaggio, Charlie Gehringer, Jimmie Foxx, and Hank Greenberg—a formidable lineup for the 1937 American League All-Star team. *Harris & Ewing Collection (Library of Congress).*

able to get as much as $100,000 from a major-league club for his contract, even at the height of the Depression. The Yankees were able to get him for only $25,000, a journeyman major leaguer, and three minor leaguers because he badly tore up the cartilage in his right knee stepping out of a taxi and missed about half the 1934 season, in which he nonetheless batted .341. The deal stipulated that DiMaggio play another year in San Francisco so the Yankees could be sure they were not getting damaged goods on account of that knee injury. DiMaggio came back better than ever in 1935 to play a full schedule of games and hit .398 for the Seals. Next stop for the dynamic Mr. DiMaggio—New York City.

Indicative of the kinds of foot injuries that would harass him throughout his career, the start to DiMaggio's much-anticipated big-league career was delayed by nearly three weeks because he was badly burned receiving heat therapy for an ankle injury in spring training. Starting in left field and batting third ahead of Gehrig in his first major-league game on May 3, 1936, at Yankee Stadium against the Browns, DiMaggio went 3-for-6 with a triple. He went home that night a .500 hitter. Not once thereafter in his 13 major-league seasons did Joe DiMaggio ever go to sleep at night with his career average under .300. He finished his rookie year batting .323—third highest on a team that hit exactly .300 for the season. Of his first 206 big-league hits, 88 were for extra bases. He had 29 homers and drove in 125 runs. He started the year in left field, then moved to right. It wasn't until August that Joe DiMaggio became the Yankees' center fielder.

The 1937 DiMaggio was even better. He hit .346 and led the majors with 151 runs scored, 46 homers, 418 total bases, and a .673 slugging percentage. His 167 RBIs were second in the majors and his 215 hits second in the American League. With those numbers as ammo, DiMaggio pressed the Yankees for a higher salary than they were willing to offer and threatened to hold out all season to get what he wanted. It was not until the end of April, after his club had already played 12 games, that DiMaggio was back in the Yankees lineup, having to settle for what he was originally offered. He batted .324 with 32 homers and 140 RBIs. DiMaggio won back-to-back batting titles in 1939 and 1940, hitting .381 and .352, and the first of his three Most Valuable Player Awards in 1939. Then came 1941. DiMaggio led the league with 125 RBIs and 348 total bases while batting .357, not to mention his iconic 56-game hitting streak and his second MVP trophy. It was also his fifth consecutive year hitting at least 30 home runs. And in 1942, DiMaggio played in every game—the only year in his career he did so—while batting .305 and driving in more than 100 runs for the seventh straight season.

For Joe DiMaggio, his wartime call-up could not have come at a more inopportune time. He had played seven years in the majors, his career batting average stood at .339, and he had 219 home runs to his credit while striking out just 196 times in 4,418 plate appearances. Just five of those strikeouts came in his 247 plate appearances during the 56-game hitting streak. DiMaggio was now 28 years old, in the prime of his career. It was also obvious that this was not going to be a war of short duration, meaning he was likely to miss out on perhaps most of his remaining prime years before the inevitable decline that comes to most elite ball-players by the time they reach 30. And in fact, Joe DiMaggio would not return to the Yankees until 1946 when he was 31 years old. He remained one of baseball's elite players for the next five years, but he was not quite as superb as he had been the first seven years of his career. Nor could he necessarily expect to have been for those years even if there was no war, given his closing in on 30; the point is simply that Joe DiMaggio's war-time service cost him three years of his prime that might have enabled him to approach, although probably not reach, 500 home runs for his career.

DiMaggio shared the Yankees outfield in his rookie year primarily with George Selkirk and Jake Powell. First called up to the Yankees in August 1934, Selkirk was the departed Ruth's replacement in right field in 1935. His days as a core regular came to an end when he broke his collarbone in July 1937. Once he recovered, Selkirk moved into a reserve role but nonetheless started in at least 60 percent of the Yankees' games each of the next three years, sometimes as a substitute for DiMaggio when the Yankee Clipper was injured. In only his second big-league season, Powell had come to the Yankees in June 1936 in an even-up trade with Washington for Ben Chapman, a Yankees star since his rookie year in 1930. As good as he was, however, Chapman had a combative, volatile temperament that was not—most definitely, not—what McCarthy wanted of his players. Now that he had DiMaggio, center fielder Chapman was expendable.

Powell never became the player McCarthy hoped he'd be. It didn't help his cause when he gave a pregame interview to a Chicago radio station in 1938 explaining that he stayed in shape during the offseason using his billy club against black persons as an officer of the law. Even for a time when segregation was still the norm and most white Americans did little or perceived no need to disguise their racism and prejudice against their fellow citizens who happened to be black, Powell's comments were beyond the pale. He was suspended by Commissioner Landis for 10 days, forced to apologize to New York's black community by Yankees owner Jacob Ruppert, and played just 59 more game as a Yan-kee before being sold to the San Francisco Seals in December 1940. While it was true he was often injured, Powell's inappropriate remarks sabotaged his career with the Yankees.

The two players most associated with DiMaggio in the pre–World War II Yankees outfield were Tommy Henrich and Charlie Keller, although neither was a core regular for more than one of the Yankees' four-and-four-in-four championship years. Henrich was a gift to the Yankees, granted free agency in 1937 after the commissioner agreed with his in-person complaint that the Cleveland Indians, in whose farm system he had played since 1934, were burying him in the minors rather than giving him a legitimate shot at competing for a big-league job. The Yankees quickly swept in to sign him and brought him to the Bronx. But the player who would become known as "Old Reliable" because of his clutch hitting had less than reliable knees at the beginning of his career, limiting him to fewer than 100 games in 1939 and 1940. After surgery to repair his knee at the end of the 1940 season, Henrich had a breakout year in 1941 as the everyday right fielder, hitting 31 home runs in a year DiMaggio hit just 30, and in 1942 he played in all but two of the Yankees' games through the end of August before his draft board sent him his letter of "Greetings!" As a result, Tommy Henrich, unlike the great DiMaggio, never played on a Yankees team that lost a World Series, since he was in the US Coast Guard while Joltin' Joe and his teammates went down in defeat to the 1942 Cardinals.

While Ted Williams was baseball's rookie sensation in 1939, Charlie Keller had an outstanding first season himself that year. He batted .334 with 11 homers and 83 RBIs in 111 games, then starred in the Yankees' sweep of the Reds in the 1939 World Series. The seminal highlight of that Series was Keller knocking Cincinnati catcher Ernie Lombardi senseless in a collision at the plate in the 10th inning of the final game. He scored and DiMaggio, whose single started the sequence of events, came charging home behind him while Lombardi lay insensate. Not for nothing did the powerful and physically imposing Charlie become "King Kong" Keller. The next four years, until he began his wartime service with the merchant marine in 1944, Keller was one of baseball's most fearsome sluggers. Like Gordon, Keller had a relatively short career—only six years as a regular before chronic back problems beginning in 1947 prematurely ruined his career—but unlike Gordon, his playing days were too abbreviated to test whether he might have merited Hall of Fame consideration. Keller certainly seemed on the way to Cooperstown, averaging six wins above replacement in his first six years in the big time between 1939 and 1946, which takes into account his wartime absence in 1944 and most of 1945.

* * *

As for the Yankees' pitching, McCarthy had been using a determined four-man starting rotation since 1935, with a fifth pitcher as a spot starter for doubleheaders and other exigencies. Lefty Gomez and right-handers Red Ruffing and Monte Pearson were his top three starters in the Yankees' four-and-four-in-four years; each year, he employed a different fourth starter. Ruffing and Gomez had the second and third most cumulative pitching wins above replacement in the five years from 1935 to 1939, after Lefty Grove. Ruffing's only four 20-win seasons were instrumental to the Yankees winning four straight pennants from 1936 to 1939, during which he won 71 percent of his decisions. Gomez's best five-year stretch, by contrast, was 1931 to 1935, before the arrival of DiMaggio. He won 20 games three times those five years, including a league-leading 26–5 record and 2.33 ERA in 1934. The best year of Lefty's career, however, was 1937, when he went 21–11 and once again led the league with a 2.33 earned run average. Although averaging six fewer starts per year than Gomez and Ruffing, Pearson had the highest winning percentage (.718) of McCarthy's primary starters in the four-and-four-in-four years.

Gomez's absence for virtually all of 1940 with an ailing shoulder may have been the single biggest reason why the Yankees did not extend their pennant streak to five in a row in a year they came up two games short. Pearson going down with an injury in late July didn't help, and he was traded after the season. Gomez's left arm had little left to give, and the Yankees let him go after he struggled through 13 starts in 1942. Ruffing also left the Yankees after the 1942 season to serve in the army, despite being in his late 30s. Ruffing was 7–2 in 10 World Series starts, including a victory in the 1932 Series, back when Ruth was still being Ruth, at least with the bat. Gomez was undefeated in six decisions for the Yankees in seven World Series starts, including one in the 1932 Series. Pearson made just one start in each of the Yankees' four straight World Series, won them all, and gave up just four earned runs in 35⅔ innings.

Notwithstanding the perennial strength of his starting pitching, McCarthy was astute in recognizing the value of having a dedicated reliever to win or to save close games. Unlike other managers of his day, McCarthy rarely used his top four starters as relievers. Instead, he routinely carried three (sometimes four) pitchers he used almost exclusively in relief. McCarthy was the first manager to specifically groom a quality pitcher for the role of relief ace since Washington's Bucky Harris did so with Firpo Marberry in 1924—an unorthodox move no other team seemed willing to follow despite Marberry's success—and Johnny Murphy was his man. A 25-year old rookie in 1934, Murphy started 20 games and relieved in 20. He was better in relief. McCarthy made clear to him that his road to success was in the unglamorous role of dedicated relief pitcher. Johnny Murphy became both the Yankees' "fireman," coming in late in the game with runners on base to douse the flames of an opposition rally (and, indeed, one of Murphy's nicknames was "Fireman" in obvious appreciation of his value to the team), and their "closer" (to use today's terminology), coming in specifically to save games.

McCarthy employed Murphy judiciously and efficiently. Murphy appeared in as many as 38 games in relief only once (in 1939) and relieved in 35 games or more only four times in the 12 years he pitched for McCarthy. But Murphy's relief appearances were invariably productive. Working about two innings per outing, Murphy pitched 262 games in relief for the Yankees from 1936 to 1943, when they won seven pennants in eight years. His record was 60 wins and 34 losses with 88 saves, meaning that Johnny Murphy figured directly in the outcome of the game in nearly 70 percent of his total relief appearances. McCarthy was clearly using Murphy when it mattered the most.

Where Did These Guys Come From?

Except for the veteran alumni Gehrig, Lazzeri, Crosetti, Dickey, Ruffing, and Gomez from the last time the Yankees won the pennant with Ruth in their lineup in 1932, nearly all of the players who were core regulars on the 1936–42 Yankees were developed in the Yankees' farm system, which by the mid-1930s was the most robust of any major-league franchise except for the Cardinals'. DiMaggio and Henrich were the exceptions. For most of the rest of the 1936–42 Yankees newcomers, the top franchise affiliate across the Hudson River in Newark, New Jersey, was their finishing school.

Nearly all the core regulars on the 1920s Yankees—including Ruth and all their top starting pitchers—had been acquired in cash or player transactions from other major-league clubs or prominent minor-league franchises. This is not to suggest that the Yankees did not come up with a few gems in the 1920s on the amateur market. Most famously, legendary Yankees scout Paul Krichell discovered and signed Lou Gehrig out of Columbia University. Krichell was one of a cadre of exceptional talent scouts that Ed Barrow assembled for the Yankees after he took over their baseball operations in 1921. Notwithstanding finds to be had like Gehrig, Yankees scouts were focused primarily on following, assessing, and acquiring minor leaguers rather than beating the amateur or semiprofessional bushes for talent. This worked very well for the Yankees at the time because nearly all minor-league clubs were independently owned, and Barrow, using Ruppert's money, was able to outbid most other major-league teams for high-quality players they were interested in. Beginning in 1925, moreover, the Yankees developed a close working relationship with the American Association team in St. Paul, Minnesota, after one of their elite scouts, Bob Connery, assembled an ownership group that bought the franchise. Yankees manager Miller Huggins, with whom Connery had a long personal relationship going back to their days with the Cardinals, was a silent investor.

The St. Paul Saints at the time were one of baseball's top minor-league teams. They played the pennant winner of the International League in the Little World Series between the top two minor leagues three times in five years from 1920 to 1924, beating the powerhouse Baltimore Orioles in 1924. Although Connery was explicit in stating that, despite his past on Ruppert's payroll and his friendship with Huggins, the Yankees would have no special consideration when it came to making deals for possibly major league–ready players on the Saints, the Yankees were in fact able to benefit from the relationship. In 1925, the year the Yankees nosedived to near the bottom of the American League standings, they acquired shortstop Mark Koenig and catcher Pat Collins from St. Paul to shore up their club for the immediate future. Both were core players on the 1926–28 Yankees that won three straight pennants. The Yankees also sent a number of players they signed to St. Paul for seasoning, including George Pipgras, Leo Durocher, and Ben Chapman.

Financially flush and with strong ties to a quality minor-league club that was not an affiliate (*not*, in the sense that St. Paul owned all of its players except those belonging to the Yankees who were there to gain experience), Ruppert and Barrow were viscerally opposed to what Branch Rickey was doing for the Cardinals, which was building a farm system to develop players they controlled. But while spending significant dollars to purchase Earle Combs and Tony Lazzeri from minor-league franchises landed the Yankees' two future Hall of Fame players who played key roles in their remaining pennants during the Babe Ruth era, there were also some expensive busts that by 1931 had Ruppert thinking there might be merit to Rickey's approach.

In 1927, most notably, the Yankees shelled out $125,000 to Oakland in the Pacific Coast League for shortstop Lyn Lary and second baseman Jimmie Reese, both of whom appeared to be rising stars. Both stayed with Oakland for another year of seasoning after becoming the property of the New York Yankees. Lary made it to the Yankees in 1929 and was their regular shortstop the next two years before losing his job to Crosetti, and Reese made it to New York in 1930 and was the backup second baseman for three years. Neither player came close to Barrow's expectations when he bought their contracts. It was perhaps their misfortune that their limitations, at least in the Yankees' world, became apparent only once the US economy was mired in the Great Depression, making their price tag seem all the more outrageous. Barrow later said he regarded his monetary outlay for the two players among the worst deals he ever made. Ruppert also felt burned when he had to pay $40,000 to St. Paul for infielder Jack

Saltzgaver in 1931, a player whose contract the Yankees thought they already controlled.

The Yankees also had not won a pennant since 1928, and it probably was not lost on Ruppert that the Cardinals had just won back-to-back National League pennants with a roster of core players they had developed in their minor-league farm system. Controlling players through their years of development was a much cheaper investment than the Yankees' approach of paying for established major league–ready minor leaguers. Among the Yankees' most recent minor-league player purchases, both transactions with San Francisco in the Pacific Coast League, were $45,000 in 1929 for Lefty Gomez and as much as $75,000 for shortstop Frankie Crosetti in 1930. Gomez was sent to St. Paul for further seasoning after struggling in his first three months with the Yankees in 1930, and Crosetti stayed another year in San Francisco before being called to New York to replace Lary at shortstop in 1932. While both were core players on the 1936–39 Yankees, their acquisitions as polished minor leaguers cost the Yankees much more than the Cardinals' development in their farm system of star players like Dizzy Dean, Joe Medwick, and Pepper Martin.

Going against Barrow's continuing skepticism, Ruppert decided he would rather invest in player development than rely so much on costly transactions for quality minor leaguers. Moreover, by now the success of the Cardinals' farm system had changed the paradigm of player development, and most other major-league clubs were moving in that direction. The Depression was another motivating factor; the survival of many minor-league clubs was dependent on cash infusions from major-league franchises, whose executives understood that, the merits of farm systems aside, their financial solvency was essential for there to be a pipeline of players to the major leagues. If hiring Joe McCarthy in 1931 as field manager was Ruppert's first impactful move to reset the Yankees' course in the pending post-Ruth years—the Babe was 36 in '31—his next was spending $250,000 to buy the Newark franchise in the prestigious International League in the aftermath of his club having missed out on the American League pennant for a third straight year. The Yankees opened the 1932 baseball season with five minor-league affiliates.

With Ruppert's commitment to invest in building a highly competitive farm system that would rival that of the Cardinals', at least in developing talent if not in breadth of affiliates, Yankees scouts became more focused on identifying and signing prospects. That, of course, did not mean passing on outstanding minor-league players like Joe DiMaggio should they become available at a reasonable price, as DiMaggio did because of concerns that his knee injury would compromise his obvious ability. Indicative of his new player-development priority, Ruppert hired highly esteemed minor-league executive George Weiss to run and grow the Yankees' farm system. Weiss, most recently of the International League Baltimore Orioles, was skilled in building winning ballclubs—a fact not lost on Jacob Ruppert.

The Newark Bears quickly became the crown jewel of the Yankees' system. The Yankees' best prospects were sent to Newark to prove their major-league worth before being promoted to New York. Newark's proximity to New York City made it easy for Barrow and McCarthy to occasionally take in games of their top affiliate to assess the would-be Yankees of the future. Other than Gehrig, Dickey, DiMaggio, and Henrich, all the key contributors to the success of the 1936–42 Yankees played for the Bears before becoming Yankees. And that does not include future major-league stars like Dixie Walker, George McQuinn, Tommy Holmes, and Wally Judnich who were seasoned by the Yankees in Newark before being sold or traded elsewhere because there was no room for them on the Yankees' roster. And there were many more besides them who made it to the big leagues on teams other than the Yankees without necessarily being star players. Ruppert expanded Yankees holdings at the top level of minor-league play by adding Oakland in the Pacific Coast League in 1935, although that affiliation ended after three years, and Kansas City in the American Association in 1937. Phil Rizzuto would be the Yankees' most prominent graduate from Kansas City.

Aggressive scouting backed by Ruppert's dollars helped make the Newark Bears such a formidable club it was said they were better than most of the major-league clubs with losing records, and even some with winning records. The Bears won International League pennants in each of their first three years as a Yankees affiliate. The 1937 and 1938 Newark Bears are considered two of the best single-season minor-league teams in history. Like all of McCarthy's great Yankees teams, the Bears those two years excelled at every facet of the game and completely dominated the International League. The first of those years they won 109 to finish 25½ games in front, then made history by overcoming a three-games-to-none deficit in the Little World Series to beat the Columbus Redbirds—the Cardinals' top affiliate—with four straight wins on the road to become champions of the minor-league baseball world. The 1938 Bears were nearly as good, winning 108 to finish first by 18 games, overcoming a three-games-to-one deficit to advance through the first round of the International League playoffs, easily winning the second round, and then facing off against—and losing to—the Yankees' other top farm club, the Kansas City Blues, in the Little World Series.

The Yankees' farm system was so imposing, particularly with regard to the competitiveness of its teams, that Washington owner Clark Griffith proposed in the 1938 winter meetings that minor-league affiliations be scaled back to just one club for each franchise at each classification level. It hardly seemed fair that the Little World Series that year was a contest between the top two Yankees affiliates—one in Newark, the other in Kansas City. The Cardinals had three affiliates at the top minor-league classification—one in the International League (Rochester), one in the American Association (Columbus), and one in the Pacific Coast League (Sacramento). Griffith's Senators, along with both Philadelphia franchises and Boston's Braves, did not have the resources to fund an extensive scouting network, let alone much of a minor-league system. His proposal to limit the size of farm systems so that franchises with fewer financial resources could compete with the Yankees and Cardinals in player development failed to get traction, however, because most clubs valued the control over prospects that dedicated farm systems gave them as they advanced through the minor leagues.

Griffith tried a different tack in the 1939 winter meetings. With the Yankees having just won their fourth straight American League pennant by a 17-game margin and seemingly poised to win decisively every year, in part because of the quality of their minor-league system, Griffith proposed that no American League club be allowed to engage in player transactions with the Yankees, either in currency or trade. This was a curious position to take because the Yankees had not acquired a player who made a significant contribution to their success from another major-league team since 1936, when they dealt for Washington pitcher Bump Hadley and Cleveland pitcher Monte Pearson. Whether by the Yankees' choice or implicit collective agreement by all other American League franchises, the only new player on McCarthy's 1940 opening-day roster to come from another team was southpaw Lee Grissom, acquired from the *National League* Cincinnati Reds in exchange for Newark right-hander Joe Beggs. Grissom lasted a month before being put on waivers. As fate would have it, the Yankees did not win the American League pennant in 1940. That effectively put an end to any concerted effort to keep the Yankees from being so good. It was the enduring strength of their farm system, however, that helped the Yankees to their seventh pennant and sixth World Series championship in eight years in 1943 despite the loss of DiMaggio, Ruffing, Henrich, and Rizzuto to the war, and that would keep them the most formidable club in the American League until the mid-1960s.

27

TRYING TO CATCH THE YANKEES

The New York Yankees were not the best team in the American League when Joe DiMaggio donned pinstripes for the first time in spring training 1936. That would be the Detroit Tigers, winners of the two previous pennants under the guiding hand of their all-star catcher and player-manager Mickey Cochrane, although it might have been Babe Ruth had the aging slugger played his cards differently.

Cochrane had just had perhaps the best year of his playing career for the Philadelphia Athletics in 1933 when Connie Mack sold him to the Detroit Tigers for $100,000 in December. Attendance at Philadelphia's Shibe Park had plummeted from the previous year and at slightly over 297,000 was fewer than half the 627,500 fans who came to see Cochrane, Grove, Foxx, Simmons, and their teammates try to win their fourth straight pennant in 1932. They didn't, and the depth of the Depression wasn't helping fans to see how paying to see a ballgame would ease their economic suffering. Connie Mack could no longer afford his star players, at least not most of them. The fiercely competitive Cochrane—he wasn't known as "Black Mike" for nothing—was not only an outstanding catcher both offensively and behind the plate, but a born leader. Frank Navin's club was in need of a new manager after the 1933 season, so Navin sent a feeler to Ruth about his interest in managing Detroit, but the Bambino was embarking on a lucrative barnstorming tour to Japan and declined to meet. Navin decided that Black Mike was perfect for the role of star-player-manager. Cochrane turned 31 eleven days before the 1934 season began.

The Tigers had been mostly a midpack team in the seven years since Ty Cobb left after 1926. They had a winning record only twice and finished in the first division just once. Notwithstanding their fifth-place finish in 1933 with a losing record, the Tigers had a nucleus of core players that made them a potentially formidable ballclub. Their only established star player when Cochrane took over was Charlie Gehringer, about to begin his ninth year as Detroit's second baseman, but he anchored an infield that was set with Hank Greenberg at first, Billy Rogell at shortstop, and Marv Owen at third. Cochrane also inherited a quality pitching staff led by veteran ace Firpo Marberry, Tommy Bridges on the cusp of becoming an ace, and Schoolboy Rowe and Eldon Auker coming off promising rookie seasons. All four were right-handers. The biggest weakness Cochrane had to address was their outfield. Contrary to Detroit's history of exceptional outfielders, particularly when it came to hitting—Crawford and Cobb, Veach and Heilmann, even Heinie Manush—none of their three primary outfielders in 1933 had a player value exceeding two wins above replacement, the minimum performance standard expected of a starting position player. Nine days after Cochrane came to Detroit, the Tigers dealt for Goose Goslin, who had just helped Washington to the pennant, to bolster their outfield.

As Detroit remained in the grip of the Depression's devastating impact on the automobile-manufacturing industry, the Tigers gave the city much to cheer about in 1934. Six of their core regulars batted better than .300. Greenberg, Gehringer, and Goslin drove in more than 100 runs, and Rogell with 99 RBIs and Owen with 98 just missed. Greenberg's breakout to stardom included 63 doubles, seven triples, and 26 homers accounting for nearly half of his 201 hits. The infield came to play every day; Gehringer, Rogell, and Owen started every game, and Greenberg missed just one. Rowe went 24–8 and Bridges was 22–11. Auker and Marberry, used by Cochrane in both starting and reliever roles, each won 15. As for Black Mike, he had a typical first-rate Mickey Cochrane season, batting .320 and edging out Gehringer for American League Most Valuable Player honors.

Three wins in four games against the Yankees in mid-July helped Detroit move ahead of New York in the standings to stay, but it was a 14-game winning streak from the end of July into mid-August that gave the Tigers separation. From July 4 until August 7, the Tigers played 26 games with first place directly at stake, and won 21. The Yankees' last chance to overtake the Tigers was when they came into Detroit in mid-September for a four-game series trailing by 5½ games. The Tigers shut out the Yankees in the first two of those games, beating Lefty Gomez and Red Ruffing, to seize a 7½-game advantage, effectively ending the pennant race. Detroit finished the season seven games ahead of New York with 101 wins, an impressive 26 more than the previous year. It was Detroit's first return to the World Series since 1909, a quarter century before, when Ty Cobb was still in his youth. The Tigers had yet to win a

World Series, having lost three in a row from 1907 to 1909, and 1934 would not change that fact; player-manager Cochrane's Tigers lost to player-manager Frisch's "Gashouse Gang" Cardinals in seven games.

The Tigers won again in 1935. Once again it was a two-games-to-one series victory against the Yankees in mid-July that put Detroit ahead of New York in the standings for good. After boosting their lead to 10 games with three weeks left, the Tigers coasted to the finish, their final winning margin of three games hardly indicative of their dominance. Once again, Greenberg and Gehringer were sensational. Gehringer's .330 average was fifth in the league. Greenberg's 168 RBIs were far ahead of anybody else in the majors, and he tied Jimmie Foxx for the league lead in homers with 36. Once again, nearly half of Greenberg's 203 hits were for extra bases. Greenberg was the unanimous selection for MVP. Goslin drove in 111 runs. Bridges won 21, Rowe won 19, and Auker 18. And Cochrane? He hit .319 with a .452 on-base percentage. It was the eighth time in his now-11-year career that Cochrane hit over .300.

Facing the Cubs, the Tigers finally won the World Series on their fifth attempt. Although it was 28 years later, Detroit had some measure of revenge for having lost both the 1907 and 1908 World Series to Chicago. Their victory, however, came at a significant cost. Hank Greenberg, who had homered earlier in the second game, badly hurt his wrist trying to score in the seventh inning. Greenberg did not play in the rest of the Series, but more seriously, the wrist was still not fully healed when he reinjured it in only the 12th game of the 1936 season in a collision at first base. The injury sidelined him for the rest of the year. The Tigers finished a distant second, 19½ games behind the Yankees.

Aside from the loss of Greenberg and the Tigers being blown away by the Yankees, the 1936 season was also very difficult personally for Mickey Cochrane. Part of his reward for having brought two pennants and a World Championship to Detroit was being named de facto general manager of the Tigers in addition to being both their catcher—the most demanding of positions—and their manager. The stress of now holding three such responsible positions proved too much, and Cochrane went on a mental-health sabbatical for six weeks in June and July to recover his emotional stability.

The next year was even worse for Cochrane. It was only 29 games into the season. The Tigers were running third, 2½ games behind the Yankees, and they were at Yankee Stadium for the start of a three-game series on May 25, 1937. Cochrane had caught all but two of the Tigers' games and was batting .306 when he came to bat against Bump Hadley in the fifth inning. Hadley pitched up and in. Cochrane was hit in the face. His skull fractured, Black Mike was near death for nearly a week. He did *not* become only the second player to die after being hit by a pitch, but

Cochrane never played another game. Mickey Cochrane finished his playing career with a lifetime average of .320 and was recognized by many at the time as the best catcher to ever play the game, although the Cubs' Gabby Hartnett and Yankees' Bill Dickey had advocates as well. Cochrane returned in August to manage his club for the rest of the season. The Tigers once again finished second to the Yankees. Although he was back in the dugout in 1938, Cochrane was released as manager in August after four consecutive losses dropped the Tigers below .500.

The Detroit Tigers hardly mattered in 1938. They finished fourth. And after winning the 1937 batting crown and five straight 200-hit seasons from 1933 to 1937—something only Willie Keeler, Al Simmons, and Chuck Klein had done before him—the 35-year-old Gehringer was beginning to slow down, and Goslin was gone. Hank Greenberg, however, had his hallmark season chasing Babe Ruth's record of 60 home runs. Going into the final month, his 46 homers had him ahead of Ruth's pace. Two home runs at home against Cleveland on September 23 gave him 56 for the year with nine games remaining. Four days later he hit two more against the Browns, tying Jimmie Foxx's 58 homers in 1932 as the closest anyone had gotten to the Babe's record. Having hit 12 so far in September with five games still to be played, it looked like Greenberg had a good shot at getting at least the two home runs needed to match Ruth, and perhaps three (or even more) to set a new record. The Tigers scored 32 runs in those five games, including a game in which they were shut out, but Greenberg did not hit any more homers. In the Sunday doubleheader in Cleveland that ended the season, he went 1-for-4 against Bob Feller in the opening game and 3-for-3 in the second game, scoring five runs in the Tigers' doubleheader sweep, and driving in one. He had a double off Feller, but all his other hits were singles.

* * *

Just when it seemed that "abandon ye all hope" was the annual prognosis for the seven other clubs in the Yankee-dominated American League, there was a real pennant race in 1940. If any team seemed likely to take advantage of Yankees stumbles, it was the Boston Red Sox. Tom Yawkey, arguably a spoiled rich kid who loved baseball, had spent lavishly on trying to restore the Red Sox to competitiveness since buying the club as a 30-year-old in February 1933 during the height of the Depression. The Red Sox had finished last nine of the previous 11 seasons when Yawkey made the investment that defined his life. They were one of baseball's worst teams offensively, and they were hardly much better on the mound. Yawkey's inclination was to buy—*buy*, since the Red Sox had virtually no quality players to trade—established stars to right the ship. Yawkey's cash transfusions for star players helped other clubs—

particularly Connie Mack's Athletics—navigate tough Depression times. None helped put the Red Sox into contention.

Yawkey's first big buys came soon after the 1933 season got under way. In the space of three days in May, he purchased Rick Ferrell, one of baseball's best catchers, from the St. Louis Browns and sent $100,000 to the Yankees for pitcher George Pipgras, an integral member of three World Series championship teams, and rookie infield prospect Billy Werber. The 1933 calendar year ended with Yawkey spending $125,000 to get Grove from Connie Mack, along with Rube Walberg, another southpaw, and second baseman Max Bishop. Soon after the 1934 season began, Yawkey paid $25,000 to Cleveland to acquire Rick's brother Wes Ferrell, whose four consecutive 20-win seasons with the Indians came undone in 1933 when shoulder problems limited him to just 11 wins. When the 1934 season ended, Yawkey sent $225,000 to the Senators for their manager and star shortstop Joe Cronin. In December 1935, he bought Jimmie Foxx from Mr. Mack for $150,000. Less than a month later, another $175,000 went to Mr. Mack for outfielder Doc Cramer.

In acquiring Grove and Wes Ferrell, Yawkey was envisioning his Red Sox throwing a potent lefty-righty combination of aces at opposing clubs. It didn't work out quite as Yawkey planned. While Ferrell pitched well with a 14–5 record and 3.63 earned run average, Grove had a disastrous first year in Boston, going 8–8 with an unsightly 6.50 ERA in 1934 as it was his turn to battle arm problems. Despite Ferrell being their only starting pitcher with a winning record, the Red Sox did finish in fourth place with 76 wins balanced against 76 losses. It was the first time since they won it all in 1918 that the Red Sox did not end a season with a losing record. Now in his mid-30s, Grove no longer had the blazing fastball he possessed when he was the Athletics' ace. Grove's speed was already in decline before his arm troubles with Boston in 1934; after having averaged six strikeouts per nine innings in his first eight seasons, Grove's strikeout ratio dropped precipitously to 3.7 per nine in 1933—his last year with the Athletics—but nonetheless went 24–8.

Yawkey got what he hoped for the next year when Ferrell won 25, Grove won 20 and led the league in earned run average, and the Red Sox finished with a winning record for the first time since 1918. In 1936, Ferrell had his sixth 20-win season in eight years and Grove won 17 and led the league in ERA again (and for the seventh time in 11 years), but Yawkey's club once again had a losing record. Pitching poorly in the first two months of the 1937 season, Ferrell was traded to Washington in June, along with his brother, for a pair of veteran players. Wes Ferrell never got to pitch in a World Series. His brother Rick never got to catch in a World Series. Brother Rick, who caught 18 years in the majors, made it to Cooperstown in 1984, courtesy of the Veterans Committee; Wes, with a

193–128 record and 4.04 career earned run average pitching entirely in a hitters' era, did not. As for Grove, even if his fastball had lost some of its renowned zip, he remained one of baseball's premier pitchers through the end of the decade, victorious in 64 percent of his decisions after his abysmal 1934 season and winning two more ERA titles. And that was despite Fenway Park supposedly being very tough on left-handed pitchers because of its close-in left-field wall.

Joe Cronin and Jimmie Foxx were Yawkey's prime offensive acquisitions. Cronin was not only the league's best shortstop when he came to Boston in 1935, but as player-manager in Washington he won the 1933 pennant his first year in charge, so Yawkey made him his player-manager. Maintaining an excellent relationship with the owner, Cronin would manage the Red Sox for 13 years, the first seven as their regular shortstop. Red Sox players, even if they respected his abilities as a ballplayer, questioned his acumen as a manager. Cronin was disliked by many of his players, especially the pitchers. Neither Ferrell nor Grove cared much for Cronin. Foxx was in his late 20s when he came to Boston in 1936. The change from Shibe Park to Fenway Park as his home grounds did not diminish Jimmie Foxx as a formidable power threat. In 1938, the year Hank Greenberg matched the 58 home runs Foxx hit in 1932 as the closest anyone had come to Ruth's 60, Foxx became just the second player after the Babe to have multiple 50-homer seasons; he hit exactly 50, while leading the league in batting (.349) and runs batted in (175).

After pacing the American League for most of May and half of June in 1940, Boston gradually fell out of the running even as the Yankees suddenly remembered they were the Yankees and surged into contention after falling 11½ games behind in early August. Hitting was not the problem; Foxx hit 36 homers and drove in 119 runs, Cronin had 24 homers and 111 RBIs, and the Red Sox had the phenomenal Ted Williams in his second season. Other than Grove, who nonetheless made only 21 starts, the Red Sox pitching was the third worst in the American League in giving up runs. The closest Grove came to pitching a meaningful late-season game since coming to Boston was on September 10, 1940, when he hurled a 13-inning complete game to beat the first-place Tigers, bringing the fourth-place Red Sox, hanging at the margins of the pennant race, within four games of the top. The next year, on July 25, Lefty Grove won the 300th game of his career—32 of which were as a reliever—in his 451st start. He made six more starts in 1941 without another victory and retired at the end of the season with exactly 300 wins, 105 with Boston. Foxx left Boston in 1942 after being hurt; he was second all-time with 524 home runs, 222 of them for the Red Sox. He hit only 10 more in his career.

* * *

With the Red Sox missing out on their best chance to take advantage of the Yankees' swoon, the 1940 pennant race came down to New York, Cleveland, and Detroit fighting for supremacy in September. Having finished fifth the previous year, and with Gehringer another year older, Tommy Bridges getting more days off between starts and Schoolboy Rowe struggling trying to come back from missing virtually all of '37 and '38 with arm problems, the Tigers' chances looked equally dim going into 1940. Greenberg, however, was still in his prime and an elite player, and Detroit had another young slugger named Rudy York, whose 88 home runs in his first three seasons made him a must-have bat in the lineup. The problem was, York was in search of a position. He had been a catcher up till now, also playing third base and filling in for Greenberg at first on occasion, but Birdie Tebbetts, far more agile and skilled defensively, was manager Del Baker's preferred choice behind the plate. The decision was made to put York full-time at first base and move Greenberg to the outfield. It proved to be a masterstroke.

At the end it was the Tigers on top, the Indians second, just one game behind, and the Yankees third, two back. Despite having to learn to play left field, which was an adventure, Greenberg had another MVP season, leading the league in home runs (41), total bases (384), and RBIs (150) while batting .340. York had an outstanding offensive year at first base, with 33 homers and 134 RBIs, and was second to Greenberg in both RBIs and total bases. Gehringer had his 13th and last .300 season. Rowe was 16–3 and Bridges 12–9, but Bobo Newsom was the workhorse of the Detroit pitching staff in 1940. A big right-hander, Newsom was an itinerant major leaguer. In the six years since making the grade for good in 1934 with the Browns, Newsom had also pitched for the Senators, Red Sox, and Browns again before the Tigers traded for him early in the 1939 season. His 21–5 record in 1940 was the second-best winning percentage in the league after Rowe, but his 264 innings were nearly 100 more than Rowe threw. It was also the third straight year Newsom was a 20-game winner. He would change teams 10 more times in the 10 years he had left in his big-league career.

The Tigers won by beating both their pennant-race rivals head-to-head in September. Going into Cleveland for the final weekend of the season, Detroit needed to win just one of three to clinch the pennant. York's two-run homer off Cleveland ace Bob Feller in the fourth inning was all the scoring in the first game; that they lost the next two didn't matter. They were at their best when they had to be, winning six of nine against the Indians and two of three against the Yankees in the final month. Feller was a 27-game winner that year, but the Tigers beat him all three times he faced them in September. The 1940 World Series with Cincinnati went seven games, with Newsom being outdueled by Paul Derringer in the Series finale, 2–1, to send the Tigers back to Detroit having lost in the fall classic for the fifth time in six tries.

* * *

Losing out to Detroit in 1940 was a tough blow for the Cleveland Indians. Since winning their first pennant in 1920, the closest the Indians had come was their stirring start-from-way-behind run against the Yankees in 1926—Tris Speaker's last year as both player and manager in Cleveland—which came up three games short mostly because, beginning from 11 games back in early August, they had fewer than 50 games remaining and ran out of time. The intervening years were a frustrating time for Cleveland fans. The Indians were in many ways like the Pittsburgh Pirates in the other league during the 1930s—solid and at the cusp of being competitive. They had some top-flight players and were a consistently good ballclub, finishing either third or fourth virtually every year. Some of those years they probably would have been a factor in the pennant race except for one thing—the New York Yankees so dominated the American League that no other club had a chance.

The Indians' most prominent position players during the 1930s were Earl Averill and Joe Vosmik, who played six years together in the outfield from 1931 to 1936, and first baseman Hal Trosky, a teammate of the first two from '34 to '36. All three were top-tier offensive threats. In the decade between the end-of-career wind-downs of Speaker and Cobb in 1926 and the arrival of Joe DiMaggio in 1936, Averill was arguably the best center fielder in all of baseball, with only the National League's Hack Wilson and Averill contemporary Wally Berger having a reasonable case to make otherwise. Trosky was an afterthought when it came to baseball's best first basemen because Gehrig, Foxx, and Greenberg were contemporaries in his league, and Johnny Mize and Dolph Camilli in the other. And Vosmik's .348 batting average in 1935 turned out to be one hit short of Buddy Myer's .349. While both Averill and Vosmik had left Cleveland by 1940, Trosky was an established seven-year veteran in a young infield that included 22-year-old second-year shortstop Lou Boudreau and, at third, the year-older Ken Keltner, in his third season.

Pitching was a team strength throughout the 1930s. Willis Hudlin, a 15-game winner five times between 1927 and 1935, and Mel Harder with eight straight years of at least 15 wins, highlighted by back-to-back 20-win seasons in '34 and '35, were steady and reliable, if understated, mainstays. And Indians fans got to watch right-hander Wes Ferrell put together four 20-win seasons between 1929, his rookie year, and 1932, compiling a 91–48 record. Only Lefty Grove, who was 104–25, pitched better those four years. Shoulder problems limited him to an 11–12 record in 1933, so mostly for the money Ferrell was sent to Boston, for whom he won 59 games over the next three years.

But they were nothing compared to Bob Feller, who introduced himself in dramatic fashion as a 17-year-old by striking out 15 St. Louis Browns in his first major-league start in August 1936. Just five starts later, in mid-September against the Athletics, Feller set a new major-league record by striking out 17 in a game where he also walked nine batters. It didn't matter that the Browns and Athletics were the two worst teams in the American League, the kid's fastball was soon being compared to Walter Johnson's and Lefty Grove's in their prime, even if he still needed to master his control—which, of course, made him a scary proposition for opposing batters in an era before batting helmets. Feller finished the year before his 18th birthday with a 5–3 record that included four nine-inning complete-game victories, in every one of which he fanned at least 10 batters.

At the age of 19 in 1938, Feller led the majors in strikeouts for the first of four consecutive years—a streak that came to an end only because he volunteered to fight for his country after the attack on Pearl Harbor. His 240 strikeouts were the most since Dazzy Vance whiffed 262 in 1924. Feller's most dominating strikeout performances were arguably in 1938 and 1939 when his ratio of strikeouts per nine innings was 26 percent better than the runner-up. His strikeout ratio would have been even better had he not had such difficulty controlling his overwhelming fastball and increasingly sharp curve. His 208 bases on balls in 1938 made Feller the first pitcher since 1898 to walk more than 200 batters—something no pitcher has done since—contributing to his 4.08 ERA and likely keeping him from his first 20-win season; he finished with a 17–11 record. Feller became a 20-game winner for the first time as a 20-year-old in 1939 when he went 24–9. Substantially reducing his walks to 142 while pitching nearly 300 innings resulted in his first sub-3.00 ERA. It was the first of three consecutive 20-win seasons before he voluntarily gave up baseball to join the wartime navy. Even with the Yankees having an uncharacteristically poor season in the McCarthy era, and by far their worst since DiMaggio's debut in 1936, the Indians would not have been in the hunt for the 1940 pennant were it not for Feller's 27 wins.

While Cleveland stayed in the thick of the 1940 pennant race until the very end, their season was at significant risk of unraveling in early June because of a player rebellion against the manager. Ossie Vitt, a former tough-guy infielder on the Tigers in the Ty Cobb era, was hired as manager in 1938 as an antidote to his predecessors at the helm—Roger Peckinpaugh from 1928 to 1933, Walter Johnson from 1933 to 1935, and Steve O'Neill from 1935 to 1937—all "nice guys" who were considered to be not as successful as they perhaps should have been because they were too close to their players. To the extent this was thought to be why the Indians had not contended for the pennant, it ignores just how good the American League winners were in every one of those years, especially the Yankees. Whatever the merits of Vitt's tough-guy managerial approach, it included sarcastically second-guessing and belittling his players in the clubhouse and the dugout and criticizing them to baseball scribes. Because he was not shy about telling the front office to mind its place, Vitt's relationship with the Indians' executive management team was also strained.

The crisis hit when Cleveland went to Boston in the second week of June, tied for first with the Red Sox. A rainout gave Indians players nothing to do but sit around the hotel lobby complaining about Vitt. Their manager's overreaction to Feller being knocked out by the Red Sox in a 9–2 loss the next day, and to losing big the day after that, motivated a delegation of 11 Indians players, including the aggrieved Feller, to confront team owner Alva Bradley about their opposition to Vitt when they returned to Cleveland. They wanted Ossie Vitt gone. Even though he was one owner who was highly regarded by his players, Bradley was unwilling to do that, most likely to avoid the appearance, feared and suppressed by every owner, of players calling the shots. Vitt stayed to manage the pennant race to its bitter end. Cleveland players, while backing down, did not make peace with their manager, but nonetheless got down to the business of playing winning baseball, although often ignoring Vitt's instructions. The story of their insurrection got out, however, including the players' specific grievances against their manager, and the Cleveland Indians had to endure persistent taunts about being "crybabies" everywhere they played for the rest of the season, sometimes even in their own park.

Immediately after the players complained to Bradley, the Indians won 12 of the 15 games in their homestand to take a 2½-game lead. They stayed in first place until mid-July, spent the next month hanging a close second with occasional forays into a first-place tie with the Tigers, and returned to the top by themselves when Feller won his 20th against Detroit on August 12. The Indians extended their lead to 5½ games over the Tigers on August 21, but from then till the end of the season had the third-worst record in the American League at 18–19, which included two meaningless victories after Feller's loss to the Tigers eliminated them from contention in the first game of their season-ending series. In their 40 years of history, the Cleveland Indians had won just one pennant, which they followed up by winning the World Series. That was 20 years before in 1920. But in all that time, they had only 12 losing seasons and finished last just once. Cleveland's fate in the baseball world seemed somehow destined to always be, good teams . . . just not good enough.

Vitt was let go as soon as the season ended, his chances not at all helped by the Indians' desultory final five weeks, and replaced by Peckinpaugh for 1941. Feller had another great year with 25 wins and Boudreau solidified his standing as perhaps the best all-around shortstop in the game. The highlight of their season was the two fantastic plays Ken Keltner made deep behind the bag at third to rob Joe DiMaggio of hits that would have extended his 56-game hitting streak that came to an end in Cleveland on July 17. The Indians finished fourth with a losing record, after which Peckinpaugh stepped down as manager and moved up to become general manager.

Lou Boudreau was still only 24 with only three seasons and 357 games in the major leagues under his belt when he threw his baseball cap into the ring as the front office was contemplating who should be the next manager. Several veterans on the club whose careers dated back to the mid-1930s, if not earlier, had also expressed interest, including Hal Trosky. Boudreau's undeniable on-the-field leadership and his presumptuous moxie in asking to be considered certainly raised eyebrows, but also changed the debate. Some of the Cleveland players were contemptuous of the decision to name Boudreau player-manager, particularly on the pitching staff. Except for rookie backup catcher Jim Hegan, Boudreau—who would turn 25 in July—was the youngest player of any consequence on the Cleveland roster. He was in fact the youngest player to be made a manager in the major leagues since 1914 when 23-year-old shortstop Roger Peckinpaugh, for whom Boudreau now worked, was named manager of the Yankees.

Aside from clubhouse resentments, Boudreau's first years as player-manager were handicapped by Bob Feller going off to war in 1942. That left Boudreau as both the undisputed star player of the Cleveland Indians and the face of the franchise. None of his teams competed for the pennant during the war years, and likely would not have even had there been no war and Feller, along with all of baseball's best players, stayed in the game. The Yankees and the Red Sox—who by now had Ted Williams, Bobby Doerr, Johnny Pesky, Dom DiMaggio, and Tex Hughson—would have been far superior teams. As if to prove the point, the Indians were not competitive in either of the first two years that Feller, along with all of baseball's other wartime veterans, was back in the game once the war was over. With Boudreau having probably the best season ever by a player-manager and Feller still their ace, even if no longer their best pitcher, the Indians finally won their second pennant in franchise history in 1948.

28

THE MCKECHNIE SCORECARD

Improving the Braves, Winning with the Reds

Joe McCarthy's 1930s National League counterpart for most respected manager was Bill McKechnie, although not till the end of the decade was McKechnie finally able to manage his team to the World Series. Then, of course, he had the bad luck to go against McCarthy's 1939 Yankees and watch his Cincinnati Reds be dismantled in four straight. That was McCarthy's fifth World Series—he won them all—in the nine years he had managed the Yankees, and his sixth overall, including his 1929 Cubs. Before coming to Cincinnati, McKechnie had managed the Boston Braves for eight years from 1930 to 1937, with 106 more losses than wins to show for his efforts. McCarthy's teams during those same years, including the 1930 Cubs before he was fired days before the season ended, won 313 games more than they lost.

If that was all to his record, Bill McKechnie would hardly have been thought of as a successful manager, notwithstanding that his Braves were not very good through no fault of his own. It was still rare in Major League Baseball that a manager with such little competitive success would last as long as eight years, still less be so highly regarded as a manager, if those had been his first years at the helm. Lucky for him, they were not. Before the Great Depression cast its pall on America shortly after the 1929 World Series, McKechnie had already won two National League pennants—with Pittsburgh in 1925 and St. Louis in 1928—in five full and two part seasons managing in the majors. His career, however, had been star crossed. He was axed by the Pirates a year after he won the 1925 World Series for alleged insubordination because veteran players on his club were in open rebellion over Pirates vice president Fred Clarke's interventions in the dugout, and he was demoted to the Cardinals' top farm team in Rochester, trading places with Billy Southworth, in 1929 apparently due to Cardinal owner Sam Breadon's embarrassment about his club being crushed by the powerhouse Yankees in the 1928 World Series.

That was the Series where Ruth hit .625 with 10 hits in 16 at-bats, scored nine runs, and walloped three homers in the final game. Breadon reputedly was upset that his manager chose to pitch to the Bambino rather than pitch around him; only once in the Yankees' four-game sweep did the Babe draw a base on balls. If those were Breadon's specific gripes that cost McKechnie his job, they were misplaced. For one thing, the equally dangerous Gehrig batted behind Ruth in the lineup, and he hit .545 in the Series and was walked six times by Cardinals pitchers. For another, in 10 of Ruth's plate appearances he came to bat with nobody on base, either to lead off the inning or with outs already in the scorebook. It would have been highly unusual at the time for McKechnie to order his pitchers not to throw strikes even to Babe Ruth with the bases empty, especially because the guy coming to bat next was Lou Gehrig. Eight of Ruth's hits came with nobody on base, including all three of his homers, which was why he had only four runs batted in for the Series. Gehrig drove in nine. Ruth came to bat seven times with runners on base, walked once and got two hits, one of which drove in a run. Cardinals pitchers got him out four times with runners on, once getting him to ground into a double play.

Whatever the actual reason for dismissing McKechnie, it took Breadon half the 1929 season to realize he had made a mistake. Southworth was alienating many of his players, perhaps because at 36 and just one year removed from being their teammate, he was trying too hard, in sharp contrast to McKechnie's strong and confident steady hand. Breadon sent Southworth back to Rochester and brought McKechnie back to St. Louis. Although St. Louis was a much better ballclub and could reasonably be expected to contend in the years ahead, which they in fact did, McKechnie turned down Breadon's offer to return as manager in 1930, signing a four-year contract with the Boston Braves instead. After being sent to the minors despite winning a close pennant race in 1928, McKechnie was loath to trust Breadon with his future and preferred the security of a long-term contract, even if it was with a terrible team. Unlike the Cardinals, the Braves were a joke in the National League—if for no other reason than in 1929 they not only finished last, but their manager was their owner; Judge Emil Fuchs, whose professional training was in the law and had no professional baseball experience, thought he was perfectly capable of managing the team himself. Clearly, he wasn't.

* * *

The Boston Braves had not had a winning season since 1921, the year after George Stallings resigned as manager and star shortstop Rabbit Maranville was traded away. During each of the next three years, 1922 to 1924, they lost exactly 100 games. By now Fuchs, who earned the title "Judge" as a New York City magistrate in the teens, owned the Braves. An attorney for the New York Giants at the time, Fuchs bought the club in 1923 at the suggestion of John McGraw, who also offered that Christy Mathewson might be interested in running the Braves' baseball operation. Mathewson, already stricken with the tuberculous that would claim his life in 1925, became team president. They inherited Fred Mitchell as manager. Although Mitchell already had the Cubs' 1918 pennant on his managerial resume, back-to-back 100-loss seasons in 1922 and '23 as the Braves' manager caused Fuchs and Mathewson to replace him with short-stop Dave Bancroft in 1924. Mitchell's was the typical fate for managers of bad teams in those days, even those who already had won pennants. The change did not make the Braves more competitive, and after four years Fuchs fired Bancroft as manager and released him as a player.

Between Stallings's departure in 1920 and McKechnie's arrival in 1930, the Braves' roster, both position players and pitchers, was constantly being reinvented. Virtually every year, the Braves were one of the two lowest-scoring teams in the National League, while their pitching and defense typically gave up the second or third most runs in the league. When he took charge at Braves Field, Bill McKechnie likely had realistic expectations that competing for the pennant was at best a long-term goal, but nonetheless expected his team to play better within the limits of his players' abilities. Well aware of the Braves' financial limitations, McKechnie also believed that being signed for four years would give him time to recast and turn around a losing franchise. A strong proponent of making all possible plays in the field, McKechnie prioritized improving the Braves' defense, which was among the worst in baseball before he took command.

He soon returned the Braves to a modicum of respectability. In 1932, McKechnie brought the team its first .500 record in 11 years. For the next two years, the Braves had winning records and finished fourth both times. In 1933, they even went into September in second place, thanks to a superb 22–6 month of August. The Braves' three consecutive years from 1932 to 1934 without a losing record were their first since Stallings's 1914–16 Braves. The Braves' much-improved defense made them a much better ballclub than they deserved to be, because their pitchers— forgotten names like Ed Brandt, Fred Frankhouse, Socks Seibold, and Ben Cantwell—were always in the bottom half of the league in strikeouts,

Braves manager Bill McKechnie (left) and Dodgers manager Max Carey flanking Brooklyn's borough president throwing out the first ball of the 1932 season. Carey starred on McKechnie's 1925 World Series champion Pittsburgh Pirates. *New York World Telegram and the Sun Newspaper Photograph Collection (Library of Congress).*

meaning they had to rely on more fielding outs, and their offense was one of the least productive in the National League.

McKechnie then had to endure the fate of Sisyphus when the rock he was pushing up the steep hill of the National League standings came crashing down on him in 1935. It didn't help that Judge Fuchs added the additional weight of Babe Ruth's managerial aspirations onto that rock. Fuchs lured the Babe back to Boston—the city where his career began—hoping to boost his club's attendance. McKechnie wasn't consulted, and Ruth was under the impression he would *first* serve as assistant manager and eventually become *the* manager. Within a week of hitting the last three home runs of his career—all mammoth blasts at Pittsburgh's Forbes Field on May 25, 1935—giving him the iconic total of 714, Ruth spitefully quit on the Braves, accusing Fuchs of double-crossing him. With or without Ruth, the season was already shaping into a disaster for the Braves. They were 9–25 when Ruth played his last game in the big leagues and finished with an abysmal 38–115 record, 61½ games out of first place. Fuchs sold the club in July. The next year, with McKechnie still in charge and Ruth gone, Boston's Braves were now called the Bees, perhaps with the hope that a name change would make what happened in 1935 go away. Maybe the new team name worked; the "Bees" nearly doubled their victory total to 71 in 1936, and in 1937—McKechnie's last year in Boston—they were back over .500 with a 79–73 record.

Unlike the 1920s, when there was a new combination of starting players every year, the Braves under McKechnie were more settled on their core players. Greater lineup stability did little to improve the Braves' offense during his tenure, however; they were last or next to last in scoring every year but one in the eight years of McKechnie's reign. Wally Berger was the only player in his lineup who menaced opposing pitchers. Beginning his career with 38 homers in 1930 that set a rookie record unmatched until Frank Robinson also hit 38 in 1956, and unsurpassed for more than half a century until Mark McGwire belted 49 in 1987, Berger hit 199 home runs, scored 651 runs, drove in 746 runs, and batted .304 for the Braves before being traded in 1937. Berger by himself accounted for 42 percent of his team's total 468 home runs and was directly responsible for 27 percent of the Braves' runs during his time in Boston. Three times he crashed more than 30 homers, and he had four 100-RBI seasons. In 1935, when the Braves won just 38 games, Berger led the league with 34 homers and 130 RBIs. No other Braves player hit more than 16 homers or had more than 86 RBIs in the eight years McKechnie was their manager. Although his career was obscured by the fact that the Braves were never competitive when he played for them, Wally Berger was the best center fielder in the National League during the 1930s.

McKechnie's last year in Boston, 1937, perhaps best reflected both the frustrations and the successes of his time managing the Braves, or the Bees, as they were called that year. Just two years removed from their horrid 38-win 1935 season, the '37 Bees finished fifth with a 79–73 record despite scoring the fewest runs of any team in the majors. But they also gave up the fewest runs and managed to outscore their opponents by the modest margin of 579 to 556, even with the lowest batting average, on-base percentage, and slugging percentage of any big-league club. Superb defense helped the Braves to the most complete games (85), most shutouts (16), and lowest ERA (3.22) in baseball even though they had by far the fewest strikeouts (387), accounting for less than 10 percent of their outs. The 1937 Bees featured two 20-game winners, both rookie right-handers in their 30s—Lou Fette (20–10) and Jim Turner (20–11)—who also are not much remembered today, if they are remembered at all.

Turner's 2.38 earned run average was the best in the league, and Fette's 2.88 was fifth.

Bill McKechnie could not have been better positioned for a new managerial opportunity than he was right now. His contract was up, the Braves' new owner thought McKechnie had stayed long enough, and he had suitors. Although nearly a decade removed from leading the Cardinals to the 1928 pennant, rather than having sunk into baseball oblivion for not having managed a competitive team in any of his eight years in Boston, his masterful job of managing the Braves had, if anything, enhanced his stature. *The Sporting News*, baseball's bible, named him "Manager of the Year" in 1937 for getting the most out of a "mediocre team," especially the pitchers, to bring them home fifth. He was probably the most respected manager in the game outside of McCarthy, whose Yankees had just won their second straight pennant on their way to four in a row—the fourth of which would be against the Cincinnati Reds, managed since 1938 by Mr. McKechnie.

* * *

The Reds were a worse team than McKechnie's Braves during the 1930s. Their last winning season was 1928, 10 years before McKechnie came to Cincinnati, when they finished fifth with a 78–74 record. The next year was an embarrassment, and not just because they collapsed to seventh, losing 22 more games than they won. Their season highlight was a lowlight—a baseball brawl with the Cubs in Chicago on July 4 that was resumed later at the train station as both teams were waiting to go to their next destination. When called to account for what happened by the league president, Cincinnati manager Jack Hendricks's version of events didn't exactly align with the irrefutable facts of what had transpired. For Hendricks, who had managed the Reds since Pat Moran's untimely death in 1924, this hardly helped his case to remain as manager, certainly not when they finished so low in the standings. The Reds went through five managers over the next nine years, finishing last five times and next to last twice.

A positive turning point for the franchise came at the end of the 1936 season when owner Powel Crosley, a wealthy local entrepreneur and regional radio-station magnate who bought the club in 1933, hired Warren Giles to be the general manager. Giles had long experience as a minor-league executive, including running the Cardinals' top farm team in Rochester, heading the Minor League Executive Committee, and serving as president of the International League. Although the Reds had just completed their best season since 1928, with a 74–80 record, Giles did not believe the club was on a winning trajectory, nor did he think that Charley Dressen, their manager since late in the 1934 season, was the guy to get them there. Giles was proved right on both counts. The 1937 Reds lost on Opening Day, lost 20 of their first 30 games, and never came close to .500. Giles dismissed Dressen with three weeks remaining and hired McKechnie soon after the season ended.

Like the Boston team McKechnie inherited nine years before, there had been little continuity of core regulars over successive seasons in Cincinnati since their last winning season in 1928. Catcher Ernie Lombardi was their only position regular for at least five years between Hendricks's departure and McKechnie's arrival. Lombardi was an exceptional hitter who hardly ever struck out. In his first six years in Cincinnati from 1932 to 1937, he batted .316 and fanned in just 4 percent of his plate appearances. Making Lombardi's batting averages more remarkable was that he was very slow; he not only was unable to get infield hits, but teams were able to cut down many hits through the infield by playing their infielders farther back, even on the outfield grass. Heavyset and less than agile, Lombardi also lacked day-to-day endurance and was frequently hurt. He had started less than 60 percent of the Reds' games since 1932—the only year he was in the starting lineup more than 100 games (he started 105)—and the most consecutive games he started in any season was 11, just twice.

The only pitchers to start 20 or more games over any five-year period the previous 10 seasons were Red Lucas and Paul Derringer, both right-handers. Lucas won 19 in 1929 and led the league in complete games three times before being traded to Pittsburgh after the 1933 season having pitched eight years in Cincinnati. Derringer, picked up in the May 1933 deal that sent Leo Durocher to St. Louis, lost 25 games with his new team, on his way to a league-leading 27 losses. It wasn't that Derringer pitched badly—his ERA was 3.23 in 33 games—it was that the Reds, the worst-hitting team in the majors, scored three or fewer runs in 25 of his 31 starts, 22 of which he lost. In seven of his starts, the Reds did not score at all. From August 16 to September 2, the Reds were shut out in four consecutive Derringer starts. After 21 losses the next year, Derringer won 22 in 1935 to become Cincinnati's first 20-game winner since 1926.

Even though Cincinnati had just finished last, McKechnie had a much better core of players to begin with the 1938 Reds than he had with the 1930 Braves. Besides Derringer and Lombardi, there were two other established players in the Cincinnati lineup he could build around, each entering his fourth big-league season—shortstop Billy Myers and right fielder Ival Goodman. McKechnie was also counting on hard-throwing southpaw Johnny Vander Meer, whose 1937 rookie year was marred by control problems, to add pitching depth, and a pair of rookies—first baseman Frank McCormick and center fielder Harry Craft—to strengthen his lineup. Just prior to spring training, Giles purchased infielder Lonny Frey from the Cubs, and in June acquired outfielder Wally Berger from the Giants and right-hander Bucky Walters from the Phillies. Although Berger was nearing the end of his career, McKechnie considered him a valued veteran to solidify both the Reds' batting order and the outfield. McKechnie resurrected Frey's stagnating career by moving him from shortstop, where his arm was not the strongest, to second base, where his quickness and agility were an asset, and Frey soon eclipsed Billy Herman as the best second baseman in the National League. Walters, freed from the hapless Phillies, became one of the best pitchers in baseball.

McKechnie's Reds were a much better team his first year at the helm, finishing fourth. With a much more potent offense and significantly better defense and pitching, the 1938 Reds were 84–66, compared to an abysmal 56–98 the year before. Lombardi, who hit .337 the three previous years, although with never more than 387 at-bats, started 122 games behind the plate, came to bat 489 times, and won the batting title with a .342 average while driving in 95 runs. McCormick's .327 batting average was third in the league, and his 106 runs batted in were fourth. Goodman's 30 homers trailed only Mel Ott for most in the National League. Reunited with his former manager, Berger hit .307 in Cincinnati, and the Reds, just two games above .500 when they acquired him, were 12 above the break-even point the rest of the way. Derringer was 21–14; Walters 11–6 after coming to the Reds; and Vander Meer was 15–10, including no-hitters against the Bees and the Dodgers in back-to-back starts. Still grappling with control problems, Johnny Vander Meer's second no-hitter in Brooklyn was notable, in addition to being unprecedented, for his surrendering eight walks.

The 1939 Reds moved into first place for good in just their 25th game of the season, went into August with a 12-game lead, and successfully held off the surging Cardinals down the stretch to win the pennant by 4½ games. McCormick was the batting star, leading the league in hits for the second straight year. His .332 batting average was second in the league, and his 128 RBIs the most of any National League batter. While the Reds had the league's second-best offense after St. Louis, it was the excellence of their pitching and defense that brought Cincinnati its first pennant in 20 years. They had the lowest team ERA, made the fewest errors, and had the best ratio of defensive outs on balls in play. Walters won 27 and Derringer won 25. Vander Meer's career was set back by chronic arm problems that limited him to just 129 innings, a 5–9 record, and a 4.67 earned run average.

Unlike 1919, when the Reds' beating the heavily favored White Sox in the World Series was besmirched by the Black Sox scandal that was apparent to many observers even as the games were being played, Cincinnati did not win a single game against the heavily favored Yankees in

1939. They lost the first and fourth games in heartbreaking fashion. Derringer went into the ninth inning of the opening game in New York having allowed the Yankees just four hits, but surrendered a triple to Charlie Keller and a game-winning, walk-off single to Bill Dickey to lose 2–1. And in the ninth inning of Game Four in Cincinnati, the Reds held a 4–2 lead with Walters on the mound in relief of Derringer, needing just three outs to avoid a Series sweep, only for Keller and DiMaggio to lead off with singles and come around to score, the second and tying run unearned. In the 10th, DiMaggio came to bat with a runner on third and Keller on first with one out. In one of the most famous plays in World Series history, DiMaggio lashed a single into right field to drive in the go-ahead run, and Keller, taking advantage of right fielder Ival Goodman misplaying the ball, came barreling into home just as catcher Lombardi was reaching to grab Goodman's throw. Keller bowled over Lombardi, the ball rolled a few feet away from the stricken catcher, and DiMaggio slid past the prostate Lombardi with the third run of the inning.

The play became known as the Schnozz's snooze. In addition to never being able to outlive the "Schnozz" nickname because of his big nose, Ernie Lombardi is forever remembered for lying in the dirt and doing nothing to grab the baseball just a few feet away, when in fact he had been flattened and knocked nearly senseless by the hard-charging, physically imposing Keller. Lost in the imagery and narrative of the story is that DiMaggio's run, and even Keller's for that matter, were in fact not decisive, even if they did provide the Yankees a three-run cushion to get the final three outs. The go-ahead run had already scored on DiMaggio's hit, and the play may not have unfolded at all had Goodman fielded the hit cleanly. As it happened, after the first two Cincinnati batters in the bottom of the 10th singled off Yankees relief ace Johnny Murphy, the still-woozy Lombardi, longtime veteran and now-outfield-reserve Al Simmons, and Wally Berger all came to bat as the tying run. Murphy retired all three.

* * *

Cincinnati's chance for redemption came the next year. Bucky Walters (22–10) and Paul Derringer (20–12) once again were 20-game winners. Right-hander Gene Thompson, in his second season, added 16 wins, and Jim Turner, acquired over the winter from the Bees, won 14 for his at-once former and current manager. Frank McCormick became the first player in history to lead his league in hits in each of his first three big-league seasons. Johnny Pesky (1942, 1946, and 1947) and Tony Oliva (1964–66) are the only other players to match McCormick's feat, and Pesky's string was interrupted by three years in World War II.

Despite coasting to the pennant after July and finishing 12 games ahead of the competition with exactly 100 wins, while the Detroit Tigers did not clinch the American League pennant until their 152nd game, the Reds went into the World Series with a significant handicap. Two of their cornerstone players—Lombardi and Lonny Frey—were injured shortly before the season ended and were day to day, at best, for the World Series. Lombardi badly injured his ankle with only two weeks remaining, did not play the rest of the schedule in hopes of recuperation come the World Series, and was not physically capable of starting in the Series—except, gamely, in the third game. Even though the often-banged-up catcher played only 109 games, Lombardi's loss took away one of Cincinnati's primary power threats. With his primary backup—Willard Hershberger—tragically committing suicide at the beginning of August and third-string catcher Bill Baker an inexperienced rookie, McKechnie was forced to activate 39-year-old Jimmie Wilson, a valued coach whose catching career had come to an end in 1936 when he was in his third year as a player-manager. Wilson caught only 16 games and had just 37 at-bats during the season, but started six of the seven games in the 1940 World Series, batted .353, and was the only player on either club to steal a base. With just three days left to the season, Frey broke his toe in a dugout accident, effectively sidelining him for the Series. In his stead at second base, McKechnie started Eddie Joost, a light-hitting middle infielder still trying to survive in the big leagues.

Replacing Lombardi and Frey with Wilson and Joost were managerial decisions of necessity. Not so was McKechnie's decision to start only right-handers in the World Series against a Detroit lineup that included three dangerous left-handed hitters—center fielder Barney McCosky, batting second, the American League leader in hits and triples while batting .340; veteran second baseman Charlie Gehringer, batting third, who hit .313 and drove in 81 runs while hardly ever striking out (only 17 times in 629 plate appearances); and Bruce Campbell, batting sixth, a .284 hitter who was platooned in right field with the right-handed-batting Pete Fox. Backup catcher Billy Sullivan also hit left-handed, but his .309 average in 57 games persuaded Detroit manager Del Baker to start him over regular catcher Birdie Tebbetts in four of the seven games.

That McKechnie opted for all righties to start against the Tigers probably was no surprise since right-handers had started all but seven of the Reds' 155 games during the regular season. No other major-league team had as few starts by lefties. Southpaws accounted for only 110 of the 1,407⅔ innings thrown by the Cincinnati staff all year, and only four of the Reds' 100 triumphs went into the win column of a left-hander. McKechnie, however, did have a potential left-handed ace in the hole for the World Series in none other than Double-No-Hit Johnny Vander Meer.

His back-to-back no-hitters in 1938 a distant though still living memory, Vander Meer had been sent back to the minors in June to recover his control and effectiveness after a tough start to the season. After the lefty had gone 6–4 with a 2.40 ERA in 14 minor-league starts, McKechnie worked Vander Meer back into the starting rotation with five starts in September. Vander Meer pitched well in the final month, with a 3–1 record, two complete-game victories, a 2.97 ERA, and 32 strikeouts in 39⅓ innings. Vander Meer was the winning pitcher in the game that ensured at least a tie for the pennant, going 12 innings to earn the victory in just his third start after coming back to Cincinnati.

The Reds' World Series experience the previous year should have been an object lesson on the potential consequences of starting only right-handers against a team with good left-handed batters. Although south-paws Vander Meer and Lee Grissom both started 21 games for the 1939 Reds, neither got a start in the World Series as McKechnie went with only right-handers against a Yankees team whose left-handed batters included Bill Dickey, Charlie Keller, Red Rolfe, and George Selkirk. McKechnie used right-handers for all but 1⅓ innings in the '39 Series, and the Yankees' left-handed hitters were the driving force in their four-game sweep. Keller, who hit .438 in the Series with three home runs and six RBIs, demolished Cincinnati pitching all by himself, and Dickey had two homers with five runs batted in.

Giving Vander Meer one or two starts in the 1940 Series would have forced Detroit to adjust from right-handers, but McKechnie also had to consider Vander Meer's continuing problems with control. Despite his winning record in September, Vander Meer walked 28 batters in his 39⅓ innings of work—a rate of 6.4 per nine innings—which probably was appalling to his manager. Particularly with it apparent that neither Lombardi nor Frey would be available for the Series, except for bit parts, McKechnie was likely not inclined to rely on a starting pitcher with serious control issues. He was surely aware that Detroit batters drew the most walks in the majors, and that the likes of Hank Greenberg and Rudy York, first and second in the American League in RBIs, and first and third in home runs, capitalized with runners on base. The whole point of his emphasis on pitching and defense was to minimize runners on base, and the possibility of Vander Meer issuing so many bases on balls surely would have undermined that essential McKechnie philosophy.

A further consideration was that the lack of throwing arm diversity among his starting pitchers hardly mattered to the Reds, who won 100 games throwing right-handers game after game after game. Derringer, Walters, Thompson, and Turner—right-handers all—started 82 percent of the Reds' games, winning 72 while losing only 38, and walked only 2.4 batters per nine innings in the 1,014 innings they pitched during the 1940 season. Derringer started three games against the Tigers, Walters two, and Thompson and Turner each started once. Vander Meer threw three shutout innings in the fifth game after the Tigers had already broken the game open with seven runs in the first four innings, as opposed to none scored by the Reds. He walked three batters and gave up two hits, but the Tigers were unable to add to their lead with Johnny Vander Meer on the mound.

The Game Seven showdown for the championship turned into a pitching duel between Paul Derringer and Bobo Newsom, whose father died of a heart attack the day after his son won the Series opener. The Tigers scored once in the third inning. The Reds tied the score in the seventh and had the go-ahead run on third with one out when McKechnie sent Lombardi to bat as a pinch-hitter. Lombardi may have been injured and virtually immobile—(some would uncharitably say, with good reason, that Lombardi was virtually immobile even when healthy)—but he was nonetheless an extraordinarily dangerous batsman. Deciding discretion was the better part of valor, the Tigers intentionally walked the lumbering Lombardi to set up a double-play situation. McKechnie countered by sending Lonny Frey in to run for Lombardi despite the injured foot that had limited him to pinch-hitting. A sacrifice fly to center scored the run, Cincinnati now led, 2–1, Frey stayed in the game to play second base—his first appearance in the field in the Series—and had the distinction of fielding the groundball that turned into the final out of the World Series, sealing the Reds' victory in seven games. This time there was no question their World Series championship was legitimately earned; there were no Black Tigers anywhere in the Detroit jungle.

That was the high point of McKechnie's nine-year tenure in Cincinnati. The Reds quite simply were not nearly as talented as the Brooklyn Dodgers and St. Louis Cardinals battled it out in epic pennant races each of the next two years. Less crippled by core players being drafted into World War II than the Dodgers, the Reds rose to second in 1943, but were effectively out of the running by the Fourth of July as the Cardinals outpaced everybody. After finishing third in 1944, the Reds began a stretch of 11 consecutive losing seasons. Considered by the Cincinnati front office at the age of 60 to be out of touch with the modern player in postwar Major League Baseball, McKechnie was fired as manager as the 1946 season came to an end.

What the last six years of McKechnie's managerial career demonstrated was that, for all the importance of pitching and defense—which remained Cincinnati strengths—scoring runs matters a lot. Unlike the Braves when he was their manager, consistently one of the worst offensive teams in baseball, the Reds in his first three years as manager were a good-hitting club. Thereafter, his team was undermined, as his Braves had been, by one of baseball's least productive offenses. Lombardi, at 33, was traded to the Braves in 1942 and promptly won a second batting title. McCormick did not play up to the level he had in his first three seasons and was sold to the Phillies after the 1945 season, having hit .300 in his eight years as the Reds' first baseman. Frey was drafted into the service in 1944. After being second in runs in 1938 and '39, and third in 1940, the Reds were one of the lowest-scoring teams the next six years, even as they continued to be one of the stingiest in surrendering runs.

* * *

Bill McKechnie managed a total of 24 years in the National League. Winning pennants in Pittsburgh, St. Louis, and Cincinnati, McKechnie became the first manager to lead three different teams to the World Series. And with the Pirates triumphant in 1925 and the Reds in 1940, he was the first manager to win the World Series for two franchises. Had he opted to accept Breadon's offer to manage the Cardinals in 1930, McKechnie would probably have retired with at least six National League pennants on his resume because the Cardinals won both that year and the next, even assuming he might not have been around for their 1934 pennant but would still have managed the Reds in 1939 and 1940.

Like John McGraw, McKechnie had very few poor years as a manager, which are not to be confused with losing seasons. McKechnie for most of the last 17 years of his managerial career did not have good ballclubs, but still had only six losing seasons from 1930 to 1946—four in Boston, and his last two years in Cincinnati. Like George Stallings and Pat Moran, McKechnie's biggest strength was his ability to substantially improve the teams he managed. Inheriting teams in both Boston and Cincinnati that were not contenders, McKechnie focused on the things that would make them better. And like Joe McCarthy, McKechnie was an excellent strategic manager fashioning a team to his liking, schooling his team to minimize mistakes on the field, preparing his team for a long season, and motivating his players to maximize their success as a team. Perhaps befitting his nickname—the "Deacon," implying reasoned, responsible stewardship of his disciples (players)—McKechnie not only prized stability and emphasized the importance of laying a firm foundation (defense, in particular) that would be constantly reliable through the slumps to which hitting and pitching are prone, but was relatively conservative in his in-game maneuvers.

When managing in Boston and Cincinnati, it wasn't so much that McKechnie disdained aggressively trying to force the action as much as he was pragmatic in assessing situations, weighing his options, and choosing strategies based on an intuitive calculation of the prospects for success. Bill McKechnie was much more Joe McCarthy than John

McGraw. Both McCarthy and McKechnie had a relatively minimalist and conservative approach to managing the game. Their restrained managerial style—letting each game find its natural course and intervening with specifically visible player or strategy maneuvers at key moments of criticality—was typical for the time. It being the second decade of a hitters' era marked by the power game, small ball strategies to set up runs were in remission. Their restraint, however, should not be mistaken for indifference, lack of attentiveness or initiative, unwillingness to force the action or take a risk, or not having a killer instinct. Indeed, their conservative approach to managing the game on the field and making few visible decisions was indicative of McKechnie and McCarthy being confident in their team's preparation and skills and in the "baseball intelligence" of their players knowing what to do as the game developed and situations presented themselves. Many of the decisions a manager makes in any given game are not apparent in what happens on the field, not to mention numerous occasions during games when a manager considers the situation, ponders his options, and perhaps decides to stay his hand. For McCarthy and McKechnie both, the premium was in managing the flow of the game and knowing when to intervene.

Their conservative approach applied also to roster management from game to game and within games. Bill McKechnie is quoted as having said that if you take care of the percentages, the percentages will take care of you. This was common baseball wisdom. But other than when he managed the Pirates in the 1920s, when platooning was widespread, McKechnie with both the Braves and the Reds did not seek a percentage advantage against opposing starting pitchers by platooning a left-handed with right-handed batter anywhere in his lineup. In his 17 years managing Boston and Cincinnati, McKechnie platooned at a position only twice—in 1930, his first year with the Braves, and in 1946, his final year with the Reds.

Nor, despite his belief in percentages, did McKechnie make many position-player substitutions during games. He managed according to "the percentages" primarily by pinch-hitting for pitchers, not for position players, and appears to have rarely made defensive substitutions, including double switches to account for pitching changes. But with rare exceptions, this was typical of managers in the 1930s. One of the rare exceptions was McCarthy at the beginning of his Yankees reign replacing Ruth in the outfield in the late innings to give the overweight Babe's aging legs a break. Once Ruth was gone, McCarthy rarely substituted for position players in his starting lineup. The same was true for McKechnie. In all three of the years McKechnie made more than 100 position substitutions in the field—1931, 1935, and 1946—his team was last in scoring, probably motivating him to pinch-hit for starting position players in an effort to ignite or sustain rallies more often than he would have preferred.

In addition to the two World Series he won as a manager, Bill McKechnie played an instrumental role in the Cleveland Indians' 1948 championship season. The Deacon's calm demeanor, big-picture approach, and intuitive grasp of the flow of the game was exactly what new Cleveland owner Bill Veeck was looking for when he concluded before the 1948 season that, while his shortstop-manager Lou Boudreau was not really up to the manager part of his job, he could not be demoted to being just a star player because of his personal stake in the dual position and his enormous popularity with the Indians' faithful. Veeck hired McKechnie to be, in essence, Boudreau's "bench coach," and his stabilizing presence assuredly made the difference in a tight pennant race that ultimately was decided in a one-game playoff against Boston's Red Sox, and in the Indians' six-game World Series triumph over Boston's Braves.

29

UNLUCKY *NOT* TO BE A YANKEE

Dykes, Stengel, McCarthy, and the Difference
a Great Team Makes

In 1946, Joe DiMaggio published the first take of his autobiography. He titled it *Lucky to Be a Yankee*, the point being that his career was as blessed as it was because he played for such an outstanding organization. In truth, DiMaggio was a great player and would have been recognized as such even if he had not played for the Yankees. He might have been "lucky to be a Yankee" in the sense that being the best player on a great team with other outstanding players made him a national icon. Of course, there were some players for whom it was *unlucky* to be a Yankee because they were unable to crack the starting lineup, which they might otherwise have done on other clubs. Myril Hoag, for example, was a Yankees outfielder for seven years, only twice playing in as many as 90 games—including batting .301 in 106 games and 362 at-bats, his most as a Yankee, in 1937—before finally getting the opportunity to be a regular in 1939 at the age of 31 *after* he was traded to the St. Louis Browns. His teammate on the Browns that year, first baseman George McQuinn, age 29, got a late start to his big-league career because he was buried in the Yankees' farm system when Lou Gehrig was playing every game of every season for the parent club. And then there were some who were lucky *not* to be a Yankee—namely, Bronx resident Hank Greenberg, who knew that Gehrig was still in the prime of his career when the Yankees tried to sign him, and latched on with the Tigers instead.

One who was truly "lucky to be a Yankee" was Joe DiMaggio's first manager in the major leagues—Joe McCarthy. In DiMaggio's first seven seasons before being drafted for World War II, McCarthy managed the Yankees to six pennants and five World Series championships. And even with DiMaggio and other core players suddenly in wartime service in 1943, McCarthy managed the Yankees to a seventh pennant and sixth World Series banner in eight years. In large part, perhaps even entirely, based on that record, Joe McCarthy was already being considered one of the greatest managers in history. He had won eight pennants—the first in 1932—and seven World Series in his first 13 years managing the Yankees. Counting 1929, when he managed Chicago's Cubs, McCarthy's resume featured nine pennants in 18 years through 1943 as a major-league manager. Connie Mack also had nine pennants to his credit, and John McGraw had 10, but neither got to nine as quickly as Joe McCarthy.

Industrial automation was still in the dark ages, but Americans knew enough about it to know exactly what Jimmy Dykes meant when he famously tried to push McCarthy's button by calling him a "push-button" manager. Dykes's inference was clear, even if he said that without intent to disparage the master of the Yankees' universe. How could he not be a great manager with the incredible New York Yankees teams he managed, particularly from 1936 to 1943—the most dominant team in baseball history? Dykes was one to know; he had been managing in dugouts opposite McCarthy for 22 games a year since becoming Chicago White Sox manager in 1934. Jimmy Dykes was unlucky *not* to be a Yankee— specifically, he was unlucky not to be managing the quality team Joe McCarthy had in New York. Had he done so, there is no reason to believe he would not have been a Hall of Fame manager.

* * *

Dykes was a baseball lifer who played 17 full seasons in the majors, beginning with Philadelphia's Athletics in 1920 and ending with the White Sox in 1936 as a player-manager. As a player, his greatest value was being able to play virtually any infield position, wherever grandmaster-manager Connie Mack happened to need him from one season to the next. Mack, meanwhile, had been grooming Dykes to be his eventual successor—should that day ever come, which seemed like it never would because he was owner as well as manager of the Athletics. At the end of the 1932 season, Mack did his protégé a favor by selling his contract to the White Sox, and it was in Chicago that Jimmy Dykes got his first opportunity to manage, 16 games into the 1934 season, when he took over a last-place team with only four wins.

Dykes became the seventh manager of the White Sox since Kid Gleason, the man in charge when they won the 1919 American League pennant, stepped down following a seventh-place ending to the 1923 season. The franchise, reeling from the disgrace of the Black Sox scandal when

Gleason left, had still not recovered when Dykes was given the reins. They had resided entirely in the bottom half of the league standings since 1920, including five times finishing seventh and twice winding up last. Despite their lackluster performance, however, attendance at Comiskey Park almost certainly benefited from Chicago being the second-most-populous city in the United States. Until 1929, the White Sox were always in the top half of American League clubs in drawing fans to their ballpark, most often ranking third in attendance. But beginning in 1926—the year McCarthy took over as Cubs manager and it became clear the north side team's competitive future was looking bright—the White Sox began losing their battle for the affections of Chicago baseball fans. While attendance surged at Wrigley Field, it began declining precipitously at Comiskey Park. The continuing competitiveness of the Cubs amid the economic realities unleashed by the stock market crash in October 1929 didn't help White Sox attendance in the early '30s.

In contrast to other clubs going through fallow times, the White Sox had maintained a fair amount of continuity among their core regulars since losing most of their team when the Black Sox scandal broke in 1920. Veteran second baseman Eddie Collins and catcher Ray Schalk, both of whose reputations were enhanced by not being part of the conspiracy to throw the 1919 World Series, first baseman Earl Sheely, third baseman Willie Kamm, and outfielders Johnny Mostil and Bibb Falk carried through as White Sox position regulars for most of the decade. Their pitching centered around the veteran Red Faber in the first half of the decade and newcomer Ted Lyons in the second. After back-to-back 20-win seasons in 1921 and '22, and leading the league in earned run average both years, Faber began an extended fade-out pitching for a mediocre team that ended in 1933 with him as a reliever. By 1930, Lyons had three 20-win seasons to his credit in seven years and was one of the league's best pitchers, only to be derailed the next year by persistent shoulder problems that forced him to adjust his repertoire. Never a hard thrower to begin with, Lyons spent the first half of the 1930s learning to master the knuckleball, which he mixed with an assortment of other off-speed pitches to extend his career to 1942.

The most impressive pitching performance for the White Sox in the 1920s was by right-handed rookie Charlie Robertson on April 30, 1922, in Detroit against a lineup that included Ty Cobb, Bobby Veach, and Harry Heilmann batting third, fourth, and fifth. Robertson was making only the fourth start of his career and had just one major-league win to call his own, but he not only shut out the Tigers, 2–0, on this day, he not only did not surrender a hit—he pitched a perfect game, striking out six batters. That game notwithstanding, Charlie Robertson had an undistinguished career which ended in 1928 without him ever having a winning season. His perfect game, however, would be the last in Major League Baseball for 34 years until Don Larsen pitched his in the 1956 World Series. There would not be another in the regular season for 42 years until Jim Bunning pitched a perfect game in 1964, and it wouldn't be until Catfish Hunter in 1968 that there was another regular-season perfect game thrown in the American League.

After four consecutive seasons with at least 92 losses, the 1933 season seemed to portend a positive change in direction. The White Sox lost only 83 games, down from 102 the year before—the first 100-loss season in franchise history. But they staggered badly to start the 1934 season, causing owner J. Louis Comiskey—son of Charles, who had passed away in 1931—to fire the incumbent just three weeks in and make third baseman Dykes the new manager. Dykes, however, could not prevent the Sox from having their second-worst year in franchise history. It didn't help that shortstop Luke Appling, an emerging star, missed more than a month with an injury. They finished last with 99 losses.

Starting anew in 1935, Dykes secured his future by leading the White Sox into fifth place with a 74–78 record. The biggest difference was that Chicago's pitching was substantially better—a staff ERA of 4.38, compared to 5.41 the previous year—as Lyons (15–8) led the team in wins and rookies John Whitehead (13–13) and Vern Kennedy (11–11) had strong debut seasons. The next year, the White Sox won 81 for their first winning season in 10 years and finished in the top half of the standings for the first time in 16 years. Appling's .388 batting average led the American League, and Kennedy's 21 wins were the most by a White Sox pitcher since Lyons won 22 in 1930. The White Sox were even better in 1937, finishing third with 86 wins for their best season since the Black Sox scandal. Thirty-three-year-old right-hander Clint Brown's 18 saves not only led the league, but were the second most in history after Firpo Marberry's 22 in 1926.

* * *

By now, however, the Yankees were in the second year of the DiMaggio era and in the habit of winning American League pennants every year by sizable margins. From 1936 to 1943, while McCarthy had the pleasure of celebrating seven Yankees pennants in eight years, Dykes managed the White Sox to five winning seasons, although never with more than 86 wins, and another year when they finished with an exactly .500 record. The best they did in the standings was third in 1936 (tied), 1937, and 1941. The Yankees won 794 games those eight years and averaged 101 wins in the seven years they finished first, while the White Sox won 624 and averaged 82 wins in the six years they did *not* have a losing record. Including their two losing seasons (1938 and 1942), the White Sox' overall winning percentage of only .513 was the equivalent of about 79 wins over a 154-game schedule.

Although his club did not spend a single day in first place, the 1940 season was probably Jimmy Dykes's best as a manager. With nearly half the season done, the White Sox had a 34–39 record in mid-July and occupied fifth place, 11½ games behind the league-leading Indians and six behind the struggling fourth-place Yankees. The rest of the way, however, no team in the American League had a better record than Chicago's 48–33, which was 2½ games better than Detroit and 4½ games better than Cleveland, who would finish first and second. The only team to keep pace with Dykes's White Sox after July 14 was McCarthy's Yankees, who *tied* Chicago for the league's best record the final two and a half months in their desperate surge to compete for the pennant. They had a six-game cushion over the White Sox to begin with, however, which is why New York had a chance to get to the World Series and Chicago did not.

The Dykes White Sox were never going to be ready for Yankee prime time. While the Yankees (except for 1940) always had their way with the rest of the league, his club struggled for relevance. Indicative of the significant difference in talent between the two teams, the 1936–43 White Sox won exactly half of the 320 games they played that were decided by blowout margins of five runs or more, compared to McCarthy's Yankees, at 286–101, winning nearly 75 percent of theirs. Blowouts are arguably a truer indicator than one-run games of the relative capabilities of teams because their outcomes are not determined by happenstance, luck, or any specific managerial decision, even if one of those factors contributed to opening the floodgates for good or bad fortune. The fact that 36 percent of the Yankees' victories were blowouts, compared to only 26 percent for the White Sox, reflects McCarthy having a much more formidable lineup. Conversely, the fact that the White Sox *lost* 58 percent more games by blowout margins than the Yankees shows their greater difficulty keeping games from getting out of hand.

Even if Al Capone, in his own way for his own purposes, knew how to handle a baseball bat (at least as depicted in the 1987 movie *The Untouchables*), Dykes's Chicago mob was never particularly threatening with theirs. Likely because his team was one of the most offensively challenged in league context, Jimmy Dykes was a managerial practitioner of playing for one run. Pitching and defense, on the other hand, were a team strength; the 1937–42 White Sox were the American League's second or third stingiest team every year, in three of which they still managed to be outscored for the season because they were last in runs scored. While the Yankees were outscoring their opponents by an average of 260

Yankees manager Joe McCarthy and Giants manager Billy Terry shake hands before the 1937 All-Star Game. *Harris & Ewing Collection (Library of Congress).*

runs a year between 1936 and 1943, the White Sox scored only 32 more runs than they gave up the entire eight years.

Unlike McCarthy's terrific team, particularly before DiMaggio and several other core regulars went off to war in 1943, the White Sox were hardly star studded. Twelve different players, including four pitchers, accounted for 31 Yankees who were among the American League's 10 best position players or five best pitchers in any given year from 1936 to 1943 based on single-season wins above replacement, including DiMaggio seven times, Gordon five times, and Dickey and Keller four times each. The White Sox those same years had just one position player who was ever among the 10 best in the league—shortstop Luke Appling, five times—and five pitchers among the top five in any given year—left-hander Thornton Lee, who had the league's best pitching WAR in 1938 and 1941, Johnny Rigney in 1940, Eddie Smith in 1941, and Ted Lyons in 1942. Rigney married the boss's daughter in 1941—the boss being Grace Comiskey, who became owner of the White Sox when Louis Co-

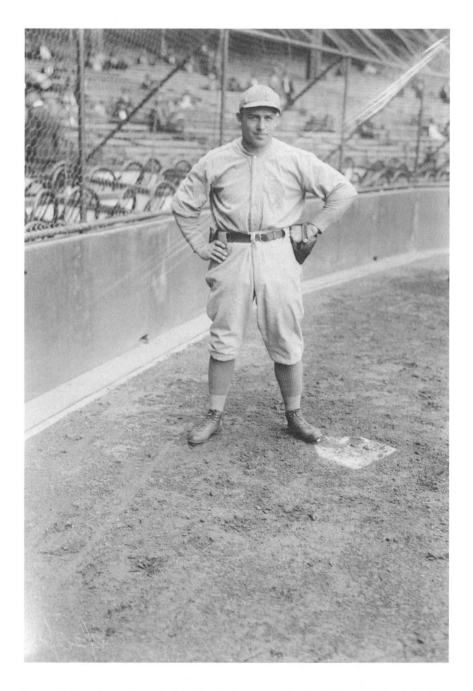

Jimmy Dykes, shown here during his playing career in the 1920s with the Athletics, is best known for managing the White Sox from 1934 to 1946. *George Grantham Bain Collection (Library of Congress).*

miskey, her husband, died in 1939, and the daughter being Dorothy Co-miskey, who wound up succeeding her mother as owner in 1956 and promptly named Johnny Rigney, *her* husband, the White Sox' general manager.

Appling, the best shortstop of his generation in the American League, was the White Sox' only position player of consequence. His cumulative 39.7 wins above replacement alone accounted for 37 percent of the combined WAR of White Sox position players from 1936 to 1943, during which he batted .323 and reached based in 41 percent of his plate appearances. He won a second batting title in 1943 when he hit .328, started every game, and played virtually every inning. Most frequently batting fifth in the order, Appling is perhaps most famous in baseball lore for his ability to persistently foul off pitches, in part for the purpose of wearing out the pitcher, but mostly to get the one pitch he wanted to hit. And every year, including playing on 36-year-old legs in 1943, he was one of the 10 best defensive players in the league. Although many believed his career had come to an end when he was inducted into the army in 1944, Appling was back at shortstop at the age of 39 after the war and played another four years before leaving the game in 1950 with 2,749 hits and a .310 lifetime average. Had he not lost two years of his career to the war, Luke Appling quite likely would have been the eighth player to reach 3,000 hits.

Ted Lyons was at the beginning of a long, graceful end to his distinguished Hall of Fame career when Dykes became manager. From 1935 to 1942, Lyons typically started about 22 games a year, most often on six days of rest. Getting by on an economy of pitches, averaging just two walks and 2.8 strikeouts every nine innings, Lyons completed over three-quarters of his 176 starts, winning 98 while losing 69. Lyons might be most famous for his 1942 season, when he made 20 starts (the only games he pitched all season), almost exclusively on Sundays—usually the first game of a doubleheader—pitched 20 complete games, won 14, lost six, and led the league with a 2.10 earned run average. Then he went off to war, enlisting in the US Marines at the age of 42.

* * *

In the pantheon of also-rans to McCarthy's 1936–43 Yankees, Jimmy Dykes arguably did more with less on the Chicago White Sox than the other American League managers vying for their teams' position in the first division below New York. Unlike Detroit's Tigers, Boston's Red Sox, and even Cleveland's Indians, the White Sox were never mistaken for potential contenders. The Tigers' best players from the mid-1930s to 1940 included power hitters Hank Greenberg (a Hall of Famer) and Rudy York; the best all-around second baseman of his generation, Charlie Gehringer (another Hall of Famer); and accomplished pitchers named Tommy Bridges, Schoolboy Rowe, Eldon Auker, and journeyman turned ace Bobo Newsom. The 1938–40 Indians featured Hall of Fame center fielder Earl Averill (in 1938), first baseman Hal Trosky, third baseman Ken Keltner, and (debuting in 1939) Hall of Fame shortstop Lou Boudreau in their batting order, not to mention Mel Harder and Hall of Famer Bob Feller in their starting rotation. The 1938–42 Red Sox had Jimmy Foxx, Bobby Doerr, Joe Cronin, Ted Williams, and Lefty Grove—Hall of Famers all, although each of their best years were mostly either before or after this time frame. Chicago's only comparable players of note were Hall of Famers Luke Appling and Ted Lyons, and Lyons was in late-career survivor mode. The Red Sox with 21, the Tigers with 20, and the Indians with 16 had many more players count among the 10 best position players and five best pitchers in the American League between 1936 and 1943, based on single-season wins above replacement. The White Sox had just 10.

It should come as no surprise, then, that the White Sox, with a 152–216 record, won only 41 percent of their games against the league's best teams from 1936 to 1943. In head-to-head matchups against McCarthy's 1936–43 Yankees, the White Sox were 64–111 for a lowly .366 winning percentage, and it was that high only because they went 10–12 against them in 1943 when DiMaggio and several other core Yankees were in the service. The White Sox had a losing record against the Yankees every year except 1940—the year McCarthy's team failed to win the pennant—when the two clubs split their 22 games. Just as Jimmy Dykes was named manager after the White Sox got off to a terrible start in 1934, so he was let go following a terrible 10–20 start in 1946. He was dismissed on May 24, perhaps ironically just a day after Joe McCarthy stepped down under duress as Yankees manager. The White Sox won 899 games with Dykes in charge, and lost 940. The Yankees won 1,460 games and lost just 867 during McCarthy's tenure, which began on Opening Day in 1931. They went to eight World Series, the first in 1932, and won seven.

* * *

If not John McGraw, most baseball historians consider Joe McCarthy the greatest manager in the game's history. But, as Dykes pointed out with his "push button" observation, McCarthy had one of the greatest teams in the game's history. No White Sox manager to this day has had a longer tenure at the helm than Dykes's 12 years from May 1934 to May 1946, and he went on to manage the Athletics for three years and the Orioles for one in the first half of the 1950s before concluding his managerial career in charge of the Reds, Tigers, and Indians for parts of four different seasons. But Jimmy Dykes is all but forgotten today despite his longevity as a big-league manager because he managed mostly mediocre and a few very bad teams. Third place on three occasions with the White Sox was the best any Dykes-managed team did in the standings.

And then there's Casey Stengel, a contemporary of both McCarthy and Dykes in the 1930s and '40s who managed mostly very bad and a few mediocre teams. Stengel might have lived on in baseball anecdotes for some of his witticisms when managing those clubs, but he, too, would likely be forgotten for his managerial prowess had he not gotten a chance to reboot his career as manager of a very good team—the New York Yankees, from 1949 to 1960, which won 10 pennants under his guiding hand.

Stengel, a journeyman outfielder who played for four National League clubs in a career that began in September 1912 and ended in May 1925, became a disciple of McGraw's when he was with the Giants and honed his craft managing six years in Toledo in the American Association from 1926 to 1931. He won a pennant in his second year on the job there, but otherwise had mixed results. As is the lot of even minor-league managers, he was fired after his club lost 100 games for the second time in three years, even though he had invested his own money in the club and was a part owner. This was the Depression, the Toledo Mud Hens fell into financial trouble and needed to be bailed out, and Stengel lost both his investment and his job. The Brooklyn Dodgers, for whom Stengel had his best years as a player, hired him as a coach in 1932, apparently in part for the entertainment value they remembered he provided when he played for them. Two years later, after the Dodgers lost 88 games in 1933, Stengel was their manager.

He lasted three years in Brooklyn. They were not successful seasons. While the Dodgers improved in his first year at the helm in 1934, they nonetheless lost 84 games and finished sixth. The next year the Dodgers rose to fifth place, but with a worse record, and in 1936 they ended up seventh with an even worse record. In the three years Stengel managed the Dodgers, only three of his players—pitcher Van Lingle Mungo, twice, and catcher Al Lopez—made the National League All-Star team among the 62 players chosen. The only one of his players to actually play at an All-Star level of performance, defined as five wins above replacement, was outfielder Len Koenecke in 1934. Koenecke ate himself out of shape over the winter, however, was a heavy drinker, did not play up to Stengel's expectations and was benched, and then in September 1935 got unruly on a plane flight, became violent, apparently tried to take over the controls, and was beaten to death by the pilot.

After being paid not to manage in 1937 and watching the Dodgers finish with their worst record since 1912 under new manager Burleigh Grimes, Stengel was hired to replace Bill McKechnie as manager of the

Boston Bees—the name the Braves were known by from 1936 to 1940—
when McKechnie left to take on the challenge of the Cincinnati Reds.
Although McKechnie left the Bees a much better ballclub than when he
first took over in 1930, Stengel did not inherit a competitive team. And
they got worse under his command. Stengel stayed in Boston six years.
The Bees, who were back to being the Braves by the time he left in 1943,
never finished last, but the best they did was fifth place in 1938 when he
was still working with McKechnie's team. That was also the only year
Stengel had a winning record in Boston, and the Bees were just two
games over .500 at 77–75. The rest were all losing seasons—four straight
seventh-place finishes ahead of only the much worse Phillies, and a sixth-
place ending to what seemed like might be the end of his major-league
managerial career.

The 1943 season began badly for Stengel when he was hit by a taxi
crossing a street in the rain and missed the first eight weeks of the season
with a broken leg. Pittsburgh manager Frankie Frisch sent cheeky condo-
lences that Stengel's attempt at suicide to escape having to manage the
Braves didn't succeed. Boston's most provocative and, hence, most read
baseball columnist, "Colonel" Dave Egan, perhaps less cheekily suggested the cabbie was a hero for running down the loser Braves' loser
manager. Their interim manager while Stengel was hospitalized led the
Braves to a 21–25 record—a .457 winning percentage; the team did not
play as well the rest of the season after their injured manager returned to
the dugout, winning just 44 percent of their games. Stengel was fired
once the season was over.

Stengel's predecessor, Bill McKechnie, also got nowhere with the
Braves. Unlike with Casey, however, there were no doubts about
McKechnie's managerial ability. He had won pennants for two National
League franchises in the 1920s, including a World Series, and did not
have a losing record in any of his seven previous years as a manager
before he took on the thankless task of managing Boston's hapless Braves
for another eight years in the 1930s. Stengel had no such record of accomplishment before he took on the equally thankless task of managing
bad National League teams, and because they were bad teams his managerial reputation became one of . . . loser. At this point in Stengel's
career, his quirky personality merely reinforced the view that he was not a
"winning" manager.

As was the case in Brooklyn, Stengel's Braves were a team of mostly
mediocre major leaguers. It didn't help his club's winning prospects that,
with the Depression still effecting the US economy, the "Beehive"—as
Braves Field was colloquially called when the Braves were the Bees—
was hardly abuzz with fans, certainly compared to attendance at Fenway
Park, home of the improving Red Sox (although that didn't help them

take on McCarthy's powerhouse Yankees). The Bees were the National League's third-lowest draw in Stengel's first year in charge in 1938, and next to last in the league and third worst in the majors the year after. With the franchise in financial trouble, the Bees' owners began a fire sale that, by mid-June 1940, had them say good-bye to most of their best players, primarily for cash. Among those they surrendered, Jim Turner helped pitch the Reds to the 1940 pennant; multiposition regular Debs Garms won the 1940 batting title with Pittsburgh; and first baseman Elbie Fletcher, sent to the Pirates in a separate transaction, became one of the league's best players until he was drafted into World War II in 1944.

The Braves' offense remained one of the worst in baseball under Stengel, and the quality of their pitching and defense, except for the shortstop position, deteriorated after 1939. The pitching staff was in constant flux. Right-handers Al Javery and Jim Tobin were the only two pitchers to make 20 starts in three consecutive years. Of the 157 National League players chosen for the All-Star team between 1938 and 1943, only eight played for Stengel's Bees/Braves, just two of whom—outfielder Max West in 1940 and shortstop Eddie Miller in 1942—started. The year West made the All-Star squad was not one of his better seasons; Miller, an excellent defensive shortstop, made five consecutive All-Star teams beginning in 1940, the last two when he played for McKechnie's Reds.

As manager of both the Dodgers and Braves, as would be most apparent with his 1950s Yankees, Stengel valued versatile players who could play different positions, giving him flexibility in setting his lineup and managing game situations. Although Stengel rarely employed a lefty-righty platoon in his starting lineup at any one position, he was much more aggressive than other managers in pinch-hitting or substituting for his starting position players if he felt there was an advantage to doing so, or just playing a hunch. Perhaps it might be said that Stengel made as many position substitutions as he did because so many of his core regulars were, at best, marginal big-league players, that they were desperate ploys by a desperate manager—please work, please! As a student of McGraw's when he played for the Giants, however, Stengel was observant and learned from the master when it came to employing his bench players for effect. Casey Stengel, of course, became famous when he resurfaced as manager of the Yankees for resurrecting platooning and widespread position player substitutions as game-management strategies that had fallen by the wayside.

* * *

The standard of dominant excellence set by McCarthy's Yankees—they were barely challenged in any of their pennant-winning years—

makes it tempting to say that any manager could have won with that club, particularly the DiMaggio years from 1936 to 1942 before he was drafted into World War II, perhaps even a managerial neophyte like Judge Emil Fuchs. The fact that Fuchs was a professional lawyer with no substantive background in the game who happened to have the financial resources to be owner of the Boston Braves from the mid-'20s to the mid-'30s did not prevent him from making himself manager of the team he owned in 1929. They finished last. But the Braves were a very bad team that would likely have finished last under any bona fide baseball manager.

It would have made an interesting thought experiment, whether the superb 1936–42 Yankees would have done as well as they did if someone like Judge Fuchs had been their manager instead of Joe McCarthy. This is the equivalent of asking whether the Yankees were so good that anybody, even somebody off the street, could have managed them to championships. After all, there are many tales of players calling the shots on the field because they lost confidence in or disrespected their manager—as the 1940 "crybaby" Indians did, for example, in rebelling against manager Ossie Vitt—although in the area of pinch-hitting and pitcher and position player substitutions, which are decisions only the manager can make, that would have been problematic. But perhaps as manager of the DiMaggio Yankees, a neophyte like Fuchs would have been smart enough to know what he didn't know and to rely on an experienced "bench coach" to make the decision or advise him on what to do when.

This thought experiment, however, would surely have hit the rocky shoals of the reality that professional baseball at all levels—particularly in the major leagues—is not a recreational pickup sport on the sandlots. It is a game of complexity, strategy, and nuance. The 1936–42 Yankees might have been so good the players didn't need any manager at all to excel, but even if that debatable proposition is true, they would have never tolerated such a rank amateur as their manager, even if he was their owner. McCarthy, of course, was not, and the executives in the Yankees' front office—owner Jacob Ruppert and general manager Ed Barrow— would have never even considered putting an amateur in charge. They didn't even give Babe Ruth the time of day when he wanted to manage the Yankees, and it is not as though the Babe didn't know baseball.

Joe McCarthy may have seemed impenetrable as a personality, but he had consummate managerial skills in evaluating the talent and personalities of his players; in organization, preparation, and attention to detail; in sustaining a killer—go for the jugular—instinct for his teams; and in preventing extraneous events and circumstances from becoming a diversion. He was a master at recognizing and exploiting the weaknesses of opposing teams and making sure his players were aware of them as well. He was a quintessential chief executive officer and chief operating officer combined, with a sensitive hands-on touch that was enough to be fully engaged and in control without being onerous to the point of micromanaging every move by his players. This was what made his great Yankees teams so dominant, so relentless, so seemingly unbeatable.

A particular strength was McCarthy's intimate familiarity with the skills and innate talents of his own players. An astute observer of character and shrewd in how he motivated, instructed, and made his expectations known, McCarthy often used indirection to make a salient point, sometimes doing so by making specific observations within earshot of the player who needed a lesson learned. He was also direct when he needed to be. No matter how talented the player, McCarthy did not tolerate slackers or players unwilling or unable to learn the nuances of the game. Baseball was not a game to McCarthy, it was a profession, and he expected his players to master their profession. Like McGraw, McCarthy insisted his players have baseball intelligence, not simply master the fundamentals of the game. There is a difference. Playing the game right—mastering the fundamentals—is, of course, fundamentally important. Every good manager and organization schools their players in playing fundamentally sound baseball. Baseball intelligence is players understanding the flow of the game, being in the right place, making the right play that might be the difference in winning a ballgame. Baseball intelligence is instinctive anticipation and reaction that takes into account precisely the action on the field as it is happening. Every experience is a learning experience, and there is always—*always*—something new to be learned and ingrained.

Even though he generally disdained "small ball" tactics because his Yankees always had a potent lineup—they were the Bronx Bombers, after all—McCarthy was hardly one-dimensional when it came to managing the Yankees' offense. McCarthy took advantage of the different abilities of his players; when he had guys with speed who were high-percentage basestealers, he was willing to use the running game to set up runs, within limits. In his 15 full seasons as their manager, a New York Yankee led the league in steals five times, and four other Yankees were in the top three. This hardly comports to the historical perception of McCarthy relying only on his very potent lineup to drive in runs. In his first three years as their manager, when the Yankees were still powered by Ruth and Gehrig, McCarthy allowed fleet-footed outfielder Ben Chapman to run often enough that Chapman led the league in stolen bases all three years, including 61 in 1931. Chapman was successful in 68 percent of his attempts, compared to the league average of 57 percent, so McCarthy was taking an informed calculated gamble. Moreover, Chapman's place in the batting order was typically *following* Ruth and Gehrig, so it was not as though his getting caught stealing took away scoring opportunities with the big boys coming to bat. In 1938, shortstop and leadoff hitter Frankie Crosetti (with DiMaggio and Gehrig batting third and fourth, or fourth and fifth) was the league leader with 27 steals in 39 attempts. And in the war years of 1944 and 1945, when the Yankees' most explosive firepower was at war, Snuffy Stirnweiss, Joe Gordon's replacement at second base, was successful 76 percent of the time in stealing 88 bases and leading the league twice in steals.

Although Yankees pitchers led the league in complete games seven times during his reign, including all but two of their eight pennants, McCarthy was a master at using his bullpen to win and save games, particularly after he persuaded Johnny Murphy that his best career option was to be the Yankees' "fireman" in the pen. McCarthy's 1937, '39, and '42 pennant winners led the league in both complete games *and* saves. That has happened only five times in Major League Baseball since 1900, three times by Yankees teams managed by Joe McCarthy. It had been done only once previously in the twentieth century, by the 1928 Cardinals, and has happened just once since, by the 1988 Los Angeles Dodgers. (The 1891 Boston Beaneaters also accomplished the feat, but those were in the days long before dedicated relief pitchers.) The significance of this hardly needs be said; at least until the 1990s, when complete games plummeted to less than 10 percent, managers with starting rotations that pitched well enough to lead the league in complete games did not need to go to relief pitchers so often that their pitching staff also led the league in saves. McCarthy was more than astute in how he employed his pitching staff—he was a genius who gave his starting pitchers every opportunity to complete a victory, but was intuitive enough to know when it was Johnny Murphy time.

Sure, Joe McCarthy was blessed to manage arguably the greatest team in history—the 1936–42 DiMaggio Yankees. And it is difficult to separate the specific impact of a manager on a team of such extraordinary accomplishment. Entertaining the idea that the DiMaggio Yankees would have been as successful under Judge Fuchs as they were under Joe McCarthy is completely unrealistic and, hence, pointless because Fuchs was hardly a baseball professional. The more pertinent question is whether the DiMaggio Yankees were so dominant—all six pennants essentially decided by the beginning of September—that they would have won the same number of pennants under any bona fide major-league manager like, say, McCarthy contemporaries Jimmy Dykes, manager of the fair-to-middling and occasionally quite bad Chicago White Sox, or Casey Stengel, manager of bad Brooklyn Dodgers and Boston Braves teams. We can never know the answer to that question, of course, but based on what he accomplished as manager of a team significantly inferior to the "push-button" Yankees, the answer is—almost certainly, yes. Had it been

Dykes or Stengel as manager of the DiMaggio Yankees, they would have won the same six pennants they won by blowout margins for McCarthy, although perhaps with a few less wins every year.

Stengel, after his purgatory managing in Brooklyn and Boston, was lucky to become a Yankee, going on to become one in a line of great Yankees managers that extends from Miller Huggins through McCarthy ultimately to Joe Torre, another manager of losing NL clubs before he got to the Bronx. All three are in the Hall of Fame for their years managing extraordinarily successful Yankees teams—each of them, some of the greatest teams in baseball history.

And had fate been different and Jimmy Dykes been given the opportunity to manage those New York Yankees—which he wasn't, and which was never in the cards—he surely would have gone down in history as one of baseball's greatest managers ever and would be in the Hall of Fame today. Conversely, if Joe McCarthy had been manager of Dykes's Chicago White Sox, he most likely would be acknowledged as a very good manager by baseball historians (same as Jimmy Dykes today), but would not be in the Hall of Fame, nor remembered by the casual fan.

Part IV

Baseball, War, and Society

30

PATRIOT GAMES

Major League Baseball in Two World Wars

There is a scene in the 2006 movie *Flags of Our Fathers* where "the heroes of Iwo Jima"—three of the six US soldiers (the others since killed in action) immortalized in the iconic photograph taken of them raising the American flag on Mount Suribachi on the small but strategic island of volcanic ash called Iwo Jima during one of the bloodiest battles in the Pacific theater during World War II—are honored before a ballgame at Washington's Griffith Stadium as part of a drive to inspire Americans to buy more war bonds to help fund the end of the war. The event occurred on April 20, 1945, the Senators' home opener against the visiting Yankees. Nazi Germany was in its death throes, but notwithstanding the success of America's island-hopping strategy in driving the Japanese armed forces back toward their homeland, the war in the Pacific was far from over and the presumed necessary invasion of Japan promised to be long, arduous, brutal, bloody, and costly. The presence of the three wartime heroes at a baseball game was an appropriate public relations move to kick off a summer "buy bonds" campaign where they would be the featured stars.

Nothing was as American as baseball, and baseball was nothing if not patriotic. And not merely symbolic of American patriotism, but an "institution"—to quote Judge Kenesaw Mountain Landis in another context—that was itself patriotic to the core. America's national pastime lent itself to the ideal, indeed self-identified with the ideal, of what it meant to be an American, not just the celebration of the good times, but also the sacrifices that the country's endeavors might require.

* * *

Major League Baseball's first brush with war began as a bit of an awkward dance between the game's owners and the federal government about whether the mobilization of the country to enter the bloody fray in Europe during the First World War left room for baseball at all during wartime. It ended with Major League Baseball as an institution fully embracing the patriotic ethos of America at war, to the point where some owners were critical of some of their own players who opted to serve in US defense industries rather than in the US armed forces fighting overseas.

Life continued with little interruption in the United States when war broke out in Europe in 1914. As the two sides bogged down into ferocious trench warfare along the front lines in France with mind-numbing casualties, including from the introduction of armored tanks, relentless pounding by heavy artillery, the insidious use of poison gas, all for incremental gains and losses for years on end, the United States was inexorably drawn into the conflict that most Americans at first preferred for their country to avoid. The German U-boat menace to merchant shipping in the Atlantic was a major catalyst to changing public perceptions and to President Woodrow Wilson's ultimate decision to go to war alongside principal allies France and Britain. Congress declared war in April 1917. Within weeks of doing so, Congress passed the Selective Service Act, establishing a draft as necessary to build an army of sufficient capacity to fight in a war of unprecedented scale. By June, the first American troops had arrived in Europe. By late October, the American Expeditionary Force was fighting in France.

Although a few players—most notably, Braves catcher Hank Gowdy and White Sox right-hander Jim Scott—enlisted in the armed forces soon after the United States declared war, baseball for the most part was unaffected in America's first year at war in 1917. The star of the "Miracle" Braves' sweep of the powerful Philadelphia Athletics in the 1914 World Series, hitting .545 with five of his six hits going for extra bases, Gowdy was the first active major-league player to volunteer for combat overseas. Gowdy reported to duty at the end of June, having played in 49 games, and was fighting in the trenches in France by the time his teammates were gathering for spring training in 1918. Scott had been a core member of the White Sox pitching staff since 1909, including 20-win seasons in 1913 and 1915. Like Gowdy, Scott was sent to France in 1918. Unlike Gowdy, who returned from the war in 1919 to play seven more years, Jim Scott, although just two years older, never pitched again in the major leagues.

Gowdy and Scott were virtually alone in volunteering for service, and the baseball season went on without them, uninterrupted. Players dutifully registered for the draft, but major-league owners lobbied the War Department for an exemption for their players from wartime service by arguing there was a national interest in keeping up morale on the home front. Many teams got into the spirit of a nation mobilizing for war by hiring drill instructors to put their players through military parade drills in front of the fans before games. Their bats substituted for rifles. Some owners contributed a small percentage of gate receipts to support the war effort. "Liberty bonds" to help finance the United States at war were sold at ballparks. The Chicago White Sox added an American flag patch to their uniforms. But as the country mobilized for war and the War Department figured out how to implement conscription, Major League Baseball escaped unscathed in 1917, playing a full 154-game schedule with very few players called into the service by way of the draft.

That would not be the case in 1918. By now the United States was fully engaged "over there," but the entry of fresh American troops and extensive resources had yet to break the interminable, bloody stalemate on the western front. Major-league owners were grappling for an appropriate "patriotic" response other than giving up on the season. They shortened spring training and debated a proposal by American League president Ban Johnson to reduce the season schedule to 140 games, a move supported by Brooklyn owner Charles Ebbets. The majority of owners rejected the idea of shortening the season, but once again showcased their patriotism with pregame military drills by the players, with some teams now outfitting their players with real uniforms and guns. Patriotic music was played before games.

Draft-eligible players, however, were soon faced with the War Department's "work-or-fight" order issued in May 1918, which meant every able-bodied American male was expected to serve his country by either working in defense industries—the most important of which was shipbuilding because of the need to ferry tens of thousands of troops and massive amounts of supplies to Europe and to defend the sea lanes—or fighting in the war. Shoeless Joe Jackson almost immediately volunteered to work in shipbuilding, leaving the White Sox after just 17 games. Particularly since US defense plants had company ball teams and he could continue to play baseball on his off hours, Jackson was quickly vilified by White Sox owner Charles Comiskey and by the press for choosing to "work" rather than "fight." The same went for his teammates Lefty Williams and Happy Felsch, also star players with the 1917 World Series champions, when they followed Jackson's example and took the defense-industry route of service for their country.

Major League Baseball's hand was finally forced in July when the War Department clarified that the work-or-fight order did not exempt professional baseball. Almost immediately, the minor leagues shut down for the season. Knowing full well their players had no alternatives, franchise owners debated when to end the year. Ban Johnson proposed ending the season right then and there, but had no backing. Although President Wilson in late July gave his blessing to the major leagues continuing their season, he did not overrule the edict that "work-or-fight" applied to baseball. As more and more players, including core regulars, volunteered to fight for their country—the avenue chosen by most as their patriotic duty, perhaps in some cases motivated by the unrelentingly harsh public criticism of Jackson and his teammates—and left their teams to do so in July and August, franchise owners agreed to terminate the season in the beginning of September and to play the World Series immediately thereafter. Most teams played between 126 and 130 of their originally scheduled 154 games.

With attendance having declined dramatically in 1918 from 5.2 million the previous year to just short of 3.1 million, and the likelihood of the war continuing for at least another year, baseball's powers-that-be debated whether there should even be a 1919 season. Factoring into the debate was the fact that by the fall of 1918 many of baseball's biggest stars were in the service, even those who had played the entire season, including the likes of Ty Cobb, Tris Speaker, Grover Cleveland Alexander, and Eddie Collins. (Comiskey made a point of favorably contrasting the service of Collins and young pitching ace Red Faber in the *armed* forces with that of Jackson, Williams, and Felsch in wartime *industries*; Faber enlisted in the navy and missed nearly all of the 1918 season, while Collins played almost the entire season before leaving for his tour of duty in mid-August.) It was debatable, with the war raging and all able-bodied men expected to do their patriotic duty, whether the major leagues could even field credible teams. Johnson, for one, recommended that the major leagues should peremptorily cancel the next year.

And then . . . the American Expeditionary Force made a difference. The German lines were breached. On November 11, 1918, an armistice agreement officially ended the fighting. There would be baseball after all. There being considerable uncertainty, however, surrounding the national issue of demobilization and the baseball issue of how ready traditional fans were to return to the national pastime, the owners decided to set the 1919 schedule at 140 games. They called it "retrenchment."

* * *

The United States lost more than 116,000 soldiers in World War I. According to data compiled by Gary Bedingfield on his website, Baseball in Wartime, 17 minor leaguers were killed in action or died in Europe in the service of their country. Only three who had played major-league baseball were among the American soldiers killed in action. None were active players. The German-born Bun Troy, who was the losing pitcher in the only game he pitched for the Detroit Tigers in 1912, and Tom Burr, who had a "Moonlight Graham" *Field of Dreams*–type cameo by playing two innings in just one game as a defensive replacement in the outfield for the 1914 Yankees without ever coming to bat, both died in France in October 1918.

The first major-league veteran to die in combat in any foreign war was Eddie Grant, killed in action on October 5, 1918, in the Argonne Forest during the offensive that ultimately broke through German lines and hastened the end of the war. Grant was killed two days before Troy died from battlefield wounds and a week before Burr's death. Although hardly a star player, one whose name would otherwise be forgotten but for his sacrifice, Eddie Grant remains to this day the most accomplished major-league player to die on the field of battle for the United States of America. Grant played in 990 big-league games, mostly at third base, and batted .249 in a career that began in 1905 when he played two games for Cleveland, and ended with him playing 87 games for the Giants in 1915. In only four of those years—1908–10 with the Phillies, and 1911 with the Reds—was Grant a regular.

Baseball's biggest-name casualties in World War I, however, were two of the greatest pitchers in history—Christy Mathewson and Grover Cleveland Alexander. Mathewson's pitching career had ended in 1916 with 373 victories. In 1918, he was in his third year managing the Cincinnati Reds when he enlisted for the war effort, even though, at 38 years old, he was not subject to the work-or-fight order. Volunteering to serve in an army chemical warfare unit deployed to France whose members included Ty Cobb and, at a more senior rank, Cardinals executive Branch Rickey, Mathewson got a dose of the mustard gas used by both sides in the war during a training exercise that went horribly wrong. His respiratory system severely compromised as a result, Matty's bodily defenses proved no match for the tuberculosis he contracted during the winter of 1920. Christy Mathewson finally succumbed to the disease on October 7, 1925—the day of the first game of the 1925 World Series, as it happened—at the age of 45, just shy of seven years from when he was inadvertently gassed in France.

At 31, Alexander was at the upper age limit of the work-or-fight order when he was called into service in May 1918. Coming off three straight 30-win seasons, Alexander was just beginning his first year with the Cubs, having been traded in December after seven stellar seasons pitching for the Phillies. By July, he was in France, soon to be on the front lines with an artillery unit under constant bombardment from enemy forces. He returned home from the war a wounded warrior, recovered from shrapnel wounds but still having to deal with post-traumatic stress, then more popularly referred to as "shell shock." His wartime experiences almost certainly exacerbated the alcoholism and epilepsy that plagued him for the rest of his life. "Old Pete" still had a long way to go in his baseball career. Grover Alexander went off to war with 192 major-league wins. After his return in 1919, Alexander won 181 more games over the next 11 years to finish with 373 victories—tying Mathewson for the most wins by a National League pitcher, a record that stands to this day. He had 315 victories on the day Matty died.

The war to end all wars . . . didn't.

When the First World War ended, America came home. Like it or not, America was now a world power, but isolationist sentiment remained strong and the country as a whole focused inward. Good times, or at least the appearance of good times, were at hand. There was the matter of Prohibition, which helped to fuel localized organized crime syndicates such as Al Capone's in Chicago, and there was the reality of inequity and labor unrest and perceived anarchist and Communist threats, but at least until the October 1929 stock market crash, America was flourishing and not having to deal with the consequences of World War I that were sweeping Europe. Germany was embittered and impoverished, paving the

The Phillies' Grover Cleveland Alexander in 1917, his third straight 30-win season. The next year he was serving his country on the battlefields of France in World War I. *George Grantham Bain Collection (Library of Congress).*

way for Hitler and his Nazi ideology. Russia was embroiled in the remaking of society and political culture by Lenin and Stalin, who imposed a ruthless will to power in the name of a utopian radical ideology and renamed their country the Soviet Union. The collapse of the autocratic Austro-Hungarian and Ottoman Empires led to a proliferation of unstable new states in the territories they had ruled. Europe's two liberal democracies, Britain and France, were emotionally and materially spent, not up to the challenge of directly confronting Nazi Germany, Mussolini's Fascist Italy, or Communist Russia as the European continent careened toward war in the 1930s. And in Asia, Japan had invaded China in 1931 and was eyeing Southeast Asia.

Protected by oceans on either side and grappling with the Great Depression, the United States was for the most part disengaged from the world's problems. But America could stay aloof for only so long. Despite powerful political resistance, President Franklin D. Roosevelt was maneuvering and preparing to take sides in the European war that broke out in September 1939 when Germany invaded Poland from the west in coordination with the Soviet Union, invading from the east. By the end of 1940, France had fallen, the Battle of Britain—mostly an air war—was raging, and FDR had begun the first peacetime draft in American history knowing that it was just a matter of time before America would be back in a world war. The first established major-league player to be drafted was Philadelphia Phillies right-hander Hugh Mulcahy, twice a 20-game loser for a terrible team the three previous years. Mulcahy missed the entire 1941 season and would not return to baseball until the end of August 1945, by which time—having lost nearly five full years serving his country in wartime—his career was essentially over.

The first major-league star to be drafted was Detroit Tigers slugger Hank Greenberg. That Greenberg should be drafted so early, before the United States was officially at war, was ironic because he was Jewish. The world already knew that Nazi Germany was persecuting Jews, including sending German Jewish citizens to work camps. Soon enough the country would learn about the fate of 6 million Jews in Germany and Nazi-occupied Europe. Greenberg himself not only had to endure anti-Semitic taunts as a Jewish ballplayer, but played in a city where one of its most prominent citizens and major employers, Henry Ford, was not shy about his anti-Semitic beliefs, and another, Father Coughlin, a Catholic priest, broadcast anti-Semitic rants on his weekly radio program that reached millions of listeners. In 1938, when Greenberg stayed stuck on 58 homers the last five games of the season in his pursuit of Ruth's record 60, there were insinuations that opposing pitchers gave him nothing decent to hit because he was Jewish. There was no evidence to suggest this was so, and Greenberg dismissed the suggestion. Greenberg played in the

Tigers' first 19 games of the 1941 season before reporting to duty. The only two homers he hit in 1941 came in his last game in a baseball uniform that year, on May 6, helping to defeat the Yankees. Hank Greenberg now had 249 home runs in his big-league career. He was 30 years old.

The prospect of America going back to war seemed inevitable, but the country was still not in the fight. While Greenberg was serving his country in 1941, Joe DiMaggio hit in 56 straight; Ted Williams batted .406; Bob Feller won 25 and led the majors in strikeouts for the fourth consecutive year; the Dodgers won their first pennant since 1920; and the Yankees won their fifth pennant and their fifth World Series in six years. Two months and one day after the Yankees put a wrap to the season, on December 7, 1941, Japan attacked Pearl Harbor. The war was on. Greenberg had served the commitment required of him, but he, along with Bob Feller, were among the first major leaguers to enlist in America's fighting forces as the United States went to war. Neither returned to Major League Baseball until the summer of 1945—Greenberg in the beginning of July, and Feller in late August. Upon his return to big-league action, Hank Greenberg picked up where he left off, hitting a home run in his first game back. So, too, did Feller pitch as though he hadn't been gone, striking out 12 Detroit Tigers in a complete-game victory in his very first game back, including Greenberg as a strikeout victim twice; he beat Tigers' ace Hal Newhouser, who had already won 20 while Feller was still in the navy.

Hank Gowdy, the first big-leaguer to volunteer for World War I, now going on 53 years old and coaching for Cincinnati, tried signing up for a *second* world war in 1942, but was rejected because of his age. Patriotic and undaunted, Gowdy tried again at the start of the new year and this time was accepted. He entered the army in 1943 as a captain and was eventually promoted to major. Serving entirely stateside, Gowdy was responsible for physical fitness programs for army draftees sent to Fort Benning, Georgia, for training. He also directed the fort's expansive Infantry School baseball league. Gowdy returned to the Reds as a coach in 1945.

With the country now at war, the issue from World War I about whether baseball should continue for the duration was revisited. Commissioner Landis asked the president what baseball should do. FDR replied that the decision was baseball's, but offered the opinion that "I honestly feel that it would be best for the country to keep baseball going" because it would be a huge boost on the home front—"a definite recreational asset to at least 20 million" Americans "that in my judgment," said the president, "is thoroughly worthwhile." Although some players were drafted and others enlisted, Major League Baseball continued pretty much unscathed in 1942, all teams able to stay mostly intact before wartime exigencies demolished major-league rosters the next three years of the worldwide conflagration.

Two of baseball's best players, Feller and Washington's Cecil Travis, saw extensive combat—Feller as a naval gunner in the Pacific, Travis in tough battles to liberate Europe. Travis's teammate Buddy Lewis flew military-supply missions over the Burma Hump in Southeast Asia, where Greenberg also served. Many of them wanted to serve in combat roles in the global war against tyranny that their country fought. Ted Williams became a first-rate naval aviator whose mastery of piloting and aerial gunnery skills led to his being assigned stateside to train other pilots for war. A significant number of big-leaguers, however—Joe DiMaggio the most prominent among them—served most of their time stateside or at relatively secure rear bases engaged not only in administrative or logistical military responsibilities, but also playing baseball on army and navy service teams. Some of the service teams were in essence "major-league" teams; DiMaggio, for example, played alongside Yankees teammates Joe Gordon and Red Ruffing on an army–air force team in Hawaii that also included Cardinals pitcher Johnny Beazley. Both the army and navy sent teams featuring multiple major leaguers to play an exhibition tour in the Pacific theater in 1945. There was some criticism that such prominent athletes had military assignments that seemed intended to allow them to play ball rather than serving, as millions of their countrymen were, in the line of enemy fire. But their games were enormously popular with soldiers and sailors. They were a reminder of home and peaceable times. They were a morale boost.

Minor leaguers, on the other hand, got few such considerations. Players for whom big-league success was still a dream saw combat, just like countless other young Americans with dreams yet to be fulfilled. Warren Spahn, a promising left-handed pitcher in the Boston Braves system who had a taste of four big-league games in 1942, fought in the Battle of the Bulge, was involved in intense fighting to keep retreating German forces from destroying the last intact bridge across the Rhine River into the heart of Germany, was wounded in action, and received a Bronze Star for heroism. Hoyt Wilhelm, a 19-year-old kid who had just begun his professional career in 1942 when he was drafted, also participated in fierce fighting in the Battle of the Bulge and was wounded in action. Yogi Berra, whose path to the Yankees was put on hold after one year of minor-league experience in 1943 as an 18-year-old, was present at the D-day landings on small craft providing fire support for the troops storming the beaches of Normandy. At least 145 minor-league players died in World War II, most killed in action, according to Gary Bedingfield's research, including in the Japanese attack on Pearl Harbor.

By contrast, no active major leaguers and only two who had ever played in the big leagues were killed in action during World War II. They were outfielder Elmer Gedeon, who had just turned 27 when the aircraft he was piloting on a bombing mission against German V-1 rocket sites in April 1944 was shot down over France, and catcher Harry O'Neill, killed in March 1945 shortly before he would have turned 28, on the volcanic rocks of Iwo Jima less than two weeks after the "flag of our fathers" was raised atop Mount Suribachi, the battle for control of the island still to be won. After playing two years in the Washington Senators system, including five games with the big club as a September call-up in 1939, Gedeon had left baseball behind for the army in 1941, before the attack on Pearl Harbor, but at a time the country was already mobilizing for war. O'Neill had his own Moonlight Graham moment, playing just one inning behind the plate without getting an opportunity to come to bat in July 1939 for the Athletics. Signed directly out of college and brought straight to Philadelphia, that game was O'Neill's professional baseball debut. He played part of the next season in the Pirates' minor-league system before concluding he had no future in professional baseball and enlisted in the marines after the United States entered the war.

* * *

Meanwhile, back on the home front, Major League Baseball made do. Schedules were not shortened as had been were during World War I, but start times were adjusted to accommodate war-industry workers. "The Star-Spangled Banner" was played before games—a tradition that outlasted the war and continues to this day. Teams urged their fans to buy war bonds, organized blood drives and collection drives for materials that could be funneled into wartime uses, conducted civil defense drills at their ballparks, and dedicated the receipts of selected games to support the war effort. Players were role models for donating blood and participating in war-charity events. For the duration of the war, major-league teams, beginning in 1943, held spring training close to home rather than in the warmer climates of Florida and California to minimize nonessential travel, as all Americans were being asked to do in order to conserve gasoline and to ensure adequate space on regional and cross-country rail lines for essential military-related transportation of men, supplies, and equipment. Spring training became a sometimes-punishing ordeal as players had to prepare for the season in unaccustomed cold weather, often holding practices in gymnasiums to get out of wintry conditions.

During the war years, teams had much less flexibility in their rail-travel options between cities and were forced to cut back on the number of rail cars used to travel to their next destination, making for much less comfortable and more exhausting trips than they were used to. Because teams were forced to adhere to more rigid train schedules, some end-of-series games were suspended in order for teams to make their out-of-town train, and by 1945 teams often had to split up onto different trains for travel to their next series. The government's request to avoid nonessential travel on the rails caused baseball to cancel the 1945 All-Star Game slated for Boston's Fenway Park.

Baseball also felt the impact of the national imperative to conserve strategic materials for military purposes. The manufacturer of official baseballs for the 1943 season could no longer use high-grade cork and rubber to make the central core of the ball because both materials were essential to weapons production. The substitute materials used to replace them resulted in baseballs with less bounce and resilience. It was, in effect, back to the Deadball Era, at least for that one year. In 1944, the major leagues were able to introduce a livelier ball using synthetic rubber, which was invented in one of the government's crash programs to solve the problem of scarce resources and produced in large enough quantities to meet not only military requirements, but to share with the national pastime. The 1943 deadball resulted in a major-league power outage, causing home-run totals to drop from 1,071 the previous year to 905—the fewest hit in the majors since 863 in 1926. The impact was greater in the NL, whose batters hit 432 compared to 538 in 1942, than in the AL, where home runs declined from 533 to 473. Curiously, while the new baseballs with their "livelier" synthetic rubber core contributed to a re-bound in home runs in the National League the next two years, over-the-fence drives continued to decline in the American League to 459 in 1944 (when 575 were hit in the NL) and 430 in 1945, nearly 150 fewer than the 577 by NL batters. For having been the dominant power league since 1930, the American League was hardly recognizable.

Baseball's World War II years, and the 1943 season in particular, are a convenient bookend to the World War I years to mark off the Lively Ball Era that Babe Ruth kicked off more than two decades earlier. That offensive era, however, may have already been coming to an end by the time wartime exigencies resulted in an exodus of major leaguers into the service and the wartime baseballs of 1943. Beginning in 1941, after a decade in which the home-run surge of the 1920s went into overdrive, particularly in the American League, which had more of baseball's premier power hitters, there was a nearly one-third drop from the then-record 1,571 homers hit in the two leagues combined in 1940 to 1,071 in 1942. The effect was most pronounced in the American League, where home-run totals dropped from 883 in 1940—a new AL record that came within nine homers of the NL mark set 10 years earlier—to 734 in 1941, the lowest AL total in six years, to just 533 in 1942. The last time American League batters had hit so few homers was in 1928, and National League batters had hit fewer home runs than that just twice since 1928.

* * *

The most important impact, of course, was the absence of so many of baseball's best players. The three years that major-league rosters were most affected by wartime player losses—1943 to 1945—could perhaps best be characterized as ragtag baseball. Not all of baseball's established stars volunteered or were drafted into service; a surprising number, given that major-league players were presumably among the most fit and physically capable men in America, were draft exempt or even denied entry into the military for physical reasons, many on account of injuries suffered in their athletic endeavors. Most notably, some of baseball's best shortstops were deemed ineligible for wartime service, which seems counterintuitive given the skill and athleticism required not only to play the position but to be among the best. Phil Rizzuto, Pee Wee Reese, and Johnny Pesky—three of baseball's best at the position, all at the beginning of their careers—lost three years to World War II, but star shortstops Lou Boudreau, who had severely arthritic ankles; Marty Marion, because of a bad knee and a childhood leg injury; and Vern Stephens, who also had endured a serious knee injury, were all physical rejects for military service despite their youth. Boudreau, Marion, and Stephens played all three war seasons with their big-league clubs instead of on service teams.

Notwithstanding being able to hold on to some very good ballplayers for the duration of the war because of situations that precluded their ability to serve in the armed services, major-league teams were constantly scrambling to replace player losses. As the war slogged on and military manpower needs became greater, the armed forces became less discriminating about physical limitations. Players who had been exempted, including for family-support reasons, or not otherwise called to duty one year might be called up the next. The pool of minor leaguers to replace them grew smaller because they were young men of prime warrior age. Indeed, player losses resulted in the minors being reduced from 44 leagues in 1940 to just 12 by the end of the war. The average age of starting position players and pitchers on many clubs was over 30, as players in their mid- to late 30s who were not called into service because of their age—war is a young man's burden, after all—extended their careers. They provided the necessary ballast to provide a semblance of major league–quality play as teams filled out their rosters with more and more players who were not major-league ready.

By 1944, and especially 1945, many of those in the majors were career minor leaguers who would never have made the big time if not for the war, or youngsters awaiting their military call-up who, even if they were genuine prospects, still needed considerably more seasoning in baseball's bush leagues. A few had more serious physical limitations keeping them from military service than guys like Boudreau, Marion, and Stephens. Most famously, one-armed left-handed outfielder Pete Gray played 77 games for the Browns in 1945, mostly as a platoon player against right-handers. He hit .218.

In both 1944 and '45 there were a handful of teenagers, some as young as 16 and 17, who found themselves playing major-league baseball. Among those who went on to have respectable careers were Eddie Yost, who played seven games for Washington in 1944 as a 17-year-old before going off to war the next year; Eddie Miksis, also 17, who played 26 games for Brooklyn in 1944 before he, too, was drafted into the service; Carl Scheib, who pitched six games for the Athletics as a 16-year-old in 1943 and 15 the following year; and Tommy Brown, who was the Dodgers' starting shortstop in 44 games in 1943 at the age of 16 and in 52 games the following year. Joe Nuxhall pitched in one game as a 15-year-old for Cincinnati in 1943, got bombed, and then spent seven years in the minors after the war before finally getting a legitimate call-up to the Reds in 1952, when he was 23. He went on to have a solid career that lasted until 1966.

The shortfall of qualified players looked like it might become a crisis for Major League Baseball as the 1945 season approached. Just when it looked like victory, at least in Europe, might shortly be at hand, the German Army launched a stunning counteroffensive in December 1944, what became known as the Battle of the Bulge, to stymie the Allied advance toward Nazi Germany. And the war in the Pacific continued to rage, with American forces island-hopping toward Japan and the Japanese giving every indication they would fight with fierce fanaticism to the bitter end. The country was exhausted by war, wartime shortages were becoming more severe, and manpower needs appeared to be insatiable— especially if the war was to continue for more than another year. There were increasing questions as to whether the major leagues should continue to play under these conditions, including a proposal that perhaps the American and National Leagues should be dismantled and their teams reconfigured into eastern and western leagues to cut down on travel. There was also reassurance from the president that he was in favor of baseball continuing on "so long as you don't use perfectly healthy people that could be doing more useful work in the war."

And then the US Army broke the German Army's back in the Battle of the Bulge and swept into Germany. US Marines captured Iwo Jima, helping to set the stage for what was presumed would be a long and bloody invasion of the Japanese home islands. The 1945 season started as scheduled. It was the last wartime season, as Nazi Germany surrendered in

May, two atomic bombs were dropped on Japan in August, and within days Japan surrendered without US forces ever having to invade the island nation.

The country—and baseball—would return to normal in 1946.

31

AL WARTIME TURNS OF FORTUNE

If any American League team seemed poised to take on the Yankees for a real pennant fight at the time World War II began impacting Major League Baseball, it was the Red Sox. Boston had finished second to New York three times the four previous years, and in 1942 the Red Sox finished number two to the Yankees yet again. But not once when they finished second were the Red Sox a threat to the far more formidable Yankees. The closest they came as the runner-up was 1942, when Boston finally breached the 90-win barrier for the first time since 1917 and finished nine games behind. Owner Tom Yawkey had little so far to show for his considerable expenditures on proven veterans like Grove and Ferrell, Foxx and Cronin, not to mention Doc Cramer, hardly the impact player in Boston he was expected to be. By virtue of their scouting on the West Coast, however, the Red Sox now had three California kids and one from Oregon in place as the foundation to compete with the dominant-in-every-way New York Yankees.

The California kids, all signed out of the Pacific Coast League, were second baseman Bobby Doerr, a "splendid splinter" (because he was tall and very thin) of a hitter by the name of Ted Williams, and Joe DiMaggio's younger brother Dominic. The Oregonian was shortstop Johnny Pesky, discovered in a semipro league. Doerr made it to the Red Sox in 1937, Williams in 1939, DiMaggio in 1940, and Pesky in 1942. Pesky was so impressive playing for Boston's top farm club in 1941 that player-manager Cronin ceded his shortstop position to him the next year. All four were exceptional players in their own right. Williams, of course, would lay claim to be the "greatest hitter" ever, and Doerr also played his way into the Hall of Fame. Perhaps as important for their legacy as their ballplaying skills, however, is that Williams, Doerr, Pesky, and DiMaggio forged a deep and abiding friendship that long outlasted their playing careers. In many ways, particularly as time passed, this band of Red Sox brothers, whose loyalty to each other embodied the ennobling characteristics that have been ascribed to the "greatest generation" of Americans who fought in World War II, leavened the reputation of the Red Sox clubhouse being a country-club environment of spoiled, self-centered, ballplaying brats.

Ted Williams was the headline grabber, and not only because he was by far the best player. He was also controversial, a perfectionist who did not suffer fools gladly—and, as far as he was concerned, baseball scribes and opinioned fans were fools, especially if they expected him to comport to their standards of behavior. In his first four major-league seasons, all Williams did was twice lead the league in homers, twice lead the league in runs batted in (including his 1939 rookie season), and twice win the batting title. He slammed 127 home runs, had a .356 batting average, and reached base in 48 percent of his plate appearances. In 1942, the Splendid Splinter won the Triple Crown, got on base by a hit or a walk almost exactly half the time he came to the plate, and *wasn't* named the league's MVP.

And, oh yes, Ted Williams hit .406 in 1941. Nobody has since batted .400. His .553 on-base percentage that year was higher than any achieved by Babe Ruth and set a new major-league record that lasted until 2002 when Barry Bonds reached base in 58 percent of his plate appearances. Unhappily for Ted Williams, 1941 happened to be the same year Joe DiMaggio hit in 56 straight, during which the Yankee Clipper batted .408. DiMaggio on the season, however, hit *just* .357, meaning he would have needed 27 hits more than the 193 he got in his 541 at-bats to have matched Williams's .406 batting average. Williams already had the reputation for being an indifferent fielder and a selfish player; DiMaggio's reputation was the opposite. Even though his career outlasted the Yankee Clipper's by a decade, Ted Williams could never escape the shadow of Joe DiMaggio, to whom he was almost invariably compared . . . unfavorably.

The Red Sox may have been set to give the Yankees a tough time in the immediate future, but the United States was already at war. And so, too, were Williams, Dom DiMaggio, and Pesky in 1943. Without them, the Red Sox plummeted to seventh place. They moved back up to .500 and fourth place in 1944, when rosters were further depleted by military call-ups, but lost Doerr to the war for the last month of the season and all of 1945, when they once again fell to seventh. The war years were not kind to the Boston Red Sox.

* * *

If the Red Sox were badly hurt by player losses, so, too, were the Yankees, and perhaps even more. Like the Red Sox, the Yankees lost two-thirds of their starting outfield in 1943—the incomparable DiMaggio and Tommy Henrich—and a budding star shortstop, Phil Rizzuto. Unlike the Red Sox, the Yankees had enough depth on their roster and more minor-league talent to make up the difference, at least for the first year of wartime baseball. Top-tier veterans Bill Dickey, Joe Gordon, Charlie Keller, Spud Chandler, and Johnny Murphy were still in Yankees uniforms, and all five had outstanding seasons. Thirty-five-year-old Chandler, having endured a succession of injuries since breaking in with the Yankees in 1939 that kept him from joining the ranks of reliable workhorse starting pitchers, was superb; his 20–4 record and 1.64 earned run average were the best in the league. Johnny Lindell and Bud Metheny replaced DiMaggio and Henrich in the outfield, rookie Snuffy Stirnweiss and veteran Frankie Crosetti played shortstop instead of Rizzuto, and Billy Johnson took over at third base, Red Rolfe having retired. Lindell, Metheny, Stirnweiss, and Johnson were all high-performing prospects who had years of experience in the Yankees' vaunted minor-league system, including their top club in Newark. The first edition of the wartime Yankees won another convincing pennant and then avenged their 1942 World Series loss to the Cardinals by doing the same to St. Louis in five games.

Wartime-depleted rosters caught up with the Yankees in 1944. Dickey, Gordon, Keller, Johnson, Chandler, and Murphy were all off to war or working in defense industries. Manager Joe McCarthy was able to rally his team from a sizable 9½-game hole in mid-August into the heart of a heated three-team pennant race. Their weaker roster too much to overcome, however, the virtually unrecognizable Yankees could not sustain momentum. The Yankees would not have gotten as far as they did without strong performances from Stirnweiss, Lindell, and first baseman Nick Etten, acquired in a trade rather than brought up from Newark. Replacing Gordon at second and unfit for military service because of ulcers, Stirnweiss led the league in runs, hits, triples, and stolen bases. He led the league in all those categories again in 1945, when his .309 batting average was also the best. Lindell, whose offseason employment as a shipyard worker kept him out of military service, led the league in total bases. Etten's 22 homers topped the league, which he followed up with the most RBIs the next year. Once the war ended and major-league veterans returned, Stirnweiss and Etten faded rapidly in performance, suggesting that both had capitalized on the diminished quality of wartime baseball. Lindell remained an important role player for the Yankees until 1949.

* * *

At one level, that the Detroit Tigers were one of the two other teams to contend in 1944 was not too surprising given they had been the only team to interrupt the Yankees' string of pennants that began in 1936 with one of their own in 1940. Whatever slim hopes Detroit had in 1941 of preventing New York from returning to the top—slim, because the Yankees were a superior club and 1940 was an anomaly—were shattered when Hank Greenberg, the reigning American League MVP who made all the difference in their winning the 1940 pennant by one game over Cleveland and two over the Yankees, was drafted into the service even before the United States was at war. Without Greenberg's bat in the lineup, the Tigers fell flat in 1941, finishing fourth with a losing record. They dropped to fifth in 1942 and were fifth again in 1943 when they also had to do without catcher Birdie Tebbetts, center fielder Barney McCosky, right-hander Al Benton, and several valuable bench players, who were off to war. Detroit's prospects hardly looked any better going into 1944 because veteran right-hander Tommy Bridges, by now a "Sunday" pitcher who typically pitched the second game of doubleheaders, and the emergent Virgil Trucks were called up for military duty.

But this was in the middle of World War II. Major-league teams were hemorrhaging players to the war effort, including the two most formidable American League clubs in New York and Boston. While most of the core regulars on the 1941 and '42 Yankees and Red Sox were playing on military diamonds in 1944, if they were playing at all, the Tigers still had slugging first baseman Rudy York and veteran third baseman Pinky Higgins in *their* uniform, not army fatigues, and McCosky had been replaced in center field by veteran outfielder Doc Cramer. Higgins and Cramer were both well into their 30s and exempted by age. Although he was in his late 20s, York was not considered suitable for military service because of an unstable knee. His "loose knee," however, did not prevent him from missing just three of the 621 games the Tigers played from 1940 to 1943, and in 1944 he played in all but five. In Greenberg's absence, York was the most feared batter in Detroit's lineup. Coming off the 1943 season when the "dead" ball in use did not prevent him from leading the league with 33 homers and 118 runs batted in, York's totals dropped to 18 and 98 in 1944, still good enough for third in home runs, four short of the league lead, and fifth in RBIs, just 11 behind the league leader.

Despite no longer having Trucks and Bridges, pitching was the principal reason the Tigers stayed in the 1944 pennant race. Right-hander Dizzy Trout, in his sixth year, and southpaw Hal Newhouse, in his fifth, were exceptional, combining for 56 of Detroit's 88 victories. Poor eyesight kept Trout out of the war. Newhouser avoided military service because of a heart condition. Neither man's physical debilities prevented them from being top-tier pitchers. Trout became the Tigers' ace in 1943 with 20 wins, and in 1944 he was superb with a 27–14 record and the majors' best ERA (2.12) while pitching 352⅓ innings, the most since George Uhle's 357⅔ 21 years earlier. Newhouser's 29–9 record and the majors' second-best ERA (2.22) were totally unexpected from a southpaw whose career record was 34–52 coming into the season, including 8–17 the previous year.

Trout's 7–1 record in July kept the Tigers relevant, even if they remained mostly in fifth and sixth place, and his 8–0 run in August fueled the Tigers' surge into contention from nine games behind and a game under .500 at the beginning of the month to just three off the pace going into September. He completed 14 of 18 starts, threw five shutouts, and had a 1.99 ERA those two months. By the end of August, Trout had already thrown far more innings than he had in any prior full season of work. He made nine starts in September, but by now was worn out and was just 4–5 with a 2.99 ERA in 72⅓ innings the final month as the Tigers took their pennant race down to the final day. His last four starts of the season came in nine days, the first three on two days of rest, and the season finale—which he lost—on just one. Trout gave up 10 runs in the 13 innings he worked in his final two starts.

If Trout was August's hero for the '44 Tigers, Hal Newhouser was virtually untouchable in September, winning eight of nine decisions and throwing three shutouts as Detroit fought for the top spot. Each of his last six starts was a game where first place was directly at stake. He won all six, including his final start to send the Tigers into the last day of the season tied for first place. Even though they were up against last-place Washington, the Tigers were unable to win on the final day because a weary Dizzy Trout was outdueled by Senators' ace Dutch Leonard.

Lest anyone think Newhouser's 29–9 record in 1944, and 25–9 mark and league-best 1.81 earned run average the following season, and Trout's 27–14 and 18–15 records those two years were attributable mostly to this being World War II baseball, both pitchers went on to show they were not merely wartime wonders once the game's best hitters returned from the war in 1946. Trout's best years were indeed during the war, but he was 17–13 with a 2.34 ERA in 1946 and remained a mainstay on the Detroit staff until 1951. For Newhouser, the fact that he now had to pitch to the likes of Williams and DiMaggio didn't matter; he had the best cumulative pitching WAR among American League pitchers in the five years *after* World War II, beginning with a 26–9 record and league-leading 1.94 ERA in 1946. Even though Bob Feller's 348 strikeouts were the most since Rube Waddell fanned 349 in 1904, it was Newhouser's 8.46 strikeouts per nine innings—275 Ks in 292⅔ innings—that set the new major-league record for strikeout ratio since 60 feet, 6 inches was set as the distance from the pitcher's rubber to home plate in 1893.

* * *

The team that beat out the Yankees and the Tigers in 1944 clearly would not have done so had the Yankees, Tigers, and Red Sox not been stripped of so many of their core regulars because of the Second World War. They were the St. Louis Browns. The Browns had still not won a pennant. They had not even competed for the top spot since 1922, when they lost out by one game to the Yankees.

Few players of historical renown had passed through St. Louis to play for the Browns since the days of George Sisler, Urban Shocker, and Ken Williams. None stayed for long. Hall of Fame outfielders Heinie Manush, from 1928 to June 1930, and Goose Goslin, from June 1930 to 1933, both spent two and a half years of their careers in St. Louis; they were traded for each other in June 1930. Manush had the best season of his 17-year career with the Browns in 1928, when his .378 batting average was second to Goslin's .379. Manush was just two hits shy of winning the batting title, but played every game and had 182 more at-bats than Goslin, playing for Washington, who missed 19 games because of injuries. Hall of Fame catcher Rick Ferrell began his career with the Browns in 1929, attracted the attention of new Red Sox owner Tom Yawkey, and was gone to Boston early in the 1933 season. The closest the Browns came to having another pitcher approaching Shocker's stature was Alvin "General" Crowder, whose days in their uniform were as short lived as for Manush and Goslin. Acquired from the Senators in July 1927 and sent back to Washington as part of the Manush-for-Goslin deal in June 1930, Crowder was one of the American League's best pitchers in the six years bridging the 1920s and 1930s, beginning with his league-leading 21–5 record in 1928 that helped propel the Browns from seventh place and 94 losses into third place with 82 wins.

The Depression years were a particularly bleak period for the Browns. They did not have a single winning season in the 1930s, and when they did finish as high as fifth in 1931, it was with 91 losses. The Browns began the decade with four straight 90-loss seasons, and ended with four straight years losing at least 95 games. Third baseman Harlond Clift, overlooked in historical context precisely because he played for the St. Louis Browns, was by far their best player in the 1930s. Despite being probably the American League's best third baseman in the 1930s—the Yankees' Red Rolfe, his rival at the position, was not as potent an offensive threat—Clift made just one All-Star team and never got the recognition he deserved.

Considering how awful they were in the 1930s, by 1942 the Browns had the makings of a decent team, though hardly one thought likely to compete with top-tier teams in the American League, and certainly not with the all-powerful Yankees. Their three most significant players were first baseman George McQuinn, a solid veteran since coming to the Browns in 1938; center fielder Wally Judnich, who hit 24 homers in 1940, his rookie season; and shortstop Vern Stephens, a hard-hitting shortstop who drove in 92 runs as a rookie in 1942. Both McQuinn and Judnich were groomed in the Yankees' farm system and became available because there was no room for them in the Bronx. Perhaps most important to the Browns' future, however, was the hiring of Luke Sewell to be their manager in June 1941. Sewell, the brother of Hall of Fame shortstop Joe Sewell, had a long career as a catcher, and his reputed excellence working with pitchers was attractive to general manager Bill DeWitt because the Browns had the majors' worst team ERA since 1936. The Browns were in seventh place on the day Sewell took charge, and they had nearly twice as many losses as victories. While their position in the standings didn't change, the club improved dramatically in the second half of the season; their 43–34 record after mid-July was bettered only by McCarthy's pennant-winning Yankees.

Their strong finish to the 1941 season aside, the Browns were on life support in St. Louis. They had been last in American League attendance every year since the start of the Depression, and last in the majors in every one of those years except 1940, when only Philadelphia's Phillies drew fewer. And they could not compete with the Cardinals for the affections of St. Louis citizens in the ballpark they shared. Only slightly more than 176,000 fans went through the turnstiles at Sportsman's Park to watch the Browns play ball in 1941, while nearly three times as many came to see the pennant-contending Cardinals. The Redbirds were on the rise, having just fought—and lost—a great pennant race with the Dodgers.

In desperate financial straits and faced with the harsh reality that, while the Cardinals looked to be competitive for the top of the National League, the best they could hope for was avoiding the very bottom of the American League, the Browns were planning to ask the league's permission to pull up stakes in St. Louis and move to Los Angeles. At a time when the railroads were still the primary means of cross-country transportation, however, and with St. Louis as far west as the major league's geography reached, a move to California would have complicated scheduling for American League teams. However realistic the Los Angeles move might have been, it all became moot after the attack on Pearl Harbor. Rail transportation would be a national security priority for a country now at war, not a priority for transporting baseball teams across the country.

Staying in St. Louis, the Browns surprised the league, and perhaps themselves, in 1942 by finishing third with their first winning record since 1929 and their most wins (82) since 1928. Judnich was the Browns' best player, leading the team in batting, on-base percentage, and slugging percentage. Clift had his last productive year at the age of 29. Outfielder Chet Laabs, in his fourth year with the Browns, hit 27 homers—second in the league to Ted Williams—and also led the club in runs batted in. And the arrival of Stephens to buttress the lineup proved a shot in the arm. The Browns broke even or had a winning record against every other club in the American League except the Yankees, who crushed them by winning 15 of their 22 games.

Then came wartime baseball. The Browns were not hit as hard by wartime player losses in 1943 as the real contenders in the American League—the Yankees and Red Sox—but it was not as though they had many top-tier players. Two of their best, George McQuinn with a bad back and Vern Stephens with bad knees, were deemed unfit for Uncle Sam. Their most significant loss was Wally Judnich, for whom three years of wartime service proved too much to overcome; he was not nearly as potent when he returned to the Browns in 1946. Without Judnich, the Browns stumbled back to a losing record and sixth place, in the midst of which they parted ways with Harlond Clift.

Despite still having McQuinn and Stephens, the Browns did not look to be competitive in 1944. They had the oldest roster in the league. Six of their starting position players were over 30, as were three of their five core starting pitchers and their relief ace, 36-year-old George Caster. Chet Laabs's playing time was limited to weekends and night games because of his job in a war industry. But the defending champion Yankees seesawed between winning clumps of games and losing clumps of games; the Tigers got off to a rugged start, finding themselves in seventh place as late as July 9; and the Browns took advantage by building a lead that reached seven games in mid-August. Then it became a real pennant race. Nine games back as late as August 10, the Tigers closed in a hurry as the Browns stumbled through the month with a losing record. After Detroit won six of eight from St. Louis in the space of 11 days, the Browns' lead was down to a half-game on September 3, and the next day they were no longer on top.

The season ultimately came down to the final weekend, which began with the Tigers protecting a one-game lead over the Browns. Detroit was at home for four games against Washington. The Browns were at home for four against the Yankees. Despite being three games behind Detroit, the Yankees still had live pennant prospects—provided they swept their series in St. Louis and the Tigers lost at least three of their games. As it happened, the Browns swept the Yankees and the Senators split with the Tigers. With the Yankees already eliminated, Detroit and St. Louis began the final day deadlocked at the top. While the Tigers were losing to

Washington, the Browns overcame an early two-run deficit to New York on Laabs's two two-run homers, the first tying the game at 2–2 in the fourth, and the second putting them up 4–2 in the sixth. Stephens iced it with a home run in the eighth. Starting from 1½ games down with less than two weeks to go, the Browns won 11 of their final 12 games. The St. Louis Browns were American League champions . . . for the first and only time in their history.

The Browns almost certainly would not have won the 1944 pennant under normal circumstances. Even with their competitors having lost many more of their top players to the war, the Browns were still a relatively mediocre ballclub. They won almost entirely on the back of Vern Stephens and solid wartime pitching from a no-name staff. Stephens, now in his third season, had a terrific year. His damaged knees may have kept him out of the war, but they did not prevent him from playing the starring role in the Browns' pennant drive. He hit 20 homers and led the league with 109 runs batted in. Nine of his homers and 39 of his RBIs came in the last two months, when the Browns were trying to stay on top and then to reclaim first place. His 5.2 wins above replacement accounted for about half the total player value of the Browns' position players.

Heretofore lightly regarded Nels Potter (19–7 for the year), Jack Kramer (17–13), Bob Muncrief (13–8), Sig Jakucki (13–9), and Denny Galehouse (9–10) pitched way beyond expectations. In the final four games against the Yankees that clinched the pennant, Kramer beat them, 4–1; Potter pitched a 1–0 shutout, allowing six hits; Galehouse hurled a 5-hit shutout, winning 2–0; and Jakucki won the finale, giving up just two runs, one unearned. Galehouse with 258 career starts, Kramer with 215, and Muncrief with 165 were all legitimately major-league pitchers, but that's about all that can be said of their level of talent and ability. None of the three had a winning career record, although Muncrief at 69–67 did win more than he lost in the seven years he pitched for the Browns (1941–47) before finishing his career elsewhere. Neither Potter nor Jakucki, however, would likely have been pitching in the major leagues were it not for so many players being drafted into the war. Potter was in the minors, a failed major-league pitcher with four years of experience and a 5.82 ERA, when the Browns gave him another chance in 1943 because experienced pitchers were in short supply and his history of knee injuries exempted him from military service. Jakucki, whose prior big-league experience way back in 1936 did not go well—20 earned runs on 32 hits and 12 walks in 20⅔ innings—had not pitched in Organized Baseball since 1938 when the Browns invited him for a spring-training tryout in 1944. As good as they were during the war years, Potter (44–23 from 1943 to 1945) returned to being a mediocre pitcher at best when baseball's wartime veterans returned, and Jakucki's career was done as soon as the war ended despite his 25–19 record in '44 and '45.

Although Stephens had another outstanding year, leading the league with 24 homers, the Browns were shown to be overachievers when they

Right-hander Nels Potter of the pennant-winning 1944 Browns might not have been pitching in the major leagues if not for the roster impact of players called to serve during World War II. *National Baseball Hall of Fame and Museum.*

followed up their trip to the World Series by finishing third in 1945, a season when the wartime quality of Major League Baseball was probably at its worst. The 1945 pennant race came down to two teams. The Detroit Tigers, who had come so close the year before, were one, bolstered by the July 1 return to baseball action by Hank Greenberg. Having spent four and a half years in the army's air corps, it took him a full month to shake off the rust, even if he did hit a home run in his first game back—off the Athletics' Charlie Gassaway, the majority of whose 39 major-league appearances were in 1945 when legitimate major-league pitching was in short supply. After batting just .209 with only three homers and seven RBIs in July, Greenberg found his footing in August, hitting .366 for the month with five homers and 25 runs batted in. Despite the superb pitching of Newhouser and Trout and having been on top every day since mid-June, the Tigers were unable to pull away even after Greenberg recovered his stroke to make his comeback an inspirational story line to the season. The Tigers' lead was down to just a half-game on September 15 when they began a five-game series on the road against the one team still breathing down their neck. With just 12 games remaining on their schedule, the outcome of the pennant race could rest on the outcome of those five games.

The club Detroit was facing with first place on the line, the pennant potentially at stake, was of all teams . . . the Washington Senators. But these were not the same Washington Senators who were dead last in 1944 and who did the Browns a huge favor by defeating the Detroit Tigers on the final day of the season.

Like the 1944 Browns, the Senators in 1945 were working on their own could-only-have-happened-in-wartime pennant. Since going to the World Series in 1933, Washington had *not* gone back to "first in war, first in peace"—although the first two were certainly true—"and last in the American League" only because the Browns and the Athletics were really bad teams most of those years. Instead, the Senators ended most of the 11 seasons since they were last the best team in the American League in either sixth or seventh place. They had a winning record only twice—in 1936 when they finished third, although 20 games behind the Yankees, and in 1943 when they finished second, 13½ games behind the Yankees, in the first year that rosters were decimated because of the world at war.

In 1935, Senators owner Clark Griffith brought back Bucky Harris to manage for a second time in Washington, but unlike when he won the 1924 and '25 pennants, he had little to work with. The only core regulars from Washington's 1933 pennant-winning team to stay for more than a few years afterward were first baseman Joe Kuhel, until he was traded in 1938; second baseman Buddy Myer, until he was injured in 1939; and Ossie Bluege as a reserve infielder, until he retired in 1939. Myer won the batting title in 1935 with a .349 average, one hit better than Joe Vosmik's .348. Washington's two best players when Pearl Harbor was attacked were Cecil Travis and Buddy Lewis. Both were in the first wave of the very few major-league stars who served in 1942, a year before most of baseball's big names began being drafted.

Travis's career was on a Hall of Fame trajectory until he lost four years to the war. Starting out at third base as a rookie in 1934 and moving over to shortstop two years later so Lewis could play third, Travis went off to war having just had the best year of his career in 1941, leading the league with 218 hits and batting .359—just ahead of 56-game-hitting-streak-star DiMaggio's .357 average. Unlike many other major-league stars called into service, Travis actually *did* go off to war, enduring not only fierce fighting but bitter cold in the Battle of the Bulge. Losing much of the feeling in his feet from frostbite, Travis was unable to regain the footwork, agility, and strength necessary to resume his baseball career at anywhere near the level of his skills before he was drafted. At least, that's the story. Cecil Travis went off to war with a .327 career batting average. Returning to the Senators in early September 1945, having turned 32 exactly one month before, Travis played just 226 more games before retiring in 1947, his lifetime average brought down to .314. He did not make it to Cooperstown.

A rookie in 1936, Lewis was nothing if not consistent before going off to war in 1942. Playing his first four years at third base and the next two in right field, Lewis batted in the .290s three times and in the .310s three times. The highlight of his career might have been not *on* the ball field, but flying low *over* Washington's Griffith Stadium after a year of state-side training as an army–air force pilot to say good-bye to his teammates before he was shipped out in 1943. Like Greenberg in Detroit, Buddy Lewis returned to baseball in July to participate in the 1945 pennant race. Lewis started in all but two games the rest of the way, hitting .333. He got at least one hit in 55 of the 69 games he played, and batted .347 in the crucial last month when the Senators matched the Tigers win-for-win to stay in the race till the last day.

Washington had not been competitive even with Travis and Lewis. Without them in 1942, the Senators dropped from sixth to seventh and seemed to have no hope for whatever the duration of the war would be, even with a change in managers in 1943 from the burned-out Harris to Ossie Bluege. The War Department's ever-changing criteria affecting who got drafted when, however, enabled Washington's Senators to hang on to more of their "high-performance" core regulars for longer than most other teams—including outfielders George Case and Stan Spence; first baseman Mickey Vernon and second baseman Jerry Priddy; and pitchers Dutch Leonard and Early Wynn. But "high performance" is a relative term in comparison to the average player on their teams, not necessarily the league.

Although Wynn would have a Hall of Fame career and Vernon nearly one in the postwar years to come, none of Washington's "high-performance" core regulars during the war years were star players in contemporary context. They were good enough, however, to give the Senators a competitive advantage over most other clubs struggling to replace wartime losses of so many of their own "high-performance" core regulars. In baseball's first war-ravaged year in 1943, the Senators were able to rise from second worst to second best in the AL standings. Wynn had a breakout season with 18 wins; Case led the league in stolen bases for the fifth consecutive year with a career-high 61; Spence led the team in homers and RBIs and was their best all-around player; and Priddy looked like he was developing into the player the Yankees expected him to be before McCarthy gave up on his attitude. There being perpetual roster uncertainty exacerbated by changing requirements for the various exemptions from being called into military service, such were the vagaries of wartime baseball that the Senators followed up their successful 1943 season with a 1944 plunge to the basement. America's escalating manpower needs for fighting an all-out global war caught up to Vernon, Priddy, and catcher Jake Early. It didn't help that Early Wynn regressed, going from 18 wins to 17 losses.

After that dismal performance, Washington hardly figured to compete in 1945, especially since their two best players so far during the war years—Spence, who had just hit .316 with 18 homers and 100 RBIs, and Wynn—were finally called up to serve. Yet compete they did, in large part on the strength of their pitching. Roger Wolff, a right-hander who might never have pitched in the major leagues had the country not been at war, had an exceptional year with a 20–10 record and a 2.12 ERA. Already 34 years old in 1945, he pitched his last game in professional baseball in 1947. The Italian-born Marino Pieretti, whose country of origin made him exempt from US military service in a war where Mussolini's Fascist Italy was an enemy, was a key contributor with a 14–13 record in his rookie season, which likely would never have happened but for the war.

The Senators' 1945 pitching staff, however, was led by 36-year-old right-hander and master of the knuckleball Dutch Leonard—first name Emil, so as not to be confused with an earlier Dutch Leonard, first name Hubert, who was a star pitcher in the teens. Since being picked up by Washington on the cusp of 30 in 1938, Leonard had become one of the best pitchers in baseball—not in the same top tier as Bob Feller, but a legitimate ace nonetheless. A 20-game winner in 1939, Leonard had averaged 32 starts a year since coming to Washington, except for 1942 when he broke his ankle in only his second start and wound up pitching just six games. It was his four-hit mastery of the Tigers on the final day of the 1944 season that denied Detroit a chance for a pennant playoff with the Browns. Leonard was 16–7 with a 2.17 earned run average in 29 starts in 1945, and added a win and a save in his two relief appearances to finish at 17–7 with a 2.13 ERA.

It was Leonard who took the mound for the Senators with first place on the line in the first of the five-game series in mid-September when Detroit came to Washington with a mere half-game lead. The Senators had stayed close to the Tigers all summer, but had not spent a day in the lead since winning their opening game. With the next five of their remaining 10 games against the very club clinging to the slimmest of leads, now was their best chance to take the lead in the pennant race. The Tigers sent their best, Hal Newhouser, already with 22 wins, to face Leonard. Things went badly for Leonard when he hurt his shoulder in the second inning and had to come out of the game with Newhouser due to bat. Interestingly, with Washington's ace taken out, Detroit manager Steve O'Neill decided to remove his own ace in favor of a pinch-hitter so he could send Newhouser back out to the mound the next day against Wolff, who had 18 wins on his way to 20. The Senators lost both games of their doubleheader that day to fall 2½ behind, split another doubleheader the next day, with Newhouser ironically losing to Wolff, and salvaged the fifth game of the series with Leonard getting the win—his 17th and last of the season—in relief. That left them down by 1½ games with just five to go.

The Senators' hopes centered not only on their own performance, but on how well the Tigers did in their final games. When they wrapped up their schedule with a victory in Philadelphia, the Senators trailed by a game, but there was still hope because Detroit had four games officially left to play. The Senators had the burden of having to wait a full week with no games to play while every other American League team played makeup games to complete their schedules. After splitting two against Cleveland, the Tigers were off to St. Louis for a season-ending makeup doubleheader. Losing both games would have forced the Tigers into a one-game playoff for the American League pennant with the Senators.

As improbable as a Hollywood ending to a feel-good story about the uncertainties facing a war veteran returning home after more than four years of selfless sacrifice, Hank Greenberg came to bat against Nels Potter, the Browns' best pitcher, with the bases loaded in the ninth inning and his team losing, 3–2, in the first game of the scheduled doubleheader. Given the unimaginable horrors that were only just surfacing about death camps in Germany and the territories the Nazis had conquered—and specifically that Jews had been singled out for systematic terror and extermination—there was no more appropriate a baseball hero to the end-game of the 1945 season than the Detroit Tigers' great Jewish slugger, Hank Greenberg, hitting a grand slam to win the pennant. The next year, Greenberg's 44 homers were the most in the majors and his 127 RBIs tops in the American League, after which, having just turned 36, he was unceremoniously sold to Pittsburgh for $75,000. Greenberg retired after the 1947 season with 331 home runs, falling 169 short of 500—a coveted total he might, but also might not, have attained had he not missed 673 of his team's games because of World War II.

* * *

In 1946, with star players like DiMaggio and Williams finally back from the war, the St. Louis Browns returned to being the Browns of old, the Washington Senators went back to being the Senators, and the Boston Red Sox and New York Yankees picked up where they left off in 1942. The Browns fell to seventh and, beginning in 1947, never lost fewer than 90 games or finished higher than sixth—just once—in their remaining years in St. Louis, which ended with them going east to become the Orioles in Baltimore, instead of west to Los Angeles, as their 1941 California dreamin' had it before the attack on Pearl Harbor came as a rude awakening to the country. The Senators, with a losing record, finished fourth. The year 1945, it turned out, was their last run for a pennant in Washington before moving to Minnesota and becoming the Twins in 1961. They finished "last in the American League" five times, and would have a winning record in Washington just twice more.

Boston came back from the war years with a vengeance, determined to prove they could take on the Yankees. They won 23 of their first 27 games, and the rout was on. Their final margin of victory was 12 games over second-place Detroit. The Yankees were far back in third, 17 games behind. The Red Sox went to their first World Series since 1918. Not that anybody was talking about their being cursed, but they seemed on their way to moving past having sold the Babe and contributing to the making of the Yankees' forever dynasty.

The 1946 Red Sox got impressive pitching performances from right-handers Dave "Boo" Ferriss and Tex Hughson. Ferriss followed up his 21–10 rookie season in the last war year of 1945 with a 25–6 record and the best winning percentage in the majors, and back-from-the-war Hughson won 20. It was the bats, however, that spoke loudest at Fenway. In addition to having Williams, Pesky, Dom DiMaggio, and Doerr back, Boston now had Rudy York at first base to bat behind Williams and Doerr because Detroit preferred having Greenberg at first base instead of left field. Williams, York, and Doerr finished second, third, and fourth in RBIs. Pesky proved both that his outstanding 1942 rookie season was not an anomaly and that three years away from the major-league game had not diminished his skills by batting .335 with a league-leading 208 hits. But Boston's indisputable star and most valuable player, and also, finally, the American League MVP was Ted Williams.

Ted Williams relished being back in Boston, even beginning the season without showing his usual antagonism toward the sporting press, which may have helped in the MVP voting at the end of the year. He hit .346 his first month back, .344 his second with 28 RBIs in 29 games, hit .369 in June with 11 homers to give him 20 for the year, and on it went. Perhaps the most entertainingly dramatic moment of the season came at Fenway Park in the All-Star Game when Williams timed Pittsburgh right-hander Rip Sewell's high-arching eephus pitch perfectly and blasted it into the seats for a three-run homer in the eighth inning to finish the scoring in the American League's 12–0 rout of the National League. It was his second home run of the game, in which he went 4-for-4 with five runs batted in. In the final month of the season, by which time the Red Sox had the pennant well in hand, Williams prepared for the World Series by hitting .400. His comeback from three years away was a tour de force. Ted Williams finished the year second to Greenberg in homers and RBIs and second to Mickey Vernon in batting, but was number one in runs, on-base percentage, total bases, and slugging percentage.

This was the season the "Williams shift" instituted by Cleveland shortstop-manager Lou Boudreau became famous. Such shifts were not unheard of, but Boudreau's overload of infielders on the right side of the diamond against the lefty slugger Williams was more extreme than usual. As fate would have it, Boston's Splendid Splinter was hit in the elbow during an exhibition game to prepare for the World Series. Whether because the St. Louis Cardinals often shifted against him, or because his elbow injury affected his ability to drive through the ball, Ted Williams was just 5-for-25 with no extra-base hits and just one RBI in the only World Series he ever played.

The '46 Series would be a sore point not just for Williams, but for the Red Sox, helping fuel the Curse of the Bambino excuse for why they hadn't won a World Series since 1918. Babe Ruth, Boston's superstar back then, was 51 and ailing; a month after watching the team he had first pitched and hit so ably for lose the 1946 Series, he learned he had cancer. Although it had been 28 years since the Red Sox last won the pennant, they had won every World Series they played until 1946, when the Cardinals beat them in seven games.

The outcome pivoted on a pivot—specifically that by shortstop Johnny Pesky, who went out into short left-center field to take a relay throw from the center fielder on a two-base hit that had the Cardinals' Country Slaughter racing from first around second to third with two outs and the game tied in the bottom of the eighth in Game Seven. Except that Dom DiMaggio was no longer in center field because he was injured sliding into second base on his two-run double that tied the game at 3–3 in the top of the eighth. His defensive replacement, Leon Culberson, was no Dominic DiMaggio, or even close, in defensive prowess. Slaughter knew that, and also seeing that Culberson was playing the hit cautiously so as to avoid the ball getting by him on the notoriously bad outfield terrain at St. Louis's Sportsman's Park—home to two major-league teams, after all— he kept going at full speed. Precisely because his trying to score was so counterintuitive to the situation, Pesky (and the Red Sox) were caught by surprise. Pesky did not expect to have to throw home, and his very slight hesitation in doing so as he quickly sized up what was happening was all that Slaughter needed to score what would be the winning run. The first two Boston batters in the ninth—York and Doerr—singled, the Red Sox got the tying run to third with one out, but rather than a Williams, a Pesky, or a DiMaggio coming to bat, it was their eighth and ninth batters. Two weak outs later, and the Red Sox had stranded the runner on third. The World Series was over.

Boston fans never held it against the popular Pesky personally. Johnny Pesky remained a beloved figure at Fenway, indeed throughout New England, until his dying day 66 years later. It took the Boston Red Sox another 21 years before they got back to the World Series, once again against the Cardinals. They didn't win that one, either.

* * *

The end of the war and the return of the Yankees' best players in 1946 promised both the roster stability Joe McCarthy had lacked the two previous war years and the possibility of the Yankees picking up where they left off in 1942. It didn't happen that way. Phil Rizzuto, unlike Pesky, did not play as though three years in the service were more like three days; Joe Gordon also struggled upon his return, hitting just .210; and DiMaggio, like Gordon now over 30, was hitting just .271 with 17 homers in early July when he was forced out of the lineup for a month with one of his frequent injuries. Although he came back strong in August, 1946 was the first year in his now-eight big-league seasons that Joe DiMaggio did not hit at least .300 (he batted .290) or drive in at least 100 runs (he had 95 RBIs). The Yankees' front-line starters were not the same as in 1942, except for Spud Chandler, whose 20–8 record in his first year back since '43 made him by far the best pitcher on the staff.

More significantly, however, 1946 was the end of the McCarthy era. The proud franchise had persevered and continued to flourish, at least competitively, under the firm hand of Ed Barrow in the front office and McCarthy in the dugout since owner Jacob Ruppert's death in January

1939. Ruppert had bequeathed his ownership of the Yankees to two nieces and a longtime female acquaintance, but he had also accrued significant debt against the franchise that was held by a trust company. By the end of the war, the Yankees were up for sale to pay off Ruppert's obligations. Larry MacPhail, who had previously run baseball operations for the Cincinnati Reds and Brooklyn Dodgers, recruited Dan Topping, wealthy by inheritance, and Del Webb, a developer and construction magnate out west, to buy the Yankees as a threesome. The deal was consummated in 1945, and MacPhail became president of the New York Yankees.

MacPhail made no secret that the division of labor prevailing under Ruppert, where the owner gave great latitude to Barrow to run the administrative side of the Yankees' baseball operations and Barrow in turn did not interfere with McCarthy's managing of the team on the field, was not his management style. Barrow voluntarily retired. McCarthy chafed under MacPhail's incessant meddling and not-so-subtle character assassination that the man who had led the New York Yankees to eight pennants and seven World Series championships in his 15 years as their manager had grown out of touch with the game and its players, and that he was drinking too much besides (as if MacPhail was one to talk about sobriety). Thirty-five games into the 1946 season, even though the Yankees were second with a 22–13 record, McCarthy resigned as manager. Nobody was going to catch the 1946 Boston Red Sox, but the Yankees did not play as well the rest of the year after McCarthy "resigned."

32

CARDINALS-DODGERS PAS DE DEUX

While the Second World War *might have* preempted a mid-1940s Yankees–Red Sox rivalry that was *perhaps* emerging by 1942—it is debatable whether Boston could have closed the competitive gap with New York to fight for a pennant deep into September anytime soon—it *actually did* interrupt a Cardinals-Dodgers rivalry that had witnessed two close and exciting pennant races between them before wartime decimated baseball rosters. Cardinals player losses did not prevent them from being the best team in baseball during the war. Then the war ended, all the players returned, and the St. Louis Cardinals and Brooklyn Dodgers resumed their rivalry in a pennant race so tight it ended with the two clubs tied for the best record in the league, requiring the major leagues' first ever playoff to determine which team would go to the World Series.

Before Boston and their Red Sox, before Chicago and their Cubs, it was Brooklyn that endured the bittersweet community angst of rooting for a perennially hapless baseball team, seemingly forever. In truth, the Red Sox hadn't been to a World Series since 1918, two years before the Dodgers—then known as the Robins—were last in, but they had won all four Series they played. Brooklyn, on the other hand, lost the 1920 Series to Cleveland, which included the indignity of surrendering the first grand slam in World Series history in the same game they were victimized by the only unassisted triple play in World Series history. And while the Cubs had not won a World Series since even before that—1908, to be precise—they had been to six since then.

St. Louis had also once been a city of abject baseball failure until the Cardinals' Branch Rickey began assembling a farm system that led to five pennants and three World Series in nine years between 1926 and 1934. They had not finished first since then, however, and by the end of the decade had faded into middle-of-the-pack obscurity. Replenished by players developed in their minor-league system—including first baseman Johnny Mize and Enos Slaughter and Terry Moore to join veteran Joe Medwick in the outfield—the Cardinals were poised once again to compete as the decade turned, finishing second to the Reds in 1939. Expectations for a move to the top the next year were dashed when the Cardinals got off to a horrid start, losing 24 of their first 38 games. Having seen enough, Rickey promoted Billy Southworth from managing their top farm club to take over in St. Louis. Here was his chance to say thanks.

Southworth's baseball odyssey began as a journeyman outfielder for four National League teams in a playing career that stretched from 1918 to 1927, the last two years with the Cardinals. His claim to fame as a player came with the Pirates in 1918 when, after being credited with the batting title (he hit .341) despite playing in only 64 of his team's 126 games and having just 246 official at-bats, league authorities took the honor away by ruling he had not played enough to qualify. Playing for John McGraw and the Giants in 1924 and 1925 set Southworth up for his ultimate calling as a manager—but this was a career that came very close to being derailed. After just one year managing their top affiliate in Rochester, he was promoted to St. Louis in 1929, switching places with Bill McKechnie, the man who had just led them to the pennant. His promotion was clearly premature; the Cardinals floundered under his leadership, and by midseason Southworth was back managing Rochester, again swapping jobs with McKechnie. Southworth spent most of the 1930s in the Cardinals' system mastering the craft of managing while also having to overcome his debilitating drinking problem. When he was called back to St. Louis in June 1940 after 11 years in minor-league exile, here was his chance to say thanks. The Cardinals were next to last with nearly 30 percent of the season already done, seemingly not going anywhere, on the day Southworth assumed pride of place in the dugout. Perhaps energized by new leadership, St. Louis came within a half-game of the best record in baseball the rest of the way to finish third behind Cincinnati, now managed by the man whose fate had been so intertwined with his back in 1929—Bill McKechnie. They were no longer in a funk. They were genuinely competitive. Also coming out of a funk in 1940, and genuinely competitive, were the second-place Brooklyn Dodgers.

* * *

Once Wilbert Robinson retired in 1931, the Brooklyn Robins became, for a time and until LA, the Brooklyn Dodgers. To their faithful who attended games at Ebbets Field, followed their fortunes in New York City's many news dailies, and by the end of the 1930s were listening to their games on the radio, they were simply . . . "Dem Bums." If there were head-smacking what-the-heck-was-he-thinking plays made, they were by "Dem Bums." If there were unusual, even creative, ways to blow a lead and lose a game, "Dem Bums" would find it. "Dem Bums" made Ebbets Field feel like an amusement park, where something unexpected happening was in fact expected. Casey Stengel, who hit .272 in 676 games for Brooklyn during the Deadball Era in primarily a platoon role, managed "Dem Bums" for three years from 1934 to 1936, enlivening the proceedings with his observations about how well "Dem Bums" were playing, or not. He was fired after the Dodgers finished next to last in 1936.

If the good citizens of Brooklyn felt their town—large enough by itself with more than 2.5 million residents to be the third-most-populous city in the United States—was not treated with sufficient respect as a borough of greater New York City, "Dem Bums" mirrored that sentiment in the city's baseball wars for relevance. While the Dodgers in Brooklyn were mired in the second division, the Yankees in the Bronx went to five World Series in the 1930s, and their National League rivals in Manhattan, the Giants, went to three.

In truth, much of their heralded incompetency was exaggerated—at least as far as being a daily occurrence—because the Dodgers were, after all, a major-league ballclub. They just were not a very good major-league club. But they weren't terrible. They took up seemingly perpetual residence in sixth place, but never finished last. They did not have a winning record between 1933 and 1938 and had little continuity among their core position players for most of the Depression years. The lyrically named Van Lingle Mungo, a hard-throwing righty with control problems who walked more than 100 batters three times to lead the league, was the only Dodgers pitcher with longevity during the decade. Mungo won 18 games in both 1934 and 1936, led the league strikeouts in 1936, and had his league's best strikeouts-to-innings ratio three straight years from 1935 to 1937.

The Dodgers' fortunes began to change in 1938 when Larry MacPhail was enticed to come to Brooklyn to repair the team's precarious financial position and build a competitive club. It probably didn't take much to entice him since he had been out of the baseball business for a year, and he loved the baseball business. MacPhail was a self-promoter with genuinely creative ideas and a strong entrepreneurial bent. In 1930 as a prominent local businessman in Columbus, Ohio, MacPhail inquired of Branch Rickey whether he might want to invest in the city's American Association club, brokered the sale that gave the Cardinals a second affiliate in the highest Double-A classification of minor-league baseball, and was rewarded by being named team president. Before long the two men were clashing over Rickey's calling the shots for MacPhail's club—it was part of the *St. Louis* system, after all—and in 1934, Rickey resolved his problem and promoted MacPhail's career by recommending him to Cincinnati owner Powel Crosley as just the man to reverse the arc of the Reds' dismal recent history. As a larger-than-life personality, however, MacPhail clashed with Crosley, as he had with Rickey. Other than introducing night games to Major League Baseball, it was not apparent he was having any success turning the Reds around. He left Cincinnati after their last-place finish in 1937, back where they were when he first came to the Queen City.

MacPhail wasted little time making his presence felt in Brooklyn in 1938. In spring training, he made a deal with Philadelphia's cash-strapped Phillies for their power-hitting first baseman, Dolph Camilli, who had just hit .339 with 27 homers. In April, MacPhail signed outfielder Pete Reiser, one of the six dozen Cardinals' minor leaguers granted free agency by the commissioner after his investigation revealed subterfuge in Rickey's farm system operation. In July, MacPhail acquired the rights to 30-year-old right-hander Whit Wyatt, who was having a standout season for Cleveland's Double-A affiliate trying to revive a career that had been disappointing at best and beset by arm problems. The Brooklyn Dodgers would not have won the National League pennant three years later without these three players.

The most remarked-upon move MacPhail made in his first year in Brooklyn occurred in June, just after his bringing night baseball to Ebbets Field was made all the more dramatic by the Reds' Johnny Vander Meer throwing his second consecutive no-hitter against the Dodgers. That's when he hired Babe Ruth to be the Dodgers' first-base coach. This was clearly a gimmick to promote attendance, especially since the Babe, four years removed from his last year with the Yankees, could still reach the seats during batting practice, which just added to "Dem Bums" sometimes seeming more like a clown show than a baseball team. Since the Dodgers finished seventh and it was no secret Brooklyn manager Burleigh Grimes would not be returning, Ruth probably harbored secret hopes that he would finally get his chance to manage in the major leagues. He almost certainly knew, however, that that was not going to happen.

It was shortstop Leo Durocher, in a stroke of genius, whom MacPhail wanted as manager. Durocher was a scrappy overachieving shortstop for the Cardinals in the 1930s, one of the Gashouse Gang, whose mouth was bigger than his talent and contributed to his being traded to Brooklyn after the 1937 season. Now in his 30s, Leo's average had sunk to just .203 that year—a new low even for the "All-American Out," as Ruth once called him. Durocher was named the Dodgers' team captain, rebounded with a better season in 1938, and his on-the-field leadership made a compelling case that he could be an effective manager. In addition to naming Durocher player-manager, MacPhail selected right-hander Hugh Casey in the minor-league draft and picked up outfielder Dixie Walker on waivers from Detroit in July. Walker (the son of a former major-league pitcher also called "Dixie") had had a star-crossed career in the American League that began with the Yankees in 1933, included a breakout season with the White Sox in 1937, and culminated in a 1938 trade to the Tigers in an exchange for their popular outfielder Gee Walker. Dixie played well in place of Gee, but was never popular with Detroit fans. His popularity quotient would change after he got to Brooklyn, where before long he became the "People's Choice." Durocher's first year as manager was a success; the vastly improved Dodgers finished third.

In 1940, Pee Wee Reese arrived in Brooklyn to play shortstop. Durocher was sufficiently astute as a manager, and not too proud of his own playing talent, to step aside in favor of the superior player. Boston Red Sox shortstop-manager Joe Cronin, on the other hand, had not been willing to do the same when Reese was starring for their minor-league affiliate in Louisville, and thus did the Dodgers acquire the greatest shortstop in their history. (Cronin would not make the same mistake come 1942, when Johnny Pesky was ready to play shortstop in the major leagues.) In June, MacPhail traded with Rickey for Cardinals outfielder Joe Medwick and pitcher Curt Davis. The Dodgers were leaders of the NL pack as late as July 6, but were still not quite ready for a pennant drive. They had a losing record the rest of the way, ending the season a distant second to the Reds. Soon after their summer swoon began, the Dodgers in late July brought Pete Reiser to Brooklyn. The MacPhail-and-Durocher Dodgers were now a competitive team.

* * *

Brooklyn and St. Louis squared off against each other in each of the next two pennant races, their rivalry becoming fiercely competitive. Both started strong in 1941, with the Cardinals at 31–11 holding a one-game lead over the Dodgers at 30–12 through the end of May. The two clubs were tied at the top on August 10 when a season-ending injury to Country Slaughter changed the dynamic. At the time his season ended abruptly because of a broken collarbone suffered when he tried making a tumbling catch, Slaughter had started every game and was batting .312 with 13 homers and 76 runs batted in. Even though the Cardinals continued to play well after Slaughter was hurt, going 28–18 the rest of the way, the Dodgers were 2½ games better at 32–17 to win the pennant. Slaughter's injury may have cost St. Louis the pennant.

Regardless of the impact of Slaughter's injury on the Cardinals, the Dodgers more than earned their pennant with 100 victories. Pete Reiser, in his second year, led the league in total bases, doubles, triples, and batting average. Dolph Camilli led the league in home runs and runs batted in. Medwick and Walker both hit over .300, and Reese excelled defensively at shortstop even if his hitting was still a work in progress. Whit Wyatt had a superb season with a 22–10 record and 2.34 ERA. Curt Davis was 13–7. These were all MacPhail pickups from other clubs in his first three years in charge of the Dodgers' front office. And MacPhail made two more in preparation for the season, and one soon after the season began, that were just as consequential in his club outlasting Rickey's for the National League pennant. And make no mistake, Larry MacPhail's rivalry with Branch Rickey was personal, not just competitive, and he measured his success against him. The first two were the offseason acquisitions of catcher Mickey Owen from the Cardinals and pitcher Kirby Higbe from the Phillies. Owen, the St. Louis catcher since 1937, was now disposable in Mr. Rickey's world because Walker Cooper, a much better hitter, was set to take over after seven years working his way up the Cardinals' farm chain. Leaving the woeful Phillies behind, Higbe went from 19 losses the previous year to tying Wyatt for the league lead in wins with 22. The third came in May when MacPhail addressed the Dodgers' one position of weakness—second base—by dealing for the Cubs' outstanding longtime second baseman, Billy Herman.

As manager, Durocher made a move on his pitching staff of no small consequence when he shifted Hugh Casey from a spot-starting role to full-time in the bullpen in late July. Casey was 9–7 at the time and the Dodgers were trailing the Cardinals by two games. In his eight starts since the beginning of June, Casey had an unsightly 6.08 ERA, but Durocher calculated that because he threw hard, he could be very effective coming late into close games for the win or to protect a lead. Durocher used him in relief 11 times in September, which began with the two clubs tied for first, and Casey was nearly flawless, giving up just three runs on 12 hits in 21⅓ innings. For the year, Casey was 8–4 with seven saves and a 2.14 ERA in 27 relief appearances, and 6–7 with a much less tidy 4.81 ERA in 18 starts.

Casey, however, lost his touch in the Dodgers' five-game defeat to the Yankees in the 1941 World Series. With the Series tied at one game apiece, Casey was the losing pitcher in Game Three when he was called into a scoreless game in the eighth inning and promptly surrendered two runs on four consecutive singles. The next day, he and catcher Mickey Owen etched their place as goats in World Series lore when, with nobody on base and two outs, Owen failed to catch Casey's strike three on Tommy Henrich for the final out of a supposed 4–3 Dodgers win that would have evened the Series. Whether Owen just missed the pitch, was crossed up on what pitch was thrown, or Casey threw an erratic spitter, the ball rolled toward the backstop, Henrich raced to first, and the Yankees went on to score four unearned runs to win the game and take a commanding lead in the Series. Wyatt lost a close 3–1 game the next day. The Brooklyn Dodgers in three World Series appearances had yet to win one.

* * *

The Dodgers looked certain to repeat in 1942. They got off to a fast start and already had a 9½-game lead over everybody else on the Fourth of July. The second-place Cardinals kept pace at that distance for the next month, but could not make up any ground. In fact, on August 5, Brooklyn enjoyed a 10-game lead over St. Louis and was on a pace to win 110 games. From then until time ran out on the season, however, the Cardinals won a phenomenal 83 percent of their games, going 44–9, to snatch the pennant from the Dodgers. Brooklyn did not play badly; it was 30–20 the rest of the way to wind up with 104 wins, a total not reached by any National League club since the 1910 Chicago Cubs. Previously, only five NL clubs had surpassed that victory total—the 1904 and '05 Giants, the 1906 and '07 Cubs, and the 1909 Pirates. But in 1942, there was a sixth. The St. Louis Cardinals won 106 to finish two games ahead of Brooklyn in the standings, giving the Dodgers the dubious distinction of being the first National League team since the 1909 Cubs—and the first major-league team since the 1915 Tigers—to win 100 games and *not* win the pennant.

The Cardinals won two critical series against the Dodgers as the season was fast approaching its end, first taking three of four in St. Louis in late August to whittle Brooklyn's lead from 7½ to 5½ games, and then sweeping their remaining two head-to-head games in Brooklyn on September 11 and 12 to go from two games down into a first-place tie. A doubleheader loss at home to the Reds the next day dropped the Dodgers out of first place for the first time since the fifth game on the schedule. Brooklyn rallied to win 10 of their last 12, including eight straight to end the season, but it was not enough to reclaim first place because St. Louis won 12 of their final 14 games to finish two ahead of the Dodgers. In their direct matchups, the Cardinals won 13 and the Dodgers nine; a split of the season series would have ended the 154-game schedule in a deadlock. If the previous year the Cardinals were hurt by a season-ending injury to Country Slaughter, the 1942 Dodgers were not helped by Pete Reiser's propensity to get hurt on the field of play. Three times he missed more than a week of action because of injury.

Healthy again, and playing virtually every game (in contrast to Reiser playing in only 125), Slaughter had the best year of his career, which may have been decisive because Johnny Mize was no longer a Cardinal. In one of his rare miscalculations, Rickey traded him to the Giants during the offseason for virtually nothing in return. If he did so thinking Mize was at the beginning of his declining years, Rickey turned out to be wrong. Mize remained one of the most dangerous hitters in baseball until 1948, even missing out on three years during the war. Only then did he enter the downslope of his Hall of Fame career. Even without Mize, the Cardinals were a formidable offensive club, leading the league in runs, batting average, on-base percentage, and slugging percentage. Terry Moore in center field and Marty Marion at shortstop gave the Cardinals superb defense up the middle. And Stan Musial emerged as a new star, hitting .315 with 10 homers and 72 RBIs. Perhaps because he was still a rookie, Southworth platooned the left-handed-batting Musial in the outfield all season, starting him almost exclusively against right-handed pitchers. Musial started only nine games against lefties, although he was typically brought into those games if a right-hander took the mound in relief.

Billy Southworth went on to seal the 1942 Cardinals' lore in baseball history by outmanaging Joe McCarthy to stun the powerful and favored Yankees in five games in the World Series after losing the opener. It was considered an improbable World Series championship because the Yankees had not lost any of the eight World Series they had played since 1928, the last six under McCarthy. After their remarkable run to the National League pennant, however, and with 106 wins—three more than the Yankees—the Cardinals really should not have been thought such a decided underdog in the Series. Musial started every game, perhaps only because all the Yankees' starting pitchers were right-handers. Although he hit only .222 in the Series, Musial's two-out eighth-inning single in Game Two driving in Slaughter from second base broke a 3–3 tie and evened the Series at one game apiece. The Yankees did not win again.

* * *

Building on that success, St. Louis completely dominated the league in 1943 and 1944, winning 105 games both years without ever being really challenged. But these pennants were won in commanding fashion while US involvement in World War II was taking a heavy toll on major-league rosters. In 1943, their 18-game margin of victory was the biggest by a National League pennant winner since the 1906 Cubs beat out the Giants by 20 games. And in 1944, the Cardinals were never not in first place after the eighth game of the season on their way to finishing 14½ games ahead of all their competition. After having lost the 1943 World Series to the Yankees, the Cardinals beat their fellow tenants at Sportsman's Park—the St. Louis Browns—in the 1944 Series.

The war years were not kind to their archrivals in Brooklyn. The Dodgers fell to 81 wins and third place in 1943 and collapsed to seventh, 42 games behind St. Louis, with just 63 victories in 1944. Durocher had to manage through the war years without his third baseman (Cookie Lavagetto, already gone in 1942), shortstop (Reese), center fielder (Reiser), and relief ace (Casey) for three years; second baseman (Herman) and a starting pitcher (Higbe), both gone in 1944, for two; and his catcher (Owen, called to serve in 1945), for one. Core 1942 Dodger regulars Camilli, Medwick, Wyatt, and Arky Vaughan, the former great Pirates shortstop for whom Brooklyn had traded to replace Lavagetto in 1942, did not go off to war, but none of them were still with the club by the time the war ended. With Branch Rickey, having replaced MacPhail in the Brooklyn front office, adhering to his philosophy of trading star players for value just at the cusp of their declining years, both 31-year-old Medwick and 36-year-old Camilli were sent to the Giants in separate July transactions during the 1943 season. Rickey took considerable abuse in New York newspapers for letting them go. Since coming to Brooklyn in 1938, Dolph Camilli had become a fan favorite at Ebbets Field. Refusing to play for the hated Giants, Camilli spent the year in the Pacific Coast League and was out of baseball a year later.

Vaughan parted ways with the Dodgers in 1944 because he refused to play any longer for Leo Durocher, and in 1945 the Dodgers parted ways with Wyatt because the veteran pitcher was 36 years old with an ailing arm. The precipitating incident that Arky Vaughan could not abide was Durocher suspending journeyman veteran right-hander Bobo Newsom for not following the manager's directions on how to pitch to a certain batter during a game in early July, then telling reporters that Newsom was insubordinate, and shortly thereafter trading him to the St. Louis Browns. Nursing a 9–4 record at the time he disobeyed his manager, Newsom had the most victories on a club that was in second place, just 3½ games behind the Cardinals. An angry Vaughan tossed his uniform at Durocher, said he would quit, but played out the season anyway, leading the league in both runs and stolen bases. Without Newsom, Brooklyn had a losing record the rest of the way and ended up 23½ games behind St. Louis. Vaughan went on the voluntarily retired list after the season rather than return to the Dodgers.

Right fielder Dixie Walker, whose past baseball injuries made him unfit for military service, and pitcher Curt Davis, in his late 30s, were the only key players from the 1941–42 Dodgers who stayed in Brooklyn for the duration of the war years. Walker's .357 batting average was the best in the major leagues in 1944, as were his 124 RBIs in 1945. The Dodgers also benefited from outfielder–first baseman Augie Galan's .305 batting average and .421 on-base percentage during the 1943–45 war years, and in June 1944 the Dodgers acquired Eddie Stanky from the Cubs to replace off-to-war Billy Herman at second base. The lingering effects of a beaning in his very first major-league game in 1943 kept Stanky out of the service. Stanky led the league in runs and walks in 1945.

The Cardinals, by contrast, were less hobbled by wartime call-ups of their core players when they far outpaced the rest of the National League in 1943 and '44. Pitchers Mort Cooper and Max Lanier, catcher Walker Cooper, first baseman Ray Sanders, shortstop Marty Marion, third baseman Whitey Kurowski, and outfielder Stan Musial all had physical, medical, or family-responsibility exemptions. St. Louis, however, did lose two-thirds of its starting outfield for three years beginning in 1943—right fielder Country Slaughter and center fielder Terry Moore. These were significant losses. Slaughter was by now one of the best players in baseball, and Moore, in addition to being a top-flight defensive outfielder, had improved substantially as a hitter in recent years. Unquestionably Brooklyn lost more important players to the war than St. Louis, but the Cardinals, like every other team, did have holes to fill as a result of wartime players becoming soldiers. Although Cooper and Lanier provided experience and continuity, the St. Louis pitching staff was particularly hard hit by the war. Johnny Beazley, 21–6 as a rookie in 1942, wore Uncle Sam's uniform the next three years; southpaw Ernie White, who tied for the team lead with 17 wins in 1941, missed much of the next two seasons with a sore arm and the two after that in the service; and Al Brazle and Howie Pollet both served two years just as they were on the verge of becoming established major-league pitchers.

The Cardinals' luck ran out in 1945. Gone that year were Musial, both Coopers, and Lanier. Mort Cooper contributed a 20-win season to each of the Cardinals' three consecutive pennants from 1942 to 1944, and his brother Walker was probably the best catcher in baseball those three years. Lanier contributed 45 wins to the Cardinals' three in a row, highlighted by his going 15–7 and leading the league with a 1.90 ERA in 1943. Both Lanier and Walker Cooper were called to duty very early in the 1945 season. Shortly thereafter, following an ugly salary dispute with Cardinals owner Sam Breadon, Mort Cooper was traded to the Boston Braves. Walker had joined his brother in complaining about Breadon's parsimonious ways and was no sooner released from the service than he was sold to the Giants for $175,000 in January 1946.

It was the wartime call-up of Stan Musial, however, that almost certainly cost the Cardinals a fourth consecutive pennant in 1945. Musial was 23 years old and had been able to play the two previous years because he was the father of one child and his local draft board could meet its wartime manpower quota without having to call on him. After being platooned in left field in his rookie year, in which he hit only .219 in games started by southpaws, the left-handed-batting Musial moved to right field when Slaughter was drafted in 1943, played in every game, and started all but two regardless of who the opposing starting pitcher was. Lefty or righty didn't make much difference to Musial, whose .335 average in games started by southpaws contributed to his leading the league in batting (.357), hits (220), doubles (48), triples (20), and total bases (347) to win the 1943 National League Most Valuable Player Award. In 1944, Musial's .347 average was second in the league, and he again led the league in hits (197) and doubles (51). For the second year in a row he was the best position player in Major League Baseball, based on wins above replacement. Marty Marion, however, was voted the National League's MVP in 1944, recognized mostly for his exceptional defense and on-the-field leadership.

Without Musial, the Cardinals got off to a sluggish start in 1945 and were unable to put together a hot streak until after they had fallen seven games behind the Cubs in mid-August. It was then that Harry Brecheen stepped up to become an ace. Nicknamed "The Cat" for his unimposing stature and athletic quickness, Brecheen helped stabilize the Cardinals' pitching staff during the war years, but was not one of the top three Cardinals pitchers in innings pitched in any of those years. After going 9–6 in 1943 and 16–5 in 1944, Brecheen battled through arm problems and relative ineffectiveness in the first half of 1945. He threw only 40⅔ innings and had a 5.53 earned run average through June, then pitched only 16⅓ innings in July. When he took the mound against the Giants at the Polo Grounds on August 9, his record was 6–2 with a 4.12 ERA. From then till the end of the year, however, Brecheen made 11 starts, completed 10, won nine, lost just two, and had a superb 1.56 earned run average. Three of his wins and both of his shutouts were against the league-leading Cubs, the team St Louis was desperate to catch. He finished the season with a 15–4 record for the best winning percentage in the National League, and his 2.52 ERA was third in the league. Paced by the Cat, the Cardinals won two-thirds of their remaining games in the last six weeks of the season. Their furious finish, however, was not enough to close the gap. They finished three back of the Cubs.

* * *

Being swept by the Yankees in the 1938 World Series for the second time in seven years was a demoralizing blow for Chicago's Cubs. Whether because of that, or because they were losing their competitive edge after winning four pennants in 10 years and contending for the honor virtually every year for a full decade, the Cubs dropped out of the National League picture in 1939 and remained out of sight until the last war year. The best they did was 1939, when their NL-title defense ended in fourth place, 13 games behind the Reds. They had a losing record each of the next five years and never finished closer than 25½ games behind. By

1943, when World War II began having a big impact on major-league rosters, the only core regulars remaining from the 1938 Cubs were third baseman Stan Hack, who had just had the three best years of his career; first baseman–outfielder Phil Cavarretta, still struggling to live up to his hyped-up potential as an 18-year-old rookie in 1935; and Bill Lee, a 20-game winner when the Cubs won the 1935 and 1938 pennants.

Nearly 30 players on the Cubs' major-league roster served in the war. If it seemed they did not lose any impact players the likes of the Cardinals' Slaughter, Moore, and eventually Musial, or the Dodgers' Reese, Reiser, and Billy Herman, that was because the Cubs had relatively few impact players on their roster. The most prominent Cubs to avoid military service entirely were Hack, Lee, and Claude Passeau, all three approaching their mid-30s; Cavarretta, exempt from military service because of an ear ailment; and right fielder Bill Nicholson, who had once wanted a naval career but was rejected for military service because he was color blind. A left-handed batter, Nicholson was one of the league's premier sluggers in the three years before wartime call-ups seriously degraded big-league rosters, and during the war years he led the National League in homers and RBIs in both 1943 and 1944. Passeau had become one of the best pitchers in the league since coming to Chicago from the wretched Phillies in 1939.

With Charlie Grimm returning as manager, the Cubs finished fourth in 1944, four games under .500 and 30 games behind the runaway wartime Cardinals. But St. Louis lost two starting corner outfielders (Musial and Danny Litwhiler), their starting catcher (Walker Cooper), and their top two starting pitchers (Mort Cooper and Lanier) to the war in 1945, while Chicago turned to the new season with their 1944 club intact. And they even had one core player back—outfielder Peanuts Lowrey, in the army in '44, but back to play in '45 on the "weak knees" that made him unfit for military duty. Even taking into account the number of established players missing from baseball action because of the war, the 1945 Cubs were a legitimately good team. Cavarretta led the league in batting and won the MVP Award. Hack was fourth in batting. Second-year center fielder Andy Pafko, unfit to serve because of high blood pressure, was third in the league in RBIs. Nicholson, however, hit just 13 homers after five straight years with at least 21.

Half of Chicago's starts were by pitchers older than 35. Thirty-six-year-old Passeau was 17–9 with a 2.46 earned run average; 38-year-old Paul Derringer, acquired from Cincinnati in 1943, was 16–11 in what would be his last big-league season; and southpaw Ray Prim, also 38, who most likely would not have been pitching in the major leagues but for so many big-leaguers and minor-league prospects being called to war, was 13–8 and led the league with a 2.40 ERA. Hank Wyse, a 27-year-old right-hander deemed unfit for military service following his draft physical, was 22–10 with a 2.68 earned run average. It was Wyse whose 8–1 record in nine starts in July led the Cubs' 26–6 surge from fourth place and five games behind at the end of June to a 5½-game lead going into August.

With the city of Chicago's pennant fever stoked by the Cubs' hot hand in July to take over first place from the Cardinals, owner Phil Wrigley went for the kill on July 27 by spending $97,000 to buy right-hander Hank Borowy from the New York Yankees. Borowy, whose winter job working in defense industries was his contribution to the war effort, had a 56–30 record with a 2.74 ERA since being called up from Newark in 1942, but the Yankees now had him on the waiver wire despite his 10–5 record so far in the 1945 season. They were in third place and not playing well, and Borowy's recent starts were not helping. Pitching through a sore arm, he had won just two of his last six decisions and had given up 24 earned runs in 28⅔ innings in five starts in July. Whatever was ailing him seemed cured by his move to Chicago. Borowy made 14 starts and was 11–2 with a 2.13 earned run average for the Cubs the rest of the way, including 10 complete games in his first 10 starts with his new team. Including the Yankees, 1945 was Borowy's only 20-win season. Borowy made seven starts in September and was 6–0, including 3–0 against the Cardinals. The Cubs went to the World Series for the first time since 1938.

The Cubs played in nine previous World Series and had won just two. None were seven-game affairs. Not so, the 1945 Series against Detroit. Because of wartime travel restrictions, the first three games were played at Briggs Stadium in Detroit, and the last four at Wrigley Field in Chicago. The two clubs alternated victories in the first four games, the Cubs winning the opener behind Borowy's six-hit shutout, and Passeau pitching a one-hitter—Rudy York singled in the second—to shut out the Tigers in Game Three. Borowy was the losing pitcher in his Game Five start, which put the Cubs in a three-games-to-two hole, but pitched four innings in relief the next day to win Game Six and even the Series. After an off day, Grimm asked Borowy to face off against Tigers ace Hal Newhouser in the Series finale, even though he had just one day of rest after having pitched nine innings the two previous games. Newhouser would be starting with two days of rest. Laboring with fatigue, Newhouser wasn't anywhere near his best—he gave up 10 hits while pitching a complete game—but Borowy clearly had nothing left. He faced just three batters, all of whom singled and eventually scored in a five-run first. Borowy was the losing pitcher.

The Chicago Cubs had now gone 37 years without winning a World Series. If that seemed a long time, Chicago hadn't seen nuthin' yet. Much has been made of the "Billy Goat Curse" leveled by the owner of the Billy Goat Tavern, whose real-live goat was denied admittance despite having a ticket to Wrigley Field for Game Four, as the reason why the Cubs did not return to the World Series for the remainder of the twentieth century—did not, in fact, until 16 years into the twenty-*first* century. Perhaps more should be made of manager Charlie Grimm's decision to start a weary Hank Borowy in Game Seven. It would not be until 1969 that the Cubs even competed for a pennant again.

* * *

With the end of World War II and the return of Musial, Slaughter, Moore, and Pollet to the Cardinals, and Reese, Reiser, Higbe, and Casey to the Dodgers, the Cubs could no longer compete and the St. Louis–Brooklyn rivalry was back on. Billy Southworth, however, was no longer the Cardinals' manager, having been recruited by the Boston Braves to turn their fortunes around. Southworth's .661 winning percentage between 1941 and 1945, when he led the Cardinals to a 508–261 record, is the highest over a five-year period for any manager with the exception of Frank Chance with his 1906–10 Chicago Cubs (.693). Not even Joe McCarthy with his great Yankees teams had a winning percentage as high for any five-year period. Replacing Southworth was Eddie Dyer, who had a long gestation period in the Cardinals' farm system, winning nine minor-league championships in 14 years as manager of various St. Louis affiliates. Dyer's resume also included serving as president of two of those affiliates and as a regional director.

Inheriting Southworth's team, Dyer had to deal with the turmoil caused by the defections of superb southpaw Max Lanier and promising second baseman Lou Klein to the outlaw Mexican League, and the nearly successful courting of Musial to do the same. A rookie in 1943, Klein was returning from two years in the service, and Lanier went 57–37 for the Cardinals from 1941 until being drafted into the army in May 1945. Lanier pitched brilliantly for St. Louis in the first month of the 1946 season, winning all six of his starts by complete games, allowing only 58 baserunners in 56 innings, and pitching to an ERA of 1.93, before he and Klein departed for Mexico. Second-year outfielder Red Schoendienst replaced Klein at second base. Musial turned down the Mexican money and stayed. In early June, Musial moved from playing left field to take over at first base because rookie Dick Sisler was struggling to find his big-league footing as the intended replacement for traded-the-day-before-opening day Ray Sanders, the Cardinals' first baseman since replacing Mize in 1942. Marty Marion and Whitey Kurowski, both of whom played through all the war years, continued on at shortstop and third base.

Meanwhile, Leo Durocher was happy to welcome back Pee Wee Reese and Pete Reiser to join Eddie Stanky and Dixie Walker in the Dodger lineup. Reese reestablished himself as the best shortstop in the National League, Stanky led the league in on-base percentage, and Walker was third in batting and second in RBIs. Kirby Higbe returned from two years at war to go 17–8, and Hugh Casey, back in the bullpen after three years away, was 11–5 with a 1.99 earned run average. With Dolph Camilli now long gone, Durocher platooned at first base; both his first basemen were marginal major leaguers at best. Catcher Mickey Owen, like the Cardinals' Lanier and Klein, was enticed by the large salaries and bonuses offered by the Mexican League and not deterred from playing south of the border by the threat of major-league blacklisting—which, in fact, all players who jumped were until 1949. A pair of rookies took over for Owen, neither of whom proved an adequate replacement. Brooklyn got off to a fast start and held a seven-game lead on Independence Day, but four straight losses in St. Louis in mid-July brought the Cardinals to within a half-game of first and ignited a pennant race that ended with the two clubs having exactly the same record after 154 games—a first for Major League Baseball. The Cardinals won the three-game playoff format favored by the National League to claim their fourth pennant in five years. The Dodgers' inability to do well against the Cardinals cost them the pennant; including their playoff losses, their record was 8–16 against St. Louis.

A major factor in the Cardinals' face-to-face dominance of the Dodgers was Stan Musial, who hit .418 against Brooklyn with three homers and 18 RBIs in their 24 games, including the playoff series. At Ebbets Field, he batted .408 against them, building a reputation for manhandling the Dodgers in their home grounds that within a few years would earn him the nickname "Stan the Man" derived from the frustration and admiration of a Brooklyn native toward what "that man" was doing to his beloved Bums. But Musial wasn't just picking on the Dodgers. He led the league in runs, hits (228), doubles (50), triples (20), batting average (.365), and combined on-base and slugging percentage (1.021) on his way to a second MVP Award. Musial got all the first-place votes save two, and those went to teammate Country Slaughter, whose three years in the service did not much diminish his baseball ability. Slaughter hit an even .300 and led the league with 130 runs batted in.

Howie Pollet came back from two years of military duty to lead National League pitchers with 21 wins and a 2.10 earned run average. His 21st victory gave the Cardinals a big one-game advantage in the first playoff game to determine the outcome of the pennant. Murry Dickson, also back from two years in the service, won two days later when the best-of-three series moved to Brooklyn to secure the pennant for St.

Louis. It was only his 19th start of the season in 47 appearances, but his 15–6 record was the best winning percentage in the National League. Now the Cardinals' go-to ace as a result of his superlative pitching in their ultimately failed attempt to overtake the Cubs in 1945, Harry Brecheen made 30 starts and worked more than 200 innings for the first time in his career. While his record was so-so at 15–15, Brecheen's 2.49 ERA was the league's fifth best.

The Cardinals went on to defeat the Red Sox in a close-fought seven-game World Series. Brecheen and Slaughter were the heroes. Harry the Cat limited Boston to just one run in 20 innings—a 0.45 ERA—and won three games, including a shutout in Game Two, a complete-game victory in Game Six, and Game Seven in relief. Although Brecheen gave up a double to Dom DiMaggio that allowed two inherited runners to tie the score in the top of the eighth, he became the winning pitcher thanks to Slaughter's aggressive baserunning to score from first on a plunked double into center field in the bottom of the inning.

* * *

The St. Louis Cardinals with four pennants and three World Series championships in five years from 1942 to 1946 were one of the most successful clubs in baseball history. Had Musial not been in the service in 1945, it's not too much of a leap to believe that the 1942–46 Cardinals— and not the 1949–53 Yankees—would have been the first team in major-league history to win five consecutive pennants. Nor should it be forgotten that the Cardinals' 97 victories in 1941 would have been more than enough in most years to win the pennant, but because Brooklyn won 100, St. Louis finished 2½ games behind. The Cardinals' 606 wins from 1941 to 1946, an average of 101 per year, is more than any other major-league team ever in six years except for the 1906–11 Cubs, who won 622. The most any of the great Yankees teams won over six seasons was 599, from 1937 to 1942; the Yankees won 598 in six years from 1936 to 1941.

How much should the depleted rosters around Major League Baseball owing to World War II discount the 1941–46 Cardinals' accomplishments, especially their overwhelming dominance of the National League in '43 and '44? On the surface, it appears as if St. Louis was not harmed as much by player losses to the war as other teams. Of their core regulars during this run, only Slaughter and Terry Moore spent as many as three years—1943, 1944, and 1945—in the service. But looking more broadly at the top National League players who lost two or more years to the war, the Cardinals' loss of Slaughter and Moore was actually about comparable to the losses of similar-caliber players on most other teams. Only the Dodgers were hit appreciably harder than the Cardinals, with Reese,

Reiser, Herman, Higbe, and Casey being comparable losses of talent to Slaughter and Moore.

Although it is true Brooklyn was hit harder by the wartime service of core players than St. Louis, the 1941–42 Cardinals were a young team getting better, while the Dodgers were older and quite likely plateaued out. Five of the Dodgers' regular position players and two of their three pitchers with 20 or more starts were 30 years or older in 1942, compared to only one core regular—Moore, 33 years old—on the Cardinals. Back then, unlike today when professional baseball players are so much better conditioned and benefit from the marvels of modern medicine and surgery to keep them going longer, being 30 was to be on the precipice looking toward the end of one's baseball career. It seems unlikely that Brooklyn's aging veterans would have kept pace with the younger Cardinals even if there hadn't been a war.

Given their core of young players, especially Musial, it seems highly plausible, if not likely, that the Cardinals' achievements in 1941 and 1942, when they and the Dodgers were by far the best teams in the league, would have given them greater momentum into the years ahead, even if both teams had been able to keep their cores intact. Once the war was over and major leaguers turned soldiers returned to being players, Brooklyn had Reese, Reiser, Higbe, and Casey back in 1946, but other core players on the '41 and '42 Dodgers—Camilli, Herman, Vaughan, Owen, Wyatt, Davis, Medwick, and starter-reliever Larry French—all of whom, except for Owen, were 30 years or older in 1942, were either no longer on the club or no longer effective players. Of the seven core regulars on the Dodgers before US entry into World War II who were 30 or older, only right fielder Dixie Walker—who was not called into service—was a regular on the 1946 Dodgers.

Excelling in every facet of the game—they led the league in scoring three times, in fewest runs allowed four times, exceeded 100 victories three times, and twice won the pennant by eight games or more—the 1941–46 Cardinals dominated the National League as no club had since the 1906–10 Cubs. Half of this record was built during the war years, but 1941, '42, and '46 were *not* war years, and the Cardinals were an outstanding baseball team all three of those years, winning two pennants and just missing out in 1941. And finally, here was a National League team that could not only get to the World Series, but win most of the ones they were in. They won three of their four World Series, losing only to the 1943 Yankees. Perhaps their 1944 World Series championship might be considered tarnished because they beat the St. Louis Browns, a team that probably would not have been there had it not been for war-ravaged American League rosters, but the 1942 Yankees and 1946 Red Sox, whom the Cardinals also bested in the World Series, were genuinely outstanding ballclubs.

* * *

In mid-September 1941, Rickey's next-to-last year in St. Louis, the Cardinals called up 20-year-old Stan Musial from their Double-A affiliate in Rochester for the final 13 games of the season. The Cardinals trailed the Dodgers by 1½ games at the time. Musial started in all but two of those games and pinch-hit in one. He finished the year with 20 hits, one a home run, and seven RBIs in 47 at-bats and went hitless in only one of the 11 games he started and in his pinch-hit appearance. Calling up the kid didn't enable St. Louis to catch Brooklyn, but Stan Musial made an impression. He was going to be great. Musial went 2-for-4 in his first game, driving in two runs. He went home that night with a .500 batting average. Like Joe DiMaggio, Stan Musial would not spend a single day in the major leagues at the end of which his career batting average was below .300. He played 22 years and retired with a .331 lifetime average.

Similarly, in 1946, Rickey, now the brains of Brooklyn's baseball operation and with his team in a fierce fight for the pennant against the club he used to work for, had a hotshot minor-league prospect playing for the Dodgers' top farm team who might have made a difference as a September call-up. He was a dynamic player, once a shortstop and now a second baseman, who hit .349 with Triple-A Montreal that year and stole 40 bases. While the Dodgers had second base and shortstop covered with Stanky and Reese, their infield was weak at the corners. Indeed, the Dodgers had been platooning for all or part of the season at both first and third. Rickey was determined, however, that however helpful he might be to the Dodgers' pennant cause, this player was not yet ready for the major leagues. Some in retrospect—years later—wondered whether the Dodgers might have won the 1946 pennant outright, without need of a playoff, had Rickey called this outstanding young player to Brooklyn for the September stretch. Rickey knew, however, that promoting this particular player to Ebbets Field in the heat of a pennant race would likely have been far more disruptive to Brooklyn's cause than welcome in the clubhouse. He would not have been welcomed, except perhaps by a few, and especially he would not have been welcomed by Brooklyn's "People's Choice"—Dixie Walker.

The player's name was Jackie Robinson.

And Branch Rickey had a plan.

A plan that even the exigencies of a taut pennant race were not going to derail.

33

BASEBALL'S ENDURING LEGACY OF RACISM

After persevering through the tough economic times of the Great Depression and forging through the wartime years as both a needed diversion on the home front from the mobilization of all the country's resources to defeat the Axis powers and a lifeline to home for soldiers on the front lines, a reminder of peacetime America, Major League Baseball had every reason to expect a promising postwar future. It was the national pastime, after all. But for all the country had just been through—417,000 American soldiers killed fighting on behalf of their country's principal ideal of freedom from oppression—there remained an indelible black stain on baseball's ledger. And that was that black Americans were not given the opportunity, because they were not allowed, to play in the major leagues no matter how exceptional their talents. And some black players were so exceptional that knowledgeable white fans knew who they were—Josh Gibson, Cool Papa Bell, Buck Leonard, Satchel Paige. It was discriminatory. It was racist. And it necessarily must discount to some degree the accomplishments of the many greats who played when Major League Baseball was whites only and they did not have to compete with and against a subset of great players who happened to be black.

Major-league owners and Commissioner Landis always insisted that there was no policy specifically prohibiting blacks. But had there been, the legal underpinning would have been the Supreme Court's 1896 decision in *Plessy v. Ferguson* that established the doctrine that "separate but equal" was OK by the Constitution. The Justices ruled by 7-to-1 that a Louisiana statute mandating that blacks be segregated from whites in their own cars on railroads was a matter of public policy that did not infer racial inferiority to blacks because the law did not deny blacks equal rights and equal protection as guaranteed in the post–Civil War 14th Amendment. Calling the Louisiana law a "reasonable regulation," the seven justices specifically mentioned that separation of the races in schools, theaters, and railway carriages did not interfere with the political equality of black Americans. By implication, states as a matter of policy could do so in any public arena they chose—including racial segregation in sports.

By insisting there was no specific policy prohibiting blacks from "Organized" Baseball, since no black players were given a chance to play in the minor leagues, either, the commissioner and the owners could also have drawn sustenance from wording in the *Plessy* decision that went beyond jurisprudence to make the point that "if the two races are to meet upon terms of social equality, it must be the result of natural affinities, a mutual appreciation of each other's merits, and a voluntary consent of individuals." This in effect validated segregation and the legal foundation of "separate but equal" as socially and even politically acceptable; if whites did not wish to associate with blacks in schools, on buses, in business, playing sports, then so be it. Using tortured reasoning that seemed to contradict the 14th Amendment on equal rights for all Americans and at least the spirit of the 15th Amendment on black suffrage, since matters of public policy (including voting rights and regulations) were left to the states, the *Plessy* decision is now almost universally considered to have been wrongly decided.

The Supreme Court ruling was made in the context of the political demand for reconciliation between the North and South following the upheavals of Reconstruction. In the spirit of reconciliation, letting southern whites maintain their self-perceived dignity after their defeat in the Civil War inevitably meant demeaning the black population, which could be justified because they now had inalienable rights conferred by two constitutional amendments. It would not be until 1946 that the Supreme Court, in a 6-to-1 decision, ruled in *Morgan v. Commonwealth of Virginia* that segregation of the races in interstate commerce, in this case, rail transportation, was unconstitutional. But they did so under the interstate commerce clause of the Constitution, not the equal protection clause in the 14th Amendment. The decision left intact segregation based on separate but equal under state laws. It was not until 1954 that *Plessy v. Ferguson* was overturned in a 9-to-0 blowout by the justices in *Brown v. The Board of Education*.

In October 1945, just two weeks after the final out of the World Series, the Brooklyn Dodgers upended the segregationist order of the baseball universe when Branch Rickey announced the signing of Negro League Kansas City Monarchs star infielder Jackie Robinson. There was, after all, no specific policy—"formal or informal . . . subterranean or otherwise"—against blacks in white Organized Baseball. Those were the words of Commissioner Landis himself, said in 1942. Rather than come straight to Ebbets Field, Rickey's plan was for Robinson to begin the integration of white Organized Baseball in Montreal playing for the Dodgers' Triple-A affiliate in a city north of the border known for racial tolerance. Rickey's message was clear, however—Major League Baseball's refusal to let black players compete at *any* level could no longer stand, and unless Robinson failed in Montreal, there would soon be a black man playing on a major-league team.

In 1896 when *Plessy v. Ferguson* was decided, there were no blacks in Major League Baseball. Indeed, Organized Baseball at all levels was an all-white affair and had been, with very few exceptions in the lower minor leagues, since catcher Moses Fleetwood Walker was quietly dumped, because he was black, by the major-league American Association's Toledo franchise in the face of relentless pressure from other teams in the league about a month before the 1884 season ended. (Walker's brother, Welday, an outfielder, also played briefly for Toledo that year.) Earlier in the season, Chicago White Stockings star first baseman and manager Cap Anson refused to play an exhibition game—Chicago being a National League team—in Toledo if Walker was behind the plate. Anson backed down rather than lose the revenue, but made no secret of his disdain for the idea of blacks in Major League Baseball.

* * *

Even at that time, more than a decade before *Plessy v. Ferguson* made its way to the United States Supreme Court because Homer Plessy, of mixed-race Creole ancestry, had the temerity to challenge the Louisiana statute that segregated blacks from whites, Jim Crow laws were widespread across the country, especially in the South. Separation of the races was *the* social construct in the United States of America, notwithstanding the trauma of a Civil War fought to end slavery, the adoption of the 14th Amendment in 1868, and the high-mindedness of "all men are created equal" as a "self-evident" truth in the preamble to the Declaration of Independence a century earlier.

Blacks were as enamored by the game of baseball as whites, but finding no place for them in the organized structures—the major and minor leagues—established by white men, they were left to their own devices. The very recent legacy of slavery, which meant black Americans started their lives as free and equal citizens with virtually nothing, ensured that black players and business entrepreneurs interested in establishing leagues did not have the financial resources or connections to build the kind of infrastructure necessary to support *and sustain* credible black Organized Baseball. In addition to just the money needed to run a league operation, the now legally enforceable Jim Crow laws restricted where blacks could play, where they could eat and sleep on the road, even how they could travel. These were significant impediments to the complex logistics required to make a success of a league, which relied on the sanctity of the schedule. Persistent insolvency, or the threat of not being able to meet expenses, meant there was also no sanctity to contracts. Blacks could, and would, have their own leagues, but they would never be as self-sufficient, as coherent, as credible, as big-time, as "equal" as white Organized Baseball.

From the 1880s to about 1920, professional black baseball played more like a traveling circus, and the choreography worked. There were many black teams, some very good, and a few inchoate leagues were formed and dissolved. For the most part, however, teams engaged in what were essentially barnstorming tours, playing other established teams and any and all takers in locales throughout the South and Midwest. Their games, whether league games or exhibitions, brought black communities together, in celebration of themselves as well as the game—which was the national pastime for all, white and black, black and white.

Most of the prominent black teams were established in northern cities, even though America's black population was still primarily south of the Mason-Dixon Line. And many were organized and bankrolled by white entrepreneurs recognizing there were profits to be made in black baseball. Although there was no specific requirement for having the best record in any particular league to play in one, the best black teams often met in "championship" series for big paydays, the enjoyment of fans, and to showcase baseball. But perhaps more important, in the context of baseball's indelible black stain, these teams in the same cities as major-league franchises proved they played a serious game. They couldn't help but draw the attention of big-league players and, especially, managers. They were *that* good. And however much the overwhelmingly white-majority population might have wanted to believe otherwise, there were many black players who had the talent to play alongside whites in the major leagues—except, of course, they were excluded.

The premier black stars of the day included the likes of shortstop John Henry "Pop" Lloyd and pitcher "Smokey" Joe Williams, both of whom broke in with black professional teams in the mid-1900s. Both were soon turning the heads of major-league observers, and of major-league players. Lloyd drew comparisons to Honus Wagner for his exceptional defensive abilities at short and his clutch hitting, and Wagner himself said it was a privilege to be compared to him. His effortless delivery, exceptional control, and the speed of his fastball made Williams somewhat of a Walter Johnson type in the black leagues. And indeed, Johnson and Grover Cleveland Alexander both lost games to Smokey Joe in postseason exhibitions where white teams played against black clubs. Williams was also said to have struck out 20 in an exhibition game against the 1917 National League champion New York Giants after their seasons were done, although there appears to be no actual record of his having done so.

The most consequential black star in the early twentieth century, however, was Rube Foster, and not just because he was an outstanding pitcher in his own right for the Chicago Union Giants in the 1900s. Not to be confused with the Rube Foster (first name George) who pitched for the Red Sox in the 1910s, the Rube Foster (first name Andrew) we're talking about is considered one of the best ever to pitch in exclusively black professional leagues, although he was not the equal of Joe Williams. Foster earned his nickname by defeating the Philadelphia Athletics' outstanding southpaw Rube Waddell in a 1905 exhibition between all-black and all-white teams; Foster was "the black Rube." In 1902, he is said to have won 44 consecutive games pitching mostly for the Philadelphia X-Cubans.

Notwithstanding his pitching excellence, Rube Foster was most important in baseball history—not just black baseball history—as a manager, a relentless self-promoter, and a man with a strong entrepreneurial bent, including networking with influential white baseball power brokers. In 1910, Foster put together his own club in Chicago, raided his former team and the rival Philadelphia Giants for their best players, formed a partnership with Charles Comiskey's son-in-law, and presided over a team that not only was the best that black baseball had going in the teens but should be in the argument for one of the greatest teams in history, period. Foster recruited both Pop Lloyd and Smokey Joe Williams to play for his American Giants in Chicago. Every year during the 1910s except the World War I year of 1918, Foster's American Giants played in a championship series of some sort. In any given year there might be three or more different such series among black baseball teams, often pitting the acknowledged best team from the East against the best team from the Midwest, usually the American Giants.

It did not go unnoticed by Foster that his great team could never play for an officially recognized national black baseball championship, like the World Series, because there was no equivalent "major-league" superstructure in black baseball. Instead of structured leagues, black teams in the East played within a loose affiliation of a league that was run largely by white promoters more like a booking agency to showcase black teams and players. Black teams in the Midwest were typically run by African American entrepreneurs as more independent operations that arranged games against each other. Different philosophical approaches to the economic viability of their enterprises, and the fact that the better-financed eastern teams had the leverage both to decide which teams played in the

East and to entice players from the midwestern teams to defect for a better payday, was a significant divide. By 1920, Rube Foster was ready to remedy that failing.

With Ban Johnson among his contacts, and the American League that both Johnson and Comiskey had been instrumental in establishing as his model, Foster took the lead in organizing eight of the best independently operated black teams in the Midwest into a formal league. The Negro National League that Foster pioneered was an important milestone in the history of black professional Organized Baseball. It was the foundation of what became known as the Negro Leagues. But it was no easy ride. In 1923, Eastern-based black clubs organized into the Eastern Colored League and enticed several Negro National League stars—including veteran star players Oscar Charleston and Pop Lloyd—to come east.

The most prominent black teams in the 1920s were Foster's Chicago American Giants and the Kansas City Monarchs in the Negro National League, and the Philadelphia Hilldale Giants in the Eastern Colored League. The Monarchs were first organized as a semipro combination baseball team/traveling vaudeville show by a white entrepreneur, John Leslie Wilkinson, in the early 1910s. Then called the All Nations, the ballplayers and entertainers comprised different ethnic groups—whites, blacks, and Native Americans. By the midteens, the All Nations were devoted to baseball, but remained independent until Foster came calling to organize the NNL. By this point they were an all-black team, settled in Kansas City, and renamed the Monarchs. With Bullet Joe Rogan their ace, the Monarchs won three consecutive NNL pennants from 1923 to 1925 and had the best record in the league in 1926, although they lost the playoff series between the first- and second-half winners for the right to go to the Colored World Series. Rogan had a confirmed record in Negro League play of 73–30, according to research by John Holway. His 26–2 record in 1925 included four victories in the nine-game NNL playoff, which he capped with a 3–0 shutout that sent the Monarchs to the World Series. Similarly, Hilldale began in the first decade of the century as an amateur club in Philadelphia before becoming an independent professional team playing against other black teams in the East. Led by their star third baseman, Judy Johnson, Hilldale won the Eastern Colored League's first three pennants. Johnson had begun his career playing for barnstorming teams and was widely regarded as a heady practitioner of what John McGraw called "scientific baseball."

From 1924 to 1927, the two league champions squared off in the Colored World Series, but that ended in 1928 with the financial collapse of the Eastern Colored League, whose various franchises played on as independently operated teams outside a league structure. A few years later, with the country in the grip of the Depression, the Negro National

League also disbanded. Foster's descent into mental illness in 1926, possibly after exposure to some kind of toxic agent, was the beginning of the end of the league he had founded because the other owners lacked his administrative skills and organizational discipline, both of which were essential for a league in perennial financial straits.

The Negro National League was rebooted in 1933, organized this time mostly around eastern-based teams, at the initiative of a new cohort of black entrepreneurs, a few of whom were notorious for operating on the illicit margins of the economy. Foremost among them was Gus Greenlee, the founding father of the new Negro National League, whose involvement in shady dealings was an open secret. Black professional Organized Baseball did not, and indeed could not, enforce a standard that would have precluded power brokers with gambling or racketeering interests from participation. Capitalization was a persistent, often acute problem for the Negro Leagues, and the original Negro National League had seen several franchises come and go. Only after a rival Negro American League came into being in 1937, with clubs mostly in the Midwest and South, did the collective Negro Leagues enter a period of relative franchise stability. By 1942 the two Negro League pennant winners were holding an East-West World Series.

* * *

Just as the Yankees were masters of the white major-league universe in the 1930s, so were the Pittsburgh Crawfords in the Negro Leagues. Beginning as a local semipro team, the Crawfords emerged as a power-

The Kansas City Monarchs of the Negro National League before the opening game of the first Colored World Series in 1924. *Gladstone Collection of African American Photographs (Library of Congress).*

house after Greenlee took ownership in 1930, turned them into an independent professional ballclub, and proceeded to recruit some of the best black players in the country—most notably Oscar Charleston, Cool Papa Bell, Judy Johnson, Josh Gibson, and Satchel Paige. The Crawfords were a charter member of the new NNL that Greenlee was instrumental in organizing in 1933. From 1932 to 1936, the Crawfords had a confirmed record in Negro League play, including 1932 as an independent club, of 237–126, which translates into a .653 winning percentage—the equivalent of 101 wins in the 154-game schedule played in the white major leagues. All five of their star players were together in four of those five years; Paige left to pitch for the Monarchs in 1935 before returning to Pittsburgh. Given that the Yankees won pennants in only the bookend years of 1932 and 1936, the Crawfords for those five years were quite possibly the best team in *all* of baseball, black or white.

The Crawfords were succeeded as the preeminent team in Negro League baseball by the other black professional team in Pittsburgh—the Homestead Grays, which also began in the late 1920s as a local semipro club, and whose owner, Cumberland (Cum) Posey, would be as high profile as Greenlee. Gibson, Charleston, Johnson, and Bell all played for Homestead before being enticed to the Crawfords, and it was Greenlee's decision to trade Gibson back to the Grays in 1937 that precipitated the beginning of the end of the Crawford dynasty. Greenlee was tired of Gibson's incessant lobbying for a salary more commensurate with the value his prodigious power production brought to the Crawfords.

Greenlee's outstanding ace Satchel Paige, meanwhile, was enticed by Dominican strongman Rafael Trujillo to raid Negro League spring-training camps for star players for the Generalissimo's pet project of starting a new baseball league in his country that would play in the spring in direct competition with US professional leagues. American baseball players, black and white, were already playing winter ball in Caribbean leagues, including in the Dominican Republic. Clearly not understanding Trujillo's intimidation-and-threats-based philosophy of governing, Paige took many of his teammates with him to the dictator's new league, including Bell and Gibson, who decided to go to the Dominican Republic instead of reporting to Homestead. It turned out to be a frightening experience for players who took up the offer. Once the 1937 Dominican season was over, Gibson returned to Pittsburgh to play for the Grays, where he teamed with Buck Leonard, their star first baseman since 1934, to give the Homestead Grays a formidable lineup. They became "The Thunder Twins" and formed the core of a team that won the Negro National League championship every year from 1937 to 1945, compiling a 294–136 confirmed record in Negro League play for an outstanding .684 winning percentage. Beginning in 1939, the Homestead Grays played their home games in both Washington, at Griffith Stadium, and Pittsburgh, at Forbes Field.

The first years of the Negro American League were dominated by the Kansas City Monarchs, for whom Paige went to pitch beginning in 1939. The Monarchs won seven pennants in 10 years and defeated the Grays in the first East-West World Series in 1942. It was for the Monarchs that Jackie Robinson played in 1945 after being discharged from the army, and in Kansas City where he impressed the scouts Branch Rickey had sent out to find the one black player who had both the talent and the fortitude to break the color barrier in Major League Baseball. Satchel Paige was a teammate.

* * *

The 1920s and 1930s were the heyday of the Negro Leagues, notwithstanding the freewheeling enterprise that was professional black baseball. Contracts were close to meaningless, with players frequently leaving for a better deal elsewhere—often with independent teams not in the Negro League structure—which might be only for a short time and quick money, and sometimes not in the United States. Many black players dipped in and out of the Negro Leagues to play in Caribbean leagues, mostly in the winter, particularly in Cuba and the Dominican Republic. Schedules were made and kept, for the most part, but Negro League teams played many off-league games for the money and exposure. The keeping of official statistics was haphazard and not always accurate. Not all scheduled games were even officially scored.

They were not the major leagues, but in the spirit of *Plessy v. Ferguson*, as far as white Organized Baseball was concerned, the Negro Leagues were the major-league equivalent for black professional baseball. Separate, yes—it was good for blacks to have their own leagues—but as far as the white major leagues were concerned, hardly equal in talent and performance. Such was the line of the unofficial mouthpiece of Major League Baseball, the influential *Sporting News*, particularly as the clamor grew, including in influential mainstream newspapers, for giving blacks the opportunity to play in the majors. Indeed, when in the aftermath of World War II the unequal treatment of America's black citizens could no longer be concealed, major-league owners were all but forced into making the disingenuous argument that black ballplayers, good as they might be in the Negro Leagues, were not good enough to play in the big time. It is important to note, however, that the white major leaguers who played against them did not necessarily argue that blacks would fail playing in the major leagues.

One generation of black baseball stars blended into the next, turning heads, including among major-league players. Oscar Charleston was the

Negro Leagues' most transcendent star in the teens and '20s, frequently changing teams before settling with the Crawfords in the 1930s. Baseball historian Bill James has noted that "*lots* of people said he was the greatest player they ever saw," including John McGraw, better even than major-league center-field contemporaries Ty Cobb and Tris Speaker. And Philadelphia during the 1920s was said to have two excellent catchers—the Athletics' Mickey Cochrane, and Biz Mackey of the Eastern Colored League's Hilldale Giants. Just as the great Yankees catcher Bill Dickey was said to have "learned" Yogi Berra all his "experience," to plagiarize Yogi-speak, the same was true of Mackey as a mentor to a young Roy Campanella, Berra's major-league contemporary in the 1950s. Mackey recruited the high-school-age Campanella for the Baltimore Elite Giants, the Negro American League club he was managing, in the late 1930s. Cool Papa Bell, whose career spanned nearly three decades beginning in the early 1920s, including playing for the Crawfords in the 1930s and the Grays in the 1940s, was almost more an ephemeral notion in the baseball world because of his exquisite speed and proficiency with the bat. Power-hitting Turkey Stearnes, who played in the 1920s and '30s, reminded some of Mel Ott. Grays first baseman Buck Leonard was called the "black Lou Gehrig" when they were contemporary players in the 1930s, but of course he was never allowed to play in the same league. And that's just to name a few.

In addition to Bullet Rogan of the Monarchs, the Negro Leagues during their prime-time years were witness to excellent pitching from the likes of Willie Foster—Rube Foster's half brother—Leon Day, and Hilton Smith. And that's just to name a few. Willie Foster, whose career was centered in the mid-1920s to the mid-1930s, mostly with the Chicago American Giants, has the most confirmed victories in Negro League play with 157 and was praised by major-league umpire Jocko Conlan for having exceptional control. Among his many notable achievements was winning 26 consecutive decisions in 1926, against both league and non-league competition. Day pitched primarily for the NNL's Newark Eagles in the 1930s and early 1940s and was said to have won about 300 games in the Negro Leagues, in Caribbean winter leagues, and with traveling black all-star teams. Smith pitched for the Monarchs in the late 1930s and early 1940s and was considered by some to be even better than his teammate Satchel Paige. His Hall of Fame plaque notes that he won 93 of 104 credited decisions in Negro League play for the Monarchs between 1939 and 1942—an .894 winning percentage—including a 25–1 record in 1941.

Black Hispanics from Cuba were also prominent in the Negro Leagues, whereas virtually no white Hispanic Cubans played in the majors, only one of whom had any prominence—Dolf Luque, "the Pride of

Havana," with the Reds in the 1920s. There had long been a symbiotic relationship between African American baseball and Cuban baseball. Many American Negro League players went to Cuba for winter-league baseball, and Cuban players were among some of the best in Negro League history. Jose Mendez, who pitched for professional black independent teams in the 1910s and was instrumental to the Monarchs' success in the 1920s, was said by John McGraw to remind him of a combination Walter Johnson/Grover Cleveland Alexander. Before Josh Gibson was called such, Cristobal Torriente became "the black Babe Ruth" after he starred in a nine-game postseason exhibition series in 1920 where his Cuban team defeated the visiting New York Giants, who had added the real Babe Ruth to their roster for the tournament. A contemporary and rival for excellence with Oscar Charleston, Torriente's exploits contributed to Chicago's American Giants winning the first three pennants in the new Negro National League beginning in 1920. A contemporary and rival for excellence of both was Martin Dihigo, who broke in with the New York–based Cuban Stars of the Eastern Colored League in 1923—the year that league was organized. Much of his career in the 1930s and 1940s was spent playing in Caribbean and Mexican leagues rather than in the American Negro Leagues. Late in his career, even though he also was a craftsman on the mound, Dihigo's hitting and grace in the field called to mind Joe DiMaggio in the eyes of many observers.

These mentions omit many other great players who played in the Negro Leagues in the '20s and '30s. None, however, reigned more supreme in the baseball conscience than Josh Gibson and Satchel Paige. Gibson never played in the white major leagues, and Paige did so only when he was a shadow of what he had been at his peak. Yet both their names are as recognizable even among casual baseball fans today as the major-league greats of any era, before and after integration. Only Babe Ruth, and perhaps a small handful of others like Mantle, Mays, Aaron, and, of course, Jackie Robinson can really claim the same.

Josh Gibson was the preeminent Negro League slugger of his day, and a solid catcher besides. He had prodigious power, belted more than his share of impressive "tape-measure" home runs, and would have been as worthy of having his blasts called "Gibsonian clouts" as the Babe was for his "Ruthian clouts." And some of his longest blasts came in the "House That Ruth Built." Before Mickey Mantle in 1956, Gibson in a Negro League game played in 1937 reportedly came the closest of any batter to hitting a home run out of Yankee Stadium, when he belted one some 580 feet that missed clearing the top of the left-field bleacher wall by just two feet, according to a *Sporting News* retrospective account 40 years later. His plaque in Cooperstown mentions he won four batting titles and blasted nearly 800 home runs in his career. Many believe Josh Gibson to have been the best all-around catcher and one of the greatest right-handed batters to ever play the game, white or black.

And Satchel Paige must be in the argument about the best to ever take the mound. He was poised and efficient. He had a terrific fastball and exceptional command of his pitches in and around the strike zone. His easygoing mechanics blessed him with an exceptionally long career. He was a master of his craft, but never took himself too seriously, which meant he was as lively and fun as he was a relentless, in-it-to-win-it competitor. Nobody knows how many games Satchel Paige actually won, for his record in Negro League games was only the half of it, and perhaps less than that. He jumped teams liberally for a better payday, or maybe just because he got bored, and starred in Caribbean baseball as he did in the United States. He suffered numerous personal setbacks and was certainly mindful of blacks' place in what was Jim Crow America the entirety of his career, notwithstanding the three innings he pitched for the Kansas City Athletics in 1965, a year after the Civil Rights Act was passed. No matter his setbacks, Paige was resilient. Through it all, his experiences and infectious personality made him the fount of perceived wisdom, because he seemed so balanced about life, all the more so because he aged so well. Don't look back, he'd say, something might be gaining on you.

* * *

Since the earliest days of black professional baseball at the beginning of the twentieth century, the best major-league players in particular were typically ambivalent or silent about the matter. Many, in fact, recognized the best of the Negro League stars as great players. Honus Wagner and Frank Chance testified to the excellence of Rube Foster. In later years, Dizzy Dean, from Arkansas, was effusive in his praise of the black all-stars he competed against in barnstorming tours. And they had reason to know, because while black players were barred from Major League Baseball, exhibition games between black teams and white "all-star" teams were not uncommon, and the black teams often prevailed. Their hitters sometimes battered the most dominant major-league pitchers, their pitchers sometimes dominated the major league's best hitters, and of course, it was also the other way around.

If Chicago deserved to be considered the capital of baseball in the middle of the first decade of the twentieth century, a big reason was not just the success of the Cubs and the competitiveness of the White Sox in the two white major leagues, but also because the Chicago Union Giants, often called the Leland Giants after their owner, were an outstanding black team—perhaps the best in black baseball at the time. It was for them that Rube Foster pitched. All three teams drew large crowds. After having defeated an "all-star" team of white players after the 1907 season had ended, the Union Giants challenged the world champion Cubs to an exhibition series for bragging rights as the best team in Chicago and, by implication, all of baseball. Perhaps fearing the outcome, the Cubs refused. They refused again in 1908 after winning another World Series. In 1909, however, after their 104 wins were far too few to match the Pirates, the Cubs accepted the Union Giants' challenge to play a three-game series. While the Cubs won all three games, each decided by only one run, sportswriters covering the series were impressed by how good the black club was, and the Cubs in subsequent years refused to play another exhibition series for Chicago bragging rights with either the Union Giants or Foster's Chicago American Giants.

Black and white teams routinely played against each other in postseason exhibitions. In the first two decades, tournaments between actual league teams were relatively common, although some players on major-league teams chose not to participate and players from other clubs were occasionally added to the squad. The results were sometimes embarrassing for the major-league club. The 1909 Detroit Tigers, having just won their third straight American League pennant, were crushed by racially mixed teams they played in Cuba, winning only four of 12 games. Ty Cobb, the "Georgia Peach," did not play in Cuba that year, supposedly because the Cuban teams included blacks, but he did the next year, with the Tigers this time winning seven of their 11 decisions. The World Series champion Philadelphia Athletics followed Detroit to Cuba in 1910 without Eddie Collins and Frank Baker, their two best hitters, and left the island nation with a 4–6 record. Chief Bender and Eddie Plank both lost three games. Even though Collins and Baker did not make the trip, the fact that the best team in the major leagues was roughed up by an integrated team, outscored by 40 to 33 in the 10 games, caused American League president Ban Johnson to declare Cuba off limits in the future to the teams in his league. The implications of those losses were just too fraught for what it meant to deny blacks any opportunity to play in the major leagues, or at any level of white Organized Baseball.

After the mid-1920s, major-league teams no longer played postseason series against Negro League teams, almost certainly because they were unwilling to risk the possibility of defeat by a black team even if such series were loudly proclaimed as just exhibitions. The winners of the major-league and Negro League World Series never met in a tournament for bragging rights. After the Detroit Tigers split an exhibition series and both the St. Louis Browns and Philadelphia's Athletics lost theirs to black teams in the fall of 1923, Commissioner Landis dictated that players could no longer use their big-league team name or uniform in postseason tournaments and barnstorming tours.

Through the end of the decade, however, singular Negro League teams, none of which was a championship club, did face off in exhibition series against white major-league "all-stars." Research by John Holway shows that the Negro League clubs beat the major-league "all-star" teams almost every postseason, probably contributing to the end of that practice. It wasn't until the mid-1930s that a Negro League team vs. major-league team series took place again, and then only in spring training when any big-league embarrassment from losing a series could be explained away as working out the kinks before the start of the season. Leo Durocher's defending 1941 National League champion Brooklyn Dodgers were nonetheless dismayed by losing three of five to a mixed-race team the next spring while preparing for the 1942 season in Cuba.

White squads playing against black squads in barnstorming tours organized by star players or promoters were common, although Landis tried to crack down on major leaguers barnstorming as a matter of principle, even if they just played against white teams. Barnstorming teams usually included any number of minor-league and even amateur players to round out teams headlined by star players. Babe Ruth loved barnstorming tours; in 1920, he led an all-star team that was shut out in a game against the Hilldale Giants. In the 1930s, star major-league players, including southerners Dizzy Dean, Lon Warneke, Johnny Mize, and Cecil Travis, had no problem playing competitive games in barnstorming tours against some of the Negro League's best players, if for no other reason than the money.

Whether exhibition series or barnstorming tours, games between white and black "all-stars" were well attended and well worth the extra payday for the players involved. And they were competitive. It was an opportunity for black players to prove they could play against some of the best of the white players, although some compelling star-player matchups did not occur despite the opportunity. In back-to-back years in 1922 and 1923, even though he was the manager, Cobb chose not to play when his Tigers took on Negro League teams that included the great player sometimes referred to as "the black Cobb"—Oscar Charleston. Neither did Cobb rival Tris Speaker, from Texas, ever play against Charleston.

* * *

Black players earned the respect of the white all-stars they played against, but could only wonder how they might have fared had they been allowed to actually play in the major leagues—perhaps even on all-black teams against all-white teams, so that white teams themselves did not have to be integrated at a time when "separate but equal" was constitutionally acceptable. If integration on teams was not possible because of the social and political climate of the times, racially segregated white and black teams playing as "equals" in Major League Baseball would have been a big step forward in Jim Crow America. But that, of course, was never in the cards.

Just because major leaguers, especially star players, almost universally respected the ability of the black players they competed against in barnstorming tours or more formal exhibition series did not mean they were willing to play *with* blacks. Right or wrong, racist and discriminatory or not, their attitudes were not inconsistent with most likely the majority of Americans at a time when segregation of the races was the norm, and at a time when advocacy for desegregation and true equal rights seemed to be the agenda primarily of leftist, typically Communist-inspired, political agitators. And if the best major leaguers were generous about the major-league ability of the best in the Negro Leagues, they could afford to be. Even had there been a move toward integration in the 1920s and 1930s, they were not going to be displaced. Acknowledging that many Negro League players could have played in the major leagues was more problematic for white players with *average* big-league ability, some of whom might have lost their jobs to more-talented black players.

Indicative of this dynamic, it is perhaps not surprising that managers seemed more open to the idea of blacks playing in the major leagues. Managers, of course, are interested in whatever it takes to win, including the best available talent. In spring training in 1901, as manager of the Baltimore Orioles in the infant American League, John McGraw tried to pass off an outstanding young black infielder named Charlie Grant as a Native American until called out by Charles Comiskey, one of the founding fathers of the new league. Throughout his managerial career, McGraw would praise the excellence of the Negro League players that impressed him, leaving little doubt he thought they could be stars in the major leagues, and kept a log on the black players he would have signed had Major League Baseball been inclusive. Connie Mack thought Judy Johnson was good enough that he could have virtually named his price in Major League Baseball, were it not that he was black and, hence, out of bounds. In 1939, when asked by Wendell Smith, a prominent black columnist for the *Pittsburgh Courier*, an African American newspaper, and an activist for baseball integration, if they would accept black players on their teams, seven of the eight National League managers said yes . . . if, of course, it was possible to do so. The Giants' Bill Terry, born in Georgia and known as Memphis Bill, was the one manager who said he would not. And in 1942, Dodgers manager Leo Durocher said he would not be averse to blacks in the major leagues, a comment for which he was called to account by Commissioner Landis, who then insisted there was no policy to exclude black players. It didn't help that Durocher's comments were made to the *Daily Worker*, a Communist Party newspaper in New York City.

Even before the war years and Durocher's remarks, the issue of integration had begun to surface. Washington Senators owner Clark Griffith, in whose ballpark the Homestead Grays with Josh Gibson and Buck Leonard played, remarked as early as 1938 that the time was coming soon when "colored players" would play in the major leagues. But when push came to shove, not only was Griffith opposed to Branch Rickey's integration initiative, he was one of the owners holding out the longest against integrating his ballclub even after Jackie Robinson and Larry Doby had proven their ability, and their mettle, at the big-league level. Pittsburgh Pirates owner William Benswanger, in whose park the Grays with Gibson and Leonard also played, said in 1940 he would be open to blacks playing in the major leagues. Both Washington and Pittsburgh toyed with trying out Negro League stars during the war, but ultimately decided not to, almost certainly because they understood how fraught with controversy such a move would be. And Bill Veeck claimed in his 1962 book *Veeck— as in Wreck*, that he intended to field an all-black team in the major leagues had he been allowed to purchase the woeful Philadelphia Phillies in 1942, only to be derailed by Landis and National League president Ford Frick when they got wind of his plan. Given that he made this claim in the postintegration era, this may have been Veeck's attempt at one-upmanship of Rickey, to whom is given all the credit for courage and conviction in defense of a righteous cause.

The influential black newspapers and white liberal activists calling for an end to segregation in baseball were dismissed by major-league powers-that-be as agitators. Indeed, "agitators"—the word in vogue to describe Communist Party members—is exactly how baseball executives were inclined to regard those who, in the spirit of the ideals for which the country fought a world war, were increasing the pressure on major-league clubs to at least give tryouts to Negro League stars for the opportunity to play in the big leagues. *The Sporting News* explicitly used the word "agitators" in its infamous 1942 editorial seeking to short-circuit—indeed, outright strangle—the call for integrating Major League Baseball. Both the major leagues and the Negro Leagues, the editorial insisted, preferred things the way they were—separate, but equal.

But the American experience in World War II was making it increasingly awkward to defend such a manifestly racial status quo, and political pressure for integration in Boston and New York could not be so easily deflected. In Boston, the Red Sox finessed the issue by inviting three black players, famously including Jackie Robinson, to Fenway Park for a tryout just as the 1945 season was about to get under way. It was a sham. The Red Sox had no intention of being a trailblazing team. In New York, antidiscrimination legislation that threatened fines and even jail time for businesses that refused to hire nonwhite employees was signed into law about a month before the 1945 season started. The new statute upped the political ante on New York's baseball teams to integrate. Branch Rickey certainly welcomed the new law, but he was already moving to sign a black player in the Negro Leagues to play ultimately for the Dodgers . . . in Brooklyn . . . in the major leagues. Established Negro League greats like Monte Irvin, Willard Brown, Ray Dandridge, and Roy Campanella were just entering or still in their prime and would have been obvious choices. Instead, Rickey settled on Jackie Robinson.

* * *

The two racial narratives in popular culture that underlay America's social construct where segregation was thought to be both natural and desirable were becoming morally and politically untenable as a result of the US experience in World War II. The first narrative, epitomized by D. W. Griffith's 1915 epic film *Birth of a Nation*, depicted blacks as uncivilized, primitive, racially inferior. This was, in fact, the underlying premise of Jim Crow laws. The second narrative, epitomized in Margaret Mitchell's epic 1936 novel *Gone with the Wind*, which became an epic Oscar-winning film starring Clark Gable and Vivian Leigh in 1939, portrayed blacks not just as racially inferior, but as innocents content in subordinate roles, implying that white paternalism was beneficial to their development.

The first narrative was, by now, discredited to all but racist bigots. The second narrative, while all but discredited, still had some resonance for those who wanted to argue that equality wasn't the issue, but community was. As major-league owners looked on with apprehension, probably bordering on horror, at Branch Rickey's Jackie Robinson initiative, they adopted the paternalistic attitude that they knew, regardless of what black and white civil rights "agitators" were saying, that professional black baseball players were not only best off in their own Negro Leagues but would be happier there. If they wanted to make a living at the national pastime, black players should prefer their own professional league, "separate" and "equal" to the majors, because it seemed unlikely many, if any, could compete at the major-league level. Jackie Robinson would prove them wrong, soon enough.

BIBLIOGRAPHY

BOOKS, BLOGS, AND WEB PAGES

Adler, Richard. *Mack, McGraw and the 1913 Baseball Season*. Jefferson, NC: McFarland, 2008.

Alexander, Charles C. *Breaking the Slump: Baseball in the Depression Era*. New York: Columbia University Press, 2002.

———. *John McGraw*. New York: Viking, 1988.

Appel, Marty. *Pinstripe Empire: The New York Yankees from Before the Babe to After the Boss*. New York: Bloomsbury, 2012.

Armour, Mark L., and Daniel R. Levitt. *Paths to Glory: How Great Baseball Teams Got That Way*. Washington, DC: Brassey's, 2003.

Asinof, Eliot. *Eight Men Out: The Black Sox and the 1919 World Series*. New York: Henry Holt, 1963.

Bak, Richard. *Cobb Would Have Caught It: The Golden Age of Baseball in Detroit*. Detroit: Wayne State University Press, 1991.

Baldassaro, Lawrence. *Beyond DiMaggio: Italian Americans in Baseball*. Lincoln: University of Nebraska Press, 2011.

Barber, Red. *1947: When All Hell Broke Loose in Baseball*. New York: Da Capo, 1982.

Carney, Gene. *Burying the Black Sox: How Baseball's Cover-Up of the 1919 World Series Fix Almost Succeeded*. Washington, DC: Potomac Books, 2006.

Cohen, Stanley. *Dodgers! The First 100 Years*. New York: Birch Lane, 1990.

Creamer, Robert W. *Stengel: His Life and Times*. New York: Simon & Schuster, 1984.

Curran, William. *Big Sticks: The Phenomenal Decade of Ruth, Gehrig, Cobb, and Hornsby*. New York: Harper Perennial, 1991.

———. *Mitts: A Celebration of the Art of Fielding*. New York: William Morrow, 1985.

Deford, Frank. *The Old Ball Game: How John McGraw, Christy Mathewson, and the New York Giants Created Modern Baseball*. New York: Grove, 2005.

Dewey, Donald. *The 10th Man: The Fan in Baseball History*. New York: Carroll & Graf, 2004.

DiMaggio, Joe. *Lucky to Be a Yankee*. New York: Rudolph Field, 1946.

Dixon, Phil S. *Andrew "Rube" Foster, a Harvest on Freedom's Fields*. N.p.: Xlibris, 2000. E-book.

Durso, Joseph. *The Days of Mr. McGraw*. Englewood Cliffs, NJ: Prentice Hall, 1969.

Ehrgott, Roberts. *Mr. Wrigley's Ball Club: Chicago and the Cubs during the Jazz Age*. Lincoln: University of Nebraska Press, 2013.

Feldman, Doug. *September Streak: The 1935 Chicago Cubs Chase the Pennant*. Jefferson, NC: McFarland, 2003.

Fleitz, David L. *Shoeless: The Life and Times of Joe Jackson*. Jefferson, NC: McFarland, 2001.

Fountain, Charles. *The Betrayal: The 1919 World Series and the Birth of Modern Baseball*. New York: Oxford University Press, 2016.

Gay, Timothy M. *Satch, Dizzy & Rapid Robert: The Wild Saga of Interracial Baseball before Jackie Robinson*. New York: Simon & Schuster, 2010.

———. *Tris Speaker: The Rough-and-Tumble Life of a Baseball Legend.* Guilford, CT: Lyons, 2007.

Gilbert, Bill. *They Also Served: Baseball and the Home Front, 1941–1945.* New York: Crown, 1992.

Goldman, Steven. "1908 National League: A Foolish Inconsistency." In *It Ain't Over 'Til It's Over: The Baseball Prospectus Pennant Race Book,* edited by Steven Goldman, 99–128. New York: Perseus Books, 2007.

Goldstein, Richard. *Spartan Seasons: How Baseball Survived the Second World War.* New York: Macmillan, 1980.

Goldstein, Warren. *A History of Early Baseball: Playing for Keeps, 1857–1876.* New York: Barnes & Noble Books, 1989.

Golenbock, Peter. *Bums: An Oral History of the Brooklyn Dodgers.* New York: Putnam, 1984.

Halberstam, David. *The Teammates. A Portrait of a Friendship.* New York: Hyperion, 2003.

Heidenry, John. *The Gashouse Gang: How Dizzy Dean, Leo Durocher, Branch Rickey, and Their Colorful Come-from-Behind Ball Club Won the World Series—and America's Heart during the Great Depression.* New York: Public Affairs, 2007.

Hogan, Lawrence D. *Shades of Glory: The Negro Leagues and the Story of African-American Baseball.* Washington, DC: National Geographic Society, 2006.

Holway, John. *The Complete Books of Baseball's Negro Leagues: The Other Half of Baseball History.* Fern Park, FL: Hastings House, 2001.

Hornbaker, Tim. *Turning the Black Sox White: The Misunderstood Legacy of Charles A. Comiskey.* New York: Sports Publishing, 2014.

Hubler, David E., and Joshua H. Drazen. *The Nats and the Grays: How Baseball in the Nation's Capital Survived WW2 and Changed the Game Forever.* Lanham, MD: Rowman & Littlefield, 2015.

Huhn, Rick. *Eddie Collins: A Baseball Biography.* Jefferson, NC: McFarland, 2008.

Jaffe, Chris. *Evaluating Baseball's Managers: A History and Analysis of Performance in the Major Leagues, 1876–2008.* Jefferson, NC: McFarland, 2010.

James, Bill. *The Bill James Guide to Baseball Managers: From 1870 to Today.* New York: Scribner, 1997.

———. *The New Bill James Historical Baseball Abstract.* New York: Free Press, 2001.

James, Bill, and Rob Neyer. *The Neyer/James Guide to Pitchers: An Historical Compendium on Pitching, Pitchers, and Pitches.* New York: Fireside Books, 2004.

Jordan, David M. *The Athletics of Philadelphia: Connie Mack's White Elephants, 1901–1954.* Jefferson, NC: McFarland, 1999.

Juliano, William. "100 Years of Ronald Reagan and Baseball." *The Captain's Blog.* February 6, 2011. captainsblog.info.

Kaese, Harold. *The Boston Braves, 1871–1953.* Boston: Northeastern University Press, 2004. Originally published in 1948.

Kahrl, Christina. "1934 National League: Learning to Trust the Man in Glasses." In *It Ain't Over 'Til It's Over: The Baseball Prospectus Pennant Race Book,* edited by Steven Goldman, 310–25. New York: Perseus Books, 2007.

Klein, Maury. *Stealing Games: How John McGraw Transformed Baseball with the 1911 New York Giants.* New York: Bloomsbury, 2016.

Koppett, Leonard. *The Man in the Dugout: Baseball's Top Managers & How They Got That Way.* Philadelphia: Temple University Press, 2000.

Lamb, Chris. *Conspiracy of Silence: Sportswriters and the Long Campaign to Desegregate Baseball.* Lincoln: University of Nebraska Press, 2012.

Leavengood, Ted. *Clark Griffith: The Old Fox of Washington Baseball.* Jefferson, NC: McFarland, 2011.

Leerhsen, Charles. *Ty Cobb: A Terrible Beauty.* New York: Simon & Schuster, 2015.

Levitt, Daniel R. *The Battle That Forged Modern Baseball: The Federal League Challenge and Its Legacy.* Lanham, MD: Ivan R. Dee, 2012.

———. *Ed Barrow: The Bulldog Who Built the Yankees' First Dynasty.* Lincoln: University of Nebraska Press, 2008.

Levy, Allen H. *Joe McCarthy: Architect of the Yankee Dynasty.* Jefferson, NC: McFarland, 2005.

Lowenfish, Lee. *Branch Rickey: Baseball's Ferocious Gentleman.* Lincoln: University of Nebraska Press, 2009.

Lynch, Mike. "1923 and the June 15 Trade Deadline." *Seamheads.com* (blog). January 2, 2009. http://scamheads.com/blog/2009/01/02/1923-and-the-june-15-trade-deadline/.

Macht, Norman L. *Connie Mack: The Turbulent and Triumphant Years, 1915–1931.* Lincoln: University of Nebraska Press, 2012.

———. *Connie Mack and the Early Years of Baseball.* Lincoln: University of Nebraska Press, 2007.

Marshall, William. *Baseball's Pivotal Era, 1945–1951.* Lexington: University Press of Kentucky, 1999.

Mathewson, Christy. *Pitching in a Pinch: Baseball from the Inside.* New York: Penguin Classic, 2013. Originally published in 1912.

Morris, Peter. *A Game of Inches: The Stories behind the Innovations That Shaped Baseball.* Lanham, MD: Ivan R. Dee, 2006.

Mulligan, Brian. *The 1940 Cincinnati Reds: A World Championship and Baseball's Only In-Season Suicide.* Jefferson, NC: McFarland, 2005.

Murphy, Cait. *Crazy '08: How a Cast of Cranks, Rogues, Boneheads, and Magnates Created the Greatest Year in Baseball History.* New York: Smithsonian Books, 2008.

Nemec, David. *The Great Encyclopedia of Nineteenth Century Major League Baseball.* Tuscaloosa: University of Alabama Press, 1997.

Pietrusza, David. *Judge and Jury: The Life and Times of Judge Kenesaw Mountain Landis.* South Bend, IN: Diamond Communications, 1998.

Rains, Rob. *The St. Louis Cardinals: The 100th Anniversary History.* New York: St. Martin's, 1992.

Ribowsky, Mark. *The Complete History of the Home Run.* New York: Citadel, 2003.

———. *A Complete History of the Negro Leagues, 1884–1955.* New York: Birch Lane, 1995.

Ross, J. Brian. *Baseball's Greatest Comeback: The Miracle Braves of 1914.* Lanham, MD: Rowman & Littlefield, 2014.

Ruck, Rob. *How the Major Leagues Colonized the Black and Latin Game.* Boston: Beacon, 2011.

Rymer, Zachary D. "The Evolution of the Baseball from the Dead-Ball Era through Today." Bleacherreport.com. June 18, 2013. http://bleacherreport.com/articles/1676509-the-evolution-of-the-baseball-from-the-dead-ball-era-through-today.

Sarnoff, Gary G. *The Wrecking Crew of '33: The Washington Senators' Last Pennant.* Jefferson, NC: McFarland, 2009.

Seymour, Harold, and Dorothy Zanger Seymour. *Baseball: The Early Years.* New York: Oxford University Press, 1960.

———. *Baseball: The Golden Age.* New York: Oxford University Press, 1971.

Sigman, Shaya M. "The Jurisprudence of Judge Kenesaw Mountain Landis." *Marquette Sports Law Review* 15, no. 2 (Spring 2005).

Silver, Nate. "1944 American League: The Home Front." In *It Ain't Over 'Til It's Over: The Baseball Prospectus Pennant Race Book,* edited by Steven Goldman, 326–62. New York: Perseus Books, 2007.

Soderholm-Difatte, Bryan. *The Golden Era of Major League Baseball: A Time of Transition and Integration.* Lanham, MD: Rowman & Littlefield, 2015.

Sowell, Mike. *The Pitch That Killed: Carl Mays, Ray Chapman, and the Pennant Race of 1920.* New York: Macmillan, 1989.

Spatz, Lyle, and Steve Steinberg. *1921: The Yankees, The Giants, & the Battle for Baseball Supremacy in New York.* Lincoln: University of Nebraska Press, 2010.

Spink, J. G. Taylor. *Judge Landis and Twenty-Five Years of Baseball.* New York: Thomas Y. Crowell, 1947.

Steinberg, Steve, and Lyle Spatz. *The Colonel and Hug: The Partnership That Transformed the New York Yankees.* Lincoln: University of Nebraska Press, 2015.

Stout, Glenn. *Fenway, 1912: The Birth of a Ballpark, a Championship Season, and Fenway's Remarkable First Year.* Boston: Mariner Books, 2012.

———. *The Selling of the Babe: The Deal That Changed Baseball and Created a Legend.* New York: Thomas Dunne Books, 2016.

Swaine, Rick. *The Integration of Major League Baseball: A Team by Team History.* Jefferson, NC: McFarland, 2009.

Thorn, John, and John Holway. *The Pitcher: The Ultimate Compendium of Pitching Lore.* New York: Prentice Hall, 1987.

Tygiel, Jules. *Past Time: Baseball as History.* New York: Oxford University Press, 2000.

Vance, Mike, ed. *Houston Baseball: The Early Years, 1861–1961.* Houston, TX: Bright Sky, 2014.

Weeks, Jonathan. *Baseball's Dynasties and the Players Who Built Them.* Lanham, MD: Rowman & Littlefield, 2016.

Weintraub, Robert. *The House That Ruth Built: A New Stadium, the First Yankee Championship, and the Redemption of 1923.* New York: Little, Brown, 2011.

———. *The Victory Season: The End of World War II and the Birth of Baseball's Golden Age.* New York: Back Bay Books, 2013.

Weisberger, Bernard A. *When Chicago Ruled Baseball: The Cubs-White Sox World Series of 1906.* New York: Harper, 2006.

Wittenberg, Eric J., and Michael Aubrecht. *You Stink! Major League Baseball's Terrible Teams and Pathetic Players.* Kent, OH: Black Squirrel Books (Kent State University Press), 2012.

Zinn, Paul G., and John G. Zinn. *The Major League Pennant Races of 1916: "The Most Maddening Baseball Melee in History."* Jefferson, NC: McFarland, 2009.

ARTICLES

The great benefits for baseball researchers of membership in the Society for American Baseball Research include SABR publications, the *Baseball Research Journal* and the *National Pastime*, and access to historical archives (1908 to 1920) of the *Baseball Magazine*, which was published between 1908 and 1957. SABR also sponsors a baseball biography project (BioProject) of players, managers, and executives throughout major-league history, as well as others who made a significant contribution to the sport. The following are research articles from SABR publications used in the writing of this book:

Allardice, Bruce. "'Playing Rotten, It Ain't That Hard to Do': How the Black Sox Threw the 1920 Pennant." *Baseball Research Journal* 45, no. 1 (Spring 2016).
Caborn, Rod, and Dave Larson. "The 1906 Cleveland Naps: Deadball Era Underachiever." *Baseball Research Journal* 41, no. 1 (Spring 2012).
Haupert, Michael. "William Hulbert and the Birth of the National League." *Baseball Research Journal* 44, no. 1 (Spring 2015).
Hershberger, Richard. "Chicago's Role in Early Professional Baseball." *Baseball Research Journal* 40, no. 1 (Spring 2011).
Johnson, William H. "The Crybabies of 1940." *National Pastime*, 2008.
Knopp, Japheth. "Negro League Baseball, Black Community, and the Socio-economic Impact of Integration." *Baseball Research Journal* 45, no. 1 (Spring 2016).
Lamb, William. "Jury Nullification and the Not Guilty Verdicts in the Black Sox Case." *Baseball Research Journal* 44, no. 2 (Fall 2015).
Levitt, Daniel R., Mark L. Armour, and Matthew Levitt. "History versus Harry Frazee: Re-revising the Story." *Baseball Research Journal* 37 (2008).
Macht, Norman L., and Robert D. Warrington. "The Veracity of Veeck." *Baseball Research Journal* 42, no. 2 (Fall 2013).
McMurray, John. "Babe Ruth, Brooklyn Dodgers Coach." *Baseball Research Journal* 44, no. 2 (Fall 2015).
Morante, Tony. "Baseball and Tammany Hall." *Baseball Research Journal* 42, no. 1 (Spring 2013).
Peterson, Todd. "May the Best Man Win: The Black Ball Championships, 1866–1923." *Baseball Research Journal* 42, no. 1 (Spring 2013).
Ruane, Tom. "Modern Baseball's Greatest-Hitting Team: The 1930 Phillies' Opponents." *Baseball Research Journal* 38, no. 2 (Fall 2009).
Ruzzo, Bob. "Braves Field: An Imperfect History of the Perfect Ballpark." *Baseball Research Journal* 41, no. 2 (Fall 2014).
———. "Fate and the Federal League: Were the Federals Incompetent, Outmaneuvered, or Just Unlucky?" *Baseball Research Journal* 42, no. 2 (Fall 2013).
Schuld, Fred. "Alva Bradley: Baseball's Last Purist." *National Pastime*, 2008.
Soderholm-Difatte, Bryan. "Connie Mack's Second Great Athletics' Team." *National Pastime*, supplement, 2013.
———. "Dazzling Dazzy Vance in the 'K-Zone.'" *Baseball Research Journal* 44, no. 1 (Spring 2015).
———. "The 1914 Stallings Platoon." *Baseball Research Journal* 43, no. 2 (Fall 2014).
———. "The Stallings Platoon: The 1913 Prequel." *Baseball Research Journal* 45, no. 2 (Fall 2016).
Steinberg, Steve. "The St. Paul–New York Underground Railroad." *National Pastime*, 2012.

ARTICLES FROM *BASEBALL MAGAZINE*

Emslie, Robert D. "Ramblings of an Umpire." November 1908.
Johnston, Samuel M. "Good Natured Joe Connolly: The Man Who Always Smiles." February 1915.

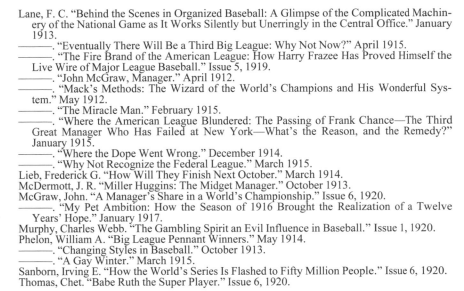

Lane, F. C. "Behind the Scenes in Organized Baseball: A Glimpse of the Complicated Machinery of the National Game as It Works Silently but Unerringly in the Central Office." January 1913.
———. "Eventually There Will Be a Third Big League: Why Not Now?" April 1915.
———. "The Fire Brand of the American League: How Harry Frazee Has Proved Himself the Live Wire of Major League Baseball." Issue 5, 1919.
———. "John McGraw, Manager." April 1912.
———. "Mack's Methods: The Wizard of the World's Champions and His Wonderful System." May 1912.
———. "The Miracle Man." February 1915.
———. "Where the American League Blundered: The Passing of Frank Chance—The Third Great Manager Who Has Failed at New York—What's the Reason, and the Remedy?" January 1915.
———. "Where the Dope Went Wrong." December 1914.
———. "Why Not Recognize the Federal League." March 1915.
Lieb, Frederick G. "How Will They Finish Next October." March 1914.
McDermott, J. R. "Miller Huggins: The Midget Manager." October 1913.
McGraw, John. "A Manager's Share in a World's Championship." Issue 6, 1920.
———. "My Pet Ambition: How the Season of 1916 Brought the Realization of a Twelve Years' Hope." January 1917.
Murphy, Charles Webb. "The Gambling Spirit an Evil Influence in Baseball." Issue 1, 1920.
Phelon, William A. "Big League Pennant Winners." May 1914.
———. "Changing Styles in Baseball." October 1913.
———. "A Gay Winter." March 1915.
Sanborn, Irving E. "How the World's Series Is Flashed to Fifty Million People." Issue 6, 1920.
Thomas, Chet. "Babe Ruth the Super Player." Issue 6, 1920.

WEBSITES

Websites indispensable to the writing of this book include baseball-reference.com; retrosheet.org; and Gary Bedington's baseballinwartime.com, which includes data on major- and minor-league players who died during World War I and World War II.

Population data for US cities drawn from US Census Bureau statistics can be found on the website census.gov/population (Population of the 100 Largest Urban Places by decade). US unemployment statistics for the years of the Great Depression can be found on the website u-s-history.com. Unemployment data for the recession of 1914 are from a 1937 report published by the Social Security Board of the US government's Economic Security Committee and can be found on the website ssa.gov/history.

The complete text of the US Supreme Court's seven-justices-to-one decision in "Plessy v Ferguson (1896) No. 210, Decided May 18, 1896," including Justice John Marshall Harlan's dissent, can be found on the website caselaw.findlaw.com. The phrase "separate but equal" derives from the 1890 Louisiana statute being challenged in court that required railroads to provide "equal but separate accommodations for the white and colored races." The complete text of "Morgan v Commonwealth of Virginia (1946) No. 704, Decided June 3, 1946" can also be found on the website caselaw.findlaw.com.

INDEX

ABOUT THE AUTHOR

Bryan Soderholm-Difatte is a member of the Society for American Baseball Research and a regular contributor to the *Baseball Research Journal*. He is the author of *The Golden Era of Major League Baseball: A Time of Transition and Integration* (Rowman & Littlefield, 2015). Soderholm-Difatte is a former senior analyst for the Central Intelligence Agency and the National Counterterrorism Center.